Contemporary Authors
Autobiography Series

ISSN 0748-0636

Contemporary Authors

Autobiography Series

Joyce Nakamura

Editor

volume **12**

 Gale Research Inc. · *DETROIT · NEW YORK · LONDON*

EDITORIAL STAFF

The paper used in this publication meets the minimum requirements of American National Standard for Information Sciences—Permanence Paper for Printed Library Materials, ANSI Z39.48-1984.

Copyright © 1990
Gale Research Inc.
835 Penobscot Bldg.
Detroit, MI 48226-4094

Library of Congress Catalog Card Number 84-647879
ISBN 0-8103-4511-0
ISSN-0748-0636

Printed in the United States of America

Published simultaneously in the United Kingdom
by Gale Research International Limited
(An affiliated company of Gale Research Inc.)

Contents

Preface

Each volume in the *Contemporary Authors Autobiography Series (CAAS)* presents an original collection of autobiographical essays written especially for the series by noted writers. *CAAS* has grown out of the aggregate of Gale's long-standing interest in author biography, bibliography, and criticism, as well as its successful publications in those areas, like the *Dictionary of Literary Biography, Contemporary Literary Criticism, Something about the Author, Author Biographies Master Index,* and particularly the bio-bibliographical series *Contemporary Authors (CA),* to which this *Autobiography Series* is a companion.

As a result of their ongoing communication with authors in compiling *CA* and other books, Gale editors recognized that these wordsmiths frequently had more to say—willingly, even eagerly—than the format of existing Gale publications could accommodate. Personal comments from authors in the "Sidelights" section of *CA* entries, for example, often indicated the intriguing tip of an iceberg. Inviting authors to write about themselves at essay-length was the almost-inexorable next step. Added to that was the fact that the collected autobiographies of current writers were virtually nonexistent. Like metal to magnet, Gale customarily responds to an information gap—and met this one with *CAAS.*

Purpose

This series is designed to be a congenial meeting place for writers and readers—a place where writers can present themselves, on their own terms, to their audience; and a place where general readers, students of contemporary literature, teachers and librarians, even aspiring writers can become better acquainted with familiar authors and make the first acquaintance of others. Here is an opportunity for writers who may never write a full-length autobiography (and some shudder at the thought) to let their readers know how they see themselves and their work, what carefully laid plans or turns of luck brought them to this time and place, what objects of their passion and pity arouse them enough to tell us. Even for those authors who have already published full-length autobiographies there is the opportunity in *CAAS* to bring their readers "up to date" or perhaps to take a different approach in the essay format. At the very least, these essays can help quench a reader's inevitable curiosity about the people who speak to their imagination and seem themselves to inhabit a plane somewhere between reality and fiction. But the essays in this series have a further potential: singly, they can illuminate the reader's understanding of a writer's work; collectively, they are lessons in the creative process and in the discovery of its roots.

CAAS makes no attempt to give an observer's-eye view of authors and their works. That outlook is already well represented in biographies, reviews, and critiques published in a wide variety of sources, including *Contemporary Authors, Contemporary Literary Criticism,* and the *Dictionary of Literary Biography.* Instead, *CAAS* complements that perspective and presents what no other source does: the view of contemporary writers that is reflected in their own mirrors, shaped by their own choice of materials and their own manner of storytelling. Thanks to the exceptional talents of its contributors, each volume in this series is a unique anthology of some of the best and most varied contemporary writing.

Scope

Like its parent series, *Contemporary Authors,* the *CA Autobiography Series* aims to be broad-based. It sets out to meet the needs and interests of the full spectrum of readers by providing in each volume about twenty essays by writers in all genres whose work is being read today. We deem it a minor publishing event that twenty busy authors from throughout the world are able to interrupt their existing writing, teaching, speaking, traveling, and other schedules to converge on a given deadline for any one volume. So it is not always possible that all genres can be equally and uniformly represented from volume to volume, although we strive to include writers working in a wide spectrum of genres, including fiction, nonfiction, and poetry. Like most categories, these oversimplify. Only a few writers specialize in a single area. The range of writings by authors in this volume also includes drama, translation, and criticism as well as work for movies, television, radio, newspapers, and journals.

Format

Authors who contribute to *CAAS* are invited to write a "mini-autobiography" of approximately 10,000 words. In order to give the writer's imagination free rein, we suggest no guidelines or pattern for the essay. The only injunction is that each writer tell his or her own story in the manner and to the extent that each finds most natural and appropriate. In addition, writers are asked to supply a selection of personal photographs, showing themselves at various ages, as well as important people and special moments in their lives. Barring unfortunate circumstances like the loss or destruction of early photographs, our contributors have responded graciously and generously, sharing with us some of their most treasured mementoes, as this volume readily attests. This special wedding of text and photographs makes *CAAS* the kind of reference book that even browsers will find seductive.

A bibliography appears at the end of each essay, listing the author's book-length works in chronological order of publication. If more than one book has been published in a given year, the titles are listed in alphabetic order. Each entry in the bibliography includes the publication information for the book's first and most recent printings in the United States. Generally, the bibliography does not include later reprintings, new editions, or foreign translations. Also omitted from this bibliography are articles, reviews, and other contributions to magazines and journals. The bibliographies in this volume were compiled by members of the *CAAS* editorial staff from their research and the lists of writings provided by many of the authors. Each of the bibliographies has been submitted to the author for review. When the list of primary works is extensive, the author may prefer to present a "Selected Bibliography." Readers may consult the author's entry in *CA* for a more complete list of writings in these cases.

Each volume of *CAAS* includes a cumulative index that cites all the essayists in the series as well as the subjects presented in the essays: personal names, titles of works, geographical names, schools of writing, etc. The index format is designed to make these cumulating references as helpful and easy to use as possible. For every reference that appears *in more than one essay*, the name of the essayist is given before the volume and page number(s). For example, W.H. Auden is mentioned by a number of essayists in the series. The index format allows the user to identify the essay writers by name:

Auden, W.H.
Allen **6**:18, 24
Ashby **6**:36, 39
Bowles **1**:86
Burroway **6**:90
Fuller **10**:120, 123
Hall **7**:58, 61
Hazo **11**:148, 150
Howes **3**:143
Jennings **5**:110
Jones **5**:121
Kizer **5**:146
Major **6**:185-86
Rosenthal **6**:282
Shapiro **6**:307-08
Simpson **4**:291
Sinclair **5**:272
Symons **3**:383, 385
Wain **4**:327

For references that appear *in only one essay*, the volume and page number(s) are given but the name of the essayist is omitted. For example:

Stieglitz, Alfred **1**:104, 109, 110

CAAS is something more than the sum of its individual essays. At many points the essays touch common ground, and from these intersections emerge new mosaics of information and impressions. *CAAS* therefore becomes an expanding chronicle of the last half-century—an already useful research tool that can only increase in usefulness as the series grows. And the index, despite its pedestrian appearance, is an increasingly important guide to the interconnections of this chronicle.

Looking Ahead

All of the writers in this volume begin with a common goal—telling the tale of their lives. Yet each of these essays has a special character and point of view that set it apart from its companions. Perhaps a small sampler of anecdotes and musings from the essays ahead can hint at the unique flavor of these life stories.

Peter Barnes, relating a hazard of modern medicine: "It is true, like everyone else, I have had a number of crises in my life. In 1978 I fell off the stage at the Roundhouse Theatre whilst directing a production of 'Bartholomew's Fair' and smashed my right knee. It was replaced with a plastic one and I resumed rehearsals within four days. I wish someone would have said, 'My God, he's a brave little beggar,' and I could have said, 'My God, I am a brave little beggar.' Instead, the surgeon who performed the operation assured me that my new knee would outlast the rest of my body. If, for some reason, in the future, they opened my coffin, they would find on top of a neat pile of dust one solitary plastic kneecap, slightly mildewed but still intact. It was no turning point in my life, though it did convince me I should insist on being cremated."

Leslie Epstein, confronting his own identity: "What happened to me in Israel was at once common enough, and most bizarre. Instantaneously, virtually on the docks, the wall between myself and the world, that membrane, dissolved. Before my eyes hustled Jewish porters, policemen, soldiers and sharpies and sellers of pretzels. Osmosis cannot take place, nor can one live on the margin, or be expelled, when there are Jews in solution inside and out. The idea that I had grown up with—that the very word *Jew* was awesome, sacred, terrible, not to be thought of, never mentioned—became ludicrous on these shores swarming with the usual run of big shots and bums. What made Israel so appealing to many Jews like me (and so repugnant to the zealots of Crown Heights and the Mea Shearim) was the promise of the ordinary, the prospect of the mundane. Only in the Holy Land could the Jews escape being a holy people."

George Hitchcock, recalling early impressions that later influenced his poetry: "Our new house was built on the banks of the Willamette River, which meant canoeing in the summer and vast floods almost every winter. My parents, I am sure, became very tired of waking up to acres of turbid brown water on all sides of them; to me, of course, it was a source of perennial delight. School was impossible, and the dogs had to be kept inside where they whimpered with fear. My father's morning preoccupation was with measuring the ebb and flood of the menacing waters; how many million acre-feet would it take to rise that last six inches and cover our floors with mud? Out on the central current, chicken coops, trestle timbers, and armadas of upswept stumps and piratical snags sailed by. The housemaid, her basement room hip-deep in café-au-lait, had moved back to her Swedish family, and all the firewood so laboriously stacked in July now floated to every corner of the cellar. The lawn was eradicated, the furnace filled with mud. And then the floods fell as mysteriously as they had arisen, and after school every afternoon for weeks I slogged about in the basement cleaning up. After these spring floods, summer generally limped onstage and the river once again became the friendly refuge of chubs and watersnakes."

Bohumil Hrabal, reviving his creative energy at his favorite pub: "Those conversations around the tavern table allow one to cope with the stress of daily life; even idle chatter is a kind of coping; perhaps, when one feels worst, the best cure is a banal conversation about trivial matters and events; sometimes, I sit there and stubbornly refuse to say anything; usually during the first beer I make it clear that it is unpleasant for me to reply to any query whatever; I look forward so much to that first beer; it takes me a while to get used to the tyrannical loudness of the tavern, to adjust to so many guests and so many conversations; it is as if everyone wanted the entire tavern to hear what he was saying, as if everyone in this tavern believed the very thing he was saying to be so remarkable that he had to yell his banal message; I also belong to these screamers; after the second beer, I, too, think what I am saying is so very important that I start to shout: I seem to see more, and naively believe that what I have to say must be heard not only by my table, but perhaps also by the entire world."

Arturo Vivante, describing his uncle's legacy: "In the early thirties, when my two brothers and I were children, if we saw an airplane flying over our house we would wave, then run into the house to tell my mother about it. 'It was flying really low,' we would say, hoping to stir her. 'Perhaps it was Uncle Lauro.' We would watch her. But her face wouldn't brighten. Her eyes, which we had known to be so lively, looked at us dully. The fascists had done this to her, we told ourselves, and hated them with a rich, deep hate. In October 1931, Lauro de Bosis, her youngest brother, thirty years old, had taken off from the Côte d'Azur in a small airplane and scattered antifascist leaflets over Rome. From the terrace of his home on the top of an apartment house near the Piazza di Spagna, his mother—my grandmother Lillian—had watched the plane flying around and around, and the leaflets showering down from it, some falling on the terrace itself. She knew it was he both from the leaflets, which she had helped print, and from the manner of the enterprise. She had seen people on the street below eagerly picking them up, reading them, folding them, and putting them in their pockets. Then the plane, in the twilight, had headed west, toward Corsica, and no one ever saw it or my uncle again."

These brief examples can only suggest what lies ahead in this volume. The essays will speak differently to different readers; but they are certain to speak best, and most eloquently, for themselves.

Authors Forthcoming in *CAAS*

Ai
American poet

Mulk Raj Anand
Indian novelist, nonfiction writer,
and critic

Russell Banks
American novelist

Franco Beltrametti
Swiss-born poet, novelist, and translator

Hal Bennett
American novelist

Algis Budrys
American science-fiction writer and editor

Ed Bullins
American playwright

Malay Roy Choudhury
Indian poet

Cyprian Ekwensi
Nigerian novelist and short-story
writer

Paul Engle
American poet and educator

Philip José Farmer
American science-fiction writer

Charles Gordone
American playwright, actor, and
director

Daniel Halpern
American poet and editor

John Hollander
American poet

Elizabeth Jolley
Australian novelist

Nettie Jones
American novelist

Etheridge Knight
American poet

Matthew Mead
English poet and translator

Aharon Megged
Israeli novelist

Jessica Mitford
English essayist and journalist

Bharati Mukherjee
Canadian novelist and short-story
writer

Fernand Ouellette
Canadian novelist

Harry Mark Petrakis
American novelist and screenwriter

Alastair Reid
Scottish poet, essayist, and
translator

Carolyn M. Rodgers
American poet

Edouard Roditi
American poet

Antonis Samarakis
Greek novelist and short-story writer

Sonia Sanchez
American poet

Robert Sward
American poet

Anne Waldman
American poet

Frank Waters
American novelist and nonfiction writer

Acknowledgments

We wish to acknowledge our special gratitude to each of the authors in this volume. They all have been most kind and cooperative in contributing not only their talents but their enthusiasm and encouragement to this project.

Grateful acknowledgment is also made to those publishers, photographers, and artists whose works appear with these authors' essays.

Photographs

Peter Barnes: pp.1, 14, Ivan Kyncl.

Charles G. Bell: p. 17, Marianna Cook; p. 37, Sydney Brink/*Albuquerque Journal.*

James Broughton: p. 41, © 1988 Becket Logan; p. 51, Sonya Noskoutale; p. 54, Harry Redl; p.56, © 1974 Photograph by Art Freedman.

James B. Hall: p. 120, Fleshman-Wain.

Ihab Hassan: p. 137, H. Wolfsbauer.

George Hitchcock: p. 167, Lysa McDowell; p. 169, #3-37a, Historical Photograph Collection, University of Idaho Library, Moscow, Idaho.

Bohumil Hrabal: pp. 183, 184, 186, M. Jankovic; p. 191, Susanna Roth; p. 192, Jan Burgan; p. 193, Hana Hamplova.

Herbert R. Lottman: p. 197, Bruno of Hollywood.

Larry Niven: p. 211, © 1988 M. C. Valada; pp. 212, 216, 223, © 1978 Richard Todd; p. 214, John William Upton/Independent News Service © 1989; p. 219, Photograph by Jay Kay Klein; p. 221, Beth Gwinn.

Natalie L. M. Petesch: p. 241, Calligraphy by Susan Dubisch from *The Odyssey of Katinou Kalokovich.* Copyright © by Natalie L. M. Petesch.

James Schevill: p. 260, George H. Kahn.

Vladimir Voinovich: p. 303, Isolde Ohlbaum.

Paul Weiss: p. 335, Zabarsky/Boston University Photo Service.

Jonathan Williams: p. 339, Roger Manley; p. 340, Francine du Plessix; pp. 343, 344, 347, 348, Jonathan Williams; p. 345, Vincent A. Finnigan; p. 352, Ray Williams; p. 354, Alex Harris; p. 354, David Lebe.

Contemporary Authors

Autobiography Series

Peter Barnes

1931-

What are words using me for?

Living writers hide themselves. When I write I am disguised. So how can I write an autobiographical article? Everything can be communicated but even if we have access to all the necessary information we never manage to know ourselves. But, then, why try? Why worry about an author's life since all authors have been declared dead by Roland Barthes and nothing remains but texts and readings? But flaws are built into texts and they can be made to mean anything. Words are arbitrary signifiers scratched on paper which obscure the truth. So writing itself becomes a central problem.

Autobiography even more so. Yet it is a booming genre since the decline of the confessional and the rise of the couch. Autobiography quickly shades into the pathology of grandiosity. It is not a mode I am happy in. All those "I's." Sweating to make oneself interesting and the problem of events meaning more to the writer than to the reader. Most autobiography is pseudoliterature, literature that has failed to transform itself.

I once heard a mental patient say, "A black Chinaman taught me karate, they're the best you know," but nothing very dramatic has happened to me. It has been like living in Canada. That's what I mean when I say words write me. Why should I write "Canada"? I've never been to Canada and, come to think of it, I've never heard the Baskerville hound baying in the great Grimpen Mire either. All I've done is struggle with language which like religion is a way of organising reality and channeling behaviour.

What happened in my life? Nothing much. I can make it up of course, but in truth, the difference between one lost day and the next seems no more dramatic than the tide going out at Eastbourne. The years have passed like a dream.

According to Berkeley's philosophy, from the logical point of view you can prove there is no outside world and life is indeed a dream. So what? It does not get you very far. It is no basis for life. You can't live in this dream as a dream. You must treat the dream as

"They say men of my age are back in style,"
Peter Barnes, London, 1989

reality, which it might very well be in any case. There is no practical difference between actually being in reality and knowing it to be a dream yet treating it as reality. Dream or reality, I still have to make a living and my hair keeps falling out. Even in a dreamworld there are people, things, causes, phenomena. So if the world is a dream it is a real world whilst we are dreaming it. Anyway that is my excuse.

One of the reasons I prefer drama to the novel is because it is a more democratic form. There is no obvious God-like "I" writing the play, or if there is, he or she must try not to reveal themselves. Most novelists own the words, dramatists don't, they give them to others. The art often lies in not explaining things. Explaining is usually scientific, philosophical, or moralistic. That is why it is difficult to write an autobiography when there is so much explanation and so few interesting events that aren't parochial, or personal.

It would probably be more exciting to write about what I did not do than what I did: the plays never written, the castles never built, the triumphs never experienced, the melodies never played, the ideas dying before they were born. But that is hardly a practical proposition. There are too many things I do not know didn't happen. And it would turn into a depressing catalogue of missed opportunities, or worse, of unknown opportunities missed.

As it is, despair is a sin ever at the door. The Jews of Babylon chose indifference and were punished for it. It was an indifference springing from despair. As a socialist I know there is no rational basis for revolutionary optimism given our human weaknesses, our fear and brutality. We try to lay the foundation of a better future without any certainty we will succeed. Either mankind destroys itself one way or another, or else the revolution succeeds in creating something new—a society in which all powers are done away with because every individual has full power over himself. To believe that will happen in the long term, you need faith.

In England '89 despair is the easiest sin to fall into if you believe in a better world. We still flaunt the Edwardian values of greed, ostentation, and selfishness coupled with the Victorian ones of meanness and hypocrisy, whilst Eastern Europe emerges from one darkness in order to return to vicious nationalism and age-old intolerance.

Still miracles happen. Look at Disraeli. I've looked at him, now it's your turn. He was able to rise to become Prime Minister of England despite being a Jewish levantine, bisexual novelist, and opium addict, in a racist, Conservative party dominated, as ever, by semiliterate, heterosexual drunks. So anything is possible, even writing an autobiography of sorts.

Obviously it cannot be a chronicle of nonevents and as for facts, for every fact there is a contradictory fact equally true, equally untrue. They would be manipulated to paint a coherent picture when there is no coherence. Or if there is I cannot see it or describe it. I feel I am never able to say what I think or think what I say, and if a true word escapes me I wrap it up with so many words it suffocates.

So in lieu of a lyingly coherent narrative I will present some fragments, anecdotes, and texts so readers can create their own biography.

For example, in 1987 numerous, dubiously prominent people in Britain were asked to contribute an essay for a book entitled *Winning Through* showing how they overcame a personal crisis. The book was to be in aid of a charity so I agreed to write a piece. Unfortunately I did not know the project was sponsored by the Church of England and naturally was expected to have a degree of moral uplift. Not surprisingly my contribution was rejected.

On the face of it my article would seem to have to be purely autobiographical but it did not turn out that way. I managed to be evasive even there. For anything personal in it has to be gained by inference beneath, around, and beyond it. It is a performance like everything else.

Text 1

To describe a crisis in one's life and how it was overcome is difficult. Only colossal personalities can benefit society by drawing attention to their own lives. The nineteenth century saw the last of them, which is why I try to avoid the autobiographical. Besides, asking artists, of any kind, to provide moral

"I used to think I was mysterious—now I'm just baffling," San Francisco, California, 1963

lessons seems dangerous when you remember that Wordsworth deserted his mistress and daughter and opened his letters with a dirty jam knife, Gauguin left his wife and children to give a succession of underage Polynesian girls syphilis, Degas was a virulent anti-Semite, Rimbaud a slave-trader, and Wagner all that and more. Would you like your sister to marry one of them?

Of course, one should be optimistic in the face of life's "downers" and win through. But the mendacity of the media, the hypocrisy of the law, the merciless stupidity of politicians, the inhumanity of mothers, the brutishness of fathers, and the last sunset fast approaching, makes optimism a touch facile. And what do writers know about winning? They are all heading for Dump City. If they can write a page with all the words facing the same direction, they consider themselves ahead.

It is true, like everyone else, I have had a number of crises in my life. In 1978 I fell off the stage at the Roundhouse Theatre whilst directing a production of "Bartholomew's Fair" and smashed my right knee. It was replaced with a plastic one and I resumed rehearsals within four days. I wish someone would have said, "My God, he's a brave little beggar," and I could have said, "My God, I am a brave little beggar." Instead, the surgeon who performed the operation assured me that my new knee would outlast the rest of my body. If, for some reason, in the future, they opened my coffin, they would find on top of a neat pile of dust one solitary plastic kneecap, slightly mildewed but still intact. It was no turning point in my life, though it did convince me I should insist on being cremated.

In 1981 I found myself depressed in a hotel room in Philadelphia. That's very easy in Philadelphia. Then I opened the inevitable Gideon Bible left on the bedside table and read the inscription on the flyleaf: "If sick, read Psalm 18. If troubled, read Psalm 45. If lonely, ring 5284738 and ask for Wanda."

Much as I would like it to have been, I have never found religion much help at such times, though I shall always be personally grateful to the Church of England for keeping Christianity at bay for so long. Miracles are rare. Remember the story of the member of the congregation who rushed up to the Priest shouting, "Father, Father, a cripple just came into church and as he reached the altar threw away his crutches—I saw him." "It's a miracle," cried the Priest, "where is the man now?" "Lying unconscious in the aisle, Father, fell flat on his face."

Whenever disaster strikes I always feel the urge to shout with Balthazer Ginsberg, "Run for your lives! The dam has broken and the waters are coming down from Lahore."

Setbacks are depressing and do nothing to strengthen your character. That is one of those wholesome adages which the authorities think up for their own profit, like the so-called virtues of patience and hardwork. What sensible person does not want knowledge without difficulty, success without effort, progress without sacrifice? Some have the priceless ability to laugh at the misfortune of others and it keeps them happy twenty-four hours a day, despite all afflictions.

In 1978 my play *Laughter!* about state tyranny opened and almost simultaneously closed and it took me seven years to get my next play produced. We do not become stoics because reality is good and rational but because we feel powerless to affect events. Those of us who work in the theatre quickly come to believe that free-will is an illusion, not because the threads of fate are manipulated by half-mad gods or even madder stage-directors but because chance alone runs the show. It is action without cause, reason, or excuse. We invent causes, reasons, and excuses later in order to assign responsibility and guilt.

It is as well to remember the public will always applaud others and not oneself, not because it is stupid or misguided but because statistically it must be on the side of the ordinary. There are so many of them, and they naturally want to hear about themselves. After all why shouldn't they? It is not a matter for gloom. And if it is, then one thinks of one's own heroes and heroines and draws comfort. I have many.

There is the woman who hired a hearse and drove it around Westminster and the Houses of Parliament shouting, "Bring out your dead!"; the Irish performer who entered in black-face, kilt, and orange fright wig singing "Danny Boy"; Machiavelli who after being tortured wrote to a friend, "I acted so well that I felt a certain tenderness towards myself"; Hugh MacDiarmid who wore a fur coat to keep out the sun and having polled only 127 votes against Sir Alec Douglas Home's 16,659 in a by-election took his opponent to court for being a zombie; Robert Damies who tried to kill Louis XV with a penknife and when he was sentenced to have his right hand burnt off and boiling pitch poured into his wound and then to be torn apart by horses commented, "It's going to be a hard day"; George Serge who after a lifetime dedicated to the Revolution died in Mexico with the soles of his shoes tied with string; the courtesan Phyone prosecuted on a capital charge, and seeing that the judges were sure to condemn her, ripped open her blouse to show her breasts during the summing up and was acquitted.

There is no substitute for style. William Saroyan's last words on his deathbed were "Now what?!" Life's what we do and what is done to us, but style can help make it bearable. That survives and feeds the centuries. I just wish I had a little more of it.

Peter Barnes. Born 10 January 1931, Bow Road, London. Educated at Stroud Grammar School and Clacton-on-Sea Grammar School. This is true as far as it goes. I *was* born in Bow, within the sound of Bow Bells which makes me an authentic Cockney. But I never heard them ring. My family left London when I was a baby and I grew up in Clacton-on-Sea, a down-market, schizophrenic seaside resort on the east coast. I write schizophrenic because it was packed with holiday-makers in the summer and deserted in the winter when the wind howled through empty beach huts and forsaken putting greens.

My parents worked in amusement arcades and later owned two cafes on the seafront along with the cockles and whelks stalls, the beach chairs, Punch and Judy booth, and sand artists. These would draw, with a pointed stick, elegant compositions in the wet sand usually of a patriotic nature, Union Jacks and lions rampant, when the tide was out. They worked next to seafront photographers who would charge for taking snaps when they actually had no film in the camera. Then there were the fishermen selling freshly caught fish on the water's edge which they had bought earlier that morning from the town fishmongers. Along with the cries from the passers in speed boats and on the helter-skelter were those from contestants in the national newspaper competition yelling at strangers, "You are Lobby Lud, and I claim my £10 reward!"

One of the amusement games on the pier operated by my father consisted of a wooden railway sleeper with large nails. The customer paid sixpence and had three chances to knock the nail in so the nailhead was flush with the wooden surface. This is more difficult than it sounds. The blows have to be exact as well as strong otherwise the nail goes in crooked. The game was popular and the spectacle of men paying sixpence for the privilege of frenziedly banging a nail into a block of wood in order to win a prize they would never have considered buying remains a potent image of human futility and cupidity. Or perhaps an image of the writer himself forever banging away at a nail and always missing. You have to hit it just right to win a prize. And when you do the

prize turns out to be something you did not want in the first place.

Much is made of this colourful background as an explanation of the carnival aspect of my plays with their characteristic mixture of songs, dances, music-hall jokes, and routines. It fits into one of those pigeon holes that critics need to make sense of the messy inconsistencies of artists who are rarely all of a piece in their work or their lives. My pigeon hole for what it is worth seems to be that of a maverick intellectual with roots in popular culture. Of course one cannot be responsible for faulty perception. Certain Royal Shakespeare Company directors who went down to Nottingham to see my first major production, *The Ruling Class,* came with the impression I was some untutored farmhand from the provinces. But they have never been noted for their grasp of reality or artistic insight ever since one of them believed he actually bumped into Leavis on his way to a lecture.

The problem with my carnival background is that it is both true and untrue. Those sights and sounds of the sea and amusement arcades, donkey rides, Punch and Judy shows, ice-cream salesmen, dodgem rides, speed-boats and sailing boats were all there, around and about me. That is me capturing a world in words as if they were enough, as if that were all there was to it. But I saw and heard very little of it. I was always reading. I tried to ignore what was going on around me and I usually succeeded. The outside world of the seaside resort even in summer was always dim. I am conjuring it up now more vividly than I experienced it when I was actually living it.

The power and glory of reading comes from moments of illumination when it clarifies the life one is living. All the clarification I had in my youth came from books and films—or rather movies. There is a difference. Films are a literary concept, movies are the real thing.

During the hottest days of the summer I would be in one of three local cinemas. More important to my development as a writer would be the movies of the late forties and early fifties than the sights and sounds of a small insignificant seaside resort on the east coast of England.

After leaving school I spent a couple of years as a local government official in London. I wrote film criticism for the local in-house magazine before becoming a freelance film critic for *Films & Filming* and other magazines.

The great advantage of being a reviewer in the 1950s was that at most of the press screenings, the film company would provide free food and drink.

"I like the Eiger, it has authority," Cornwall, 1967

The screenings took place, Monday to Thursday, mornings and afternoons on a good week. So with any luck I would eat well and cheaply—that is to say free—at the expense of MGM, Rank, or RKO, and they could afford it. If memory serves, and it usually doesn't, MGM provided the best lunches, Warners the best movies.

Another text: a short story published in *The New Reasoner* in the winter of 1958—this was—is—a left-wing magazine of political theory which sometimes published short stories. This is as near an autobiographical piece as I ever wrote. Only the names are changed to protect the guilty.

Text 2

A SAFE JOB

My uncle Nathaniel was the man who threw a brick at Churchill in '29. He always regretted that he missed.

It happened when Churchill was making a campaign speech in the East End. The crowd got out of hand and tried to lynch him. Beating a hasty retreat to a waiting car, the politician was helped on his way by jeers, catcalls, and a badly aimed brick. My uncle threw it. He had been an active Socialist all his life.

This story was one of his favourites. There were others. Marching around Brixton Prison singing Socialist songs and waiting for George Lansbury to appear at one of the barred windows; getting Attlee elected the first Labour Mayor of Stepney; the pitched battles with Mosley's thugs. He made it all sound rowdy, colourful, and yet remote; something that had happened long ago, in another age, on another planet.

All my relatives were connected with the Young Labour Movement. There was nothing unusual about this. Anyone whose family lived in the East End during the years between the wars had similar memories. It was natural, like breathing, to belong to a Socialist Party of some sort. You were involved, because you were alive; a member of a community.

Uncle Nathaniel helped to create the Labour Party. You will not find his name in any of the histories of the period, but he, like thousands of other unknowns, sacrificed himself for the Movement. He gave it his complete devotion and love.

He knew Attlee and always spoke of him with respect. Morrison he never "took to"; I do not think he ever really trusted him. Bevin he grudgingly admired; Lansbury he adored. Like most East End Socialists, 39 Bow Road, Poplar, was an address he never forgot all his long life. For years, Uncle Nathaniel campaigned on endless, windy street-corners and in draughty, half-empty halls, on their behalf. Now, those that are still alive do not even remember his name. But then, why should they? There were so many just like him in those early days. They did not expect recognition. What they did, they did for the Movement.

For a short time, Uncle Nathaniel was a member of the Stepney Borough Council. He never spoke about it much, except to mention he was on the Library Committee and made sure that the Borough Library was one of the best in London. He was not a particularly avid reader, except of the novels of Jack London, whom he had known personally. But he believed that books, and for him books meant education, were important.

He lived most of his life in a poky four-roomed house behind Charrington's Brewery, just off the Whitechapel Road. The whole area is being pulled down now and the quiet back streets are deserted. But in my uncle's day it was a teeming community. Every morning for over sixty years he was awakened by the rattle of beer barrels over cobble-stones and the clatter of sliding hoofs as massive drays trundled off with their loads.

In 1939 the war came and England changed. Everything changed. My uncle gave up active political work. Naturally, if the local Party asked him for help, he gave it willingly. But for the rest, he would leave it to the youngsters.

When Labour came to power in '45, he was happy. So they did not do all that was expected of them: Uncle Nathaniel was too old to expect miracles. Besides, there was his son Harry to think of. The boy was going up to University and my uncle doted on him.

As the years passed, he took less and less interest in politics. He knew none of the new Party men; the men from Winchester and Eton. Who were they anyway?

"White collars and white hands," he would snap. "Never done a day's work in their lives."

But the beliefs of a lifetime could not be destroyed. When the Tories slithered back in my uncle spat disgustedly and moped about the house for days. Years of Tory rule did not soften his attitude.

Three weeks ago I saw Uncle Nathaniel for the last time. He seemed to have grown old, all at once. All the years I could remember, he had been a broad, robust man, well over six feet in height, with iron grey hair and strong, nicotined fingers. Now he had shrunk. The skin around his neck and under his chin hung in wrinkled folds; old man's skin.

He sat in his favourite armchair in the small over-furnished living room, which had not changed much in sixty years except that there was now a television set stuck in one corner. On the cluttered mantelpiece stood a picture of his son Harry, in Air Force uniform.

My aunt brought in two cups of tea and then left us alone to talk.

I opened the conversation with, "Unemployment's rising. Things are beginning to look bad." I knew he still liked to discuss politics.

"What do you expect? They're in aren't they? This is what they like. They've been afraid to do it up till now. Now they don't care."

He took a large mouthful of hot tea and swallowed it with noisy enjoyment. Uncle Nathaniel liked it hot and sweet.

"How are things with you, Uncle?" He was still working as a timekeeper in the docks.

"Bad. Forty stood off last week. There'll be more."

I grunted.

"How's Harry?"

Uncle Nathaniel did not answer at once. He finished his tea, put the cup and saucer on the table and wiped his mouth with the hardened palm of his hand.

"Anything wrong?"

"No, why do you say that?"

"Thought there might be. Harry's all right, isn't he?"

"Yes, yes. He's a Flying Officer now, you know?"

"Really? Where's he stationed?"

"Germany. Just outside Munich. But we get letters from him from all over the place . . . all over the world. He's doing some sort of scientific work. It's all very hush-hush. Won't tell me anything about it. Still, he likes the work. His Ma and I miss him though."

"He'll be out soon. What is it now? Three, or is it four months to go?"

Uncle Nathaniel shook his weighty head deliberately.

"No. He's signed on for another seven years. Didn't you know?"

"When did this happen?"

"A couple of weeks ago."

"What—did he do it without you knowing? I mean . . ."

"No, I knew all about it. So did his mother. We had a long talk about it. He left the final decision to me. He's a good boy like that . . . They'd got this good job waiting for him if he signed on. You know, it's a fine life in there now if you're a regular."

"Um . . . ," I said doubtfully. "Does he really like it then?"

"Yes, he does. That's the point. He'd made up his mind to stay in anyway. But I suppose if I'd said no he'd have . . . well . . ."

Uncle Nathaniel paused and lit a cigarette. He began coughing violently. It was a real smoker's cough, harsh, dry, and rasping, but he affected not to notice it. After the paroxysm had past, he continued.

"Everything's done for him. He's got his own batman. He doesn't have to lift a finger. Then there's free transport all over the world. He'll get to see places you and I'll never see.

"It's a good secure job," he added emphatically.

I was still doubtful.

"Yes, I suppose so. I hated it, of course. But if he really likes that sort of life . . ."

Uncle Nathaniel interjected quickly.

"Just what I said . . . And it's a safe job, that's what's important. It doesn't matter what happens outside. At the end of it he'll have a good pension and still be young enough to start something else."

I smiled slightly. I understood what he meant. My own parents had drummed that into me since childhood; get a safe job, one that was permanent, with a pension at the end.

"A safe job. You should hear my mother on that subject," I said ruefully.

Uncle Nathaniel growled, his heavy head jerking forward angrily.

"It's not funny. If you'd tried raising a family before the war you'd know what it means to be out of work."

He leaned back in his chair, his weak eyes focused mistily on the wall mirror just above my head. Of late he had become addicted to oracular pronouncements of various sorts. This could be easily excused. He was nearing seventy.

"It's coming again. Mark my words. I know the signs. 'Recession'—what does that mean, eh? Words, words, that's what it always starts with. First there's just a few out of work, like now. Nothing to worry about they say. I've heard that before! Then a few more get pushed on the dole. So it goes on. You watch 'em start bleating about 'trade balances' and

'bank rates.' Words, words, that's all they are. Now they're forcing us to strike. That's a sure sign of what's coming. We've had it all before."

His gritty voice rose sharply.

"It's going to be like it was before! Those bastards'll see to that!"

I was frightened. I did not like to admit it, but I was.

"Christ, you really think it might . . . no, it can't happen . . . not now . . . not like it was in the thirties."

"You don't know. You don't remember."

He stopped and looked straight at me.

"Anyway, that's why I told Harry to sign on. Whatever happens he'll be all right. He'll have three square meals a day and a pay cheque at the end of every week."

Recovering from my panic I muttered uneasily:

"Yes, I know how you feel. It's just that . . . well, you know what I think of the Services."

Uncle Nathaniel finished his cigarette and flung the stub into the grate. He rubbed his watery eyes heavily with his left hand. Suddenly he looked small and grey; a wizened old man.

"Me too," he said slowly. "All my life. The army—that's what we've always been against."

He began reminiscing.

"I told you what it was like in the First World War. That was bad enough, but then there was the General Strike. You don't remember that, of course. They brought in the army to break it you know. A lot of those soldiers were working-class lads too, the bastards! I remember one young officer, thin as a rake he was . . . he carried a riding crop or something . . . kept bending it between his hands. Anyway, he ordered an army lorry to drive straight through one of our picket lines. A couple of our lads got badly hurt. I think it was all a big game to that young officer. I'll bet he enjoyed himself . . ." He trailed off.

"Anyway, Harry's in the Air Force," I said encouragingly.

"Yes, but . . . I feel the same as you. Have done all my life. But it's a safe job. I've got to think of the boy's future."

He slapped the arm of his chair violently.

"It's a safe job! That's what's important!"

Suddenly I wanted to leave.

"Well, time to push off. Train to catch you know."

Uncle Nathaniel called into the kitchen.

"Mother! Peter's leaving!"

My aunt hustled in.

"Oh, so soon? We don't see enough of you."

I said awkwardly: "Why don't you come down to my place one evening? It'd be like old times and Janet'd love to see you."

My aunt smiled.

"Yes, we might do that. It gets a bit lonely, just Dad and me."

As I stood at the open street door saying good-bye, Uncle Nathaniel came hurrying out of the living-room carrying an old, clothbound book. Handing it to me he growled:

"This is the one you asked for."

I looked at the title: Jack London's *The People of the Abyss.*

"Yes, that's the one."

"There's an inscription inside," he muttered proudly.

On the flyleaf, scrawled in faded red ink, were the words: "To my youthful guide through the abyss. With love and respect, Jack London."

"It's very fine, Uncle. Don't worry. I'll look after it. You can have it back the next time I see you. I promise."

"No, I want you to keep it."

"But . . ."

"Take it. I said I wanted you to," he insisted testily. I knew he meant it. There was no point in arguing so I thanked him and left.

My aunt and uncle stood waving to me as I walked away from the house. At the end of the street I turned for a last look. The gaunt figure of Uncle Nathaniel now remained alone in the open doorway. I waved to him and he nodded slightly in response.

From far away I heard the muffled rumble of another old house falling. A thick cloud of dust rose slowly above the distant rooftops.

Clutching the book tightly, I turned the corner and hurried away.

Film story-editors read written works of all description for potential movie material. Such works, novels, plays, original scripts, have to be synopsised for the producers into a page or less. Producers rarely have time to read anything over a page, unless it is a contract.

During my period as story-editor for Warwick Films I would get through at least two novels a day

"I'm innocent, Your Honour, I was led to believe I was above the law," Canterbury, 1973

plus assorted scripts. This was done by speed-reading the centre of each page, and the blurb on the dust cover. Film companies are not interested in style, only plot and character. The better the material the longer it took it to read and the less suitable it was for filming. It is roughly true that pulp fiction makes for a better movie than literature. Sometimes the only difference is that one is hyped by the publicity departments, the other by academic departments.

In Robert Parrish's charming volume of memoirs *Hollywood Isn't What It Was* there is a chapter called "Good Cop and Bad Cop." It deals with the two executive producers of Warwick Films, Cubby Broccoli and the unnamed but unmistakable Irving Allen. Parrish points out the contrast between the two men, Broccoli quiet and understanding, Allen loudmouth and boorish. This was true as far as it went—about five linear feet. Broccoli was a most sympathetic producer but Allen was something more than an uncouth philistine.

He had made one of the first antifascist documentaries before it was fashionable to be antifascist. After the war Allen and a few American film technicians formed an independent production company to make a number of small budget movies. One of them which Allen directed called *Strange Adventure* with Eddie Albert was a romantic adventure story set in the Pacific. It was a movie of great purity and grace and, perhaps as a consequence, was a commercial failure and Allen, perhaps because of it, became a hard-nosed, commercial producer. Yet *Strange Adventure* showed a poetic talent, unfulfilled. Human beings aren't all of a piece and they remain unknown to others. And we can only know them from the outside—which is why I remain a dramatist. Allen suffered from a severe case of the Faulkner syndrome. So many American artists play the hard-drinking macho man to cover up artistic sensitivity which could be considered effeminate.

Another chapter in Parrish's book deals with the film *The Marseilles Contract* on which I did a couple of days rewriting. Parrish is very funny about an unnamed studio agent's obsession with toilet paper. The man in question is a producer friend of mine—witty, talented, ironic. I am sure he was as aware of the absurdity of the toilet paper mania as Parrish was. But it only shows the truth of the old saying—try not to use irony, people mistakenly take it at face value.

On leaving Warwick Films in 1959 I devised, as Programme Director, a huge comedy season for the National Film Theatre called "100 Clowns." This is the introduction for the season:

Text 3

100 CLOWNS

This Season will survey the work of some of the screen's greatest international clowns from Mexico, Sweden, Czechoslovakia, Hungary, America, and Britain. The achievement of comics as diverse as W. C. Fields and Cantinflas, Nils Poppe and the Marx Brothers, Voscovic and Werich, and Laurel and Hardy, will be compared and contrasted.

Except for the lucky few, the work of most comedians, however good, is usually relegated to the bottom of the film critic's weekly review. For some reason comedy can be dismissed in a few patronising lines whilst a "serious" film, however routine, must be dealt with at length. Yet comedy is as difficult to achieve as tragedy. Both are aristocratic forms requiring immense self-discipline.

Comedy does not just happen. To become a true clown demands years of selfless devotion to the Comic Muse. When we see the inspired antics of a Buster Keaton, a Harry Langdon, a Will Hay, we laugh but rarely marvel. Yet it is marvellous that certain men, by so mastering a few basic techniques, can make us laugh at our overweening pretentions and conceit. The clowns must always be here to remind us that however high we aspire there is something basically ridiculous about mankind lost in a world they themselves have created.

The masters of comedy give us more, much more, than laughter. They show us a lost world of innocence, a world of tolerance, grace and wit. Their art is life-giving and true. We need them very much.

I then became a freelance scriptwriter. The mythical British Film Industry was going through one of its illusionary rejuvenations. Britain makes films but never has had and never will have a film industry. It doesn't take movies seriously.

I wrote a series of low-budget second-feature thrillers for Beaconsfield Studios. There is nothing to say about them. I learnt a craft progressing to first features and American mainstream comedies. I received credit for some of these and for others I did not. It is a familiar story. There is no point in naming the films in question, they crop up from time to time on late-night television, rising like a bad conscience to haunt me. No, that is not true. I reject them but am not ashamed of them. A writer has to learn his craft somewhere unless you are a Rimbaud, and look what happened to him.

It soon became apparent that the cliche that film is a director medium is true. One of the irritating problems about so many cliches is that they are true. That is why they are used so often. I would have liked to have become a film director, for one thing the power given them is intoxicating. And naturally it is an easy job. I mean it is easy to direct a film, you have so many experts protecting you from yourself. It is not easy to direct a great film but how many do that?

In my case it did not happen, though I had a postcard from Luis Buñuel signed Archibaldo de la Cruz. I interviewed the great Don Siegel when my tape recorder broke down so he invited me out to lunch instead and John Ford said I looked like an Irishman; I think he meant it as a compliment. Despite all these encouraging signs I did not become a film director—the stars were retrograde—until some thirty years later in 1989 when I directed two plays for television. That was on video of course, but near enough. I wonder what would have happened if . . .

But instead of the cossetted life of a film director—the studio cars, the paid trips, the secretaries and assistants, the hype and the hypocrisy—I began writing for the theatre. Even there, the director's life is made easy. I once asked the then director of the RSC, Trevor Nunn, when was the last time he rode in a bus or a subway train? He could not remember. But he knew about ordinary people didn't he? He saw them every morning and evening through the window of his chauffeur-driven car as he passed to and fro from the rehearsal room. Most stage and film directors know as much about ordinary people as D. H. Lawrence knew about sex, which is next to nothing.

I love lists and distrust adjectives and exclamation marks. I look for the similarity in opposites, the swirls of smoke over the Battersea Power Station and the whirls of a ballerina's skirt, the eddies of an estuary and the vectors of an iris.

My first play, *Time of the Barracudas* (1963), a black comedy about two professional murders, opened in San Francisco and closed in Los Angeles. Years later John Huston made a very successful film on the same theme called *Prizzi's Honor*. The only thing to be said about the production was that Laurence Harvey, in the lead, was absolutely right and everything else was absolutely wrong. The one positive thing that came out of the trip was that I met Stan Laurel. After talking to him, I at last knew what they meant by "grace."

My next piece, *Clap Hands Here Comes Charlie*, has never been produced. At the time it was considered too radical. Now I think it is too conservative. I had offers, particularly from actors who wanted to

play the lead but I have consistently refused to have it performed: a dubious decision smacking a little of arrogance. But I've always sincerely believed that all my plays are the best. That way I have survived some of the worst drama reviews. At least they seemed the worst to me. But if *Clap Hands Here Comes Charlie* finally saw the light of day and was greeted with the usual Hallelujah chorus of jeers, part of me would say maybe this time they are right though they've never been right before. *Clap Hands* is a monster one-character play where Charlie eats up everything in sight, including the play itself. It would only work in context: an early piece contrasted perhaps with something more mature, if that were possible. I have regrets. Charles has never been given the chance to live. Perhaps one day he will be let out to roar.

The spluttering start to my career as a dramatist continued with *Sclerosis* (1965), a comedy about a British torture unit in Cyprus directed by Charles Marowitz at the Traverse Theatre, Edinburgh, then transferred down to London for a Sunday-night club production for the RSC at the Aldwych Theatre.

The British Theatre censor was still in power so it had to be a private-members-only show. During it I heard the sound to which I was to become familiar during the coming years, that of seats being tipped back and customers shuffling out muttering angrily to themselves.

It had been different in Edinburgh. At the opening night the Traverse Theatre had, for some extraordinary reason, invited the Lord Provost. Afterwards he cornered me to talk about the play. I expected the worst, what with the stage beatings and torturing it was hardly Lord Provost material. But he said, "Good play. And true. They did that—and more."

"Who?" I asked.

"The English Army. They did that for years to Scotland. We know, don't we?"

Drama is a cooperation between the actor and the audience to recreate imaginatively an experience by the author. I became a recognised dramatist with *The Ruling Class* (1969), which took me a year to write. *The Bewitched* took two, so did *Laughter!* Years and years in the Reading Room of the British Museum, 10:00 A.M. to 5:00 P.M. Saturdays included. Has it really been worth it? What a mess . . .

You need patience as well as talent to write, a lot of patience and a lot of talent to write well. I needed the patience then. I was creating whole worlds, stone by stone. Now I try to tell stories. Which is one of the reasons why this autobiography of sorts is getting too anecdotal. It needs a stiffening of analysis and theory.

"When I speak, I expect people to listen and they don't," The Bewitched, *1974*

Like part of my notes from the publication of *The Real Long John Silver* (1986).

Text 4

Writing, not so much an expression of subjectivity but a search for new knowledge, new ways of seeing.

Writing which has a moral purpose in the service of politics; not politics as propaganda but, rather, teaching by example.

Writing in which reality's concreteness is worked on, but not dissolved by making it abstract or butchered to fit some preconceived ideology. For that which lives by subject matter alone, quickly dies with it.

Writing to convey a knowledge which is not empirical information which the author possesses but judgement which he or she has gained by writing; a judgement which perhaps provides within itself the capacity for action, if not immediately, then later.

Ultimate complexity of thought and language with absolute clarity of expression.

The fear that might hold me back from going too far in a sentence is only another example of unconscious control and therefore artistic stupefaction.

A drama of extremes, trying to illuminate the truth as contradictory. Instead of eliminating those contradictions as untrue, they are emphasized; melancholy and joy, tragedy and comedy, the bathetic and the sublime are placed side by side. The similarity of such opposites is shown by such juxtapositions. What we call tragic or comic are, in fact, their opposites, for it is a principle of dialectical logic that what seems on the surface one thing, is essentially its opposite. So incompatible and widely contradictory elements are superimposed on each other till they are transformed into reality, which is itself made up of similar contradictory elements also existing side by side with each other.

Quotations taken out of their original context mean something different, placed in a different setting. This is one way to discover the new within the old.

To scrutinize certain concrete and conceptless details of life in such a way as to show their transcendental meaning, without for once leaving the empirical living world or forgetting the facts of life.

The value of art, which is other than given reality, must depend on how fitting the artistic form is to the content or idea which it expresses.

Why is there always a gap between the words and the things they conjure up?

A play has to be translated from the written text into sounds and movements, which means it has to be thought through and interpreted in order to exist. In the reproduction of a drama on stage, two moments of creation and interpretation exist simultaneously.

Theatre should be a passion for knowledge.

Writers in the process of imitating brute matter transform it so that it can now be read as an expression of social truth . . .

I have very little desire to actually go to see a new production of *The Ruling Class.* It is the only one of my plays I feel this way about. I could not see it done better; different yes, but not better. Productions of subsequent plays had their glories, some surpassing *The Ruling Class,* but they also had their abysses. *The Ruling Class* unlike human beings was all of a piece.

It was all pure chance, for when the cast assembled on that first day of rehearsal at Nottingham Playhouse and looked out of the window they saw the potential star, Christopher Plummer, stepping graciously into his chauffeur-driven car, and gliding silently away. He had gone and we were left without an actor to play the Earl of Gurney.

Then someone told the director, Stuart Burge, that Derek Godfrey had been seen at the theatre the previous evening. He was doing a radio programme nearby and had come to visit a friend. Derek was contacted, given a script, and started work next morning. Chance, pure chance.

I was going to write the rest is history. It is not. The play was a critical success and Derek gave an extraordinary performance in the lead. One of my stage directions had him entering playing a flute. Only Derek went one better and entered playing it through his right nostril. The irony is that the audience and of course the critics never noticed.

Some artists make it look too easy. They are too good for their own good. In truth Derek had a fault—one I recognise only too well. He wanted to be famous but was unable to make the compromises needed. He expected fame to just happen, as a reward for boundless talent. It does not work like that. Virtue is never its own reward, drums have to be beaten, trumpets blown—your own if necessary—but

Derek was always too fastidious to shout. It is always easier if you have a product that has nothing to do with who you are, but for an actor—and others—fame only comes when you can market yourself. Derek could not, all honour to him. But the consequence was that Peter O'Toole did the movie of *The Ruling Class.* It's a hard go.

In contrast to Derek Godfrey and myself, Charles Marowitz, the director of *Leonardo's Last Supper* and *Noonday Demons* (1969) and *Laughter!* (1978) had an awesome flair for publicity. When he married for the first time he told the press he had met his future wife in the toilet of an aircraft halfway across the Atlantic. It was not true so the Press printed it. Charles was a man of great gifts but none for friendship.

I will write about Anthony Jacobs, the actor who took over the part of Leonardo da Vinci in *Leonardo's Last Supper* at the last minute. The original had, like Plummer, walked out. Jacobs looked like Leonardo, believed himself to be Leonardo, and lived and slept in the Open Space Theatre so as not to lose the aura of Leonardo.

Later he would appear in Buddhist saffron robes and tell of a holiday where he lived alone as a hermit for weeks in the Black Forest, only coming out to get food and drink. One day he stumbled across a deserted castle. Going inside he saw on a table in the hallway a copy of a script *The Bewitched* by Peter Barnes.

It turned out later that Stuart Burge was spending a week's holiday as the guest of the owners of the castle and had left a copy of the script for them to read. Life is full of such seeming mysteries: world conspiracies can be built on them and they destroy reason. Jacobs died, where I do not know, we lost touch. He was, I think, too frightening.

I love actors. That is not as obvious a statement as it sounds. Many dramatists distrust them and the majority of directors dislike and fear them.

In 1979 I adapted and directed two plays of John Marston's, *Antonio and Mellida* and *Antonio's Revenge,* for Nottingham Playhouse under the title *Antonio.* In the middle of the first preview, one of the leads, Paul Hardwicke, had a heart attack and I found myself in a speeding ambulance, accompanying him to the nearest hospital.

The ambulance assistant suddenly leaned over and whispered, "Is he an actor?"

Now as Paul was lying on a stretcher in thick makeup and full Jacobean costume, it would have been difficult to guess what else he could have been.

"Yes, he's an actor," I said.

"On the stage, is he?"

"Oh, yes."

"On television?"

"Yes."

At that moment Paul rose from his stretcher and croaked, "I'm on the cover of this week's *TV Times,"* and fell back.

The ambulance assistant shouted excitedly to the driver, "Get a move on, he's on the cover of this week's *TV Times!"*

That's why actors are so splendid. Rain or shine, life or death, they always get their priorities right.

Though I am a comic writer I have always been uneasy about the comic muse. The easy generalisations about comedy being life-giving, and good for what ails the world, are just that, easy generalisations. Perhaps comedy is just another drug to make us bear those injustices we should eliminate and not bear. Laughter is for losers.

I sometimes feel like a man who stays up late every night reading and writing at a window lit by a solitary lamp. The lamp guides a gang of thieves up a rocky path outside to rape and murder.

After *The Ruling Class, Leonardo's Last Supper,* and *Noonday Demons,* I thought it would be easy to get my plays produced. Not in England, friends, where never is heard an encouraging word and the skies are cloudy all day. In Europe, writers prove themselves once. On this offshore island, once is never enough and is soon forgotten. That's why TV is such a truly English medium, it is forgotten even as it is being broadcast.

This is about the time my relationship with the RSC really began. *The Bewitched* (1974)—together with *Lament for Armenians and Grey Viruses* (1984)—contains some of my best work. At least I think so. I am probably wrong.

I know in writing it I was fully stretched. It's an ocean, rich with plankton. If I was less lazy there would have been more such plays. But to what purpose? *The Bewitched* was, after all, greeted with calls for the Government to withdraw the RSC's subsidy.

It was my first production with the RSC and my relationship with them has always been fraught. Is that the word? When I say "with the RSC" I really mean with the artistic directors Terry Hands and, to a lesser extent, Trevor Nunn. I never met any of the other directors. It was hardly surprising. When it was suggested that, as most of them had been with the company twenty years or more, it was time for them to move on, I commented that if they were driven out of the RSC they would probably starve to death. I

mean, where would they go? How could they support themselves in the style to which they had become accustomed? Poor devils. Besides being a home of the drama the RSC was also a home-from-home for directors, a combination alms-house and charity ward. Out in the real world they would turn white and die.

After waiting seven years—that's easy to write but hard to endure—*Red Noses* (1985) was finally produced at the Barbican Theatre by the RSC. But it was only accepted, at last, because the actor Anthony Sher agreed to do it. Without his muscle the script would still be in some drawer, its edges nibbled by mice. As it was, the production was only given twenty performances and then taken off. Hardly a ringing endorsement.

The original Ur-text was called *Red Noses, Black Death* but after it had passed through the winter of Terry Hands's personality it became *Red Noses.*

My radio work sustained me artistically and was helpful too financially over the years. The adaptations of various foreign and Jacobean plays kept the dramatic muscles supple. The film director John Ford when asked how did he find new projects to film said that if he had any difficulty he just remade his old films. "The thing is to get down to the studio every morning and work." Good advice.

The short radio plays *Barnes' People* sprang out of a certain bloody-mindedness. Critics always complain of the length and complexity of my major works—"Long, and with such huge casts." So I did the opposite. What could be shorter and with a smaller cast than twenty-minute monologues?

I once asked in print some questions which I thought were pertinent to my work. Amongst them, where do the correct political tendency and the correct artistic tendency converge and is the purpose to produce valid art or to change society?

I answered the last question by saying that it was not a question because these were the same thing. However if the artistic technique is at fault does it mean that the revolutionary message is invalid? Does the purity of the artistic technique in itself correspond to its revolutionary message? In fact, is truth not just *what* is said, but *how?*

I had avoided television, or rather television had avoided me. I had written nothing for television since my apprentice days. I was none too eager and they had never asked. Until 1988, that is, when both the BBC and Channel 4 asked me to write and direct two plays, *The Spirit of Man* and *Nobody Here but Us Chickens.* They turned out to be two comedies cut from the same cloth as my stage plays.

What is the woof and warp of that cloth? I had best quote from the preface to my *Collected Plays* (1981). It can be Text 5 and a good way to end this article. I am becoming tired of writing about myself.

I have discovered writing even non-autobiography is like having your photograph taken. You lose part of your soul—it's being stolen from you. A thousand reading eyes know too much about you and you grow weak.

When you see or read a Barnes play you get the best of him. Not as he is, but how he would like to be: his aspirations and his dreams. That is what you are entitled to, the rest is trespassing.

Remember it is all lies. But the best lies, the truthful lies, are in the plays.

Text 5

Write what you know is good advice for journalists. I write what I imagine, believe, fear, think.

If there is one certain way of achieving absolute unpopularity it is by writing against the prevailing modes and pieties. With each new play I presented to disinterested parties I felt I was always starting from scratch. Here, the fact one may have written a number of major plays over the years counts for very little. I always had to persuade theatre directors, producers and agents that I knew what I was doing. They did not know. For them the theatre was a job, not their lives. Unfortunately I am passionate about it. And it *is* unfortunate. Fish trust the water and are cooked in it. Sometimes I'm not smart enough to be an idiot. Passion is an emotion you must never show if you want to be effective in England. Play it cool, understate, pretend to be an amateur who has just wandered into the arts by mistake. It is what puts the damp in walls and white hair on old men.

At the start I believed that it was enough to write well, everything would follow. It is not enough and it never has been. Few know what a well-written page is, with all the words looking in the same direction.

So what was I trying to do in these plays? I wanted to write a roller-coaster drama of hairpin bends; a drama of expertise and ecstasy balanced on a tightrope between the comic and tragic with a multifaceted fly-like vision where every line was dramatic and every scene a play in itself; a drama with a language so exact it would describe what the flame of a candle looked like after the candle had been blown out and so high-powered it could fuse telephone wires and have a direct impact on reality; a drama that made the surreal real, that went to the limit, then further, with no dead time, but with the speed of a seismograph recording an earthquake; a

drama of "The Garden of Earthly Delights" where a Lion, a Tinman, and a Scarecrow are always looking for a girl with ruby slippers; a drama glorifying differences, condemning hierarchies, that would rouse the dead to fight, always in the forefront of the struggle for the happiness of all mankind; an anti-boss drama for the shorn not the shearers.

The theatre is a thermometer of life but our theatre is a theatre without size or daring; a theatre without communion. It contains no miracles. The bread is never changed into flesh or the wine into blood. It is a theatre of carpet slippers.

"Well, change it then? Nothing's impossible."

"Have you tried juggling soot?"

There is no creativity, only discovery. If I return again and again to the same themes, like a child to the fire, it is because they are essential and I still owe them something. But whatever forms I use, whether it is the drama or the song lyric it is still, above all, *information*.

To strike out, to launch repeated bayonet attacks on naturalism, to write rigorously against the prevail-

"I'm making it, but not quite far enough,"
London, 1989

ence, history, fiction, and poetry), of some god-rapt human imperative.

So my Delta schoolmate Walker Percy wrote me, when he was working on *The Last Gentleman,* I on *The Half Gods* (having described his attempt as firing a precision rifle with telescopic sight): "We come from the same town, but we ain't plowing the same field. To foul the metaphor: yours is a very big gun with a massive charge of powder and I hope you can deliver on target without laying waste the surrounding countryside."

My thirty-year scrimmage with the Infernal Revenue of the United Snakes of America affords a comic example. One summer stay at Yaddo (retreat for musicians, artists, writers) I was prompted to explore the old reservoirs where fish swim through fanwort and milfoil. I bought the required gear, accomplished the mission, produced and sold a poem, "Rainsong of Fish and Birds" (see the *Five Chambered Heart).*

Next spring—with other expenses of teaching, travel, entertainment and study-groups, books, art books, scientific journals, music in score and phonograph records, photographing slides, recording tapes and keeping up equipment—I of course deducted the mask and snorkel. It seems to have been the straw that broke the auditor's back. I was summoned to a fat chestnut worm in Baltimore who had no notion how to be a thinker, teacher, universal writer, multimedia lecturer, yet believed he could disqualify for me all costs clouded by his ignorance. At the climax of a hot session, he hit on the diving mask: "Well, Mr. Bell, what is your profession? You're surely not a diver?"

I knew it was ill-advised, but I let him have it: "My profession is *being* Charles G. Bell, and there is almost nothing I do that does not contribute immediately and essentially to the carrying out of this important calling." His jaw as I spoke dropped lower and lower; and for twenty years thereafter I was continually investigated, to accumulate whole notebook files of no less ridiculous and ironic episodes.

What is the history of my fond attempt (Ulysses' "folle volo"—"mad flight") to bring all realms of knowledge into creative cognizance?

My Kentucky grandmother's great-great-uncle was Daniel Boone, from whom I have a powder gourd. My present task is to lead, as deftly as I can, over the Cumberland Gap of a life-road.

If I go back two generations, I find myself spanning the poles of Mississippi. My mother's family draws me to the washed-out Faulkner hills. My father's to my own cotton-rich and supposedly enlightened alluvial Delta.

No doubt I owe as much to my mother as to the Bells—her Norman Olivers and Archers come through Virginia to the slash-pine slopes in the northeast part of the state. Her father, Captain Archer, who fought in the Civil War (for States' Rights, he told her, his slaves freed), was at least represented in our library by his sword. But both he and the mother had died when Nona Omega, "ninth and last," was young; so she had scant memories of them. Thus of all her kin she only enters here, as by miracle—a spring from the clay of those gullied fields, backward towns, hard-hit relatives. In the polarity of my birth her elements are air and water, cloud reflections on a mysterious pool.

But the activity, characters, tales, the tragicomic energies, swirl around the Greenville house where my father and Aunt Bessie were reared by my musing grandfather (who died before I was born) and his driving Kentucky firebrand of a wife. He had been a photographer before the Civil War in the Ohio basin, with an earlier family. When that broke up, he worked, after the war, with a portable studio, up and down the Mississippi, until, in a Kentucky river town, he won that child beauty, come for her portrait (as Fra Lippo Lippi finished his novitiate model with the picture), and took her down river to Greenville to set up house and studio.

In *The Married Land,* reversing the roles of male and female, he becomes the yielding mystery of air and water, she the drive and hardness of rock and fire. Let a picture pair (figures 1 and 2) revive the story of the old photographer, often harried to collect rents on her squalid properties—until once water took his part, time of the spring rise; when she came home raging against river, flood, destinies, above all that husband: "the most useless hulk of a man God ever sent to cumber the earth. While you sit here rocking and dreaming, our houses have gone in the river, that whole Poplar street row of houses. And the miserable sheriff, who was there watching, had the effrontery to tell me there was nothing he could do. Will you get up and go down there and act like a man, and make him do something? Do you understand me? The houses have caved off, gone in the river."

But the old man sat smiling and rocking, intoning to himself (though she heard and was brought to explosion): "Thank the merciful Lord; thank the blessed, merciful Lord."

How from that crossed engendering could a son (my father) but love more the ineffectual bearded photographer with the detached smile of art—love but fear to be like him, his life-ambitions formed and fired by the daemonic will of the mother? His maturation claims a photo pair (figures 3 and 4): from poetic dreamer, who had hoped in college he might become a scholar, thinker, writer; to lawyer politician, brought back by family debt to venture his idealism in the battle for power.

Now his elements are earth and fire; he searches the state, country, even abroad, and chooses for generative nexus (Sylph and Ondine memory of a dreaming father?) my nature-mystic mother (figure 5)—costly for him, but for the protagonist of *The Married Land,* ideal. A snapshot of me (figure 12) from the summer of 1947, when I was teaching at Black Mountain College, may conclude this series with the stamp I bear of that androgyny—treated, before *The Married Land,* in *Delta Return.* Thus "Gulf Memories" poises the mother, "Spirit of the South"—

In these clay hills my mother was born, like
A spring to flow through the Delta south to the
    sea—

against that "Spirit of the North," "the father-well of force." His trials shadow "The Columns," those "Faustian towers, crumbling of their own weight." Here the picture is of our house (figure 7), built for a wife who did not ask such outwardness:

Promethean father, child of the westward pride,
You beckon from these columns, white on red
Behind the green oak shadows—you whose end
Was bitterness, beckon and smile. And I climb
    the wide
Porch stairs under a roof tall and blue like the
sky.

From my earliest awareness of the creative polarity my life and thought must manifest, I tied its delight (Odyssean? Heraclitean?) to that tensile bonding of mother and father in my blood. Though the order of the joining should also be specified: in my fictional self the father's drive is embraced in a mother's quiet; in my brother's toss of the same coins

(tails, tails), her estranged sensibility meets the father's unrest.

Of my birth I cannot tell much, but that it occurred on Hallowe'en, 1916, at the height of the First World War. My cheerful state, perhaps a year and a half after, is exhibited in figure 6. My first memory cannot be from much later; since, as in the picture, I can just, by propping myself on my arms and shoulders, lean over and stare (it is late at night) into the flushed toilet of my mother's bathroom. The experience is not at all scatological but cosmic. What I see is a foaming vortex, clue to a Book of Knowledge quest of tornadoes, whirlpools, spiral nebulae. Surely it was the wonder of science which so imprinted my consciousness. Leonardo: "the sea at Piompino, all foaming water."

Despite that earlier recall, I have no memory of learning to read. When my mother, who taught us all before we went to school, began with my sister (at a normal age), I (though two years younger) joined in. When that sister, at six, went to first grade (we had no kindergarten), I tagged along; it seems no one could stop me. Though I wouldn't be five until Hallowe'en, I could read and write; at my father's suggestion the superintendent let me stay. Then my sister said she wasn't going to sit in the first grade with her baby brother; so she began in the second and skipped the third. Three years later, it was my younger brother's turn to take up the family tradition, though it didn't work as pleasantly for him as for me. I enjoyed singularity, was always adoring some tall long-haired girl, and the boys, very brotherly, treated me as a mascot.

Still, I came to a crisis by my second or third year. The cause was my father's saddling us with his unrealized life-ambitions. He had gone to the University of Mississippi when he was fourteen, and had graduated four years later with every honor. When family finances required his help in Greenville, he was made high-school teacher and, soon after, superintendent of education. Meanwhile he taught himself law (besides a lot of literature and history), was admitted to the bar, and over the next years served, mostly by appointment, as state representative, chancellor of the circuit court of appeals, and then as state senator. Dreaming no doubt of Washington and the White House, he resolved to clean up Mississippi by running, on his own, for governor, against Bilbo and his faction—Bilbo, "the very Gyves and Shackles of the State":

We heard a speech he made once in full-dress.
"You folks think I'm gettin rich in Jackson," he
    said;
"But I tell you, I'm so poor" (histing his tails)
"I have to patch my pants." He spun his rump:
In the new cloth were patches of bright red.
The crowd roared, and one spat, shifting a
    quid:
"That's a slick bastard; I'm going to vote for
    him."

(Delta Return)

It was the wreck of my father's public (and financial) hopes—of which, unwittingly, he made us legatees.

The first move was to keep our grades straight A's—what he called "passing." After sitting all day in the schools, we were to come home and prepare tomorrow's assignments, which he would hear when he returned that evening from the office. My sister and brother found no way out, though it was a terrible drag on body and spirit—even on the brain, since the teachers taught for the dullest, and if you knew the stuff already, you were being trained to waste time. Both of them got fat, unexercised, allergic, short of wind, physically incapacitated.

I was in despair, when an angel voice addressed me from the sky: "You can give him today's assignment as tomorrow's." That was all it took to make our public education stimulating. From the third grade through high school, I used the classes as they should be used. There was no time to waste. I ran to school. No more dawdling in the halls. I flung myself into my seat while the others were goofing off. Under desperate motivation I tried to do the lessons, solve the problems, memorize the poetry, before the teacher could discover I hadn't done my homework. I found I could read a poem two or three times and know it by heart. Of course such industry was conspicuous; a teacher would catch on now and then that Charley was doing the assignments in class. The daily grade would be marked down and, in a pinch, I might be given a note to apprise my father that I had come unprepared.

I walked home down an alley of old stables, garages, chicken-coops. There was a knothole in a

Figures 3 and 4. *Father, Percy Bell, as dreamer . . . as politician and judge*

Figure 5. *Mother, Nona Oliver Archer Bell*

clapboard structure where I filed those messages over the years. "Old Judge Bell, independent as a hog on ice" was hardly to be buttonholed by a teacher.

Afternoons I was free to run and play, climb trees, pore over *The Book of Knowledge* or, as I got older, take up my Tom and Huck heritage of the river and swamp woods. At night my father would hear what he thought was for tomorrow. When reports came in, the daily grades brought him to boil: B's, B minuses, a C plus sometimes. But the exams were always A. He couldn't fathom it. As I went to bed I would hear his voice from the study, addressing my mother in the high style of Southern oratory: "Suffering mother of God, that I should be cursed with an imbecile son! He seems to know the stuff at night; he must forget it before morning. But then how does he pass the exams? That's a mystery that won't bear looking into." Smiling like Adam "with superior Love," I fell asleep—and never told a soul.

Until I was finishing Virginia after three years, with all A's and a Rhodes Scholarship awarded—

when I thought my father might enjoy my stratagem. Misprision! Never was a man so keelhauled: "That you could have deceived me all those years." I claimed necessity, and that it had been for the best, that I had acquired will and independence, not to speak of a healthy running, swimming, and tree-climbing body. He groaned, "But to have lied to your father!"

All that time, when he had urged me to read Dickens and the rest, from a library rivalled in the state only by Will Percy's, while I pursued the passions of science—astronomy, physics, evolution—there was one author we supremely shared, Mark Twain, those river books, more real to me than life. Of course I remembered the time Huck marvels (never having been in such a situation before) whether the truth, for once, might not be safer than a lie.

Another groan. "To have lied . . ."

"Tell it to Huck Finn!" I said. My father knew the passage as well as I. He could only laugh, and that was the end of that.

Though reading *Tom* and *Huck* (and even the lugubrious Poe) until I knew them by heart, would hardly have prepared me for the speed-browsing I was going to need in college. But about the time I discovered the Tarzan books and began to go through our great oaks more like an ape than Weismuller could dream of, I also became aware of the erotica in my father's library. After exhausting Boccaccio, *Moll Flanders,* de Maupassant, I hit on the twenty-four-volume Burton translation of the *Arabian Nights* (with its footnotes). For years I went through it on the sly, perceptively searching and brain-filing what was relevant—practicing, without intention, that scholarly skill.

Years later, at my father's death, I inherited the set, and when my new wife, Danny, and I were at the University of Chicago, it was shelved high in the oak-paneled Tudor library. I wrote there after everyone else was asleep. One night I wanted to refer to the story where a lady goes into the woods to couple with a bear. I climbed to the shelf and pulled out volume four. For the first time it opened to the back flyleaf, and there in my father's scratchy hand was a row of figures, all the page numbers of all the passages I had sifted so long and laboriously to cull. The same with every volume. What if I had hit on that in adolescence? I wouldn't have been ready for college, and my life would have been incalculably otherwise. If what education needs is motivation, no wonder I have written so many poems in praise of Eros:

Neighborly

She's like an apple tree
　　that leans
　　　　over the wall;

She belongs to him
　　but her fruits fall
　　　　to me.

What that Delta boyhood brought to the ambivalence of my blood is hard to assess: the passions of a symbolic landscape, cloud-heaped sunsets over the River, the Great Flood of 1927, when through the long cold wait on the levee for a barge, I curled up like a dog in a small box, slept, and waked fresh when everybody else was worn to a frazzle—an ease of relaxation natural to me. To which add the energy of our classes, races, Blacks, the drama of heroes and villains in the battle of right against Klan; the ferment which produced, in that little circle of my coevals, Shelby Foote and Walker Percy; the telescope and astronomy books I got before I was fourteen, and pursued for years, night after night, so that the sky still surprises me with the love and knowledge of worlds in space. And there was the fortune which taught me before 1933 the complementarity of light, as formulably both particle and wave—a creative opposition archetypal to my being, thought, and action. In comic support of which there was our old English teacher Miss Hawkins, called "Hawkeye," who to every searching question would answer "Well, Yes; and then again, No." She proved mostly right in the end. As I have later phrased it: "A question well suspended is worth twenty badly answered."

At the age of sixteen I went to the University of Virginia, where my boyhood battle for my own way turned somehow to the discipline of books. When, at the end of the fall term, I got on the dean's list and had, by the gentleman's privilege of the university, no required class attendance, but only to stand quizes and exams, I knew that by taking more and more courses, I could finish college in three years instead of four. I had only to stay up all night before tests, memorize everything, and so make a hundred. I would even have time to spare. But I didn't know how much the first course I added would cost me in life-devotion.

It was Stringfellow Barr's History of the Ancient World, which his lectures turned into the provocation of Spenglerian cycles in world culture—a thing he deplored but could not answer and so unloaded onto us: "If you can't disprove it, then (as Spengler says) 'bare your necks to the blade!'"

After a week or so I went up to argue with him, citing the Century of Progress Fair, which I had just seen in Chicago, as proof of a new culture, new philosophy, science, architecture, even the thrilling art of the color-organ. In three minutes Barr performed the most concentrated piece of teaching on record: The buildings, he said, were mostly of cardboard; so the architecture smacked of Alexandrian pleasure pavilions. "As for the color-organ, it's a fad; but Bach is real; Beethoven is real." He summed it up: "You can't argue about history unless you know the artifacts."

So I had to know them. It wasn't that I knocked under to Barr and Spengler; I joined the battle on both sides. Mississippi politics and the Depression had raised such doubts. My last year in high school I won first prize in the state with a yellocution on what Roosevelt had called the "Forgotten Man"—mine

Figure 6. *Charles G. Bell III, Spring 1918*

the manifesto of a socialism I thought I had invented. There the cyclical wheel had shared with the formative arrow (time only to be conceived as a clockwork recurrence reaching from the garnered past to a creative future). Anyway, the day I tackled Barr my life was changed, opened from the usual sciences to a total science (and poetry) of cosmic and human action. Barr had fired me to such a life-search, I no longer seemed to need even his classes; though I would always honor him as my teacher.

On top of the quiz and lab work required for my accelerated bachelor of science, I now followed a program of my own. I read two books a week from a pamphlet listing world literature. For art I began to visit that section of the library and to put on my walls such prints as I could acquire (Khafre of the Old Kingdom against Ikhnaton of the New). For music I went to the Carnegie Room to hear requested records and grope my way through the scores. By my third year, against the adagios of late romantic indulgence, I had set Beethoven, Mozart, Haydn, the great counterpoint of Bach and (lately discovered) the mystery of Solesmes Gregorian. For writing I not only took composition every year, with other English courses to relieve the math and physics, but kept a journal in which I recorded what I was experiencing without and within. I would stay up all night two or three times a week—for exams, on principle; for my own reading, from pleasure.

I would start one of Shakespeare's plays about midnight, when I had done my other work, and finish it as dawn poured robins' song in the bowl of Albermarle. When I opened Milton I was so caught by the roll of heroic verse that I read all that night, all the next day (but for one meal) and most of the night following, absorbing, at a sitting, *Paradise Lost, Paradise Regained,* and *Sampson Agonistes.* For years after, when I tried to write serious prose, it would come out iambic pentameter; and friends still inquire why my recorded shows slip so often into blank verse.

Meanwhile, for my natural exercise, I ran and walked in the Ragged Mountains, declaiming the poetry I had memorized—most of an anthology, from Middle English down, but especially Milton, Coleridge, the odes of Wordsworth, Keats, and Shelley. For gym I submitted, as my father urged, to fisticuffs. I had been dieting for years, not to be fat like the rest of my family, and now, living on one meal a day, plus milk and apples, I used to weigh in at about 117 pounds. I could not tell until I got on the scales the fate of that day. Below 118 I was Bantam and sparred with a little Creeping Jesus even slighter than I, whom I would beat around. Over the mark it

was Featherweight, and I was paired with a heavier and tougher Italian who could pound me to a pulp. Every boxing day was like a Last Judgment weighing of the soul. How well such libration attuned me to the unaccountability of divine will.

As may be inferred from my telling, Virginia was perfect for me. I left at nineteen, with a B.S. in physics, a little library of books read, a start at writing prose and verse, boundless motivation, and the grades that took me to Oxford.

At this point in my second novel, *The Half Gods,* a chapter on sex appears, called "In the Liver Vein" (*Love's Labour's Lost*) occasioned by a college-magazine purity test, on which a friend and I achieved so virginal a score that we ventured a two-weeks race, to see who could lose the most points in all categories. I won pants down. The story is extant (as Hamlet might say) and writ in choice English; so I do not retell it here. Yet something should be said of where I stood in the cloven matter of life's central drive.

On the purity test we had not counted kid-games. Of course little girls had come to our secret houses to make overtures with their apertures, and we boys had responded in our small way: five-year-old Ginny, thrown back, dress raised, insistently pointing, "Put it in! Put it in!"—while we stare in baffled inadequacy.

On the other hand, and with other girls, I hardly remember a time when I was not in love. One spring evening after school, my father found me sitting with a braided blond under a mulberry tree, singing (he said) some adoring composition of my own. The rift was already there, to be widened in that South to an ideal worship estranged from touch. Thus Victorian morality and the bawdy house, without which I could hardly have won the sin race. But where was the clue to a love-passionate mating procedure? What was required (as everywhere) was to knit the poles in a fabric of skill and luck, control and abandonment.

My scholarship was in physics. When I had settled in Exeter College, got my trunk and bags and warmed my feet a bit, I presented myself to a dour tutor appointed me in Magdalen. I told him of my Virginia experience, how I had carried physics with my right hand and the whole of culture with my ambidextrous left; that this being my great chance at languages, music and art, I aimed to do the same.

"Eauo, Mr. Beyuh," he told me, "deaun't be fadish. Physics is a demanding subject. You will spend all your time in the laboratory." I told him I would spend my vacations on the Continent pursuing my

Figure 7. *"Our house on Washington Avenue, Greenville, Mississippi"*

heritage. We parted. I petitioned to change my subject to English, the only other school I was prepared to read in. To celebrate my liberation, I bought a Nonesuch Blake and an Italian Dante at Parker's bookshop just below my window. Next day I had the luck of getting Nevill Coghill, in my own college, as tutor.

I took to him from the start. He had the large Medici print of Botticelli's *Spring* on the wall; his shelves were full of books I wanted to read, records (as of the late Beethoven quartets) I was just beginning to know. He set me to compare Chaucer's *Criseyde* and Boccaccio's *Filostrato* in the parallel text, and to write a paper for our next week's meeting. Day and night I revelled in it. He had me read the paper, smoked and smiled and said, "Very well. For next week try the Book of the Duchess." That glowing Chaucer time, I was also working, on my own, to fathom Dante's Italian.

About Thanksgiving, the woman who would become my first wife, my "married virgin," Mildred, appeared *en famille;* we fell in love and I read her, voicing and translating, the pocket tragedy of Paolo and Francesca. For Christmas, however, I went to

Florence, and fell in complementary love with the city, its art, language, the Palazzo Alberti with its pensione-daughter Gabriella, who began to teach me, in her gentle way, at once Dante and sublimation. (In the latter I was pretty well practiced.) My two novels, not to mention the unfinished *Third Kingdom,* have variously scrambled this history. A measure of my need, that I had hoped to persuade one love or the other, married or unmarried, to travel with me for the summer (and as I have written of the Florentine: "How could I tell her: / If you love me recklessly now, / You will have me for as long as husband?"); but before that, my younger brother, a freshman at Sewanee, had taken cyanide. So I spent the summer at home.

At your death I was abroad; I crossed
The ocean to a sad home. A grief unhouseled,
As from beyond the tomb, settled upon me.

I found myself at odd times sketching figures
For poetic lines: "Bound on a wheel
Of fire . . . tears like molten lead . . ." So I
Received your spirit. Brother of my blood,

Figure 8. *"Soul Freed,"* by Percy Bell, Jr., 1936

You haunt not this house only, world-wounded shade.

(Delta Return)

I had of course been absorbing my brother's poems and watercolors; here I set his death-love "Soul Freed" beside the "Soul Bound" I drew from Lear's lines (figures 8 and 9). Meanwhile I was probing for Coghill the tragic and comic tangles of Shakespeare, Donne, and the Restoration. For my health I swam across our partly diverted Mississippi (and back) every day. On my fall 1937 return, I wrote Coghill a paper on tragedy. It was the same "Mr. Bell" who read it to him, but he hailed me now as never before: "That's a first class paper! Let's drink a glass of sherry, and you call me Nevill and I'll call you Charles." I had witnessed another example of teaching.

That year, reading everything from Anglo-Saxon down, I also wrote poetry, much of a verse play, and went beyond my depth in Barr's project of correlating culture, though still without benefit of Medieval or Renaissance music. So I fell, on my own, into Nietzsche's blunder (though it makes no sense) that music must lag centuries behind everything else. Norrie Frye joined our group and we blazed our way through the glories of art from Graeco-Roman to the Renaissance. Blake, however, I was determined to crack for myself.

Easter, I went for Gregorian chant to Solesmes, seeking a form which had outlived the fall of Rome and might help in our foreseen destruction. There I met Simone Weil, and shared in a mystery of "Angel Boy" and "Devil Boy," which I thought to explore in the Mansard Window chapter of *The Half Gods,* though it remains insoluble. Summer term, my married love (now widowed) joined me, and then my mother and sister.

I took the B.A. exams so charged with assumed relations of literature to music and art, that I crossed out the printed questions to propose and answer my own on cultural history, which got me a begrudged third. Despite that, I was granted the graduate year, and with Edmund Blunden as advisor, did research and a thesis on Edward Fairfax, translator of Tasso and writer of eclogues (mostly lost), a fine poet, whom I have since done too little to refurbish.

European politics all this time was rising toward war through successive crises crucial to my later fiction. September 1938, we returned from Italy on troop-crowded trains over restless borders to England and the Sudeten crisis—a sporting ad in the London *Times* announcing: "You can still reach Czechoslovakia before the shooting season begins."

Christmas vacation 1938–39, it was up the Rhine from the glass-broken gutted synagogues of Cologne, I practicing German by haranguing everybody—emptying a room in the Karlsruhe Gallery, where Teutonic admirers of Grünewald's *Mocking and Crucifixion of Christ* heard my raised and warning voice: "Er ist eine Jude." And scrammed. The next day, inspecting the Siegfried Line constructions at Breisach on the Rhine, I was arrested at gun point and held five hours by bull-necked questioners, goaded by my jesting ironies—as if I had schemed it all for *The Half Gods,* to be published thirty years after.

Though what has won out over politics was the sudden expansion of *Symbolic History* when, returning through Paris, I went at 9:00 A.M. to the best record store and asked the attendant to set me up in one of those airless and windowless basement listening booths, with all the records by Anthologie Sonore, Lumen, L'Oisseau Lyre on which (I had learned) treasures of Medieval and Renaissance music had at last been explored—mostly by two expatriate Americans, Safford Cape from Missouri and Guillaume de Van (Billy Van) of Texas. "All of them, sir?" he queried. "Yes," I told him. "If they are what I hope, I'll buy the lot and take them back to England."

So I played through stacks of musical revelations, from the tenth into the seventeenth century—for which, correlating the arts and literature, I had searched five years in vain; and there they were: Leonin, Perotin, the Franconian, Ars Nova, Dunstable, Dufay, Ockeghem, Josquin, and all the rest. Every piece I played scored its character, name, and date into a cognizance long readied to receive it. I was fanning out from the great Gabrielli through the European radiants of his Venetian style, and had the whole scaffold of music history once and for all in my head, when the attendant reappeared, saying (in French): "I'm afraid you'll have to leave; we're closing now." —"What!" I cried, "You don't close for lunch?" —"Lunch, sir? It's five o'clock." The eight hours in that airless cubicle had been as vibrant as any in my life. It was right there that the fifty-year project of *Symbolic History,* conceived of Barr's spermatic logos, was born.

I took the records to Oxford and began playing them for everybody. Mildred had found me great digs in the gardener's cottage of Worcester College. Soon the history don of Worcester, Vere Somerset came, then brought a class to hear selections, with my burning discourse on resonances: Landini, with Petrarch and Boccaccio and the school of Giotto. He told me I couldn't go back to the States; I must stay with these treasures; he would get me a fellowship and I could do my work. But I was promised in marriage and had accepted a job at the Illinois bottom of the world from that Europe and Gothic; I could not change. It was long after, reading in Gordon's book *Eliot's Early Years,* that I felt the magnitude of my refusal. There Somerset is mentioned as one of the friends who sponsored the poet of *The Waste Land* at the baptismal font.

That last spring Mildred and I joined a French cruise to Greece, where my cyclical studies reached a

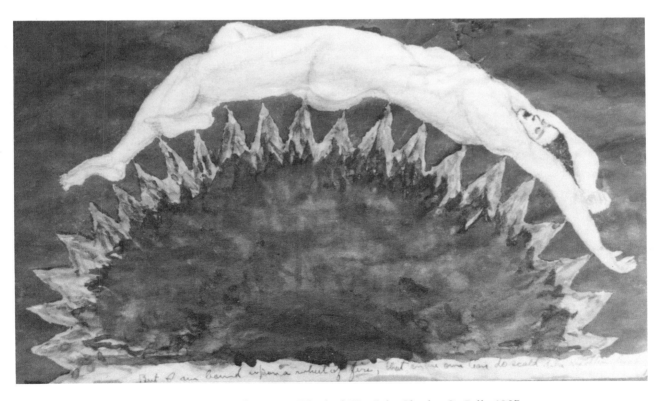

Figure 9. *"Bound upon a Wheel of Fire,"* by Charles G. Bell, 1937

kind of climax. A tour companion was Rolfe Humphries. I never caught names, and wrote him down, for his bald dome, as "The Man with the Head." Encountered twelve years later in Chicago, he would prompt and guide me toward publishing my poems.

Summer, as I waited for the oral on my Fairfax thesis, Mildred and I cycled over England on a tandem (tantrum, really). Then I got another degree and we made New York—though the German boat almost turned around in mid-Atlantic. What ensued was the train to Mississippi, Poland attacked, war declared, that first marriage celebrated, heedlessly consummated, then fructified, in Illinois: "Low light in the land of the living have ye, plainsmen, luckless plight."

The job I had been handed by Rodney Baine, my Rhodes friend who did not want it himself, was at Blackburn Junior College in Carlinville, Illinois—unlikely place for a world-historical aspirant. I taught English like a geyser and loved it, though only for a year. They had written of their need for culture, and surely I brought it; but need becomes a measure of the prompting to get that wise guy out of there. Happy when both can say: "The Lord giveth and the Lord taketh away; blessed be the name of the Lord."

The year gave me at least a signal boost. Kodachrome had just been released, and I began to make slides from all the art reproductions I had brought back from Europe, using them to accompany those records of early music Americans had not yet learned to listen to. I have been told when colleagues or friends would call, day or night, I would greet them, seat them; the shades would go down or the lights off, and for an hour or so I would play Gothic music with quotations and projected images. Light would be restored; I would shake their hands and tell them how good it was to have seen them. Before long, I was asked to give a lecture course (1939–40) for adults in the Springfield state library. *Symbolic History* had been conceived and born before; now it took tottering steps toward actuality—I, working the old toggle projector, groping in the dark to put on related records, quoting and improvising to tie it all together. I kept notes on what went well.

We spent the summer in the Delta—a saturated one hundred degrees where everybody wilted, but I rallied to the old motion of breast stroke, and walked and ran everywhere, eating figs down all the alleys. My father had always had devoted friends and enemies (typical, he had lately taken a Black sharecropper's case to the Supreme Court, and won it). When I gave a talk about politics and the Sermon on the Mount to his Bible class, it set the barber shops of Greenville buzzing with "Young Bell, Communist, Nazi, Pacifist, Nigger-lover" (the last two accusations not unfounded). Klan and Legion questioning secured me an FBI record which later prevented my lecturing in occupied Vienna. Though a friend who weathered the war in that Bureau has assured me my voluminous file is scrawled across the top: "Harmless crackpot."

September, Mildred and I went with little Nona (see figure 13) to the ample corn plains of Ames, Iowa. Such a winter bore down as I had not known before. How could it but thrill the spanner of antinomies?

Ten below is a good cold, the tread snow
Rings to the sole sheer crystal song . . .

Kenneth Boulding was a lively Quaker pacifist there. We read Augustine together in Latin. Among teachers and refugees I formed an Italian group for Dante; German for Goethe and Hölderlin; French for Racine and Baudelaire. I was photographing furiously in the art room of the library. Stringfellow Barr, with whom I was still in touch, had sent from St John's the study list of Great Books. At last I dove deep into philosophy, reading what stirred me to write my own. Not to mention my poetry, and now sketches for an autobiographical *War and Peace*. Meanwhile I graded 120 partly illiterate Freshman Comp papers every week. I was ordering microfilm scores of unrecorded old music and copying them for singing groups in which I played the recorders I had brought from England. I am still staggered at how much I did. No wonder that marriage was put to a strain. When the going was dark, I would bed down, long after midnight, with *Don Quixote*, read, and smile into blissful sleep.

No doubt Aristotle ripped off the Pre-Socratics; but to read searchingly is to digest and transform. So Pascal's vertiginous retreat from the contradictions of reason (as Kant's from his antinomies) became for me (after Blake and the wave-particle formulation of light) a Heraclitean celebration, Creative Paradox, a new discipline of thought, action, worship. Thus from the meditations of those years came the unifying polarities of my later works:

(1941) The life of humanity is a mansion too large for all parts to be kept in repair. Who would raise one wall must draw from the ruin of another. Thus creation destroys and destruction builds, and of every action there will stand opposing views, both, just and sound.

A point of departure for the tensile dramatizations of *Symbolic History.*

So from the March thunderstorms of 1944, my journal brought the core of an organic physics:

I walked into the woods and climbed a large oak, clouds boiling above, the batteries of lightning bursting around; sat with my shoulder to the twisting trunk and pondered the astonishing world. Having perceived the dilemma of Newton's laws, that mass resists motion only by moving, inertia and acceleration counterfaces of the same stress; having extended this through all realms of energy, observing the self-contradiction of Carnot's law of decay except as met by its validating antithesis, a creative will buttressing energy against its own fall and weaving from smaller ephemerids more embracing wholes, it came to me in that wind and downpour, that here was the key, the universal field in which man and world were strung. Returning home I wrote:

All matter, systems, worlds and living things express the need of energy to buttress against its own decay. In this sense cosmic history is a heightening and unfolding of the perceptive ambivalence of energy: that its activity is the fall by which it dies, its life in time a transcendence, using and used by the destructive urge.

After Pearl Harbor, Navy V-12 units were sent to Iowa State for schooling, and I was detailed to teach them physics. A limited assignment; yet the return to the classical laws in the light of my larger inquiry, heightened my philosophy of science as of history. I saw my life work in the form it has not veered from: a great organic tree. At the base was the philosophy of antinomy, with a methodology and outline of science. From that root system and resonant with its dialectic, *Symbolic History* was to rise, the unfolding of consciousness, attested by thought and the arts. From its last branchings a trilogy of novels must leaf out, symbolic transformation of experiences I had undergone or could appropriate. The whole

should be surrounded by a poetic mantle where the same metaphysical discourse would flower in things, acts, and images. At the volcanic and tornadic center, let the transformational epic of man and cosmos be the crown of my age.

From then until now I have worked at all these levels, though concentrating where patronage or publication seemed to offer some likelihood.

The return to science brought me an offer from Princeton University—it turned out, to do research on telemetering (at Ames I had done what I could for Atanasoff's first electronic computer). I left my family of Mildred (and as I told the draft board, two-and-a-half children) to explore the site. The first day, Sunday, I popped into the Parnassus Bookshop, as it would appear, unacknowledged cultural center of Princeton. Keene and Anne Fleck ferreted out that I was writing philosophy, poetry, fiction, and cultural history. They asked me for dinner, a walk by Carnegie Lake, and then for a piano rendition by some great European of Bach's *Art of Fugue.* I launched into German with a couple speaking it beside me. He proved the high-domed Frankl, art historian, who had distinguished Romanesque from Gothic as "Additiv" from "Divisiv." During intermission I discussed history as a causal probability, like the final four-subject fugue we were to hear, destinate where completed, indeterminate where Bach had dropped it. I asked them to join me in a German reading of Hegel's *Philosophie der Geschichte.* Next day we met at their house.

They told me, as the Flecks had, of Erich Kahler, who had just published *Man the Measure,* a great book in my line. Next night the European community was to meet at his house; they had spoken to him; I would be welcome. I went, talked with the host; he seated me by Einstein, idol of my earlier days. An old rhapsode intoned corny nineteenth-century ballads, where I had hoped for Goethe and Hölderlin. I told Kahler as much. He invited me for a quieter occasion. Though I begrudged any great work standing in my path, I took the pulse of Kahler and chose him for my Princeton father.

Research was dull, stalled at the end of a vacuum tube. But there was idle time. I had my papers and wrote reams: philosophy and fiction. I was not working on the bomb, although since the neutron one knew of the possibility. In *The Half Gods,* however, my alter ego discovers he is doing just that, and so enacts what all pacifists contemplated; he goes to jail in protest and expiation.

For me, the war ended and I was invited by Gerould, a gentle scholar, into the English department. My family of course had arrived from Iowa; that "half child" Deedie had joined Nona and Charlotte (see figure 13); and we had rented a house just across the street from Einstein, where my children would go to play, to the delight of the genial sage. With him, Frankl, and Kahler, I shared in a committee to win the Peace, one of those admirable attempts that never got the postwar gradient. As Einstein had broken with Heisenberg's dice-game, so he did with the dark probabilities of my "Studies in the Future" (unpublished). Yet Kahler could espouse a vision at the same time that he saw the blackest potentialities of Stalin and free enterprise cold war.

As if symptomatic of such shift of loyalties, my wife found and bought a fine old run-down house on Nassau street; we moved from opposite Einstein and found ourselves next door to the Kahlers, Erich and Lili.

I could go on with the congeniality of the great Europeans: Hermann Broch, who lived in Kahler's attic and asked me to help him with his first English writing, an Introduction to Bespaloff's *Homer;* Hermann Weyl, Kantian mathematician who had a poetry group at his house and from whom I have wonderful letters about the philosophic essays I sent him later in Switzerland; the Oppenheim-Erreras, who graciously invited us for the entertainment of visiting celebrities. And there were the art historians: Otto Benesch, who did the Rembrandt books and so much more, my closest friend after Kahler; Charles de Tolnay, Michelangelo man, who (with his wife) joined a Dante reading group which I had persuaded Giuliano Bonfante to lead; and of course there was Panofsky, whom I admired, but who hated the others so much that even I could not quite juggle the ambivalence.

Of Americans, Berryman and I were ironically close, though I let him affirm my Blake-mad cultural synthesis, without troubling him about my poetry, which was sure to outrage him. Bill Merwin was a student who came in the first weeks to read me his poems. "Don't ask what it means," he told me of the "Soldier Aristotle" misprint in Yeats; "feel the flow!" I felt with wonder Merwin's flow (since deepened and distilled by a life of poetic concern). Then Galway Kinnell appeared, more immediately attuned to my circuit. He hit on a poem of mine and, moved, showed me his first (Wordsworthian) sonnet, of which the closing couplet went off like a Vesuvius fountain

Figure 10. *"Professor swinging in a back-campus beech," Princeton, 1946*

in the room. "Anybody who could write that couplet," I said, "is a genius. You can do anything you're a mind to."

I had built up my slide collection fivefold by photographing in the Marquand Library; now I began to give shows at the Parnassus Bookshop, where Berryman used to read his poetry, complaining when hoarse of his "physical organ." My first audience included almost all the people I have mentioned, from Einstein down, and they seemed excited. I have never much needed an audience thereafter, having once enjoyed a great one.

But I was teaching in the English department, where no one shared in these foreign vagaries any more than in my tree climbing (figure 10, professor swinging through a Princeton beech). The sensitive Gerould had given way to Stauffer, who told me, trembling all over: "Your larger studies constitute a liability in this department." I pointed out that I had published (from my Fairfax thesis) as much as most of them lately; besides (though I did not mention it), I was admired as a teacher. But nothing could compensate for my not wasting time in the English club (I knew English already), or worse, arrogating beyond my competence in the shows (as if anybody had a secure competence in anything).

So I went hog wild, and when it was my turn to address the English faculty, instead of presenting some normal Fairfax criticism, I gave them (without benefit of slides or music) the densest abstract of my Philosophy of Paradox, with its overflow into an Outline of Period Styles. Old Root, who read his lectures from notebooks falling to pieces, left, crying: "Bell is mad!" Though I was not half as mad as I needed to be.

Kahler and John Berryman, however, were so moved that we went to Erich's and drank wine and talked much of the night; and John, without sleeping, got on the train and went to New York to tell the John D. Rockefeller people, whom he knew, that they had to give me a postwar grant, which they did, without my even applying. It was the spring of '48 before I took it and went abroad, photographing,

Figure 11. *"Idyll of Danny and Charles,"*
Little Pines Farm, 1948

now from the originals, for *Symbolic History*. And it was on the boat coming home—my first marriage long falling apart—that I met Diana Mason, to be celebrated as Lucy Woodruff in *The Married Land*. On account of which I have always been indebted to both those Johns.

But I have leapt ahead. The summer of '47 Erich got me invited to Black Mountain College to give my slide and music lectures. Galway took some of his navy stipend to follow me. I have treated all that in *The Married Land*, by my rule, of boosting the factual to the symbolic. Memory strips it to a moment, as I stood in line for a blood test, and when the nurse needled me, the plunger broke and blood spurted over the room. "You see," said a friend beside me, "you can't even give blood like a normal person, but there has to be a mix-up and explosion."

That fall, in Princeton, I was much with Galway, and in the spring I went abroad. The souring of marriage had stamped me with such hunger that through all the Rockefeller wandering I was caught in the magnetism of looks—only to back off, determined to weather and regain my family. So Danny and I on the boat settled for amity. We said good-bye as if forever. But Mildred had been wiser; she knew the union was irrecoverable. At the start of that last Princeton year, when she told me to leave the house, I stopped at the Parnassus bookshop and the Flecks rented me their attic, with board. I recalled the other address, Little Pines Farm, Maryland. So I began to move to firmer ground. Here a poem and a photo (figure 11) from that autumn:

Woodbird softly trilling from the maple spray
Red leaves above quiet waters
In the webs of sun.

This fall is my spring: down lost forest ways
Your frank eyes guide, the daughters
Of laughter run.

When I forget, my love, image of the light and
  spray,
Forget, eyes, earth and waters
And lose the sun.

But it was a long winter, with all the pangs of legal action and inaction. When Galway brought a sweetheart up to my heaped attic to meet the professor, she looked at the book-stacked bunk and refused to believe I lived there. "Where do you sleep?" she asked. "There, on that cot," I told her; "I clear the books off at night." She thought she had

Figure 12. *Charles G. Bell, Black Mountain, 1947*

me: "Where's your pillow?" she demanded. I never used a pillow those years; but what I said was: "My pillow is care." Galway told me that when he took her home she ran into the house crying: "O Mother, Mother, I've met a man whose pillow is care."

Meanwhile I had pulled my early poems, with a commentary on the model of Dante's *Vita Nuova,* into an autobiographical setting, a kind of Old Life, called *Sparks of Ego.* It would have been accepted by Erich's friend Kurt Wolff, but a smart American told him: "Wait for his Catholic conversion"—thinking a search like mine must end there. If that's the condition, the work will not be published. Also, with a contract from the University of Chicago, I had translated Goethe's *Elective Affinities,* but that too came to nothing.

My metaphysical genetics, however, got hammered into a dense little piece, "The Mechanistic Replacement of Purpose in Biology," showing such science analytically necessary and fruitful, though for synthesis, reductive and misleading:

Our axiom is only this, that the sum of any interacting, organized thing from the electron to the cosmos, transcends as a unity the parts which construct it, and, examined rationally, must be found to exist as well *in toto,* in essence, in spirit (a shocking word) as in the no more solid particles relationships and dependencies. If this is metaphysics, make the most of it. It is only what physics presents us in a world where, without this, not only we ourselves but the universe throughout dissolves into nothings within nothings, every substance to the last electron melting into mystery, a trail of manifestations, essential void crowning a phenomenal field.

That essay was published, January 1948, in *Philosophy of Science.* It won me friends from whom I received almost the only patronage of my life. John Vincent, of the old Chataqua line, had outgrown our orthodox genetics. He wrote, and hearing I was to embark, with no means, on a new marriage, invited me with Danny, children, and friends to use a farmhouse he had bought near his summer home in New Hampshire; we would meet from time to time over drinks to talk philosophy; meanwhile, the farm and a postwar Jeep were ours for the summer. It was a fine time: Galway came, great Europeans came, Aunt Bessie came from the Delta, and of course my three children from Princeton. Then it was farewell; Danny and I were headed for another place.

Typical of our universities that when I had overstepped my Princeton department, the only offer came from Chicago, Hutchins's undergraduate college of Aristotelian inquiry—free-shopping students rallying to a teacher who roused them, crowding a likely class with intense discussion—exciting indeed, but with twice the load of the Ivy League.

John Vincent, that summer, had asked where we planned to live. We had no notion. He told us the whole lower floor of the house William Rainey Harper, first Chicago president, had built on Woodlawn Avenue was empty, and that his sister, Isabel Vincent Harper, could let us have it for a song—her infinitely precious friendship thrown in. We took up residence. Isabel's daughter Jane, with the great George and small Overtons, lived above. How such a place and such life-friends eased our seven year affair with the begrimed, though still challenging, city of the Century of Progress.

Also in Chicago were Great Europeans, in touch with their Princeton peers. Of many, I was closest to the old Giuseppe Antonio Borgese, writer of Italian and English prose and poetry, who ought still to be known. His wife was the youngest daughter of Thomas Mann, Elisabeth, whose special earlobe the father loved to stroke in "Disorder and Early Sorrow." Their apartment was a meeting place for everyone from Hutchins down. It was there, at a party when Hutchins was resigning Chicago to be one of three directors of the Ford Foundation, that Borgese thrust out his lower lip and delivered a prophecy: "Well, Bop, when the elevator girls took us up to that top floor of yours, they would say: 'to God's office.' Remember what happened to God when he allowed himself to become one of a trinity—he was crucified!"

Borgese ran the Committee to Frame a World Constitution, with its journal *Common Cause,* in which he published two of my ambitious essays, thus bridging the way for others to appear in the six-language *Diogenes* sponsored by UNESCO—though the collection of such ventures in all disciplines, "See It Whole," has still to search for a publisher.

Our second year, when T. S. Eliot came to lecture on runcible spoons, it was from my Oxford tutor Coghill that he brought greetings. At the thronged reception, I thought to persuade him that the crown of his poetic career should be a translation of *The Divine Comedy.* Had he not given the best English sample of the mood and meter in his fourth *Quartet?* And unbelievably no translator has had a clue to Dante's shifting from what we would call pentameter to the Gothic lilt of four-stress endecasyllable:

　　　Con angélica vóce in súa favélla . . .

Eliot answered: he did not think he should do it, and for two reasons, one of humility and the other of pride. "Yes?" I said. —"Of humility: I don't know enough Italian." I doubted that: "You know as much as Pound!" —"And of pride," he pursued. —"Yes?" —"I think I might have better things to do."—"If you mean writing original poetry, I quite agree; if giving lectures on runcible spoons, I have to dissent." Then I asked him for lunch with some colleagues, in the oak-panelled Harper hall. He came; but I got nowhere with luring him to compare "Gerontian's" "Christ the Tiger" with Yeats's "what rough beast."

When Rolfe Humphries was scheduled to read, I went by chance and found "The Man with the Head" from the Greek cruise. He produced my name, came to supper, and took up my so far rejected poems. Their concentration stirred him, and he began to instruct me how to send them out and get them published. Our third year Bergstraesser chose me for guest professor in the exchange with Frankfort, where I taught American literature, wrote, and renewed my languages. I returned to a year-long Ford Grant, on which I struggled with *Symbolic History* (still thinking it had to be a five-tome word-hoard, instead of a sixty-hour set of multimedia shows). When that got slow, I yielded to poetry and had the satisfaction of placing most of what I wrote. In fact I sold so much poetry that year that Oscar Williams, visiting Isabella Gardner, called *me* commercial!

Truly my *Songs* and especially the *Delta* poems, seemed popular. The editor of *Ladies' Home Journal* (who within her range chose as perceptively as Rago of *Poetry*) bought, among others, my *Delta Return* mother poem; *Harper's* was running a picture-spread of three; even the *New Yorker* would have taken "The Gar," if I had let them cut the poor fish up as they wanted to. But I got tired of running such a stock exchange. Then the *Saturday Evening Post* (reputed to pay more than anybody) closed the comedy. They apologized, after keeping a bunch of those twenty-five-line *Delta* pieces a month or so; said they liked them, had hoped to work them in, but their rule was to use nothing in verse longer than thirteen lines (to squelch sonnets, I guess); and that besides being "too long," these pieces were also "too wide," and unfortunately "they had not quite overcome this double handicap." Small wonder I began to give up unsolicited submission.

All this while Galway Kinnell had been sending me his poems, which I sprinkled with suggestions and assurances of his power. Now he joined us and was made head of the Downtown Liberal Arts Center. Our working closely together was a boon to us both. I finished my first volume, *Songs for a New America,* and published it in 1953 with Indiana University Press. That summer I went to see my mother in the Delta, riding the bus to Greenville, then back to Little Pines Farm in Maryland, and so by train, with Danny and our girls, to Chicago. The whole way I was scribbling the sketches of what would form itself into *Delta Return.* As I added to the foreword of the revised edition:

Some days after we were settled again on Woodlawn Avenue, I opened the barely legible bundle to a page about our old servant Lethe, and saw that what had been jotted down as prose fell into pentameter, and that five lines revealed themselves in each of five stanzas. Now I studied the other scrawls and found that every one bore in latency the same shape; moreover, when they were arranged in the order of the journey, they formed five groups of five poems . . . Starting with five feet to the line, it was an array of five to the fifth power . . . By the next spring, teaching, and writing mostly after midnight, I had completed a triangle, or Delta, of such five-by-fives—more knit and philosophic, with a middle section like a dialectical pillar for the whole.

Since I had realized what my larger synthesis required (and modernity has commonly rejected)—a controlled poetic discourse, I chose for the title page a motto from Paul: "I will sing with the spirit and I will sing with the understanding also." Like all my claims, a bridged antinomy. The crux of life, thought and art: to precipitate the poles, and embrace both.

That finishing of *Delta Return* occupied the fifth Chicago year. Meanwhile, from the humanities-science link which Champ Ward, college dean, had hoped I would cultivate (and I tried; but Joe Schwab, another Mississippian, as jealously hostile as he was brilliant, blocked that), my teaching had gravitated to the synthesizing history of McNeill and Mackauer, fine men, and a searching course, but so disparaged in that Scholastic setting, that it was ominous to come to roost there. And the stir which followed my Michelangelo lecture, first garnered fruit of *Symbolic History,* attested how radically I had come to roost.

To my creative solace, the Clearing, on the wooded limestone bluffs over Green Bay in Wisconsin, invited me, several of those summers, to lead adult classes, for which they provided housing and meals—for us and our five daughters. You may see the daughters perched on Isabel Harper's porch rail (figure 13), as we head north from Chicago. And it was at the Door County retreat that I met Ann Markin, who would give her life in epistolary memoirs to Daren Leflore of *The Half Gods.*

Our seventh Chicago year was spent on loan to Puerto Rico. The chancellor of the University at Rio Piedras, was, like many of us, a fan of Hutchins; he wanted to found a Chicago program on an island where language skills (English or Spanish) were not up to the level of those books. So every year we were sending them a helper. The last had been Jim Gilbert (of the Humanities group around Gladys Campbell and Hal Haydon), one of the wonders of the college, an artist admired by a few and since his death neglected (though two housefuls of important paintings wait discovery)—Gilbert, our living old master, whose works have enriched my walls and life ever since. Born 1899 on the upper Mississippi and first trained in Chicago—when he wanted to go abroad and everyone was going to Paris, he paddled a canoe down river to New Orleans, sold it, and worked his way on a freighter to Spain. He painted in the Prado, absorbing into an American realist base Velàzquez and Goya. It put him afoot with Manet and early Cézanne. When he was on the street, painting a bold scene, an urchin observed him for some while. Gilbert's spirits rose, until the boy spat and saying, "Cago en la cara de Dios" (I shit in the face of God), walked away. For all that, Gilbert stuck to what may be called the Cézanne problem: how to interplay surface and depth, visible objects and abstract color forms. His conspiring to be neglected has been treated in *The Half Gods;* what is relevant here is that Gilbert preferred me as his Puerto Rican successor. He knew Spanish; I had to rape my Italian; it worked well enough, but Italian never forgives. I went down, took the blaze of sunlight on the palms, ate mangoes (akin to poison ivy) until my mouth swelled, while I searched out a place for my family.

My job was to build a Chicago honors program in Mayaguez, where the former College of Agriculture and Mechanical Arts was being upgraded. Besides classes, I taught teachers how to stir up Great Books seminars. With a few others I worked pretty hard; though everybody partied at beach joints on blood sausage and land crabs, drank beer or rum and danced the Cha-cha-cha with the secretaries. I grew up where the Blacks were dancing wild, but I never broke from ballroom formality until that year. It came easy therafter. I also invested loads of time, with flippers, mask and snorkel, on near and far reefs, become to all intents and purposes a sea-beast—one of life's great experiences. In spare moments I tried to seduce the tropics into short stories.

And now, for the first time the power-circle sought my continuance. We were having a marvelous year, but were leery of staying. The few books I had brought down were being tunneled by termites, and to move my library from the States seemed appalling. Moreover the little dive-bomber mosquitoes who carry elephantiasis were always active in the screenless houses; and when they zoomed under the table where I was trying to work, I dropped everything to swat them. To Kahler in Princeton I wrote it all, with my doubts about returning to Chicago, where the independents had lost ground. By the up-or-out system I had a year to fight for tenure, but it would have been against a competing friend; and my mother had taught me Landor as a boy:

> I strove with none, for none was worth my
>   strife;
> Nature I loved, and next to Nature, Art;
> I warmed both hands before the fire of life,
> It sinks, and I am ready to depart.

(Though I used to tease her by saying "it stinks.")

Let William Carlos Williams, with his plucky wife, Floss, bridge the span from Chicago to the future we were anxiously debating. We had met them there, late in our stay. He was recovering from one of his speech-and-motion-impairing strokes, and had come to read in the Rockefeller Chapel—where he would battle his handicap to a cheering ovation. At a crowded lunch in his honor we were somehow seated at a table where he was being harassed (fruit of that Carlos heritage) by a Jesuit whom Williams's halting enunciation could not exorcise. For quite a time I had been reading and teaching theology from the Fathers down (with Dante besides), especially at that Baptist University where, it was said, Atheist professors taught Catholicism to Jews. I pitched in like Socrates, and before long had that priest as tangled in contradiction as a bluebottle meshed in an orb spider's web—a rescue for which Williams proclaimed himself my friend for life, and indeed we wrote, visited, and were fond of each other until his death.

The next meeting was in Puerto Rico. Casals had been invited for a memorial playing in the Mayaguez house where his mother was born. We were there; though instead of the Bach last cello suite I was wild for, the master gave a tearful rendition of "Songs My

Figure 13. *Five Bell girls at Isabel Harper's Wind Farm: Sandra, Corola, Debra, Charlotte, and Nona, Summer 1954*

Mother Taught Me." I had learned that Bill Williams's mother also came from Mayaguez, apparently from the same neighborhood. We contrived that he and Floss should be brought down for readings—and, as it happened, splashings off coral beaches in cerulean seas.

Later he would come to Annapolis, and whenever I passed New York, headed anywhere, I would take a bus to East Rutherford, spend the night, with an evening and morning of food, reading, and talk. Floss steered him through my *Delta Return,* on which he wrote helpful reviews; then through carbons of *The Married Land,* for which he provided a jacket blurb. Finally he took up mythic residence in *The Half Gods;* as Richard Ramon Richards, he lived, wrote, and died there.

At this juncture Erich sent my Puerto Rican letter—termites, mosquitoes, and all—to his friend Zuckerkandl at St John's in Annapolis, a place I had been in touch with, before Barr and Buchanan bailed out. Zuckerkandl took it to Jascha Klein, dean, another of the great Europeans, though a shrewd administrator. He read it and is reported to have said: "We've got to get that boy out of there." So I was invited for an interview.

I saw no need of jumping from the frying pan into the fire. I had to meet them honestly—no more mistakes in identity. When I sat with the Instruction Committee, doubt was expressed about my writing. Most of them thought teaching the Great Books was enough. Someone voiced the question: "Do you like to teach?" I said my life-devotion left no other premise; I enjoyed—had even been thought good at it. But I knew it was a pleasure which could be overindulged and might prove habit-forming. They gasped. I left the room. In a few minutes they called me back to say they wanted me.

So I came to the most challenging program of my career. The talents of Princeton, Galway Kinnell, Bill Merwin, Arrowsmith, were harder to find; there was not the almost daemonic intensity of Joe Schwab's Chicago, where I saw a girl, pounced on for an answer, leave puddles as she fled the room; and if Chicago had asked more hours than Princeton, St John's asked more again than Hutchins's College. But I could teach anything in the program, to the benefit of what Stauffer had deplored as my larger studies. From an essay of that time, "Incarnate Fruits" (unpublished), I quote a St John's experience:

Early in my career at our Platonic Academe,
I was teaching at once Greek mathematics

and modern chemistry. As we were working in the laboratory exploring combinations of sulphur (while I had fled to the window to catch a breath of air), one of my brightest students came coughing through the fog to put a question to me which Plato also might have proposed: "Why at this college, where we are expected to give our souls to philosophic inquiry, must we waste our time on these stinking experiments?"

I had come from the pure forms of Euclid; here I stood like Faust in the witches' kitchen, or a medieval alchemist in his den, the very smoke flaunting some satanic relation. We were working with the stuff of probability, and I was supposed to give an answer to such an imperative why. In my poetry group we had just read Yeats. I quoted:

> A woman can be proud and stiff
> When on love intent;
> But Love has pitched his mansion in
> The place of excrement;
> For nothing can be sole or whole
> That has not been rent.

The answer baffled him. "Why?" I said. "Because the changeless One took flesh in a stall, to become among beasts a pattern for the Western world." The student, muttering his protest, went back to the crucible and flame.

No doubt I was at St John's as disturbing as elsewhere; but they gave me tenure, gave me a community, almost a family (loving and hostile) of ancient reason. I never thought I would profit by going back to departmental Belles Lettres.

We had hardly moved into a house on Spa Creek, where I was building shelves late at night for my books, when I cracked a neck vertebra and crushed a disk, for which, in motion, I wore a racking frame, or at my typing table, was hoisted like a hanged man by a cord over pulleys to a weight. For the first time—as if I had gone through death—I got outside myself. At last my Wolfian fiction could be cleaned up. I was as conscious an egoist as ever, my subject the experienced life and cosmos of protagonist Bell. But as the Greeks donned masks for tragedy, my halter gave me a distance. I published some Puerto Rican stories, then took forceps to the novel in its birth throes. It asked more deaths than my own symbolic one. Danny's rebel Quaker father, dead, her matchless English mother, dying, had left invaluable memoirs. So from my dead father came *A Child of the Delta*, from my failing mother, poems and letters. "'Gainst death and all oblivious enmity" these assumed the searching suspension of a union bridging opposite shores—the dry rot and fire of the broken South, the stable order of the Quaker East—for which *The Married Land* took its title-page motto from Augustine's *City of God*: "The beauty of the course of this world is achieved by the opposition of contraries, arranged as it were by an eloquence not of words but of things."

Meanwhile another of the Princeton circle, Max Knoll, who had come with my best man, Erich Kahler, to the wedding at Little Pines Farm, he, inventor of the electron microscope and now director of the Munich Institute for Electronics, got me a Fulbright, to broaden his graduate students with my slide-music-word lectures and a seminar on Ambivalenz (both in German). I took the novel sketches with me—though photographing, and composing the Teutonic prototypes of my later shows took most of my time. Indeed, I thought I had lost the novel altogether.

Driving back through France, we went to Versailles and parked while I took thrilling shots with my Exacta. When we returned to the station wagon the tailgate had been opened and a satchel containing the irreplaceable sketches had been stolen. I have not been gloomier in all my life. Here, it was Chicago friends who came to the rescue. We were visiting Lulix and Otto Simpson, he then working for UNESCO. With horror Lulix heard of the loss. It turned out she knew a composer who gave the best musical program on the French radio. "Everybody listens to him," she said. "We'll go tomorrow and he'll announce it on the air." He greeted us at the Radio Diffusion Française. The devastating story was told. "I lost my first symphony the same way," he cried. "Gone, forever! I'll be on the air again this afternoon. I'll spread the news."

Our schedule took us to London. We were staying with Danny's relatives when Lulix phoned. The "grief-case," rifled of a little money, had been tossed over a Versailles wall into the garden of people who heard the program. We were sailing at once to the States. I had almost despaired of taking up an intended residence at Yaddo. What could I do with nothing to write? Now the scribbled bulk would be there waiting for me. Though even with such favor from the gods, the through-writing took two more years, 1959–61.

I finished at Yaddo the cold January of Kennedy's inauguration, when Galway and I, in next-door rooms, would work until midnight, and then go for a run round the forest road, the forty-below air at each breath piercing the chest like a knife. Pati Hill, sensitive stylist, was also there. She had been dumbfounded by the tangle of my Delta chapters (as in fishing, when you snag a line and drag up the whole bottom of the lake). The night I typed the close she phoned her agent, protesting scion of the Yeats circle, Diarmuid Russell, universally and rightly admired. Next day, going home to Annapolis, I took the MS by his office in New York. He promised to read it that night. How he did it I don't know; but the morning after, he phoned that he was sending it to his friend Craig Wylie at Houghton Mifflin, who was sure to like it. Indeed, it seemed not long, before Craig came to spend the night and discuss publication.

Walker Percy being then ascendant (with Shelby Foote and others) Craig was staggered by the phenomenon of Greenville, and asked if I knew of any other writers down there. I happened to have by my bedside the typescript of a first novel just sent me by Josephine Haxton, wife of my brother's best friend, Kenneth, himself the town composer, with an amazing body of work. Craig grabbed *A Family's Affairs* like manna from heaven. By morning he had read it and decided not only to publish it, but to give it the Houghton Mifflin award. (He might have been considering me before, but I would joyfully have given it to Josephine—her pen name, Ellen Douglas.)

About this time, Danny bought us into a Vermont farmhouse, great for pulling burdock, and reunions with children, relatives, and friends, though for a Mississippian, creatively remote.

There and elsewhere I revised *The Married Land* four times; but by 1962, with hardly a break for philosophy or poetry, I had begun the vaster *Half Gods*.

By now it was clear that my old biographical stages had yielded to the Kingdoms of Joachim de Flores: the first of the Father (thus the ancestral focus and stability of *The Married Land*); the second of the Son (the institutional quest of *The Half Gods*); then *The Third Kingdom*, of Spirit, the Beat and Hippy dreamers of the next generation, talking in tongues, the fire burning on their foreheads. Of these the third was interrupted by *Symbolic History* and is still to be completed.

For my office at St John's, I had moved into the great windowed octagon of the bell tower over the college and tree-banked city between creeks and bay. Tower poems sprinkle the *Five Chambered Heart:* "March Snow" and "From Height and Silence," on love; "Resonance of Towers," claiming with Milton, Yeats, and Jeffers that all-night legacy. Though it would take twenty years and the expanse of the West to complete the lyrics of that volume, and, by a symbolic array, turn them to world-discourse: twenty-five waves, each moving through five archetypal states of love: LOVE as such; love narrowed, as in wit or LUST; attached to things, EARTH; by attachment spoiling its ground, WASTE; no way back, only up or down, transcendence, SOUL. Twenty-five times around, LOVE, LUST, EARTH, WASTE, SOUL: the sequence begins to say something.

Sometimes in the tower, Jim Gilbert, who had joined us at St John's, would sketch me in oils, as I heaped up typescript for *The Half (Baked) Gods.*

My novels, as extensions of world history, had to forge the stuff of the actual into symbolic paradigm. *The Married Land,* dialectic of a love-union essentially Danny's and mine, took its facts from our lives, with the records of family and friends. Though Dan Byrne is not me, he stands in my shoes. For *The Half Gods,* a political allegory, I had to seat my alter ego in another family, assembled from Greenville memories, plus oral and written contributions from willing victims. Nor was that all. I hit on an actual house a wife had rented in Ellicott city; there I went through all seasons to observe and record. As if living and writing were one, I called on participants to join me in our book-haunts or send details of theirs. Thus Cecil Roberts, British charmer, fighting for liberal causes in the deep South, gave me her memories, for the fiction some fools took for fact and turned to scandal. A clumsy way to compose a novel; but my larger aim did not admit of easier invention. Various of these debts are detailed in the acknowledgments.

The result was a file of papers so formidable that it took me more than a year living on a Worcestershire farm near Danny's *Married-Land* cousins (and on funds gleaned from such forebears) to melt it down and through-write it as *The Half Gods.* Though for the reading public, that made little difference; since the challenge of the book, with the voiced communism of LeFlore's wife Anna, got it dropped from the shelves as if it had never been there.

Meanwhile, St John's College had planted a colony in Santa Fe. I spent a last eastern spring protesting Vietnam, and as guest at the University of Rochester, often with Norman O. Brown—Nobbie, proofing *Love's Body,* while I revised *The Half Gods,* he

demanding as we read to each other: "Why do you try to hold so much? Why don't you let go?" Then Danny and I went west, as if for a year, climbed the fall mountains, looked over the wilderness and said: "We'd be fools to go back East, just for the smell of dead languages." So we bought, on a ridge above Canyon Road, the ugliest house in seven states, tore it to pieces and rebuilt it with luck (and Bill Lumpkins) into a luminous space, fit for life and work. Here, with intervals in San Cristobal, Chiapas—photographic outings to the vanishing Lacandon rain forest with Trude Blom—twenty years have passed.

Though large parts of the third novel were sketched, and a story, *Prodigal Father,* pulled out and published, most of that terminal toil has gone into the Winkie Barr project, *Symbolic History, Through Sight and Sound,* forty recorded slide-tape programs, now videoed (figure 14)—as if I had conceived a stage for the actual voices of time (art, music, poetry and thought) to enact the tragedy of consciousness—the only great tragic action left, of man and world.

Yet perhaps it will not be so terminal. I am seventy-three; I run and walk the mountains; in good weather (to use arms and shoulders) I swing a bit through these inadequate trees. At a party when people have drunk enough to expect some catastrophe, I may fall dead forward, catch myself on my hands, and bounce through twenty push-ups. I work most of the day, and at nights until twelve. As for sleep, health, and memory, here is my doctrine:

What's in my shows I mostly have by heart or I couldn't have made them; also much of the poetry I once memorized. I keep up the imprint by silent recitation when I wake at night, which makes waking a pleasure. Insomnia is a plot of petty demons. When they rouse you, you have only to cry: "Thank God, I can read," or "I can recite poems." So pick up Aristotle or go through "Lycidas." Those fiends are thrown off the track; they leave you to sleep when you will.

Viruses are subtler demons, but not gods, or I wouldn't arrogate against them. Strategy is best. When others are sick and you feel queasy, drink a quart of water, go to bed, put the smile of a possum on your face, and doze off, sure the body is producing virophage, called interferon, and that the killer cells are liquidating invaders. You wake clear of taint.

No doubt, running, climbing, leaping, you (or I) may pull a muscle, sprain a joint. The purple sawdust sags down to the ankle. Get tough with the brain: "See here. You tell those cells (for you're in touch

Figure 14. *Videoing* Symbolic History, *1988*

with them) not to go into shock; it's counter-productive." And when kin, friends, doctors, push this or that pain killer, wave them off and say (though they'll pronounce you crazy) that the possum-smile will do it. And it does.

But all this subserves a purpose: to keep alive for the whole work—of which certain tasks remain. First is *Now,* final double show of the multimedia prodigy. From the frenzy of today (racing present of merely physical time), it rounds to the rooted eternal of formative self, world, cosmos. The making and videoing of this prophecy must not overreach the present summer. Next, the philosophy of paradox, from axiomatic antinomies to the contours of reality, physical, organic, intellectual and spiritual—felt out through generations of sketches, articles, lectures—is to be articulated within the covers of a book. Also *The Third Kingdom,* lurking in boxes of notes, must raise the trilogy from love and politics to spirit. There remain essays, translations, and, if it should prove imperative after *Symbolic History,* the long delayed Earth Poem.

(The ironic "I AM" of this close may be caught in Marianna Cook's 1989 portrait of Charles Greenleaf Bell, opening photo.)

And should I finish these things before I die, surely I will remember Goethe: "If I am restlessly active to the end" (and it was near the end) "nature is obliged to find me some other form of being, when this one breaks down under my spirit." Whether that obligation was fulfilled, we have small evidence, unless one of us should prove a case in point. But when and if my own organon should be completed, how long would I (with Mozart) not have been asking: "What will the little ones do when Don Giovanni has gone under?" To which the opera gives ready answer: "Noi buona gente . . ." "We good little people will sing the old familiar song."

BIBLIOGRAPHY

Songs for a New America (poetry), Indiana University Press, 1953, revised edition, Norman S. Berg, 1966.

Delta Return (poetry), Indiana University Press, 1956, revised edition, Norman S. Berg, 1969.

The Married Land (novel), Houghton, 1962.

The Spirit of Rome (film), Encyclopaedia Britannica, 1964.

The Half Gods (novel), Houghton, 1968.

Five Chambered Heart (poetry), Persea Books, 1986.

Other:

Symbolic History Through Sight and Sound (forty slide-tape shows or studies), 1970-1990; also available on videocassettes.

Contributor of poems to numerous magazines, including *Harper's, New Yorker,* and *Atlantic Monthly.* Contributor of critical study to *Modern Age.* Contributor of short stories and articles to literary and philosophic journals.

James Broughton

1913-

BECOMING A POET

James Broughton, 1988

I am a third generation Californian.

My grandfathers were bankers, and so was my father.

But my mother wanted me to become a surgeon.

However, one night when I was three years old

I was awakened by a glittering stranger

who told me I was a poet and always would be

and never to fear being alone or being laughed at.

That was my first meeting with my angel

who is the most interesting poet I have ever met.

The above paragraph prefaces a collection of my poems, *A Long Undressing* (1971), and is spoken on the soundtrack of my autobiographical film, *Testament* (1974). It is a simple statement of fact. Yet there are persons otherwise tolerant who refuse to believe it. Even my first psychiatrist, an Adlerian coffee addict, scoffed: "A pretty fantasy! It shows how weak your sense of reality has always been."

Poets should be advised to give analysts a wide berth, or at best a narrow margin, unless they want to get into troubled waters. Poets never lie, they only embroider. A poet's business is to clarify the unknown and celebrate the unmentionable. In this endeavor my angel has been a luminous collaborator, as he has been equally a boon companion in my secular follies.

He must remember as clearly as I do that our first encounter took place at Thanksgiving time of 1916 on a night when my mother was experiencing premature labor pains from my yet unborn brother (he who would not choose to join the family until December 13). This major epiphany of my life occurred in the San Joaquin Valley town of Modesto at 1015 Sixteenth Street, an airplane bungalow that is still standing: it has housed the Baird Photo Shop for the past forty years.

Even if they had witnessed that angelic visit, my parents would not have believed it either. So I never told them. Actually I didn't have an opportunity to confide much of anything to my father: he died two years later, just after my fifth birthday, in the fierce influenza epidemic at the end of World War I. I inherited, I was told, his complete sets of Rudyard Kipling and Robert Louis Stevenson, as well as his stamp collection. But before I was old enough to look into any of these books my mother had sold them.

"Irwin Broughton was the handsomest grandest man I ever met in my entire life," said a hostess pouring tea for me at a charity auction I attended in 1959. She had been my father's classmate at Berkeley in 1909. On the other hand my mother, whose name was Olga and who had never attended university, had this to say: "Your father drove me crazy. I never had any idea what he was thinking." My own memories of him are permeated with an aura of sadness, even of inappropriate despair on supposedly cheerful excursions like a ferris-wheel ride or a merry-go-round. Years later I discovered in my grandmother's bookcase what must have been one of his favorite books: a well-thumbed underlined copy of *From Job to Job around the World.* I later learned that it had been written by another of his classmates and a fraternity brother.

My mother, when she read at all, preferred popular romances and fashion magazines. She had an innate sense of style, an idolatry of the rich, and stern moral prejudices. She venerated surgeons because they could cut the bad out of one. I had to keep many secrets from her for fear she would have me operated on regularly.

I was born under a Scorpio sun in November of 1913, the year of *Le Sacre du printemps, Swann's Way,* and *Nude Descending a Staircase.* My birth trauma proved to be no trauma at all, for both mother and child were said to have enjoyed an easy, felicitous,

and joyful experience. Apparently the world began for me not with a bawl but a chortle. Almost immediately I was nicknamed Sunny Jim. This must have been caused by my naturally cheery disposition and my sense that the world is an amusing place. When I saw the inscription on Sterling Hall at Yale, "He was born with the gift of laughter and a sense that the world is mad," I took it as my own birthright. Then I was reminded that it was written by a favorite author of my twelfth year, Rafael Sabatini.

I was named James Richard after my paternal grandfather. This has always pleased me, since he possessed unshakeable integrity, a twinkling eye, and the dense fragrance of an oak tree in midsummer. Invariably he signed himself J. R. Broughton, even in letters to me, although he was familiarly called Dick, for reasons never clear to me. In my early years I had to bear the appellation of Jimmy Dick.

J. R. was president of the Modesto Bank of Stanislaus County, in which he had worked his way up from janitor. He stood ramrod erect, his white beard slightly browned from cigar smoke, and always dressed in three-piece suits that would have looked correct on Abraham Lincoln. He kept chickens in the backyard, loved to play pinochle, tell jokes on women, and brag about his youth as a vaquero. I moved in devoted awe of him: he was the strongest father of my life and a vivid link to the past of the United States.

His father, Job Broughton, had been a scout with Fremont before the Gold Rush and had settled in the Almaden of Santa Clara County. Behind that ancestor was a long history of pioneering quest. The Broughton ancestors had come from England to the Carolinas in the early eighteenth century, moved on to Virginia, where one of them was a captain in Washington's army, and another gave birth to Daniel Boone. From St. Joseph, Missouri, his mother had come west with her parents and met my great-grandfather in San Jose. When I fled Stanford in April of 1935 and hitchhiked eastward across the continent I was not unaware of how the restless searchings of my ancestors buzzed in my own bones.

An even more intimate connection to the westward ho of my forebears was another James of the family, Uncle Jim Hammond. He was in fact an uncle of my grandmother Broughton and still lived in the abandoned mining town of La Grange on the Tuolumne River. As a boy he had been brought across the plains in a covered wagon and his memories of it were still immediate and thrilling. He was a spry and wiry bachelor in his eighties and I was a boy of six when he held me on his knee and regaled me with stories of Indian raids, buffalo herds, flooding rivers, and the death of a beloved brother in the desert of Nevada. Eidolons of American history surrounded us in that old clapboard house when he squeezed me on his lap and sang "Oh Susannah" in a low lilting tenor.

At other times Uncle Jim would demonstrate for me gold-digging equipment, arrowheads, coal-oil lamps, and corsets in the general store called Hammond & Bates across the street. It was now the only store on the deserted main street of that ghost town, but when Jim and my grandmother's brother George Bates had opened it in the mining days it had been a humming place. Now the two of them spent their days sitting on the front porch of the store, while George's wife, Aunt Gussie Bates, ran the post office and the telephone exchange alongside the cash register. When Uncle Jim's will was probated in 1924 his bequest to me amounted to $17.31. My mother snatched the check away with a contemptuous snort, but I valued it as a substantial legacy of the adventurous spirit of my James lineage.

My grandmother herself had been born Jennie Bates in the Mother Lode town of Sonora when it was a booming center for the mines. She was a gracious, soft, and pious lady, fond of quoting Elbert Hubbard, embroidering samplers, and entertaining the Episcopal bishop. Her ancestors from Somerset had been founders of Springfield, Massachusetts, in the seventeenth century, later moving west to establish Springfield, Illinois. From there they had come to California in search of gold, bringing Uncle Jim with them. Jennie's mother, however, could not stand the roughness and the boredom of mining life: she ran off to Chicago with a dude gambler. All her life Jennie spoke righteously on the subject of loose women, never overcoming her conviction that sex led to lamentable and inevitable disaster. One summer Saturday when I asked if I could go to the matinee of a Ronald Colman movie called *One Night of Love,* she replied with a shudder, "Absolutely not!"

The greatest tragedy in her life was the death of my father at age thirty-five, for Irwin was the big darling of her heart. However irrationally, she blamed my mother for his death because Olga had taken him away from Modesto. Olga had loathed the small town, their modest home, the heckling of her neighboring mother-in-law. She continued to be homesick for San Francisco, where she had been raised in a large lap of luxury: the three-story mansion of her immigrant grandfather, Nicholas Ohlandt, who had come from Prussia with seven dollars in his pocket and had recently died, president of the German Savings Bank and the National Ice Company.

James with his parents, Irwin and Olga Broughton, 1914

In the summer of 1917, with money from Mr. Ohlandt, Olga persuaded my father to move us to a big house in the city, where he would work for the Federal Reserve Bank. But a year and a half later, just when I had been initiated to kindergarten, he was stricken and died within twenty-four hours. For the remainder of her life in Modesto Jennie kept a fresh rose in front of Irwin's photograph and almost always wore the lavender of Lent.

My brother and I went to visit in Modesto, especially at Thanksgiving, Easter, and Fourth of July. I loved my grandmother unreservedly, not so much for her generosity with cakes and candies but primarily because she indulged and admired my appetite for the arts: my passion for dressing up, declaiming, practicing jetés, stringing beads, cutting out paper dolls, all the things that horrified my mother. Above all I longed to be a dancer, a great dancer. If that should prove impossible—if I lost my legs, for instance—I vowed to be a dramatic poet, for I loved the magic of words and everything about the theater.

There were poems, homilies, and miscellaneous poetry volumes in soft leather bindings all around Jennie's house. That was how I first read Longfellow, Whittier, and Omar Khayyàm. But the first poem I memorized hung on the wall beside my brass bed in that house. It was illustrated with grinning goblins clambering over the text:

There is so much good in the worst of us
And so much bad in the best of us
That it hardly behoves any of us
To talk about the rest of us.

Perhaps there is some connection between this homily I learned as a child because I looked at it every night and the printed broadside I acquired when I was sixty from Rimpoche Tartang Tulku, the Tantric Buddhist of Berkeley, for I look at it every day also and know it by heart. This perches above my toilet, where one has to read it if one stands to urinate:

Since everything is but an apparition
perfect in being what it is,
having nothing to do with good or bad,
acceptance or rejection,
one may well burst out in laughter.

This is credited to *The Natural Freedom of Mind* by Long Chen Pa, whoever he might be.

A poem can have a lasting effect on one's life. At my baby bedtime my mother often got her kicks by wiggling each of my toes in turn as she intoned, "This little pig went to market," beginning with the big toe and ending with, "This little piggy went squeak squeak squeak all the way home." As a consequence I have ever since relished having my feet played with.

Did this tootsie-wootsie game in my crib inspire the poem I wrote years later, after I had first sampled Freudian theory?

Papa has a pig.
And a big pig too.
Papa plays a piggy-toe that I can't do.
O Papa has the biggest pig you ever did
 see.
He gave only ten little piggies to me.
 Papa has the star of all the swine,
 Papa shines stern in the sty.   &c.

This was actually written about my stepfather, who was the biggest pig I knew as a child. The poem was published in 1947 in a magazine called *Wake* edited by José Garcia Villa, a vatic Philippine poet with intense black eyes and a passion for commas who disappeared from the literary scene in the late fifties after being overpraised by Edith Sitwell. Michael McClure remembers reading the poem in *Wake* when he was a teenager in Kansas. He still quotes it.

Other than piggy toes I do not remember my mother teaching me any poems. She did make us sing *Stille Nacht* and *Tannenbaum* on Christmas Eve, and

she sometimes checked whether we had said our prayers before we got into bed, the way she checked whether we had moved our bowels before going to school.

What a big nose Mrs Mother has,
the better to smell her dear.
Sniff sniff sniff it comes round the door,
detective of everything queer . . .

Unlike my grandmother Jennie, who sent me a missal and a hymnal bound in soft leather, my mother never showed any serious interest in my prayers or my philosophic questions. In Olga's family the prime usefulness of the Almighty, if mentioned at all, was to help one make money.

Born on Potrero Avenue in San Francisco, my mother had been orphaned by the age of thirteen and raised by her mother's parents in the big house on Steiner Street. This Queen Anne pile, with an entrance hall large enough for weddings and receptions, plus a third-floor ballroom reached by an elevator, is nowadays a home for alcoholic Episcopalians. There is irony in this. The only son of the family never did anything in his life but drink, gamble, and play practical jokes until he died of acute alcoholism. His sisters were more interested in jewelry and social climbing.

Upright in corseting and veils, my widowed great-grandmother Ohlandt used to arrive in her Locomobile town car with a basket full of stale bread to take my brother and me to Golden Gate Park to feed the ducks. More than the ducks, I was impressed by her thick German accent, her Queen Maryish toques, and her extraordinary vehicle: a dark enclosed cab the shape of a hansom with roses in cut-glass vases, lap robes, and gray silk window shades. The chauffeur out in front could be directed by way of a tube one shouted into. Alas, by 1920 the Locomobile and the mansion were sold, for she too was dead.

In that year my mother was a still-young widow bent on acquiring a rich husband, despite the handicap of having two small boys. She had moved us to a flat on Pacific Avenue across the street from Ulysses S. Grant Grammar School. The best thing about our new home was its huge attic playroom, large enough for all our games and bloody fights. There I set up my toy theater, my magic lantern, my Oz books, and my stage for theatricals. There with congenial schoolmates I acted out my pastiche versions of everything I had seen on Saturday afternoon at the Orpheum vaudeville or on Sunday afternoon at the silent movies. Aunt Marion from Indianapolis, the widow of my alcoholic great-uncle Henry, was the one who provided these regular treats for my imagination. She was the generous mother of my entertainments.

But perhaps the favorite mother of my childhood was Mother Goose, who has remained a good mother to me all my life. She is the merriest poet in the English language, she and her bastard son Anonymous. She takes delight in follies and forays, obsessional antics, and the widespread silliness of human beings. Her rhymes and her craziness have inspired many of my wisest whimseys.

One reason I enjoyed living in London in the 1950s was to listen to the delightful nonsense the English speak all the time. I deplore solemnities about life, as much as I deplore those who are revolted by frivolity. I agree with J. K. Galbraith: "It is a far, far better thing to have a firm anchor in nonsense than to put out on the troubled seas of thought."

The British often quote one of Mrs. Goose's sophisticated offspring, Lewis Carroll. When I lived on the island of Ischia during the summer of 1955 and saw Wystan Auden every evening at Maria's cafe on the piazza of Forio, he would chastise me for any uncertainty I expressed by saying: "Remember what Alice's friend Mabel said: 'Keep your toes well turned out, if you don't know the English words use the French, and *always remember who you are.'*"

I have appreciated that for Edward Lear nonsense was the norm of life, and I confess to plagiarizing his forms. For example, The Alan of Watts for the Akond of Swat. Then there are Lear's limericks with his cast of loony actors. Limericks are a schoolboy's raunchy delight. Every poet tries his hand at them, and philosophers too. Alan Watts, when he was my neighbor in Marin County, invented scurrilous ones about prelates and gurus. I wrote a Zen limerick for Alan that was, though enlightened, a bit lame:

> Said that nasty old man in the road
> as he set down his unpleasant load,
> Since I now plainly know
> there is nowhere to go
> I'll just nastily sit in the road.

When I sailed to Japan on a cargo ship in the summer of 1934 I received a surprising bon voyage gift, presented to me by my Stanford professor, Dr. Margery Bailey, Shakespeare scholar and formidable disciplinarian. She had taken a commonplace autograph album from Woolworth's and on each page calligraphed a different limerick. The first of these I have never forgotten:

> There was a young scholar of Greenwich
> who lived on baked apples and spinach.
> His terrible tool
> he kept on a spool
> and let it out in-itch by in-itch.

My father's sister, my aunt Esto Broughton, was the only one who consistently read poetry to me when I was a child. She must have recognized that I was a social anomaly like herself, since she too was looked upon as an embarrassing freak in the family: she was dwarfed, walked with a limp, and was unmarried. But she had defied the small-town frumps, obtained a law degree from UC Berkeley, gone into politics, and become one of the first women elected to the state legislature. She brought me my first Mother Goose collection, as well as Eugene Field, and *A Child's Garden of Verses* with the Jessie Willcox Smith illustrations.

This aunt also had a passion for the theater, which led her eventually to the staff of the Pasadena Playhouse in its heyday. When I was seven years old she took me to a matinee of *The Merchant of Venice* with David Warfield playing Shylock in the Belasco production that included a real ship for Antonio in the first scene, splashing fountains for Portia's garden at the end, and a lavish Venetian carnival in the middle. This was my awakening to the enchantments of Shakespeare, who proved to me that everyday life is more understandable when observed poetically. He became my first literary guru: he taught me to think poetically, to keep imagination articulate and alert, and to relish human diversity. At that *Merchant* matinee, in the midst of the long moonlight scene of the lovers ("On such a night . . ."), my little brother piped up, "When's that old Jew coming back?" to the considerable disruption of the audience around us.

One winter in the late thirties when I was stranded penniless in Bermuda I borrowed from the library in Hamilton the Oxford edition of the *Complete Works* of W. S. and prowled through the entire book, all 1352 pages of double-column small print, beginning with *The Tempest.* Though I had studied some of the plays in college I now reveled in the whole parade of the agonies of kings and the innocence of lovers. I basked in song, soliloquy, and the ravishments of language. If a poet is not enraptured by language he might as well write obituary notices for a newspaper.

Shakespeare became so intimate to me on Bermuda that I engaged in long chats with him, sat close beside him as he worked, watching the concentration

With father, grandparents J. R. and Jennie Broughton, and aunt Esto Broughton, Modesto, California, 1916

of his face and the rhythms of his body. He told me then to call him Will. He also taught me to regard human life as a theater, wherein each of us may try out for any of the parts, but no matter how deftly we may enact them, we remain deluded fragments of the whole show. I cycled the coral byways of that supposed isle of Prospero's, memorizing "When daffadils begin to peer, / With heigh, the doxy over the dale!" and "Merrily, merrily shall I live now, / Under the blossom that hangs on the bough."

My own spring songs are tributes to Will:

Come dally me, darling, dally me with kisses,
loiter me with lingers while the Romes all
    burn . . .

and

Spring   spring   runs round a green riddle,
follows a round robin cruel and gay.
The virgins of April heed the call of the
    leapfrog
and go on a roundtrip till the middle of
    May . . .

The Tempest has always been my favorite of the plays, probably because it is the one most obviously about a poet's magic. It is also the only one of the plays in which I have performed. And even that comprised only one scene from the play, presented as a term project at the Hitchcock Military Academy in San Rafael, California, in 1924. I had been shipped off to that strict school when I was ten years old, at the insistence of my stepfather, to be cured of my passion for poetry and ballet. In such a macho environment it was probably not surprising that I should have been the cadet selected to play Ariel.

In the scene chosen I was supposed to be invisible to Trinculo and Stephano during their drunken buffoonery. The only words I had to say, several times, were two: "Thou liest." But I was so panicked by stage fright that I peed in the wings, leaving a puddle to puzzle the stage manager. Years later at Stratford, in the summer of 1951, I watched Alan Badel perform Ariel to the Prospero of Michael Redgrave. He was naked, silver white, slender as a magic wand, gracefully powerful enough to carry out any astonishment a poet might require. He reminded me so much of my own glittering guardian that I

them meant as much to me as Whitman. Living in his Manhattan, and like him striving to make a living as a journalist while writing poems at odd hours, I felt Walt to be my companion and cohort. Often he walked the streets with me or sat with me in the automat as we watched the human variety show passing by. Walt confirmed time and again what I had learned with my boyhood comrades: that sexuality is the closest thing to the divine and that poetry is an act of sexual joy.

In the marrow of my soul I knew that I was a poet and always would be, but there were times when I did fear being alone and being laughed at. The war years were particularly hard to bear. Not that I suffered in combat—I was classified 4-F—but "war effort" was not my kind of effort.

The first sentence of my book *Seeing the Light* (1977) reads: "When I was 30 my greatest consolation was the thought of suicide." Readers familiar with my present-day blithe spirit cannot believe that I ever stood at such a brink. But in 1943, when I was living in a creaky dark room in the back of the old Hotel Brevoort I dined on my thirtieth birthday in a

San Francisco, 1940

clattering cafeteria, my only company a copy of Rilke's *Journal of My Other Self* (as his *Brigge* was titled in its first translation). "People come here to die . . . ," it says in the first sentence. With war headlines screaming constant disaster there seemed to be no space for poetry, no time for comedy, no mobility for a free life in the arts.

Five years later I was back in San Francisco, back in the arms of poetry, celebrating the publication of my first book and the premiere of my first solo film.

In the New York years I tried to betray my poet angel. I tried to write the Great American Prize Novel. Then I tried to write a smash-hit Broadway play. I did my best to conform to the unpoetic values of American success. I had a potent need to be publicly accepted, a foolish desire for fame. Fortunately the novels I wrote were never published. And though I studied playwriting with John Gassner and John Howard Lawson I could only think in self-contained scenes, in vignettes, rather than in plot and what is called characterization. I had only the poet's aptitude for visions of momentary essence. This has proved invaluable to the method of my short films, but it was useless in Times Square.

Yet it was the success of one of my untypical short plays that brought me back to California for the summer of 1945. The Dramatists Alliance of Stanford had bestowed a prize on a work of mine and planned to produce it for a summer festival. The play, called *Summer Fury,* was the small tragedy of a Chicano boy in Los Angeles victimized by prejudice and police. It was well-enough manipulated melodramatically to earn it inclusion in the *Best Short Plays* of that year. If nothing else *Summer Fury* expressed my sense of being a victimized outsider in a world of destructive madness.

Back in California I no longer had any family home. My mother had died of cancer in August 1939, her prophetic last words to me being: "Don't worry, dear, there won't be any war." My stepfather was relieved never to see me again. My brother had not yet left the Conscientious Objector camp in San Bernardino County. I had intended to return to New York at the end of the summer, but as it turned out it was five years before I got back to the Hotel Brevoort to retrieve the trunks I had stored in its basement, only to find a brand-new apartment tower standing on the site. What kept me in California were two memorable explosions: Mr. Truman's bomb on Hiroshima and my encounter with the Brotherhood of Light.

Once the war clouds had cleared, imaginations were free to proliferate again. Pent-up creative energies burst into bloom. In a liberated Bay Area I met the poets and artists who would become friends, lovers, and colleagues for many years to come. The creative camaraderie that we enjoyed I have called the Brotherhood of Light. In my book *Seeing the Light* I used the term specifically in reference to cinematography and the craftsmen of cinema, but the term should also include all light-bringers and light-readers, all servants of illumination.

The period from 1945 to 1952 was labeled "The San Francisco Renaissance" by local commentators, while in New York magazines like *Harper's* it was titillated as "Sex and Anarchy." In the poetry scene of those years there were four major figures, poets who advanced the cause of poetry as an expressive oral art.

Madeline Gleason organized the first public poetry readings, bullying museums, galleries, and bookshops into sponsorship of her gala events. An incandescent redheaded lamplighter and a superlative reader herself, Madeline loved song forms and organized readings like song recitals. She would present four, six, even eight poets on a program when each poet would function like a soloist performing a musical selection. She called these events "festivals" and they proved resounding successes both with audiences and with aspiring poets.

Kenneth Rexroth, on the other hand, held weekly readings in his flat where poets read to other poets, and where Kenneth told them what was politically correct and what to do about it. Robert Duncan, being a minstrel intellectual, had a loftier coterie in Berkeley, where he encouraged the young voices of Robin Blaser and Jack Spicer. The fourth leader of the movement, a special kind of master of poetry recitation, was William Everson, whose thundering oratory of rage and confession derived from Jeffers and was even more impressive in later years when he wore the Dominican robes as Brother Antoninus. Madeline and Duncan were my special close friends the rest of their lives, but all four of these guiding spirits had potent effects on my writing, and perhaps most of all on my perception that living poetically is as vital as writing good poems.

Beside his vigorous verbal style Everson set another example for the blossoming poets of the region. He was a poet who printed his own poems by hand on his own press with great elegance and technical perfection. It became a dream for each one of us: to have a press of our own that we could print our work on. Before coming to live in San Francisco Everson had begun hand-press work at the Conscientious Objector camp at Waldport, Oregon. Among

James Broughton, Madeline Gleason, and Robert Duncan, San Francisco, 1949

his disciples there were Adrian Wilson and Kermit Sheets.

In the autumn of 1947 Adrian proposed the printing of a sheaf of my poems for Christmastime. This proved to be an Opus One for both of us. It was a folder of poems, not a book: a dozen verses, each printed on a separate sheet of a different-colored construction paper and each one embellished with an antique woodcut. In the chilly evenings of early December Adrian printed on a borrowed temperamental press stored in a potting shed behind a dilapidated mansion on O'Farrell Street. The separate sheets were collated and inserted unbound into a larger cardboard folder. The collection I called *Songs for Certain Children,* there were only seventy-five copies and we gave them all away to friends. Hence this item is now the rarest in my bibliography.

When Pauline Kael was selling art books at Brentano's in San Francisco she introduced me to Kermit Sheets, who was in atlases and reprints. This was both a momentous and an ironic meeting:

momentous because Kermit became my active collaborator for the next eight years, ironic because he shortly replaced Pauline as my roommate.

Since Kermit was an experienced actor and theater director he helped me produce my films, mounted my plays over the years in his own theater, and created the memorable figure of *Loony Tom, the Happy Lover* in my film of that title. Beyond these attributes Kermit was the one who printed my first books. And he did that on our very own press.

I was thirty-five when my first book was published. At thirty-five Whitman published *Leaves of Grass,* Mozart wrote *The Magic Flute,* Byron finished *Don Juan,* and Buddha was enlightened. For me, in the year 1948, it was a verse play called *The Playground.*

I had written this satiric allegory after Hiroshima and it had been published in *Theatre Arts* magazine. Its original title was *The Condemned Playground,* because the play dealt with the threat of total disaster to a society which preferred not to notice a Last Judgment that disrupted its habitual childish games.

"What shall we do with the Ostriches?" and "What are you taking into the Dark Ages?" begin two speeches in the play.

After the original script was performed at Mills College in dance-drama form, I rewrote the text. Kermit Sheets much admired the play and said it ought to be in book form. He added, "Why don't we acquire a press and print it ourselves?" "Why not?" said I. And that briefly is how the Centaur Press came into being. Our intention was to print books of poetry by me and by our friends.

Kermit located an old clam-action monster of a letterpress which cost less than a hundred dollars. We installed it in the basement of the building on Baker Street where we shared a flat. For this an extra five dollars was added to our twenty-five-dollar monthly rent, and we were in the business: the business of making a hardbound book from scratch. We purchased a font of Centaur type, which gave the press its name. From that point on we learned everything the hard way.

Anaïs Nin presented us with the font of sans-serif type she had used during her own self-publishing days in New York. She advised me to set my own poems in type, saying, "Every writer should feel the weight of a word in his hand." I admit this discipline proved fruitful. Setting the letters of each of my words by hand taught me forever after to keep in any line only what was essential.

Putting one's own book together provokes quiet amazement. Ever since that first one I have most cherished the books that I have taken part in shaping physically. When *The Playground* came back from the binder we invited everyone we knew to a publication party, where we sold enough copies to cover the costs of the book. There was such a crowd in our small flat that John Cage and Merce Cunningham never made it up the stairs.

The Playground contained a vision germane to all my work following. The subjects of my writing and my filming tend to take place on some platform or in some corner of that "playing field" where the human comedy parades by in all its odd variety. My major films from 1948 (*Mother's Day*) to 1983 (*Devotions*) occur in some microcosm of "the world as play," usually taking the form of Theme and Variations. The film of *The Bed* (1968) makes use of a wrought-iron double bed in a pasture for its kaleidoscope of enacted fantasies, illuminating my argument: "All the world's a bed and men and women merely dreamers." The longer film of 1970, *The Golden Positions,* is performed in an indoor playspace: a playroom reminiscent of the childhood attic where I devised my first spectacles.

For me "play" is a key word in the language and a key to all my work. Without play there is no wonder, no merriment, no love. Making poems is my favorite form of play. I have never been a realist, except of the imagination. I have never been political, except that I want nothing less than a sexual and spiritual revolution in the name of love.

> Only when I wing
> am I dancing on the ground
> Only when I fly
>   am I I
> Only when I sing
> am I quietly profound
> Only when I glee
>   am I me

After the praise for our first publication Kermit and I were ready to tackle other projects. Our second Centaur title was Robert Duncan's *Medieval Scenes.* That was followed by Madeline Gleason's *The Metaphysical Needle,* and after that came *Orpheus,* by Muriel Rukeyser. At that time Muriel was living near us in San Francisco, arranging to have a child. Another New Yorker living nearby, Anaïs Nin, offered us Volume One of her famous diaries after she had altered the dates in it to make herself younger, but she withdrew it at the last moment. I was pleased that Kermit's handsome design of my second book, *Musical Chairs,* earned him a national Fine Book award.

Along with the Press we were involved in theater work and in sixteen-millimeter filmmaking. By 1951 I had completed four short films, comprising an hour's program. Their titles, using a production logo of Farallone Films, were *Mother's Day, Loony Tom, Four in the Afternoon,* and *Adventures of Jimmy.* Of these the first to use poems of mine on the sound track was *Four in the Afternoon.* This practice I have continued over the years, my most recent film, *Scattered Remains* (1988), using as many as ten poems with my own voice.

I submitted my first films to the Edinburgh Film Festival of 1951 and I received an invitation to attend. We sublet our flat to Robert Duncan and Jess Collins and in August Kermit and I sailed to South-ampton in the smallest cabin on the *Nieuw Amsterdam* of the Holland-America Line. To our great surprise we remained abroad until Thanksgiving of 1955, living in London, Paris, various parts of Italy, and on the Andalusian coast of Spain.

In England the first poets I met were Hugh MacDiarmid in a kilt, Stevie Smith in a fret, and Dylan Thomas in a pub. Dylan and I had already become friends in California during his reading tours of the States. One weekend we had been together in Big Sur when Dylan, beer bottle in hand, delivered a thundering extempore ode to the Pacific Ocean. If Jeffers taught me not to be afraid of consonants, it was Dylan who taught me to enjoy sibilants. I also relished his impish wit ("Oh, isn't life a terrible thing, thank God?") as I was equally awed by his incantatory style: the rush of his line, the soaring music, the forceful pitch of his voice.

It was therefore the more astonishing when I observed his agony in London at the ICA Gallery in the winter of 1952. Before getting up to read his poetry that night he sat trembling and sweating and gulping till I thought he would be physically ill. He was suffering extreme apprehension, while I, sitting beside him, did not feel a single twitch, even though I was scheduled to read right after him. Dylan had arranged for me to be on the program with him and Vernon Watkins. I was a nobody to that audience, while Dylan's fame was already secure. Despite my brashness and my eagerness to make an impression, a thick and reeking pea-soup fog slowly filled the hall and by the time I had finished reading I could no longer see the audience.

Thanks to John Lehmann I had some poems published in London quarterlies and my story of "The Right Playmate" was issued by Rupert Hart-

With Kermit Sheets, San Francisco, 1957

Davis with pictures by Gerard Hoffnung. But the most prestigious opportunity offered me came from the British Film Institute. I was invited to make an independent film entirely of my own devising for which they would raise the money. My sponsoring committee at the institute, composed of Basil Wright, Gavin Lambert, Paul Dehn, and Denis Forman, adopted the production name of "Flights of Fancy."

Beginning it in Capri and finishing it in Dieppe I wrote a screenplay with Kermit's help that I called *The Pleasure Garden.* Subtitled *A Midsummer After-noon's Daydream,* it was my tribute to Puck, poesy, puritanism, and the delicious silliness of British solemnities. Filming was planned for the summer of 1952 in London. Two discoveries had clinched the idea of the film in my mind: 1) seeing Hattie Jacques perform the role of an absentminded fairy godmother in a Christmas pantomime, and 2) being shown the board-ed-up ruins of the Crystal Palace Gardens in Syden-ham by Mary Lee Settle and Douglas Newton. These gave me the star actress and the ready-made location, the latter a peculiarly Old World playground fallen into romantic disrepair.

I was blessed to have Lindsay Anderson as my producer and Walter Lassally as cameraman, plus many professional actors who performed for the lark of it. The filming took place during July entirely outdoors amid fallen statues, overgrown balustrades, and grand staircases leading nowhere. I poured my full energies into visualizing this masque as a triumph of love over repression, utilizing every trick I had learned in the theater and my study of cinema. In one sense the film was a kind of experimental musical comedy. Dialogue was kept to a minimum, the story being told mainly by action and song.

The Pleasure Garden was sent to the Cannes Festival of 1954 as an official entry from Great Britain. There, to everyone's surprise, especially my own, it won a special jury prize for *fantaisie poétique.* Cocteau, who was chairman of the jury, told me mine was a very French film for an American to have made in Britain. I told him that his *Beauty and the Beast* had opened my eyes to the possibility of a cinema of the poetic imagination. He kissed me on both cheeks.

In the United States, on the other hand, *The Pleasure Garden* was denounced as "psychopathological" by the National Board of Review and New York audiences demanded their money back. Not till the hippie years did the film acquire a reputation as a precursor of the "Underground" film movement of the 1960s.

Because of the Cannes prize I received an offer from England to direct feature films. But when I learned that I would work only with scripts by other authors, I felt my angel tap me on the shoulder: "Would you abandon the hazards of poetry for the agonies of movie business?" To answer him I returned in due time to California and to the life he had prepared for me in the beginning. Pauline Kael told me that this was the greatest mistake I ever made.

Since I have in this memoir emphasized my coming of age as a poet and my encounters with other poets, I cannot deal here in any detail with the complex incidents and the many personalities that colored my parallel career as a poet of cinema. It is a separate story to tell of Sidney Peterson, Frank Stauffacher, Maya Deren, Jerome Hill, Stan Brakhage, and the many other American artists who enriched my explorations of the medium. I would only make the point here that I am not a

Filming a scene for Erogeny, *1976*

James Broughton during the filming of Testament, *1974*

"moviemaker" who happens to write poetry. I am a poet whose poetry has expanded into many fields of action. My films derive from my poetry as my poetry embellishes my films. It once amused me to think of my films as illuminated manuscripts like Blake's.

My years in Europe were rewarded with another Brotherhood of Light, during the time I lived in the sixth arrondissement of Paris. The Café Tournon, near the Sénat at the upper end of the rue de Tournon, became in 1953 and 1954 a lively hangout for expatriating American writers taking refuge from Senator McCarthy's vendettas and from the war in Korea. Since I lived across the street in the modest Hôtel de Tournon I spent many an hour inside or outside of the cafe. Its regulars included Jean Garrigue and Stanley Kunitz, Evan Connell, Christopher Logue, Daisy Aldan, Alfred Chester, as well as novelists like Richard Wright, Max Steele, and James Baldwin.

It was in that cafe that I first met Jonathan Williams, who has since published three books of mine, most notably my collection *A Long Undressing* (1971). There also George Plimpton and Bob Silvers prepared the early issues of the *Paris Review* (its tiny office was around the corner) while Alexander Trocchi and Austryn Wainhouse edited their magazine *Merlin* at another table. The *Merlin* boys published my book of love poems, *An Almanac for Amorists,* in 1955. Over the making of this book Kermit came to blows more than once with the unsympathetic printer in the rue de la Harpe.

Merlin was a subsidiary of the larger Olympia Press of Maurice Girodias, for whom many of the expatriate poets, in order to stay alive in Paris, ground out hard-core pornographic novels. Girodias paid a set sum for every raunchy hastily written manuscript and marketed the books largely among the British navy.

A more gracious and more discerning patron of poets was Princess Marguerite Caetani. She came to Paris often from her palazzo in Rome to seek new writing for her hefty multilingual quarterly, *Botteghe Oscure.* She nourished (with huge luncheons) many a budding young author, paid handsomely for their contributions, and cared about their well-being. When I came down with dysentery after a trip to Morocco she took care of the doctor bills, and when Kermit and I moved to Italy she offered us haven in her abandoned castle at Sermoneta. Prince Caetani had inherited the title Duke of Sermoneta from his recently deceased elder brother. It was amusing to behold unpretentious American-born Marguerite, with her sweaters and sensible shoes and Back Bay accent, being addressed both as *Principessa* and *Duchessa.*

Marguerite encouraged me to complete the major dramatic poem *True & False Unicorn,* which I had been working on for three years, so that she could publish it in *Botteghe.* This, my "portrait of the poet as a unicorn," was the literary culmination of my years abroad. In 1957 Grove Press issued it in a volume that also included the *Almanac* poems.

By this time I wanted to touch my roots again. I was forty-two and feeling the need of a more settled identity. After I recovered from the culture shock of returning to the U.S.A. I recognized that I belonged to Northern California. Most of my growing had been lived in and around San Francisco. Now it was to become my "main stage" playground for the rest of my adulthood. It is where I have thrived in theaters and in the schools where I have taught (most happily at the San Francisco Art Institute until my retirement in 1981). It is where I married and raised a family, where I have received honors from my peers and my neighbors, and where I have experienced the most rapturous glories of my heart. It is also where I have moved through a bewilderment of literary groups, both formalist and informal.

When Kermit and I came back to live on Telegraph Hill we found a second San Francisco Renaissance in ferment, the one that came to be known as the Beats. Lawrence Ferlinghetti, a neighbor on the hill, had opened his City Lights Bookstore, which became a center for the Beat poets, for browsing, and for gossip. Allen Ginsberg had just mimeographed his first version of *Howl* and he recited it wherever he went. He was also notorious for taking off his clothes at any polite social gathering.

When Allen came to dinner he brought along Peter Orlovsky, who put his feet into the butter dish on the table. "Think nothing of it," said Allen, "Peter is a saint." Peter called me Brautigan that night and has continued to do so for thirty years. "No," Allen will say to him every time we meet, "this is Broughton, not Brautigan."

With Gregory Corso, Philip Whalen, Gary Snyder, and Jack Kerouac, Allen formed a lifelong gang that enlivened North Beach days and nights. Their public readings were more political and more outra-

geous than those of ten years before. Those of us in the older avant-garde—including Rexroth, Duncan, Everson, and even Josephine Miles—were swept onto the Beat roller coaster along with unique younger talents like feisty Jack Spicer and ecstatic Michael McClure. It was an effervescent time, and American poetry has never been the same since.

But I have never been identified with any one group for very long. My body of work has never been able to wear any easy or convenient label. Maybe I am unclassifiable. Maybe it is because I have been as faithful as I could be to my peculiar vision and to my special craziness.

> Even if I never arrive
>   I shall keep departing
> I believe in the unreachable
> the unlikely and the unmentionable
>
> Anywhere that I await
>   my traveler's alert
> I rely upon the dimensionless
> the immediate and the imperishable
>
> Wherever I may be landing
>   or hoping for takeoff
> I swear by affection
> exuberance and clarity

SELECTED BIBLIOGRAPHY

Poetry:

Songs for Certain Children, Adrian Wilson, 1947.

Musical Chairs: A Songbook for Anxious Children, Centaur Press, 1950.

The Right Playmate, Hart-Davis [London] and Farrar, Straus, 1952, revised, Pearce & Bennett, 1964.

An Almanac for Amorists, Collection Merlin [Paris] and Grove, 1955.

True & False Unicorn (includes *An Almanac for Amorists*), Grove, 1957.

Tidings, Pearce & Bennett, 1965.

The Water Circle: A Poem of Celebration, Pterodactyl Press, 1965.

Look In Look Out, Toad Press, 1968.

High Kukus, Jargon Society, 1968.

A Long Undressing: Collected Poems, 1949-1969, Jargon Society, 1971.

The Androgyne Journal, Scrimshaw Press, 1977.

Seeing the Light, City Lights, 1977.

Odes for Odd Occasions: Poems, 1954-1976, ManRoot, 1977.

Graffiti for the Johns of Heaven, Syzygy Press, 1982.

Ecstasies: Poems, 1975-1983, Syzygy Press, 1983.

A to Z: 26 Sermonettes, Syzygy Press, 1986.

Hooplas: Odes for Odd Occasions, 1956-1986, Pennywhistle Press, 1988.

75 Life Lines, Jargon Society, 1988.

Special Deliveries: New and Selected Poetry, Broken Moon Press, 1990.

Films:

(With Sidney Peterson) *The Potted Psalm,* 1946.

Mother's Day, Farallone Films, 1948.

Adventures of Jimmy, Farallone Films, 1950.

Loony Tom, the Happy Lover, Farallone Films, 1951.

Four in the Afternoon, Farallone Films, 1951.

The Pleasure Garden, British Film Institute, 1953.

The Bed, Farallone Films, 1968.

Nuptiae, Farallone Films, 1969.

The Golden Positions, Farallone Films, 1970.

This Is It, Farallone Films, 1971.

Dreamwood, Farallone Films, 1972.

High Kukus, Farallone Films, 1973.

Testament, Farallone Films, 1974.

The Water Circle, Farallone Films, 1975.

(With Joel Singer) *Together,* Farallone Films, 1976.

Erogeny, Farallone Films, 1976.

(With Joel Singer) *Windowmobile,* Farallone Films, 1977.

(With Joel Singer) *Song of the Godbody,* Farallone Films, 1977.

Hermes Bird, Farallone Films, 1979.

(With Joel Singer) *The Gardener of Eden,* Farallone Films, 1981.

(With Joel Singer) *Shaman Psalm,* Farallone Films, 1981.

(With Joel Singer) *Devotions,* Farallone Films, 1983.

(With Joel Singer) *Scattered Remains,* Farallone Films, 1988.

Plays:

Summer Fury (one-act), first produced at Stanford University, 1945, published in *The Best Short Plays of 1945,* edited by Margaret Mayorga, Dodd, 1945.

The Playground: A Play for Precarious Grown-ups, first produced by the Interplayers, San Francisco, 1949, Centaur Press, 1949.

Where Helen Lies, first produced at Playhouse Repertory Theater, San Francisco, 1957.

Burning Questions (four-act), first produced in San Francisco at Playhouse Repertory Theatre, 1958.

The Last Word (one-act), first produced at Playhouse Repertory Theatre, 1958, Baker's Plays, 1958.

The Rites of Women (two-act), first produced at Playhouse Repertory Theatre, 1959.

Bedlam (one-act), first produced in Waterford, Conn., by Eugene O'Neill Theatre Foundation, 1969.

Poetry on cassette:

Songs from A Long Undressing, Syzygy Press, 1977.

Graffiti for the Johns of Heaven, Syzygy Press, 1977.

Ecstasies, Syzygy Press, 1977.

True and False Unicorn and Other Poems, Syzygy Press, 1977.

Work is represented in anthologies, including *Faber Book of Modern American Poetry,* edited by W. H. Auden, Faber, 1956, *The New American Poetry,* edited by Donald Allen, Grove, 1960, *Erotic Poetry,* edited by William Cole, Random House, 1963, *Mark in Time,* edited by Nick Harvey, Glide, 1971, *A Geography of Poets,* edited by Edward Field, Bantam, 1979, *Sparks of Fire,* North Atlantic, 1982, *Practicing Angels,* Seismograph Press, 1986, and *Whitman's Wild Children,* Lapis Press, 1988.

Leslie Epstein

1938-

I was born in 1938, in May, the same month Germans began sending Jews to Dachau. Germans? Jews? Dachau? I saw the light in Los Angeles, and for all I know the nurses in St. Vincent's wore the starched headgear of nuns. One of my earliest memories has to do with that sort of mix-up. I must have been four at the time, maybe five, and was sitting with my playmates around the edge of the Holmby Avenue pond, waiting for tadpoles to turn into frogs. The topic for the day seemed to be religion. At any rate, one of these contemporaries turned to me and said, "What are you?" Here was a stumper. All of the possible answers—a boy, a human, a first-grader—were common knowledge. While I stalled and stammered, one of the others took over:

"I know what I am! I'm a Catholic!"

That rang a bell. An historical tolling. Over a half-century before, and close to a century ago now, my grandfather had stood in line at Ellis Island, wondering how he could translate the family name—Shabilian, one way, Chablian if you're in the fancy mood—into acceptable English. Just in front an immigrant was declaring, *Mine name it is Epstein!* My grandfather, no dummy, piped up, "Epstein! That's my name, too!" Now, on the far side of the continent, his grandson provided the echo:

"Catholic! That's it! That's what I am!"

I must nonetheless have had my doubts, which I brought home that night. That's when I first heard the odd-sounding words, *Jewish, Jew.* "It's what you are," my mother informed me. "Tell your friends tomorrow."

The next afternoon, while the polliwogs battered their blunt heads against the stones of the pond, that is what I blithely proceeded to do. I do not think that, almost fifty years later, I exaggerate the whirlwind of mockery and scorn that erupted about me. I can hear the laughter, see the pointing fingers, still. What horrified my companions, and thrilled them, too, was not so much the news that I was a Jew—surely they knew no more about the meaning of the word than I—as the fact that I had dared to switch sides at all. "Religion changer!" That was the cry. "He changed his religion!" *Vanderbilt:* what if the gentleman, the

Leslie Epstein

greenhorn, ahead of my grandfather had said that magic name? Or Astor? Or Belmont even? What then?

From that day to this, the word *Jew*, especially in the mouth of a Gentile, has remained for me highly charged, with the ability to deliver something like an electric shock—rather the way the touch of a sacred totem might be dangerous to a Trobriand Islander, or the image of God forbidden, awesome, to the devout of my own tribe. The irony is, I doubt whether, through the first decade of my life, I heard the word mentioned within my family at all. In this my parents, the son and daughter of Yiddish-speaking immigrants, were not atypical. The second generation, emancipated, educated, was as often as not hell-bent on sparing the third the kind of orthodox regime they had had to undergo themselves. Still, I imagine the situation of my brother and myself lies beyond the norm. For we were brought up less in the faith of our, than the founding, fathers: that is to say, as Deists, children of the Enlightenment, worshipers before the idol of FDR.

This minimifidianism sprang in part from the fact that our parents had settled in California while still in their twenties. Eastern shrubs in western climes. More decisive, I think, was the reason they'd made the move. Phil, my father, followed his identical twin brother, Julie, to Hollywood, where both began (and Julie yet continues) distinguished screenwriting careers. Now the figure of the Jew, on celluloid, had undergone any number of vicissitudes (my source on the subject is Patricia Erens's *The Jew in American Cinema*); but by the advent of the talkies, particularly with *The Jazz Singer* and *Abie's Irish Rose,* the puddle in the melting pot, the stuffing in the American dream had pretty much taken on, at least insofar as the Jews were concerned, permanent shape. In the latter film, for instance, Abie Levy and Rosemary Murphy have to undergo three different marriage

ceremonies, Episcopal, Jewish, and Catholic. As Erens points out, the title that introduces World War I reads like this:

> *So in they went to that baptism of fire and*
> *thunder—Catholics, Hebrews, Protestants*
> *alike . . .*
> *Newsboys and college boys—aristocrats and*
> *immigrants—all*
> *classes—all creeds—all Americans.*

Moreover, one can easily determine, by the treatment of the descending generations in this film, from the bearded, accented and quite money-minded grandparents on, the ingredients for this Yankle stew: acculturation, assimilation, intermarriage; followed by blondness, blandness, and final effacement. These last three traits are meant always to apply to the third generation. Thus *Abie's Irish Rose* comes to a close with the birth of something like a genetic miracle—twins: Patrick, the lad; the girl, Rebecca. Once established, the movies rarely deviated from this recipe, which Erens calls "the tradition of casting

The author's uncle (left) and father, screenwriters Julius and Philip Epstein,
at Warner Brothers, 1944

Jewish actors as parents and Gentile-looking actors as their children.'' The point I wish to make is that my brother Ricky and I were firmly a part of that tradition.

Make no mistake: my father and uncle were proud of their Jewishness. Hank Greenberg and Sid Luckman were two figures followed with special attentiveness in the Holmby Hills. Indeed, Julie and Phil wrote the script not only for *Casablanca* (whose first word is ''refugees''), but for what I believe is the *only* wartime film that dealt with domestic anti-Semitism. That, of course, is *Mr. Skeffington,* about which The Office of War Information complained, ''This portrayal on the screen of prejudice against the representative of an American minority group is extremely ill-advised.'' Moreover, it should be pointed out that Jews of a certain stripe—the American Jewish Committee, for instance, or the Anti-Defamation League—have, from the days of Griffith's *Intolerance,* through *Gentleman's Agreement* and beyond, been no less zealous than government bureaucrats in trying to expunge the image of the Jew from the screen. Ostrich-ism, not ostracism.

In this atmosphere, is it surprising the real-life children of the film community should suffer the same fate as the Rebeccas and Patricks their parents had created? That my brother and I should, in a sense, be acted by, or inhabited by, Gentiles? Or that, since the word *Jew* had been banished from American popular culture from the beginning to the end of World War II (''If you bring out a Jew in film, you're in trouble'': Louis B. Mayer), it might for the duration disappear from the households of those engaged on that particular front? Remember, the success of *The Jazz Singer,* whose theme was the repudiation of anything resembling ethnicity, turned Warner Brothers into a major studio: the Epstein twins had been writing for Jack (''See that you get a good clean-cut American type for Jacobs'') Warner pretty much from the start of their careers. How could Julie and Phil, busily creating the American dream in a film like *Yankee Doodle Dandy* (don't look for their names in the titles, they gave the credit to a needy friend), not allow their own children to become part of that great national audience of upturned, white, anonymous faces? Would not we, no less than Paul Muni (né Weisenfreund) or Edward G. Robinson (Manny Goldenberg of yore) or John Garfield (another Julie—Garfinkle), become transformed? ''People are gonna find out you're a Jew sooner or later,'' said Warner to Garfield, ''but better later.''

Meanwhile, the lives of the Deists went on. The great ceremony of the year was Christmas. I never lit a Chanukah candle in my life until, mumbling the words of a phonetic prayer, I held the match for my own daughter, my own twin boys. The Chanukah miracle is pretty small potatoes compared to the star in the heavens, the wise men and their gifts, the manger filled with awestruck animals, and finally the birth of the little halo-headed fellow before whom all fall to their knees. Rest assured that when all this was acted out for me, year after year, by the students of the public schools of California (I may well have donned a beard myself, and gripped what might have been a shepherd's crook or wise man's staff: either that, or I am once again adopting the guise—*that's what I am!*—of my friends), the *J*-word was never mentioned.

What most sticks in my mind, however, is the Christmas trees: giant firs, mighty spruces, whose stars—emblematic of the supernova over Bethlehem—grazed our eleven-foot ceilings. There were red balls and silver cataracts of tinsel and strings of winking lights—all strung by the black maid and butler the previous night. Mary and Arthur were there the next morning, too: she, to receive her woolen sweater; he, his briar pipe. Of course my brother and I were frantic with greed, whipped up by weeks of unintelligible hymns (*myrrh,* for instance, or *roundyon* from ''Silent Night,'' or the Three Kings' *orientare*), by the mesmerizing lights and smell of the tree itself, and the sea of packages beneath it—and perhaps above all by the prospect of the rarest of all Epstein phenomena: the sight of our parents, in dressing gowns, with coffee cups, downstairs before the UCLA chimes struck noon.

Hold onto your hats: there was Easter, too. Not a celebration. No ham dinner. No parade. But there was no lack of symbols of rebirth and resurrection: the ones we dyed in pale pastels, the ones we hid under the cushions of the couch, or others, pure chocolate, that we gobbled down. The eggs I remember best were large enough to have been laid by dinosaurs, covered with frosted sugar, with a window at the smaller end. Through this we could see a sylvan scene: bunnies in the grass, squirrels in the trees, and birds suspended in a sky as perpetually blue as the one that arched over the city of the angels. Aside from Christmas and Easter, which created a special sort of pressure, there were ordinary Sundays, when it was my habit to lay late in bed, listening to the radio. More than once, twisting the dial between a boy's piping voice, ''I'm Buster Brown! I live in a Shoe! *Arf! Arf!* That's my dog, Tyge; he lives in there, too!'' and the genie's growl, ''Hold on tight, little master!'' I'd linger at a gospel station. At which point Mary would appear at my bedroom door. "That's right," she'd declare, with a broad smile. "You going to be blessed!" She was at least more subtle than the All-American rabbi in *Abie's Irish Rose,* whose words to a dying soldier the sharp-eyed Ms. Erens quotes as follows:

Have no fear, my son. We travel many roads, but we all come at last to the Father.

Let's make a crucial distinction. Muni Weisenfreund turning into Paul Muni is one thing. Saul of Tarsus becoming Saint Paul is quite another. Everyone knows what happened after the local priest gave his Easter sermon. Those are not chocolate eggs the peasants of Europe have been hunting these hundreds of years. The Jews who were rounded up the month I was born would have gone free, just as the millions who were soon to be gassed in ovens or shot at the edge of ditches would have been spared if Constantine the Great—*religion changer!*—had not seen a flaming cross in the sky: that is, if Christianity had remained, as I dearly wish it had, a minor sect and not become a major heresy. Nonetheless, those performances at Brentwood and Canyon Elementary had done their work. How appealing to a child those dumb donkeys! Those cows of papier-mâché! The mumbo jumbo of *inexcelsisdeo!* Few films have moved me as deeply as Pasolini's *Gospel According to Saint Matthew,* which I sat through twice in a row, weeping at the figure of Jesus, the babe in the grade-school manger, broken now on the cross.

Inconceivable that the whole of the Second World War could go by without leaving a trace. Nor did it. But the truth is that for us, in California, in sunshine, the conflict was more a matter of Japanese than Germans and Jews. I doubt very much whether I noticed when the Orientals in nursery school and kindergarten disappeared. Almost certainly I paid no heed when the same fate befell the old gardener who smoothed our flower beds with his bamboo rake. Odds are I was too distracted by the exciting talk of submarines off the coast, or bombs falling by parachute over Seattle.

There was never any question that the threat to us would come, as it already had at Pearl Harbor, from the Pacific. I can still remember the barrage balloons, like plump brown eggs, tied off the local beaches. My brother—aged what? Three? Four?—saw them from the end of Santa Monica Pier, and began to whimper. A trick of perspective, the sharp sea air, the taut lines gathered on buoys or barges,

Leslie, with his father holding his brother, Ricky, about 1941

made it seem that these fat blimps, a mile offshore, were street corner balloons. "Want one! Want one!" Ricky cried, stamping his feet, throwing himself onto the planks of the dock. For the loss of this toy he would not be consoled.

Throughout the house on Holmby, half-smoked cigarettes, my mother's Chesterfields, bobbed in the waters of the toilet bowls. Sitting ducks, they were, for my stream of urine, which would sooner or later burst the zig-zagging hulls, sending thousands of tiny brown crewmen over the side, to drown next to their floundering transports. Even after the war, when we moved to a yet larger house on San Remo Drive, my fantasies remained fixed upon the Far East. And on nautical warfare. We'd purchased a surplus life raft, yellow rubber on the sides, blue on the bottom, which was initially, thrillingly, inflated by yanking a lever on a tube of gas. In this vessel, on the smooth waters of our swimming pool, I floated for hours. Through the windless afternoon. Under a pitiless sun. The downed airman. With a metal mirror, also surplus, I signaled every passing plane whose silhouette did not resemble that of a Zero.

Naturally my imaginative life was shaped by the movies. The jump from the cartoon festivals I attended each Saturday at the Bruin theater to the war films showing everywhere else seemed a normal progression, just as the cartoons themselves were an innate part of the animism of a child's world. If a discarded pair of pants could become, in the dim light of one's bedroom, a slumbering crocodile, or a breeze in the curtain a masked intruder, then there was little to wonder at when barnyard animals, creatures of instinct much like ourselves, began to dress up, sing like Jiminy Cricket, or scheme for a piece of cheese. Also: murder each other, poleax their enemies, chop them to smithereens, or flatten them, under the wheel of a steamroller, as thin as a dime. All victims, it seemed, had nine lives. No death was unresurrected. It was this, I suppose, along with the white-hat, black-hat morality of the westerns, with their thousands of expendable Indians, that eased the transition to *Winged Victory* and *Pride of the Marines*. Now the enemy were mowed down like ducks, or blown, as Tom was by Jerry and Jerry by Tom, sky high. *Yankee Doodle Mouse*. 1943.

The early immersion in cartoons may help explain why, since I probably saw as many movies about the war in Europe as I did about the fighting in Asia, my attention remained firmly fixed upon the Pacific Theater. The Germans in movies were simply too adult, real smoothies like Conrad Veidt, witty, cunning, prone to understatement and reserve. Even the Prussian stereotypes, the smooth-shaved head, curled lip, and glinting monocle of a Preminger or von Stroheim, possessed a kind of refined sadism worlds removed from the clear-cut cruelty of a mouse handing a cat a sizzling bomb.

There was no problem of reticence in the movies that dealt with the war in the Pacific. Here the violence was full bore. More crucial, the enemy, like the Indians, were a different race—no, almost a different species, like the talking animals we already knew. Indeed, when these short, comical characters—yellow-skinned, buck-toothed, bespectacled—did speak, they had something of the stammer of Porky, or Woody's cackle, or the juicy lisp of Daffy Duck. Thus the most forceful images of war remained, for me, those of death marches, jungle patrols, palm trees bent under withering fire, and kamikaze pilots with blank faces and free-flowing scarves.

What made such pleasure possible was the certainty that nothing I saw was real. I was, remember, a Hollywood child. Towering over the lot at Twentieth Century-Fox was a huge outdoor sky, painted so much like the real one, white clouds against a background of startling blue, that whenever we drove by I had to look twice to see which was which. The decisive moment came when I visited a sound lot, probably at Warners, where a pilot, one of our boys, was trapped inside his burning plane. A cross section of the fuselage rested on sawhorses; the actor's legs protruded beneath it, standing firm on the floor. Also on the floor, flat on their backs, were two civilians, one with a flame-throwing torch, the other with a plain wooden stick. *Action!* shouted the director. At once the pilot began to beat on the inside of his cockpit. The torch shot gobs of fire in front of the white linen background. And the fellow with the stick banged at the fuselage, so that, bucking, shaking, it seemed about to break apart. Finally the pilot managed to pry off his canopy and thrust his head into the wind-machine's gale. *Cut!*

The ambiguity of both that Magritte sky and desperate scene, indeed the tranquil unreality of the war itself: all that concluded one afternoon at Holmby Park. What I remember is my father running pellmell down the avenue, snatching me off the playground swing, and then dashing back up the hill toward our house. "The war is over!" he shouted. Either that, or, "The president is dead!" I have a scar, hardly visible now, under my lip, from the time I fell off that very swing. Possibly it's that catastrophe I recall—the same sense of urgency, the same excitement, the elation at flying along in my father's arms—and not Roosevelt's death, or the bomb-burst that brought the war to an end.

Not long afterwards we moved to the house with the swimming pool. Already my missing schoolmates—the plump, pleasant James Wada, was one—were starting to return. So did our gardener: or someone like him, arriving like a comical fireman in an old truck covered with hoses and ladders and tools. He tended lawns set with cork trees and fig vines and eucalyptus. The property was surrounded by lemon groves, which perfumed the air and filled it, two or three times a year, with canary-colored light. We weren't the first movie people in the neighborhood: Joseph Cotten's place was catercorner, on Montana, and a block or two over, toward Amalfi, were Linda Darnell, Lou Costello, and Virginia Bruce. Down the hill, our school bus made a loop into Mandeville Canyon to drop off the son of Robert Mitchum. Not the first film folk, then: but among the first Jews. For when the former owner of our house, Mary Astor, changed her name, it wasn't from Manny or Muni but the proper Lucille. The Gentile who disguised himself as Phil Green in *Gentleman's Agreement* was none other than our neighbor, Gregory Peck. The closest we came to a refugee was the sight of Thomas Mann, walking his dog along San Remo Drive. The Epsteins were the pioneers.

That meant my friends had such names as Warren and Sandy and Tim and John. We used to build forts together, ride our bikes through the polo fields, and use our Whammos to shoot blue jays and pepper the cars on Sunset Boulevard with the hard round pellets that grew on the stands of cypress above. We also camped out on each other's lawns. The smear of stars in the Milky Way is the prime text for Deists. All is order, beauty, design. The ticking of the master clock. Yet our gaze, once we closed the flap of our pup tents, was lower. In the new sport of masturbation one kept score by palpable results. A drop. A dollop. At one such tourney, the champion posed in our flashlight beams, his member bent at the angle of a fly rod fighting a trout. At precisely the midway point in twentieth-century America, the rest of us, the slow pokes, saw that something was amiss. Uncircumcised. Here was a rip, a rent, in the universal design. From this common sight I drew a skewed lesson. I may have been in the immediate majority, hygienic as any in the crowd. Yet I knew as gospel that the one who had been torn from the true course of nature was not he, the victor, our pubescent pal, but I.

Which is to say that, over time, we discovered differences. This was palmy Pacific Palisades: no crosses were burned in yards, no swastikas were scratched on lampposts. In our half-wilderness—polo ponies in the fields below, and, above, hills covered with yucca, prowled by bobcats—there were not even lamps. Why, quail sang in our hedges and stood on the lawns! The bus for Ralph Waldo Emerson Junior High School picked us up at a vacant lot on Sunset near Amalfi. Wheat seemed to be growing in it, and fiddleheads that tasted like licorice. One morning I arrived to find that the usual allegiances had shifted. My friends greeted me by throwing clods of dirt, sending me back to the wrong side of the boulevard. They arched their bomblets over the traffic. Their cry was "Kike! Go Home! Kike! Kike!"

Now this was not, in the words of the old transcendentalist, the shot heard round the world. Certainly the incident was a far cry from the kind of warfare the Epstein boys had engaged in, circa 1921, on the Lower East Side. There, you had to battle your way, against the Irish, against the Italians, just to get to the end of the block. On the other hand, while my schoolmates had never learned Emerson's pretty rhyme—

*Nor knowest thou what argument
Thy life to thy neighbor's creed has lent—*

I knew what a kike was. *Not,* as in Salinger's story, something that goes up in the air. Thus I went home, as commanded, from which sanctuary Arthur drove me to school in the Buick.

Once a year farflung branches of the family gathered for the Passover Seder at my grandfather's house in Santa Monica—a time warp away, hyperspace distant, from Białystok. "Say, der!" we called it, gazing with some dismay at these strange, gawky relations, mole-covered, all thumbs. The only cousins who counted were Jimmy and Lizzie, who, since they were Julie's children, and Julie and Phil—bald from their college days, two eggs in a carton, peas in a pod—were identical twins, were therefore my genetic half-brother and sister. Jim (later a starter at Stanford) and I made a point of throwing the football around the backyard and bowling over the pale kinfolk as if they had been candlepins. During the ceremony itself, which droned on forever, Jim and I would sit at the far end of the table, arm wrestling amidst the lit candles, the bowls of hot soup, the plates of (here is a title for a novel, or a memoir like this) *Bitter Herbs.* The empty chair, we were told, the untouched glass of wine, were not for yet more distant cousins, missing in Europe, unheard from since the start of the war, but for Elijah, who was fed by ravens and departed the earth in a chariot of fire.

The "Seder Boys"—Epstein with cousin Jimmy, about 1983

That was the extent of my religious knowledge. Not once had I set foot in a synagogue, or been exposed to so much as a page of the Bible. I knew more about gospel music—*You going to be blessed*—and Christmas Hymns—*Glo-or-i-a-a, or-or-i-a-a, or-or-i-a-a, oria!*—than I did about the songs concerning grasshoppers and boils that my relatives chanted while thrusting their fingers into the sweet, red wine. Bar-mitzvahed? Perish the thought! Yet the idea must have occurred to someone, because, for perhaps three weeks in a row, I found myself in a Sunday school class of glum Jews whose dogma was so reformed in nature as to hardly differ from that of Franklin and Jefferson and the other founders. About this trial I remember little. Bad food, for one thing. And a distinctly dubious rabbi. My fellow sufferers seemed unlikely to be interested either in the fortunes of the Hollywood Stars—not the film colony, but our Triple-A franchise—or pup tent pleasures. Before I left, or, more likely, was asked to leave (the issue being my habit of roller-skating between the pews of the temple), I did pick up the fragment, the refrain, of one new song: *Zoom-golly-golly-golly,* so went the nonsense syllables, *Zoom-golly-golly!* Then I zoomed off myself, on my eight little wheels, back to the rhapsodies of secular life: *Sha-boom!* and *Gee (love that girl),* by the Four Crows.

I got ice-cream! Every flavor! Chocolate! Coffee! Vanilla! Strawberry! Lamb chop!" That speech, from a little Cub Scout play, was the first line I can remember writing. I suppose it was in the cards I would try my hand at the craft. Phil and Julie, unique among studio employees, did their writing at home. Once, Jack Warner cracked down about this, pointing out that their contract called for them to be at work on the lot by 9:00 A.M., just as bank presidents had to. "Then tell a bank president to finish the script," said one or the other of the twins, and drove off the premises. It wasn't long before Warner had another such fit, demanding that the boys, as they were habitually called, show up at the stipulated hour. They did, and at the end of the day sent over the typescript. The next morning Warner called them in and began to shout about how this was the worst scene he'd read in his life. "How is this possible?" asked the first twin. Concluded the second, "It was written at nine." So it was that I'd often lie upstairs, on the carpet, outside the closed library door. From the other side I'd hear a muffled voice—maybe Julie's: *yattita-yattita-yattita,* it would declame, with rising inflection; then another voice, let's say Phil's, would respond, *yattita-yattita-yattita!* Then both

Playing tennis at Webb School, 1955

would break out together, indistinguishably, in their crystal-shattering laugh. It seemed an attractive way to live one's life.

Still and all I don't think I wrote a story until my first year at University High. What I remember of it, more than three and a half decades later, is a public plaza, a milling crowd, a feeling of excitement, anticipation. There is, in the description of the square, the clothing, the mustachioed faces, something of a South American flavor. The snatches of dialogue, while not Spanish, must have been accented somehow. Buenos Aires, then. There was no real plot, only the waiting, the crush of numbers, the electric expectation. Finally, when the tension was as great as a fourteen-year-old could make it, that is, when all the upturned faces had turned in the direction of the tall brick building, when all eyes were focused upon the high balcony that jutted out over the square, the closed doors of the palace open. A small figure, unprepossessing, clean-shaven save for his mustache, and dressed in plain uniform, moves into the open. A sudden hush falls over the crowd. The man, not young, aged in fact sixty-three, steps forward. He leans over the balcony's wrought-iron rail. Then, suddenly, he stands upright and raises his right hand in the air. A great wave of sound, long suppressed, breaks from the crowd. It is half a sigh, half a shout. *"Viva!"* That is the cry. *"Viva,* Hitler!"

Where on earth, or at any rate in California, with its blue skies, from which the sun shone in winter at much the same angle it did in July, did this vision of evil incarnate come from? Had I, after all, noted something hidden, unspoken in those wartime films? Or heard a few whispered remarks around the Seder table? Or seen, in newspapers, a blurred early image of what would later become such familiar photos: bulldozers at work on piles of bodies; heaps of spectacles, sheared hair, shoes; wraithlike figures in striped pajamas; the lamp shades, the ovens, the showers, the ditches? The answer is no, and no, and no. Rather, an answer of yes would be superfluous here. The truth is I had always known—in the same way that one knows, from childhood on, the laws of gravitation. What goes up must come down. From childhood? I might have been born with an innate grasp of the fate of the Jews. What a person learns later, the facts of physics, the formulas about the mass of objects and the square of their distance, only confirms what he carries within like the weight of his bones. Hints, hushings, inflections, a glance: these pass from Jew to Jew, and from child to child, by a kind of psychic osmosis. So it was that history passed molecule by molecule through the membrane that held me apart from my fellows, and apart from a world long denied.

That's not the end of the story. Indeed, there was a second piece of fiction written for that same freshman class. The time, the present: that is, 1953. The place: the American Southwest. We see an old man, a prospector perhaps, a desert rat, dragging his way across the alkali flats. He pulls his burro behind him. The plot, hazily remembered, involves the way he had tricked everyone into thinking he had left the area, when in fact he had no intention of quitting the spot. It may be he was about to make his big strike. Or might have remained from cussedness alone. In any case the ending goes something like this. As the man and beast turn eastward, away from the setting sun, the sky lights up in a fireball, which grows larger and larger, lighting up the white sands, the tall cacti, the quartz hills, brighter than any day.

I mention this tale not because its subject, like that of its companion piece, was, for the frosh squad, so portentous, but because it indicates that in matters of war and peace my gaze was still out over the Pacific. How could it be anywhere else? The year before we had exploded a hydrogen bomb on the atoll of Eniwetok, and now the Russians had replied in kind. The weapon that had leveled Hiroshima, and killed a hundred thousand Japanese, served as a mere trigger, a kind of spark, for these giant explosions. The very air, it was thought, might catch fire. At University High we drilled for the moment the bomb would fall. There were three levels of strategy. The first, which assumed we had something like an hour's

notice, involved a brisk march through the hallways and down the stairs to the fallout shelter in the boy's locker room. Not much different than a fire-drill, really, except that instead of milling outside we waited for the all-clear with our backs against the green metal doors. An imminent attack was indicated by a pattern of bells. The teacher lowered the blinds against flying glass while the students filed into the hall: silent, we were, in the dim light, the endless corridors. But the maneuver we practiced over and over occurred when there was to be no warning at all. A student might be in the middle of a recitation, *Tomorrow and tomorrow and tomorrow* from *Macbeth,* when suddenly, from nowhere, the teacher would bark out the word, "Drop!" There would be a rustle, a rumble—falling books, falling bodies, a flutter of paper—as we hurled ourselves under our desks. We tucked our heads into our laps and clutched our knees, like the little crustaceans, the tightly coiled sow bugs, we unearthed from our lawns. The main thing, the great thing, was not to look out the windows. The light would blind us. It would fry the whites of our eyes.

Silent in the hallways, silent in the nation at large. Dumbstruck. Numb. This is how my brother and I entered the fifties. Ricky had already taken the measure of this world: he knew an illusion, a veil of Maya, when he saw one. Hence he drew inward, toward the realm of the spirit. That is to say, he drifted yet further toward the East—specifically toward the gardens and incense clouds and priests of Vedanta. I am certain that Ricky's sudden, but lifelong, interest in Karma, the way one's actions determine his destiny in past and future incarnations, the hope of rebirth on a higher plane, the dream of final release from the endless round of being—that all this was precipitated by the death of our father in 1952.

Even then we did not enter a synagogue. What rabbi could hope to match the vision of Nirvana preached by the followers of Vivekananda? Or compete with the scenes—Alec Guinness scrambling down the Eiffel Tower, clutching his ill-gotten gains—in the movie we attended instead of the funeral? A comedy, no less. There might be an echo, in our laughter that afternoon, of the afternoons at the Bruin. No death, to a child, is irrevocable. Cartoon critters pop up living and breathing. Why not our father, in the guise of his identical twin? Retake. Double exposure. Remember, though, that at the end of *The Lavender Hill Mob* Guinness is punished for his thievery and led off in chains. The doctrine of Karma is no less strict than the Hollywood

Production Code. Our crime, those hours distracted, the glee, may yet lead to a lower form of existence— as Republicans, say, or reptiles—in the incarnation to come.

I cannot say whether Ricky was aware of the Holocaust, or, if he was, whether the knowledge had anything to do with his withdrawal. I do think that what little the country had discovered—in newsreels, mostly—about the destruction of the Jews of Europe, and the consequent erasure of those same mental traces, may have had no small part to play in the symptoms of paranoia, the deep, dumb shock, that characterized the decade. I do not mean to say the national hysteria had more to do with denial of the Holocaust than apprehension about the role of the Soviet Union in Europe and its testing of the same kinds of weapons we had already used. But those quick glimpses on the Movietone screen were not altogether ineradicable. That they left a mark could be determined from the kinds of comments people allowed themselves at the time. "How could these things happen in *Germany?*" was the most common remark. So clean. So enlightened. So civilized. Now we know better. It was the very modernity of German culture, its mastery of technology and the means of mass communication, that made it, with its glorification of violence, its infatuation with death, not our century's aberration, but its paradigm. Hence the chill that fell over the land. All the values of modern life had been given an ironic twist, a mocking echo. Belief in cleanliness? Here were bars of human soap. The quest for light? Here were lamp shades of human skin. What we feared in the fifties was not only communism, it was ourselves.

Throughout the nation, of course, the fear of fascism and the Yellow Peril had long since been replaced by that of the Red Menace. The hysteria was greatest in Hollywood, which, as Adolphe Menjou told the Committee, "is one of the main centers of Communism in America." If I had been older, and less sheltered, I might have found an example of resistance, one full of insouciance and dash, within my own family. When, in the late forties, Jack Warner testified before the House Un-American Activities Committee he produced a ludicrous list of subversives, largely consisting of those with whom he had contractual disputes. It included Philip G. and Julius J. Epstein, Roosevelt Democrats, on the grounds that they always seemed to be on the side of the underdog. Little wonder, then, that when Martin Dies took over the Committee he should send them a two-part questionnaire. The first question was, *Have you ever been a member of a subversive organization?* The second

Yale graduation photo, 1960

was, *What was that organization?* To part one the boys dutifully answered, "Yes." To part two they wrote, "Warner Brothers."

But I, no less than Ricky, or the country, joined the ranks of the silent, the stunned. After my quick start in the freshman year at high school, I withdrew. That is to say, I did not write any more stories, or playlets, or imaginative prose of any kind, until my undergraduate years in New Haven were drawing to a close. Why not? While the answer is complex, I think it fair to state that in the course of the decade I was, all unwittingly, willy-nilly, coming to a decision: when I was ready to write, it would be as a Jew; or, better, when I was a Jew, I would be ready to write. There was, however, a long way to go.

Among the newsreel pictures in my own mental gallery—wasn't there a crowing rooster in the old Pathé titles, much like the roaring lion in MGM's?— are shots of crowds dancing about piles of burning books and young, grinning soldiers cutting the beards of learned men. These images, together with what I soon read about the music the Nazis banned from their concert halls and the paintings they mocked in their Exhibition of Degenerate Art, convinced me that the war against the Jews was in some measure a war against the nature of the Jewish mind. Absurd, I know, to claim that by exterminating the Jews the Germans were in fact attempting to eliminate Jewish art: but it is far from senseless to claim that the oppressors had come to identify the Jews with some quality of imagination, and in creating a world without one they were attempting to confirm that it was possible to live without the other.

In a sense the Third Reich had no choice. An aesthetic of Blood and Kitsch must, by its very nature, try to undo that embodied in Abraham and Isaac: that is, imaginative reenactment, the metaphorical power of words, the inseparable link between act and consequence, and the symbolic prohibition of human sacrifice. Specifically, what fascism repudiates in the ancient tale is the power of faith, the recognition of limits, and trust in the word of God. Enter the Jews. It was they who took the greatest imaginative leap of all, that of comprehending, out of nothingness, an empty whirlwind, the glare of a burning bush, the "I am that I am." In spite of much backsliding, in spite of having been warned by a jealous God (in a commandment they have rebelled against ever since) not to make likenesses, this people have continued that "repetition in the finite mind of the eternal act of creation" that Coleridge defined as the essence of imagination. In an age when such faith was no longer tenable, when the supreme fiction, *which is that we matter,* became a rebuke to the countervailing belief, *which was that everything is possible,* then those finite minds, with their dream of the infinite, had to be eliminated.

These are the thoughts, or half-thoughts, I entertain now. The lesson I drew at the time, however, was little more than the proven adage: hard to be a Jew. And dangerous, as well. Once, in the mid-fifties, traveling back to California for summer vacation, I found myself on a New Orleans bus. A pleasant-looking lady leaned forward from the seat behind. "See that? See him there?" she asked, pointing out the window to where a motorcycle policeman sat on his machine, hidden behind a billboard. I nodded. The belle of the south lowered her voice. "The Jews put him there!" Now I knew how Gregory Peck felt, but—the Jew as Gentile, not the Gentile as Jew—in reverse. He had a swell speech for the occasion. I held my peace. A smile sufficed, and a nod.

Nonetheless, within me the ice was breaking. For one thing I had wheels. The friends with whom I cruised Hollywood Boulevard in the latest model of the Buick turned out—to my surprise: no, to my shock—to have names like Alan and Robbie and David and Dick. Similarly, the books I was reading, and the stories in the *New Yorker,* were written by fellows like Norman and Saul and Bernard and, soon enough, Philip. Not to mention J.D. I saw new kinds

of movies: *Night and Fog, The Diary of Anne Frank,* and, best of all, Renoir's *La Règle du Jeu.*

So beneath the calm surface much was in turmoil. The symptom was this: no matter what situation I found myself in, I moved to the verge, the very edge. More to the point, having already been thrown out of the Jewish temple, I now proceeded to get myself banished from the citadels of Christendom. First, was the Webb School, where I'd been sent, with several dozen other products of broken or unhappy homes, two years after my father's death. *With the cross of Jeee-suus,* these were the words I mouthed in compulsory chapel, *going on beeeforrre!*

"What's this?" asked one of the preppies, as the turnips were plopped on his plate.

"The week's profit," sweetly said I.

Gone. Rusticated. Dismissed. Expelled. In the land of the *goyim,* however, what is done may, through contrition, repentance, and a good deal of breast-beating, be undone. The suspension lasted only three days. Perhaps my goal was not so much to draw the wrath of the Christians as to bask in their forgiveness. Better a prodigal son than no son at all. A more likely explanation is that, at loose ends, in limbo, I was pushing myself toward becoming that marginal figure, the wisecracking Jew.

Then the scene shifted. Off I went to college in the cold cloudy East. My instructions from Uncle Julie were as follows: when in New Haven buy an overcoat at Fenn-Feinstein; when in New York, eat the free rolls at Ratner's. There I was, a freshman again, at Second Avenue and Fifth. My coat, three sizes too large, was reddish-brown, with hairs sticking out of the lining. On my head, a snappy hat. Round my neck a Lux et Veritas tie. After studying the menu I raised a finger to the waiter. "I'm not electric," he said, hobbling by. A quarter of an hour later a second old man shuffled over.

"What's this *ma-ma-li-ga?*" I inquired.

Said he: "Not for you."

At about the same time I first met my maternal grandparents, who lived off the Boardwalk in Atlantic City. What drew me to them, through the last half of the fifties, and into the sixties too, was the way the aged couple clung together, whereas my own family had always gone their separate ways. A dead cigar in his lips, Herman would bicycle through the streets of the black ghetto, collecting rent. Our favorite restaurant—Clara, bedridden, was not to know—was a place that fried up forbidden crab cakes. Once I was at their shabby flat watching the evening news. "Nixon!" Herman said, grabbing his nose. "P! U!"

The waiter was right. Not for me. Not yet. It was still the era of the deaf and dumb. But things were soon to change. One afternoon at Yale, where the quota for those of the Mosaic persuasion was 10½ percent, I was standing on High Street when the Mayor came out of Fenn-Feinstein and stepped into the barber shop next door. "What's the Mayor doing?" asked my current straight man, as His Honor emerged from the doorway and moved toward the entrance to Barrie Shoes.

"Wednesday. 2:00 P.M.," I replied, not quite *sotto voce.* "Collection time."

We were, remember, still in the fifties. The next thing I knew I had been thrust up against the side of a car, had handed over my wallet, and been told to be at the Dean's office the next morning at 10:00 A.M. By eleven, I was no longer a Son of Eli. Historians may yet come to note that this injustice, together with the response it provoked, represented the true birth pangs of the counterculture. I did not, as demanded, return to California. I spent a pleasant fortnight in nearby Hamden, strolling to the campus each evening to be interviewed by various senior societies, Manuscript, Elihu, Scroll & Key. Meanwhile, enough of a flap had developed—beginning with mimeographed notes on bulletin boards and ending with an interesting call from the *New Haven Register*—to bring about my reinstatement. Thus did the balance of power between the student and administrative bodies begin to tip. Some years later, after my years at the Drama School, the quota had been abandoned, Bobby Seale was camped on the New Haven Green, and the knock on the Elihu door was answered by—her blouse unbuttoned, a babe at her breast—a co-ed. *Après moi, le déluge.*

Oxford, or "Oggsford," as my coreligionist Meyer Wolfsheim is made in *The Great Gatsby* to call it, proved a tougher nut to crack. What do you do with people who, when asked to pass the salt, say, "Sorry!"? My boorish crowd used to hang out in the taverns and try, with comments on the weather and the bangers and the temperature of the beer, to drive the locals out. The low point (or pinnacle, depending) of this campaign occurred in the dining hall of my College, Merton (a place so stuck-in-the-mud that its library, as old as Bologna's, turned down the gift of T. S. Eliot's manuscripts because he was not yet dead). Let me paint the scene. On the floor are a series of long tables, upon which sit pots of marmalade made from the very oranges Richard the Lion-hearted sent back from Seville. Huddled on long benches are the undergraduates, shoveling down peas and gruel. On a platform, perpendicular to the

masses, the Dons are drawn up at high table. The crystal, the flatware, shine. The chef, a Frenchman, has made a *poulet en papillote.* Even down in the pit, we can hear the puff of the little paper bags as they are punctured by the professors' tines. Time for the savory. The Dons tilt back their heads, dangling asparagus spears over their open mouths. But what's this? A stir on the floor? Where the Americans sit? In the Jewry? Indeed, at the moment, friend Fried, out of New Jersey, is about to be sconced.

Sconce, says the OED. *At Oxford, a fine of a tankard of ale or the like, imposed by undergraduates on one of their number for some breach of customary rule when dining in hall.*

The first infraction, 1650, was for "absence from prayers." Fried's folly, however, was making a serious remark, since the aforesaid rule forbade any conversation about one's studies, about politics, or anything that might be construed as an idea. That left the girls at Saint Hilda's and cricket. No sooner had Fried made his point about Marxist dialectics that gleeful cackle broke out among the Brits. Instantly a waiter appeared, sporting the usual bloodshot cheeks and bushy mustache. In his arms he held the foaming chalice that untold numbers of Merton men—including, surely, the animated Eliot—had raised to their lips. Fried, deep in his argument, paid no mind. The ruddy waiter—in his white apron he looked the kosher butcher—tapped him on the shoulder and held up, with a grin and a wink, the tankard. Fried whirled round.

"What am I supposed to do with this?" he asked, as if unaware that custom dictated he drink down the contents and order an equal portion for all those at table. "Shove it up your ass?"

Immense silence. Everything—the Dons with their buttery spears, the students balancing peas on their knives, the thunderstruck waiter—was as frozen, as still, as the twelfth-century fly caught in the marmalade amber. Then, as if a howitzer had been fired, a sudden recoil. The students shrank away on every side, their hands to their mouths. "Oh!" they cried. "Oh, God!" Meanwhile Fried had turned back to his interlocutor, out of California, and together they resumed their argument about the merits of Marx and Freud, a sort of mental arm wrestling not much different from that at the end of the Seder table.

Clearly if Fried was not rusticated for this, I had my work cut out for me. To make a long story short I found myself on the telephone with the head of my department, Dame Helen Gardner. I fear that in so many words I told her that she ought to deposit her Anglo-Saxon riddles and Middle English charms (how to get honey from honeybees, for example, or cows out of bogs) where my compatriot had suggested placing the tankard of ale. Then, having resigned the major, I packed my bags, determined to leave the university at the start of the next term.

The two best things about an Oxford education are the length of the vacations and the relative proximity of the Mediterranean Sea. I'd already been to Greece, Spain, Italy, and Southern France. Now, on a broken-down freighter, the *Athenai,* I chugged right across the greasy, gray waters. Easy enough in the lurching bowels of this vessel to imagine that you were your own grandparents, storm-tossed, debating whether it was permitted to survive on a scrap of pork. Never mind that this journey lasted only two days, and that the welcoming landmark was not the Statue of Liberty but the golden dome of the Bahai temple, high above the harbor at Haifa.

What happened to me in Israel was at once common enough, and most bizarre. Instantaneously, virtually on the docks, the wall between myself and the world, that membrane, dissolved. Before my eyes hustled Jewish porters, policemen, soldiers and sharpies and sellers of pretzels. Osmosis cannot take place, nor can one live on the margin, or be expelled, when there are Jews in solution inside and out. The idea that I had grown up with—that the very word *Jew* was awesome, sacred, terrible, not to be thought of, never mentioned—became ludicrous on these shores swarming with the usual run of big shots and bums. What made Israel so appealing to many Jews like me (and so repugnant to the zealots of Crown Heights and the Mea Shearim) was the promise of the ordinary, the prospect of the mundane. Only in the Holy Land could the Jews escape being a holy people.

The impact of that part of my trip (the fact that I now kept track of Sandy Koufax on his way to mowing down 269 of the *goyim*) was altogether banal. But there were eerier forces at work, and they involved the history of the Germans and Jews. Of course I visited the memorial at Yad Vashem and the smaller museum, with its cases of torn scrolls and striped pajamas, on Mount Zion. At the center of everything, dominating each day, was the spectacle of a well-guarded German, Eichmann, pleading for his life before a court of his former victims. What was odd about these things was that I saw them in the company of someone who belonged to the last generation of Germans to feel, if not guilt, then more than a twinge of shame. This was Katrin, an architect

from Munich, whom I had met aboard the *Athenai.* Everything you need to know about her background may be inferred from the fact that the name on her passport read Karen and had been changed by her parents to avoid what became, in the Third Reich, the most fashionable Aryan moniker.

Our relationship ("Don't tell Clara" was Herman's reaction upon hearing the news) was to last five years. When it ended I met—and was eventually to marry—a young woman who had also been a passenger on the *Athenai,* just one week before Katrin and I. That we had both suffered seasickness on that old Greek tub and had quite likely rubbed elbows in one museum or the other was but one of a series of near misses. Here was an image in a flawed mirror: an identical twin herself, and not the offspring of identical twins; a mother dead in childhood instead of a father; years on the beaches of Florida instead of California; Christmas celebrated, but without servants, carols, trees.

All this had to be sorted out in the future. At present fate had more tricks in store. My plans to leave Oxford were suddenly abandoned when Khrushchev put up the Berlin Wall. Waiting for me in England was a letter from my draft board stating that I would be inducted the moment I set foot on native soil. "Agriculture": that was the first degree-granting program listed in the University Bulletin, which I'd dashed the mile to the Bodleian to read in only a little over the landmark 3:59.4 that Roger Bannister, my fellow Oxonian, had set a few years before. *Better boot camp,* I decided. *Better Berlin.* The Bulletin's second entry was "Anthropology." The wise guy set out to talk his way back into yet another institution of learning. *Dip. Anthro. Oxon* reads my laconic degree.

But it was the beast in man I studied, while pretending to solve the kinship system among the Nuer. Nor was it the wall in Berlin that occupied me, but the one the Berliners had erected in the streets of Warsaw. In brief, I spent my second year in Oxford reading everything I could about the Holocaust, including the story of the Elder of the Łodz Ghetto— one paragraph in Gerald Reitlinger's important book *The Final Solution.* I turned down that page in my mind. When I wasn't reading, I was writing. The subject, at last, was myself.

This story, my first as an adult, was called "The Bad Jew," and in it the title character—a cool Californian, aloof from the faith of his fathers, unmoved by the traces of the Holocaust he sees about him—is nursed through an illness by two aged

With wife, Ilene, about 1983

survivors. While recovering he comes across a long letter from one child in a death camp to another. The key passage deals with the time the writer, Jacob, gave way to despair and attempted to smother himself beneath a pile of dirt in Bergen-Belsen. He is foiled, first, by the sensation of an earthworm moving up his leg, and then by the fear that the slightest movement on his part will crush that little creature. The right thing to do, he realizes, both for himself and the Jews, is simply to wait. At this point a shift occurs in the tone of the story. The burden of irony, of detachment, is shifted from my alter-ego to the survivor, the mother of the dead Jacob. The crisis takes place when, on a bus trip across the desert, she turns in disgust from a group of dark-skinned Sephardim and says to the hero, *"Schvartzers!* Look at them! *Schvartzers!"* The Angelino, while no angel, is no longer the bad Jew.

The story has never been published. While it was making the rounds I returned full circle, to the sunshine, to the Pacific, in order to study Theater Arts at UCLA. Even then I sensed I owed this much to that city and those climes: if I had grown up there as a Jewish child, that is, if there had been nothing to

search for, no vacuum to fill, I would never have become a Jewish adult. Now Ricky and I lived in an empty flat on Fountain Avenue. He burned his incense in one room. I wrote in another. The year sped quickly by. I was jogging with a friend, my old pal Alan, when the Cuban Missile Crisis was at its worst: no way to fast talk my way out of that one. Koufax, I noted, was on his way to winning 25 games and striking out 306. Marilyn Monroe died, and so did Pope John.

Adolf Eichmann, of course, had already been hanged. In the course of that year the work that affected me most was Hannah Arendt's account of his trial. What so angered her critics—her claim that the Jewish leadership in Europe had been so compromised, so woeful, that the Jews themselves would have been better if they had had no self-government at all, and had merely run—seemed to me then, as it does now, so obvious as to be almost a truism. How on earth could things have been worse? The second half of her thesis, concerning the banality of the *Obersturmbannfuehrer,* and of evil in general, was not welcome news either. Clearly her readers, Jews and Gentiles, were more comfortable thinking of Eichmann and Himmler and Goebbels and the rest as either subhuman, or superhuman, monsters, beasts, psychopaths, and not as human beings much like themselves. What struck me most about her argument—that evil was a kind of thoughtlessness, a shallowness, an inability to realize what one is doing, a remoteness from reality, and, above all, a denial of one's connectedness to others—was how much radical wickedness resembled a defect, and perhaps a disease, of imagination.

That malady, whose symptom, a stunned silence, was as prevalent in the sixties as in the fifties, could only be healed by the writers and poets whose special responsibility was to show the world what those plain men had done. As Arendt maintained, only those who have the imagination to recognize what they share with the force of evil—in her words, "the shame of being human . . . the inescapable guilt of the human race"—can fight against it. And only that fight, it seemed to me, that fearlessness, could give meaning to the suffering of the Jewish people and, in that narrow sense, bring the millions of dead back to life.

With daughter, Anya, 1971

Grandiose thoughts, granted. I cannot claim to have entertained them, or worked them through, at the time. But it was partly under Arendt's spell that I spent the academic year writing a play. It doesn't take a prophet to guess the subject. An Ivy Leaguer, living abroad, first initial L., falls in love with a German heroine, first initial K. In spite of some humor ("An American Jew is someone who thinks a *shiksa* is an electric razor"), this is a tortured piece of work, haunted ("I have the feeling, when I think of Europe, of what happened here, that I ought to be dead") by the destruction of the Jews. Somehow, it won a large prize, the Samuel Goldwyn Award, and persuaded Yale to let me in yet again—this time to the School of Drama.

The award ceremony provided a kind of Hollywood ending. Certainly it drew many loose ends together, completing a kind of cycle. Goldwyn (né Goldfish) was the producer of one of my father's last films. Uncle Julie was in the audience. So was his ten-year-old son, Philip, named for his identical twin. Jimmy and Liz, grown-up, were in the auditorium, too. Alfred Hitchcock, for the Christians, gave a speech and handed over the prize. Thus did the film industry, which had played such a large role in making my childhood *Judenrein,* now bestow upon me—and for a play so Jewish it would make *Abie's Irish Rose* look like a crowd-pleaser at Oberammergau—its imprimatur.

Still, there were no happy endings. Katrin was in Munich, recovering from a recurrence of tuberculosis she had contracted during the war. I was already preparing for my trip to the East. Little did I know I would not return—at least not for more than a few days at a time—to the West Coast again. "Include me out": that is not just a wacky Goldwynism. It is a description, canny to the point of genius, of the lives that Jews lived on the screen, and beneath the white clouds and peacock blue of the painted sky.

But I was back for good beneath the changeable vault of the East. I spent two years at the Drama School, feigning sore throats so I would not have to act in my own plays. None of these works had a Jewish theme or Jewish characters. It may or may not be a coincidence that this time I was not expelled. Immediately after completing my residency I started work at Queens College, where I was to remain for the next thirteen years. Apart from my marriage and the birth of my three children, two significant things happened during those years: I came to love the city that the Reverend Jackson quite accurately called Hymietown; and I began to write fiction. This work, on its own, it seemed, willy-nilly, veered back to what appears to be my natural subject. The first story dealt with an article from the newspapers—a Yeshiva playground under attack by a group of blacks; the second was about an exiled Romanian who had spent his entire life attempting to prove that Mozart was a Jew. Because both were immediately accepted for publication I wrote others. It was momentum, then, that drew me from the theater, though I have never stopped staging plays, sometimes of full chapter length, inside of most of what I've written since.

I finished my first novel under the thatched roof of a house in Holland, where I was teaching on a Fulbright. I can easily remember lifting, or half-lifting, its last words from what I recalled of *Little Dorrit*: ". . . they passed up and out of the courtyard itself, into the sky, like dandelions blown over the domes and towers and hot busy people of Moscow." Then I walked into our little Dutch garden and looked up at the real sky, which in the late afternoon was half pink, half blue, as if stitched like a flag down the middle. A writer isn't likely to forget such a moment—or the one, some months later, back in my windowless Queens College cubicle, when my agent called to say that an editor had accepted *P. D. Kimerakov* for publication. Here's a rarity: I've had the same agent, Lois Wallace, and the same editor, Joe Kanon, through thick and thin ever since.

For my next project I gathered five of my published stories into a book, *The Steinway Quintet Plus Four*. The only class I ever had in writing fiction occurred when Joe, his two assistants, and I sat late one night with the manuscript all about us, scissoring out paragraphs, crossing off passages, pasting, rearranging, and smearing with pizza sauce some eighty thousand words I had always assumed to be sacred. Even then I was beginning to think about my second novel. For some reason I found myself going back to the battered Reitlinger volume (I have it, in pieces, still), which fell open to that same page 63 I had turned down in the winter of 1961–62: "At Łodz, however, the Germans chose a president in October, 1939, who suited their purposes for nearly five years. Mordechai Chaim Rumkowski . . ."

For the next year I spent every day at the YIVO Institute for Jewish Research, Fifth Avenue and 86th Street, reading everything I could about this man. The library itself was on the second floor of what must have once been a mansion, and the requested books came up the dumb waiter inside the librarian's flowered purse. The oddest, and in retrospect most frightening, aspect of this year was the way my heart, instead of skipping a beat, or stopping, at these accounts of misery and woe, pumped merrily along, essentially undeflected. I think I must have sensed soon after I began my research that if I were to get through such material at all, to say nothing of being able to think about it and shape it, I would have to draw a psychic shutter between myself and these tales of the fate of the Jews. Thus I sat through long winter months, wrapped in my overcoat, calmly, callously reading.

Finally, one day in spring, I looked up from my text. Sunlight shone from the west, lighting up the window box. The top of the trees in the park had already started to bud. *I'm going to be punished for this,* I thought. *I'm going to have nightmares.* Then I dropped my eyes to the book. In it a German officer was putting his ear to the side of a bus in which Jews were being gassed. "Just like in a synagogue," he says, of the wailing from within; and that, word for word, is how I recorded the line in my notebook and the novel to come.

There were no nightmares. I started work on my book, not looking back. "In the winter of 1918–1919, on a day when the wind was blowing, I. C. Trumpleman arrived in our town." Wait a minute! Who's talking here? Why so jaunty? So homey? So familiar? I stopped. More solemnly I started again. Before I was done with page 1, I'd described another window box, "through which you can see clouds and birds and the lemon-colored lozenge of the Polish sun." Worse still! That "you," as if the speaker felt he could just come up and drop his hand on your shoulder; that sun like a cough drop. What nerve, what cockiness! Again I halted. High seriousness I wanted—not high spirits. Yet no matter which way I turned it, the material kept coming out in a tone so lighthearted and glad-to-be-alive—so much that of the reader's friend—that I had no choice but to surrender to it.

What, then, of the punishment I'd as much as promised myself? The nightmares that never came? One has only to wait. True, it did seem for a time there might be no price to pay at all. *King of the Jews* was more successful than I had dared hope: nominated for awards, translated into many foreign languages, still in print after more than a decade, it has come to look like a classic book on the Holocaust. The trouble started when, just before publication, I moved to Boston and began work on my next novel. It proved almost impossible to write. Everywhere I looked in this new manuscript I saw pain and death: amputations, autopsies, disinterments, acts of torture; whole armies crossed rivers, like Caesar's men, on the backs of their fallen comrades. I realized that all the horror I had kept from the pages of my Holocaust novel was now returning, as if in a reflex of revenge. Thousands of missing corpses were pressing round.

Clearly enough, I'd been made the butt of a joke, of an ironical trick I'd played on myself. It was as if I'd made a pact with my emotions not to feel, not to respond, but had forgotten about what might happen when the pact came to an end. This was the working out of one of the great archetypes of the culture, the bargain whose deepest meaning is never grasped by the bargainer: the man who asks for immortality but neglects to request perpetual youth; the figure who puts on a mask he can't remove; or a version of "The Sorcerer's Apprentice," in which the very powers sought for—to animate, to imagine, to control— become the source, through sheer repetition, of one's own demise.

Over the course of the next decade I continued my work on *Pinto and Sons.* Twice I came to a complete halt and wrote, rather quickly, two other books of fiction—*Regina,* a novel, that deals most explicitly with my interest in drama; and *Goldkorn Tales,* three novellas about Leib Goldkorn, the character of whom I am most fond. Always and ever I returned to the recalcitrant story of Adolph Pinto, and his adventures in the new world. Why was his tale so difficult to tell, and so filled with horrors? Part of the explanation is simplicity itself: the terms of the writing game had changed. The attention given to *King of the Jews* would now be refocused on me. My next large book had to be as good as the one that had come before. I was self-consciousness, self-critical, in a way I had not yet experienced. But this is a happy hurdle, really, and one that any real writer (that is, an author who has more than one good book in him, just as a genius is someone with two great ideas) is only too eager to jump.

Nor do I think the emotional censorship I practiced at YIVO could by itself account for this large-scale return of what I believe is called the repressed. When, at what other time, had I purposefully turned my back on my feelings? Recall, if you will, the day after my father's death, when Ricky and I laughed our heads off at *The Lavender Hill Mob.* What kind of bargain, I wonder, was I making in my thirteen-year-old mind when I said I did not wish to attend the funeral? First, probably, that my refusal would not be allowed; the far-off beginnings of the

Mother, Lillian, and stepfather, Erwin Gelsey, about 1980

"En Famille: Anya, Paul, and Theo"

ironical joke may lie here—in the way halfhearted words are taken at full value. Or perhaps this: if I ignored the proof of my father's death, he might return to us (remember those cartoon characters with nine lives?) in the guise of his identical twin. What were those gold statuettes that Alec Guinness had in his suitcase? Miniature Eiffel Towers? Or Oscars? My father's Academy Award?

"No Dancing on the Graves of the Dead!" That is the slogan of the young resistance fighters in *King of the Jews.* They're warning the residents of the ghetto not to go to a play (*Macbeth,* as it happens) while their people suffer. Was this meant to be a flag waved in my own direction? For going to the movies on the day my father was buried? For writing a novel about these millions of victims, in some sense ancestors too? For my laughter on both occasions? For the voice of that narrator, our jaunty friend? One would have to be a resistance fighter in a different, Freudian sense to untangle these knotty questions, though no less heroic for that.

It didn't take heroism, only grit and stubbornness, to complete *Pinto and Sons*—well over eight hundred pages in the first draft. Time, the one true

critic, will determine whether the ten-year effort was misplaced. I can say this: the book only began to move, the logjam to break, when I overcame my written-in-stone objections to allowing any Jewish element into its pages. By the time I was done, my immigrant, a long-nosed and high-minded Austro-Hungarian, had taken over title and text. In a sense the writing of this book was a recapitulation of the journey I had taken from a *Judenrein* childhood to the discovery of the Jew.

And next? Well, as yet another Hebraic gentleman says at the end of *Regina,* "Lots of things, in my opinion, have got to be a secret." Not that one isn't allowed a couple of clues. Because the new book will be set in Hollywood, and in the forties, we again come round full circle. Who knows? Maybe Julie will be in it, and Phil. Certainly there will be some of the characters, the emigrés and refugees, I glimpsed as a youth. Not to mention the writers and actors and agents who hung round our pool. The war will be in the background. Up front, the city, and the busy workings of its chief industry. And everywhere, of course, the flat, unchanging sunlight, the blue of the real and brush-stroked sky. During the task—and for how many years?—I won't budge from my study at Brookline, Massachusetts. The wings of the imagination are, for me, the best way home.

BIBLIOGRAPHY

Fiction:

P. D. Kimerakov, Little, Brown, 1975.

The Steinway Quintet Plus Four (short stories), Little, Brown, 1976.

King of the Jews: A Novel of the Holocaust, Coward, 1979.

Regina, Coward, 1982.

Goldkorn Tales (three novellas), Dutton, 1985.

Contributor of stories, articles, and reviews to periodicals, including *Atlantic Monthly, Esquire, Nation, Antaeus, Playboy,* and *Antioch Review.*

Nicolas Freeling

1927-

Bitterne Manor, 1935. "Typically exuberant, Nancy clutches both her child and her handsome French lover. My father's polite distance is as characteristic."

Finding that one has passed sixty is a jolt, which should be salutary. There is the sense of wingèd chariots: how often one has got up and gone, it seems immediately, to bed again. The future is still interesting while the past is only the last time one brushed one's teeth. This time of year beheld is that in which childhood begins to be remembered vividly, while last week has faded into last year. Childhood shaped us, and we should look at it; our time lost and our time regained is also our work of art.

My own filled the classic conditions for a writer: the jaded psychiatrist tosses a languid head, paws with a halfhearted hoof. It begins in the Royal Free Hospital, Grays Inn Road, London, in what was then the Borough of Saint Pancras, a dingy and downtrodden neighbourhood. What was she doing here?—but Nancy was both Hon and Rebel; original, funny, and a trial to her family. She lived in France, but was in London to have a Communist baby.

She was not pretty but the witnesses agree, highly attractive. A cloud of lovers hung about, but platonic; it is probable that they were mostly homosexual. This was the Cambridge, Bloomsbury world. Nancy had been a pillar of the 1917 Club, was (like dear Vanessa) guru to many tiresome young men paint-and-ink-spotted, and (like dear Virginia) didn't much enjoy sex anyhow. The well-known anecdote of Strachey pointing to the stain on the girl's frock, sternly asking, "Sperm?" is true as far as it goes; one need not take it too seriously.

Childbearing was serious, indeed earnest. The lovers wrote many postcards, in musical notation— Handel's "Unto us a son is given." Ridiculous since Nancy knew nothing of music, but very Bloomsbury. My father, in France, might have asked, "Who's this Us?" but for knowing the lovers, and Nancy, better. He had been a biologist, at Cambridge, but no longer worked; his heart was bad. They lived, in France, on small inherited incomes, a commonplace in the twenties when life there was cheap. Nancy had run away with him from her boring and musical husband, a humourless soul as was shown in later years when he solemnly proposed that my father marry his own mistress: this would make the situation reputable. One does not quite grasp why she had ever married him. On a rebound, I expect; she was a bolter by temperament.

Back we went to France. There was no Nanny, for she believed in bringing up children herself, in a comic mix of progressive theory and Victorian prac-

Highland dance in 1930 France. "The tartan would be of the well-known Harrods clan."

tise. There was thus a goat, milk for the sort of child that is sick over everyone. I am also to be glimpsed with long hair, high-buttoned boots, and a sailor suit from Daniel Neal, a Proper little English boy. How English? That is difficult to answer. A disrupted background made further rootless by two homes in France and three more in England up to 1939, when my father died. It seems sufficiently traumatic.

Sadly, and painfully, I never really knew him and know little of him. A solid family of Norfolk squires which I suspect spewed him out on Nancy's account; a righteous lot? I never met any of them. He did not speak of it. A few anecdotes survive, of Mr. Betts, a neighbouring farmer who got in such a rage when carving the Sunday beef. "Everybody eating, and me not begun yet." He was a good cook, and from him I have a love of food's good, solid raw materials. In Le Croisic he went out fishing and learned landscape painting; gardened, read aloud—well—and loved natural history. He had been a gifted athlete. He was proud of his son; it was a sadness that I should have no aptitude for rugby, cricket, or botany. Now that I too love natural history it is too late. A hideously sad story. I see him, now, in my own sons. He loved to shoot, to fish, to sail. He should have stayed in Cambridge. Why did he . . . ? There is a novel there, perhaps a crime novel, but it is not mine to write. I have never been in Norfolk. Once my son went. Yes, said the archivist at Kings, here's your grandfather, but we lost sight, you know, we don't know much. It is perhaps better so; a love story left in peace. Nancy never told it either.

But her I know well: her I most resemble, her name I carry. A flashing, splendid girl of great vitality, much intelligence, no common sense. One can see great gifts there, and a fatal silliness. She is Englishly eccentric; Freelings indeed are often farcical. Upperclass families knew their genealogies and hers went back to William the Norman: it thus appears that I am related to Barbara Cartland, but so are lots of people who aren't aware of it. The tree is all in the female line, which interests me; one would like to know more of the Fair Maid of Kent or Celia Fiennes. Halfway down it looks quite muddy and provincial, if better than the present Queen: there are none of those crook Tudors, though John of Gaunt is no great credit either to a family.

Freelings appear lateish: the first is a crony of the Prince Regent, sounding in Harriet Wilson's book a nice if silly boy. It is just after Waterloo. (Harriet says that Wellington looked like a rat-catcher.) I think they may have been Belgian or north German: the name occurs there, and not in England. There is a subsequent row of rackety and drunken baronets, now extinct, given to vagabondage and popping up in odd corners of the globe. Aunt Annie, herself permanently flown with claret, made Nancy promise never to Drink. She never did; though I Do.

It is an uneven childhood: the houses were original and funny, like the comet herself full of character, full of books, some good, full of pictures, mostly bad by Bloomsbury artists; almost anything by Vanessa is a good illustration of Nancy-with-a-child. One—Bitterne Manor, Southampton—was pure magic, by me transformed into Masefield's Seekings, where Kay Harker lived. No music, to subsequent sorrow. A solitary childhood, halting and lacking, peopled and enriched by imagination. In 1931 Nancy had bolted back to England, worried about schools. She had made the transition from virulent Communism to a yet more narrow and fanatical Catholicism, quite a commonplace but it posed problems, though not to her. She never realised the damage caused: no detachment, despite a sense of the ludicrous.

One story will do for these times. On pilgrimage to Saint Francis, her favourite guru, around 1935 in Assisi, taken-short, she was conducted to the only lavatory in the guesthouse by an unselfconscious Italian Father, who finding the door barred turned to her smiling. "Won't be long, Signora. I can hear the paper." Really it is the story of my life. From early childhood the favourite present would be an exercise book, of paper to be listened to before being written upon. Indeed we will reach a moment when Nicolas, spending time in the municipal jail of Amsterdam, will start writing his first novel on lavatory paper.

In 1939 Nancy would bolt again. In August too, but war was far from her thought; she was no coward. It was fortunate in that a year later Bitterne Manor House was to be totally destroyed by a Nazi bomb, but like most of her caprices it was fraught. I must forgive her: my father died. Among her Childers cousins, pillars of wide Yorkshire fields, of the Doncaster racecourse, of Gladstonian government (plushy sinecures like Lord President of the Council; what does he do?), the most extravagant, worst thought of, and thus most sympathetic to herself, was her cousin Erskine. Who abandoned his own sinecure (he was Clerk to the House of Commons, and a keen yachtsman: he wrote *The Riddle of the Sands*) for the cause of Irish nationalism, a fervour after Nancy's own heart. He used his boat to run guns for Sinn Féin, was secretary to the Irish delegation which signed the Treaty, ran unhappily afoul of Griffith and Collins, who both distrusted an Englishman and disliked the doctrinaire manner; espoused the Repub-

lican cause in the civil war which followed—and got shot for it. One has respect, and can have love, for this awkward, cranky man of high principles and noble ideals. To de Valera, a man of similar nature, Erskine was a trusted confidant. One is glad to say that the Free State postponed his execution so that he could see the sun rise, and that he shook hands with each member of his firing squad: one has to understand the tortuous Irish character, the devotion to legalistic chicanery which could show generosity and chivalry.

Twenty years later de Valera was head of the government and Erskine's son a minister (who would become—ironic footnote—President of the Republic). Fertile ground for a great emotional fling; nearly Nancy's last, for she was to die in Ireland. I can find nothing now for which to blame her, nothing to forgive. But the twelve-year-old boiled with resentment among an alien people, and played the sullen. I have never fallen in love with Ireland but these teasing, flirtatious ironies, at the most vulnerable moment of adolescence, would eventually teach lessons in metaphysics. In a last throw of dice I would meet my wife there and this time it would not be ambsace.

Debits: Englishness died with my father and was gone for good. There would be no scholarship to Kings College; no network of position, club, and privilege through which the Englishman obtains wealth, ease, and civilised company. Deuce-ace again? How to tell? I have learned detachment, and if these ashes, stirred, make me sneeze, I will blow my nose, and avoid lechery.

Credits: in Dublin as in Lisbon was freedom from wartime rhetoric and hysteria; laughter at spy stories; clearer visions of heroisms or treacheries: the futility of invasions, hegemonies, and military glories. Social conditions: I had seen and understood little of the depression years, and Dublin was a town of great and bitter poverty, of barefoot scant-nourished children and old drunken shawlies. Slum, and mean small suburb, but Dublin in the forties was enjoying the last, Indian summer of a town with fine urban architecture set in beautiful surroundings, before the cancer of the automobile came to eat it away and destroy it utterly. There was the love of arts too, and of civilised leisures. Nobody had money, so that money was of small worth. Save for buses, bicycles, and a few horses, the streets were empty of traffic, but not of silence, nor of dignity. Only forty years on have I understood what I owe to Baggot Street and Leeson Street, and the hills above Killiney. Such formal education as was had was hopelessly botched, but here I looked at the pictures of Jack Yeats and Paul Henry, and the Lane bequest, heard my first music, smelt my first theatres.

The war was over and the boy, now of military service age, was athirst for London, for what he still saw as his own land and people. Conscription could easily have been deferred, and the sensible thing would have been to look for a university place, but everyone had been in the army; one could not be left out. The stories of my cousins were all of idiocy and imbecility, of senseless destruction and waste, but they had immense glamour. I ran to volunteer and was posted to the Air Force. But I do not regret the army; that too taught me much. The soldiery was unwashed, uncouth and past belief ignorant, and knew everything I didn't: not least, friendship. The working man: I am, of course, a socialist but I have no sentimentalities about workers; I have been one of them. Here for the first time I would be part of a working gang under harsh conditions, and when I came to know the harsher world of restaurant kitchens in the fifties nothing there would shock or frighten me. I learned that I was a spoiled puppy who had lived an entire childhood in sheltered conditions. Today's spoiled puppy does not know it.

Two memories will serve. The first is of a Wing Commander. He cannot have been much over forty but was whitehaired. He was tall, slim, languid, and elegant. His uniform carried faded pilots' wings, and what was called "the double top" (a darts' playing term): the DSO and bar, DFC and bar. His face, and hands, were built all of distorted pink burn-tissue. He lounged, legs crossed, in the Officers' Mess, pretending not to listen to the boastings of a fat, administrative squadron-leader such as exists in every army, but exasperation forced him to turn at last. "Broadbent—if ever you were at Biggin Hill—I don't recall seeing you there—they'd surely have made use of you—to fill in a bomb crater." When I reported this to the Other-Ranks, there was jubilation. I was a mess waiter on this station, where I met air-gunners who had managed to avoid getting washed out of the turret with a hose, and also officers who had not bombed Dresden, but who said they were ready to do so again tomorrow.

The other is of Corporal Phillips, an undersized Welshman whose real claim to fame is that he once made his compatriot Anthony Powell laugh. He commanded the shithouse squad, of which I formed part, and made war upon lowered standards of hygiene and morals in the Ablutions. Some frustrated airman wrote "Wanker Phillips" on the shithouse

"Romantic. Renée on a North Sea beach,"
about 1950

door; a retreat was made upon Welsh dignity. "Mate, I do not wank. But I peg you all, see?" There we all were, upon a charge of conduct prejudicial to good discipline. The detail pleasing to Mr. Powell was that Phillips had the enjoyable task of hoisting the flag during working parades, rather slowly, while we stood at the salute. During this precious daily fifteen seconds, in my imagination, the Corporal grew from a scrawny five feet to a burly six. "Stand by your Beds," we sang. "Here comes the Air-Vice-Marshal. He's got—lots of rings—but he's only got one Ass Hole." The aircrews' favourite songs were of course all German and their favourite, "We're marching against England," marking the "Sieg-'Heil" with mightily banged beer mugs, while in sadder, more frustrated frame of mind we gathered in the pub to sing, "Salome—You—should—see—Sa-lo-mé, Standing there, With her tits all bare, Every little wiggle makes the boys all stare." I was discharged from the army in the splendid, unending summer of 1947.

In my memory these are silvered years, with every minute of our generous forty-eight hour passes, our generous yearly thirty days of leave devoted to London. I remember theatres; the ageing but enchanting Leigh and Coward, Evans and Gielgud, light-foot Massine and heavy-foot Fonteyn and the very young Richard Burton—one should at this age fall in love with older actresses, as well as the young ones. And there followed an extremely pleasant time, golden in fact as well as gilded by memory, for at twenty-one quite a smallish sum of money, the remains of my father's meagre capital, appears large when there is no prudent uncle to wag a finger about the wickedness of exceeding income. These are the last years of glorious irresponsibility, and some instinctive foreknowledge that such times will not lightly come again prompts one to every fantasy that a romantic imagination can compass. Two years is just about right for grand hotels and starred restaurants, silk shirts and opera tickets, Cuban cigars and vintage bottles, and the discovery of this Europe, so battered and dingy but which love and gold-dust could still make refulgent. It is the time to enjoy toys, in pleasure undiminished by whatever servile shopman, parasite, or greedy harlot. Only in later years will one have learned enough of metaphysics to shrug at delights which are so expensive and so cheap. Most men only earn them after much toil: it is a sad sight to watch, in some restaurant, a man of forty-five with a new mistress, so mistrustful, certain only of being cheated. When now and then a good cigar or bottle comes my way it is a benefit-forgot, rediscovered with delight in the constancy of old friends.

A good guide in those years was Ludwig Bemelmans, artist and civilised European, writer and painter and talented enough at both to be memorable, remembered now with unalloyed happiness and gratitude. Certainly, when the pocket was empty and a living had somehow to be found, it was "Life Class" that sent me into the restaurant world; initially as trainee, or "stagiaire" as it is called in French grand-hotels, but I came quickly enough to prefer the kitchens to the world of management—men, as Ludwig says, with faces like towels on which everyone has wiped his hands. Twenty years later I wrote *Kitchen Book* about this time, and would not change much of it, even today.

It was like being in the army at first, a time of boredom and learning many humble tasks, within a precise and military hierarchy: it was then a year and more, in the big brigades where staff was cheap and discipline severe, before the apprentice could even reach the grade of "second commis," while the chef-de-partie was a lordly and remote figure, master-

craftsman of ten to twenty years' standing—and still grossly underpaid for immensely long hours of narrow but precisely edged and hard-bought skills. At fifty years of age he would still be living in a tiny dark apartment on the airless back streets of Cannes or Nice, with bad teeth and impaired digestion, a wife as meagre and flat-chested as himself and a child or two, late-born; one thought twice before conceiving them. Treading twice daily a deep-rutted path to the Carlton or the Negresco. But a man of much dignity, total self-respect. Asked your trade, to throw a chest, "Suis cuisinier, moi," was a thing esteemed in this area of Europe still in mentality prewar. To say, "Chef-poissonier, au Martinez," was to be a notable, in this little, provincial town. To be even a first-commis at some temple like Point in Vienne or Walterspiel in München was to carry a badge recognised and respected throughout Europe, and such a man would be prized above rubies in the New World. It was like saying, "I am first horn, in the Gewandhaus of Leipzig."

I felt this respect, and was in awe of such men. The menus then were full of things no longer seen,

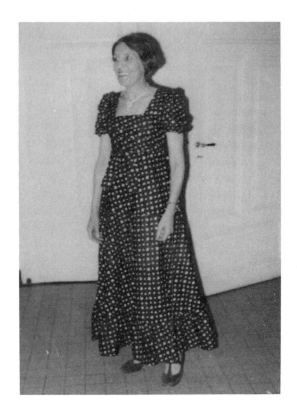

"And the classic. Renée in maturity"

"Lyrical. The child has written 'poetry' on the back."
French countryside, about 1968

delicate and difficult preparations like a sole Colbert or chicken Kiev. I was apprenticed in the larder, where such dishes were made ready for the kitchen. As the "piccolo" my task was to run with them to the designated corner. Let us say, a tournedos Rossini (today grotesquely old-fashioned, nigh uneatable) readied and handed me with a throwaway joke by the chef of the garde-manger, my master. Breathless to the sauce-cook (a great man) and shyly, "Roblin dit que le Rossini est tombé de son vélo." A quick grin. "Il s'est pas fait du mal?" Damn it—he spoke to me, instead of just kicking my ass.

D'you know how a sole Colbert is made? You will find today few cooks who do. In the larder a sole is trimmed, the head left on. Using a narrow, flexible knife the two top fillets are opened and bent back in a double bow, but not separated. The backbone exposed is cut top and bottom, with the point of the knife. The sole is bathed in beaten egg and fine breadcrumb, with care to stick down the loose fillets. In the kitchen the sole is fried in butter, the cut backbone lifted out, the cavity filled with a roundel of "Maître d'hôtel"—butter worked with chopped parsley and lemon juice. For service it is presented on a folded napkin, with lemon wedges and two sprigs of fried parsley. Ludwig says, and rightly, that this is one of the finest dishes to be found in the city of Brussels,

then as now the gourmet's paradise, but you would be hard put to find it there today. Fashion, as capricious in regard to food or medicine as over the length of a skirt, today decrees that food cooked in butter is injurious to health. Like most doctors' pronouncements this is arrant nonsense, and in Belgium they know better, but the truth is that in all but the best restaurants a dish of this sort takes too much time and is too much trouble—and in those the presentations are decreed by fashion. A starry restaurateur is a prima donna, exactly like Saint Laurent, and charges accordingly for showy novelties. The "classics" like Lasserre's duck with orange, which is the best there is, could be done at home, at a third of the price but treble the trouble, and wouldn't taste the same. The cook's real chagrin is that four of his five customers are only nouveaux-riches, there for vanity and to be noticed, and who would be just as happy with a Big Mac. Nodding wisely in their Lanvin suits, asking to smell the cork (the Haut Brion of 1929 was just nicely ripe in my best year), but the sommelier knows well that the Beaujolais Nouveau would really be more their cup-of-tea. Like—I suspect—most artists, one had rather a Burgundy to any Bordeaux, and finds a really fine boiled egg superior to mere fleisch, but vanity is there again apreen . . .

In the kitchen one got plenty of knocks, and knife-cuts; after years of learning the manual skills I remained unhandy. But became a good cook; a thing inborn and once more, my father to thank. A good professional. It is now a fine career, and that can lead rapidly to fame and fortune. A boy can go to school, hygienically and in relative comfort, can follow with three years at a good "university," Troisgros say, or Haeberlin, and at the age of twenty-seven borrow money, take up some house of decayed reputation, challenge the world. Such a notion was never mine. I can remember no ambition beyond reasonable working conditions, which were often unspeakable, a stable place, a lodging for—now—a wife and a child. A home; quite a humble aspiration, such as I had never really had. Instinct, one may believe, will often prove the surer guide than reason and experience. No conscious resolution led me to become a writer; no friendship or frequentation encouraged such a belief. The kitchens of European restaurants could not be called propitious. The way in which it came about was melodramatic and in retrospect entertaining. It has an invented, worked-up sound, of an anecdote for journalists. But it is more than a truth. It was a gift, the first occasion on which I felt the touch of the Daemon.

Vagabondage, a Freeling characteristic, led in these years through many European lands: the cook's luggage, his tools and clothes, heavy but not bulky. Obviously, they all steal food. They eat little on the premises, and in general there is a tolerance to a cutlet or a piece of chicken pocketed. Naturally too, a sharp eye is kept upon expensive materials, and we did not think of lifting foie gras or smoked salmon. Someone had been exaggerating?—for whatever reason some manager decided to show zeal, set a cop to lurk outside, captured me. Which would have been trivial enough but for zeal deciding to make an example. I found myself pushed off to the Amsterdam municipal jail and left there for three leisurely weeks while justice decided upon the turn this matter should be given. This sounds, and is, outrageous since Dutch justice is in general both liberal and expeditive, and there is no reason why a petty thief should not have been stood before a judge the following morning and given the usual choice between a fine and a day's imprisonment. I incline to believe that malignance rather than incompetence must answer, since I recall the prosecutor as both spiteful and brutal; an unpleasant combination. His name was van der Valk;

the Daemon turned him into a mild-mannered and broad-minded man, which plainly he was not.

The municipal jail in those days was primitive but not punitive. We slopped-out of a morning, and the food was mostly beans, but a tolerant warder gave me a cell to myself, suggested mildly that I do a simple task for a few hours, and did not dream of taking away the pencil in my pocket. In this cell, without in the least knowing why, I wrote the first three to five thousand words of *Love in Amsterdam*. It was something to pass the time.

The judge remarked, mildly enough, that three weeks' imprisonment seemed to him a little excessive; since they had been served such would be the sentence. The chap could now rejoin his wife, euphoric until discovery that he had also been served with a deportation order. "Mm," said the passport officer at Harwich, "hammered you then to rights, didn't they. Got no penny? Well, we can give you a rail pass to London." It took a little time before things got back into balance; something of a rush, and then time to think. With a wife and now two children staying, sensibly, in Holland, there was more to think about than writing a book. It was written, because a

"A Japanese azalea, and Nicolas in middle age"

writer who once finds his vocation has no other choice. Kitchens from that moment would only be a means of paying the rent.

It is time to talk about crime fiction. A small, indeed a very trivial injustice paid oneself has, to be sure, more impact than even a great wrong done to others. A small kitchen cut, frequent when handling knives all day, upon hands less dexterous than practise should have made them, stings sharper than the most lurid of fictional daggers.

Or when, here in our Vosges woods, it was time to teach the children to shoot (in them their grandfather's blood flows strongly), I found it impossible to keep the rifle sighted upon a living creature, one begins to see guns in a different light. The traditions in the United States governing the sale or possession of arms make as I believe for one of the two basic differences in their fiction (the other of course being the uses of language)—carriage or even simple possession of a piece is not in itself criminal. Here on the borders of France and Germany (and both peoples love to hunt) too much blood has been shed and violence too often blessed by the state. Violence is endemic to virtually all fiction save that of Jane Austen, but when I see it coming I do not write the passage with enthusiasm.

I have thus always disliked the crime label. That first book, and indeed every other since, explored crime themes: as was just noticed they are rarely absent from writing undertaken with any energy or regard for psychological truths. Paradoxically one touches here upon the basic flaw of the "Krimi" genre: they are too often merely mechanical exercises in the construction of artificial excitements, and the display of bloodshed is too often a disguise for the lack of any real energy.

Forty years ago, in a celebrated essay, Raymond Chandler pointed out that the old-fashioned mystery or detective story could not depict character because in order to create a suspense you had to cheat. This brought the crime novel—in the general acceptation of the term—down to the enfeebled level of escapist entertainment, exactly like the romance fiction of the other popular genre. As a practitioner himself, and a considerable artist in exploring the limits of the krimi, he was trapped. He could hardly point out that the whole "mystery" genre was no more than an exercise in nineteenth-century gothic, a highly stylised mannerist variation consequent upon the search after novelty. Exactly the same trend may be observed and studied in the later and weaker stages of all schools of art. The mannerism of the fifteenth-century Gothic is

Nicolas Freeling. Charcoal on paper by Markiel. Paris, 1975

echoed in the Japanese-inspired fantasies of late nineteenth-century painting. Decoration substitutes for invention. Poe and his followers had not found anything new: crime themes were developed with great originality and power from the beginning of the century, manifest in the work of Stendhal, and all the Romantics, through Balzac and Dickens and culminating in Dostoyevsky. Manner took the place of matter. The "horrid" exaggerations of mists and moonlight on the Gothic ruins are found quite early in pictorial art, and the oriental element widespread by the seventies. By the end of the century it would all be thought quite academic. Wilde or Whistler, Poe or Beardsley would no longer be shocking but seen as the minor mannerist artists they were. Conan Doyle, genuinely vigorous and inventive as he was, capturing the imagination when most English writers were turning away from the crime theme to that of class, is alas responsible for the rash of puzzle stories which proliferated up to the Second World War.

My book was sent to a reputed literary agency in London, a name known to me by hazard, for the professional book world, on the fringes of which Nancy had dabbled before I was born, was to me Kamchatka: awestruck by a formal, civil answer one could only journey as bid to London and listen dumbly to a lecture on the elementary aspects of publishing, given in the most kindly, protective manner by a woman of great eminence in this world. The book, it was said, had merit, originality, and the promise of talent; was publishable and saleable in many countries, had been sent to Gollancz and at once accepted, and would be published under the celebrated yellow-jacket imprint within the usual nine-month gestation period. There would be the usual editorial going-over, which might require a few retouches but no major changes, since the expert opinion was that it was all quite nice as it stood. (Seldom has a book of mine passed into print with so little fuss, but of these agonies I knew nothing.) "And now we are going to lunch with Mr. Gollancz who is anxious to meet you and we'll pick him up at the Savoy as usual." More than ever a matter for awe. Not to be sure the Savoy, a familiar terrain, where one ate rather badly (it had then no very good reputation among cooks . . .), but Victor Gollancz

was certainly an awe-inspiring figure, famous as imaginative, eccentric, and exceedingly astute.

Victor was charming, delightful company, and as often a bully. I pleased him by taking an interest in food—"I keep telling them how to make cucumber salad, and they don't listen"—liking his views on opera, and showing appreciation of a cigar: we got on well. Juliet was in stitches throughout lunch—"Nicolas sniffy about the food and showing Victor how to call an inattentive waiter . . ."—but Mr. Gollancz on the subject of crime-writing was a steamroller: a crushed silence while he told us that this was a detective story. Such an idea had never crossed my mind. Now the interesting character was the policeman, here quite a minor personage, so would Nicolas kindly go home smartish, forget all this kitchen nonsense, and write as quick as may be a book in which whatsisname will be the central figure.

I could find nothing to say: was not Victor a great expert? My great mistake was in allowing myself to be convinced by him, but who on earth could blame me? A few months later I had the second book, the first had been published, kindly reviewed by the "crime" pundits, and Juliet as promised had sold it to

The Freeling children. Oil on canvas by Odette Arranz, 1970

"everybody" starting with Joan Kahn, then the leading crime editor in New York. The die was cast.

Several voices can be heard at this juncture, including my own, to remark that there is nothing in the least bizarre here. The young writer (one can be thirty-three and know nothing) is plainly in excellent hands. He has nothing to complain of, having found his true bent, enjoying happiness, and making some money into the bargain: sounds like the life of Riley.

That is all true. The first three or four novels are written on a permanent high; it is the champagne time. Each is the first novel ever written; you are the first human being ever to walk upon this hill and look down into this valley. The sun rises only for you, and you are never tired. Literally true, for a summer in a seaside resort is a means of earning more and saving what one has, at the cost of a seventy-hour week. The book was written in the two-hour afternoon pause, and in five months I never set foot on the beach.

Given the expert professional advice which the wise editor keeps to a minimum these were better than competent crime stories. They acquired a faithful following among addicts, gave much pleasure, also to the writer, and culminated in the prizes with which the establishment greets those who reach the summit: the Gold Dagger, the Grand Prix, the Edgar. This caused me great delight, an immense gratitude—and all unwitting, consternation.

For in writing these books, I felt I was learning the trade of a novelist. Instead of each being an instinctive act, based on the wish to entertain and the joy of earning a living at something one was good at, they were beginning to need thought, to set problems in craftsmanship, to develop technical skills while asking a question ringing now louder in my ears: what were my intentions, and where did I think I should be heading, with this kind of work? Only two things seemed clear: that it would be a grave mistake to find oneself pinned into the purely commercial need to write the same book again and again, which is what most crime-writers do, of pure necessity and accepting narrow limits to further ambition. Dorothy Sayers—another "Gollancz" writer and a respected one—attempted to break this rigid mould, and put a rueful conclusion in the mouth of Harriet Vane—"Try something else, and your sales are apt to go down, and that's a fact." One cannot defy with impunity an established convention. So I was to find, but had not thought it already too late to make the effort.

The other thing was a growing conviction that there should be more to crime-writing than a series, especially one featuring the same principal character, which would end inevitably in facile self-parody, the stale repetition of characteristic mannerisms.

Determining thus that after ten books of this sort one could view an apprenticeship as ended, and begin to explore a more flexible vein, and one—such was my hope—with wider potential, the series was brought to an end upon, I thought, a lyrical note; one of gratitude, of regret, but also of hope: a page turned, a new horizon sought. The editor complained, as it appeared to me, in timid, conventional, and platitudinous words. Nicolas, you cannot do this; it breaks the rule. No? But I already have . . . The folly, since this word must be used, and wickedness, for so it was viewed, of this action was quickly brought home to me in the shape of markets diminished, and disappointed readers slipping away. The ways of the world take no account of an artist's convictions: to publishers, booksellers, and to, alas, a lot of readers, these are mere caprices and the expressions of a vanity which has overestimated its own talents.

Perhaps it may be so, and there is the possibility that one will not live long enough to find out.

"Grandfather," Christmas 1988

The French call this "la traversée du désert"—a theatrical phrase. To spend forty days in the desert—or months, and why not years?—is thought to be quite acceptable, and even admirable, on the condition that the U. S. Cavalry will appear in the last reel. A certain sentimentalism can be observed in—to take a famous example—the concept of Charles de Gaulle, who in a fit of pique decided that an ungrateful people did not deserve his services, and spent ten years stalking about in the park at Colombey (a fairly gloomy part of eastern France, not very far from my own home); stoically brooding upon that certain idea of France that he cherished. A better example might be found in the painter Hans Hartung: pursued, captured, tortured, and wounded by the Gestapo, he spent many lonely, tormented, and mutilated—and penniless—years in Spain, while seeing mediocrities grow rich in America, flaunting the experiments he had himself made and had no thanks for.

But these are highly talented men. From, approximately, 1960 until their death, both were fêted and rewarded by large crowds of worshippers. Rather more to the point would be the large number of men, politicians or painters, who having failed to make their mark—a mark, that is, they thought to have deserved—withdrew into no doubt a painful and embittered silence. Another anecdote recognisably sentimentalized. Plainly they pitied themselves, and thought it very wrong of the ungrateful public *not* to have brought them back in triumph to the Capitol. Certainly—I agree—between vanity, which is always both odious and ridiculous, and a self-pitying sulk (Coriolanus is neither an attractive nor a popular figure, understandably), the path is narrow. One must see these situations with humour as well as detachment.

And neither of these situations is my own. One can have successes which remain modest, and triumphs that are discreet. Fame and fortune, delightful girls at a distance, are both whores closer to. Better friends are found, and sometimes in obscurer places; and there is the discovery, hesitant and difficult, betimes painful and hard-bought, of metaphysical values. For the themes of crime fiction are only superficially those of greed and fear, and the scramble for power and possessions. Crime is above all the violent expression of our frustrations; our anguish at the barren ugliness of our world, our fundamental misjudgments that have brought us nothing but injustice and disharmony. The breaking, the poisoning, the destruction of our environment, the starvations and the massacres, the serfdoms and the enslavements, the maddened and rabid behaviour of whole populations; all our miseries and discontents are the expression of our desire for wholeness.

The moralistic view of crime as infringement of a Mosaic book of rules, threatening us with punishment for bashing Johnny's head in, bedding John's wife, breaking into Jack's bank, is not viable. Through the law courts, the State pretending to be God still punishes us for these crimes, but we do not respect the State, which we clearly see as a greater source of wrong than any individual. We ask for bread, and get stones: we are paying the price for our doctrines of irresponsibility. We want untouched, innocent islands: they are deserts. Having destroyed our planet we should like to abandon it, and reach others: the result would be identical. The physical equation fails us; the metaphysical is hardly attempted.

Plainly, this view of crime-writing covers a broader spectrum than most people will allow, in their definitions. I see the "mystery" as boring and ultimately a sterile affair: I do not try to rivalise with the work in this field. The equation is not going to be solved with pistol shots.

The use, indeed, of the pistol-shot as a device of violent, dramatic resolution is a hundred years out of date: Hedda Gabler's shot echoed round the world but the shot which concludes *The Sea Gull* is only Chekhov's clumsy way of telling us the play has ended. The sound of the axes, cutting down the cherry trees, has still a hundred years later a resonance in our deafened ears.

Today's "mystery" at its best shows brilliant and exact American skills: brief, witty, and fast-paced. They are not "novels": they are movie scenarios, the narrative pared to the basic visualisations needed for the reader who must use the page as a substitute for the screen. The heart of these scripts is in dialogue expressed in topical street-talk. European writers cannot compete with these dazzling entertainments; would be foolish to try, since they are ploddingly pedestrian in comparison. The European tradition of crime-writing is altogether different, is to be found in the central preoccupations of metaphysical art, derives from the high tide of nineteenth-century prose fiction, is based upon a firm moral pivot. Exemplified, between the wars, in the work of Simenon and Greene, visible today as stylisations nearly as narrow and mannerist as the anaemic, bloodless, unsexed decorations of Chesterton or Dickson Carr—but alive today because of their metaphysical content.

In France and in England, where the mannerist Poe school has been strongest, its influence most felt, and the interpretation placed upon "crime" fiction narrowly academic, the critical gap appears widest: it

"Grandfontaine in the sixties. Now, there is a garden . . ."

there appears impossible to write to crime themes without tripping over the prim vicarage ghosts of detectives or the gibbering gothic spectres left over from even earlier times. "British" writers are primarily interested in the nuances of pronunciation and behaviour which illustrate the subtleties of their own class distinctions, and the reader is left with an asphyxiating sense of provincial insularity. The French, in a very similar syndrome, have always found the greatest difficulty in coming to terms with the idea that a world outside France exists or is possible.

North America shows itself more fluid; I believe, more sensitive. Smugness enough there too; arrogant beliefs that the planet exists only to admire and copy a plumply self-satisfied model, reminding one of late-Victorian English attitudes . . . But one finds an open and a generous thought, that classical Greece has always contributed more towards civilisation than the materialist, mechanistic Roman imperium. Am I wrong to see this behind the fertile quickening of the best American writing?

Because of the miserable sediment of hatred and distrust left by the two world wars, it has for ninety years been fashionable to sneer at German thought and expression; a crippling automutilation. Only recently do we rediscover the German talent for metaphysics, holism in an increasingly schizophrenic world. To my mind, crime-writing is a natural expression of this. The long tradition of poetical and metaphysical writing in the Spanish-speaking world is another powerful example. Nor can one help wondering what amazements Russia, so long occulted by stalinist paranoia, has waiting for us.

As a European, but one whose medium of expression is English, I find my own position paradoxical. It is both a great privilege and grave handicap: visible in the language itself, which while it becomes the lingua franca of the "educated" world (ninety percent of European schoolchildren learn English as their first, and basic "foreign" language) degenerates progressively towards an imprecise and vulgar jargon, thicksown with illiterate barbarisms. No one pays any more attention to a floating nominative than in logic to an undivided middle. I am grateful for the few scraps of Latin and Greek picked up at bad schools, while remaining furious that it was not thought needful to teach any biology, chemistry, or physics whatever.

A further handicap has been the need, imposed by hungry mouths, to write saleable books, which once one found oneself typecast had to be "detective-stories." I have thus looked forward to the moment when with children grown and one's own needs modest I could turn to the more serious and difficult work of "true" crime-writing. In yet another paradox, publishers have now a morbid—in the sense of pathological—fear of whatever book they have themselves decreed is unlikely to sell in the narrow mass markets they have created. One cannot complain, since every musician, painter, architect, or gardener is in exactly the same boat. History teaches us only that this situation does not alter. The only truth we can be sure of—apart, that is, from metaphysical truths—is that from the beginnings of our known world the artist has paid no heed whatever to the beckonings of material prosperity. Stendhal's famous dedication "to the Happy Few" (those who could grasp metaphysical meaning in a profoundly base and boring world) is as true today as ever it was.

Grandfontaine, France. December 1989.

BIBLIOGRAPHY

Fiction:

Love in Amsterdam (also see below), Gollancz, 1961, Harper, 1962.

Because of the Cats (also see below), Gollancz, 1963, Harper, 1964.

Gun before Butter (also see below), Gollancz, 1963, published as *Question of Loyalty*, Harper, 1964.

(Under pseudonym F.R.E. Nicholas) *Valparaiso*, Gollancz, 1964, (under name Nicolas Freeling), Harper, 1964.

Double Barrel (also see below), Gollancz, 1964, Harper, 1965.

Criminal Conversation, Gollancz, 1965, Harper, 1966.

The King of the Rainy Country (also see below), Gollancz, 1966, Harper, 1966.

The Dresden Green (also see below), Gollancz, 1966, Harper, 1967.

Strike out Where Not Applicable, Gollancz, 1967, Harper, 1967.

This Is the Castle, Gollancz, 1968, Harper, 1968.

The Freeling Omnibus: Comprising "Love in Amsterdam," "Because of the Cats," and "Gun before Butter," Gollancz, 1968.

Tsing-Boum, Hamish Hamilton, 1969, published as *Tsing-Boom!*, Harper, 1969.

Over the High Side, Hamish Hamilton, 1971, published as *The Lovely Ladies*, Harper, 1971.

A Long Silence, Hamish Hamilton, 1972, published as *Auprés de ma blonde*, Harper, 1972.

The Second Freeling Omnibus: Comprising "Double Barrel," "The King of the Rainy Country," and "The Dresden Green," Gollancz, 1972.

Dressing of Diamond, Hamish Hamilton, 1974, Harper, 1974.

What Are the Bugles Blowing For?, Heinemann, 1975, published as *The Bugles Blowing*, Harper, 1975.

Lake Isle, Heinemann, 1976, published as *Sabine*, Harper, 1977.

Gadget, Heinemann, 1977, Coward, 1977.

The Night Lords, Heinemann, 1978, Pantheon, 1978.

The Widow, Heinemann, 1979, Pantheon, 1979.

Castang's City, Heinemann, 1980, Pantheon, 1980.

One Damned Thing After Another, Heinemann, 1981, published as *Arlette*, Pantheon, 1981.

Wolfnight, Heinemann, 1982, Pantheon, 1982.

The Back of the North Wind, Heinemann, 1983, Viking, 1983.

No Part in Your Death, Heinemann, 1984, Viking, 1984.

A City Solitary, Heinemann, 1985, Viking, 1985.

Cold Iron, Deutsch, 1986, Viking, 1986.

Lady Macbeth, Deutsch, 1988.

Not as Far as Velma, Deutsch, 1989, Mysterious Press, 1989.

Sandcastles, Deutsch, 1989, Mysterious Press, 1990.

Those in Peril, Deutsch, 1990, Mysterious Press, forthcoming.

Nonfiction:

Kitchen Book, Hamish Hamilton, 1970, published as *The Kitchen*, Harper, 1970.

Cook Book, Hamish Hamilton, 1972.

Isaac Goldemberg

1945-

(Translated from the Spanish by David Unger)

Isaac Goldemberg, "right after the publication of The Fragmented Life of Don Jacobo Lerner," *1977*

would be no way to explain the sweltering heat, the vast amounts of fruits, and those downpours that were like fists beating upon us. And the Andes? Cajamarca wasn't too far off; moreover, the Andes crisscross the whole of Peru both physically and spiritually.

Yes, I was born in Chepén in the bosom of a family that was questionably Catholic. From my maternal grandfather I inherited a bloodline whose roots were unclear: there was talk of English, Italian, and Basque ancestors who came to Peru in the middle of the nineteenth century, amassed a great fortune for the better part of fifty years, only to find themselves bankrupt by the twentieth century. As a result, my great-grandfather Carlo Bay Miani ended his life by putting a bullet in his head. From my grandmother, a native of the Andean town of Cajamarca and a folk healer by trade, I inherited a stream of blood no less confused: Andalusian on one side, Indian on the other. From my father, a Russian Jew who immigrated to Peru in the thirties, I only inherited—at least for the first eight years of my life—the weight of his shadow.

Life in Chepén, my family's history, the yearning for my absent father, the environment in my maternal grandfather's house, the blending of my two ancestries—all were re-created in my first novel, *The Fragmented Life of Don Jacobo Lerner,* translated by Robert S. Picciotto:

I don't know why Grandfather stuffs himself while we're half-starved. I sure would like to eat that steak and fried eggs with the mound of rice on the side since I don't like soups and stews very much. True that sometimes Bertila takes me to doña Chepa's restaurant and then I really get my fill of dishes so good we don't even get them for Easter at home; Grandmother says it is because there is no money, but Grandfather has such a steak every day that Iris, Ricardo, and I drool. Doctor Meneses says Ricardo needs vitamins, or maybe he said it about me, I don't really remember. But don't sing that tune to Grandfather. The truth is, I don't like wine very much but I

Nineteen forty-five: Born in Chepén, a small village in northern Peru, about an hour and a half from Trujillo. My memory of the town is rather hazy, made more so by the fact that time, distance, and my imagination have transformed it little by little. I think of it now as a lush area hemmed in by the desert, the ocean, and the Andes. What's certain is that Chepén wasn't on the coast, although it wasn't far from the sea. Our sea was the railroad tracks. And I'm also sure that the town was flanked by tropical vegetation. If it weren't, there would buy myself an Orange Crush for lunch and another one for dinner, because then I would have two bottle tops a day, fourteen a week and sixty a month, and there would be no one in school with more bottle tops than me. I would even give a few to Ricardo if I felt like it, but I am not going to give them to him if he keeps on bothering me. Yesterday he hid my reading book from me and Miss Angelita screamed at me in front of everyone because I didn't know my lesson. But then all the money is gone, and Bertila says what are we going to do? Again chick-peas with the rice and not any butter at all, not even for breakfast, and I'm not going to have my bread with just sugar. I drink my chocolate not too hot, because if I burn my tongue I won't be able to speak again. Grandmother says Bertila spends all the money on crap instead of giving her enough to buy some chickens; then we would have fried eggs every morning, turned over so that the yolk is hard and mealy.

One of these days Grandfather is going to die and leave us the money in his strong-box and we're

The author standing in front of what was his father's store in Lima, Peru, now a Chinese restaurant

going to have to bury him wrapped up in his blanket. The only one who loves me, after all, is Aunt Francisca, even though she scolds me and makes me read the catechism every night before I go to sleep. I tell her if I die, bury me in a shoe box with my bottle tops, but her eyes light up bright and her chin shakes and she says that only pure souls go to heaven; God doesn't protect boys who don't behave and don't say their prayers at night and don't go to church on Sundays to be blessed by Father Chirinos. Aunt Francisca must be the only saint in the family because my other aunts are lost souls who don't even go to mass any more and they haven't confessed their sins for years. Aunt Irma ran away last year with a sergeant of the Republican Guard whose spurs jingled when he came to visit her on Sundays. Grandmother says that they live as lovers in Pacasmayo and that they are going to burn in the fires of hell. Beatriz and Zoila are younger than Bertila. They're gone the whole day and late at night they come home drunk, with their hair all messed up and their dresses like crinkly cellophane. Zoila is the prettiest of all my aunts. Last year she was the queen of the carnival and the druggist is in love with her. She was so pretty with her ribbon tied in a bow she looked like a Spanish lady, and Grandfather is very happy because the druggist has a lot of money and he says that he is a serious man. When the royal carriage went by the sidewalks were covered with red and white flowers and with confetti that people tossed from their balconies. Grandfather is always asking Zoila when she is going to get married, and telling her to watch herself, not to be like Bertila, who let herself be had, and look at her now. Once Zoila had a pink silk dress and a crown of shining pearls; she looked like a princess in one of the fairy tales that Iris tells me.

Aunt Francisca gets so mad she almost has a stroke every time she sees Beatriz and Zoila go out all painted up "as if they were whores." She says they are staining the name of the Wilsons, who were recognized and respected by everyone when they lived in Cajamarca in their father's house, even if now they're not. I don't know whether I am a Wilson or an Alvarado. Grandfather says "they arrived to this land in the last century, respectable, industrious, decent people," and Grandmother says "we have no need to envy those bland, long, thin, English people." When I ask Aunt Francisca if Grandfather is my father, or whether it is Uncle Pedro, she answers that I have no father, that he died seven years ago, before I was born. She doesn't remember too well, she says, but it seems that his store burned up, and he died in the flames the same as if he had been in hell. I'm not going to die like my father because I am a good boy who goes to mass every Sunday, and I go to confession, and I collect images of saints. Father Chirinos promised to give me an image of our patron, Saint Sebastian, who died shot through by the arrows of barbarians who adored a different god than ours. But Jesus Christ is the only true god, and I have to believe in him, or I will die and be condemned for sure, like Matilde's son, who was born with two heads so that they didn't let him be buried in holy ground. They say they took him to some other village and buried him in a cardboard box, with his bottle tops. When I get the image of Saint Sebastian, the biggest one of all and in colors, I will have fifty-two, and I am going to put it on the wall above my bed. But I'm going to have to wait because Father Chirinos doesn't give it away just like that. You have to really earn it, being very good and learning all the prayers by heart, before he gives it to you, and for me it's very difficult because sometimes, like when I have to say the Our Father, I am thinking of other things, like my father, who is not in heaven but burning slowly in hell. Grandmother says that he was a heretic son-of-a-bitch who brought perdition to our house. *Blessed be thy name* . . . My name at home is Efraín, but in the street and at school they call me little Jacobo, though the teacher only knows me as the grandson of don Efraín Wilson or the son of Bertila who a few years back made a big mistake and believed a lot of lies. Bertila didn't leave the house for two years and even tried to kill herself like a fool one night when she went into the deepest part of the river without knowing how to swim. She was half-drowned when they pulled her out and screaming they should let her die because she was so ashamed and would never again set foot in the street. *Thy kingdom come; thy will be done in earth as it is in heaven* . . . how could she stand it, she said, now that everyone knew what had happened to her? That night Grandfather cursed the Jew, the whore that gave him birth, and all his ancestors. . . . And Grandmother, like a fury, blaming Grandfather, calling him a shitty old man. Where the hell was he when they were fucking his daughter? Where was she? She also blamed herself for having done nothing, as much of a procuress as the old man, even though she had known that nothing good could come from those Sunday visits. Francisca had already warned doña Jesús that Bertila was headed on the wrong track. What kind of example was that for her daughters, who were already grown enough for the devil to tickle their bodies and make their insides feel warm, with Bertila crying at night like Iris when she lost her little Chinese doll, not

letting me sleep . . . *Forgive us our trespasses as we forgive those who trespass against us.* I hate to hear her speak of her misfortune because afterward I have horrible nightmares of a witch with a long nose and hair all over her face, and eyes like those of a snake, who fries me in boiling oil. All my screaming bounces off the walls of the house as if I were inside a deflated ball. Bertila can't hear. Bertila never hears, always minding her business locked up in her world. Sometimes it is very peaceful: stories from the Bible where everything is pretty, bicycle rides by the river, fig trees and acacias, white clouds and skies as blue as the cloak worn by the virgin in the church . . . *lead us not into temptation* . . . But some other times Bertila looks at me with bloodshot eyes and keeps staring at me while she curses practically everyone, and then I shiver all over and I am afraid even of going to sleep because I know I am going to dream that they chop my head off and that Father Chirinos throws me in the river so the crabs will eat me. Aunt Francisca says crabs are just like devils with steel claws and white sharp teeth to reach straight for the heart. I never call Bertila then, because I know that she never comes, and I try to hold onto a rock to save myself. But the rock is covered with thick slime that is very slippery, and the current sweeps me away while the rock stays behind laughing like a giant face that I do not recognize. It has a mask painted on, like the clowns that come to the village with the circus. Everything gets darker. I fall deeper and deeper in the well that is full of Jews who are also something like devils, with long, sharp tails they use like wasps against Jesus Christ, who Father Chirinos says is the Savior of the world, Son of God, and Father of all Christians. I can see him whenever I want, because his hands and feet are nailed to the cross so he can't leave the church. Father Chirinos says the church is our house as well, but Bertila never comes with us on Sundays to see him. Aunt Francisca says it's because she has the devil in her body, and it is going to eat her up little by little, until only a shadow is left, and then not even that. So I have to go to mass by myself and not only that, when I told her that Father Chirinos had made me an altar boy, she started to laugh like crazy and said it was really the living end, she would like to see the Jew's face now, to find out what he thought of having an altar-boy son. I didn't know who she was talking about, whether it was about the devil or about Mr. Mitrani, who is the only Jew I know. But that lame old man could not possibly be my father, because I would die of fright and shame. Besides, Aunt Francisca has told me that I shouldn't even get close to him, because he grinds up little boys and bakes them into pies.

It's better if I don't think of these things, because when I do I get dizzy and shake, and I know I won't be able to sleep the whole night. I hope Ricardo doesn't sleep. I would like to ask him whether he knows if there are any other Jews in the village besides Mitrani. Mitrani is nothing more than a crazy old man who spends his Sundays preaching in the square in front of the church about the end of the world that is near. He says the river will flood the houses, that we will all drown, that the anger of God will fall on our heads like a sword, that no one in this village will be saved because we are all damned . . .

If the end of the world comes, perhaps I'll see my father . . .

and Father Chirinos gets so angry because more people are out in the square, listening to the rantings of Mitrani, than in church. I like to be inside, surrounded by those smiling and silent saints and the cherubs, round and rosy like Iris' doll. They watch very carefully. You can't stick your finger in your nose, or scratch where you itch, or pinch the legs of the daughters of Polo Miranda, even if they give themselves airs because their father has a lot of money and owns the mill at Santa Fe . . .

and Father Chirinos begins the mass. I like to kneel and raise my eyes to Christ on the cross who looks a little bit like Mr. Mitrani, with the same nose and the same long, wavy eyelashes. Of course it can't be true because Mitrani is a heretic, like my father was. I like to look at the Virgin, who protects us from all evil, even from the voice of Mr. Mitrani, who is still shouting outside the church. I have no father. My only father is Jesus Christ, who is in heaven with the Holy Family. My family is not holy. They are all a bunch of whores and procurers, except Aunt Francisca, who is a real saint.

Like when Bertila tells me not to wait for her at night, that she is going to visit Irma in Pacasmayo and won't be back until the next day, and Aunt Francisca has to take me to her house to sleep. She has some flowers in a vase on top of the dresser and they have a smell that goes deep inside my head. It makes me sleepy and makes me think of cemeteries. When the druggist's mother died, Zoila took me with her when she went to leave some red flowers on the grave. It makes me sleepy, lying on the bed with the lumpy mattress and the bedbugs that I feel crawling on my body.

Aunt Francisca wakes me up, in the middle of the night always, and drags me, dying of fear, to wash my fingers in the basin because they are all sticky. She says I am already grown and have to stop doing that. Only swinish men do that, she says, not good boys.

When I sleep with Iris, Iris says nothing. She comes closer to rub herself against me and she puts her hand between my legs. The next day she avoids looking at me, as if she were ashamed.

I guess I won't be able to talk to Ricardo until tomorrow, in school. I don't know whether I'm going to go. I didn't do my homework, and Miss Angelita said she's going to ask us questions about the Inca empire. It's a story all about a man called Manco Kapac, who is the father of all Peruvians, and comes out of Lake Titicaca with his wife, and that's all I remember. I think he might have something to do with the god of the sun and a rod of gold that was stuck in the hill as if by magic, but I don't really know because I haven't looked at the book. The book has nice pictures in color of men with beards riding horses. Those are the heroes who made the country. There's also a picture of the flag and another of the national seal. I remember a crown of laurel leaves, and a flame, and a very green tree, and against a red background a horn-of-plenty full of golden coins. I have to read that tomorrow. I'm going to do it instead of going fishing in the river with Ricardo.

I'm getting dizzy, but it's better if I don't say anything. It would only make Grandfather angry, like last night, at dinner, when I asked him again and Bertila gave me the usual answer: "You are the son of the rock." And Grandmother said, "That's some stone that you drew! It would be much better if you went to live with the Jew!" And Aunt Francisca said, "Shut up! The only innocent one in this whole mess is the boy!" And Grandfather said "The only important thing is that the Jew goes on sending you money every month."

Here's one fact that may be of interest: my birth date, November 15, and Cajamarca, the town where my grandmother was born, share a curious connection. According to history, on that very date four centuries earlier, the Spanish priest Valverde entered the town's main square, where the Spaniards and the Incas had gathered, and gave the Inca king the Bible saying: "Here is the word of God." Atahualpa took the book, put it to his ear, and tossed it into the air shouting: "I don't hear a thing." At that moment, the Spaniards opened fire, scattering the Indians in all directions, and captured Atahualpa, who, after he was granted the privilege of baptism, was condemned to the garrote.

1946: My family gives in to the parish priest's missionary zeal and has me baptized. Years later I would discover that, though my grandparents had ten children, I was the only person in my family ever baptized. From then on, the parish priest becomes my father and the church a second home. This father-home-church-town relationship would appear time and again in a dream which I recounted, years later, in my second novel, *Play By Play,* translated by Hardie St. Martin:

Yes, ladies and gentlemen: Marcos has had an extraordinary prophetic dream : and, thanks to the miracle of Peruvian television and to the ever fresh, always delicious Motta fruitcakes, you will have a chance to enjoy it step by step on your screens : And so we see Marcos's dream taking him into a church : In the background we can make out the figure of Christ without His cross : Yes, without His cross : arms dangling at His sides : naked : circumcised : suspended in the air like a battered old rag doll : Kneeling at His feet, an old man with bent head rocks back and forth, chanting a prayer : his thick mane of silver hair glistens : he's coming to his feet now : turning to watch Marcos : does he have grandfather's face? : Father Camacho's? : eyes with a blue gleam in them : an extremely aquiline nose : and a beard that seems out of place on his face : a tangle of strands hanging down to his feet like the branches of a weeping willow :

And here he is now, suddenly stepping to the right as the doors of the temple swing open with a tremendous bang : he pierces Marcos with his eyes, beckons, and the boy comes toward him obediently : Trouble in Peruvian territory : where a grand stairway comes into view at Marcos's feet : the old man takes him by the hand : the two of them go down the steps quietly peering at the road ahead : Suddenly, out of nowhere, the small town comes into sight : The stairway ends inside Marcos's house : the place is deserted and run down : its walls flaking : ceilings caved in : covered with a shroud of cobwebs and dust : The playing field is in terrible shape, fans! : But nothing can hold up this game : They're up to midfield. looking for a way out : going down a passageway crowded with ghosts : they fight their way out, arms flailing, but the Brazilians are marking them very closely : They cross into the penalty zone, a deserted spot, with rubble everywhere : Yes, folks, it's his hometown : only the church is still standing, off there on that hill of sand that looks like ashes : and suddenly the figure of the old man, crouching like a cat, appears outside the church : he motions to

Marcos : who makes a desperate run toward him : but the sand gives under the soles of his feet : he falls : and the sand sucks him, head reeling, toward the door of his house : And when he looks up, the hill is gone : only the church is still standing there and in it the old man beckoning once more : But before the boy can react, the old man spins gracefully, turning his back to him, and the doors slam quickly shut : And look at the temple rising into the air, higher, higher, higher! till it soars out of sight and leaves a gray cloud trailing in the sky.

The images in this dream—the destruction of the town, the church disappearing in a cloud of smoke, my grandfather's house turning into rubble—prophesied the loss of that "sacred space" which was my childhood years, the years in my village. That's why I wasn't at all surprised when, after returning to my hometown in 1977, I found out what the word Chepén meant. This word is derived from the joining together of the Mochica words *chep*—dust—and *en*—mother and/or house. Therefore, Chepén means mother or house of dust.

1948: One day an old man comes to the house claiming to have been sent from Lima by my father. He brings me a pile of gifts as if he were one of the Magi. One gift catches my eye: a six-pointed gold star. The old man ceremoniously places it around my neck while he says in a voice choked with emotion: "Don't ever take it off. You're one of us now." A few days later, the star ends up at the bottom of a river. I weep over it all afternoon and I remember being plagued night after night by awful nightmares in which an old gypsy, eyes ablaze, comes into my room and asks me what happened to the star.

1950: I learn to read from two sources that, at first glance, seem contradictory: the Catholic missal and Hollywood movies. That's how I become the priest's helper during Mass and the cinematographic reader of the family. Practically illiterate, my aunts and uncles take me to the movies so that I can read the Spanish subtitles to them. A conflict develops: I'm not sure if I want to be a priest or an actor when I grow up. The Mass, as well as the other rituals in town, becomes, for me, a kind of small drama: town life is a chain of processions, funerals, festivals, births, carnivals in which we all are actors and audience at the same time. From that experience, I developed a liking for a special kind of literature: the type that celebrates the joys and sorrows of life. Literature as a collective experience. Literature not as the expres-

"This is the river in Chepén, where I lost the Star of David that my father sent to me"

sion of a solipsistic "I," but rather as the universal expression that articulates the thoughts and feelings of a people.

1951: I read my very first book, the New Testament, and I also learn to write. I write my first book: I copy the Gospels word for word, letter for letter. My favorite is the Gospel According to John which starts off: "In the beginning was the Word."

1952: For the first time in my life, I get a close look at death. After several days of painful agony, my aunt Amalia dies at the age of nineteen. Until the moment they place her in the coffin—three or four hours have passed—I stay at the foot of her bed watching her. A lovely smile lights up her face and I cannot accept her death. We hold a wake through the night, and the following morning we carry her to the cemetery. I "saw" her again twenty-two years later in New York's upper Manhattan when, as I was about to begin writing my first novel, she appeared at the foot of my bed one morning with the same smile with which she had died and wearing the same clothes she was buried in. That same day I began working on *The Fragmented Life of Don Jacobo Lerner.*

1953: First exile: I leave my village for Lima. My father awaits me there and 5,700 years of Judaism fall on me like a ton of bricks. In addition, my encounter with a large city takes place. The late-night taxi trip to my new house is actually a journey through time: from the center of town, garbed in a Baroque colonial style, we enter a long neoclassical avenue and then cross a wide nineteenth-century promenade that every ten minutes is interrupted by beautiful, small medieval-like plazas that house winged statues erected to commemorate national heroes. My house is in the Jesús Maria district and I walk into it knowing that my true home isn't here, but in the town that I have left behind. (And now it occurs to me that I never lived in the same house in Lima for more than three years, a fact that has deeply affected the character of my work in which a recurring theme is the absence of roots and home.) Soon I discover that my father is a Jew and that his world stretches beyond Peru's borders. I begin to ask myself who am I, what am I. I hunt around for mirrors to see if I can recognize myself. No luck. I am alone confronting my own fragmented image. I've got to be someone, I tell myself, and that someone is my father. I must become what he is: a Jew. But in order to be a Jew I must erase my past. Thus, my second exile: from myself. I have to stop being in order to be. In my new environment, that of the Jewish community in Lima, I begin to discover that its members are living a marked schizophrenic existence. My new Jewish friends feel Peruvian, but also something else as well, something that in time I myself learned to feel. It so happened that we found ourselves, my friends and I, vacillating back and forth between Jewish and Peruvian culture. For that reason, a large part of my work deals with the attempt to reconcile both these roots and histories. The following poem illustrates this attempt:

Chronicles

Then I set out on my journey through history
and now I remember that heroes—I mean
    those
who thought about life as they were dying
flashed their ghostly claws

And it so happened that in the end
I couldn't forget Mariátegui's seven poems
that even though my head had been cut off
I still kept in my pocket
(the left pocket)
two cents worth of patriotism

Then I took the road that neither began
nor ended in Jerusalem or Cuzco
finally I discovered that Confucius
    Jesuschrist
    Karl Marx
were scheming to put out a new edition of the
    bible
and that the earth's navel
could be found inside a barren woman

Solomon ordered that the son of my conscience
    be cut in half
and that the head be handed over to the
    Western mother
and an ass with two legs to the Eastern mother
and that's how a lie the size of a nose
began growing on our culture

A parched, dying voice revealed to me that
civilization began when Cain committed his
    crime
who cared if Wiracocha was born in a
    Bethlehem manger
or if Jesus was Lake Titicaca's son
we didn't need sperm tests
but tests of conscience

in the end I, the offspring of Abraham's rape of
    Mama Ocllo
paternal step-brother of David the Hebrew
    Pachacútec
spun my roots in the Spanish-Jewish wool of
    Tahuantinsuyo

Poets: don't waste your words
today the word is no longer the prophet's sword
and reason, in this age, further removed than
    ever
from the mystery that the universe weaves
    around us
is only reflected in the stubborn silence of our
    dead

It's necessary, however, if you are looking for
    pseudonyms
to understand that it makes no difference to be
    called a lion
        a horse or a cat
that heroes' names already smell like
    parchment
and that's why it's better to be called ram than
    Abraham
lamb instead of Jesus
    or llama instead of Manko.

1954: I begin attending León Pinelo, a Jewish school. It's the first day of school for me. I know no one, and in comes the teacher. He picks up a piece of chalk, scribbles some very weird symbols on the blackboard, from right to left. Then he turns around and pronounces a few totally incomprehensible words. What's worse, the class then begins to repeat the teacher's words in a kind of litany. I sit there nailed to my chair wondering if I am going crazy. After four months of playing an invisible role in the class, I finally realize that they have been speaking Hebrew all along. That year I write my second book: an exact copy of a book of stories from the Old Testament in Hebrew. Writing those Hebrew letters placed me in a kind of trance—they were full of magic. I felt that a secret was hidden inside them, that these characters—and by extension, all writing—could be used to decipher the world. I wasn't a bit surprised to discover many years later that the following three words have the same root in Hebrew: *sefer* means book; *sipur*, narration; and *mispar*, number—that which contains and measures all things.

That same year I began reading my fourth book, the Bible in Spanish. We read through it with the rabbi in my religion class. Those classes and my own reading of the Bible taught me that the history of a people is also its myth. This lesson has shaped my writing: I do not treat Judaism as a purely historical process, but as something from which to retrieve a series of myths still latent in Judaism.

1955: I join *Betar*, a club of young Zionists linked ideologically to Israel's Herut Party, which advocates a Jewish homeland on both sides of the Jordan. Little by little Peru starts receding into the background: we study Peru's history, geography, and customs in school, but it's as if we were studying a foreign country. The Jewish community resembles a small Israeli ghetto nailed to the heart of Lima and, at the same time, it is also like a small Jewish village in Eastern Europe. For the first time I suffer an identity crisis when both my Jewish as well as my Peruvian friends ask me: "If Peru and Israel went to war, who would you fight for?" I tell my Jewish friends for Israel and my gentile Peruvian friends for Peru. That year I write my first original work, a lengthy narrative poem that tells a story of love and abandonment. The autobiographical link is clearly there: an Inca king conquers a foreign land, falls in love with a princess, and then returns to his kingdom not knowing that the princess is carrying his child.

1956: My father and I move into the house of a friend of his who had immigrated with his family to Israel. It has an unbelievably huge library, full of books by French, Russian, and American authors. Peruvian writers stand out by their very absence; there are, however, an abundance of books by classical Jewish writers, especially those written by Sholem Aleichem.

Little by little I begin to learn what it means to be a Jew, what makes us different from other people. To begin with, I am told that the Jews are the Chosen People. There's an additional burden: the most important men in history, from Moses to Freud—so it seems—have been Jews. Many years later, perhaps to relieve myself of the burden of this historical responsibility, I wrote a poem entitled "The Jews in Hell":

As the story goes,
the Jews bought for themselves
a private spot in hell.

In the first circle,
Karl Marx sits on a wooden bench
using his hand as a fan.
The prophet Jeremiah
fights off the heat by singing psalms.

In the second circle,
Solomon carefully studies

The author (standing, second from right) with friends from the Jewish school, León Pinelo, 1957

the stones from his Temple.
On some yellowing rolls of paper,
Moses draws hieroglyphics.

Christ dreams of Pontius Pilate
in the third circle.
Freud's clinical eye
follows every move he makes.

In the fourth circle,
Jacob wrestles with a devil.
Cain and Abel
treat each other like brothers.

In the sixth circle,
Noah rides drunk on a zebra.
Einstein searches for atoms
in the space between rocks.

In the final circle,
Kafka tilts his telescope
and bursts out laughing.

1957: First rite of passage: I become an official member of the Jewish people by being circumcised in the clinic of my father's doctor. That same night, half a block from the clinic, the film *The Ten Commandments* premieres and almost all the Jewish community of Lima attends. My father and I miss the opening night. A week later, when I return to school, I no longer have to avoid my friends when I go to the bathroom. Now I can proudly show them that I, too, am a Jew. The events surrounding my circumcision are narrated, as if they were part of a dream, in *Play By Play:*

Marquitos Karushansky's circumcision, or rather his bris, took place on the same day as the opening of *The Ten Commandments* at the Tacna movie theater. What's more, Dr. Berkowitz's office, where the operation was done, was only half a block from the theater. Marcos was operated on in the afternoon, some time between five and seven, and the show was to start at eight. But he and his father missed the opening. The saddest part of it, old Karushansky said, was not being able to see the film together with the rest of the Jewish community of Lima. They had to see it four or five days later, sitting among Peruvians, and it wasn't the same, it wasn't the right atmosphere, what did those *cholos* know about the Bible, anyway?

It had all started when his father announced, like a patriarch in the Old Testament: "Next year you be ready for Bar Mitzvah but first is necessary you have bris." Marcos remembered his eyes wandering to the smudgy windowpane, and then his voice, mocking and at the same time trying to reassure him, he shouldn't worry, they had also snipped off the foreskin of Jesus the Jew.

They showed up one day in Dr. Berkowitz's office where the physician, very professional, very freckled, explained: "Bris is an extremely simple operation. All it amounts to is cutting off the prepuce, the end of the skin that folds over the head of the penis and covers it. Then it's much easier to keep the glans clean. No sebaceous matter collects around it and this reduces the risk of catching dangerous infections." Marcos didn't know what he was talking about and went back with his father to the doctor's office the next day. The nurse had already left and they were greeted by a silence like the Sabbath's in the homes of Orthodox Jews. Before he knew it, Marcos was stretched out on his back on the operating table. Dr. Berkowitz was standing beside it, scalpel in hand, arm poised, and his father, sweat running down features drawn tight in pain and disgust, his father was lying across his chest, pinning his arms, papa's chunky body on top of his, would he ask him for a camphor liniment rubdown later? Every night at bedtime the ritual of the rubdown would begin and Marcos would massage him furiously, as if he wanted to tear off his skin, as if he were trying to draw blood

from the heavy body with an oval head. He would pass the palm of his hand down the slope of the thick short neck, up the incline of the shoulders with their overgrowth of hair, matted like the fur on a battered old grizzly, his body stripped of every shred of nobility, letting out low grunts, soft moans of pleasure.

His penis had been put to sleep but not enough to kill the pain from the clamp holding on to his skin as if it would never let go. Then the doctor—warning him not to exaggerate, because too much anesthetic could leave him paralyzed for life—raised the needle to eye level to make sure he had the right amount in the syringe. His whole body shuddered when the needle entered his glans. His father pressed all his weight down on his chest, and on his lips and chin Marcos could feel the rough beard, soaked with sweat and tears. Now his penis was a soft mass, a spongy mushroom, an organism with a life of its own, capable of tearing free with one jerk and slipping all over his skin, looking for a way into his body, or capable of dissolving and leaving a smelly, viscous fluid on his groin. He knew his penis was already in the open and he tried to imagine its new, hoodless look. In his mind, he compared it to the image he had of his father's member, its extreme whiteness, the perfect distribution of its parts, the scarlet crest topping the head of the sleepy iguana, with its vertical blind eye. He wanted to examine his phallus, to hold it above his eyes like a flower, to fall under the spell of the rosy calyx snug around its neck, to weigh it in his hand and stroke it warmly back to the familiarity it had lost. He was conscious of the small pincers clutching his foreskin tight: they were fierce little animals with fangs, beady eyes, and metallic scales on their backs. At the same time, he felt the pressure of his father's dead weight on him as a reproach, the embodiment of all the insults he had ever had to take. He thought about how, when he went back to school, he wouldn't have to hide from his friends in the bathroom. He would be able to piss casually now, to pull out his prick, take his time shaking it out, boldly pressing hard to squeeze the last drops out and then turn around defiantly and show it to the others, to all his schoolmates at León Pinelo, proudly, now let's see who is man enough to say I'm not a Jew.

The doctor left them alone in the back office: he told them he'd return in half an hour, they'd have to wait for the anesthetic to wear off, and Marcos watched his father nodding yes. Then the old man started to pace with his hands clasped behind him. He marched up and down next to the operating table, eyes straight ahead, without bending his knees, swinging each leg sideways slowly in a semicircle, before setting his foot down on the tiles. The controlled stiffness of his body, the deliberate halt after each about-face, before he started pacing again, reflected all the misery and resignation stored up in him. But Marcos knew every detail of this tactic his father had used, over the past two years, to put a certain amount of distance between them, to make him understand that behind this temporary withdrawal, all the things he had ever silenced were crying out, louder than words, against his bad luck and his unhappiness. If he had had any hope of crossing into his father's world, he would have asked him to come over to the table, dry the sweat on his forehead, take his hand in his, and help him clear away the skein of solitude unraveling endlessly in his chest. But he was sure the old man would avoid his eyes, as he did whenever he pounded on him with his fists, only to feel sorry afterward and break down like a vulnerable Mary Magdalene.

His senses had become dulled. His father looked older now: his beard had taken on a grayish tint and a hundred wrinkles had formed around his eyes. He tried to think of his mother but he couldn't retain a solid image of her behind his eyes. He had closed them and felt himself rushing down a toboggan run, rolling over and over without being able to stop. Only his father was solid; all the objects in the room had melted into ribbons of vapor swirling around him, and only his father's presence kept him from turning into a gaseous substance too.

He didn't move a muscle when the doctor's voice burst into the room like a garble of voices and sounds, and asked him if he was feeling better. He nodded without unlocking his eyelids, and the doctor and his father helped him off the table. His eyes were still closed, he staggered as if whipped by a blizzard, and the weight of his nakedness embarrassed him. The mere brush of the doctor's gloved hands on his member, the slight pull of the threads sticking out from the skin under the glans, made him feel wretched and he had the urge to piss. He guessed the pain this rash move would bring on and stopped himself just in time; the doctor was fitting a jockstrap stuffed with wads of gauze on him and he had the sensation that he was pissing inward. His bladder was tightening up and his inward-flowing urine plunged through his ureters, was picked up by the renal tubes, flooded his kidneys like a winding current, and was pumped, bubbling and humming, into the bloodstream. He felt that he was burning up inside, explored by the fine probe of an intense blue flame. The doctor's voice jolted him back to reality. A sudden smile lit up the doctor's face as he put out his hand in an outlandishly formal way and made a big show of shaking Marcos's father's hand, saying: "Mazel tov, Señor Karushansky, congratulations, mazel tov . . ."

1958: I am now a writer. I begin to write a novel entitled *The Miser,* set in my hometown and based upon my maternal grandfather. And yet, the landscape I describe is Russian, not Peruvian, and Chepén is quite a faithful reproduction of Kasrilevke, the mythical town created by Sholem Aleichem. I don't get beyond chapter three. That same year I discover César Vallejo's *Trilce* and Ciro Alegría's *El mundo es ancho y ajeno* [Broad and Alien is the World], books written by writers born in La Libertad, my native province. I am particularly moved by those poems in *Trilce* that speak of family and home life. In Vallejo I find a familiar voice, a voice filled with echoes of my hometown. It is a voice—obviously, I wouldn't discover this until years later—that not only reveals the poet's innermost conflicts but actually extends to the very roots of the thoughts and feelings of his *mestizo* race. I'm also deeply influenced by one of the central themes of Ciro Alegría's book: the world is a huge place, there are many areas to explore, but it will always be a foreign land for the Indians. Couldn't the same have been said about the Jews of the Diaspora?

1959: My Bar Mitzvah is celebrated early one Thursday morning. No more than twelve very old, wrinkled, and somber men show up at the synagogue. The ceremony lasts five minutes, just enough time for me to stammer through the two prayers I had memorized. Twenty years later I write a poem about this experience which attempts to reconcile my two religious traditions:

Bar Mitzvah

My father comes to see me on Friday night
He cleans my ears
brushes my smelly suit
and drops two vitamins down my mouth
On Saturday he shows up with sleepless eyes
makes breakfast
polishes my shoes
and takes my best shirt out of the closet
He grabs my hand
and we quickly pass by a church door
Hunched over almost touching the ground
we walk back and forth down endless streets
chasing off flies as they land on our faces
Three old men a tray of sardines and tomatoes

wine and a loaf of bread wait for us at the Breña
  Synagogue
The rabbi makes me climb up to the *bimah*
the old men smile at me
praying through their beards
The rabbi nods for me to start the prayers
instead I kneel down
ashamed my father blushes
an old man points to a few words in the Torah
I begin to stammer
I see my father out of the corner of my eyes
my old grey father celebrating this rite
      curled up like a fetus

In April of that year, my father takes me out of
the León Pinelo School and puts me in the Leoncio
Prado Military Academy. I'm the only Jew in the
whole school and, for the first time in my life, I come
face-to-face with anti-Semitism. There's no point in
behaving like a good Peruvian Catholic from Chepén.
My first and last name give me away, and I find
myself forced to defend my Jewishness with my fists.

1960: I read for the first time José María Arguedas's
novel *Los ríos profundos* [Deep Rivers]. It's the story
of a boy in search of his identity or, actually, in search
of a way to reconcile his Western and Indian roots.
The boy wanders through a not very clearly defined
world, caught between two cultures that clash not
only on the surface but in the very heart of every
Peruvian. The story is told in a richly lyrical language

Goldemberg (left), Leoncio Prado Military Academy,
1961

and all sorts of mysterious and magical occurrences
take place, the kind of writing that foreshadows what
was later to be called "magical realism" and which
pervades the work of García Márquez and Juan
Rulfo. This book by Arguedas would be vitally
important to me and would spur me to examine a
similar problem in my own writings: the cultural and
racial crossbreeding in Peru, incorporating history
and myth.

1962: Third Exile: I finish high school and my father
sends me to Israel to study agronomy. Before leaving,
I go back to Chepén to say goodbye to my past. My
return forms part of the epilogue of *Play By Play:*

Some weeks before his grandfather died, Marcos
showed up in town. Ten years after leaving, he
was returning not only to say goodbye to his mother
but also with a strange mission his father had given
him: to go to the home of the priest (he and old
Karushansky had been close at one time), ask him for
a crate of avocados, and take it back with him to
Lima: "Following the river you get there in ten
maybe fifteen minutes. If you wait till sun sets, you
can walk in shade of eucalyptus trees."

After almost twenty years of absence, his father
still remembered that the best avocados in the area
grew in the priest's orchard: "They are gems. No
others like them in thirty maybe forty kilometers
around. If he offers them free, take and thank him;
otherwise pay him. Here's some money."

Marcos went to see him. Having retired a few
years back, he lived with a sister, who had never
married, outside of town on the road to the old ice
and storage house. He had been his childhood parish
priest but Marcos did not recognize him. With his
crown of thick white hair, and wearing his old
cassock, the priest, who was sprawled out in a rocking
chair whose back looked like the bridge of a ship,
seemed to be floating in the dim light of the room. He
had lost most of his vision and his memory was almost
as clouded as his eyes.

"What did you say your father's name was?"

It was the fourth or fifth time he had asked this
question.

"Karushansky. Don Yehuda Karushansky."

"A tall, hulking, red-faced man who worked at
the Las Cruces mill and lived on Arequipa Street?"

Marcos said no.

"Then it must be the man who had the barber
shop. It was in the Plaza de Armas and got burned
down."

"No. Not him either," the boy said.

"Ah, then it has to be the Hungarian who was found knifed at the bottom of the river! Of course, he left a string of children all over the place . . ."

But Marcos said no again. And before he could say anything else, the priest broke in: "Shhh! Don't tell me, I'm starting to remember."

And he sank deeper into the rocking chair: a frown on his face, as if he were straining hard to sort out his memories. And so as not to drive them off, he stayed in the same position a long time, stretched out, holding his breath. At last he raised his head and tried to rivet Marcos's eyes with his own dull whitish ones. The boy started. He turned his eyes away. The walls were reflecting the last strands of the evening sun. He felt sticky sweat crawling down his back like spider legs. And then he heard the priest's voice, coming from far away. Like the river's rumble. As if he were saying a prayer. But he did not look at him. And with his eyes half closed, not stopping to look at anything, he felt his way out of the house. Only later, when he got back into town, did he remember the avocados. He had not mentioned them to Father Camacho, because of that famous orchard his father remem-bered as a second Garden of Eden, nothing remained, not even a shadow.

As I get off the boat in Haifa, I'm astonished to find that the dockworkers as well as all the people swarming around the piers are Jewish. An under-standable reaction, if you consider that I was part of a community of barely five thousand Jews among fifteen million Peruvians. I live on a kibbutz for a year, and then I spend another six months in a Haifa boarding house run by an Argentine woman. In that house I discover Borges and Kafka, two contempo-rary cabalists and prophets living in a world devoid of memories.

1963: I leave for Barcelona to study medicine. A month later I receive word of my father's death in Peru; he died without me getting to know him, and from that moment on, he will only be a ghost in my memory. I give up my medical studies, become an insurance salesman, and go back to work on the novel I had abandoned when I was twelve. It's still called *The Miser,* but now the book is actually set in Peru. Again, I get nowhere and I put it aside after writing

Goldemberg (left) with his father, "on the day I left for Israel," 1962

three or four chapters. Eleven years later I would finally realize that if I wanted to write the book, I would have to make my father's world part of it.

1964: I return to Peru. All ties with my family, on both sides, have been broken. I'm married by now and my wife, a girl from New York that I had met in Israel, is about to give birth. I'm unable to get any work, and I feel estranged from my native land. My trip to Israel and return to Peru, after a two-year absence, figures prominently in another poem, also entitled "Chronicles":

On the thirteenth day I set out on my journey
I pass a good share of the nights on the lookout
About a month into the voyage
We sight land
Without having endured major calamities:
We've reached the Old World
I live in a crummy hotel in Genoa
The landlady wouldn't even feed me
Or let me use the telephone
I spent my whole visit buying ties on the street
Within the week I was off to Venice
obligatory rites:
Crossing the canal in a coffin
A visit to St. Mark's Square
Small talk with the pigeons
The next day we plough across the Adriatic
Stopover in Greece
What my friends told me was absolutely true:
The Parthenon doesn't resemble an Inca
    fortress in the least
We enter into the Strait of Corinth
At the other end: Haifa
I start off living with a family
For the longest time
Mother and daughter treat me like a brother
That first week they take me sightseeing by car
The hills make my hairs stand on end
We finally reach the Dead Sea
Before the month's out I'm in bed with the
    daughter
Her mother hovers over me knife in hand
I pack my bags and abandon ship
I spend two months plagued by hunger
They finally send me a ticket to Lima
The boat makes stops in places none too
    friendly
Friends and relatives come to meet my boat in
    Callao
They ask me about my trip
I decide to beat a fast retreat

Our first child, David, is born and our financial situation grows worse each day. Fourth Exile: my wife convinces me that we should go live in New York. A month after our arrival, I enroll in college and, from 1964 until 1969, all I do is work and study. I do find time, however, to write two books of poetry. The first dies a quiet death at the bottom of a drawer. The second book, *Tiempo de silencio* [Time of Silence], is published in 1970 by a small press; the title is perfect, given the response it receives: not a word is written about it. That same year I begin teaching in New York University's Department of Spanish and Portuguese.

1969: Our second child, Dina, is born.

1973: My second book of poems, *De Chepén a La Habana* [From Chepén to Havana], is published in New York. I treat personal experiences in the book and I begin to explore Jewish themes for the first time. A few critics review the book, one of whom discovers a strange, exotic voice in my poetry. "The poems in this book," he said, "comprise a kind of journey in search of a traveler: the father. The poet is the prototypical uprooted man, traveling against the current of history as he searches for his roots. How can this be done? By delving into the stranger that was the poet's father and changing the familiar Jewish myth into a personal story that is neither a fable nor an epic." Already in this book of poems was the seed that four years later would give fruit to my first novel.

1976: The mother of my children and I separate. A year later we divorce.

1977: My novel *The Fragmented Life of Don Jacobo Lerner* is published in an English translation. Using autobiographical material, it brings together the most important experiences of my childhood: my early Catholic upbringing, the experience of exile, the clash between Jewish and Peruvian culture. On the one hand, the novel establishes a sort of counterpoint between the short history of the Peruvian Jewish community and the much broader national experience. Yet, this reality plays against a much larger world: the five thousand or so years of Jewish history. To a large degree, the story of the novel—Jewish immigration to Peru in the 1920s, the life of Jacobo Lerner, etc.—is only a backdrop for the re-creation of an experience that is at once historical and mythical: the Jewish exile. One critic claimed that I had written a documentary novel. Nothing could be further from the truth: the novel does not depict the true history of the Peruvian Jewish community, but instead fictionalizes a particular Jewish experience in which the historical is lived through certain remembered myths.

1978: *The Fragmented Life of Don Jacobo Lerner* is published in the original Spanish in Lima. The majority of readers, public and critics alike, claim that I have used an idiom, a mode of expression, and a "sensibility" that is foreign to Peruvian letters. Since this was also the reaction of my readers in English, I feel that I have been classified as the author of a Jewish novel written, as if by accident, in Spanish. Since I had not intended to write a Jewish novel, I ask myself the following questions: What makes a novel Jewish? What makes it Peruvian? Is it the subject matter? Is it the language in which it is written? If it is the subject matter, then my novel is both Peruvian and Jewish, since it deals with both realities. But if the "nationality" of a novel is defined by the language in which it is written, then my novel is definitely Peruvian. Why, then, did Peruvian readers detect a mode of expression—both syntactical and cultural, that seemed alien to Peruvian Spanish? By way of explanation, I am only able to come up with more questions: Does culture exert an influence on language or does language shape culture? Can a particular culture produce a sort of meta-language even if that culture, as in the case of the Jewish experience, expresses itself in different and often unrelated languages? Is there such a thing as a Jewish collective unconscious with its own unmistakable mode of expression? I find myself unable to come up with adequate answers to these questions.

1981: *Hombre de paso/Just Passing Through,* my third book of poems, is published in a bilingual Spanish/English edition. It includes several poems from *From Chepén to Havana* and is a kind of poetic autobiography: the attempt to create an "I" through the process of self-examination. In a broad sense, these poems confront the human condition after it has been worn down by time; by examining Jewish and Peruvian roots, these poems manage to integrate the individual with the whole, memory with the future, and nostalgia with exile. The poetic "I" undertakes a journey that embraces a complex history, with many roots, times, and spaces. "The protagonist is 'passing through' at many levels: as someone subject to the world at large; as a victim of exile; and as the product of a process attempting to integrate his various cultural roots." Also, with this book, Peruvian critics began to notice the "Peruvian" quality of my

The author's mother in her home in Chepén, Peru, 1976

writing, a discovery that forces them to reevaluate my first novel. "Goldemberg's novel," one of them suggests, "represents the start of a Judeo-Peruvian literary crossbreeding of special significance. The Peruvian Indian, as well as the Jew, is characterized by his submissive and nomadic nature. Goldemberg's poems reveal the same outlook: they are as clear and direct as verses from the Bible. These poems have an indisputable mystical foundation, a deep and unmistakable lyricism, religious feeling, and historical and cultural concerns found in another of our poets, César Vallejo." With these words, I finally deserve Peruvian citizenship as a writer. And yet, there still remains an unasked question: What is a Jewish Latin American writer? The answer, to paraphrase an Argentine Jewish writer, is simply: a Jewish Latin American writer is what he himself is, added to what Latin America is.

1984: My second novel, *Play By Play,* is published; it reintroduces several themes that were developed in my earlier books. This novel also has an autobiographical foundation, but even I don't know where the autobiographical elements end and the fiction begins. I identify personally with the story that is being narrated because I can recognize certain events in it as real and because I've attempted to expand and unearth them, to *give* them meaning, significance. What survives all those events? What remains of those deeds that actually took place? Is there a faithful rendering of what took place? These are a few questions I've asked myself and tried to answer. A writer attempts to write an "autobiographical" novel and soon discovers that there is no memory—only what *is remembered,* and that's where fiction bursts in. Memory, then, is that which I allow to exist and the only way to grasp it is by imagining it. Although the novel, any novel, happens to be autobiographical—even when the novelist identifies completely with the events—it is still the biography of an imagined being. Using one's own life to write a novel does not prevent the use of the imagination: to write a novel the writer must place himself right in the heart of the character, which implies that he has the character's intuitive imagination. Furthermore, underneath the plot line, *Play By Play* is a meditation on what it means or what it could mean to be Peruvian and/or Jewish. Throughout the whole book, characters and readers run up against the same question: what does it mean to be a Jew and/or a Peruvian? The novel offers, in a parodic style, the following answers:

Let's see: To be Jewish and/or Peruvian is:
Ser:
Estar:
A lucky star:
It's to be from a country of sharp contrasts:
It's to let the country go down the drain fast:
It's to have a Hebe Mame:
Or a screwed-up Mom:
It's to warn a Jewish Mother:
It's to belong to a race:
To pray for belongings:
To look for spiritual guidance:
Or be a misguided spirit:
It's a people:
Not a steeple:
A religion:
It's to populate a region:
A confluence of races:
A race against integration:
It's Zionism:
Cynicism:
Nonism:
It's crazy:

A destiny:
A necessity:
Something foolish:
History:
Hysteria:
What is it?:

The novel suggests that you mark with a Cross (or a Star) the answer you—character or reader—think is correct.

1985–1988: Four trips back to Peru. The full and undeniable reencounter with my past takes place: I renew the bonds with my family and friends, I fall in love with a childhood girlfriend, and I begin writing—for the first time—love poems. These poems form part of an unpublished manuscript entitled *De amor y sueños* [On Love and Dreams]. I stop teaching and cofound The Latin American Book Fair (1985) and The Latin American Writers Institute (1987).

1989: My fourth book of poems, *La vida al contado* [Life Paid in Cash] is published in Lima. A Peruvian poet and critic had this to say about the collection: "If the poems entitled *Chronicles* are nourished by collective history, both personal and familial, the texts entitled *Origins* grow out of the history of the Jewish people or any other kind of history, to express the most basic of elemental situations, for example the relationship between a man and a woman. There are other poems in the book entitled *Inventory* or *Just Passing Through* whose purpose we can define with two words: stillness and motion. Whoever is making the inventories doesn't want to go anywhere; on the other hand, the man just passing through, as defined, goes from one place to another, and is nowhere. These two signposts, corresponding on the symbolic level with two attitudes of the Jewish people, both equally active, one can almost say genetically, in each individual: the craving for planting roots in a land that can be recognized as one's own and, on the other side, the need to be a traveller through this vast world. These two ways of being, both interconnected, has historically given the Jews the ability to adapt to any environment and, at the same time, together with an internal order of a religious nature, a firm will to return to sacred places."

With *Life Paid in Cash,* a kind of anthology comprised of about one hundred poems, some old and some new, I feel that I have completed my Jewish itinerary in Peru. Now, perhaps, I should begin to consider what it means to be a Peruvian Jew in New York. Something tells me, however, that I will only be

Chepén's main street, with the author's house on the right

able to relate this experience from the vantage point of Peru.

1990: My childhood friend Dina and I get married in New York. My life has come full circle.

BIBLIOGRAPHY

Fiction:

The Fragmented Life of Don Jacobo Lerner (translated by Robert S. Picciotto), Persea Books, 1977, published in Spanish as *La vida a plazos de don Jacobo Lerner,* Ediciones del Norte, 1980.

Tiempo al Tiempo, Ediciones del Norte, 1984, published in English as *Play By Play* (translated by Hardie St. Martin), Persea Books, 1985.

Poetry:

Tiempo de silencio (title means "Time of Silence"), Colección de Poesía Hispanoamericana, 1970.

(With José Kozer) *De Chepén a La Habana* (title means "From Chepén to Havana"), Editorial Bayú-Menoráh, 1973.

Hombre de paso / Just Passing Through (bilingual edition; translated by David Unger and the author), Ediciones del Norte, 1981.

La vida al contado (title means "Life Paid in Cash"), Lluvia Editores, 1989.

Contributor to Spanish- and English-language journals, including *Present Tense, Nimrod,* and *Mundo Nuevo.*

James B. Hall
1918-

I

"On a Sunday," my mother often said afterwards for she was much present at that time. "And far away, I heard church bells ringing."

So in that place and at that time I was born: an Ohio day at midsummer, cumulus clouds aloft, the crops almost laid by on the Hall family farms. A grandmother and two neighbor women "in attendance," hot water on the kitchen stove, Doctor Tribbets said to be on his way.

Born to Florence and Harry Hall, of Jack Oaks farm, a second child, this time a boy. At home. Silver nitrate in the eyes. No small event: an heir and assign, possibly a manager on form, on bloodlines. Boys and colts were about the same; given time, they might be of future use.

The territory of Ohio east of Cincinnati and not far from the river was by tradition very Southern, perhaps more so than Kentucky just across the river. Therefore a landowning man was obliged to all visitors. That morning they drank Harry's second-best whiskey, ate his ham from the sideboard, stayed on.

So it was: older manners, even then passing. At that time and in those ways I was born.

For my mother in the agony of birth to remember church bells while my father was in the next room with well-wishers and cronies is typical of both Harry and Florence.

She was imaginative, musically trained, loved flowers, raised five children before penicillin, was a strong personality and community leader. To Florence, the church bells were more than music.

Harry drank not much at all, but was gregarious, openhanded, and needed almost obsessively to be with others, to talk, play cards, or simply to *be* there. To him this occasion was purely secular, and when his last guest had departed—after the customary three announcements of intention—Harry would have dropped by the bedroom for a second to say affably, "When I heard you screaming, Flos, I knew every-

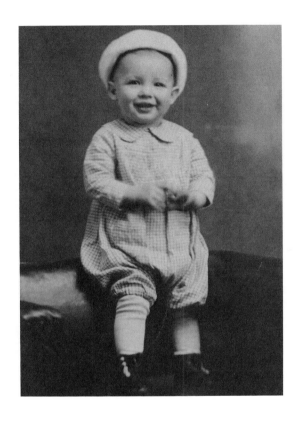

James Byron Moon Hall, two-and-a-half years old

thing was all right . . ."

Harry was a Squire-type in transition: not much inhibited by formal education, widely read, a practical drainage engineer who in his youth became a very young telegrapher and train dispatcher; a scientific farmer and landowner by inheritance; a sportsman, nearly professional poker player, informal scout for the Cincinnati Reds, agnostic, and a high Mason.

If Florence expected either public display or private sympathy she did not get it. Harry and Florence were decidedly disparate personalities, but at this time their bonds had not yet been tried.

Four highly visual, tactile, even olfactory encounters which happened when I was about three years old are vivid in exact detail even today. Whether my sensibilities were already formed, in a primitive way, or whether these key moments emerged to validate mature experience, I cannot say.

Great-grandfather Hesler had been a drummer boy and a soldier in the Civil War, the Union side. He limped from a bullet still in his heel. When very old, he died.

The funeral was "at home"; and he was laid out in a casket. I was lifted up, the better to see into his coffin. He was laid out in his customary black suit, hands folded, face artificially ruddy, and in his parted hair and full beard not one grey hair. There was an odor of roses and black suit, metallic as with an empty tobacco can of "Prince Albert." I was lowered to the floor, then toddled outside to a porch until someone came and got me.

One day in summer, in the field across the road exactly in front of Jack Oaks farm, an airplane landed, stopped just beyond the fence. I saw silver wings in reflecting sunlight, then in my mother's arms saw the curved, blue propeller. Beside the airplane, I felt the engine's heat.

Mother held me aloft, and I looked down into the rear cockpit: an array of instruments, chrome glass catching the light. There was a dusty, nitrate odor—with oil, burned. I felt a long, squirming tremor of joy for the faring of doped canvas seemed wonderfully shaped, smooth, and soft to my hands.

Later I understood this was Jenny biplane, from an airfield in Dayton, here to take passengers for a ride. On its return trip to Dayton, the biplane crashed, killed the pilot; also killed the fat man who wore a leather coat.

Then not in one day, but nearly so, the final two "key moments" are now strongly connected in memory.

Mother's hired girl took me with her to the general store in Midland City. There a railroad water tank stood on tall legs beside the tracks. At the grocery store everyone was laughing, pointing to the sky.

The hired girl pointed my arm and got me to see: atop the very tall water tower was a black automobile, tilted with the roof, a big, black thing, the windshield reflecting the sun.

I understood, laughed, and also pointed to the big thing on the top of the water tower.

Then, at home, I had taken all of the books out of a low, glass-door bookcase and crawled inside, curled snugly on the shelf, made the doors close and looked out through different, colored panes of glass:

a darkened den which smelled book-dust, smelled smooth wood, and every day I played here.

That day someone took me from my dark den, took me to the big, front-room window.

During the night, there had been an ice storm: at midmorning, the sun caught in each tree branch, fence wire, every stalk, weed, and blade of grass. In blinding detail, all ice blazed and the fields forever were drifted, ice-burning snow.

Mother remembers that even as a baby I had a long span of attention and that I stood there and then went back again and again until all of it melted.

What then, might these key moments signify?

The man with the black beard in the parlor casket was like so much of the past of this territory not far from the Ohio River. Nearby lay Fort Ancient. Here a pre-Indian people hunted, lived, built the great Ohio mounds—and others. Mysteriously they vanished, died, or were overrun in battle, their dead laid out in barrows.

At one boundary of a Hall farm the road is Mad Anthony Wayne Trail, marking the route to Fallen Timbers; before that the Indians defended, sporadically, their tribal hunting grounds, and not far away, across the Little Miami, was the "Miami Slaughterhouse."

In the Civil War this was Copperhead (Southern sympathizer) country; Morgan's Raiders were cheered. Although the Underground Railroad for transporting runaway slaves often ended in Ohio, this territory remained segregated; and only after World War II in a nearby town of three thousand—more than a village—did any black person dare remain overnight.

Thus there were always "finer" things, citizens of public spirit; in the background, intertwined, there was violence, loss, a dead man in the parlor, the bushwhacker's state of mind.

The airplane landing in a pasture field was much like the arrival of factories, machine-tool plants, tractors in every field, electricity, radios. New highways changed utterly the old dispensations of land, hogs, wheat, and clover.

A little like the Mound Builders, an older social order disappeared.

The car on the water-tank roof, and sun blazing on an ice storm are more subtle.

A man's sons were denied the use of the family Model T, so on Halloween his boys took apart their father's car, and piece-by-piece reassembled it on the giddy tower. Whereupon, vastly "sympathetic," appropriately "angry," the boys worked hard to bring their father's car back down—piece-by-piece—for reassembly. In gratitude, thereafter, the father permitted his sons to use the car to take girls for rides. Everyone except their father knew the truth of it.

This humor, practical jokes, "Folk Theatre" went on in all seasons. I do not remember a time when in someway I did not know there was a wild, even hilarious side to life—and one born every minute. Only a closely knit community can play elaborate, harmless jokes on one another, just for the hell of it.

The opposite pole of communal hilarity must be the utter dazzle of sun on a fall ice storm, nature's brute unpredictability. After an ice storm in the Middle West, summer never again seems quite the same, and a darkened bookcase with pretty, stained-glass windows is not the world.

*

At that time farm life in Ohio is conventionally thought to be the hayseed life, pastoral, early to bed, etc. etc.

In fact, our house was high-talk, musical, free-wheeling, highly emotional, fully argumentative, and possibly Bohemian. If Jay Gatsby was on Long Island, Florence and Harry in their own ways were of the Jazz Age at Jack Oaks farm.

The house itself was built in a grove of oaks, new when Florence and Harry began housekeeping. The two-acre yard, garden spaces, and room for a chicken house was simply divided from another Hall farm. At that time, of course, there was neither electricity, indoor water, bathrooms, or insulation as we know it; heat was from one stove and a range in the kitchen. The furniture was not elaborate, but the piano was large. There were no provisions at all for washing clothes, neither appropriate hot water nor a washing machine.

Being an energetic, imaginative former schoolteacher, Florence was a community leader, a 4-H Club state official, coached plays to raise money for the schools, did work with the poor, and had a wide circle of friends. To play at cards bored her, but she read a great deal, often to the children. Moreover she was an accomplished seamstress, could make elaborate costumes, played classical piano, and sometimes sang Victor Herbert songs at weddings. At the same time she could be highly emotional, given to tears, had beautiful long hair, and a trained, highly effective contralto scream of great range and anguish.

From time to time Florence had "help," but her style was to concentrate on one thing, at the expense of routine matters; then in a flurry of activity she

"caught up with everything." Thus Florence might not cook very much for weeks: it was the ever-full pot of beans on the back of the stove, and a piece of toast half-burned over the range-stove fire. When small I had to move and then stand on a kitchen chair to get my own food from the ever-full pot. Except when visiting, especially the grandmothers, I do not recall sitting down to eat very many meals of any kind, although I suppose this also happened.

Mother's great giddy moments were at Christmas. Then she boarded the train for Cincinnati, always took one child, wore her furs, had lunch at a restaurant, spent all her money on presents for others, loaded her department-store credit accounts. She was highly susceptible to elaborately decorated, lighted shop windows, and would sometimes stand transfixed. Always she tried to see a dramatic production, and if music were involved, Florence bought the scores, and then at home played them for everyone.

Harry's life was somewhat the same, but in a different key, so to speak.

In the busy seasons of farming he was out early, and "on call," actually worked. Mostly he was a "windshield" farmer, one who farms by riding around in a pick-up truck. Usually Harry managed everything important by noon, so it was lunch in town, and the afternoon at one of his fraternal order club rooms where there were nonstop card games, the news, or if no one were around he would drift on to another place, looking for company.

Harry was a very progressive farmer. For years he was on the governing board of the county children's home. Harry was broadly political, seemed always to know the current Lieutenant Governor of the state, and was said to "deliver the farm vote." I have seen him pass cash for "general expenses" to a "doubtful" vote.

In his own business dealings, Harry was generous, often to a fault. I recall a violent argument: a man had been forging checks on our father; Mother was outraged, wanted blood. Harry said, quietly, "Oh, hell, if he wants money that bad let him have it. I'll just go talk to him."

Contralto scream.

Naturally Harry was seldom home, in part because he was a near-professional poker player and typically had books "on the subject," theories; he was deceptive, a fine "psychologist," and had a retentive memory for the cards played and for a last year's hand. Early, he taught me "the game."

With all these "obligations" Harry kept irregular hours, was often home near dawn, or read until

Father, Harry Hall, about thirty: "a squire type, an intellectually inclined poker player"

midnight, oblivious of any amount of activity around the house.

Harry was the kindest of men, but had been raised as a single child, largely by hotel maids, and until almost grown had no regular room: he slept anywhere there was a vacancy. Because he had eaten always by taking what he wanted as he walked around the hotel dining-room tables, he had no very steady adult eating habits—or table manners. At dinner, in a good restaurant, he might order breakfast food, if that notion struck him.

In consequence, I saw Florence throw herself at our house: sweep, clean, mop, black the heating stove, clean the windows.

Harry might very affably return home, notice nothing different at all. When asked, *Do you see anything different?* He might say, "Why, did something burn?"

Tears. Recovery. Dramatic lecture, and review of past slights, etc. etc. Sobs.

"Well," Harry might say, "Want me to get us a bite to eat?"

Looking back on it, even though Harry was remarkably effective with men, public affairs, issues, and friendship, I think profoundly he lacked domestic imagination.

*

From my point of view, it seemed I lived among a thousand girls: Elinor, my elder, very beautiful, talented sister, something like Mother, had club, and musical, and dance friends, all girls. Likewise my cousins with one exception were girls, and my mother's 4-H Club activity was with sewing, cooking(!), gardening: "domestic science"—as they said. Very much I did not like this, felt put upon, estranged.

Because both Harry and Florence spent money fluently and neither of them kept accurate checkbooks, there was never quite enough. Each person had credit accounts, but no one "kept the books." Increasingly, late at night, there were violent arguments about money—or its surrogate—Harry's insensitivity to Mother's needs.

Against this, there was always much music in the house.

At Jack Oaks there was a great deal of reading, and much vocabulary floated around. By the time I went off to the first grade, I could read fairly well, and this I learned from Grandfather Moon.

In the evening or late Sunday afternoon, before an open fire in the grate, the kerosene lights low, he held me on his lap. While smoking his evening cigar, he read and on request reread the "Uncle Wiggly" stories from a newspaper. He saved these and then in order read each one aloud. I followed along the text while he read.

Then it was my turn to read them back to him. Grandfather put up with this for hours, and in the end would say very appreciatively, "Now what in the world will happen next to that Tommy Tittlemouse?"

The joy of being held, and rocked before an open fire, and smelling his cigar smoke, and hearing his even, manly voice hypnotized me, I suppose; and I am sure he was not "teaching me to read." It was only our bond, and I was his grandson.

Daddy Bye (Byron) also had a large repertory of poetry. If asked, he would recite American vintage work such as "Skipper Erickson's Ride," a hundred lines from "Hiawatha" or "Snowbound." He recited these and many others with gusto, made the words *rhyme,* ker-thunk! I am sure he had no notion about the worth of poetry, or that poetry was an art; he simply had a retentive memory and apparently liked the story and the sound of the words. And so did I.

*

At age six I went off to a newly completed, "centralized" school.

Possibly there were twenty students in the first grade, which met in the same room with the second grade, both taught by Miss Osborne, the spinster daughter of a local Quaker family.

I did not learn anything new, but I was not at all bored. In the more advanced grades, often I sat in the back row and read reference books, especially the *Scientific Encyclopedia*. In the fifth and sixth grades, others had pretty much caught up; I was loafing.

I rode the school bus three miles to school, in all weather, fall, winter, and spring. My father raised pet crows, all named Jim, as in Jim Crow: one pet sometimes flew above, followed our bus to school, a piece of food in his beak (his lunch). Sometimes he waited on the cross-arm of a telephone pole outside the school until it was time to follow the school bus home again.

In any event, my education was on two, loosely connected tracks: that which was taught in class; and that which I read and absorbed at home and from widely diverse sources.

Above all, however, very much I liked school and each fall I was always eager for school to begin. The local religion was basketball; by eighth grade, I was thin, not very fast, and could not have phrased it, but did not like team sports. Worse, I began to see my teachers with a terrible clarity, their weaknesses, their foibles, their pretense. Among other things, I was sometimes their "professional" test-taker: for county and state competitions. I did very well for them in a variety of subjects; but this was not basketball, so I felt the loneliness of the Long Distance Test Taker.

I cannot explain the reasons, but even in only the third grade, I liked what I was doing, but I did not like the people in authority, the Establishment.

Of course this was a generalized feeling, much as I might feel about rain, or the darkness among trees. Temperamentally, but not to my overt knowledge, I was already at odds "with the system."

*

At Jack Oaks farm some of the ebullient, open, country gaiety of the Jazz Age continued, but now the Great Party was elsewhere, in Cincinnati, in New York.

Harry's home poker parties now ended well before dawn—and the stakes were much lower. Florence's concern for "style" and clothes for the girls became subdued. She spent hours at the sewing machine, "doing dresses."

The trouble was money. In the late twenties, the Great Depression first hit farm prices. In addition, there were seasons of flood, drought, and the first dust storms. Harry had always borrowed easily at any bank, but now interest was high, and progressive farmers who had phased out horses had tractors and up-front gasoline bills. The tenants and their families were in need; as yet, there were few agencies of "relief" in place.

Some tenants, former hired hands, and the indigent began almost openly to steal sweet corn, chickens, wheat, even hogs from the pen. Both Harry and Florence knew this, were much torn or confused, looked the other way. Without knowing it, Florence and Harry were of the postwar (World War I) generation, had never before known or even in a realistic way imagined hard times.

Once I remember them sitting on the floor. All around were little piles of cancelled checks, Hers and His. From the farm; from Harry's drainage business. This man *paid twice;* but *she* denied a purchase, lied about an account at Pogues. Then two smaller children, one a toddler, picked up piles of checks, threw them up in the air.

Apparently Harry became a more serious poker player, came home at dawn, threw bills and coins on the bedroom dresser, slept until noon.

In her way, Florence needed Harry's easy, mildly extroverted ways, but no longer found this; at times she took to her bed, and cried and cried.

I suppose this house built especially for her became a kind of nightmare of her high-minded, at bottom romantic dreams.

Those years, for months, saw temperatures in the Ohio Valley to all-time, historical lows. Snowed in, with not much to eat, Harry would telephone the nearest country grocery store, and someone would carry bread and perhaps sliced dried beef in glass jars to our door.

Odd that an establishment like Jack Oaks farm had few amenities, except a cleverly decorated, outdoor privy. Even more unusual that Harry depended on his mother (Grandma Hall) virtually all her active life for his own family's milk, eggs, butter, cream, and, in summer, garden vegetables. All these from "her" farm at the village edge, across the fields from Jack Oaks. Put another way, I suppose the couple who lived at Jack Oaks farm required a great deal of support.

By this time Elinor, our eldest sister, began to be a genuine help. She became our tribal leader, a surrogate mother. She was imaginative, kind, gifted at music; she was even then beautiful, and to me seemed to have a charmed life, as though everything good happened to her. And she loved her little brother very much; not always, I suspect, an easy thing to do for I was at once jealous of her, but also protective. A difficult combination in a younger brother who seemed increasingly to tip into outrage, throw almost anything just close enough to miss.

What I must have sensed but did not fully understand was this: the blight, the bad years for landowners and farmers alike had become the depression years for everyone.

In many ways high-minded and innocent, the Jazz Age of rural Ohio was over, the card games finished, the orchestra gone home.

Almost overnight this highly social, dramatic, usually fun-loving household of means, of generous impulse, this rural Bohemia of Jack Oaks farm became a place where people not so much lived as camped out. In the end, to pay debts and raise money, that fifteen-acre dream eventually was sold.

And Herbert Hoover was president.

*

I am uncertain of the sequence, but three significant things happened: Elinor became ill: a "spot" on her lung, persistent fevers, the beginning of tuberculosis. She lay abed almost a year at Grandmother Moon's, recovered, the "rest" cure. She went then to live with an aunt in a northern city where the high school offered advanced Latin, a good cello teacher, and mathematics. In those two steps, she went away. I used to lie abed at night, too "manly" to cry, but wondered, vividly, what she was doing, *right now . . .*

Some time after that, there was a particularly traumatic night. Harry came home at about three o'clock in the morning, had lost at poker; as was her custom Florence almost literally lay in wait. As was often the case, the next hour or so was a loud review of present and past complaints—all real enough. The climax was when Florence took all her clothes out of the closet, stated how old each piece was, how little it cost.

Harry was maddeningly noncommittal through all of this, might eventually say, "Well, you about ready to turn in?" Or sometimes they would both

become enraged, scream and yell for half an hour, then go to bed and noisily make love.

Very underweight, with major ear infections, one spring day without asking permission or telling anyone at all, I packed all of my things except books in a cardboard box, walked out of Jack Oaks and across the fields towards the railroad. I had no intention of getting in a boxcar.

I went to my grandmother Hall's back door, and told her I was going to live with her.

*

Grandma Hall was a marvel of a woman: long widowed, a manager-type, she lived on her own farm, kept cows, played the foot-pedal organ, devoted one room of her house to raising canary birds, and every election she "got out the vote"—Republican, of course.

At the door, Grandma never asked a question. "Why you just come right on in, you can have the back bedroom all to yourself—and private entrance. Your bicycle can come later, just keep it on the porch. I'll just get us something to eat. And what—she said—*would you like to eat?*"

I was dumbfounded: never before had I ever been asked what I would *like* to eat.

Grandmother sat a place for me at the table: silverware, plate, napkin. A glass of water, at the correct place.

She was very motherly, and after we had eaten she laid out the program: "You help me around here, some. And you need to gain some weight. I'll see to that."

And she did.

My departure from Jack Oaks was never mentioned by either my mother or my father, nor do I imagine they said anything to Grandmother Hall.

I had made a decision, and though only twelve or thirteen, it was mine to make—and so were any consequences. I did not feel anything for my father or my mother; I just did not live there anymore. Years later Graham Greene wrote of "the icicle in every writer's heart." My icicle was not large, but it was there.

*

Grandmother Hall was a broadly sympathetic woman, hard on herself—and she understood boys very well.

She took a great interest in my lessons, and I began to see the advantages of study habits which, before, had not occurred to me. Grandma was of the "stored nut" school of learning. Whenever I solved a difficult arithmetic problem, or learned Latin verbs, she would say, "Now that will come in handy someday." I believed this to be true.

In fact I gained weight, grew taller, no longer had colds or infected ears. I felt great vitality, like a coiled spring; my bicycle was just outside my "private" bedroom door, so if I leapt into the saddle at midnight, rode for miles, came home—no one knew, or cared. But I had to be up with the cows at six o'clock in the morning.

Grandma's farm was on the edge of a town, a rail junction, with cattle pens, coal storage, railroad crewmen and maintenance crews—and one detective. Essentially, it was a market town with country grocery stores, barber and beauty shops; once there had been a dozen saloons, but only half that number of churches. I did not and no one I knew had any intimation of Midland City's certain decline.

I loafed at a well-equipped garage, where the owner and one mechanic repaired any car that could get through the door; they were tobacco chewers, and liked to spit on a boy's unwary bare feet. If a first crop of pubic hair was suspected, then a boy might be caught, the case pragmatically verified, and gasket shellac daubed on—just for the hell of it. Dried gasket shellac came off only by the use of barber shears.

I liked automobile engines very much, and they let me help by standing by, always with the absolutely correct tool at the ready.

In summer at night, I was often at Nestor's place. He was a railroad electrician, and a sophisticated builder of radio receivers. Nestor was also a friend of my father's, and the first man I ever knew who sipped whiskey—just barely enough—and smoked cigarettes chain-fashion. In a little while I could read "circuits" and sometimes he would leave soldering jobs for me while he went out to shoot pool. Nestor was very tall, very thin, a large, bulged forehead, a self-taught radio engineer before that term was used.

And there was "low life." Before prohibition ended, there were home-brew joints along a route known as "Around the Horn." A group of men, and tag-along boys, "cruised" in two or three cars, one joint to the next, at each stop entering the joint with a wild whoop. My favorite stop was the Silver Barn, probably near Georgetown. Here there were three pianos in a row, played by three black men, all of the blues, stride, riverboat, and boogie schools of jazz.

Because I played piano a little, through "Country Gardens," I marveled at their tremendous speed,

their attack, their great communal memory for almost any tune. I used to stand beside the end piano, watch closely. Sid continued to play, but also talked to me at the same time. His father, he said, once "played the riverboats," had taught Sid "all I know."

I had a strong, emotional feeling about their music, and when Sid used his left hand to play the treble notes of the next piano, I knew I could never, never in my life do that. One of the last times I was taken to the Silver Bar, Sid looked up, saw me. Did not nod or wave, but began a favorite tune, "The Little Rock Getaway."

Even at the time, vaguely, I saw the irony of it. Through illicit activity, an underage boy going with rounders to illegal home-brew joints, I heard a new music, was humbled by it; in addition, this encounter was the first sloughing away of an endemic, Ohio prejudice. I registered first Sid's talent, and later—if at all—the color of his skin.

Mother, Florence Moon Hall, about twenty-three: "a civic-minded former schoolteacher, trained in music"

My two or three years with Grandma Hall marked the time when I had money of my own—earned, put in the bank. It was a way, Grandmother said, to be "beholden to no man." She had the "stored nut" theory of money.

Attracted at first by the usually red, high-action covers, I began to read pulp magazines, mostly World War aviation: *Flying Aces, Battle Aces, G-8;* in addition, I found people who bought *Argosy, Black Mask Detective,* and *Adventure.*

By that time I read very fast (apparently) and developed the almost lifelong habit of eating crackers, and reading in bed sometimes until three o'clock in the morning. I was not a collector, a trader, or someone who remembered the names of authors; I read for the action, the heraldry, and the "way it all came out."

I liked *Adventure* and *Blue Book,* and especially a feature called "Lost Trails" where one could write perhaps to get back in touch with a buddy who "worked the high lines in Montana, Winter of '29—a real big one." I had a firm sense of being a part of a close, manly audience; to read, among other things, made me "one of the stiffs." Nearly always, I entered wholly into the spirit, the tone of these publications. When an Ace returned to the field, saw the aerodrome beneath his lower wing, was downwind, heard "the under carriage rumble on the tarmac, was home . . . ," literally, I perspired, was weak; but though exhausted, reported to the Adjutant, who looked up from the papers on his desk and said, "Dammit, Bostick, you are supposed to be dead. Again." "No such luck," the Ace replied. "Jerry is back over Amiens. They have got a new airplane. It's a triplane, surely a Fokker. It's fast. Deadly."

At some time I began to read, even reread those stories, and felt I *could do that.* I was very sure I could write almost as good a story. At first, I thought to cut out the best passages of several stories, then change the parts a lot, and then paste them back together and somehow get the "new" story typed. Literally, I knew no one who typed, and I had never known anyone who typed. But I began to read the want ads in the local paper, perhaps to find a cheap, used typewriter.

And this I did. An Underwood "Standard," for twenty dollars. With a new ribbon.

*

Except for an almost overnight transition, at about sixteen, from a show-off, somewhat "wild" bicycle rider to automobiles and almost at the same time motorcycles, I think the essentials of my personality were at least tentatively in place.

This involvement with automobiles and what was more clandestine, motorcycles, was in some ways explainable, and in some ways still mysterious.

Even as a very young boy I had been around two generations of farm machinery. A wheat binder (my job to ride the rear seat, dump the sheaves) and then a wheat combine, are complex machines; they were pulled first by Fordson, then by Farmall tractors. The Farmall, for example, was rigged with corn plows, four or six rows at a time; when the corn was only two inches high, the tractor driver developed a delicate touch. Besides, something always "broke down." Repairs in the field were essential; always we worked against time, darkness, the season. Soon one developed a rough-and-ready attitude about machinery, a combination of great respect and appreciation and the field saying "If it ain't broke, don't fix it."

Naturally I could drive almost any automobile by the time I was twelve, but only in barnyards, to a far corner of a field (to bring someone a wrench). At sixteen I was "road legal" with an adult aboard; no one much cared about the adult for a good local driver was known. What an older two generations knew about their horses, care, feeding, habits, precepts, and worth, I knew in the same detail about internal combustion engines and all local machinery.

In the Middle West, auto racing and motorcycle racing were highly developed. The Memorial Day race at Indianapolis was the major event, but I never attended. On that day, there were also races for lesser drivers, at smaller tracks.

I was drawn to these local events, often at small town or county fairground horse tracks. The motorcycle owners put up some money in a purse (and from admissions); then it was once slowly around the track in a loose gaggle, and out of the last turn in a "flying start."

Locally, I was a "speed merchant," on country roads and in the streets. The Cartmel brothers had a 1931 Ford roadster, the engine "hotted up," and "juice" brakes. Some Saturday nights we took turns, might drive 125 miles around the county, leaving four long, controlled skid marks at many curves. We were somewhat "scientific" about this, would not have remotely thought of having a beer. "Red" became a long-distance truck driver, and when very young was killed in a small town when at two o'clock in the morning a drunk ran a red light. Red took the rig into and through a drugstore to a brick wall, was crushed by his load.

If speed close to the ground was an obsession, I knew what I was doing, felt I was very good at it, a little cocky. Deeply, I liked the actual or implied applause, the indirect but very real admiration of others. And it was compensatory, for in a community addicted to baseball and basketball, I seemed temperamentally incapable of playing any team sport.

Moreover, to choose between a baseball game or to drive a hundred miles each way to an air show was easy. It was the air show every time: pylon racing, and free-fall parachute jumps with an open sack of flour which left a long, white exclamation mark down the sky. At terminal speed, I heard the cloth explosion of a chute opening above the crowd.

I was the one—the fan—who managed to be near the aircraft, or not far from the packing table when they rigged the chute and the jumper and got him in the cockpit for takeoff. I liked this very much, listened to everything they said.

*

In a remarkable show of healing, of a delayed but real cooperation, Florence and Harry seemed to emerge again, this time on a more realistic, useful, and solid plane.

They "emerged" from a series of make-do rental houses, a shabby make-do life. Because Harry was a self-taught engineer, and excellent manager of men, had been or still was "important," he was appointed county road engineer: pick-up truck, salary, long hours in summer, or in times of flood. In that way he held the farms together, kept the tenants on, embraced adversity.

When the Great Depression thawed only a little, Florence and Harry moved "to the country," to the "Pansy farm," four miles to the nearest market town, twelve miles to the county seat.

At that time Florence began a remodeling project which lasted for some years. By then I was a sophomore in high school, and moved from Grandmother's back "home" for the advantage of a larger school: with Latin, algebra, advanced chemistry, music of several kinds, and dramatics. Oddly, it was the same high school my mother attended, but instead of eight or nine miles by school bus, she had commuted on the train, the Baltimore and Ohio railroad.

At Pansy farm I was at home with two younger sisters, and my much younger, very independent younger brother. During this time, I worked when needed on the farm, to include the threshing ring.

A young man sixteen or seventeen could make money in two ways: on the farm, by taking over the cows, by raising chickens, sheep. Harry was easy about land, and would say to almost any proposition, "If you lose your ass, don't come running to me." Despite the rhetoric, he was both interested and proud when any of our "ideas" succeeded, but Harry scarcely knew how to be appreciative of children.

Or a young man might "cash crop" in town, as Harry might say, "An entirely different proposition."

In town I "hoed" at the chain-grocery, Krogers; the starting salary was twenty cents an hour, and at least sixteen hours each Saturday. My first task was to sort about fifty bushels of half-rotted potatoes.

In early supermarkets, a customer ordered (from a list); asked innumerable questions on price, quality; the clerk fetched, totaled the bill. This store had hardwood floors; we were expected to trot (and slide) all that market day. Then it was "bring in the front," sweep the store, secure it for Monday.

On the farm my best idea to make money came about when I came across an old, horse-drawn tomato planter, gone "to staves" in an old man's toolshed. Once this area had grown tomatoes, but the cannery had burned down. Then the nearest cannery was too far for horses and wagons; but now, with trucks, it seemed an easy trip.

With a friend, we got the barrel to hold water, and without too much trouble, made the old planter work again: a man rode on a rear seat; the machine made a hole, the barrel squirted water, the fertilizer dropped, and the operator put one tomato plant in the hole before the machine tamped it upright. This as fast as a horse could walk.

The cannery furnished the tomato plants, and I was paid by the ton. By contract, all the tomatoes belonged to the cannery. A ton of tomatoes, in boxes, is many boxes; ten tons is formidable, and three acres, picked every three or four days, is more tomatoes than . . . well, many tons.

The land my father had "given" me was exceedingly rich. I was overwhelmed by tomatoes, hired pickers, ran the truck late at night, waited in line at the cannery. The scoffers now laughed at something else: too damned many tomatoes.

For a brief time I was called "The Tomato King," but for reasons beyond production. I sold tomatoes over the fence—bring your own containers—for one dollar a bushel. To wrongfully convert tomatoes behind the back of a distant cannery was thought very promising. There was country irony—and praise—in "The Tomato King."

*

My years at Blanchester High School did not seem so and at the time I did not know so, but they were highly fragmented.

Blanchester was a much larger school than Jefferson Township Consolidated; here my class was doubled in size, all of forty-five students. Before arriving in Blanchester as a new person, I had been a nonathlete "generalist"; I read widely, in that context; I got good grades, but in many ways I was still the boy who already knew how to read in the first grade.

In Blanchester High, I continued the same pattern, but at a much more intense level. By then I had stopped playing the piano, and now played clarinet: in an octet, in orchestra, in band; then I thought of a high-school newspaper in a dedicated section of the local weekly, the *Star Republican,* published and printed two blocks from school. I convinced the editor to try it; and of course I became the high-school editor, and wrote a column most coolly called "The Observer."

Then I wrote a play—a vaudeville entertainment—and this was put on at a PTA meeting, and a great many people laughed. Some at the wrong places.

There had never been a yearbook, so the class got behind this project: sold advertising, mimeographed up each sheet separately, and then pasted in the accompanying photographs. If there were 100 copies of *The Scarab,* each glossy picture required 100 copies. Much pasting; much collation; many class-picture sessions.

Among other things, I noticed that there was a vacant space (and machine) in a typing class. I was precollege and not technically eligible, but Blanchester High was the kind of place where the teacher simply handed me a book, and said, "Oh sure, and try to catch up with the rest of them." I learned to touch-type, but characteristically, not the numbers in the upper row of keys, except the 8. I am still very good at the 8, without peeking.

For the first time, with the help of a sympathetic librarian, I began to read "good" fiction. And it was then I first read *Esquire,* read Faulkner, Hemingway, Steinbeck, Fitzgerald: "The Snows," "Ears of Johnny Bear," "The Crack-Up."

These things I read avidly, for prose style; and for the story. I also read *Esquire* for men's styles. Very much I wanted to know what "they" were wearing in New York.

"Young Jim" at age twelve

At home, in my own room, I also had the Underwood "Standard" on a desk, and began to send out pulp fiction. But it all came back, sometimes with a penciled comment, "Some good little things here." I always expected them to be published.

Probably not an easy student to have around: the wisecrack that hurt, the brittle "leader" type, the local speed merchant, one of the few boys in school who did not smoke. A tough talker, at times; tall, now, and thin; aloof, but no local resonance for anyone who intended to become a Foreign Correspondent. I knew Hemingway started that way—also, he had the trench coat.

All these diversions, activities, the drive for recognition surely diverted me from what should have been a strong, college preparation course of study.

For the first time, I met students who were apparently brighter, better organized, solidly persistent. Very much I wanted good grades, for it was assumed I would go off to college. But at that time—as with a crack of light under a closed door—in a nagging way I knew it was genuinely difficult for me to learn almost anything by rote.

Worse, it was increasingly difficult for me to be consistent, to "get organized." At home, at Pansy farm, most of the old tensions were compromised, if not gone; clearly neither Harry *nor* Florence were going to change. Their camp was simply now less an armed camp than when we lived such an emotionally shattering life at Jack Oaks.

On Saturday night, as was absolute custom, everyone at the farm, in two automobiles, drove into Blanchester. One bitterly cold, zero day, roads and streets were adrift, icy. As usual, I was at the Kroger store. Near midnight, badly, I was ready for my usual ride home, to the farm.

Everyone in two separate automobiles had forgotten about me. I was stranded; the wind cold, the moon full.

No help for it. I walked every step of the four miles home, in street shoes, a light jacket. During that freezing, stubborn, nighttime walk, I was at first furious; then I saw something hilarious about it, zany. About halfway home I knew two things clearly: this would never change, would forever be so; and that my heart was hardened against all of this. The icicle in my heart grew larger.

That spring I graduated from high school, possibly the president of the class. But our class graduated only thirty-six. Fewer than half a dozen were going on to college or a university.

Because my elder sister Elinor was now a junior at Miami University in Oxford, Ohio, was "important" on campus, was a fine pianist and cellist, and brought home her autographed yearbooks, and girlfriends, and always told me all about it, and how she would prepare a place for me, and because I loved her so much—without ever thinking anything else, that fall, I went off to college.

*

My mother thought going off to college was an important thing in a young man's life. So we went to Cincinnati, to the best men's store. She had a keen sense of style, and appropriate color. At the end, on impulse, she insisted we buy a grey, snap-brim hat, a tiny red feather in the band.

"A gentleman," she said, "may not *wear* a hat, but he should own one. In case."

So, a hat.

My father took me to Oxford in his Ford, and because he had done this for Elinor, knew the campus. We pulled up in front of a new, rather small, restored, stylishly furnished men's dormitory.

I unloaded my two suitcases, and Harry said, "So long," and drove away, left me standing on the sidewalk.

A few yards away I saw a very tall, very swiftly running man, running so fast his head seemed not far off the ground. He launched, threw himself forward, floated above the grass. Landed.

He let out an unmistakable Tarzan yell. He had captured a campus squirrel.

For certain I was now at Miami University: I had known it would be exactly this way.

With my two suitcases, wearing the snap-brim hat, I found my room. Knocked. Entered.

A blocky, red-faced, redheaded young man was stretched out on the bed. He did not get up. He did not say, "Hello." He just looked.

I said, "Good afternoon. I'm Hall."

The man who was to be my roommate began to laugh. He laughed and laughed and then did his roll-on-the-floor laugh. Finally, he went out in the hall, ran down the corridor, brought back two of his Lakewood, Ohio, high-school friends, from Cleveland.

"A hat! A hat! Look at him! He just showed up— My God, wearing a hat!"

I was stunned. The snap-brim was something my mother . . . I bolted, went to the nearest lavatory. I looked in the mirror. Saw a terrible hick. Took off the hat. I thought upon it coldly: I decided not to go back to the room and possibly kill a redheaded loudmouth. I thought to hit him, as I would a farm animal.

In a few minutes, I returned. He was there alone, sitting on the bed.

I threw my suitcase on the other bed, and said not too pleasantly to my new roommate: "You can have that side of the room. You got here first. My sister is a junior here. She says they put compatible people together. And that's you."

If he said, "hat," I knew what I would use: the desk lamp. With a solid base. I intended first to pull the lamp cord from the plug. Use the wire later as a whip.

Even now I am sure he was lucky for both of us: he did not say "hat."

He was here for the school of business, had been a high-school fraternity man; his big city high school was almost the same size as this university. In my whole life, never before had I been ridiculed.

I had brought some favorite books: Thomas Wolfe, Hemingway, Faulkner's *Pylon,* and of course my upright typewriter. He casually looked at the backs of my books, "So you can read, hey?"

As the weeks went on, it was worse. I had never thought about it, but in no house where I had lived was there inside toilets. My roommate realized that *someone* on this corridor *was not flushing.* I tried to remember, but a lifelong habit is not easy to correct. Then one day, he found the offender. Me.

It was something I could never, never live down. And he never permitted me to do so, weeks on end.

There were other good, interesting, obviously bright men on my corridor: a fine jazz trumpet player named Diz, for "Dizzy"; two premeds who worked all the time, an older "boy" who was Jewish, and who understood I was suffering, and was kind in a way that to me was new and absolute. He was the first Jewish person I ever knew and I remember him with great affection to this day. In the war, he was on air crews, blew apart with the bomb load of a B-17 at 25,000 feet headed for Schweinfurt.

Soon, I went to the local Kroger store: they needed just one good man, every Saturday. At the time I did not think work was an evasion, but that way I never went to any of "their" football games.

                              *

In some ways my semesters at Miami University were like the years that Florence and Harry spent at Jack Oaks farm, in Ohio's version of the Jazz Age. As with my parents on their not very functional farm, with their variety of unfocused interests, pride, high expectations and eventual disillusionment, so it was with me and the university.

I did not question the system, the goals, the nature of the professorate. In fact, when I read the university catalogue, I wanted to take everything; because I had no easily stated goal, I was "Undecided," so was in liberal arts. I envied the ones who could say forthrightly, "I'm going for Accounting" . . . even that.

Never for a minute did I question my "strong" background, so I signed up for courses that could "lead anywhere": chemistry, a foreign language, a history course, speech, and the required freshman composition. These classes were not outrageously large, twenty-five to forty students; everything was taught by the professors, and only the lab sections had "assistants."

In freshman composition, the professor was a Chaucer scholar. A pedant, he resented teaching his one required section of comp. His approach and assignments were said—year after year—to be identical.

We were to write but three hundred words, one page and a half. Usually my themes were six pages, sometimes more. They were imaginative, and must have displayed some talent; and, always, I wrote on the prescribed subject. But his policy was plainly stated: he read until he found three misspelled words; then he stopped, quit. Graded on what he had read to that point. The students on either side of me, young women, got A's; I got D's, and F's, and only the misspelled words circled. No other comments.

In panic, I tried for correct spelling—and used plenty of semicolons. I got other students to read my work, especially for spelling. That helped, but in the final typing—in a kind of hysteria—I made errors, did not find them in time. In a "free topic" I wrote on "Hemingway's Wound and Fitzgerald's Crack-up." The paper came back, this one read to the end: "Interesting concept. *D+*." I had managed in the typing to change correctly spelled words to misspelled words.

I saw Elinor frequently on campus: we passed, and we spoke, and I could not tell her of my shame; I lied, said, I really loved it here. The elms. The colonial architecture. The tradition. Elinor had a boyfriend, a senior. I did not like him at all, was jealous, and besides his father owned a factory which made cherry-wood furniture.

Winter became spring, and by dropping courses, taking a minimum, I had scraped by, with a *C* average: the exact edge of probation.

Elinor soon caught on, and began—directly—to help me learn to study. She soon understood I had no study habits at all. My span of attention seemed furtive. Increasingly, I felt I could not remember what I read. I became so constricted, so lacking in confidence that at study time I always wished to cry.

At the same time, I liked the library very much and there had a good place to read, soon prowled the stacks. I got an *A* in history, and the professor encouraged me to *Look further into Marx. Also Engels. Did I know the correspondence?* In that way I came to Nietzsche—was hooked, was reading a book a day. Wrote the papers and although McNiff admonished the spelling, he did not count off.

By spring I had managed to move out of the dormitory, found a much, much worse place in town. Here I kept my own hours, liked very much to hit the all-night hamburger stand at two in the morning, to see other night owls.

When I thought about the future, it seemed only a dark hole. Easily, I became engrossed in my studies, but nothing very good ever came out of it; I seemed to like the university very much, except for the whole thing. I believed I was trapped, by some fault in my brain—and I would not have said "mind." I thought upon this, heard it as a contralto scream, saw it as a tattoo, a shirt no one wanted, but that I had to wear . . . These things a young man struggling on a very friendly campus could never tell his advisor—or scarcely admit to himself.

*

On campus there was a highly developed student newspaper, sponsored by a part-time instructor whose name was R. J. McGinnis. Once he had been a foreign correspondent; his standard dress was a trench coat.

The seniors were editors (or business managers); the juniors editors, and others came along. After each issue, headline by headline, McGinnis cynically, ruthlessly, tore the edition to pieces.

I began to write for the campus paper. More people wrote stories than there was space in the paper; thus to be published was to meet the competition. I moved from straight news, to "feature" work. I was resourceful, imaginative.

I learned a great deal about newspaper work, but it did not occur to me, ever, to take classes to that end. The idea of employment after graduation (or before) seemed distant, vague. Secretly, I confessed it: I was a pretty good feature writer.

On the campus, for "advanced" people there was one class in short story writing. This was taught by Walter Havighurst, a professor of American literature, a writer of stories and a novel, and an authority on the history of the Old Northwest. Moreover, he had worked at sea, matriculated at Oxford, England, and wore Norfolk jackets. He looked for the best in new writing, and he looked hard. I submitted "representative" work, and though I had repeated freshman comp, was admitted.

Each week the best story was read, and there was class comment: an early version of a writers' workshop. Then there was a conference in Walter's office, and he was less reserved—calmly direct, but even.

He was kindly, fatherly. He had trained once to be a preacher, but gave it up. He would ask about the farms, mentioned Faulkner, whom he had met, and once asked about my grades. *What did I wish to do. In life?*

No one, no one at all, had ever asked me that question.

I told him I probably could never do anything. I catalogued my campus failures, and finally said it was my brain and I would never be able to do very much.

Walter questioned me more about this. Considered it.

"Oh," he said. "You're just very imaginative. Don't think anything about it. A lot of us are that way."

The "us" was not lost on me. Us. Us writers?

After that I wrote and wrote, and I thought people in the class liked it.

Most especially a very bright, a very good writer, named Beth Cushman. She liked my stuff quite a lot and I knew this by the way she commented: judicious, but always so right.

I asked my sister Elinor about Beth Cushman and she said, "One of the nicest, really nice, girls I know. Why don't you just call her up? On the telephone?"

I am sure I had to sneak up on myself to do it. But I did, and we began to go for long walks.

Beth, on the Miami University campus: "off to college at age sixteen"

*

I began to see more about the campus: it seemed middle class to the core, polite, a largely tea-drinking faculty. Then I understood why there were so few black students on campus. A reactionary dean of education refused to admit a black student—an understanding, with the administration. Worse, the *only* black students were those whose parents worked for the university. And these employees were nearly all descendants from slaves who came here on the Underground Railroad, in Ohio, to this high-minded university town, and now surely still were slaves, nearly all menials in this most white of institutions.

These things and others, I began to see more and more clearly; for example, the exploitation of unmarried, single women on the university staff.

I continued to read Marx, and the impacts of his thought in Russia and the revolutions of 1905 and 1917. Lenin amazed me; very much I liked Trotsky. I wrote some short papers with a "Marxist" slant, with a "realistic analysis." One paper came back with the notation, "Interesting stuff here. You are too hard on Stalin, who now seems firmly in control."

I think this sounds better than it was. I lacked focus, and as a sophomore my mind was no hard, gemlike flame; in other classes, with about equal weight, but with slack interest I read Pater, and the Shelburne essays. In fact, liked both.

If I read Bukharin a little, I also read John Reed, and about the Americans who flew for the White Army. Possibly my mind was at bottom anecdotal; in any event "radical" was not much in the campus vocabulary. By this time I worked for the university library; the books in those shelves were seldom checked out.

Spring came that year, and the campus bloomed. The aggressive "beauty" of the place, the pseudocolonial facades, the highly structured campus society (the leaders were sorority and fraternity premedia personalities) to me seemed a world I did not know. Profoundly, I was an "outsider"—and cultivated that image.

If I had a pure flame, it was hatred of so much of what I saw. In this there were three exceptions: Beth Cushman, Walter Havighurst, and my sister Elinor. And I did not know what to do about any of them.

In fact I was in an extended, extreme state. What, the end of my rope? Soon now, I would be required to fill in the lower division courses necessary for upper class status. There were laboratory courses in science, and I was too proud to go "the girl route," Botany. There was a foreign language, and though I

Sister Elinor Carolyn Hall: "so talented, and dead at twenty-two"

seemed to work through some Nietzsche in German, sometimes with a parallel English text, I seemed unable to learn vocabulary lists or recite in class: a "gentleman's C-," but I now hated the idea of a Gent. No: no hat.

These things drove me even deeper "underground" and there on this campus, oddly, I found others: chemistry majors with long, Polish names; Jewish men with no money and large, ordered rows of books, a personal library; a few renegades from out-of-state.

We of the underground talked: "How much was it okay to steal, to get an education, or just stay in school, because we were *owed* this, right?"

I was now almost totally estranged—and liked it this way. Sometimes. Nor did it remotely occur to me, simply to stop, to go back to the farm, to live there and become a writer. In the same way, I never thought of going to a place I might like to live—say New York—and there look for newspaper work. Pride was involved, and my sister Elinor seemed always to have "good ideas" about everything.

*

Then I saw a notice posted on a bulletin board of a YMCA-sponsored poolroom—which at some hours, I managed. The notice announced a scholarship, an "exchange" with the University of Hawaii, in Honolulu, T. H. (a Territory).

At once I obtained the rules, studied "the deal."

I wrote a long, well-structured application: me a Representative Ohioan, for sure; with an abiding interest in history, and most especially the impact of both religion and whaling on the (then) Sandwich Islands.

I was interviewed, awaited the good word.

Soon I told Beth and I told Elinor—and she was much pleased, for her sense of family was strong: it was a coup, for the Halls. Mother told the local newspapers, with picture.

*

A few weeks later, when Elinor was back for the summer at Pansy farm, she was driving on a straight country road; my sister Ruth was a passenger in our father's blue Ford sedan.

Where two roads crossed in the midst of farmlands, near no town at all, a huge gravel truck rammed their car. On this totally familiar road, in a moment of inattention, they drove through a stop sign.

Elinor died only a little later in the county hospital; Ruth was very badly injured, finally recovered.

On the farm, and everywhere, there was a terribly dead time. And then the funeral, and then the burial of a beautiful, very talented young woman, Florence and Harry Hall's firstborn. In those two or three days, everyone else who knew Elinor died a little.

I do not know what I felt. Because everyone else was so shattered, so much in tears, I tried to be brave.

But was never quite the same.

II

To the Islands

After his sister Elinor was killed at a country crossroads, there was a muffled, dead time long after the funeral.

More quickly than necessary, H. departed the farms, the university, and Ohio for what he thought, secretly, was forever.

His motive was beyond reproach: a scholarship to a relatively unknown place. He had bought his own one-way steamship ticket on the *Lurline,* San Francisco to Honolulu.

In his suitcase and the box of books, however, there was more of his past than he knew.

In 1938 American-flag passenger traffic across the Pacific was by either Matson or the President Lines. Honolulu was a town of fifty thousand people, and to meet an arriving vessel was a social event. Reporters came out on the pilot boat; a brass marching band played on the dock.

At the university business and then the dean's office there was a great deal less *Aloha.*

H. had his black, strapped suitcase, his outside box of books. He had thought about how he should dress: modified, college casual, just arrived from the States . . .

H. waited.

First for the registrar, then waited until both the registrar and the dean called him in.

H. had not expected a personal welcome from a dean.

For a few moments the dean and registrar looked at H. closely, as though for clues.

Finally, they put it this way: a "misunderstanding," not easily, "Ah, explained, you see?"

In fact. At least in *their* record. Ah, no scholarship. Of this nature.

By chance, did Mr. H. have something from that splendid school, Miami, in Ohio. Perhaps a letter?

"Oh, no. Not really," H. said, and he too was very puzzled, but laughed. He had, of course, asked the secretary back there for a letter, but *she* had said they would just inform the University of Hawaii direct, "And transcript."

The registrar had already checked that: there was a transcript.

H. said, "Oh, wonderful. Oh good." He could not now get money from home, because of his sister's recent death; and he had no money, *here,* to catch the *Lurline* back to the coast . . .

H. did not feel he was misleading anyone for he was absolute in his conviction that he had been awarded a scholarship. It was even in newspapers . . .

H. began to cry because he had to cry.

The dean made a decision: "Go ahead and enroll. We will take care of this locally. You can stay at Atherton House until you find another place."

Nor did H. mention that along with buying the Matson ticket, he had thought to order his transcript sent to the University of Hawaii. In case.

Not then, but many months later, at sea, H. tried to discern if indeed there had ever been a scholarship. At that time he could not say, but he did not then realize the kind of imagination which was his lot: projective, realistic in detail. The award was so "real" he had ordered both a ticket and a transcript. In addition, the "idea" of a scholarship also justified departure and brought on him public praise; the elegance of all of that appealed to H., something like tasting fine food.

The words "deceptive," "dishonest," or "cunning" did not at all enter his mind.

Much later, H. felt there was a scholarship, and he had applied. The dean and the registrar may have suspected, but they were either the most kind of men, or saw only someone in trouble too outlandish to be of his own manufactory.

In that way H. came to the Islands; in those ways he stayed.

*

In the first weeks, H. felt he was a different person: anonymous, with no past; a loner, with no obligations; and a new sense of superiority.

H. could feel this way for Hawaii was still a Territory, and the U.S. military establishments were shadow governments of vast importance; ranks and precedence were firm. By now the early missionary families and their descendants owned few Bibles, but much land.

The university was in their image; their hegemony was in a hundred ways tilted towards matriculation of their own.

Class distinctions were clear. Students from the outside islands spoke pidgin—and this H. did not hear clearly, or totally comprehend. There were "white" fraternities and sororities and to H. these students resembled planters in some exotic colony, easy on their verandas or in the surf.

Largely because he spoke unclouded, Ohio English (not pidgin), there were advantages.

*

To remain "independent" H. kept expenses at rock bottom, began at once to work for food, room, and money.

"On an LST, headed for the little-remembered invasion of Corsica"

In Honolulu, at the fringe of any enterprise were people who were useful only because they spoke English well. Or well enough. Sometimes renegades, these people had a niche just above those who labored: carpenters, longshoremen, the rapid transit drivers.

Because Hawaii was a Territory, there could be—among others—a "liquor lash-up," an informal cartel.

Between the city center and Waikiki Beach, Frankfort Distilleries had a retail store facing the street, and a warehouse and wholesale establishment in the rear. H. presented Kroger grocery experience, but was hired for his accent to wait on specialty trade: army and navy enlisted men and officers, ladies, and the odd tourist.

The important people were "outside" men, the wholesale liquor salesmen. One Japanese, one Chinese. Two—always said candidly—white men: Hawke was the older, sold the city (bars, hotels, small liquor stores, owned by whites); the second, a Pomona/Berkeley man with an M.A. in philosophy, sold to the army, navy, marine, and air force officer and enlisted men clubs.

Each salesman sold to his ethnic "following," had appropriate methods. The Japanese took his best customers and twenty-five gallons of hundred-proof whiskey to an outside Island, to "Visit the graves of our ancestors." The Hawke's method was that of "an old-time whiskey drummer": he went from bar to bar; at each place he got the bartender drunk, then wrote up a big order.

The Philosopher was a flashy dresser who "called on" generals and admirals, and hated Seagrams.

The Philosopher's single outside interest was women. He was handsome in an untrustworthy way; he was ruthless.

At Christmas (and sometimes Easter) there were large flat baskets, each one filled with Mattling & Moore, then topped off with exotic liqueurs too long on the shelves.

H. delivered these gift baskets to the homes of admirals, generals, and some to colonels or navy captains; then to the vice squad, the police chief, to detectives of rank; then to the houses of prostitution, to the Madams—matronly, outgoing, they might say, "Verne won't mind, come on in and have one."

The Madams always tipped; the police and officers never did.

Behind the whiskey business, H. saw the clandestine underbelly of Honolulu, and the Islands. The outside salesmen had a total, encyclopedic cynicism about all human beings. In this, curiously, they resembled the city detectives, for everyone, always, lied to them. There was something theatrical about their incessant gossip.

Soon H., himself, absorbed and then played back the liquor-store talk, concerns, attitudes; he too became a character, at first unconsciously, then by some effort.

*

To save money, to wear a doctor's white jacket, and to "assist," H. sometimes lived at the beach. There he slept in the waiting room of a physician who was a religious fundamentalist and a general practitioner.

Nights, H. slept in the doctor's waiting room. These offices were also the unmarried doctor's only home. After hours he closed his examination-room door, and slept on his examination table. Breakfast, always, was brought in.

The Doctor drank no alcohol, but he roamed the bars, got referrals and the news, "making his rounds," as though in a hospital.

His practice was emergency work, drunks, possible pregnancies; sunburn, soldiers or sailors who turned up with VD, but sought outside help to avoid "bad time" on their service records. In many of these examinations, H. stood in the background, in a white jacket, discreet, the "Assistant."

A great many rounders, tourists, and night people knew the Doctor's office.

At two o'clock in the morning, a cab would stop in the street below, and H.—asleep—heard them hit the stair landing. Shouts: "Doc. Doc, get up!"

It was H.'s job, for room and breakfast, to get up, get them a drink, and get them back on the street. Unknown to the drunks, Doc, himself, was sound asleep on his examining table, not ten feet away.

There was a second white-jacket kind of duty.

Every month the Doctor and H. (as assistant and bearer) "called on" every syndicate house of prostitution in the city.

The Madams were middle age, and had seen a great deal in their lives; matronly, good managers, they were selectively protective of their "girls on the floor."

The women were uneducated, often ignorant; often H. assisted in filling out credit applications, for department-store accounts, or to buy a "boyfriend" a car. Invariably the women listed their occupation as "Sales Lady."

On other jobs lasting few weeks, a month, a season, H. drove a night-shift forklift in a pineapple cannery, where the drivers called one another "Ace"; he helped repossess living-room furniture and even floor lamps from shacks where men and women could not make the payments; H. was the time clerk on-the-job for gangs of two hundred Japanese carpenters; as a joke they exchanged ID bangles, gave him false names, laughed and said, "Don't you know? We all look alike!"

In all these places and on all jobs, H. always met and got to know merchant sailors; some were full-book union men his own age, "on the bricks" or "on the board," ready to ship out "on the *Sauk City* to Baltimore, except there I'd have to buy an overcoat." They had dental work done in Japan, bought clothes in Hong Kong.

At some time during those nights and days, after a shift, after a class, H. went to a late-night movie. Because he was of long standing "antiwar," this film was of especial importance: from a novel H. had read several times and then for comparison puzzled through a parallel text in the German: *All Quiet on the Western Front.*

The film ended, and outside there was rain.

Late-night Extras were on the street: **Hitler Invades Poland**—and somewhere in Europe the war began.

The melodrama of last night's film and rain seemed far away, but everything was now changed utterly for a young man who now owned a 1929 Chevrolet convertible, with yellow disc wheels, the body-wood so rotted (unless the ropes were tied) both doors swung open on the curves.

*

All the time H. fluently left one job and got a better one, always with flexible hours and more money, he was campus-based. On the beach or at the campus edge, for the first time H. saw young people living together who were not married and did not intend to become so.

H. had no course of study firmly in mind. As at Miami, those old habits hung on; in the Islands, however, this was all right, and no one seemed to care at all. So he signed up for some "interesting courses," worked forty hours a week, some place, and continued to read, knew Miami's library was much better in nearly all respects.

After awhile H. became a philosophy major, in a small, celebrated, oriental institute (later, the East/West Centre). The instructional staff was inter-national: a platonist from Yale; the oriental staff, especially the Chinese professors, were classically trained, in oriental philosophy, culture, and especially art. The Chinese seemed especially perceptive about the inner-life, the minds of their undergraduate students.

Under their influence, H. began to take larger, both reasoned and intuited views of the world, a way of seeing not much encouraged by the occidental professors. Above all, H. liked the Taoist art, but deeply distrusted the principles of the yin and the yang.

H. learned to drink tea, was much drawn to the Chinese professors, oddly felt himself become more "philosophical."

At the same time one thing was clear: to go farther, to claim scholarships, H. would have to learn Chinese, to speak, to read, to write. This he seemed to do not easily: he could not imitate, mimic the Chinese tonal system of speech, but he learned ideographs somewhat more easily. H. understood: he was not of the highest order or promise. In some ways it was a terrible thing: to know others apparently could, but he could not make those sounds.

In parallel, in a less rarified way, H. took a journalism course from a possibly ex-alcoholic, older journalist.

Perhaps more importantly, H. qualified for and completed a CAA-sponsored ground school, the course taught by flying officers from Hickham Field. This course was demanding, military; pilot training—no charge—was to follow. He liked everything about this course, was good at it; ground school seemed to combine things much in his past: weather, engines, electricity, and promised speed.

The "Cadets" talked much about the future, over coffee: make one hundred hours flight time, head for Canada, and on to England and the RAF. As yet no one had heard of a Spitfire.

Even at the time, H. saw no contradiction between preflight and Taoist paintings and Plato's *Republic.* He could be of two minds: despite FDR and talk of registration for a draft, America would not fight again in Europe; if the draft came, there were ways to beat the system. The Territory of Hawaii also looked west, and Japan, China, and the South Seas seemed easy havens.

These things H. often heard from the international, pre-Beat students who traveled light and traveled far. H. looked to Nietzsche and Mencken, relied on a farmer, failed-crop pessimism: he would be drawn in, some way; and in some way be killed. He did not for a minute ever expect to survive the war to come. Better to die in flight, cleanly, and be remembered; and to this conclusion philosophy brought a larger vision, Tao, The Way.

From the first semester in the Islands, H. began—or continued—to write. In a formal way, he set up a work place, found another Underwood "Standard" typewriter: thirty-five dollars, ten dollars down, the balance monthly on Okay student credit.

This time, H. began to take stories downtown, to the *Honolulu Advertiser*. The editors either said, "Okay," or as H. watched, threw it in the wastebasket.

The *Advertiser* paid space-rates, and H. showed up two or three times a week with copy. Cynical, a bad speller, H. found good copy all over the university. This the editors liked, for they got only handouts from the "U-PR" office, and the campus was not important enough to assign a reporter even part-time. No byline.

Then H. found a former submarine commander on campus who also wrote short stories (about submarines) for *Collier's;* an older employee who knew Jack London when London learned to surf at Waikiki; and—too much—an account of a botched drama rehearsal.

That way, H. began to write exclusively feature stuff for the *Advertiser,* even then a large newspaper. The Sunday supplement each week carried a main feature, with pictures, byline. H. was resourceful: he presented a list of possible stories; the editor checked off a couple of interest. H. wrote on spec.: the anniversary of the Dole Airplane Race (San Francisco to Hawaii), etc. Increasingly, this copy was changed only a little.

*

That spring, in May, several things happened almost at once.

The CAA ground-school course was over, and they had toured Hickham Field, were guests at the officers' club. Flight training was laid on for summer. In the second, much more demanding physical examination, H. failed, and though no one remarked it, so did every Japanese student enrolled save one.

Initially H. had done a "yarn" matching test for colors, but for actual flight training, there was a more standard test with color plates: H. showed "marginal," red-green. Never before had H. realized this, but after a navy doctor repeated the test, he was rejected.

Oh, H. "saw" colors, but any license would be restricted for night flying. And it was also a little chilling to learn that he could never join the navy or air force, as an officer or enlisted man. But the army? Yes. Easy.

Then there were social complications, not with one woman, but two. By now H. knew merchant sailors, his age; knew that to "get out" seaman's papers were necessary, but the Coast Guard strictly controlled those passports. It was no papers, no ship; and no ship without papers.

To get a seaman's passport (papers) without a ship was the qualifying test for the profession: it tested "grift sense," an ability to lie constructively (a higher good).

H. got a seaman's passport: an introduction by a full-book steward's department sailor; for a deuce ($20.00) a union "trip ticket," this for a ship due in (and shorthanded). With the "ticket" the physical examination came about—and H. sorted the tufts of yarn, passed the color vision test.

With papers in hand, H. now turned back his "rented" trip ticket. There remained but one problem: to find a ship which was really short a hand.

So H. sold most things, stored a footlocker in someone's attic, "singled up," waited at the hiring hall daily, one suitcase of clothes, a smaller suitcase of books.

It happened in minutes: H. caught the SS *President Cleveland* to the Orient: Yokohama, Kobe, Hong Kong, Manila, Singapore, and the return voyage via Shanghai.

When the ship's horn sounded, the liner separated easily from the pier. Astern, then hull-down, Honolulu grew small, lowered itself into the sea, at last became a line of smoke—and was gone.

III

At Sea, at War, and Home

Because H. first signed aboard there, Honolulu became his home port, his own "Crossroads of the Pacific."

H. went out as a butcher's scullion (helper) so he was often deep in the ship's reefers, wearing a sheepskin coat, sorting piles of frozen lambs, sides of beef, loins, ox tails, cardboard boxes of calf's liver, pheasant, small, white, perfect little frozen piglets.

This wreckage of frozen meats was dumped by a cargo net; until everything was sorted and secured, when the ship rolled in long, Pacific swells, the tons of meat also rolled. In this sub-freezing reefer with its ice-covered pipes, in the half-light, when the meat pile rolled, H. first became seasick, vomited on sacks of frozen partridge and quail.

Back in Honolulu a full-book (non-probationary hand) bumped H., said, "Sorry, Jack," when he came aboard; said he had a movie date with a broad in San Francisco. For a full-book to change ships through the union hiring hall was that casual.

The next morning was Sunday. In the absolute leisure of a voyage ended, H. drifted to a restaurant; it was white tablecloths, a newspaper, and English spoken with casual fluency. After the shocks of the Orient, this was a curious moment of acceptance. For the first time H. accepted, fully understood, and felt grateful: in voice, in manner, and mind, he was to be forever an American. Then he saw older men in business suits, with their wives, entering this restaurant, returning from church. Always before H. felt such people were his natural enemy; now he had no reaction at all.

Mostly to get a deck discharge (certified experience), H. caught a Greek-flag (registered) freighter. Without really seeing the ship in daylight, H. signed aboard to sail at midnight. Ten days later, the *Oakalais* finally singled up, departed; the only Greeks aboard were the captain, and the chief engineer, who had a highly cultivated, white handlebar moustache.

The "OK" was a rust pot, for Kobe, loaded with scrap steel: coal-fired boilers, and a single stack. The deck and black gang were the dregs of any port: a Cockney half-wit, much retarded; a one-eyed, sinister Syrian or possibly Arab who shipped with his "punk boy," was armed, always, with a sheath knife. A Senegalese, with filed front teeth; openly a thief, he pillaged any unguarded kit box or locker.

For the first time H. came to know a trusted shipmate: a French "colonial" from Tunis, who once did casual plumbing maintenance for the hotel where his wife also sometimes worked. Unexpectedly, "Armond" came upon his wife in bed with an Italian airplane pilot; with a large pipe wrench, he beat the pilot to death.

Now a longtime fugitive, "Armond" worked junk ships, always in the Pacific; apparently he also had other passports. Even in 1940–41, the Pacific seemed trackless, exotic, anonymous, safe.

Both this ship and its crew were lucky: nearly four weeks of mill-pond weather, and a steady six knots. In Kobe, the captain paid off all hands, in gold.

At voyage end it came about this ship had been her own cargo: was to be broken up for scrap.

For H. the longest voyage was Honolulu to Manila direct, almost thirty days. Fights broke out in the mess rooms—over a bottle of catsup, or a hotcake, "too god-damned brown . . ."

Across the Mindanao Deep, the *Republic* tied up briefly in Davao City, went coastwise, anchored here and there offshore. They lightered great bales of hemp off the beach from plantations farther inland. Farther offshore H. saw the blue lanteen sails of *dhows,* Arab trading boats, or pirates of the Sulu Sea.

H. was rereading much of Conrad. This weather, the cargo, the ports had changed not much since before World War I. Lord Jim might have made one more trip offshore—on a barge loaded with hemp.

In those weeks and months at sea, and especially ashore, news of the war in Europe became a more consistent, persistent theme.

All men of draft age, in their different ways, tried to discern the future; there was no counseling, save from older men. A few sailors "got off" in the Orient: feigned sickness, or missed their ship. They "shacked," made out easily in Singapore, might move on to Batavia. A seaman's passport was valid, with few enforceable restrictions. No one remotely thought war would also take the Pacific. In San Francisco, after the crew mustered, H. could not show a draft card his first time ashore. H. had not registered: on that date, he had been at sea.

So he registered late, in San Francisco.

The draft clerk would not accept a ship or hotel, or even the seaman's YMCA as an address. So H. gave his father's name and address, and the county seat of Wilmington, Ohio, "where he could always be contacted."

Aboard the *Red Jacket,* for Boston by way of the Balboa and the Canal Zone, H. often lay on the foredeck at night, watched the mast move across the close, star-filled sky. The National Guard had been called for duty, for one year.

Without quite understanding the reason, H. felt he was leaving the Orient for good. If H. now felt more isolated, alone, this was in part because he now knew no young American women. At sea, H. understood for the first time that he liked women very much, liked to be around women, liked to hear what they said.

On that last trip, H. was a wheelsman through the Canal: four on and eight off. The Canal pilot constantly called course changes. H. steered ocean-going vessels very well; offshore he bested "Iron Mike" (the autopilot) in holding her course in heavy weather; it was a little bit like steering a Farmall down delicate cornrows. Aboard any ship, H. was a "smart" (alert) sailor; but not "salty" (tough, in any weather).

Almost due north, through Crooked-Leg Passage, the islands of the Caribbean passed abaft the beam, and Cuba for some hours seemed very near.

The final two days of that voyage the crew "dressed" the ship: moored her, finally, at a Boston pier. Very much H. liked the moment when it was all engines stop, and the vessel seemed to sleep.

A U.S. Marshal at once came aboard.

He sought two men: one a wiper in the engine room. And H.

The U.S. Marshal was firm. The ship's captain shrugged. In a few minutes H. went down the gangplank, a seabag on his shoulder, and the U.S. Marshal followed.

The Wilmington County Seat Draft Board had declared H. long overdue for induction into the U.S. Army.

At once H. understood: his name had been forwarded from the Coast, and being not present to make a case, and a seaman not being necessary to the economy of Clinton County, Ohio, H. was the first name on every list.

"I will take you to the bus station, Son. And watch you buy a ticket. Or: I will take you to the Federal Pen. Which one?"

By then H. had a practiced "Asiatic Stare," an expressionless face in the face of any authority.

"Let's go," H. said. "And take a bus ride."

In less than two weeks, H. was at an induction center in Covington, Kentucky. Defective color vision was no bar to army service, so with a line of other men, H. stepped forward, raised his right hand, and was forthwith inducted into the U.S. Army, a private, at twenty-one dollars a month.

Not many months later, all merchant sailors were declared draft exempt. By that time H. had almost completed infantry training, in Georgia.

*

The infantry training company had come off the range, and the weeks of Basic were nearly finished. They were scheduled for night hikes, in "field conditions"; then assignment to a division for summer maneuvers, the summer of 1941. In August, in Louisiana.

H. saw it clearly: once on maneuvers, it was the infantry for the duration. France and the low countries had collapsed under the German *blitzkrieg*. All these things confirmed his worst calculations: taken by the draft, and now by the infantry.

One day H. saw a long line of soldiers, perhaps one hundred men. They were in line trying to reach a square card table, set up in an outside, open area.

One officer was at the card table; his sergeant was taking names. The two officers were from Fort Benning. They wore jump boots, and the parachutist insignia; they were recruiting volunteers for a new parachute battalion. Jump pay was fifty dollars a month.

At once H. imagined they had a quota of men from this training camp; soon they would have enough men. Also they would like resourcefulness, grift sense, some daring.

H. violated every army custom, strolled directly to the head of the line. One officer who had just done a forward flip, and landed much like an acrobat, said to the men in line, "Can *you* do that?"

The officer was Edson Raff. H. motioned him to one side, as though in confidence:

"Captain, I can type very fast. And I will make you a good man."

The officer considered it, smiled at the brazen nature of it, and then said, "Okay, Soldier. Stand right over there."

And in that way H. became a member of the 504th Parachute Battalion, the third ever activated in the U.S. Army.

*

H. was away from Benning for a weekend, at an airfield in Alabama, there to visit a navigation cadet, an acquaintance from the Island, and the CAA ground school class. The cadets had their own club on base, and the party lasted late. In a parachutist uniform, H. struck an exotic note at the club. Many free drinks.

The next morning was Sunday. Slightly hung over, not chipper, H. was beside the highway, hitch-hiking back to Fort Benning, wearing jump boots and the parachutist cap—the better to get rides.

A salesman in a black Chrysler coupe stopped, opened the door. His car radio was on. When they were back on the highway, the driver said, "Well, I guess you are right in the middle of it."

Often people made this kind of remark for parachutists were "suicide" troops; their conduct outside Benning generally confirmed that estimate. The driver pointed to his car radio:

"Pearl Harbor has just been attacked. By the Japanese."

H. did not realize fully what this meant.

The driver added, "It's war. You are in a war."

At Benning, the post was on war footing.

H. could not get in, not even with good ID and his pass. Very soon, someone from the 504th arrived to identify him, and take him back to the Battalion Training. A place singularly vacant, more quiet than H. could believe.

That week, the 504th was scheduled to Qualify, but this did not happen: the aircraft at Benning had been ordered west, to defend the Coast against a strongly rumored Japanese invasion.

After random, yet efficient training, H. never did jump for the 504th.

In a few weeks an order came down from Washington: all former merchant sailors, forthwith, transferred to a coastal fort in New Jersey, there to train and sail as army mineplanter crews.

This order was abrupt, and an appeal did not keep H. in the 504th.

In two weeks it became clear: no mineplanters. They were to be built at Point Pleasant, outfitted, and then were to sail, "Under sealed orders."

To a man the sailors shouted down a "phoney" Coast Guard officer, "Fuck that! No destination. No go!"—this response in unison, like good union men.

H. saluted, without saying anything, and the young ROTC officer, probably on his first assignment, returned the salute, blushed, left.

Not even the captain, in charge of base personnel, would request a transfer back to the 504th. The captain smoked a large cigar, was an attorney in civilian life, said, "You got it good here."

In the end H. was transferred back to Georgia, this time to Camp Stewart. Another "separate" battalion was being activated, this time antiaircraft.

*

In the next months H. became a technical sergeant and, by taking a test offered all enlisted men, became a warrant officer, WOJG. Neither commissioned nor precisely an enlisted rank, the pay was equivalent to captain in the army; the specialty might be in ordinance, administration, radar, reconnaissance, intelligence. H. felt he had not compromised, had not become a commissioned officer.

Once overseas, the warrant specialties often blended into any new, necessary job that might require generally a resourceful person. In some assignments H. was like a captain; in others very much like a respected sergeant.

The new battalion of searchlights and guns trained rapidly and in the next three-and-a-half years were in North Africa, Corsica, southern and northern

France, Alsace, and finally deep into Germany, near Innsbruck.

Those days and weeks became months and seasons, but every day brought night, especially the night: weeks of rain, fog, snow. Every day the army became more fluid, and the Tables of Organization so sacred in the States became outmoded forms.

Then one day in summer, when H. was south of Munich, not far from Innsbruck, everything seemed to stop for one day, then two.

At a roadside checkpoint where American soldiers lay on the grass, looked at the tops of trees, dozed, at that time and at that place our war ended.

*

For a few days among line outfits, there was an easy, sullen, rebellious feeling: enlisted men "forgot" to salute, there were drinking parties, one folding into the next. Oddly, the GI's liked the German civilians much more than they ever liked the French.

About the war's end, H. had mixed, confused feelings. He had been in the army going on five years—formative years. And he had been in the Islands and at sea before the army, so Ohio, and the Hall farms, seemed in the distant past, gone.

Yet nothing about the present was decisive: in the Pacific the war went on, and "hot" outfits (among them the battalion) were scheduled for transhipment to Japan, direct.

Against this, there was Occupation Duty, to be announced. H. had been "superior" (an efficiency rating) all those years, and was now a chief warrant officer, but with no more future than when in desperation he had left Ohio and the Hall farms for the Territory of Hawaii—or so it seemed.

More deeply, more privately, H. was more than a little afraid to go home. And such was the cry: Bring the Boys Home.

Although H. was not to see it until much later, his emotional maturity was retarded by the service; in some ways, he was still sixteen years old; worse, though now twenty-six or twenty-seven, he felt forty.

Although it seemed far away, hopeless, two things seemed constant, good. While in a bivouac area, in the States, mostly by candlelight in a pup tent, H. had written what he thought was a short story: supply ships on the North Atlantic, "Bundles for Britain." The old freighter sank, but some of the cargo floated.

This he sent to Beth Cushman, the girl he had met in the writing class; she was obviously a warm, highly intelligent young woman who was born and raised in Miami, Florida. Beth had liked the stories, felt he had talent.

So she typed the story and sent it off to *Story* magazine, edited by Hallie and Whit Burnett. They liked the story very much, and published it. H. knew nothing of this until one day in an open field in North Africa at mail call, a brown paper envelope sailed his way: two contributor's copies of *Story* magazine.

In the chaos of a war's end, H. felt like a truck, an airplane (with air crew gone), acres of empty gasoline cans—as with these things he, also, had been used. Used up. Was scrap.

In this ruined, fallen world H. could see only two possible things open to him: back to school, any school, there to write and write; and also to return to the one person in this wide world who cared about him very much, had cared enough to wait.

About this H. did not wish to be realistic, to permit himself to believe after so many years apart they might now not know one another at all, or in memory only.

*

Without warning, orders arrived: Chief Warrant Officer H. transferred to Military Government School. "No delay en route authorized."

During the ten days of "classes" at Bad Neuheim, the situation became more clear. On his personnel card, H. was still listed as a merchant sailor, as when drafted. His German was now good enough to keep an interpreter honest.

H. had been pulled out for assignment to the American Enclave, with headquarters in Bremen, and

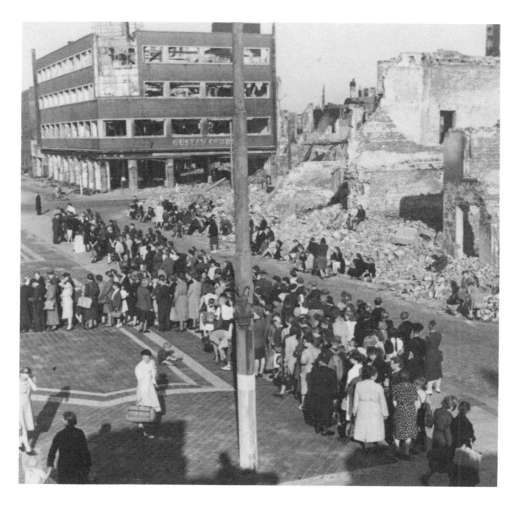

"Scene from the Labor Office's window, looking down on German people lined up for food," Bremerhaven, Wesermünde, Germany

Jim and Beth in an Ohio meadow, just married, 1946

more cogently in Bremerhaven, the port of entry (and exit) for the U.S.

In ten days, H. became an American Military Government officer, in charge of the waterfront labor offices and displaced persons in a bombed-out, virtually destroyed city, where German navy, army, marine, and Luftwaffe troops still in uniform (all insignia removed) were in the streets, along with displaced Germans, their former forced laborers, civilian employees attracted here from all over Europe—and not much food.

But there was no American policy to implement: the colonel explained the "Morgenthau Plan": Germany to become a pastoral state. At that moment outside crowds were marching past, orderly but not for long.

In rubble, in the North Sea wind, in a policy vacuum, people rioted at the former German Navy storehouses.

Russian officers appeared, came seeking "their fish," but there were no fish. And the displaced persons camps had to be managed, and Poles, Czech, Lithuanians, Russians were to be repatriated, sent home.

As the labor officer, H. presided over the first labor union meeting in postwar Germany. On the waterfront, the old union leaders exhorted their members to do more work; the *Europa* finally sailed, with denazified officers, several thousand troops, and no one knew where a German manager found all those necessary lifeboats.

In the temporary camps the DPs (displaced persons) started their own schools and often boarded trucks, ostensibly headed for home. In a day or so, most returned, had left their convoy.

Now there really was a decision to make. Being an indispensable, knowledgeable labor officer, H. could stay on in Germany, as a civilian. Or he could return to the States, to school, and to . . .

And so little came of all the rebuilding: the *Europa* lost her engines just past midpoint Atlantic. The union meeting elected members of the old Communist cell which all those years eluded the Gestapo—and now were pro-USSR, Stalinist dominated. And the displaced persons who sought their homeland found it only briefly, for when they arrived in Russia, men, women, and the children were shot.

The death penalty was for being found in Germany.

In a great many small ways, H. understood: Americans were no good at occupation. The British were ever so much better. And H. saw a long, disgraceful chapter of American history beginning, but now seldom mentioned: the Occupation Years.

Priority for leaving the European theatre was based on points: for years overseas, decorations, combat time. On one list H. saw a familiar name and number: his own. More points for discharge than any other warrant (and most officers) in the European theatre. To H. that name seemed to belong to someone else.

*

In mid-February of 1946 southwestern Ohio was covered with snow. On terminal leave, after all that time overseas, H. felt what once was an Ohio pastoral community had been changed forever by the industrialization of the war; and after Pearl Harbor the Islands and the Pacific, which he had seen with innocent eyes, were destroyed, occupied, in ruins. In a like way Europe (and especially Germany) was a bombed-out ruin under snow.

The Cold War was now beginning, but as yet it had no name. H. had seen all of these things, but now could only do what a returned soldier was supposed to do: talk to the local Rotary Club, for Harry was the program chairman.

In the way of Gatsby—in the novel he had read several times—H. made lists, sat at his old high-school study desk, stared towards the sixty-acre Hall woods. One list caused H. to cry and cry, and he could not stop.

This list was the names of men lost, killed by the war: not replacements, not strangers in roadside ditches, but good men, all known to H. by their first names.

Cal, out on the wing-root of a B-17 on fire, and no chute; Jim, a doctor, bailed out in a raging gale over Greenland; Bob, beheaded by the Japanese after the Dolittle raid; Yale Kaufman, never returned to base after a search mission.

These were melodramatic. But most of his list were killed by accidents, error, booby traps; on motorcycles, a chute malfunction, an airplane on fire at takeoff; complications from burns—and indirectly from drink, or directly by their own hands. And in this list H. did not count what was said to be Company "C" of the old 504th, dropped at night off Sicily into the sea. H. felt the weight, the burden of their loss.

At last, in a moment of clarity—almost vision—as he stared out a farmhouse window into moonlight, snowy fields, H. understood each day remaining was to be used for himself and for others, as though there was no reprieve at each day's end.

Once H. had read Thomas Wolfe avidly, had gone to Asheville and had spoken to the author's older brother. Those novels now seemed rhetorical but not empty, and H. accepted the truth implicit in *You Can't Go Home Again.*

*

In two weeks, H. went south: from Ohio and winter to Miami and the sunshine, the palm fronds, and to her arms. Miami and the white, spacious, very Southern Cushman home with mango trees and gardens was cordial, in bloom. In a church, with two families, with H. still in uniform, they were married.

Beth's parents and her mother's parents had been long in Florida, Methodist bishops, missionaries among the Seminoles, also homesteaders who claimed a square of land. Because they were civic-minded and high-minded, H. could have said he intended, now, to become a writer. But Beth was their youngest child, had stayed at home for their comfort longer than she ever, privately, wished.

So H. was general: he and Beth would use the GI Bill for graduate work at a university. And her mother replied, with what any Southerner would know was polite skepticism, "And you can always come right back to Miami. An *interesting* place."

*

At Miami University, in Oxford, the writer-historian who had first seen literary talent in words H. put on paper gave advice.

Because H. had published, Walter Havighurst felt there was a program for him at the University of Iowa. Walter had been out there, with four or five others, heads of the only established writing programs in America; he had met Wallace Stegner and Hudson Strode and a couple of others, including the local Iowa writer, a poet named Paul Engle. Why did not Jim and Beth try Iowa?

H. placed a long-distance call that Sunday morning. Someone named Paul Engle sleepily answered. Engle listened, and in a few minutes said, "Well, why don't you just come on out?"

Only then did H. consult a road map and locate Iowa City. The best way to go there was by railroad:

With an Iowa Writers' Workshop group at a Stone City quarry, about 1950: Jim Hall is second from right; Beth Hall is at left; Flannery O'Connor is at far right.

to Chicago, and the Parmalee Transfer Company, and a train to Iowa City, almost direct.

*

Paul Engle was headed for Fiction Workshop. He noted the copy of *Story* magazine.

"Come along," Engle said, and improvised easily, "we will use your story. You can read it to us."

In uniform, very tense, H. felt this was a formal interrogation; they went to a room where six or eight students were at ease, in a half-circle of chairs.

In a voice ever more tense, H. read. For quite a while in the room, there was only silence. These advanced writers knew about existentialism and saw Graham Greene as "really beautiful junk," for they were very cool.

Engle finally began the discussion, "Well, there for a minute I thought you had lost it."

After the students finished, nothing at all was left of that poor story; because it had been published, H. had expected only praise, in fact a great deal of praise.

After an hour and a half, H. was to go back to Paul Engle's office. But he went a roundabout way and, at the base of an old brick building, got in behind the shrubbery and cried.

There was a word for this type, "A bleeder." H. bled a very great deal.

On the basis of one published story, and a fifteen-page list of books H. had read—or reread—at sea and elsewhere, he became am undergraduate, a junior, at Iowa. To help GI's, some credit was given for in-service training: infantry basic, probably malaria control school (Algiers), and parachute packing. Nothing for demolition.

*

The Iowa Workshop was in its early, perhaps heroic phase. On the one hand the New Humanist ideals were still in place, despite slackness during the war years. At the same time, the influx of GI's, and a new focus on all the arts, creative writing included, made Iowa City a new Bohemia, albeit in cornfields. One goal was to train literary artists, Men of Letters.

In short there was a great deal of hard work of a new kind, literary work. But there were justly celebrated staff members, novelists, poets, short-fiction writers, translators from most regions of America, also from Britain and Europe. It was all loosely managed by Paul Engle, who kept future plans in his head and the dean in his pocket.

Among others, H. worked with such diverse people as James T. Farrell, Hansford Martin, R. P. Warren, Paul Horgan, and a most influential person, Andrew Lytle. Although H. was primarily a prose writer, he began to write and then to publish poetry and in this was helped by such visitors and teachers as Auden, Spender, Tate, Dylan Thomas, Ransom, Engle, of course, and most significantly, Robert Lowell. The official accounts of the workshop name many others, but H. worked with these.

In their first year at Iowa, things were extremely difficult, but neither H. nor Beth apparently understood this fully.

In the first place they had married, but without knowing one another very well—save by many let-

The author, from the dust jacket of his first novel, about 1955

ters. To afford postage stamps was not the same as the desperate, catch-up, competitive life at a major university.

Each week, however, things became more clear: very much, very deeply they loved one another; and about graduate work and writing there was no doubt. He also learned to respect Beth's judgment on all matters, and if he disagreed and went ahead, nearly always it was to his regret. If Beth was intelligent and very social, she was also wise.

Again, without realizing it, H. became restive, could concentrate only sporadically, more and more cried over disappointments, and had bad dreams, then nightmares, always about the war. He would become entwined in the bed sheets, thrash, lash out, scream as though falling . . . Beth had not known this violent side of him; she was more frightened than she told others.

In ways not now entirely clear, H. became an outpatient at the local Veteran's Administration Hospital, the patient of a Canadian doctor, about the same age. After a few sessions, the physician suddenly turned on H. "Look. Tell me: what really is the matter with you?"

For a long time there was only silence in the room.

The sessions went on for some months, and H. was careful to tell no one about this help, and said not much about it to Beth. There was no lack of trust, but some of the things H. began to realize about himself were so shameful . . .

In part because his now trusted friend and confidant and true physician was returning to Canada, H. never sought additional help, but one thing H. never doubted: these sessions, those insights, were one of the best things that had ever happened to him. In that way the war finally ended.

By the second year, H. was on graduate status, combining the writing program with the kind of Ph.D. program for someone who would never become a scholar. Nor did he handle ideas stringently, aseptically enough to become a critic, save at the practical level.

With that kind of self-knowledge and not until then, H. began to enjoy, to relish graduate studies. He wrote in the morning, went to school in the afternoon, read much at night, and increasingly realized he was married to a woman of great character and tenderness. And among other things, they read a great many of the same books together.

In short-story workshop, H. tried always to hand in not one, but three stories: his flourish.

In his tutorial, a writer and critic H. much admired paused for awhile, the scripts (apparently not marked) between them.

"You know, don't you," the instructor said, "*these* are very good. And *this* one," pointing to the unmarked story on top, "is publishable. Just send it out."

Without changing a word, H. sent it out, and it was published in a highly literary magazine and was named "First Lion at the Chalice." The first story, in fact, truly about his own life.

That was the day H. walked out the door of the corrugated-metal shed, a temporary building left over from wartime, walked out and into the Iowa sun.

What H. felt was relief and a sense of very pure accomplishment for at last he *knew:* at last he could do it, and that he would continue to write, as though he had been pointed towards this moment of recognition almost all of the days of his life.

Then he went to another building, to the Poetry Workshop. That day in class, in the customary mimeographed versions, they were to criticize his new poems.

What anyone in this class might say would not matter at all.

For this moment of knowledge about his future was strange, was new—and, Oh! he liked it very much, as though he had come through. But not what he had imagined, not much at all like being in a fast car or on a motorcycle and speeding close to the ground.

BIBLIOGRAPHY

Novels:

Not by the Door, Random House, 1954.

TNT for Two, Ace, 1956.

Racers to the Sun, Obolensky, 1960.

Mayo Sergeant, New American Library, 1967.

Stopping on the Edge to Wave, Wesleyan University Press, 1988.

Short story collections:

(With R. V. Cassill and Herbert Gold) *Fifteen by Three,* New Directions, 1957.

Us He Devours, New Directions, 1964.

The Short Hall: New and Selected Stories, Stonehenge Press, 1980.

Finding What Was Lost, forthcoming.

Poetry:

The Hunt Within, Louisiana State University Press, 1973.

Journals from the Ark, forthcoming.

Editor:

(With Joseph Langland) *The Short Story,* Macmillan, 1956.

The Realm of Fiction: Sixty-One Short Stories, McGraw, 1965; 2d edition published as *The Realm of Fiction: Sixty-five Short Stories,* 1970; 3d edition (with wife, Elizabeth C. Hall) published as *The Realm of Fiction: Seventy-Four Short Stories,* 1977.

Instructor's Manual for Realm of Fiction, McGraw, 1965.

(With Barry Ulanov) *Modern Culture and the Arts,* McGraw, 1967.

Instructor's Manual for Modern Culture and the Arts, McGraw, 1967.

London, Jack, *John Barleycorn: Alcoholic Memoirs,* Western Tanager Press, 1981.

Work represented in anthologies, including *Best American Short Stories,* edited by Martha Foley, Houghton, 1949, 1952, 1953, and 1954; *Poems from the Iowa Poetry Workshop,* Prairie Press, 1951; *Prize Stories: The O. Henry Awards,* Doubleday, 1951 and 1954; *Oregon Signatures,* edited by R. D. Brown, Binfords, 1959; *Midland Anthology,* edited by Paul Engle, Random House, 1961; and *A Country of the Mind,* edited by Ray B. West, Jr., Angel Island Publications, 1962.

Contributor to *Collier's Encyclopedia.* Contributor of poems to journals, including *Sewanee Review, Poetry,* and *Western Review;* contributor of short stories and articles to *Esquire, Harper's Bazaar, Epoch, San Francisco Review, Los Angeles Times,* and other magazines, newspapers, and literary reviews. *Northwest Review,* co-founder, faculty advisor, 1957–60, advisory editor, 1965–69.

Ihab Hassan

1925-

FRAGMENTS OF AN AUTOBIOGRAPHY

Ihab Hassan on Mount Fuji, 1985

I

Where begin? In the middle, of course, in that strange, glorious muddle we call human life. As a traveling man, more nomad than exile, given to bouts of self-invention, I might as well start with my most fateful journey—except the last.

On a burning August afternoon in 1946, brisk wind and salt of the Mediterranean on my lips, I boarded the *Abraham Lincoln* at Port Said and sailed from Egypt, never to return. My father gave me a gold Movado wristwatch, and waved me good-bye from a bobbing white launch. I waved back, not daring to shout or speak. Churning tugs nosed the battered Liberty Ship into the seaways. I saw the town, the minarets, the high cupola of the Compagnie de Suez, recede. I saw the sands of Sinai shimmer, fade. And gliding past the great bronze statue of Ferdinand de Lesseps, who rose from the barnacled jetty above breaker and spume, one hand pointing imperiously east, I could only think: "I did it! I did it! I'm bound for New York!"

Thus began my passage to America. New birth or false rebirth? I had not heard yet of Whitman— "Passage indeed, O soul, to primal thought!"—nor read much about Columbus.

*

But now I must set down some facts, softened by the cunning fictions of remembrance, unappeased wishes that threaten to melt reality before our eyes. I was born on 17 October 1925, in Cairo, Egypt, and though I carry papers that solemnly record this date and place, I have never felt these facts decisive in my life. I do not recall the house I was born in. Years later, driving by in our silver Packard, my grandmother would point out the house to me, still standing, tall and glum, in the now rowdy heart of the city. Its grill, its narrow doors and black shutters, seemed always closed against my gaze as if holding some riddle.

The Sphinx, *Abu'l Hol* (Father of Terror) himself, crouched but a few leagues away, as Egyptian crows fly, in its sandy hollow at Giza. Huge, pocked face, nose chipped, wild eyes staring in the wind. Still, the thing inspired no fear in me, nor stirred ancestral memories. Behind it rose that abstract wonder of the Seven Wonders, the Great Pyramid, transcendent will in desert landscape. Seen with boyish eyes, it offered no promise except that I might some day clamber up its jagged edge and so claim an end to my puberty. Yet there were a few times when, its vermillion image glistening in newly watered fields, it suddenly dissolved in the mind as if stone could become quintessence of thought.

"17 October 1925, Cairo, Egypt": strange, stubborn ciphers to conjure time and space, and appease mortality, our mystery.

*

Like other Egyptian children, I walked among the ancient gods unseeing. Amon, Horus, Set, Hathor, Nu, Mut, Khnum, Anubis, Isis, Osiris: they all haunt the world's museums. In our house they lived only as carvings on lacquered chairs, replicas of Pharaonic thrones awkward to sit on. By their side, Turkish hassocks, Arabesque tables, copper trays engraved intricately with the Koran, and European art nouveau furnishings cluttered my childhood space. The old gods with animal heads could still evoke a childish shudder in a room darkened against the midday sun. But their awful power, like much else in Egypt, had long fled.

My childhood space: it was indeed a palimpsest of styles, babel of tongues. French and Arabic were my first languages; but I like far more another which I now write; and I speak all with a slight foreign sound. Who reckons the deep declensions of Desire, inflections of the Logos, or denials of a Mother's Tongue? Does "matricide" free men into alien speech?

Roots, everyone speaks of roots. I have cared for none. Perhaps, in my case, they were too old and tangled; or perhaps they withered early from some blight, which I have long ceased to mourn. Looking as a child upon those ancestors chiseled in stone, so rigid in posture yet so fluid in line, ancestors who stared eternity down and answered to uncouth names, I bore away no kinship feelings. Still, who knows but that their Ka, uniting Life and Death in its Essential Self, did not inscribe some hieratic message in my soul?

*

Growing up in Egypt.

I stand before my uncle, Hafez Pasha Hassan, who frowns at me from his ogre's height. His white mustache twitches thinly over his lips.

"And what will you be when you grow up?"

"A warrior, a warrior," I cry, "better than Alexander or Thutmose the Third."

"A general?" he asks.

"And also a saint."

Faint smiles as I rush out of the room with hot cheeks. Barely five years old, I suffered already from an implacable shyness. More than others—or so I thought—I dreaded humiliation, and both dread and pride conspired in my need for self-creation, perpetual re-creation.

Self-recreation: a sovereign fiction that yet enabled me to resist, even to remake, "things as they are." It helped me slip through my birthrights: language and the clutching blood. Slip? We tear ourselves free. We learn murder in the family, as the ancient Greeks knew, and rehearse the pride of Oedipus before the Sphinx. With luck, courage, grace, we may shed our violence at last and, like ancient heroes, rise to myth.

But how many of us are truly transfigured in myth? I still carry childhood memories of a different kind, lapsed terrors, strange only to those, like myself, who recall few dreams.

*

My family teemed with uncles, aunts, cousins. Feckless, greedy, intemperate, spendthrift often and rarely wise, my family was insufferable as all families must seem to those born to reclusion or exile.

Habib and Faika Hassan, Badgastein, 1950s

And my parents, my own parents? Who will recall them now, if not I, their sole son? Who will speak of them? In their case, I do not know—*will* not know?—whereof I speak. Whatever passions or pains speed our childish days, we grow up to become familial ghosts, eidolons signaling to one another across darkening inscapes of memory. "Where" are my parents, now dead, where anyone, including Thutmose the Third and great Ramses, except in the shadow world of representations? Only language, simulacrum of our presence, speaks.

But really: *only* language speaks? I have never quite believed it.

*

My childhood lay, I later realised, in an invisible field of force: British colonialism. True, the phrase *El Ingileez* would sometimes catch my ear, carrying some hint of menace or obloquy. But as a child I had no aversion to the English language itself, nor to its native speakers who sometimes visited our house. Power, real power, I then sensed, rested elsewhere: in

my father's burly presence, in experiences which the body recalls before the mind.

The power of my father was, in fact, provincial. As a governor, his duties required him to walk on frayed ceremonial carpets, inspect local police troops, bestow dreary trophies at the annual *gymkhana*. Yet authority somehow adhered to him as he strode about, carrying a silver-headed cane that excited me more than all his other badges of office. For the cane concealed a rapier, stealthy and sharp, unknown to all—so I thought—but Father and myself. This weapon has etched a particular scene in my memory.

We were strolling toward evening by a field of dense sugar canes. Father held my small hand in his left hand; his right, as usual, held the cane. Suddenly a mottled yellow viper slithered across our path, then inexplicably stopped, rearing its triangular head. It swayed ever so slightly, fixing two jet, unblinking eyes on me. I shrank behind one of Father's knees while he, hesitating for a moment, stood still. Then, softly, he slid the rapier free, and in one continuous movement impaled the viper through its head, stepping on the flailing body to hold the beast at both ends to the ground. Writhing insanely for an instant, the thing terrified me as if it were still free. When the sword came finally out, red drops glistening on its steel, I felt a strange thrill. It was like a clear note trilling throughout my own blood, fear that had suddenly turned into glee.

This glee had another side, some childish compassion that did not recognize itself. I had seen playmates dismember live birds and insects, rapt as in a secret ritual, and experienced first fascination followed by active disgust. We came sometimes to blows; sometimes I fled. "You're born under the sign of Libra," an English friend of the family, whom I called Aunt Cecily, once told me, holding my open palm in her hand. "You will always defend justice. But remember, scales go up and down, and justice is like a swing." She was English; she spoke of justice; but I saw then no irony or contradiction.

*

Like some invisible worm, the colonial experience feeds on all those seeking redress for old wrongs and lacks. Self-hatred, self-doubt, twist in their bowels, and envy curls there with false pride. "*Baladi, baladi,*" Egyptians cried to dismiss someone uncouth or vulgar, forgetting that the word means "native." But Egyptians also feigned scorn for Europeans whom they strove to emulate. Was European skin a little fairer? "Allah, what difference can it possibly make? My cousin is fair.'' Was European literacy, or power, or technology, preeminent? *''Ma'lesh,* never mind. Those *frangi* perform no ablutions and eat pork. How foul!'' Thus the tacit principle of the Colonial Complex: to extol only such differences as serve oneself, other differences to deprecate or ignore. Thus, too, the Colonial Complex both constitutes and institutes its necessary bad faith: necessary for resistance, self-respect, sheer survival, yet shady, corrupt nonetheless, and self-deceiving.

As for myself, out of pride or pain, pain at seeing the legacy of colonialism maim so many around me, I resolved early never to give it a place in my politics or heart.

*

I became aware of Egyptian politics in El Mansura, capital of Daqahliya, rife in the thirties with student protest. Students believed themselves to represent the only political awareness in Egypt. Their volatile demonstrations, in which I later participated, could express sheer deviltry and fun, a carnivalesque relief from crushing studies. But their riots could also bring a government down.

At that time, the perennial grievance, British colonialism, was one that the patriotic Wafd Party, headed by Mustafa el-Nahhas Pasha, sought always to inflame. Eloquent, wily, and bold, el-Nahhas also considered himself a ''man of the people''; whenever he visited a village or town, the entire population would pour out to cheer him—except landlords. Such visits became the stuff of a governor's nightmares, sometimes the stuff of his unmaking. Pressured by the prime minister in Cairo, who would be pressured by the king in turn, governors sought to ''contain'' the junkets of el-Nahhas without actually constricting his movements, since he might someday sweep into power and avenge himself. It was a game of perilous balance, won only by consummate pols.

El-Nahhas visited El Mansura early one spring. For a whole week before his arrival, the town alternately sulked and seethed. High schools shut down; *sooks* (markets) swelled. Helmeted police, on horse or foot, patrolled the streets, wielding long supple canes or leather-strapped cudgels, carrying iron shields. But the students had cunning and surprise on their side. Once, driven home in an open *décapotable,* my father suddenly found himself surrounded by a mob of faces, black as gunpowder, ready to flare. He stood up in the car and spoke to them for an hour before they dispersed. Once, too, the son of the lieutenant governor, a boy my age, was

jostled by a gang of high school students who lay in wait outside his primary school gates. The gang had intended to ambush me; when they discovered their mistake, they gave the boy soft licorice candy and sent him home.

In the end, the bloody confrontation that my father had tried to avoid came. El-Nahhas surged into El Mansura on the crest of a roaring sea of *gallabiahs;* crowds rampaged through squares, through streets, smashing windows, hurling bricks and ordure at the police. Anger and fear mingled, and mingling turned into rage. Canes and cudgels sliced the air, people fell, trampled by hooves or boots. Police lines buckled, then broke like mud dikes before a flood. Rifles suddenly appeared, fired over the rippling crowds, then at their feet. By day's end, six people lay dead in the streets, four students in their teens. No one counted the wounded.

Was it, after all, a clash of useless passions? I confess it: on that fateful day in El Mansura, I felt my loyalties torn between my father and his foes. Three years later, Mustafa el-Nahhas Pasha became prime minister of Egypt. My father was forced to resign.

*

We lived thereafter in Cairo, in ''reduced circumstances'' as my mother liked to say. Our seven-room apartment occupied the top floor of a two-story, *fin-de-siècle* brick and grey stucco building facing the river on Shari el Nil, near El Gala bridge. No high rises then obstructed the sun, the eye. On any day, I could see from our balcony the old Semiramis Hotel across the Nile, and beyond it central Cairo, rising eastward toward El Mokattam Hills, toward the Citadel, and the mosque of Mohamed Ali with its twin, slender (too slender) minarets and great central dome. A large vegetable garden abutted on the southern side of our house, owned by a Coptic neighbor, shy and prodigiously rich. To the north, across a side street, lay a flowery, open-air café, where the Cairo Sheraton now stands. (In that café, Om Kulsoum, *el bulbul* [the nightingale] of Egypt, sometimes sang, her wailing voice pure and high pitched.) Behind the house, to the west, I practiced bicycle fights on my Raleigh in an improbably empty lot. In that house, I lived ten driven, yearning years, attending first the Saidiah Secondary School, then the Faculty of Engineering at the University of Cairo.

Dreamy, I have said, and shy, tutored at home in my first decade, I experienced much grief when I began to attend government schools. These proved intellectually demanding, socially bruising, physically dismal, proved altogether traumatic for me. At the grilled, lead-hued gate of the school, which shut at five minutes past eight with frightening finality and opened mercifully again at five minutes to four, the parental Rolls or Daimler might wait for the most privileged pupils. But once inside, these abandoned all hope. Jostling with the rest, they relied on their wits, fists, and unbreakable skulls—a quick, sharp blow with the head to the enemy's nosebridge—to absolve themselves daily of cowardice, effeminacy, or simply good breeding. In the brief recreation periods, the younger boys played *el beel* (marbles), viciously throwing their nickle leaders at a triangle full of bright, multicolored spheres. Older boys played *fudbal* (soccer) with a makeshift lump of old socks, delighting to kick each other in the shins. Lunch was a predatory affair, wolves and hyenas, the stronger or hungrier fighting for inedible gobs of glutinous matter while *el alpha* (the monitor), disdained by all, tried to establish some order of precedence around the table. (For many poorer pupils, this was their only meal for the day.) Extracurricular activities? Suspect. Character development? Absurd. The fit survived, and everyone else studied grimly or else fell by the way.

Not quite ten, I entered the lowest grade of Saidiah. The youngest boy in class, I wore short pants: a new, red *tarboush* (fez) barely concealed hair parted on one side. I sat at a rickety, sepia-colored, wooden desk, ink-splotched and carved-up by the *canifs* (pen knives) of all my predecessors. When the teacher stepped briskly into class, we all clattered to our feet and saluted, hands to fezzes, standing till he ordered us seated. The lesson began, and as in schoolrooms around the world, excitement and misery mingled in the period, which sped or dragged till a hand-rung bell struck the hour.

Directly behind me sat Tawfik, the class bully. He was fair, almost creamy of complexion, not particularly muscular. But he could glare ferociously or snarl, displaying a snaggletooth, and he fought with reckless glee. At once, he began to smile at me, making a slow, pumping motion with his hand, his thumb and index forming a circle. I smiled affably back. Afterwards, I discovered the meaning of his lewd, homosexual gesture. We fought, of course, and I lost—gashed lip, blood filling my mouth, ribs aching for a week—though not so badly as to brand myself a pansy nor so well as to discourage future strife.

That first year in school became my initiation to social reality. It certainly wrenched, remade, my character. I woke every morning with fear in my guts,

in my feet; I ended each day with an infinitesimally stronger sense of my endurance. I could not share my pain with my parents; I could not stay away from school. The year passed, the next came, the misery remained. Then one day I made a stunning discovery: I had lost my fear. I discovered also that by striking out first I could win most fights. Sensing, really believing, that I had nothing to lose, I found that I had accidentally won everything, almost everything. Suddenly, I began to excel in my school work, standing near the top of my class. Suddenly, too, I became popular: boys asked me to join their secret bands and warring gangs, practicing roughhouse pranks. I declined, my old bitterness stronger than their newfangled flattery.

Tawfik and all those boys who had bullied me for an eternity began to fade from my awareness. They also faded into a lower "form." (At Saidiah, high achievers were segregated into the same classroom or form within each grade.) But a few others—Talat, Ibrahim, Roshdy—remained within the tight, invincible circle of friendship through my school and university years, until exile, marriage, age, dispersed our ways.

Though I belonged to no racial or religious minority in Egypt, I was tormented more than if I had been a freak. What have the tormentors of my boyhood become? No doubt some have grown into upstanding men, model fathers to their sons. Were they to recall the pain they once inflicted on a boy, they might now wince and squirm. Or was that pain but some exchange for a lack they themselves as boys endured? Lack or warp, something there tempts us to indulge a nameless evil: we torture purely, like art, for its own mysterious sake.

*

Summers brought relief from the rigors of the Saidiah Secondary School. My parents sometimes traveled to Europe; sometimes they vacationed in Alexandria or Port Fuad. But much as I loved the sea, I loved best to spend my summers alone with my grandmother on our Delta estate, *el ezbah*.

Long, idle days, full of sunny projects; soft summer nights, echoing with stories and laughter; nature gracious, appeased, without sting, without those locusts descending like a black cloud from heaven in Upper Egypt. This was a time out of time, will-less and free, irrecoverable except as a charmed space, the green garden each child carries within him, perhaps to inhabit again only at the instant of death.

Our *genenah* (orchard) was the most treasured part of the estate. Rows of orange alternated with peach trees in a rectangle larger than several football fields. Two latticed vine arbors intersected over the orchard, meeting at the center in a high, octagonal kiosk, painted blue and orange, which served as a perch for sparrows, swifts, hummingbirds, doves, and hoopoes. All these fed rapaciously on ripe grapes and peaches, and like local orchard thieves had to be driven away by guards banging cymbals in the harvest season. But at other times, the orchard breathed peace, the fragrance of incipient fruit. In its dense geometry of shades, I learned to play hide and seek alone, to double myself between row upon straight row of trees, and to recognize the fluttering shape of each, startling myself as I came upon my Other around a bend.

Other times, I preferred to follow storks circling high in the immaculate blue sky, a swirling, dotted cloud which would finally glide gracefully away into some far-off space, beyond my reach or ken, leaving me with a bittersweet pang for the rest of that day. Or I would fish in one of the *ezbah* streams with a hook

Two years old

made of twisted pins, catching the whiskered *armut* (catfish), which I threw back into the muddy water in revulsion from its thick, slithery body and flat, primeval head. Or I would follow the line of deft cotton pickers in the field, singing as they plucked the long-threaded "white gold" of Egypt from its dried buds, and intervene when supervisors tried to whip, with a thin stalk, girls who left unpicked cotton in their wake. Or I would join the cooks in the kitchen, to make delicious mango or watermelon ice cream, turning by hand the syrup in a metal beater covered with cracked, salted ice, till the liquid became mysteriously gelid. Or I would sketch the twenty-room country house in which all my maternal uncles had been born, using charcoal stubs on large, rough-grained paper sheets, seeking to capture some quality of it as it rose, solemn and solitary, above the shimmering green haze of the fields, the mud village of "our" fellaheen—I never set foot in it—slung low behind the house, except for the conical turrets of pigeon houses. Or I would play Ping-Pong with Samia, a pretty, henna-fingered, barefooted, laughing servant girl of twelve, whose long earrings tinkled as she moved, and whom my grandmother forbade to accompany me anywhere out of her vigilant sight. Nothing else those summers was forbidden to me, except swimming in the *bilharzia*-ridden streams.

After luncheon, I liked to steal away upstairs and read. Since my grandmother refused to climb the steep stone steps of the house, the whole second floor remained mine. I read while others napped. In some unfurnished rooms, books piled there on books and across buckling shelves; magazines rose in teetering columns from the floor; and the scent of thick, musty paper greeted my nose, lingering in my mind long after I closed the last book. Here was the scent of words, verbal dreams. Pell-mell, I found French novels, classical Arabic poetry, English detective stories, German technical manuals, medical books in sundry languages. I found old wrinkled maps of the earth, glimmering celestial charts, inscrutable surveying deeds, spectral anatomy drawings, still lifes in ornate, gilded frames, and sepia photographs of mustachioed men and crinolined women, some with *yashmak* (veils), whose names I never came to know. Rows upon yellow rows of the *National Geographic* magazine took me around the world in an hour; and huge folios of the *London Illustrated Gazette* unfolded before me the Great War, Ypres, Chalon, Amiens, Verdun, the Marne, mud and blood filling trenches of battles that rumbled still in my family's talk.

I read riotously and consumed myself as I read. I obeyed no principle but irresistible whim, took no witness other than the lazy, afternoon flies. And I came down for supper only after my grandmother, calling from the stairwell repeatedly, threatened to close the kitchen for the night. At table, I ate silently, my head wounded, swaddled in a huge bandage of make-believe. But my grandmother would joke and scold, piling food on my plate, and menace me with the evening's game of *tric-trac,* till I returned to her side.

Strange country pleasures these, that enchanted a boy even as they sapped his will. For I endured no greater wrench, until much later, than returning to school after an indolent season at the *ezbah.*

*

Increasingly, I discovered in Saidiah an outlet for my energies. I endured its dreary, disinfected classrooms and execrable lunches because the world opened itself to me again as it had on those long, silent afternoons when I read at *el ezbah.* At Saidiah, though, the autodidact in me encountered odd and exacting masters.

Most pupils perceived only the ludicrous quirks of their teachers. One, dubbed "The Klaxon," kept tapping his hip pocket during class to check his wallet; another, called "The Clutch," reached for his crotch and glared to stress a point in the lesson; a third, nicknamed "The Bullet," fired chalk pieces with the accuracy of a high-powered rifle at nodding or chattering boys. Other teachers, however, evoke images of richer hue.

I recall Mr. Miller, who taught us the King's English, and conveyed a certain hurt radiance even to the rowdiest spirit. His pale, pinched face and distant, sunken eyes rendered all the horrors of W. W. Jacobs's "The Monkey's Paw," and his flashes of mock braggadocio infused in *King Solomon's Mines, The White Company, Montezuma's Daughter, The Coral Island, Kidnapped,* and *The Prisoner of Zenda* a delightful irony without impairing their romance. He had a taste for things Gothic, a gentle way of shaming obscenity into silence. He may have also inspired me to the first prize I ever won at school: a handsome combination desk calendar and writing pad, inscribed, "For Excellence in English."

I did well in all subjects—except Arabic. Once, my total points in the marking period earned me second place even though I had failed Arabic. The headmaster came as usual to congratulate the three top pupils in class. He called on the first, and walked up to his desk to shake his hand; he called on the third, and did the same. Then he called on me.

Pausing as if in great perplexity, he lowered his brown, watery eyes and softly asked: "Why, my son? Are you *rumi* (Greek or Roman, any foreigner really)?" I did not fail Arabic again, though I never did more than pass it.

The baccalaureate examinations of Egypt resulted annually in a national trauma. Harsh, exigent, and inflexible, more French than English in their centralized character, these exams, lasting two weeks, remain the most strenuous I have ever endured. Administered across the nation in vast, silent tents, with endless rows of numbered desks and sawdust on the ground, the ordeal—indeed its very place—exuded dread. Watchful monitors prowled the aisles of that city of the living dead, construing any communication, any whisper, as an attempt to cheat. This brought instant retribution: a red mark in the corner of the examination book, assuring failure. Punctually at the end of each exam, the head monitor screamed maniacally his command: "Pens at rest! Pens at rest!" Any delay in obeying this doomsday cry brought again the red stigma of failure. Thus we raced against time as well as each other, raced ultimately against our own selves.

Failure meant a year lost and, far worse, shame. Students who failed sometimes committed suicide; others, in fearful anticipation of the event, would flee their homes, or simply collapse. Thus the great battles of Egypt were fought not on the playing fields of its public schools but under its examination tents. Were these battles really won? I have known piercing intellects among my classmates who have either emigrated or remained to find their minds brutalized by bureaucracy. I have known others who lost hope and quietly lapsed into cynicism, sloth, sensualism. Is the school to blame for this? Is Egyptian society? In some rude, outlying districts of Upper Egypt, an intelligent school child may aspire to a world centuries, literally centuries, ahead of the world its family inhabits.

Ahead?

*

Careers. We drift into one, elect another, obey yet a different call, then wake one day to find ourselves cast on a distant shore. We work all our days to make ourselves, or remake the world, and with luck may stumble on a brilliant hour, unmaking all our pain. Mercifully, we see nothing ahead.

I received my baccalaureate in the spring of 1941. I wanted desperately to enter El Harbiah (the Royal Army Officers School), modeled on Sandhurst, and drive the British out of Egypt. Had I had my way, I might have joined Nasser's Free Officers Movement or perhaps lain in a desert grave, among the red hills of Sinai, after the first Israeli War. But my parents would not hear of it.

"El Harbiah," my father scowled. "With your grades? You can enter any faculty, medicine or engineering. Why waste your brains?"

My mother was more indignant. She hated every hint of war as much as any whisper of *déclassement.*

"Who goes into El Harbiah now? The lower orders. And some rich delinquents who can't manage anything else."

To me, El Harbiah stood for discipline, idealism, a sharp, clean edge to cut off the rot of Egypt. Radical surgery, not technocratic reform: that's what this gangrenous land needs, I thought. I was at the age of sinister purity. But my parents would have none of it. Obscurely, they sensed I struck at their mode of being, sought to undo their lives.

That summer, I sulked and skulked. My parents left for Alexandria; I stayed behind in Cairo, alone. Sometimes, I would ride a tram to the end of its line and idle about, there where the rails ended, bending back upon themselves. Sometimes, I would go out into the desert, away from the feculent city, away from the small emblems of domesticity, the soft impediments of relatives. And I would burn a dry palm leaf, past the tracks of caravans, in memory of unknown desert warriors, anchorites, ravenous saints.

When autumn came, I joined the Faculty of Engineering of the University of Cairo. Though its course would last fully five years, the degree, I consoled myself, would lead me out of Egypt.

*

Soon after my admission to the Faculty of Engineering, however, I took up religion and sports. I took up both fanatically.

In my youth, it was considered crude, even boorish, to display religious zeal. No one, of course, spoke against Islam, nor would a nominal Moslem deny its central creed: "There is no God but Allah, and Mohamed is the prophet of Allah." But the history of Egypt proved conducive to tolerance, even if each sect believed itself alone elect.

My family considered itself Moslem as naturally as it accepted a rainless day. Yet its various members drank alcohol, gambled occasionally, fasted irregularly, never visited Mecca, and seldom prayed, not to mention those other peccadilloes which human beings share in a sodality wider than any faith. For my family, for an entire Egyptian milieu, Islam simply defined a cultural inheritance, backward sometimes, sometimes uncouth, yet always a source of pride, pride that concealed its prejudice.

This prejudice took root in social rather than spiritual grounds, ultimately sinking into that clotted underground which nourishes all human fears. In Bulgaria, polyglot and polytheist like Egypt, Elias Canetti experienced during his childhood many prejudices, including the prejudice of Sephardim Jews against other Jews. In Cairo, I saw upper-class Moslems discriminate against other Moslems more subtly, tenaciously, than against Copt or Jew. Fairness of skin, in shades perceptible only to an Egyptian snob, connoted descent from Mameluke, Turkish, or Albanian ancestors, some of whom had held feudal estates since the times of Saladin. As for religious observance, not to mention zealotry, that could be left to servants and fellahin.

None of us ever knows enough to cry: "I reacted against this . . . I became that. . . ." I know only that for a year I became unbearably devout, flouting my piety, relishing my parents' discomfort. For what parent can bring himself to say: "Son, you are too virtuous for your own good or ours"? Had I been by nature an adherent, I might have joined the Moslem Brotherhood then, which Nasser later outlawed as terrorist. Instead, I fasted, kneeled toward Mecca, and gave charity to beggars with an inner arrogance that should have delighted Iblis (alias the Devil).

But was it all just adolescent revolt, way-wardness, spleen, at best young pride testing its fettle? The quest for verity, probity, justice, for an ethos to counter centuries of deprivation and defeat, the spirit's thickest sleep, was then, as it remains now, a crux of politics as of moral life in Egypt. Nor was my "Moslem Interlude," as my mother came to call it, all protest or all ascesis. I roamed Cairo in search of its legendary mosques where I could pray: Amr ibn-al-As, named after the first Arab conqueror of Egypt; El Azhar, tenth-century seat of Islamic learning; Ibn Tulun, which reputedly stands where Abraham sacrificed the ram for Isaac; Sultan Barkuk and Sultan Hassan, the last, perhaps the masterpiece of Islamic architecture in Egypt; and Mohamed Ali Pasha, highest on the Cairo hills.

Roaming those ancient quarters of Cairo, I discovered much which had been denied me. I saw the quotidian city, crowded, sordid, insistent, color-crazed, throbbing with a sensuous energy that left my senses dazed. I became a tourist, wide-eyed and fastidious, in my own native place. I walked through the bazaars, brimming with strident vendors and garish wares, fearful of some contamination I could not quite name. I evaded the bold, *kohled* eyes of street women, the fluttering touch of peddling children, the mournful frolics of cripples. I saw, as in the *Arabian Nights, el sakkah* come around the corner, bent double beneath his great water-buffalo skin, selling water for a few piasters. And I saw the merchant of *kharoub* stride among the crowds, gaily bedecked in red and white, silver castanets in one hand and bulging beaker strapped across his chest; in the beaker's mouth, a big splinter of ice cooled the crimson juice. Once, even, I saw the crowd open in a hush before the local *fetuah* (strong man). He stomped the ground and glared, veins bulging in his bull's neck. A ferruled staff—thick as his penis, someone whispered—preceded him menacingly, and a purple scar cut across his cheek and brow. An unceremonial dagger showed in his wide, braided belt.

In the *fetuah*'s quarter, his rude word made law; in the mosques, another spirit, immanent, serene, reigned. The mosques I visited appeared nearly empty, so vast their masonry and quiet their space, creating a larger inner space. Straw mats spread from wall to wall, yellow and cool beneath my shoeless feet, like desert sand at sunrise. Here I could leave behind the confusions of the bazaar. Here I could escape my own nascent prurience: urgencies of sex, anxieties of venereal disease, phantasms of menstrual blood and female circumcision. Here I would experience an intimacy of being as I performed my ablutions, feeling the soft rustle of water flowing over hands, arms, feet, over face and scalp; as I heard the high wail of the muezzin drift from the minaret: *"Allah akbar, Alla-ah akbar, Alla-a-ah akbar,"* as I kneeled, facing the sacred niche southeast, then pressed my forehead ritually to the ground, astonished by its mute immensity.

Yet even then—or do I think so only now?—a vein of hedonism laced my faith. This showed in Ramadan, season of extremes. Tempers could flash, especially in summer heat, and angry words would pass among friends. But those words soon would fade, forgiven, forgotten: *"Yallah,* it was only the hunger of Ramadan." From dawn to dusk, fasting kept the spirit edgy, lean; then, precisely at sundown, the Cairo cannon boomed, its echo rolling among the Mokattem hills, releasing all the faithful from their ordeal. Many of the poor were long inured to hunger, though in that holy month charity sometimes supplied their needs. Many of the rich pretended to fast during Ramadan, yet gorged themselves at sunset, as if breaking their fast, before laying their jowls to rest.

Hassan, Cairo, 1945

Near sundown, I sat on the balcony reading the Koran, feigning indifference to the cannon's prandial boom, while Ali, in spotless white gallabiah and broad red sash, set the dining room table for *el fetar:* literally, break-fast. (Setting it thus beforehand, my parents agreed, Ali could later eat his own meal in peace.) I read the Koran, but my mind wandered away from its visions of the hereafter, rendered in resonant verse, to things mundane. I imagined the sideboard inside, covered with walnuts, hazelnuts, almonds, and pistachios, all heaped in a bowl; figs, mangoes, grapes, and diverse, multicolored dates; or perhaps some cakes, *kahk* and *ghorayebah;* or perhaps sweets, *kunafa, esh-el-sarayah, amar-el-din,* jewelled with nuts and sugared fruits. Then I would wrench myself from esurient reveries, realizing that I profaned Ramadan, making it a gluttonous feast. Many hours later, at *el sahar* (pre-dawn snack), I would sleepily contemplate the spare tray by my bedside—bread, water, fruit—and would feel chastened again, austere. By the time Ramadan ended in the feast of *'Eed el Kebir,* with its orgies of sheep's entrails, kidneys, brains, hearts, roasted testicles, I loathed all that crapulence in the name of Allah, which I had seen and shared.

Thus began—every beginning is lost in mystery—a life-long rhythm of resolution and relapse, abstinence and satiety, puritanism with a wide sybaritic streak. Hurdy-gurdy of aspiration and need.

*

An adolescent finds rigor where he wills. I found it in religion, and found in sports a kindred tautness of spirit and gristle. I was not big for my age, but I was determined enough, determined to be determined, and agile.

I first learned to row a scull-and-four on the Nile, snatching the oar free on the beat, and twisting the blade flat from the wrist as the trolley-seat reached the end of the stroke. For months, our varnished skiff skimmed the choppy, mocha-brown river, passing full-rigged feluccas whose crews waved us over to "share their bread." (In Egypt, *uzmat el marakbyah,* the invitation of boatmen, has come to mean any ritual or impractical offer.) We darted beneath the rumbling steel bridges of Cairo which cast moist, black shadows across our bow, and circled the islands of Roda or El Gezira. One day we returned to the bobbing clubhouse, moored across the street from my home, returned awash with sweat, back and thigh muscles aching and palms raw from rowing, to learn from the trainer that we really lacked the "heft" to qualify for the team's first scull-and-four. Sheepishly we dispersed, though we had so far clung together, avoiding one another thereafter as if in mutual reproach.

I turned to other aquatic sports, where my light weight mattered little, and made both the swimming and water polo teams. In water polo, I offset my wobbly shots at the goal by a knack for stealing the slippery ball from opponents and passing it on to teammates with stronger arms. Our entire team played with less power than speed and cunning, and so won gold and silver medals inscribed with images of fearsome hippos, crocodiles, and other Ancient Egyptian lacustrine gods. We wore the medals ostentatiously around our necks, over our brief black trunks, and dove and scrambled in the pool like otters when the medals, torn off in play, sank gracefully to the blue-painted bottom.

It was in fencing, though, that I came thrillingly alive. Hardly a "sport," fencing compounded violence and ceremony, instinct and skill, engagement and distance. It demanded both grace and precision, yet its explosions of movement hinted at some

desperate finality, as if all life hung on a *botte* or lunge. There lay its subliminal message: despite their masks, pads, blunted points, men acknowledged in that instant their capacity to deal or receive death. In that instant, they also found their bond. No accident, then, that Talat, Michel, Riyad, closest friends of my university years, composed with me the Faculty of Engineering fencing team.

We practiced in the Royal Fencing Club which occupied a white villa in the Ezbekiah Gardens, across from the old colonial Shepheard's Hotel. Talat's father served as chancellor in Abdeen Palace; Michel, from a wealthy Coptic family, drove his own Ford *décapotable;* Riyad seemed vaguely related to the royal family through his divorced mother, a cultured, decisive woman who powdered her face like a Kabuki heroine. All, in short, could afford the entrance fees to the club and, excepting Talat, all spoke French more fluently than Arabic. But what we truly shared, even more than the shifting flow of friendships, was a "passion for the sword."

The Club's *Maître d'Armes* was a Frenchman called Prost, and in his *salle d'armes* he reigned more absolutely than Louis XIV. (Or was he rather like some outrageous master of *kendo* who understood that certain tyrannies refine both spirit and sword?) For six months, he permitted us only to receive from him *"la leçon";* he forbade us to fence or practice together. For a year thereafter we lived in dread lest, displeased with some awkwardness or error in us, he would order us curtly *à la douche.* He prohibited us from fencing with others till we lost all the "bad habits of our bodies." Later, even after we became collegiate champions, he ordered us out of the fencing hall whenever he sensed the slightest lapse in our skill or will. *A la douche!* Dismal interdiction, sound of scorn! Humiliated, with silent sympathy only from the old locker-room attendant who warmed our clammy canvas suits in winter—like us, he was much ordered about—humiliated and barely sweating, we would shower and return sullenly each to his home.

*

Religion and athletics could not displace forever the erotic urgencies of my youth. But where, how, might such urgencies find clarity, let alone satisfaction, in Egypt?

Yet when I see today some boys and girls touch one another casually, as if zombies hid behind their lids, I am grateful for that intense constraint which gave my temper its tilt. Seeing a woman walk ahead of me down a Cairo street shaded by eucalyptus trees, hips swaying to the rhythm of her high heels, hair tossing, I would try compulsively to fix her fleeting figure in my mind, and invent for her a voice, a name, a face. Fancy-bred, clad in romance, such images could wrack me more than any naked expressions of desire.

The first romance of my youth took place by the sea, in a summer camp pitched among the dunes of Ras-el-barr, where the Nile meets the Mediterranean, far from any city or tree. She was a sun-goldened, green-eyed Jewess, whose name I never knew. She belonged to another camp, young men and women preparing to settle in Israel after the war. At night, under an immense, star-scattered sky, their songs rose above the rumbling surf, strange, alluring to my ears. She did not surface like Cyprian Aphrodite from the foam; she first came into view riding a donkey, her bare thighs clamped firmly on the beast, smiling with her eyes. We never spoke, needed no speech. Whatever daring I showed, swimming far or jumping high, I showed to her tender amusement.

Once the two camps played volleyball, Moslem against Jew. I can not recall who lost or won; I recall only the sun-lit down on that girl's arms, the spryness in her eyes shifting suddenly into darker hues. I recall bare bodies in the sun, bright, breezy seascapes, white sand lighter than spray. And I remember an uglier shadow: the clumsy, homosexual advance of a teammate bent on breaking the spell of my summer romance.

*

False urgencies of spirit, sports, sex. They all had their shapes of excess as of ascesis, but they led me nowhere. By my second year at the university, I realized that rigor must become practical, generous—or else it stunts. I turned to work, sensing that my Great Escape from Egypt depended on professional achievement more than on existential quests. If I graduated with distinction, the Ministry of Education might award me a fellowship to study abroad.

At eighteen, I began to reproach myself for all the time I lost in erotic fantasies, time canceled in the onanistic fastness of movie houses, where I sat sometimes from noon to midnight. "You will never become a scientist or engineer that way," I admonished myself at least once a day. Then I would rush to my bicycle and race to the Faculty of Engineering, barely a mile away in Giza.

The University of Cairo, then, was a conglomerate of florid governmental buildings designed only for instruction; no student unions, cafeterias, or dorms obtained. Unapproachable professors declaimed from the podium; assistants supervised anxious students in the labs; annual examinations determined the issue. No electives, no general education, no extracurricular activities except half a dozen sports. One matriculated in a particular branch of engineering—electrical, mechanical, civil, chemical—and learned nothing besides. Such illiberal education, though exigent, deterred creativity, blunted any ethical stance. Nor did it foster a sense of community within the various faculties of the university. Indeed, the notorious student riots of Egypt may have been sparked less by political events than the need of fervent youths to meet one another in common hope.

Despite its dreary routines, however, the university could not deaden us. At times, the drudgery of study gave way to lambent visions, and the future danced like an incandescent genie caught in a will of fire. Blazing with a knowledge we did not really possess, we dedicated ourselves to vast schemes: a new Moslem Empire, extending from the English Channel to the China Sea; or a rebirth of the ancient gods, Amon, Isis, Osiris, and Set, to supplant the barbarism of Islam and usher in new mysteries; or a concept of Universal Justice, reinstating the fellah and reapportioning the land without spilling blood; or, again, some miraculous, technological plan to turn all the deserts of North Africa into a green paradise—and always, of course, the expulsion of the British from Egypt. Such were the reciprocities of history and dream, the overweening desires of youths at once too young and too old for their years.

As I approached graduation, the war neared its end. Most Egyptians, of course, considered the war as merely a struggle between factions of European colonialism: D-Day meant less to them than El Alamein. British soldiers, and even the rambunctious "Aussies," went now unnoticed on the streets. But American GIs, who appeared increasingly on Cairo streets, met with curiosity, good will. *El Yankees*, after all, had never occupied Egyptian soil, and they brought a history known better for its idealism than imperialism. (Now, alas, we know these to be all too compatible.) They arrived, as well, after a million Hollywood myths had long invaded our heads.

For me, the termination of the war meant one thing only: I could sail to America. Throughout the war, I was as little affected by it as I had been by *la crise* (the Depression) a decade earlier. To be sure, sandbags and antiaircraft emplacements appeared at various public sites—ministries, bridges, powerhouses, waterworks. And on the flat roof of our house, near El Gala Bridge, a Lewis machine gun stood idle except when I would persuade two slack Egyptian Army soldiers to let me scan the empty horizon in its sights. For a year or so, a blackout seemed sporadically in effect. We all lined our curtains, painted our windows black, and forgot to close them at night. Once or twice, the air-raid sirens shrieked. We would rush to our balconies or into the streets, pointing excitedly at the long, luminous beams sweeping the sky. Then someone would murmur: "Oh, it must have been a stray *Italiani* plane." And everyone would laugh.

What, then, did the war mean to Cairenes? Distant slaughter; armies hurtling back and forth across school maps; headlines growing larger; loud Movietone newsreels on every screen; the streets full of alien soldiers, escorting more *efrangeyas* (foreign women) than we thought Egypt held; English speech pouring everywhere into our ears, displacing French as the foreign tongue; hotels, restaurants, cafés, movie houses, alive with money and bought sex; native officials, contractors, profiteers growing suddenly rich; involuted arguments about the war, who will win, and what Egypt stood to gain or lose; above all, a sense of expectancy, waiting not so much for the end of the war itself as for a new order, a post-colonial dispensation—and, for me, the start of another life.

In the countryside, fellahs continued to draw water from the Nile with their *sakiah, shadoof, tambour.* In the provincial cafés, *el kary* recited in sing-song the Koran, and old storytellers recounted the epic of Abu Zayed El Hilali, killed at last by a blind enemy who aimed his poisoned arrow by the sound of the hero's urination. ("Allah," Abu Zayed cried, "you have only punctured my water gourd," whereupon the enemy fell dead of fright.) And in the desert, the bedouins maintained their ancient feuds, burying each other alive in the sand—or burying their children only to the neck as a cure against rheumatism.

Of the war's enormity, of its carnage and waste, few Egyptians had any sense till the very end, when images of Dachau and Auschwitz, Dresden and Hiroshima, began to appear in newspapers and on movie screens. Were Egyptians, then, like so many children at a historical play, cheering a spectacle they thought to leave behind when the final curtain fell? Did *I* look upon the Second World War with the same eyes, fantasy-glazed, that once dwelled on pictures of Big Bertha and the Red Baron's Fokker, in the *London Illustrated Gazette,* as if they were big toys?

*

In the last two years at the university, I consecrated myself to work, schooldays and holidays, mornings, afternoons, nights. To my distress, I discovered that my mind had become lax, my calculations careless, my solutions slapdash. I set about to reverse this trend, practicing logarithms at dawn till I could feel my brain purr like a balanced, well-oiled rotor. And I specialized in electrical engineering, which carried a certain cachet—long before Marshall McLuhan, Egyptians considered electronics the science of the new day.

Sometimes on weekends, though, I would snatch a day or two to read poetry or fiction. Locked up in my stale study, cross-legged in an old black leather armchair, I read for fifteen hours at a stretch, until my mother protested outside my door. I read first in the morocco-bound, gilded sets in my father's library: Corneille, Conrad, Scott, Flaubert, Thiers, Goethe, Macaulay, Dickens, Shakespeare, Gibbon, Jules Verne, books acquired long before by someone concerned with their decorative effect. Then I began to frequent the lending library of the British Council, near *Midan el Opera.* Housed in a clean, bright basement, with direct access to the street, the library smelled of unopened books, binding glue, glossy paper, and the fresh fragrance of its comely young English librarian. Still shy, I rarely spoke to her except to say "Hello" and "Thank you," though I remained conscious of her presence even as I leafed through novels on the "adventure" shelves: Charles Read, Rudyard Kipling, Charles Kingsley, Robert Louis Stevenson, W. H. Hudson, Frederick Marryat, Somerset Maugham.

The works that stormed my imagination then— like Maugham's *The Moon and Sixpence* and *The Razor's Edge*—might go begging for a place in the high canon of fiction today; but they were the works I needed, somehow, to release some inchoate idea of myself, some obscure promise. I read, at any rate, with headlong absorption, a mood that I envy now as I approach "serious literature"—let alone poststructuralist criticism—with mind frowning and pencil in hand.

After each reading orgy, bitter self-reproof. Electronics, not literature, will bring my release, I argued; once out of Egypt, I could read what I willed. I returned to my work with the single-mindedness of the Count of Monte Cristo plotting his escape from Chateau d'If. I passed my fourth year exams with the grade of "Good." I resolved to graduate in my fifth year with "Distinction." My parents now receded from my horizon; so did my spiritual quests, athletic feats, erotic reveries. I spoke only to my closest friends, spoke to them only of gausses, volts, amperes. When the phone rang for me, it was Riaz, Talat, or Ibrahim checking the solution to a problem in calculus or circuitry. I went to bed, after midnight, my head humming with numbers till I fell in Newton's sleep.

*

I graduated in June 1946 from the Faculty of Engineering, second in my class. A Catholic, Elie Aziz, placed first; two Copts, Faiz and Ibrahim, came third and sixth; and my two close friends, Talat and Riaz, ranked fourth and fifth. All six, in a class of more than a hundred graduates, received "Distinction." The Ministry of Education awarded Talat, Riaz, and me—nominal Moslems—opulent fellowships to study electronics abroad. A year later, the ministry offered similar fellowships to the three Christians.

But where should I go? England, Switzerland, America? No one in my family favored England. My mother, of course, preferred Switzerland; it was "closest, and very scenic besides." My father, though reluctant to see his son leave, argued forcefully for America. Its technology was peerless then; it held the future in its keep. As for myself, I was implacably set on studying in the United States—and set secretly on remaining there. My father and I prevailed, first over my mother, then over the Ministry of Education itself, which reserved its choice, expensive "missions" to America for graduates with political clout.

I still faced frightening medical and bureaucratic ordeals. To secure my "educational mission" and my student visa to the United States, I had to prove my health, sanity, financial responsibility, and impeccable moral character. I had to prove acceptance at a reputable American university. And I had to obtain trans-Atlantic passage at a time when returning GIs preempted both shipping berths and college admissions. But having come so close to my goal, I had no intention of faltering. Predictably, I found the medical inquisition the worst. (To this day I avoid doctors, visit them only when I am in the best of health.) Teams of Egyptian physicians (rather crude), then American specialists (somewhat cool), examined me for everything, trachoma, *bilharzia,* tuberculosis, all rampant in Egypt; for every trace of mental or physical degeneracy. For the first time in my life, someone prodded my anus, pulled painfully on my testicles; another searched my arms with a needle for a vein, almost without success; still another pounded my chest and kidneys as if practicing on a drum; yet another peered down my throat till I gagged. Blood, urine, feces, spittle were extracted from my body. Then they sent me home, with many a dark look, to await the results. These took an interminable month, my humor swinging wildly from anxiety to hope, hope to despair, despair to anxiety again. Finally, the reports came, pronouncing me fit except for some small excess of albumin, which our family doctor cured with injections and pills and the recommendation to eat a great deal of watermelon that summer.

My interview with the American consul, a brisk, crewcut Stanford man, proved more civilized. Behind rimless glasses, he quickly ascertained that I could speak English, appeared sane enough, had not practiced pimping or prostitution, and felt no sympathy for Communism. The medical reports, the police record (blank), the Egyptian Educational Mission Award, all lay on his desk: so did a letter of admission from the Moore School of Electrical Engineering of the University of Pennsylvania. The consul did not press the point about the missing trans-Atlantic ticket, having been assured by our family friend, Colonel

Electrical engineers (author at left) aboard a felucca on the Nile at Aswan, 1946

Siemen, that he would help secure my passage. In my immaculate new passport, the consul placed a student visa, stamped with the Great Seal of the United States of America, and with a combined shove and hand-shake, showed me to the next room. There, a burly U.S. Marine forcefully fingerprinted both my hands, gave me a large slab of Palmolive and a clean linen towel, and pointed silently to the wash bowl.

Colonel Siemen called a week later to say that my passage to America had been arranged on the SS *Abraham Lincoln,* leaving from Port Said in late August. He had written earlier to recommend me to the University of Pennsylvania, his *alma mater.* I do not know what prompted his improbable friendship with my parents. They met at some reception in the flush of the Allied victory, and in the untrammeled feeling of the day found in each other some baffling affinity. He introduced himself affably as judge advocate in the U.S. Army, an American Jew. Around his round, blue eyes he wore a round, gold pince-nez, and wore over his small, pear-shaped body baggy uniforms. His preternatural quickness of mind, of intuition really, seemed always generous; his gaze penetrated everyone even as it promised sympathy. I shall never know why he liked me; I know only that his intercessions proved decisive in my life.

*

In that hot, fateful summer of 1946, as I desperately waited for all the pieces of my life to fit, I walked one still evening across Kasr-el-Nil Bridge—now renamed Tahrir (Liberation)—alone, sick at heart, and sick in the stomach of those albumin pills. I had not eaten; my mouth was parched; the bridge seemed to stretch without end beneath my leaden feet. In my eyes, the lamplight shone yellow, bleary, washing down like fluid rust on the iron railings. I felt congested, clotted, like some lump of clay yearning to lose its shape in the earth. Yet there was a tightness in my mind, an edge of resolve somewhere, that would not obey the call of dust. I thought to myself: why, this must be despair—despair checked by some deeper trust.

II

It must have been trust in rebirth, stubborn intimations of a new life. I discovered America on a Liberty Ship, which had barely survived the war, lurching toward New York on its last voyage. The ship creaked continually and left in the ocean a wake of rust. During the passage, a longshoremen's strike closed the Port of New York, forcing "Old Abe" to veer south toward New Orleans.

The voyage stretched; the empty days came and went, invariable. I could fill them only with anticipation. But my severance from everything familiar, from the very languages that housed my feelings, heightened my anxieties, my senses. Sea-smells everywhere—spume, fried fish, capstan grease, oily soot floating from the single smokestack. At night, I dreamed exorbitantly. My fellow passengers—some military derelicts, a few on sick leave, a few nondescript civilians, all Americans somehow uneager to reach any port—seemed to me phantasms.

At last, one morning, the ship rounded Key West. A long night after, it began to glide through the Mississippi Delta. As a schoolchild, I had learned that the Nile was the longest, the stateliest river, the great artery of history; it flowed like "some grave mighty thought threading a dream" (Leigh Hunt). The Mississippi ranked only third in length. Yet sliding through the bayou in that strange dawn, the air thick, the horizon still clotted with darkness, I sensed hidden luxuriance and menace. Everywhere, a nameless vegetation threatened to clog the channels and ensnare the ship which slipped through like a huge sea snail. The air was humid as I had never known it in Egypt, the sky low. I had not sailed farther up the Nile than Abu Simbel, and so never felt the wild pulse of Africa. Yet knowing Conrad, I now imagined myself, like Marlow, pushing into the heart of darkness. Blacks began to appear in curious skiffs around Old Abe. And how odd! These blacks spoke English, a kind of English, wore European trousers, shirts, hats.

I had entered America, it seemed, from its secret, gloomy underside, not like Columbus or "stout Cortez." Yes, I had read the boys' books, *Deerslayer, Tom Sawyer, Atala,* but had never really believed that modern America could be anything but a romance of Europe, El Dorado civilized. I felt now, exhilaration contending with dread, that I had come to a land more extravagant than any of my dreams. A country younger than Egypt but also older, claiming the precedence of a primeval jungle over the most archaic temple. Here I was on my own at last. But what awaited me at the end of this swampy river? Liberty—or some immane power, without bounds or name?

*

*Randall Jarrell (front) with Leslie Fiedler and
Robert Fitzgerald (rear),
Bloomington, Indiana, 1952*

A decade and a half later, I wrote of America, in
Radical Innocence: Studies in the Contemporary American Novel (1961), thus:

A country without prehistory, it has suddenly entered history with the intention to rape and redeem time in its heart. A country of illimitable spaces, it has confronted men with nature in the raw, inducing in them permanent and atavistic solitude, and it has been turned by them into the most profoundly denatured spectacle on record. Conceived as a dream, it has shown that dreamers may also awake in the cold sweat of a nightmare, and sleep to dream again. . . . The curse of Columbus is still with us: everyone must discover America— alone!

Later still, in *The Postmodern Turn* (1987), I wrote:

Foreign born, he still recalls that nothing terrified him more than the prospect of repatriation. He opened every letter from the Immigration and Naturalization Service with dry mouth, clammy hand. But now his impatience with America grows. For there is a crank in him, organ-grinding Jeremiah, ill-tempered, unreasonable, uncouth—a creature twisted of dream and hope. This is how the organ-grinder rasps:

"What's wrong with us now?
A 'crisis of confidence'?
You wouldn't know it, the
way America rides on roller
skates. In the parks, the
future walks with transistors
instead of ears. The dollar's
up and down, the dollar bill
itself torn and dirty. Our
famous know-how has gone awry,
our inventiveness nearly dry.
We've become careless. Everywhere gas-guzzlers, gouged
hulks, rust-cankered. The
streets cracked, the lawns
alitter. Subways, whole cities,
reeking harm in the night. We
do love funk and horror; so,
Television and the Mafia give
us what we need. For the rest,
flabbiness like ocean to ocean
carpeting, up to the knees.
Yes, we've become a nation of
first names. Oleaginous egos,
spread thinly, like a smile or
stain. Occlusions of desire,
seeking in rage release.
Certainly we're a Superpower
still. But when did America
become a dirty word around
the world?"

I ponder now these crotchety lines written at the end of the seventies, a low American decade. And I wonder if, in aging, I reproach America for losses that are really mine.

*

New Orleans, Washington, Philadelphia: I remember boarding incredulously a great, glittering, roaring plane—my first plane ride ever—then landing in a trance, feeling an alien chill in the air, and seeing maple leaves which had begun to turn yellow and red, outrageous colors on a tree. Three days after I arrived in Philadelphia, I rented a prim little room in a greystone suburban house in Upper Darby, and commenced my graduate studies, eyes bright like a conquistador's, tongue tied like an Indian maiden's.

But already I harbored traitorous thoughts. For a year, I studied diligently at the Moore School of Electrical Engineering, a squat, pseudo-Georgian building which housed ENIAC, the world's first digital computer. To my puzzlement, I found the courses there both casual and demanding. To my astonishment, I discovered that Americans studied not to pass dismal examinations but to understand. Yes, I thought, this is knowledge. But could I ever become a scientist? I had the intellectual passion, I persuaded myself, but lacked that numinous power, mathematical intuition, which penetrates the secrets of the universe. Still, I would try: I would risk myself among the pure ciphers of creation, ignoring the jejune gadgetry of engineering.

By the middle of my first year, Papoulos had disabused me. Among the intense drudges of Egypt, as among the resolute veterans now studying by my side, I felt I could hold my own. But Papoulos, wide-browed Papoulos, was a creature of a different kind. A curly-haired, large-eyed Greek, his brow faintly hinting at the ugliness of Socrates, Papoulos took no notes, carried no books. He sat in class, a slight smile playing around his thick lips. Yet his mind could dazzle. I suspected that Papoulos had jumped ship somewhere to enter the United States. I suspected, too, that he carried the dendrites of Euclid, Archimedes, and Pythagoras in his brain.

Euclid may have "seen beauty bare," but I began to long for a human geometry with no circles or squares. How could I express in cosines or tangents vague, poetic stirrings that I now gathered in a notebook, aptly titled "The Glimmering Well"—moonshine of Decadence, Ernest Dowson, and the young Yeats. The corridors of the Moore School appeared to me intolerably drab, its labs and libraries dreary. Still, I did well enough in my engineering courses to receive an invitation from the Honorary Society of Sigma Xi—which an American fellow-student promptly mistook for the "exclusive fraternity of Sigma Chi." But my spirit chafed. I had failed in one career (theoretical science) before starting, and I had no wish to succeed in the other (electrical engineering), already begun.

My adviser, Dr. John Brainard, understood. A shy, quiet Quaker, with steel-grey eyes and a laser-sharp mind, he sent me to consult with an assistant dean of Liberal Arts.

*

In the fall of 1947, unbeknown to my sponsors or parents, I enrolled in four undergraduate literature courses at the University of Pennsylvania Extension School. From the first day, I found myself moving in a vivid world of images, intuitions, sensuous recall, evoking somehow those distant summer afternoons on our Delta estate. How different, too, were the teachers of undergraduate literature, now thundering heroic passions in class, now whispering in realms of gold. Hearing Professors Harbeson lecture on "The Eve of St. Agnes," Leach on the *Tain Bo Cuailnge,* Boll on *Great Expectations,* Laurie on *The Playboy of the Western World,* I participated in a mode of exultant being which I had never experienced in a university before.

Thus, in Philadelphia, I tried to awaken from "Newton's sleep": neither science nor engineering, but literature would be my fate. I had written stories in English in my teens. (One, entitled "The Bronze Medal," set against the Napoleonic wars, crossed Conan Doyle's *The Exploits of Brigadier Gerard* with Thackeray's *Vanity Fair.*) I began to write stories again, ransacking dictionaries, thesauruses, maps, illustrated books, copying in a ledger specific names: of armors and birds, of dogs, flowers, and gems, of trees and wines, and all the signs of the zodiac. My interest in character and narrative, though, proved weaker than in self-enamored lyrical forms. I wrote poetry. Then, reading a few lines of Marvell or Keats, I would become mute. Would I ever have wit enough and time to write one memorable poem, one irrefutable line?

My Egyptian "mission" demanded that I continue to study electrical engineering; my own imperatives demanded otherwise. I tried to compromise. I attempted to enroll concomitantly in English and Electrical Engineering at Harvard, then at Columbia. The admissions director of the first said: "You don't have Latin. We wouldn't touch you"; the second asked in pain: "Why?" I could not explain, and so returned to Pennsylvania, rebuffed, resolute.

Officially still a member of the Moore School, I went again to see Dr. Brainard—scientists at Penn were always "doctors," humanists "professors." I said: "I want to change my field. I want to study for a Ph.D. in English."

"Hmm," he said, grey eyes twinkling. "How much reading have you done in English literature? Have you read Beaumont and Fletcher?"

"No, but I have taken some literature courses in the Extension School. I've done well in them."

"Hmm," he replied, gazing out of a huge window at the blank, brick wall across the street. "Perhaps you should see Professor Baugh. He's Chairman of the English Department, and a very distinguished medievalist. I'll call him."

A few days later, I went to see Professor Albert C. Baugh in his high-ceilinged, oak-panelled office in College Hall. He wore a white, starch-collared shirt, and his voice was crisp. He came quickly to the point: "If you have the equivalent of an undergraduate English major at Pennsylvania, we'll admit you to the Graduate Program."

"Could I apply for a scholarship?" I asked, feeling the sweat gather and begin to seep through my pores.

"Not the first year." Behind their fishbowl glasses, his eyes grew icy. "But we can talk about it later."

Back in my book-strewn room, I sat down and wrote two solemn letters, one resigning my mission from the Egyptian Education Bureau, the other informing my parents that I had done so. Then I wrote a third letter applying to the Summer Writer's Workshop at the University of Wisconsin in Madison. I had burned my bridges; as a "poet," I needed no bridge to soar.

*

Starting with the spring of 1948, I lived in a series of small, linoleum-smelling, attic rooms on Chestnut, Walnut, Pine Streets. I subsisted largely on hamburgers, chips, apples, peanuts, and chocolate bars, though I could have afforded a better diet. I lived to read, to write, carrying every evening into my lair bulging packs of books which I had wrested from their shelves in the University of Pennsylvania Library. I carried the books up the back steps, gloating, ravenous, as I imagined—now that I had begun to read Old English Literature—Grendel must have dragged his victims to his cave, breathing on them the air of his hungry maw. Now I played Grendel, now Dostoyevsky's Man from Underground; I played Büchner's Lenz, Hesse's Steppenwolf, and Chatterton's Chatterton. I pitied those humdrum mortals scurrying to their jobs in the morning, shuffling home again to sup, yawn, fall into dreamless sleep.

In my autodidactic rage, I tried to make up for centuries of colonial blight, years of my young life's waste. My earlier education had left my mind a honeycomb of ignorance, fancies, and facts. Now, I sat down to read enormous works at a stretch: *The Faerie Queene* in five mellifluous days, *Paradise Lost* in four booming nights. And when a professor casually dropped the name of a "masterpiece," the *Iliad,* the *Divine Comedy, War and Peace,* I rushed after class to the library, fearful that another student might outrace me to the shelves. I cultivated in my writing style a hieratic rhythm, some exotic turn of diction, twist of syntax, that I have faintly retained. Yet I also took correspondence courses in business English to keep

my working idiom plain. In short, I tried to will myself into a foreign language as others, masters of verbal exile like Conrad and Dinesen, Nabokov and Beckett, had already done.

*

In the early summer of 1948, nothing seemed to me more crucial than to test the limits of my writing gift. How light, perishable, was it? How fragile my literary judgment? I had heard of a few Egyptian authors—Taha Hussein, Shawki, Hussein Hykal, Tawfik El Hakim—honored in my family as one might honor a whirling dervish or beached whale. But I was in America now where living authors, however suspect, enjoyed some cultural status and financial reward. Their works circulated in libraries, found their way to classrooms, sometimes sold half a million copies through clubs. (I subscribed then to both the Book of the Month and Book Guild Clubs.) These writers demanded heirs. Was I one of theirs?

Fecklessly, I had enrolled in two courses at the Summer Writer's Workshop in Madison, one in "The Short Story" with Mari Sandoz, the other in "The Art of the Essay" with Professor Fulcher. (Poetry writing I kept jealously to myself.) It was a cool, green summer and my pencil—I have never learned to type—seemed fluent. Words spread unctuously on the pages, and the scent of adolescence, in late bloom, rose from each line. I began an essay called "Down the Nile" with an epigraph from Verlaine:

Le Nil, au bruit plaintif de ces eaux endormies,
Berce de rêves doux le sommeil des momies.

Professor Fulcher said, "You may do some distinguished writing in ten years," and Mari Sandoz said, "You like ideas better than people. But write on."

Later that summer, I flew to Geneva to meet my parents on neutral ground, and announce my irrevocable decision: I would become an author.

*

Long after, I wondered about my equivocal status, neither plain critic nor true poet, not a novelist either and an essayist reluctantly. And I wondered about art. What is this agony, evasion, dementia, this unholy obsession or divine possession, this shady simulacrum of life, this wound of nature, this ecstatic promise that we call art?

At first, I believed that Art was the expiation of Matter in Form. But now I see that art contests,

Buckminster Fuller, Sally Hassan, Norman O. Brown (back to camera), John Cage,
Beth Brown, Middletown, 1969

subverts, negates itself, a "fidelity to failure" (Beckett), and form forgets itself in anti-form. "The modern Orpheus sings on a lyre without strings," I wrote in *The Dismemberment of Orpheus* (1971, 1982). Torn finally apart by the Maenads, body scattered to the winds, Orpheus sings on as his head drifts seaward in the river Hebrus. Yet who would willingly seek dismemberment, woo all the woes of art?

Perhaps will has no place in the scheme of beauty. Something speaks through all artists, something *speaks them,* and for this they endure the torments of creation. Kafka, who should know, put it thus: "Our art is a dazzled blindness before the Truth: the light on the grotesquely distorted face is true, but nothing else is. . . ." What light is this? The "pure white light of being" (Henry Miller)? Or was Brentano's poet, in "The Story of the Just Caspar and Fair Annie" closer to the mark?

A certain humiliation makes us reticent, a feeling that comes over all those who barter in free spiritual capital, the immediate heavenly gifts. Scholars are less embarrassed than poets, for as a rule they have paid their tuition. . . . But the so-called poet is verily in a bad way, because as a rule he has played truant from school to climb Parnassus.

I doubted that scholars paid, more than poets, their dues to life. Quite the opposite, I suspected, was the case; and this suspicion led me, as early as *The Literature of Silence* (1967), to an interest in the "free spiritual capital" of writers, the margins of literature and mysticism.

But who, I wondered again, taught best? The scholar, the artist, the mystic, the warrior monk? True paideia is not only martial; it enables us to grow into (human) Being. Though they have become trite—*Musashi* now a bestseller in America—Zen and Bushido once offered a way of universal attentiveness, "not my song but yours," even as the sword flashes, timeless, to carve another's flesh out of time. But Bushido is irrecoverable to us in the West. What, then, in our schools, can quicken action, hone perception, calm the self—chattering macaque on a long leash—attune us to Being? What provisional silence can cleanse ideological discourse, dead speech?

To invoke such aims in our academies is to risk, again, the charge of "mysticism." Mysticism: facile dismissal, favored by dogmatists intolerant of all but their narrow portion of reality. Was William James mystical? Proust, Einstein? Whence this academic hostility to mysticism, to its slightest aura or trace? A Marxist, Zionist, or Feminist may prove no more rational than some "mystics," yet no stigma attaches itself to their commitment. Is it because men forgive attachments to factions, fractions—*my* side, *your* side—but never to the whole? The threat of mysticism: not vagueness or unreason, but a loyalty wider than most of us can bear.

*

I flew back from Geneva on a TWA Super Constellation. The four-engine prop-plane gradually fell behind the setting sun. The sky darkened at the "rondure of the earth" (Whitman), the engines roared drowsily into the night. I thought of all that I had left behind. I though of Whitman's "Europe," its "feet upon the ashes and the rags—its hands tight on the throats of kings." That Europe had not really vanished. I saw it in Paris, in the vain grandeur of its vistas, on which had settled the recent grime of inglorious history. I saw it in London, a stubborn, blackened city, eroded by war and empire. I thought, then, of Egypt, a land triply unblessed, in its people, geography, and natural resources, despite the high splendor of Pharoahs and Fatimid Sultans. But the pall of nineteenth century colonizers—Kléber, Cromer, Kitchener—had settled upon it now, and its aged, riparian spirit promised no rebirth.

Ah, I reproved myself, these fictions of "national character" serve only to explain away the inexplicable. But how else account for differences between Egypt and Switzerland or America today? Whence these outrageous discrepancies, which rend and crack the earth more than any quake? Could a Swiss banker or American businessman begin to apprehend the barnacle existence of a slum dweller in Cairo? And why do these rifts survive *internally,* survive between the *fellah* who has never heard of Switzerland and an Egyptian dowager I had just seen in Geneva, her great chest sagging with precious stones?

Tipping back my narrow seat, I tried vainly to sleep. Marxists, no doubt, would know the answer to such desperate queries, but I found in Marxist theodicy no cheer: the State preempted salvation, purging individual sin with torture or terror, the

State enforced pastoral servitude. I was a westering spirit in any case, westering in time as in space. And as I began to drowse, I recalled something I had once read: "Start now on that farthest western way, which does not pause at the Mississippi or the Pacific, nor conduct toward a worn-out China or Japan, but leads on direct a tangent to this sphere. . . ." Was it Thoreau?

*

Philadelphia. Graduate School for four years. After my M.S. (1948) in engineering, M.A. (1950) and Ph.D. (1953). Work, work—and women. Gradually, I felt part of me grow mute. Was it penury or sloth, my own faltering ambition, that served to constrict my fate? When I completed my M.A., Professor Chester, Chairman of the Graduate Program, called me in.

"You have done excellently on your master's examination," he said, looking mumpishly away. "Do you plan to go on for a Ph.D.?"

"Yes," I said.

"Then you don't need to take the doctoral examination. Just finish your courses, write your dissertation, and defend it well."

I was stunned. I remained at Penn out of need, inertia, gratitude. Yet the sobriety of the City of Brotherly Love, like the stodginess of the University of Pennsylvania, began to dampen my ardor. I found a few inspiriting teachers there, and others whose meticulous scholarship proved exemplary to their students through the years. But of intellectual passion, of mind as a place of high debate and imagination as a deeper, more vehement life, the university was singularly spare. Sartre and Camus? Passing fashions. Heidegger? Unknown. Marx, Freud, Kierkegaard? Irrelevant to literature. The New Criticism (then at its apogee)? Young man, stop reading the *Kenyon* and *Sewanee;* read *Modern Philology, Speculum, PMLA.* No wonder that I kept my distance from the university after graduation, and the university kept an even greater distance from me.

It came to me as a shock: few academics were intellectual. Fewer still encouraged their graduate students to write fiction or poetry. I could honor the conviction of certain professors that the Muse of Scholarship brooks no sublunary rivals. But I could not concede their innate hostility to the creative act, to literature itself. What impotence there, I wondered, turns so much knowledge into refined spite? What fear shapes academic lives into learned parodies of desire? I encountered at Pennsylvania no Faust.

But I did find in Schopenhauer's *The Art of Literature* a corresponding glee: "He who holds a professorship may be said to receive his food in the stall; and this is the best way with ruminant animals. But he who finds his food for himself at the hands of Nature is better off in the open fields (like a wolf)."

There was, of course, some self-irony in my glee: my own desk drawers filled with rejected stories, plays, and poems, my wastebasket overflowed. Decidedly, the writing was not going well. Then, one day, I sent out a seminar paper called "Toward a Method in Myth." It was accepted by a scholary journal. I submitted another, on Baudelaire, and it was accepted too.

Was I, then, but another scholar, "dry-as-dust"? A literary engineer, tinkering with bibliographies and notes? Could I make of teaching a career? I went to consult the Chairman of the English Department, Professor Albert C. Baugh.

He said: "Your creative writing is not pertinent to an academic career."

He said: "There are still nonstandard elements in your speech. It will be difficult to secure a teaching appointment in America."

He said: "Though your record is excellent, we ourselves couldn't give you an instructorship here. Not even an assistantship. We have already given you all the fellowships and scholarships we can."

At last, he leaned back: "Why don't you try to combine your English and Engineering training? Technical writers are now much in demand."

I left with visions of myself writing manuals for circuit-breakers and advertising copy for eggbeaters till I died in some decently modest house in Germantown. Better, I consoled myself, than a landlord in Egypt. It never occurred to me to blame my setbacks on chauvinism, racism, "the system." Why blame?

*

"Everything is political," ideologues now like to cant, wanting to claim for politics a forced priority in the whole of life. Yet in ancient Egypt, politics remained seamless with religion, agronomy, astronomy, art; it was part of eternity and daily life. So was it in ancient Greece. Aristotle wrote on politics, wrote on metaphysics, ethics, physics, logic, rhetoric, and poetics as well. That ideological priority of politics displaces pleasures of the body and a larger civility of mind. And if indeed "everything is political," should we not still discriminate between kinds of ideology— say fascism and vegetarianism—their values, goals, and exactions, their hidden claims on our being? For

some ideologies breed totalitarians, some terrorists; others make bigots, captives, or cowards of us all.

Like Nietzsche, I assumed "it is our needs that interpret the world; our drives and their For and Against." Why else do human beings continue to disagree, pretending to make reason of their discords, and out of their desires high justice? Why else, through all history, do they rage, beyond sex, faith, or race, convinced that Truth stands meekly at their side? Call it an ontic imperative, a will to power or being, unceasing, or *dur désir de durer:* this radical oppugnancy is what politics tries to mediate, and mediating, perpetuates.

*

The life of a graduate student is surly, claustral, unpolitic. Still, I learned during those years to live in the world, to fend for myself, and to overcome, with twinges of regret, my abysmal shyness. I learned to change a car tire, shop at the supermarket, darn my socks. I took part-time jobs, stacking books in the library and teaching conversational Arabic at the Berlitz School of Languages. And I learned to dance, going to Arthur Murray Studios, and dating one of their girls on the sly.

What did I think then of American women? I had no intuition of their nature. Certainly they were the prettiest, the most fresh, uncrumpled, I had ever seen—yet somehow aseptic. Tocqueville may have been too old-worldly in his judgment: "An American girl scarcely ever displays that virginal softness in the midst of young desires or that innocent and ingenuous grace which usually attend the European woman in the transition from girlhood to youth." And Henry Miller too passionately naive: "The face of the American woman is the index of the life of the American male. Sex either from the neck up or from the neck down. No American phallus ever reaches the vital center." Still, I sensed in the women I met some elusive lack, some attenuation *both* in their dream and lived lives.

I sensed a larger lack in American men. Forthright, energetic, hale, they also seemed, if not "childish," as Europeans say, rather incomplete. Perhaps I missed in them a certain nuance of being, literacy of the heart. Perhaps I missed only what I myself began to lack: the capacity for intense, for reckless friendship such as I had known in Egypt. There was, of course, no dearth of jollity in America, of generous and cordial good cheer. But heartiness had a way of slipping easily into farce. Seeing Shriners on the street, clowning in floppy tarboushes and outlandish garb, I was offended more by their travesty of American manhood than of Oriental rite. Ah, I chided myself, you still look on your new compatriots with alien eyes.

Among my new compatriots, I did find some kindred spirits, even if I could not rush to them with the headlong trust of adolescence. But then, I had not crossed the Mediterranean, the Atlantic, seeking friendship. I simply had not liked what I foresaw of my life in Eternal Egypt. But could I remain permanently here?

*

My days in Philadelphia were filled with one large lowering concern. The annual immigration quota for all Egypt was an even hundred; I would have to wait a hundred years before entering America as a permanent resident. But there were loopholes, loopholes even in the strict McCarran Act, my bane. Some foreign students advised me, leeringly, to marry an American woman, though the law was sexist then, and accorded a lower priority to alien husbands than to alien wives. I married a Dutch woman instead, who had been admitted to the United States as a permanent resident, and had served during the war, in Limburg and Brabant, in the Allied underground. It was not a marriage of civic convenience.

I met Bolly Koten through an American friend, Helen Doerfuss, at the Philadelphia International House. Six months later, a Justice of the Peace married us simply at Upper Darby. It was a marriage of young love, but until it broke, and after it broke, it remained a marriage of unwavering loyalty. It withstood many anxieties, deprivations.

III

Until now, I had no serious prospect of employment in America. Waiting in vain for a teaching job to materialize, Bolly and I decided to spend the summer of 1952 at the School of Letters (successor to the Kenyon School) to which I had been admitted. Bloomington, Indiana, was torrid, but my classes with R. P. Blackmur and Randall Jarrell proved more hieratic, inspiriting, than anything I had experienced before. And there were the flooded quarries where the visiting faculty—including Leslie Fiedler and Robert Fitzgerald that year—came with their girls to cool off. In naive awe, I saw them swim or flirt, figures in a mythic landscape, beyond my youthful ken. I was waiting for some myth of my own.

Then, in that late summer, before the term's start, though I had quite despaired of finding a teaching job, I received a call from Dr. C. Harold Gray, Head of the English Department at Rensselaer Polytechnic Institute, requesting an interview. The interview went well, and Dr. Gray offered me a full-time instructorship in English. Where, I thought, where but in America, would an Egyptian teach American literature to natives? Seven months later, Dr. Gray wrote the District Director of the Immigration and Naturalization Service a decisive letter on my behalf.

Three months of silence. Then, one indifferent morning in the summer of 1953, seven years after landing in New Orleans, I received in my mail "The Green Card," together with a curt, printed notice informing me that I had been "permanently admitted" to the United States and would qualify for citizenship in three years. I had been granted asylum. From history? From myself?

*

For seven years, I had struggled with the specter of repatriation. Now that specter had suddenly, bureaucratically, vanished. What, then, was it all about? What had I really meant to find in America? Was it scope, an openness of time, a more viable history? Call it, simply, a chance to stretch, grow, tinker a little with destiny.

I thought of all who had flocked to America, men and women, fleeing or seeking, driven by the most diverse motives. Yet psychological exiles or true nomads stand apart, their case shadier, thicker with complicity and silent intrigue. Who are these beings, forever on the move, full of dark conceits, rushing to meet the future while part of them still stumbles about, like a blind speleologist, in caverns of the past? What urgency speaks through their "homelessness'?

No doubt, all leaving is loss, every departure a small death—yes, journeys secretly know their end. Yet self-exile may conceal other exigencies. Rilke believed that the story of the Prodigal Son is a legend of "him who did not want to be loved," except by God alone, and so nourished the "profound indifference of his heart." Such pride, demonic pride, refuses the interdebtedness of all human hearts. Had I fled Egypt out of pride, denying family, friends, compatriots, detesting the argument of kinship and blood?

I could not really answer: I knew only that, since childhood, I loved deep-sea fish and far-out swimmers, and creatures that drive themselves to the limits of their nature, there where nature waits to be remade. And I loved, many years later, Pioneer 10, which, on 13 June 1983, became the first man-made object to leave entirely the solar system.

*

In my present—probably last—job at the University of Wisconsin, Milwaukee, I write about my first at Rensselaer Polytechnic Institute. The thirty-eight years of my academic career now seem a noisy blur. Yet moments, ideas, people, places break through the blur, plain moments devoid of childhood's sheen.

Troy, New York, was then a ramshackle, Depression town, but RPI, as I learned to call it, stood high on a hill, and on a slope higher still stood the clapboard barracks and Quonset huts in which married students lived. There Bolly and I found a tight, three-room apartment heated by a black oil stove that roared pleasantly into the night. Our neighbors watched over us placidly; we had only small talk to share. I rose with the sun, infants somewhere crying, and prepared for my eight o'clock classes, all six of them.

I did not know how to teach, and so looked intently at my students' eyes, hands. I wanted their attention, their interest besides. I taught three classes of composition, and panicked whenever my idiom wavered or diction lapsed. I taught also a class of sophomore literature, in which we read *The Great Gatsby, Tonio Kröger, The Death of Ivan Ilyich,* and felt happy when I saw an emotion spread slowly over the impassive faces before me. Gradually, my confidence grew.

My colleagues in the English Department built houses with their own hands or farmed. Others, who seemed keener on literature, drank with gusto. I, too, learned to drink as I sat next to Jim Westbrook in a roadhouse—he drove an Avanti—debating the ironies of Jane Austen. And I learned to converse with Alvin Kernan, now at Princeton, who practised Latin in his spare time and wrote crisply about Jacobean drama; with Ike Traschen, who liked best to assume the role of Dostoyevsky's Man from Underground while I played Zarathustra.

In that period, I felt my old addiction to movies return, intensify. I went to movies indiscriminately, the good, the bad, and the ugly. I sat there in the dark, feet propped up rudely on the seat in front, eating ice-cream bars, impersonating an American adolescent. On the way home from the late show, I would experience pangs of intellectual remorse. The next day, I would riffle through literary quarterlies till the library closed, then force myself to write essays crafted on the example of Blackmur, Brooks, or Tate. I wrote on Paul Bowles, Jean Stafford, J. D. Salinger, and sent the articles to Ray B. West who edited the Examination of New Writers Series in the *Western Review.* He accepted them. Thus began my interest in contemporary American fiction, and my concern for good critical prose.

At the end of my first year at RPI, my contract as Instructor of English was renewed, with a raise from $3,600 to $3,800. But Harold Gray had resigned as head of English to become Dean at the Julliard School of Music in New York. His resignation affected me personally, as might the loss of a new-found father. But the shock was not simply personal. He and Mrs. Gray had spent many years in the Middle East, teaching and writing, and they had returned to America alive to the world's variousness, uncompromising in their best values. Like John Brainard before him, like Victor Butterfield afterwards, Harold Gray defined for me an idea of American integrity that has perdured, untarnished.

When Gray departed, I sensed, or perhaps simply imagined, a whiff of xenophobia in the air. Ike Traschen said he smelled a waft of anti-Semitism. We both muttered about leaving when Kernan accepted an offer from Yale.

*

I have personally encountered little prejudice in America. Perhaps I belong to a minority too marginal, too exotic, for prejudice; perhaps, anticipating no prejudice, I summon none; perhaps, unconsciously, I avert my face from the bigotry I meet. Certainly I do not permit myself to be "insulted," as some are nowadays eager to claim, by every passing oaf.

Once, in Geneva during the fifties, my father asked me: "Ihab, are American Jews hostile to you because of your name?" "But no," I answered, taken aback. "It's American anti-Semites who are the problem. They expect me to hate Jews." Then, after the Arab-Israeli War of 1973, I began to feel a certain uneasiness toward me among a few Jews. That year, at a dinner preceding a lecture I gave at a Midwestern university, a nervous academic confessed: "Professor Hassan, I must tell you. As a Jew, I found it hard to come to this dinner."

Or did that uneasiness start earlier, with the War of 1967? I recall an incident at the home of Melvin and Judy Friedman who gave a party for us when we first moved to Milwaukee. Suddenly Judy burst on me, eyes blazing with merriment: "Ihab, will you come with me? We have a dear friend who wants to meet you, but can't bring himself to walk over to an Egyptian, he says. I think he's less sore than scared."

Rage, it seems, remembers rage; a mythic paranoia infects us all. My shadow falls on another, and its touch turns him into a freak. Thus Leslie Fiedler, whom I have known for nearly forty years: "What children's books tell us, finally, is that maturity involves the ability to believe the self normal, only the other a monster or Freak." Still, though all black rivers run from the unconscious, we dwell on the plains of history. Had American anti-Semitism, then, a particular character, different from the anti-Semitism I saw in Egypt in my youth? I could not really answer, so unctuous were Egyptian hypocrisies and snobberies under Farouk.

Eugene Ionesco, Ihab Hassan, Jean-Francois Lyotard, Milwaukee, 1977

*

Chance—we also call it fate—once again intervened. In the late summer of 1954, I received a call from Alexander Cowie, then Chairman of the English Department at Wesleyan University. The Department suddenly needed a replacement, he said, and he had been talking with Robert Spiller, one of my teachers at Penn—would I come to Middletown for an interview? I knew nothing of Wesleyan, and did not like its name; but Kernan said: "You'd be crazy not to go. It's one of the Little Three." This sounded even more occult, and so to hide my befuddlement, I packed an extra shirt and drove off to Connecticut the next day.

It was a whimsical interview with three gentleman-scholars. We lingered over Gilbert and Sullivan and hurried past French Symbolism, on which I had written my dissertation—its full title was "French Symbolism and Modern British Poetry: Yeats, Eliot, and Edith Sitwell." I sensed that Cowie, having committed himself to the initiative, wanted to hire me, though he had no power to do so. At the end, he said: "President Victor Butterfield also wants to see you. I'll give you directions to his country place, out by Candlewood Lake." I drove back nearly to the New York state border, twice losing my way.

When I finally arrived at Butterfield's place, he was on top of a bulldozer, prying out huge boulders from the side of a hill. A craggy, leathery man, he climbed down casually, gripped my hand, and said: "Glad to see you. I'm building a road up that hill. Let's have some coffee." He walked to the cabin, and we stopped talking only two hours later, when the sun had set. We talked about everything, especially teaching, which he prized above all else. Fortunately, I had

just read Gilbert Highet's *The Art of Teaching,* and was able to keep up my end. But Butterfield, a preternatural listener, could draw anyone out by the sheer candor and power of his interest in liberal education. He offered me the job; RPI was not eager to keep me; Bolly and I moved to Middletown in the fall of 1954 and remained there sixteen years. These were galvanic years.

Wesleyan University was then a selective men's college, less generally esteemed, perhaps, than Amherst or Williams, but richer—in Xerox stocks—and more dynamic. After the war, Butterfield had recruited a brilliant, maverick faculty, many from the old Office of Strategic Services, and recruited the students to challenge them. The humanities faculty included a young classicist called Norman O. Brown, a historian, Carl Schorske, and a literary scholar, Fred B. Millett, who became my intellectual mentors or provocateurs.

Brown, secretive and saturnine, was not yet the great guru of the sixties, Dionysus in America; that was to come with *Life against Death* (1959) and *Love's*

Body (1966). His temperament was radical, truly innovative, mystically dark—and not wholly innocent of malice or spite. Calvin and Marx, Swift and Freud, not to mention Madame Blavatsky, shaped his insights. Our offices were in the same white, Greek-revival building, Russell House, and this led to encounters, sometimes confrontations, of every kind. Working in my second-floor office late one night, I heard his heavy step on the carpeted stairs. He opened my office door and stared at me gloomily. I started to say: "There is something . . ."; he interrupted: "There is nothing," and ran downstairs, laughing all the way maniacally.

Schorske was a child of light, a Settembrini figure, just as Brown appeared shadowy by contrast, like Naphta in Mann's *The Magic Mountain.* Clear of mind and marvelously eloquent, Schorske lacked Brown's daemonic drive, and was not immune to pomposity. I felt closer to Brown, though his sullen wit could cut deeply. As for Millett, older than either, a flamboyant New England Mr. Chips, teacher, recluse, and aesthete in equal parts, he decided with a flourish to take me under his wing.

With Millett, Schorske, and Brown, I taught in the elite Freshman Integrated Program, a triple, coordinated course in literature, history, and philosophy, from Homer to Joyce—the very best course I have ever taught, and the course that taught me, more than any other, how to teach. Later, I inherited from Millett his popular course on Major Modernists—Yeats, Proust, Joyce, Mann, Kafka, Lawrence, Eliot, Gide, etc.—a course that has not merely withstood the rancor of time, but continues to move, indeed terrify me.

But the best exemplar of Wesleyan's ethos may have been Peter Boynton. Hired from Princeton, where he refused to complete his dissertation on Conrad, he remained, preeminently, gloriously, a teacher. He did publish two uncanny novels, *Games in the Darkening Air* (1966) and *The Eavesdropper* (1969), before his premature death at fifty-two. A huge hulk of a man—he once served as an MP in the Pacific—he possessed a large appetite for experience, an agile mind, elusive intuitions, a sense of the quiddity of things—he stroked objects. He was independent, yes, but seductive too, stylish, everyone's favorite bachelor. His charisma derived ultimately from his extraordinary gift for friendship. In my flailing and thrashy years, he would look at me with a slight, quizzical smile, then ask: "And who are we nowadays?" We shared the same birthday, six years apart.

Was it a golden age at Wesleyan University or simply an excitable time for me? Call it an Athenian moment, at least for those who longed to converse or descant. The faculty may have become more "distinguished" there, and the students more diverse, but I doubt that Wesleyan has since surpassed that fervor of mind. I worked at night, and during the day sat, when I was not teaching, in Downey House sipping coffee with colleagues young and old, from every field. I learned more in Downey House, listening and talking, more that remains vital to me, than I ever did at the Universities of Cairo or Pennsylvania.

*

I reread now some of the early notebooks I kept at Wesleyan:

> I am first a man. Asked to define my philosophy or politics, I always state my name.
> But I am also a teacher, and my responsibility adheres to a vision of the human adventure, not to a canon, method, or text.
> Great teachers have something to teach. That is a given like grace, or else earned by a great effort of the spirit.
> No life wholly satisfied in literature can bring to it the highest vision. No life wholly fulfilled in criticism can bring to literature the deepest insight.

Brave words, I think, rare thoughts that even so heroic a man of letters as Jean-Paul Sartre, in his autobiography *The Words,* finds illusory.

Still, when I read now my fellow critics, sequestered like myself in academies, I want to recover part of my young ambition, callowness and all. Some professors devote themselves to ethereal Ironies; others, in desperate reaction, to prove the World exists, kick Language, thinking to stub their toes on a stone; yet others, afraid to sleep, cant Ideology into the dawn. Yeats rebuked the scholars: "Bald heads forgetful of their sins." But humanists can be scholars and more than scholars, and must recall what turbulence makes the spirit whole. Can humanists, I wonder, learn to dream again, and dreaming wake to mediate actively between Culture and Desire, Language and Power, History and Hope? And can mediation retain a measure of "negative capability" (Keats)?

I wonder, again, about knowledge, which humanists have made their own. Knowledge is virtue, Socrates said; knowledge is power, Bacon rejoined. Renaissance humanists attributed to education everything from civic virtue to sexual courtesy, from aesthetic awareness to moral insight and even eternal life. In the New World, the educational premise sustained the American Dream for two centuries, though neither dream nor premise now escapes challenge. And in "developing" countries? The mandate remains practical, technological, illiberal—or else fundamentalist, sweeping away knowledge in the name of Allah, a *jihad* against history.

Between pseudo-technocracy and Islamic reversion, what, then, can avail? Something, I think, beyond nationalism, socialism, revivalism, beyond convulsive hope and each day's dram of despair. Yes, a sense of worth, relief from need, the will to change, and, withal, reverence for life, all life, whose staggering design we have barely begun to glimpse. Also: imagination, cognitive wonder, a faith in human gnosis. For though we learn and learn all our lives only to die at the end, that labor of self-perfection passes, as if by Lamarckian inheritance, into all the generations waiting to be born. And who knows but that such ceaseless labor, unremitting gnosis, accrues to the perfection of the universe? Thus mind transforms itself even as it alters the cosmos, and this, too, is "education": *the education of creation*. In this, scientists, poets, and mystics may be of one imagination compact.

*

Violence was on the rise in America; each year in the sixties brought increase in its horrible and brilliant uses. Was violence, then, really native to the American Dream? We sue and savage one another, wrench time and ravage nature, claiming right for every expectation and might for every hope. Our needs have become absolute.

In those days at Wesleyan, I looked to the tiger for instruction, and I still believe the path of spirit traverses much strangeness and fury. But there is meanness in violence too, a saurian quality closer to the alligator than to the eagle or tiger. It has nothing of the glory I once experienced, trawling for marlin off Long Island, when the fish hit the line like dark lightning, and I felt the shock travel to the base of my skull even as the leader snapped. True, I had been in no fistfights in my forty years in America, nor had I come close to any physical harm. Yet I sensed, with the assassination of John F. Kennedy, a dread, homicidal power gather itself in the land.

I remember a conversation with Norman Mailer shortly after that dire event. It was at a faculty party at Wesleyan, in one of those desperately liberal

homes. Bland furnishings; flowered paper napkins; decent, bearded faces; Spock in the bathroom; a second-hand Volvo in the garage, somewhat battered on principle. Mailer looked grumpy, a big tumbler of bad bourbon in his hand. I tried to cheer him up, though I was not entirely clear of head or really of good cheer. We talked about violence, about Oswald.

"If I were Oswald," I said, "I would have planned everything perfectly to the last detail. I would have cocked the rifle, placing Kennedy's handsome head in my telescopic sight. And I would have held it there for five seconds. But I wouldn't have felt the need to pull the trigger, knowing that I could."

Mailer took a big sip of bourbon. The light in his irises sparked as he fired back: "You write about America, Ihab, but you still don't understand. Our history is too short: we don't have time for symbolic gestures."

I knew he was right. Still, an immigrant's hope remains exacting: I abhorred the assassin's cankered expectations, his mutilated self-regard.

Geoffrey Hassan, Great Pyramid at Giza, 1976

*

Wesleyan University had, of course, other, less enchanting aspects. Inbred, insular, intensely self-regarding, it believed itself the *omphalos* of the universe. Gradually, too, as the fifties fled before the sixties, it became a trendy, gossipy place, given to fits of radical and homoerotic chic. A fashionable fringe of the faculty began to muddle sex, style, food, politics, marriage. Petronius supplanted John Wesley, and I found myself sitting often at the former's table.

I separated from Bolly in 1960, divorced in 1966. (She lived on in Middletown, with our only son, Geoffrey, until she died in 1978.) The freneticism of the age seemed to coincide with Wesleyan's and my own. But this was also a formative period, shaping my interest in avant-garde movements, from Dada and Surrealism to Postmodern trends. I espoused disjunctive, even wrenching, change, and often found myself in running debate—say about the Beats—with more patient and worldly colleagues like Richard Wilbur and Paul Horgan. I even practised "Dadacticism," a pedagogy of surprise, welcoming the fecundity of the absurd. Still, part of me, unabashedly Romantic, continued to believe in the Imagination, that it was the teleological organ in human evolution, predicting, directing, fulfilling change.

In that same period, John Cage commenced to visit the campus. The Wesleyan University Press had published his epochal books, *Silence* (1961) and *A Year From Monday* (1967), and his influence had begun to spread in American culture. It proved in my case key. For Cage, like our mutual friend, "Nobby" Brown, took immense risks; he possessed the genial ruthlessness of the true avant-gardist. But whereas the genius of Brown appeared to me protestant, a whisper demonic, that of Cage was reconciled, almost saintly, if a touch mischievous. No one could resist Cage's open-mouthed, Zen-fool laugh, black eyes glittering with cosmic gaiety.

I owe Cage my interest in new modes of literary subversion, which I first explored in "The Dismemberment of Orpheus," *American Scholar* (Summer 1963), and "The Literature of Silence," *Encounter* (January 1967), later in two books bearing those titles. I owe him also the impulse to experiment with my own prose, in a hybrid genre of cultural criticism, autobiography, narrative, dream, and citation, which exasperated traditional scholars with my two subsequent books, *Paracriticisms* (1975) and *The Right Promethean Fire* (1980). But above all, I owe Cage, and Brown, the courage to endure disapprobation,

personal or professional, without bitterness—the imagination of risk.

Wesleyan University was ferment; it moiled continually like yeast in a sealed jar. It did not always tolerate values other than its own, being more anxious to proclaim tolerance than to practice it; but it always rewarded merit, which it recognized on its own terms. It certainly supported my work, and granted me generous sabbaticals to supplement two Guggenheim Fellowships (1958-59, 1962-63) and a Senior Fulbright Lectureship (1966-67) to France. It could even tempt mavericks to become, at least briefly, administrators. Thus I came to serve as Chairman of the English Department (1963-64, 1968-69), Director of the College of Letters (1964-66), and Director of the Center for the Humanities (1969-70), to my own incredulity.

English Departments are what they are; the College of Letters was different. It embodied Butterfield's belief in the eros of ideas, the intimacy of knowledge. For three years, students lived and worked in one of three units: the College of Letters, the College of Social Studies, or the College of Quantitative Studies. In the first year, students shared a common, interdisciplinary core of studies; in the last, they worked on theses and independent projects. Housed in handsome new quarters, the college faculties and resident students enjoyed informal relations, and soon acquired the aura of elitism, an aura they did nothing to dispel. Their real distinction, though, rested on their aversion to parochial, to narrow knowledge.

More catholic even was the Center for the Humanities. Modeled vaguely on institutes of advanced studies at Princeton and Stanford, it remains unique among undergraduate colleges. But then, Wesleyan could never make up its mind to be a university or a college. Under its director, Paul Horgan, the Center became a gracious place of learning, where faculty and students could work with distinguished fellows. These included, at various times, Edmund Wilson, Walter J. Ong, Herbert Read, Frank Kermode, Stephen Spender, C. P. Snow, Pamela Hansford-Johnson, Hans Jonas, Lucien Goldmann, Michael Polanyi, Willard Van Orm Quine, Jean Stafford, among many others. In my last year at Wesleyan, I directed the Center, and was fortunate to invite John Cage, Buckminster Fuller, Norman O. Brown (then at Santa Cruz), Harold Rosenberg, Hayden White, Frank Kermode, Richard Poirier, Leslie Fiedler, Daniel Stern, Michael Wolff, and Louis Mink as fellows. Their contributions appeared in a volume called *Liberations* (1971), which I edited.

This was for me the end of Wesleyan—and the end of the sixties.

*

I spent sixteen years at Wesleyan University. The years have an inner and ineluctable shape, moment by lived moment. They also have an outer shape, that of gratuitous retrospection. The two shapes coincide only in rare moments of grace. Such a moment came, on a day like any other day, in the winter of 1962.

The phone rang at my desk in Russell House. The speaker was my future and second wife, my present wife, Sally Margaret Greene. She spoke in a beautiful voice; I could not know she was also beautiful. She identified herself as Chairman of the Vermont Conference and a senior at the University of Vermont. Would I speak at the Conference in April? The other speakers would be the cartoonist Jules Pfeiffer and Oscar Lewis, author of *The Children of Sanchez.* I said I would. Later, I discovered that she had first called Norman O. Brown. He had said, "I'm sorry, I don't go to conferences. But there is a young man here. . . ." And he had given her my name.

Sally and I were married in 1966. All my books, after the first, have been dedicated to her.

*

My first book, *Radical Innocence,* was dedicated to my son, Geoffrey Karim Hassan. He and Sally are easy, good friends. But I experienced my greatest pain on his account, during estrangement and divorce from his mother. She was Dutch, stubborn, selfless, and brave. In the course of time, our marriage tore— I have no need to say more. In 1960, after returning from my first Guggenheim, spent in Rome, we decided to live apart. Though Bolly has died now, Geoffrey grown, other women gone their way, the white pain of those years, his childhood, has seared some parts of my brain.

I think back of a wintry day in Connecticut, 1978: deep snow, the woods stark, grey and white birches peeling against a ragged sky, the streams almost frozen, trickling blue-black beneath the ice. Dead of winter, they say, and I had come to visit

Ihab and Sally Hassan, Cassis, 1975

Bolly, a woman dying. I brought a dozen perfect yellow roses from the airport. She protested the gift, pleased, while she put them in an earthen pot she had turned. She wanted to burden no one; her self-pity, if any survived her convent childhood, remained invisible; over the years, her solitude became essential. We played a record I had also brought, sonatas for violin and clavier, in the glassed-in parlor. The winter sun filtered through the birches. I kept thinking: "Mozart and terminal cancer in one room." She bragged shyly about her "other" healthy organs. When she looked at the late light on the snowdrift outside, she said: "It's beautiful." I wondered: "What world she sees there with those slate-green eyes?" Before I left, she gave me a sliced apple "to freshen my mouth." I would not go with her, though she asked me twice, to a large Sunday brunch given by old friends in Middletown. She lies buried now in Tewksbury, having donated her body to the Harvard Medical School.

*

All writers despair. Even Flaubert throws up his hands: "We take notes, we make journeys: emptiness! emptiness! We become scholars, archaeologists, historians, doctors, cobblers, people of taste. What is the good of all that? Where is the heart, the verve, the sap?" Where the verve and sap?

Once, in Sohâg, I saw a peasant's bride alight from a camel, and the one, red rose in her veil set the street on fire.

On a steep slope in Garmisch, I glimpsed a slim apparition slalom past in a pale blue negligé—it was Fasching—the sun in her flying yellow hair, a faery in the wind.

In Trondheim, I followed to my table a hostess with mauve eyes, who moved with such easeful pride, all the queens of Europe might have whispered in her veins.

And once, in Montpelier, I saw a Vermont beauty bound across a snow-patched maple field, Proserpine in early spring, and that woman became my wife Sally.

*

My autobiography nears its end, my life still unfinished. Another chance encounter, another turn of the road.

In 1968, I ran into Melvin Friedman, an old-time friend, at the MLA Convention in New York. Such conventions are carnivals of banality, enlived by personal encounters, unconventional practices—one year, I interviewed all the candidates for my department at the Playboy Club. Melvin spoke to me of a "big professorship, lots of free time for travel and research, they call it a Vilas Research Professorship," at the University of Wisconsin in Milwaukee. A true Wesleyanite, I wondered: who is Vilas, where is Milwaukee? But I applied. And now I write this autobiographical essay from Milwaukee where I have lived since 1970.

It is an American story. William Freeman Vilas was a public citizen, benign plutocrat—timber, tanneries, vast land holdings which became Vilas County—a Postmaster General under President Cleveland, a U.S. Senator from Wisconsin and a power in the Bourbon Club during the Gilded Age. He endowed "the most cherished chair in the University system." And here I am, heir to some part of his fortune and vision, westering from Cairo, yet still some distance from "that farthest Western way. . . ."

I like Milwaukee, this spacious Midwestern city, except in its reluctant spring. I like its candid cityscape, spare population, fitful lake, forever changing colors from tan to blue-green through a spectrum of fluid shades. I like even its cold climate—let others seek their final truths in the Sun Belt. And I like its university, committed to a Wisconsin idea of practical democracy in civic as in educational life, not, like Wesleyan, to some East Coast concept of *noblesse oblige* turned into radical chic. On some days, though, I rage at the triumphant "mediocracy" that is also part of the "Wisconsin idea" in education, and in raging prove that human beings want it both ways, want it all.

Indubitably, our lives, Sally's and mine, gained some amplitude in Milwaukee, of time as of space. We travel together, I to lecture, she to write of food and far places. And as we travel, time thickens with experience—in Salzburg, Grenoble, Kyoto, Cassis, Bellagio, Munich, Tokyo, London, Canberra, where we have lived, in Marrakesh, Bergen, Lahore, Lisbon, Seoul, Milano, Istanbul, Warsaw, Delhi, Bucharest, Singapore, Moscow, Utrecht, Shanghai, Paris, Kuala Lumpur, Point Barrow, Hong Kong, Uppsala, Corinth, which we have visited—time thickens and fills, as it would not had we been reading literary theory instead.

*

Who are the nomads? What brings on the traveling mood? Though it is not always metaphysical like Ishmael's ("Whenever I find myself growing grim about the mouth; whenever it is a damp, drizzly November in my soul; whenever I find myself involuntarily pausing before coffin warehouses, and bringing up the rear of every funeral I meet . . .—then, I account it high time to get to sea as soon as I can.''), that mood moves us all.

I know counselors against travel. Thoreau boasted that he ''traveled much in Concord''; and Emerson said, ''We owe to our first journeys the discovery that place is nothing. . . . My giant goes with me wherever I go.'' True, travel may betray some insufficiency in us, a dubious need that deeper natures refuse. Still, the Koran says: ''And God hath spread the earth as a carpet for you, that ye may walk therein through spacious paths.'' Walking these paths, we learn the ways of men, and meet in ourselves the stranger we most dread to meet. We experience the world interactively, feeling the shock of differences even as we absorb them in us. Seeing how human beings vary in shape, language, custom, creed, can we hope to coax our distinctions into wider civility?

But voyages are also errancies of the soul; they whisper of the unknown. Who has not turned the corner of a strange street and come suddenly upon

With Ackbar Abbas and Peter Conrad at Repulse Bay, Hong Kong, 1988

Gautama, Cleopatra, Tamburlaine? Voyages whisper loss, departure, things thrown to the wind, and evoke that very country ''from whose bourne no traveler returns.'' In journeys, we hear the cadences of the universe itself, and endure our death, going hence, coming hither. ''Ripeness is all.''

*

Increasingly, I came to consider travel a central metaphor of our world, a condition of our planet, globalized by technologies, tribalized by local traditions and concerns. Travel is not simply motion; it is power, knowledge, aspiration, an analogue to the writing process itself, a collision of cultures, a strange, post-colonial quest. Thus I wrote in *Selves at Risk* (1990):

> This is a book about quests in contemporary American letters, and about contemporary reality. These quests are of a particular kind. They solicit adventure—I would call them ''questures,'' but we have had critical neologisms enough. They also affirm essential values even as they assay new modes of being in the world. Spirit, effort, peril constitute these journeys, in fiction or nonfiction, as does the great wager with death. Such journeys put articulate selves at risk, selves that may incur failure or folly but always spurn the glossy ironies, the camp and kitsch of our day.
>
> Still, one may ask: Quest? Adventure, in the fading glare of our century? In this era of satellites and supersonic jets, of the ubiquitous McDonald's and pervasive Panasonic? In our coddled jacuzzi culture, our cybernetic, if not quite cyborg, society of acronyms and first names, where acedia measures lives between hype and fix? Indeed, the very name of quest may strike some as quaint, lacking as it does deconstructionist brio, Marxist bravura, or feminist coloratura.
>
> Yet the spirit of quest endures, unquavering, with stiff upper lip. It endures, moreover, confident of its future and proud of its (largely British) pedigree. From rain forests, across oceans, steppes, savannahs, saharas, to the peaks of the Andes or Himalayas, men and increasingly women still test the limits of human existence. They test spirit, flesh, marrow, imagination, in a timeless

quest for adventure, for meaning really, beyond civilization, at the razor edge of mortality. And they return, with sun-cracked skin and gazes honed on horizons, to tell the tale.

My own travels, though, were largely free of risk. Still, they brought home to me some sense of Emersonian experience; of life as "not intellectual or critical, but sturdy"; of human existence as but "a tent for a night," which, sick or well, we inhabit till we "finish that stint;" of spirit as "matter reduced to an extreme thinness: O *so* thin!", yet somehow serving as "its own evidence" throughout our errancies.

But travel was not only metaphysical; it also brought people, people speaking foreign tongues, into our lives. I think of Iwao Iwamoto. I first met him when he began translating *Radical Innocence;* he ended by translating Japan for me. His impeccable courtesy of the heart—though he had experienced the devastations of Tokyo and Yokohama as a boy—his loyalty, taught me friendship anew, its clear thread unbroken, unknotted in three decades. I think of Ackbar Abbas, through whose veins all the blood of Asia flows. Born in Hong Kong—his father, a courageous Malay journalist, lies buried in Macao—Ackbar might have been born in Cairo, Lima, or Cracow, so essential his decency, natural his dignity, seamless his tact. And I think of diminutive Lu Fan in Jinan. She suffered immeasurably as a child, youth, even in her old age, and wrote her story for Sally, a tale immaculate of complaint. In her seventies now, she remains undaunted by power or pain. In the presence of these three and of a few rare beings like them, I deplore the unredeemed spiritual vulgarity of more brilliant minds I have known; I feel twinges of shame.

There are others: Hans Mayer, overwhelmingly erudite, engagingly vain, who initiated me into the dense mysteries of Central European culture; André Le Vot, proud and shy Breton, whose generosities of feeling awakened me to another France; Malcolm Bradbury, Chris Bigsby, Christopher Butler, English friends; and others—Peter Conrad, Régis Durand, Kaiser Haq, Yuan Yuan, Marc Chénetier, Malashri Lal, Danuta Zadworna-Fjellestad, Oya Başak, Brigitte Scheer, Shuichi Kato, Giovanna Borradori, Gerhard Hoffmann, A. N. Kaul, Alfred Hornung, Paul Noack, and how many more?—who flung open so many "magic casements" on our dappled, motley world.

And I think still of more colleagues, country-men, who gave and took in friendship throughout my later years: Robert Corrigan, William Halloran, Melvin Friedman, Jim Kuist, Matei Calinescu, Thomas Van Alyea, Norman Holland, Walter Abish, Marc Pachter, Jerry Klinkowitz, Murray Krieger, Paul Levine. . . .

*

Travels, conferences, reputations, careers: there is an ineluctable vanity in all this, disguised as "professional concerns." Living in Milwaukee, am I really cut off, as some friends warned, from the Eastern establishment? Who in New York, beside Elie Wiesel and Richard Poirier, has shown interest in my work? Why have references to that work been so reluctant or spare? What makes my "paracriticism" more acceptable abroad than at home? Clattering queries that any sensuous experience—say an evening at Jean Banchet's peerless restaurant, "Le Français," in nearby Wheeling—can prove nul.

Sometimes, though, sitting in Milwaukee on a moody afternoon, I try to imagine what my life in Egypt might have been. I cannot do it; an iron door clangs shut. But then, in our travels, passing through some distant provincial town—Kwangju, Lublin, Djikili, Tromsö—I have a sudden, dreadful intuition of what it must mean to exist there, from birth to death, feeling the blood, the years, leak away. I had a still nearer intuition of Egypt, passing through Athens some years ago: a stifling moment of heat, dust, noise, young men in short sleeves drifting through shabby streets, old ornate buildings, their cornices, carya-tides, peeling on hovels below—most of all, the sense of durance, merciless contraction in the gut. It was, finally, an intuition of prisons: hospitals, asylums, monasteries, dungeons, any occluded relation or caved-in self.

Such places, though, may offer a supreme spiri-tual challenge. I first felt that challenge in Egypt when I thought that my plans for leaving might miscarry. I felt it again, decades later, reading Thomas Mann's *The Holy Sinner,* in which the incestu-ous saint, Pope Gregory, clings to a tiny, bare, rock island for seventeen years in harsh penance. Then, later still, I saw in London Arnold Wesker's play, *Caritas,* concerning Christine Carpenter, a four-teenth-century anchoress who renounced the world and immured herself in a vault not larger than a roomy grave. How can spirit subsist in such stony confinement, without day or night, unless it breaks out into vast inner spaces? Was it not precisely there, in that intolerable constriction of need, implosion of

Traveling by plane, 1989

desire, that heroic destinies were clarified like dia-
monds in the burning, black bowels of the earth?

For a long time after leaving Egypt, I had a bad,
recurrent dream. I dreamt that I was compelled to go
back, complete some trivial task—close a door left
ajar, feed a canary, whisper a message. There was
terror in that banal dream, terror and necessity, and
also the sense, within the dream itself, that I had
dreamt it before, and within that feeling that each
time I dreamt the dream, something would work out:
I would no longer need to go back. The dream
became less frequent with the years, after Sally
entered my life; to my conscious knowledge, I no
longer dream it. Is that dreamlessness itself but
subterfuge? I like to think of it, rather, as a hint of
unconcern, that heedlessness or detachment which
comes, to those who seek it, in good season—I may
even return someday to Egypt.

Some things have come to me like grace: Sally, a
sane body, a few friends. Most things I strove to earn:
America, and all that America has enabled in my life.
But I am not certain that grace and effort are not
tangents to our souls, tangents meeting every night in
the dark.

When I think of the Egypt I fiercely fled, on
which the sun rose in the clear, dry dawn of history
and now has set, perhaps never to rise again; when I
think of the America to which I deliriously came, a
land violently dreaming the world into a better place;
when I think of everything real, implacable in my
existence, which neither age nor tragedy can dim—
when I think of these, I know then that Time has kept
its secret from my prying mind, and that all my
writing, this autobiography, remains vain. But I
know, too, with the deeper, stranger certainty of
faith, that such "vanity" is itself augury and sign. We
come to sentience in a universe which returns us to
signs, perhaps a larger sentience, of its own.

Some earlier parts of this essay appeared, in another form, in
the author's *Out of Egypt*, Carbondale: Southern Illinois University Press, 1986.

BIBLIOGRAPHY

Criticism:

*Radical Innocence: Studies in the Contemporary American
Novel*, Princeton University Press, 1961.

Crise du Héros dans le Roman Américain Contemporain, Minard, 1963.

The Literature of Silence: Henry Miller and Samuel Beckett, Knopf, 1967.

The Dismemberment of Orpheus: Toward a Postmodern Literature, Oxford University Press, 1971, revised edition, University of Wisconsin Press, 1982.

(Editor) *Liberations: New Essays on the Humanities in Revolution,* Wesleyan University Press, 1971.

Contemporary American Literature: 1945–1972, Ungar, 1973.

Paracriticisms: Seven Speculations of the Times, University of Illinois Press, 1975.

The Right Promethean Fire: Imagination, Science, and Cultural Change, University of Illinois Press, 1980.

(Editor with Sally Hassan) *Innovation/Renovation: New Perspectives on the Humanities,* University of Wisconsin Press, 1983.

The Postmodern Turn: Essays in Postmodern Theory and Culture, Ohio State University Press, 1987.

Selves at Risk: Patterns of Quest in Contemporary American Letters, University of Wisconsin Press, 1990.

Other:

Out of Egypt: Scenes and Arguments of an Autobiography, Southern Illinois University Press, 1986.

Contributor to *Literary History of the United States* (edited by Robert E. Spiller and others; revised edition), Macmillan, 1974. Also contributor to numerous journals and newspapers, including *American Scholar, Kenyon Review, Comparative Literature, Critical Inquiry, Journal of American Folklore, New York Times Book Review, Salmagundi, South Atlantic Quarterly, New Literary History,* and *Saturday Review.* Member of editorial board, *American Quarterly,* 1965–67. Member of advisory board, *Diacritics,* 1973—, *Humanities in Society,* 1978—, and *PMLA,* 1979–83.

George Hitchcock

1914-

SOME SKETCHES FROM A LIFE

George Hitchcock, 1987

My Churches

Today on the trailhead seventy-five hundred feet up on Mount Shasta I found a star. Neither a celestial nor a metaphoric star but a metallic paper one, exactly like the ones Miss Liljeqvist used to paste into my presentation Bible. Silver for attendance, gold for successful recitations. The star I found today was golden; what it was doing on the trail up Shasta I have no idea, unless God had placed it there to summon me back to Miss Liljeqvist and her Presbyterian certainties after sixty or more lapsarian years.

Miss Liljeqvist was *beautiful,* that much of the Lord's message I do remember. In fact I think it was

her rosy Norse beauty that led me to Presbyterianism—I know for a certainty that that was what kept me pasting silver and gold stars in the Good Book for the next year or two. It certainly wasn't their message, which I thought too gloomy by far.

My mother did not exactly encourage my attendance at Sunday school. She *tolerated* it, on the grounds that most of my peers were forced to spend Sunday mornings there and she didn't want me to grow up feeling odd or left out of normal suffering. "You can go to whatever Sunday school you like," she told me, "but never, under any circumstances whatsoever, sign anything or make any pledges that you'll regret later." Very sensible advice to a nine-year-old.

So I shopped the church directory in Eugene, sampling a number of offerings. The two I remember best were the Presbyterian, because of Miss Liljeqvist, and the Unitarian, because of Professor Barnes. Professor Barnes wore cheap dark suits seven days a week and rode a bicycle with a basket heavy with books and papers. On Sunday mornings he acquainted us with the *Dialogues* of Plato and cosmic physics. He never remembered to take the bicycle clips off his trousers and his lectures had an ethical turn but, as far as I can remember, never cited the Scriptures. That pleased my mother and suited me just fine. I don't think my father had much to say about it one way or another. His aunts in Glens Falls, New York, had brought him up in the Baptist church and, although he retained a lot of their attitudes, particularly where sex was concerned, he seemed rather more ashamed than proud of his sect. Somewhere along the line he had obviously discounted its doctrines rather severely. In any event he never suggested that I return to Baptist Sunday school after my one bored visit, perhaps because he anticipated the day I would ask him why *he* was never there.

As for my maternal grandfather, who certainly set the intellectual tone for our family, he was decidedly agnostic and very much a Darwinian, familiar as well with Herbert Spencer and Victorian positivism. In his final years he took to visiting churches, but that was because he had little taste for popular entertainment and needed the stimulus of a "capital sermon" on some social or ethical topic to get his own intellectual machinery in working order. On the other hand he did not care for Scriptural "rubbish." Sermons, my grandfather maintained, were meant to provoke thought and argument, and the details of any particular credo were, *sub speciae aeternitas* (another favorite expression of his), all brummagem anyway. What my grandmother Kate thought of his agnostic scoffing I don't know, since she showed her wisdom by never to my knowledge saying a word on the subject. Yet her father had been a Methodist pastor in Dublin, full of Wesleyan hellfire, so there must have been fireworks somewhere in the fifty years of their married life.

I should say, parenthetically, that my mother's tolerance of, or indifference to, the various churches in our community had its limits. Buddhists, Jews, Zoroastrians, Parsees, and other such exotics were welcome at her table, but for Catholics and born-again Fundamentalists she had no mercy. Our family's grudge against Roman Catholics probably had its roots in Ireland's troubles, but it was certainly reinforced by the papal hostility to birth control, which had convinced her that Catholicism could be equated with ignorance, poverty, and overpopulation—in her creed mankind's three chief enemies. As for the proselyting charismatic sects, we were brought up to view them as exhibits in a sort of raree-show, pitiable examples of the depths of human foolishness. Quite indiscriminately, they were all referred to as "Holy Rollers," with all which that epithet implied. Frenzy of any sort, whether divinely inspired or not, was never in favor with my family.

From all this it must appear that religion played a small part in my childhood. Certainly I had none of those feverish conversions or mystical seizures which are features of so many sensitive adolescences, but I did have my own religion, as rich in demons and deities as its institutionalized cousins. Unaware of its name or systemics, I was a fierce animist, endowing every toy or piece of furniture with good or evil spirits and invoking their intervention by rites of magic and incantation. Animism—there's the religion all children share until age blunts their perception and the dryads, naiads, gnomes, and grimalkins are either institutionalized in churches, adjusted out of existence in the name of psychotherapy, or executed in the name of higher education.

The chief and most feared of these gods of mine was a giant black bear, erect and menacing but by day disguised as a raincoat hung over a doorknob or a ladder-back chair draped with a bolster. Only at night did it assume its true, terrifying shape. Many times that bear came to me with punishment or vengeance in its bloody mouth. It was really and truly there; protests, screams, eye-rubbings were of no avail against its reality; all I could do was endure it with what fortitude I could until it chose to resume its old disguise. Usually, I suppose, children expect bears to maul, claw, or perhaps eat them, but with my ursine night visitor I had no specific fears—the bear was simply there; nothing more was required of him; his very presence was a judgment on me. This I take to be the behavior of a god.

The lesser gods were those which defended and comforted me. Variously, they could be stones, dolls' arms, pinecones, a treasured triangular postage stamp from Dahomey, beads, marbles, a blue pill bottle, and so on—bits of the day's detritus arranged in a charmed ring about my pillow to offer protection against the evil spirits abroad that night. The properties of each individual talisman were not important; it was their arrangement, the circle itself that made magic. Incantations were sometimes helpful; I made up a number of them, and the ones which were particularly protective were those composed of gibberish. I have forgotten all these incoherent prayers, although the attractiveness of ritual antilanguage persists with me.

But nothing, absolutely nothing, was effective against Thanatos, the black bear, on the nights he chose to enter my room and stare down at the huddled, fearful form curled under the tangled blankets.

All these reflections and memories have sprung, however circuitously, from the gold star sparkling on the tarmac far up Mount Shasta—Miss Liljeqvist's star mysteriously reborn. I must only add that on one of my subsequent trips back to Eugene I discovered that Miss Liljeqvist herself was no longer there. Her devotion to the Bible stories had become so extreme that she had begun acting them out with herself as one protagonist after another. Sadly, medical science and her family joined in having her put away. As it has for many another imaginative soul, the Bible had proved too much for Miss Liljeqvist. Dr. Barnes, who had perhaps cast himself as a provincial Socrates, was luckier. He lived into a ripe old age and died sane.

> Plato proffers universals
> Books you with the Absolute
> By any name they're but rehearsals
> For the waltz of bone to flute

This table has two empty glasses
This bottle's lost its cork
That's all philosophy encompasses
That and a two-step in the dark.

Hood River

I was born (so I am told) very early on the morning of the second of June, 1914, in the hospital at Hood River, Oregon, then a town of perhaps two thousand. My grandfather Louis F. Henderson had come there around 1911 to put in practice what he had long taught: scientific arboriculture. This may seem excessively formal language with which to describe an apple-grower, but in my grandfather's case it is appropriate. He had been a founder of the Agricultural Service at the University of Idaho before deciding, in his late fifties, to chuck it all in favor of practical ranching. I don't know what dream or delusion motivated that decision, but I do know that he came to regret it.

"My grandfather Louis F. Henderson," 1932

I spent my first six years in Hood River and returned to it annually, until my grandparents finally sold out and at seventy-two L. F. Henderson returned to academic life as curator of the herbarium at the University of Oregon, so most of my earliest memories revolve around that town and the apple orchards which ringed it. Much of the imagery of my poetry is rooted there.

In the distance Mount Hood;
above my head various sopranos
floating in spasms of miraculous
sunlight.
        There are fires on the sea
and wandering tongues in the meadow.
The telephone wires whisper together;
the white breath of the apple trees
hovers in a net of twigs.

I walk alone through the wet fields
carrying an aging life. The swallows,
felicitous surgeons, present me
with their airy sutures. I shall lean
into the calligraphy of new wheat.

Hood River has another distinction which, like my birth there, is never mentioned by the tourist office. It is the leading candidate to become the North American Herculaneum or Pompeii. Mount Hood, which towers above it less than twenty aerial miles away, is considered by seismologists the most likely of the great Cascade volcanoes to next blow its top. It last erupted nearly a century and a half ago, and the optimistic residents of its slopes had for years referred to it as extinct. What happened to Mount Saint Helens, a few leagues to the north, put a stop to that. Mount Hood is not extinct, only taking what amounts in geological time to a catnap. When it awakes, should that awakening occur on its north side, much of the Hood River Valley may be covered with magma, mud, and ash.

Meanwhile, that possibility seems to bother no one but me, and the rich soil of the subvolcanic valley continues to bring forth blossoms and fruit of dazzling beauty and sweetness. The boulders spewed out by the earth-demon are everywhere, mainly gathered into walls by the frugal pioneers but still strewn carelessly about on pasture land as if propelled there by the giant's slingshot. When it hails stones like these again, all of man's puny works shall vanish from that valley.

But from my grandfather's farm Hood was obscured by its foothills; Adams and Saint Helens were the commanding features of our daily view. The house was frame, of two storeys, set in an ancient grove of oaks. Electricity was yet to come. There was a telephone but, naturally, no radio or television. Water was pumped manually from the well after the long labor of priming. That was my first job, to ladle water onto the pump while stronger arms kept the handle moving. The plumbing was out-of-doors and the attic was full of dusty treasures. There was a timbered barn with rusting machinery—diskers, cider-presses and the like—but I recall no farm animals; I think my grandfather rented horses when he needed to plow or haul the vile-smelling, sulphurous sprayer. Then there was a packing shed where in season a gasoline donkey engine powered the endless belts on which the apples were borne to the sorters and packers. This was all hand work; each apple was wrapped in tissue paper and nested within its graded box. Hood River apples were—and perhaps still are—sold at a premium on the eastern market, and their shipping had to be given especial care.

Newtowns, Red Delicious, Winter Bananas, Gravensteins, Winesaps, and Northern Spies! I'm hard pressed to tell them apart on the market shelf, but those names reverberate in my memory as the notes of bells must to one born by a cathedral. And the sweet cidery smell of the rejected culls rotting under the conveyors! The heft and shape of the boxmaker's hatchet, entrusted to me at ten to nail shut the boxes for shipping. The pine laths soaking in a bucket beside me to avoid splitting. The odor which comes back to me at sixty years' remove. The liberating hand of memory.

When the rivers began to flow backward
he knew he was on the right track

it was only a matter of time until leaves
sprouted from his fingers and the gold coins

off the sycamores renewed his gray hair,
only a matter of time until the minstrel

of meteors came singing past the haybarns
bearing in his left hand a seven-stringed lyre

and in his outstretched right hand
a deep lake locked in glass.

Icons in the Hallway

Like most families, ours had its icons, its ancestors about whom myths collected like dust on an old hall-tree. Chief among these progenitors was Senator John Henderson of Pass Christian, Mississippi, who overlooked our family gatherings from a giant steel engraving of the U.S. Senate in 1840, the last year of Martin Van Buren's wobbly helmsmanship. The engraving was of a sort popular in the nineteenth century where the laws of perspective gave way to the claims of egalitarianism—each senator was accorded equal space in the print, an easier trick in a time when there were few more than fifty of them than it would be today. In that gallery were Clay, Webster, and Calhoun, masters of the orotund phrase and disremembered issue; but to my eyes there was none so handsome as my grandfather's grandfather, the senior John Henderson. Born of immigrant Scottish parents, he had been a river bargeman, had studied law in Cincinnati between trips, and had then emigrated downstream to set up practice on the Gulf Coast. Pass Christian (surely a name right out of *Pilgrim's Progress*) and his big house at Henderson's Point were to be the focal points of our family traditions for the next century, no matter how far the diaspora of the Hendersons carried us.

As for the old senator, at least as seen behind glass in my grandfather's hallway, he could not have fit the part better had central casting been his sponsor. Clean-shaven firm jaw over a high wing collar, thin cheeks (no sensual extravagance here!), aquiline nose, and wavy pennons of hair, eyes aflame with forensic zeal—all the classic marks of orator or actor. Indeed, there was another John Henderson, a late–eighteenth century actor termed "the Roscius of Bath," one-time rival of David Garrick's for popular favor, whose portrait would have him a brother of my ancestor, although it hardly seems probable they were connected; Hendersons sprout all over Scotland and England.

From an early age I was told that I looked like him and that I might follow in his footsteps. I was immensely flattered but never wholly convinced. The senator seemed to possess such an absolute clarity of vision—no sign of moral doubt or introversion there, while I, of course, wasn't so lucky. But he was, incontestably, my mythic role model. The famous steel engraving has since passed into the distant hands of cousins; it is perhaps forty years since I last saw it, but the senator's fearless and unforgiving gaze is as fresh in my memory as if I had run across him on the street yesterday, wing collar, cravat, and all.

Apparently no one took much notice of Senator Henderson in Washington, but when he had left to set up practice in New Orleans he managed to make the history books. He was three times tried on a federal indictment charging that he had violated neutrality statutes by supplying arms and assistance to one Narciso Lopez, a Spanish officer turned revolutionist who led a number of expeditions against the royal government in Cuba. Gunrunning, in short. At this distance it is hard to say what admixture of motives guided John Henderson—how much of it was Garibaldian idealism and how much dreams of Southern aggrandizement. The family tradition naturally stressed the former. I am told that his name can be found even today on a plaque in Havana commemorating those foreigners who helped Cuba in her long struggle for independence. No doubt he was popular, too, in New Orleans—no jury could be found to convict him, and after three mistrials in the end he went free.

Now here, to show that the tradition dies hard, some political rhetoric from his great-great-grandson:

Sketch for a Mural for the New Senate Office Building

Warriors, arising from the sands at Tropicana,
direct us to deserted urinals while,
prescient and dispassionate,
Statesmen clench the surf in scrubbed teeth
and issue maps of the inner ear.

Policemen behind the motorbarn pursue the
    pederast;
Euphoria (an outlaw) stands on the Mount of
    Love
distributing used condoms while,
driven by three nuns on spavined horses,
the Hearse of Ecstasy (its axles leaking ichor)
comes rattling down the hill.

Liberty lies on her back among the acanthus
and, silent as ice,
lifts her dress of cocaine.

When rebellion swept the South, the old senator was dead and did not have to face the hard decision which confronted so many Southern Whigs—whether to stick by the Union or go to war for secession and the slave system. Our family iconography thus shifted to his son, the second John Henderson, by now an attorney and declared Union sympathizer in New Orleans. After Louisiana was taken into the Confederacy by her officials—"kidnapped," some Unionists said—my great-grandfather fled to the North. His Boston-born wife and two sons took refuge with friends in Tennessee ("where I lived on nothing but cornbread and sowbelly for over a year," my grandfather recalled) while Mr. Henderson worked in the Union cause. In 1862 Farragut blasted the Confederate forts on the Mississippi and the Union army under General Butler reoccupied New Orleans. Presum-

ably, John Henderson returned with Butler; at any rate he was back in practice and radical politics by the war's end. Then came the other event which stamped my whole childhood with its bloody *imprimatur*.

My great-grandfather immediately took a leading role in the struggle to give blacks the vote. As a result he became chairman of a committee to that purpose and was assassinated in 1869 while, unarmed, he led a peaceable march to the hall where an inter-racial congress was to meet. Struck down by a pro-Confederate bullet, he was temporarily rescued from the bigots by the courage of a former rebel officer and friend who brought him, gravely wounded, to his home. There Mr. Henderson lingered for weeks, finally to die of gangrene from his wounds. My grandfather, a boy of fourteen at the time, was to tell me the story in vivid detail, and I was not likely soon to forget it. I have since more than once made my own pilgrimage to my great-grandfather's grave amidst the cypress and Spanish moss of the old Pass Christian cemetery. *Requiescat in pace . . .*

The Assassination

An abrupt arm raised
the lapel which leaps from the revolver
the crunch the gasp
the eyelashes in the gravel

the celebrated statue spread
on the street like a stain . . .

a red flower blooms from its mouth
a clamshell goes on opening and closing
secondhands spilling from it
like jackstraws   the sirens
are eaten by their echoes
the stub of blood is left
to burn itself out on the sidewalk . . .

My family had done with the South.

Out of the Running

In the family mythology my father was, I am afraid, a supernumerary at the back of the stage. His family was hardly ever in evidence, and then what patrilineal relatives did show up turned out, like his uncle Fred, to be rather uninteresting commercial types. The closest thing to a romantic figure was his cousin, a utilities executive, who once met my brother and me at the Portland railway station with manly handshakes and presents of ten-dollar gold pieces. Of course, my father was not strictly to blame; he had been an orphan, raised by his aunts in Glens Falls, New York, where Solomon Parks, his maternal grandfather, had been a successful paper manufacturer. His father's people, the Hitchcocks, had been small farmers and merchants in Vermont and upstate New York since pre-Revolutionary days.

After high school and a brief year at Colgate College, my father had come West in search of his fortune. His uncle Fred had gotten him a job as railway freight agent in Hood River, and there he met my mother, who had recently graduated from the University of Idaho. I know nothing about their courtship; both of them were reticent about such matters and, since the bloom of their romance didn't last very long, it was a subject their tormented children weren't encouraged to pursue.

My father was a tall, handsome, florid man, red-haired and increasingly given to girth. He looked every bit the Yorkshire sporting gentleman you might meet at a horse show. A pink skin, a close-cropped moustache, pale blue eyes bulging a bit—a whiskey-and-seltzer-water sort of a man. A man who bought, rather than sold, lumber. I think this distinction proved important to my mother. Democratic (with both large and small D's) as she was, she was snobbish about retail trade. It mattered to her that my father dealt in carload lots and went around to the sawmills with orders in his hand; I don't think she could have borne it as long as she did if he had been a mere salesman.

He wasn't cut out to be a Willy Loman, anyway, although he certainly shared a lot of Willy's values. The trouble was he was too shy and, beneath his imposing bulk, too sensitive and wary of rejection ever to be a top-notch salesman. But at doing you a favor, making a present, or buying your lumber, he had charm and ceremonious manners which were a pleasure to watch. I admired him vastly through the first years of my childhood—it was only later, when his magniloquent sense of occasion became sheer pomposity and his hatred for Franklin Roosevelt soured his natural kindliness, that I began to detest him, and then, I am sure, the fault was as much mine as his.

When I was six my father left us for his one great mythological moment. He took a job in Havana selling derrick timbers to the nascent Cuban oil industry. He was gone for a year while we lived with the Hendersons. Ultimately the Cubans failed to discover much oil, no one had any use for forty-foot Douglas fir timbers, and my father returned proudly speaking bad Spanish and with a one thousand dollar bill sewn into the lining of his coat, a sum which in

1920 matched in my imaginings the treasures Marco Polo brought back from Cathay. There was also a photo of him, very Anglo and debonaire with straw hat and swagger-stick, standing athwart the *malecón* on Havana's waterfront. He described to me the open-air cafés where he had watched Jorge Capablanca, the soon-to-be world champion, play half a dozen chess games at once. I was enthralled and began to take chess seriously. Of course, I told my schoolmates that my father had played Capablanca, which I am almost sure was a lie if not a very consequential one.

Yet from then on things began to slide. It seemed that nothing I could do could possibly please him. He began exercising the barbs of his naturally sarcastic temperament on me, and I, in turn, grew sullen and obstinate. With a few amiable *intermezzi*, we grew to be enemies and stayed frozen in that posture for many years. Of course, I did not then realize that I had become a pawn in a deadlier game, not with Señor Capablanca, but with my mother and the whole Henderson clan whose favorite I was.

But up or down my father had style, a feeling for how things were done. He liked poetry, of the Kipling variety, and had a taste for philosophizing and the thrice-baked epigram. He was an excellent cook and always at his best when it came to organizing games or festivities. He was cursed, I think, with an artistic temperament with no particular talent, a certain recipe for dissatisfaction. When I was eight we moved to Eugene and he went into the wholesale lumber business. His generosity and increasing conviviality over the bottle earned him many admirers from the commercial classes there, most of them coarse men whom my mother despised. He assumed civic responsibilities, became chairman of the chamber of commerce, secretary of service committees, a pillar of the country club, and a substantial contributor to the Republican party. For two years he was the director of the town's Pioneer Pageant, in whose parades I played a Red Indian scout and went gleefully war-whooping through the streets. Meanwhile, his marriage turned into a battleground, his sons pilfered his bootleg Scotch, and he increasingly built a wall of sarcasm and silence about himself.

I was seventeen when my parents finally separated, but their discord had long been a fact of my adolescence and must be responsible for the loathing I have since felt for the conventional American home, beneath whose well-advertised gloss so many horrors lurk. Family gatherings, their sentimentality and manifold hypocrisies, have been the particular butt of my aversion:

Group Portrait

The family is gathered here
Uncle Ted on the left smoking consonants
Aunt Beth in her mechanical night-gown
Mother on her motorbike   Father getting
refuelled   the sons and daughters busy
becoming monuments . . .

They've got style this family
they study they learn to turn leaves
into lighter-fluid they mouth forecasts
from almanacs   they become famous
flying about the room on mothwings
when they grow old they embroider
sparks and go to Victor Herbert on
Wednesday afternoons trailing innocents
behind them on umbilical cords . . .

Birth of the Magician

Bring me then if you will
  the osprey in its taffeta kaftan
  the safety-match dancing in the cathedral
  moons which sweat kerosene
  elephant salt
  and the ventilated shriek

We are in Central Oregon. The landscape has three tones—red where the soil is bare, feathery gray where sagebrush has taken over, here and there rude splotches of dark green. This last the junipers, stunted, aged, with red berries bitter to the tongue. The year is 1924 and tomorrow it will be the Fourth of July, Independence Day, the merriest of all holidays for us petty dynamiters.

From miles off the great dream-building of Deschutes City can be seen; there it stands in a sea of sagebrush, a three-storied box of a brick hotel.

Let me enumerate the features of Deschutes:
The hotel.

A pine boardwalk which connects it to a squat, brick office building housing the Deschutes Bank and the Deschutes Water Company.

A wooden shed, usually closed, offering ranch hardware and lariats.

A railway crossing sign and loading platform.
A pump-shed.
A spotted dog.

That's it. No houses, no streets, no trees. Nothing but a monstrous box of a hotel plumped down heedlessly and needlessly in the desert.

My great-uncle Frederick Stanley lives here, a solitary spider. Since the death of his wife, my father's aunt Ruth, he has no place else to live. He is a fat,

bald-headed old party with the air of a Roman prefect in an expiring empire. His only companions are his Chinese cook and two linemen from the telephone company who seem to be the only paying guests for the last decade. Who else would stay here? Deschutes is on the road to Nowhere—perhaps its prime way station.

Of course, there had once been a dream. When my father came West in 1910, Uncle Fred had been a Portland tycoon and had given him his first job. Land and irrigation canals had been the twin props to his fortune. The Deschutes River was to be harnessed and Deschutes City was to become the hub of a fertile valley of orchards and ranches. Ultimately it all took place, but half a century too late for Uncle Fred and his investors—Bend, Oregon, a dozen miles away, is today the center of just such a development as he envisaged. But Deschutes . . . ?

Hold the camera still for a moment. It is hot midsummer, 1924. The blinds are drawn on the hotel sitting room; everything is suffused in ochreous light; the tufted furniture is shrouded in dust covers. Within its glass case my uncle's show piece, a stuffed China pheasant, sleeps in its stale air. Uncle Fred dozes in his rocker by the cold grate. Upstairs in the broad square attic we've sifted through boxes of Horatio Alger and *St. Nicholas* and the *Youth's Companion*, and now my brother and I have gone outside to the embankment by the irrigation ditch. There we plot ever more spectacular explosions from the gold-and-red packages our father has allowed us in the Republic's honor. Who supplies these firecrackers I can't remember but it must have been Vulcan himself, for on one final blast I succeed in elevating a tobacco tin the full three storeys of the hotel plus the height of the chimney into which it disappears. Amazed yet triumphant, I rush into the hotel to find my somnolent uncle awakened by the clatter in his fireplace. Yes, there is my projectile, blown sky-high by the toy petard. I fish it from the ashes and bear it triumphantly away.

On Wednesday he stopped time in mid-air
and asked it to doff its cap of bees

Thursday on the moon's emery-wheel
he ground down prayers until nothing

but sparks remained   he tried
to assemble them into lightning

but it wouldn't work   Friday
was the day of voyages   the day

of the broken rudder and the compass
lost in the haystacks

It seems so improbable, in such utter defiance of the laws of dynamics, that I have often wondered if I didn't dream the whole adventure. But there it is, stark in my memory. Forty feet straight up, from the force of one child's firecracker? The perfect arc into the chimney? But even more important was the flush of power suffusing one ten-year-old sorcerer. Desert air. The inexplicable triumph. The rush of adrenalin. The pride. The magic.

Wait. There is a sequel. Thirty-five years later I went back to Deschutes, which I found only after a lot of crisscrossing of the desert. There was a railway sign stark in its simplicity: DESCHUTES. That was all—not even altitude such-and-such, population 0. Everything else was gone. Down the track a quarter of a mile there was a gravel dump. Not a stone, not a brick to show where Uncle Fred's great palace had once stood. Wiped out. Completely.

For now the Deschutes Hotel, that absurd and magnificent hostelry in the desert, exists only in my mind. Perhaps somewhere one of those telephone linemen still survives and can share its memory with me. But somehow I doubt it.

Two Ways

My mother was one of those very dangerous parents who began each piece of advice by informing you that you were completely free to make whatever decision your heart and the canons of liberal good sense dictated, although, as might be expected, this always turned out to be just what she had in mind for you to do. The advantage of this sort of guidance was that you cultivated a sense of principled freedom and moral complacency; the chief disadvantage was, of course, that you found yourself trapped by a sort of Kantian universal law extremely difficult to escape since it was totally encased—or perhaps padded—in affection and altruism.

And who could not respond to my mother's affection with love? Simply to ask the question was heretical. For she was a truly remarkable woman. Strikingly attractive in her youth, charismatic in her later years, hers was a life of achievement against heavy odds. During my childhood her passion was horsemanship; she attended and participated in many western rodeos, and each spring and fall she would convoy the string of riding horses in and out of Crater Lake National Park, a week's difficult riding through the Cascades. When she divorced my father, she moved to San Francisco and launched herself, a provincial housewife in her forties, on a new and highly successful career as a newspaperwoman for the

"With my mother," 1919

Hearst syndicate, covering many notable trials and making her byline familiar up and down the coast. Not content with these two widely separated careers, she took up another passion—small-boat sailing—and again distinguished herself by her navigational skills (at sixty she earned second-mate's papers in the merchant marine) and her extensive and much-publicized cruises in the South Pacific, which she described in numerous articles in the sailing magazines.

Indeed, if my grandfather was the prototype of the devoted Victorian scientist, my mother could well stand in for the Edwardian "new woman." In her presence I was often reminded of one of Shaw's heroines—say Vivie Warren or that charming Polish aviatrix who parachutes into the garden party in *Misalliance*—self-assured, practical, humane yet argumentative, a woman conventional at heart yet always prepared to defy those conventions she thought archaic or useless, intelligent but in no way an intellectual, a daring soul who found marriage a prison, who survived all challenges by the power of positive thinking. Her biography would be in most ways more interesting than my own, but since it is the latter I am here concerned with I am obliged to add that it was very difficult to break away from her influence. With my father I always knew where I stood—with my arms folded in the stubborn posture of the defiant son—but with my mother the issues were forever clouded over by love and admiration. It was rather like being the wayward son of Amelia Earhart (whom my mother resembled physically as well as stylistically).

The great problem for me was that my mother's philosophy was fundamentally anti-artistic. She represented the world of action, and I was struggling toward the world of *aboulia*. Everything was sunlit and clear to my mother; I gravitated toward ambiguities, idleness, and that other world of the dream kingdom.

Tao

I take my leave
of the hats &
gloves &
indecisions
the manuals for
internal com-
bustion   the tea
spoons & insomnia
& my days under
fetid glass.

The sun declares
daylight   my head
is bedizened
with garnets.

I am scholar to
feathered texts
of flight   the in-
cantation of oaks
with their barbaric
flags & strange
manifestoes   the
savage tribes
of sunflowers.

I devour rivers with
my celebrated
teeth   I ascend the
magnetic smoke
of bonfires   I visit
the acrobatic moon
& in the entrails
of winds I divine
the authentic history
of passion.

My twin lungs
the pearls of my
testicles   the puls-
ing glove of my
bowel   the courteous
flexure of knee
& elbow enter
the galaxies.

I matriculate
in holy inertia.

This sort of thinking was, I am afraid, incomprehensible to my mother; what Keats called *negative capability* she would have considered mere indecisiveness. She was an Irishwoman through and through, but the misty side of the Irish temper she had resolutely put behind her, and she viewed it with loving dismay in me; to her the world was neither more nor less than what it seemed and was there to be enjoyed and conquered. We always continued to love and take pride in one another, but I know I caused her much grief by the fitful and feverish side of my life. The truth was that her path was not my path, although it took us many years to acknowledge it. But all that was in the future.

Streams, Lakes, and Canals

Our new house was built on the banks of the Willamette River, which meant canoeing in the summer and vast floods almost every winter. My parents, I am sure, became very tired of waking up to acres of turbid brown water on all sides of them; to me, of course, it was a source of perennial delight. School was impossible, and the dogs had to be kept inside where they whimpered with fear. My father's morning preoccupation was with measuring the ebb and flood of the menacing waters; how many million acre-feet would it take to rise that last six inches and cover our floors with mud? Out on the central current, chicken coops, trestle timbers, and armadas of upswept stumps and piratical snags sailed by. The housemaid, her basement room hip-deep in café-au-lait, had moved back to her Swedish family, and all the firewood so laboriously stacked in July now floated to every corner of the cellar. The lawn was eradicated, the furnace filled with mud. And then the floods fell as mysteriously as they had arisen, and after school every afternoon for weeks I slogged about in the basement cleaning up. After these spring floods, summer generally limped onstage and the river once again became the friendly refuge of chubs and watersnakes.

Before the move to the river house there had been lakes and canals and irrigation ditches everywhere, including the one from which I, stalwart five, plucked my slippery squalling little brother, thus saving the United States Navy a future commodore and earning myself laurels for infant valor. Irrigation ditches! With their mossy stone beds, their fascinating wooden drop-gates which I loved operating, and the cascading standpipes where the cold clear water burst forth from under the roadways. And best of all their ultimate rills in the orchard, shaped by my grandfather's deft hoe, where I watched the water's paws dart through the dry clods. What horse-chestnut navies, what maple-leaf luggers we embarked on those rivulets!

Are all children as fascinated by water as I was? Is it a heritage from the universal tenancy of amniotic fluid or was it only my own crotchet?

At six or seven I came near drowning, in Lake Wenatchee, I think. My mother said it was only the luck of the Irish that kept me from coming up, when I rose for the mythic third time, under the boathouse float instead of in the comparative safety of open water. Anyway, she hauled me out, with no permanent damage. It was a close thing, but I held no resentment against the lake, as this poem will show:

Runneled, muddied, bespattered lake
take me unhesitant in your avenues,
let me set fire to the chimneys of lilies,
entangle me in your slippery gutters of trout
the boudoirs of watersnails . the alleys of pike.

Lake which among the reeds sings endlessly,
lend me your sedge voice
and permit me with your wet teeth
to devour the marsh-marigolds.

And you, old witness, comrade-in-arms
who does not forget,
will you sing with me among the rushes?
Dragon fly . water nymph,
clandestine fisher of the secret places?

and this one, a few thousand dreams later:

He awakes
in the glaucous breast of water swimming,
swimming like the Jack of Dolphins

toward some indefinable shore; he cannot
remember where he has been, he only knows
that his mouth is full of fish-eggs

and that the soft membrane between his toes flares in the sea-dappled light.

Water and swimming, then, became symbols of freedom to me, not unassociated with danger (the lurking snag, the camouflaged crocodile) but liberators all the same. Liberators from what? To answer that I must turn to those images that did stand in for Death in my child's imagining.

It was not drowning but suffocation that formed the warp of my childhood dream-weaving. Trapped underground, a prisoner of mine, subway, or storm-sewer, I gasp and grope toward an ever-receding pinpoint of light, the last hope of escape, while the shoring timbers creak above me and clods of shale and clay fall on my shoulders. This claustrophobia has pursued me all my life; though nowadays it takes some story or film to reawaken it (Flann O'Brien's vision of hell as an underground boiler-works in *The Third Policeman* brings me to a sweat, while the deadly constriction of submarine life in the German film *Das Boot* provokes palpitations of fear), in my boyhood it was a ruling image, awake or asleep. I have no doubt it has its origin in crib experiences—to this day I dread sleeping beneath heavy blankets—but, like any neurosis, once launched it took on a life of its own.

There were also frightening dreams of falling from high places—never trees, into which I ventured with impunity—and hiking or cycling up crags which became ever steeper until one could not avoid falling backward off their cliffs. The usual stuff, I suppose, but compared to these visions my encounters with water were always benign. The world of lake, river, and sea was the world of liberation.

Low Tide

I hear the music
of sorcerers
trapped
in the bowels
of herons.

I follow their
signals past
the sand icons
the prayerwheels
of bone the
frantic claws
in the surf

to the dark wells
of guitars.

Let water and wisdom
recede; I search
for the eyes which
flower at the back
of the sea.

The Twelve Gods

Every spring, walking through the hills of northern California, I stoop to pay my respects to the Western shooting-star, a lovely little wild cyclamen which is one of the earliest flowers to appear in the meadows, just after the crowfoot and bluebells make their appearance. The name of the genus is *Dodecatheon* and the species *Hendersonii.* Where the generic name, "twelve gods," came from is a mystery—perhaps the elegance of the name was irresistible to its discoverer—but its second name was bestowed on it by the great Asa Gray, systematizer of American botany and correspondent of Charles Darwin, in honor of my grandfather Louis Fourniquet Henderson. L. F. Henderson was the second son of the New Orleans martyr and one of the Northwest's earliest and most eminent taxonomic botanists. He also had a wild cow parsnip and some sedges named after him but, naturally, when I recall him I like to think of the flower of the twelve gods rather than these humbler eponyms.

One of the great gifts of a childhood in the far West was the constant ubiquity of nature; you could not escape it even if you would. The forest was everywhere, alternately menacing and revivifying a boy's imagination. Nothing is more familiar to me than the plash of raindrops on the leaves—the one glossy, the other almost of leather—of the Oregon grape and the salal; or in summer the harsh odor of the linked chains of spores on the dried bracken; the odor and viscosity of the resin which oozed from the wounded firs; and the insistent, sharp-edge clamor of blue jays. Even Eugene, then a town of a mere fourteen thousand when the university was not in session, did not escape the presence of dryads—her buttes were thickly cloaked in Douglas firs, dogwood, and vine-maple, and her flatlands by the river were home to willows, cottonwood, and a wild profusion of blooming camass, *brodiae,* and rein-orchids. Crawfish, waterskaters, newts, and fingerling trout were our splashing companions, while merely to set foot in these meadows in July was to provoke a whirring storm of green-and-redwinged grasshoppers which fell by the hundreds to the sharp eyes and practiced beaks of the meadowlarks and glistening grackle.

SHOOTING-STARS—*Dodecatheon Hendersoni,* var. *cruciata.*

"My shooting-stars"

Before the Storm

The trout undulate
in the black water.
A blade of oats
trembles, leaves stir,
the sky dark
as a meadow of violets.

Autumn filters
through doors
and cupboards.

Enormous thrushes
rise to the forest roof
in silence. The stream
turns cloudy, coils
like a snake. Mapleseeds,
crazed, whirl to the ground.

Gulfs! Abysses! Caverns!
And in the distance
dark violets.

I could not possibly have wished for a better tutor to this world of miracles and monsters than my grandfather. He had come out to the Northwest in the 1870s to teach Latin and French to the young gentlemen at the Portland Academy, but his true loves were botany and mountain-climbing. He began collecting—both peaks and flowers—in the time spared from his schoolmastering. There was no herbarium worthy of the name in Oregon, so he shipped his specimens to Gray at Harvard and, somewhat later, to Willis Jepson in Berkeley. He made many discoveries and his repute as a field botanist grew; in 1893 he was called to the University of Idaho to establish a collection there. After nearly twenty years at Moscow his work quite literally went up in smoke—a disastrous fire destroyed the herbarium—and he retired to ranching. But when I became his student and field companion, the University of Oregon had summoned him, as the senior taxonomic botanist in the Northwest, to take over and reorganize their collections. He worked in rooms in the basement of Deady Hall, the oldest building on the campus, rooms jammed with aged oak cases, microscopes, and the constant musty odor of botanical blotting paper, rooms which became very familiar to me.

I have since wondered why, with this tutelage and the example of his devotion to science, I came to stray so far from that ideal. The emotional advantages of a career in the sciences were certainly evident in his serenity and undeviating fixity of purpose. But the truth is that these qualities, however admirable in the abstract, have never been known to appeal to nascent teenagers; the names of our demons were adventure and swashbuckling sex, and at twelve, in my mind, these images were clustered about the dream figure of the journalist-traveller or war correspondent. That was what I was determined to become. For in that year my grandfather had taken me to a slide lecture by Captain John Noel, who was touring America with his account of the ill-fated 1924 assault on Mount Everest in which Mallory and Irvine lost their lives. The event had a great, I might almost say decisive, effect on me; not so much on my waking life, for although I have since climbed a number of peaks, I never achieved the mix of determination and physical skill which is necessary to a successful climber; no, the really lasting effect of that evening was on my dream life. Mountains I had long been familiar with; they surrounded my childhood on every side; but here, in Noel's photographs and verbal eloquence, they took on the aspect of life, death, attainment, and tragedy; they were suffused with

moral significance which transformed them into icons or eidolons of teenage longing. My childhood animism found new gods onto whom I could project my yearnings and vague ambitions.

> The mountains gallop
> their manes combed their saddle-cinches
> tightened the mountains have nostrils
> of ice and their eyes are glacial lakes.
> High in the moraine
>
> they're bridled by wanderers with secret
> violins in their saddlebags   dreamers
> who thirst for the nectar of stones
> pilgrims who ask forgiveness
> of their basalt teeth
> who ask the mountains where
> they're going and whether it's true
> they're the daughters of midnight
>
> the mountains don't answer
> they shake their white heads and paw
> the valleys with granite hooves
> they've ridden far these mountains
> they know a lot they keep threatening
> to turn into constellations
> and lose themselves in the vast
> pastures of the Milky Way.

Borderlines

I looked forward passionately to my twelfth birthday; there was nothing I wanted more intensely than to be done with childhood, and for some reason I thought of twelve as the magic watershed—surely from that point on my river would run in the direction of freedom! To me infancy was a state of perpetual wretchedness, and I plotted out campaigns of hypocritical behavior with the single goal of being accepted as an adult. I became discreet, silent, well-mannered; I obeyed my father's commands without so much as a sullen grimace. In short, I began to manipulate my parents like a young Machiavelli. I had read with approval of the scarifying rituals Indian lads had to undergo at puberty, so I became a stoic in the face of pain and scorned my younger brother for his whining and tears. I set myself trials, exercises in endurance and self-denial which went so far as to deprive me of the consolations of masturbation, a recent discovery. At twelve I was already over six feet tall, derided as "high-pockets" or "Ichabod," gawky, and hideously self-conscious. My school was Theodore Roosevelt Junior High, from which I cannot recall one teacher or speak with certainty of a single shard of knowledge acquired there; my club was the Boy Scouts of America, which I mostly despised but which always rewarded me for enduring the wintry tedium of their paramilitary meetings with two glorious summer weeks at their camp in the Cascades; and my friends were nearly all within the covers of books.

I began reading at five, and between eight and sixteen must have read, by a conservative estimate, over two thousand volumes. Of course, since I was omnivorous and quite undiscriminating, they were mostly trash, but the course of the addiction was set and I have never been able to break it. And, as a by-product, I did win almost every schoolroom spelling contest. When I was twelve or thirteen I was reading ten books a week and coaching my mother, who had just taken up journalism, in her spelling and punctuation. I had also run through most of the resources of the juvenile section at the Eugene public library; fortunately, my grandfather came to the rescue and secured me stack privileges at the university library. This was an unheard-of dispensation; I thought it my life's greatest achievement to date, but along with it came a battery of "intelligence" tests devised by Professor Lewis Terman of Stanford to identify and brand forever "gifted youths." I came out of them with the descriptive tag "borderline genius," a phrase which was to pursue and secretly humiliate me for years. It was bad enough to be a genius, with the heavy load of parental expectation this laid on you, but then the slightly sneering tone of "borderline" rose up to undercut the rosy prophecies. It deeply embarrassed me—if I was going to be a genius I wanted it all or nothing. Yet the test results immensely pleased my mother, who had foreseen them all along; my father said nothing but I knew he was irritated—his sarcasm took on, if possible, an even sharper edge and he identified me more openly as a Henderson. Looking back on it, though, I think the Terman description more apt than I gave it credit for—isn't "borderline genius" synonymous with "brilliant but dubious"? Which is not a bad description of my subsequent artistic career.

But what were these books I was devouring at this Gargantuan rate? Happily, time has obliterated all memory of most of them, but I do recall a few of the authors who held me under their spell. To begin with, there was George Alfred Henty, a retired Victorian officer in Her Majesty's Service, who must have written forty volumes of historical fiction, each one designed to show war and the British flag in carnival colors—dollops of history were stirred into kettles steaming with the stew of heroism. Then came Jules Verne and Edgar Rice Burroughs, ancestors of

science fiction, with their fantastic travels beneath the skin of the sea and among the bones of the earth. Next was Dumas with his musketeers and the great Revenge Symphony of *The Count of Monte Cristo,* which has never failed to enrapture fresh generations of daydreamers. But my favorite representative of the literary avengers was Davey Balfour in R. L. Stevenson's *Kidnapped.* Stevenson's far more popular boys' tale, *Treasure Island,* hardly appealed to me at all—its boy hero was much too passive and conventional for my taste—while the story of the disinherited and hunted young Scots laird brought out all my empathy. (It is worth noting that three or four years later, with growing sophistication, I transferred this empathy to Raskolnikov in *Crime and Punishment* and Julien Sorel in Stendhal's *Red and the Black,* each of whom finds in murder a way of revenging himself on a repressive society. Obviously, a deep well of hatred bubbled beneath my façade of self-control; I was to pay and pay heavily for that repression later on, but that is another story.)

My taste in poetry was rudimentary; at school we were force-fed swatches of Longfellow, Tennyson, and Felicia Hemans, but my idea of excitement was to be found in Poe, Coleridge's *Rime of the Ancient Mariner,* and, a bit later on, Wilde's *Ballad of Reading Gaol* and Fitzgerald's *Rubaiyat,* from all of which I memorized long passages, more, I think, to live up to my projected role as a genius than from any real enjoyment. I can't remember a single schoolfellow who shared my new enthusiasms; to them I was definitely becoming an odd one, an outsider.

All during this period books were virtually my only contact with human emotion. What school friendships I had could be maintained only by concealing my real thoughts, and I had been so indoctrinated in my father's notions of reticence and Puritan decorum that emotional openness was utterly beyond me. Anyway, the hostility which every day grew more oppressive between my parents did not encourage confidences. My brother, with whom I might have shared them, disliked me (probably with good reason) and found his own circle of friends, while I mentally accused him of aping our father in his conformism.

Yet on the surface we were a successful, pleasant, and somewhat original provincial family, not differing greatly from thousands of other such middle-class families in our absorption in picnics, schools, golf clubs, and Sunday nights with the radio's Firestone Hour of light music and Jack Benny and Fred Allen for comedic relief. I am sure most people thought such a childhood a fortunate one.

The author with pioneer figures, Hood River, 1989

And perhaps it was. No doubt there was a strong neurotic component in my hatred of this life and my certainty, even at that tender age, that I must find and follow a different path.

October. Under its cage
of culverts the river
dreams of drowned canoes.
Rusted axles loll in the mud.
Regattas of froth set out
on their mysterious voyages.
The butterflies are gone.
I am half asleep. I lie in my drowsy
blood, hands clenched on a book of chalk,
my mind unclothed of all ambition.

Some white morning shall I
follow the fleets of foam
to that mountain of chalcedony which
lies under Capricorn, and there
in the lungs of the sea will I
encounter the dark king of indolence
and do him obeisance.

An Epilogue of Sorts

Recollection has now brought me to my fourteenth year, where things began to change for the better, at least as far as my self-esteem was concerned. Choices opened up before me. Increasingly I got away from my family. I began to read Schopenhauer and Nietzsche and find answers to the static Platonism Professor Barnes had offered. I saw "the World as Will" (a pet phrase of Schopenhauer's) and determined to force my way into it and make waves. I entered a high school where I was allowed to choose many of my subjects and began the study of Latin (still being offered in those days); I read Roman history and discovered my own inherent anti-Christian bias wonderfully buttressed by Gibbon's great *Decline and Fall*. I made the high-school golf team and even took the desperate step of attempting to play football. I formed new and utterly nonintellectual friendships. I grew to be six feet three inches tall and weighed 142 pounds. I learned, albeit awkwardly, to waltz and fox-trot. I drank from my father's whiskey. And naturally, spurred on by the philosophy of action and a hunger to please my peers, I turned my back on poetry and magic.

These developments occupied my next five years; they could in themselves be the topics of an interesting study; but since they had nothing at all to do with my essential education or the development of my poetic vision, it is perhaps best to end here. Dylan Thomas (my exact contemporary) is said to have written an early version of every one of his poems by the time he was seventeen. I can't say the same, since I only consciously turned to poetry at an age when Thomas was already dead, but the sources of my best poetry—the images, the emotions, yes, and much of the language—are to be found in the ten years of my life I have here explored. My plays, stories, and novels have all developed out of the thoughts and experiences of adult life, but poetry, I believe, cannot be manufactured from such materials—it is either lying there, awaiting the alchemist's wand, or it is not.

And, as you can see, it is with discovering the veins where such ores have secretly crystallized that these vignettes have been concerned.

Beneath Me the Earth Forever Thinking

In the entrails of the mountain
smiths labor at their forges;
on its crest a wisp of steam,
elsewhere: cold granite.

In those hot depths leaves are broken apart
and the delicate sinews of feathers
impressed in stone. Crystals are spawned
and die in these basalt rivers. Mica
leaps like trout in the schist.

The thoughts of the earth are slow,
are pounded with gold hammers,
perdure in the gneiss, sing
in the secret jade. On the moraine above

a farmer wanders in search of his lost goat.
He does not hear the clamor of anvils
but runs home, a forecast of snow
printed somewhere in his mind.

BIBLIOGRAPHY

Poetry:

(With Mel Fowler) *Poems and Prints*, San Francisco Review, 1962.

Tactics of Survival, and Other Poems, Bindweed Press, 1964.

The Dolphin with the Revolver in Its Teeth (illustrated by Gary H. Brown), Unicorn Press, 1967.

Two Poems, Unicorn Press, 1967.

The One Whose Approach I Cannot Evade, Unicorn Press, 1967.

A Ship of Bells (illustrated by Fowler), Kayak, 1968.

Twelve Stanzas in Praise of the Holy Chariot, Kayak, 1969.

The Rococo Eye (illustrated by Anne Swan), Northeast/Juniper Books, 1971.

Lessons in Alchemy, West Coast Poetry Review, 1976.

The Piano Beneath the Skin, Copper Canyon Press, 1978.

Mirror on Horseback, Kayak, 1979.

The Wounded Alphabet: Poems Collected and New, 1953-1983, Jazz Press, 1983.

Cloud Taxis, Cafe Solo Press, 1984.

Plays:

"The Discovery and Perilous Ascent of Kan-Chen-Chomo," first produced in San Francisco by The Interplayers, 1955.

"Prometheus Found," first produced in San Francisco at Actors Workshop, 1958.

"The Housewarming," first produced in San Francisco at Actors Workshop, 1958.

"The Busy Martyr," first produced in San Francisco at Actors Workshop, 1959.

"The Magical History of Doctor Faustus," first produced in San Francisco by The Interplayers, 1966.

"The Ticket," first produced in San Francisco, 1967.

The Counterfeit Rose: A Baroque Comedy (first produced in Memphis, Tenn., at Circuit Theater, March, 1978), Kayak, 1967.

The Devil Comes to Wittenberg: A Tragicomedy, Dragons Teeth Press, 1980.

Five Plays, Jazz Press, 1981.

Fiction:

Another Shore (novel), Kayak, 1971; revised edition, Story Line Press, 1988.

Notes of the Siege Year: Eight Entertainments (stories), Kayak, 1974.

October at the Lighthouse: Tales, Jazz Press, 1984.

Travels in Remote America, forthcoming.

Other:

(Editor with R. L. Peters) *Pioneers of Modern Poetry* (satire), Kayak, 1967, 4th edition, 1969.

(Compiler and translator with Heiner Bastian) *Eight Poets of Germany and America*, Kayak, 1967.

(Illustrator) Lennart Bruce, *Observations: An Agenda*, Kayak, 1968.

(Editor) *Losers Weepers: Poems Found Practically Everywhere,* Kayak, 1969.

(Translator with Fernando Alegria) Ludwig Zeller, *Dream Woman,* Kayak, 1975.

Contributor to anthologies, including: *The Modern Short Story in the Making,* edited by W. Burnett and H. Burnett, Hawthorn, 1964; *Poets of Today,* edited by Walter Lowenfels, International Publishers, 1964; *Of Poetry and Power: Poems on the Presidency of J. F. Kennedy,* edited by Glikes and Schwaber, Basic Books, 1964; *A Poetry Reading against the Vietnam War,* Sixties Press, 1966; *Where Is Vietnam?: American Poets Respond,* edited by Lowenfels, Anchor, 1967; *The Voice That Is Great within Us,* edited by Hayden Carruth, Bantam, 1972; *A Geography of Poets,* edited by Edward Field, Bantam, 1978; *The Oxford Book of American Popular Verse,* edited by William Harmon, Oxford University Press, 1978; *Surrealism in English,* edited by Edward Germain, Penguin, 1978.

Contributor to *Chelsea, Hudson Review, Nation, First Stage, Malahat Review, Western Humanities Review,* and other publications.

Bohumil Hrabal

1914-

WHO I AM

(Translated from the Czech by Mary Hrabik Samal)

I am sitting in the tavern "U zlatého tygra" and playing with the paper coasters; I cannot get enough of the emblem; my fingers twirl the two black tigers; as always, I am unconsciously bending back the corners of the check—the first after the first beer, then the second, third, and fourth; sometimes, when Bohouš brings my first beer, he pulls a slip of paper out of his white jacket, and with a smile, in advance, he bends back one of the chit's corners; I am sitting with my party; wherever I choose to sit, there is my party; this is my ritual, and not only mine, but also of everyone who comes to drink beer; a table makes up the party, which converses. Those conversations around the tavern table allow one to cope with the stress of daily life; even idle chatter is a kind of coping; perhaps, when one feels worst, the best cure is a banal conversation about trivial matters and events; sometimes, I sit there and stubbornly refuse to say anything; usually during the first beer I make it clear that it is unpleasant for me to reply to any query whatever; I look forward so much to that first beer; it takes me a while to get used to the tyrannical loudness of the tavern, to adjust to so many guests and so many conversations; it is as if everyone wanted the entire tavern to hear what he was saying, as if everyone in this tavern believed the very thing he was saying to be so remarkable that he had to yell his banal message; I also belong to these screamers; after the second beer, I, too, think what I am saying is so very important that I start to shout: I seem to see more, and naively believe that what I have to say must be heard not only by my table, but perhaps also by the entire world. So, I sit there and play nervously with the paper coasters; I hold them like cards, sometimes ten at a time; I shuffle them, let them fall on the table; I take a sip of beer, and again I play with the coasters and the chit. I am here, but I am not here alone; I do not barge into the conversation; I merely listen. How many tens of thousands of evenings have I spent in this manner, how many tens of thousands of people have taken their turns in my taverns, how many tens of thou-

Bohumil Hrabal in one of his beloved pubs, 1974

sands of guests have I sullied not so much with my monologues as my dialogues, which sometimes turned to lectures, usually not mine but others'; then, we would all stop talking and listen to a story being told in a way that ended the tavern's idle chatter, "the inn's prattle," as Professor Václav Černý used to call it, or as Eman Frynta, one in the know, used to say, "tavern talk"; Mr. Ruis, the violist of the Dvořák Quartet, was telling us about the last concert in Bílina: how the town was sad and run-down, how neglect and the weather had taken their toll, how

The brewery where Hrabal's family lived, Nymburk, Czechoslovakia

gypsies and drunks sauntered about the main square, but how well-dressed ladies and gentlemen came to the town hall at night and Bílina was transformed into an attentive audience moved by the music. Next to me, the guests were discussing mushrooms, *Lactarii deliciosi;* I waited for them to address the essential, but nobody did, so I asked for their permission and said . . . Gentlemen, *Lactarius deliciosus* is a mystical mushroom, beautifully flame-colored; its concentric greenish circles contain the mystical mission of this fungus, because the diminishing greenish circles of each *Lactarius deliciosus* converge into a green navel, the point in the center of those concentric greenish circles, and this dot in the cap is the center of thought, what the Buddhist monks contemplate, their navel, as they thread themselves by their umbilical cords backward in time to the original sin of our mother primeval, the first woman, who had a flat stomach, the beginning of the human race; all this, gentlemen, I declare, can be read from the concentric greenish circles of the flame-colored *Lactarius deliciosus,* which contain the unalloyed and most fundamental symbols of man's origin and present existence. But, gentlemen, for those of you who like to eat, I'll give you the Spanish loggers' recipe for *Lactarius deliciosus:* a layer of sausage, then the *Lactarius,* diced green peppers, bacon, diced tomatoes, and again the sausage and the other layers; it should end with the sausage and be baked on an open fire; when the casserole is done, it can be topped with grated cheese . . . And I was shouting these two tidings because I could not be heard otherwise and because I naively thought I had to scream so this would be heard not only in Prague, but also in the entire region, country, and continent; I shout when I foolishly believe what is in me belongs to everyone . . . Mr. Ruis was telling us how in Sweden the Dvořák Quartet played only Czech music, the Dvořák quartet written when his children died and finally "From My Life" . . . all of a sudden, sobbing and crying were heard; everyone turned to see what was happening; after the concert, the wife of a doctor who had emigrated told Mr. Ruis in the dressing room that she had to return home, that she had not seen her mother, that she had to return home or die in Sweden, that, although she had everything, including a Mercedes, she had to go home, to see Prague, her mother and friends . . . Mr. Ruis related this quietly; all had fallen silent, and only Mr. Ruis's cracked, yet beautiful, voice could be heard; the conversation then was about Stravinsky and the portraits on his walls of his three musical patron saints, Webern, Schoenberg, and Berg . . . I kept waiting for an opening, for the crack in the door into which I would force my foot and relate what, I always think, should be known not only by my table, but also by the entire tavern, and not only the tavern, but also the entire town, country, and world . . . When I stuck my foot in the door, I said loudly . . . So, gentlemen, I listened to radio Vienna this afternoon, and there his son-in-law told more about Webern's life . . . As the war was ending and the American army advanced past Linz, there was a curfew . . . Webern's son-in-law, who did not know the Webern who came to visit them that evening was *the* Webern, and even Webern himself did not know that he was the famous Webern—so, the son-in-law said, "Father, I have saved you eight cigarettes. You are such an avid smoker. Here, you take them"; Webern was moved to tears: "I'm so happy," he said, "that I gave you my daughter, that I have such a good son-in-law, and that

my daughter has such a fine husband. I will light up immediately. I can't stand it." The daughter and son-in-law protested that they had children, "Perhaps, Father, you could go smoke in the hall." Webern did go into the hall, but said to himself that the smoke would penetrate the room where his grandsons were sleeping, and because his son-in-law was so good, he decided to go outside and smoke on the balcony. He went into the darkness, hungrily put the cigarette into his mouth, and struck a match; as he inhaled that first breath of nicotine and tasty smoke for which he had waited so long, a shot rang out and Webern fell; they found him dead; his first breath was also his last; it cost him dearly; because fires and lights were forbidden, some soldier on duty shot Webern . . . Attention, gentlemen, the mystical coincidences did not end here! So distressed was the soldier that he had shot Webern more or less by accident that he sought treatment when he returned to the United States; so deeply did Webern wound him; he spent three years in a psychiatric ward, and five years after he shot Webern, he shot himself . . . And Mr. Maryško was moved, and then he said to me, as we were leav-

Bohumil (center) with his parents, Francin and Maryška Hrabal, and his brother,
Slávek, around 1922

ing . . . You should not have told me that story about Webern . . . Mr. Maryško, who bad-mouthed Webern so much—Who could play him? he used to ask—but Mr. Ruis insisted that he not only liked Webern, but also liked to play him, and Mr. Hampl, a graphic artist, supported Mr. Ruis and declared that he actually loved Webern only because he did not understand him at all . . . And I am sitting in "U zlatého tygra" and looking over the guests' faces, and, yes, no babble, no tavern prattle, Mr. Václav Černý; sometimes this screaming tavern is a small university, where under the influence of the beer people tell each other of events and occurrences that wound the soul, and where above their heads, the cigarette smoke floats like a question mark of life's absurdity and wondrousness . . . I was si-lent—that *Lactarius deliciosus* with its concentric greenish circles, that green dot in the middle of the flame-colored cap, that omphalos, that navel of the world by which it is possible to travel backward into the smooth belly of our primeval mother, Eve . . . I am so lost in thought that in the middle of a conversation, which I did not register, I am transport-ed to my childhood, to my first tavern visits; these taverns so enchanted me that they became my destiny. My dad, a brewery agent, used to take me along on his Laurin and Klement motorcycle when he made the rounds of the taverns, his customers; we traveled to little towns and villages; every time, I remember, the taverns seemed deserted, so sad in the mornings and afternoons, with practically no guests; each of these village inns was dark; only the spigot, the barroom tap, gleamed faintly; Father went over the innkeeper's accounts; he used to hold forth in the kitchen, and I sat in the taproom, where it was nearly always cool, and drank lemonade, one after another, those beautiful red and yellow lemonades, which foamed in the glass; only the tipped and lifted glasses attested to the presence of the few guests sitting in the darkness; some smoked; a match was lit here and there, and I was happy in these inns; sometimes I was invited to the kitchen behind the taproom; nearly always, the tavern keeper's wife there seemed very tired to me; these wives often had a hard time walking; they leaned on the furniture and got up from chairs as if they had rheumatism; I was given soups, tripe and goulash soups, and again I had my fill of red and yellow lemonade, one after the other; on the table, the bright papers shone in front of my father; smoke filtered through his fingers—the blue smoke of Egyptian cigarettes—the only ones I was ever sent to fetch; Dad's voice was cajoling, quiet and insistent; the tavern keeper took in his advice. I did

At a photographer's studio in Brno, where he ran away and did not want to be photographed

not know what those two were talking about; it was as if they were speaking a foreign language; the tavern keeper always had something amiss in his accounts like me in my schoolwork; Dad was like the teacher; I, the student, never had the homework done right; like me, the tavern keeper looked at the ground and was afraid to look Dad in the eyes, but Father's voice gave him hope and courage; finally, they were both laughing; they shook hands for a long time and looked each other in the eyes; Father left the papers on the table, and always the tavern keeper forced a bottle or two on Dad; then the innkeeper saw us outside and helped us get the motorcycle started, and when we left, I knew, the entire inn breathed a sigh of relief that Dad was gone—my father who was the agent, because he brought a measure of sadness to the innkeeper, a measure of something that the tavern keeper feared . . . And again in the next tavern, I drank red and yellow lemonade, one after the other; a year later I was afraid to go into the kitchen, so I sat in the taproom and listened through the glass door to how Father's voice reproached and how the innkeeper defended himself; the tavern keeper would sometimes run into the taproom, down a shot, and return pale to the kitchen, where Dad put an arm around his shoulder and using his kind voice tried to talk him into something as gently as he talked to me about working harder in school and stopping all my nonsense; what would become of me if I didn't study? I liked going with Dad; I went with him after school and especially during my vacations; every day I made the rounds of the taverns in the Nymburk district with him; I knew them by heart; the most impressive tavern was "U města Kolína," near Lysa, where the tavern mistress was so foulmouthed that she made Dad blush; she would laugh, shrug her shoulders, and deflect all questions about beer and taxes; I sat in the taproom, where it was sunny and where the large asparagus plant and the sewing machine were kept; I drank one red lemonade after another, and in between a yellow one, and strained my ears to hear with great pleasure all the forbidden words used by the tavern mistress, who whenever she went into the taproom to serve me yet another still-capped lemonade would pat me on the head, and whose beautiful eyes took me all in as she looked at me. At the other taverns, I had already checked out all of the rooms for drinking, dancing, and entertainment; I used to go to the gardens where the tables were set up and skittle was played; the inn belonging to Mr. Hugo Šmolek, a Jew, really impressed me; his children had such thick hair, such thick braids, that their faces were barely visible; Mr. Šmolek had his head shaved, and his black hair grew over his forehead nearly to his eyebrows; his wife always sparkled with sweat; she gleamed as if oil or lard had been spread over her; even her dress seemed covered with grease, lard. So enamored was I of the inns and taverns that I felt out of my element when Dad took me to a restaurant with tablecloths and even waiters dressed in black; I sat there shy and ill at ease; whenever I could, I preferred to pace outside the restaurant and wait for Dad and the opportunity to go to the village taverns . . . those village taverns where they knew me so well that they considered me one of the family, where I was happy, where I had the run of the entire tavern and where sometimes I wandered into the barn and courtyard; some of these taverns, and those I liked the best, also had butcher shops; I used to get round salami there; that was my special treat, to drink one lemonade after another and eat salami . . . When

in high school, I already drank beer. Wherever I went with Dad, I was a living beer ad. Drinking one beer after another and relishing them, I kept exclaiming loudly how excellent and tasty this beer was; this amazed not only the tavern keepers, but also the guests . . . And so we made the rounds of the same taverns, I drank one beer after another, and Father in his calm voice continued with the tavern keeper to solve the problems of the quantity of beer and the fees; always something was not in order, but I sat in the taproom and after the third beer conversed with the guests. My favorite place to go with Dad was Vodvárka's in Kolín's Zábalí district. It was merry there from the very morning, and Mr. Vodvárka, man of the world, was always in a good mood. Dad did not have to point out anything or reproach anyone, because Mr. Vodvárka, as far as I am concerned, was and still is number one. When this Mr. Vodvárka came to Nymburk, Dad was always afraid of having to go to Prague with him, but for me this was a wonderful event; as soon as we arrived at Šmelhaus's, as soon as we entered the hall, Mr.

Bohumil Hrabal, from the passport he used to see the Olympic Games in Berlin, 1936

With Josef Hrabal, who became famous as Uncle Pepin and deeply influenced Hrabal's poetics

Vodvárka pressed a hundred-koruna note on the violinist's forehead; from then on, every time we entered, every three months, the band struck up "Kolíne, Kolíne" . . . as we sat there, Dad reminded us every hour that it was time to go home, but Mr. Vodvárka sang and danced, smiled at and joked with everyone; I sat there, and the more I drank the more I hugged those who came to shake Mr. Vodvárka's hand; so we made merry at Šmelhaus's until closing time; Dad was unhappy; he could not drink much because he had to drive the motorcycle, later the Škoda, home, and he wondered what a fix he had got himself into, because Mr. Vodvárka came every three months and always promised that first they would go settle everything at the brewery headquarters and only then, for just a little while, to Šmelhaus's . . . and then the musicians accompanied us down the stairs from Šmelhaus's and into the street; as we were going home at dawn, Mr. Vodvárka woke up the tavern keeper in Nehvizdy; again we drank beer and coffee; Mr. Vodvárka had the musicians awakened; they played for us, and Mr. Vodvárka also woke up the merchant and bought the chocolates he distributed to the women he had invited when he knocked at the windows to summon all good-hearted people; the musicians played, and we sang; Dad kept looking at his watch and worrying that in two hours he would again have to be in the billing room of the brewery . . . These chains of taverns from my childhood and youth, then the taverns in Nymburk where I used to go every Saturday and Sunday morning and afternoon to play billiards, Pospíšil's "Pod mostem," where I played piano and cards with the young men of Zálabí, my friends unto death, those ordinary young men from the little houses of Zálabí, the inns and taverns that I frequented as I traveled through Bohemia as a postman, and then inns where I stayed every day while traversing half of the Czech lands as a traveling salesman for the firm of Harry Karel Klofanda, the taverns where I ate breakfast, lunch, and dinner every day, the quite ordinary inns in which I preferred to sleep, and then the Prague taverns in Libeň, Žižkov, Vysočany, Malá Strana, and Staré Město I visited every day—in fact, for a quarter of a century, I have eaten supper in these inns; seldom, usually by accident, did I enter a restaurant, a hotel; I never liked being there; I felt ill at ease and came to only after entering the first tavern; here I feel good; here are my kind of people. Here are the busboys and headwaiters with whom I had made pacts of friendship; here I am at home, in my family . . .

Sitting in "U zlatého tygra," I have traveled backward through all my taverns; I have found out about myself, how it all began with Dad, as I traveled with him so that I could drink one lemonade after another and so that Dad could put together the fees and bills of those unhappy tavern keepers, who did not always have their accounts in order. So here I sit in "U zlatého tygra"; I am smiling, and for a long time I have not heard anything, as if I were sitting in the middle of a quiet forest, because I have traveled backward through all the taverns of my life to the very first one in the Nymburk countryside. Mr. Ruis, now I hear him, is saying . . . And so we landed in Copenhagen, where two cars were waiting for us; this was the first time we had accepted an invitation on behalf of the Dvořák Quartet without knowing who had invited us or who was paying us such a princely sum. The cars took us into the evening, beyond Copenhagen; the two gentlemen in evening clothes, one in each car, were calm; we came to a large building, the gate opened, the grill was lifted, and our cars drove into the courtyard; by the bars on the windows, we saw that in a few moments we would be playing in a prison. Then we visited the warden and were treated to drinks and a smorgasbord; when the time came, we entered the chapel where the prisoners were assembled and tuned our instruments . . . We performed the Dvořák concert and "From My Life"; as we played, there was silence, and we knew that we were playing for an audience the likes of which we had never had before. When we finished, they did not applaud; they just sat there, all deeply moved. We got up, started to leave, bowed, but the prisoners continued to sit there with their chins cupped in their hands or their faces hidden by their hands . . . it was our best audience, like our audience when we played in Oxford last year—all in tails, all so formally dressed—when we finished playing Dvořák, Smetana, and Janáček, the audience rose to its feet, their shirtfronts glistened, and we, also in formal attire, stood up, bowed, and started to leave; when we turned around, the audience was just standing there; they were as moved as the prisoners in Copenhagen for whom we had played the same Dvořák quartet, the one he wrote after the death of his children, Smetana's "From My Life," and Janáček's quartet; we played it in such a way, and so profound was this music, our music, that in Oxford, as in the Copenhagen jail, none of the listeners dared to interrupt their

mystical union with the music by a single hand clap. Gentlemen, what is music, by what does it affect us? In essence, by nothing . . . and everything, said Mr. Ruis; we were all moved, and so we preferred to hide our faces in a mug of fresh beer.

*

It has never occurred to me, not even in my dreams, to change, or even desire to change, the political situation in which I live. I never wished to transform the language or the world; when I cited Marx, when I cited Rimbaud, when I cited Mallarmé, I always wanted to change myself, to change the one I had within my hand's reach, me. Thus, I always consider myself a witness to my epoch, not its conscience; I never had the wherewithal for that; since childhood I have been awed by reality, which I did not create and which existed before I was; my desire is no more than to mirror it, for even the most horrendous events hold so much beauty for me. I have always been that joker in the deck of cards, the one who saunters in the sun, a jingling bell in hand, and that seeming fool's cap still accompanies me today. It was an honor to witness World War II as a train dispatcher; so overwhelming were these drastic events that I could never believe my eyes; likewise, when the war ended, I saw in myself and around me so much beautiful horror and experienced so much pain in love that even today I sleep badly from it all; my seemingly ordinary life is dramatic enough in itself. So it is an honor to live with this nation about whose virtues I have the same doubts as about my own; I am a heretic, a blasphemer of sorts, when it comes to what this nation lives for on an idealized plane, in which it places its hope, and finally what is inscribed on its standard; I doubt very much that truth conquers all; without denying the greatness of those who professed and sacrificed for truth, such as Master Jan Hus, George of Poběbrady, and finally professor Masaryk, I do question whether we are a nation which desires truth and hopes for it. Now, I live within the realm of limited sovereignty, as Brezhnev elucidated our truth, and that canon bothers me no more than "truth conquers all." I live as I have always lived, and as I would live were the representatives of the Habsburgs in the Castle. I have such a hard time with myself, steeling myself, I have such a hard time with my neighbors, that I simply have no time for any political changes whatsoever; moreover, I really don't even know what people are talking about when they want to change the political situation, because all I want is to change myself; all I wish for myself is to be able to say when I reach heaven: I am what I am . . . For the time being, I am only my own guilty conscience. What happened to me, I have always thought, happened only to me; that is why I hesitated and was so modest, why I always showed what I had begun to write and had written as if someone else had written it; my first texts caused me such trepidation that I was ashamed of them. Only after I ventured into the world, learned to bestow gifts on others, and began to delight in the pubs, the realization that what seemed to happen only to me also happened to others gave me courage; perhaps I am not so alone after all. I realized after eavesdropping for so many years that my greatest secrets, exaggerations, failures, and most tender confidences were not my secret illness; all this happens to *others,* more often and with greater intensity; it rages with greater force in entire groups of others; so I began to think what happened and was happening to others also happened to me; my joy was greatest when what happened to others also happened to me, and so I preferred to pretend that what happened to others was my own experience. Somehow, the others so strengthened me that I found the daring to step on thin ice, on the ceiling through which the soul was threatening to crash; my courage grew as I discovered in the taverns that what I had thought was only mine also happened to others. My taverns, they never were some sort of office, some sort of confessional; I did not go there to ask questions, but only to lounge around without forcing conversations, not to begin inquiries as a reporter or pollster, but only to sit, drink, eavesdrop, and wait aimlessly; suddenly, under the influence of the moment, someone would begin, as I did, when I did not want to, but suddenly was compelled to sit at my typewriter; he would begin to talk about what seemed antisocial, what seemed scandalous, what seemed repulsive, what was close to murder, fornication . . . In the tavern, at that moment, I would have the feeling that I was talking to and with myself, that my public prosecutor and confessor was addressing me, that what I thought of myself, what I thought happened only to me, was common, and finally that the narrator and author of my confession had come solely, as if he had been born solely, to help me with my aberrations, my peculiarities, my most secret desires and vices, to help me bear them . . . I am trying to reach my deep nonconsciousness by shoving, none too successfully, subconsciousness into consciousness; only now do I shine the light of consciousness onto my past life, so that I can save myself, so that enlightenment can nurse me, so that I will slowly get well. My literature and my texts

With Eliška Plevová at their wedding, 1956

are nothing other than my own remembrance of things past; the search overwhelms me, but at the same time, it amuses me; in my texts, I put much emphasis on entertainment, on how entertained I am by the difficulty of this quest. All my slowness is unintentional; I do not try to write what I know, but to reach what I do not know; so I am not yet doing what I want to do, but what I do not want; it is necessary, I know, to piss in the wind, to be burnt by what cannot be extinguished. I am standing before my tribunal, and my internal trial is a great inquisition; it is simultaneously an indictment and a defense; I am both my prosecutor and defense attorney. My manner of writing bears within itself the premature crossing of parallel lines, the interrupting of my own conversations, because it is impossible to go forward in a mechanical way; I can move forward only by the interjection of outside events into the internal monologue. In this manner, my writing is my path, day after day, month after month, year after year, but not *ad infinitum*—only to keep me in a state of creative tension up to the moment when as the last hour dawns I will perhaps receive the check, my bill, in this gigantic tavern which this world is for me. Up to now, the innkeeper has let me run up my tab; I am living on credit; all of my expenses are inscribed in the frame of the open door through which I observe the wondrously beautiful world; I transcribe from it only what I believe to be my extenuating circumstances; although I realize, all too well, that I am fooling myself, that what I think might reduce my guilt for living will get me, will nail me, and will establish my total culpability . . . In the meantime, my writing is my punishment for wandering between crime and innocence, for constantly postponing the final judgment and settlement of accounts, for becoming, at least partially, what I have always wanted to be, an accursed poet. Now, at my trial, I subpoena what lies deep in my nonconsciousness; I am horrified at myself; aware of my past, I wring my hands over myself; I cannot grant myself absolution; I am courageous at least in that I proffer, by and in my texts, my feelings of guilt. At the same time, I am cracking a smile. It is my gallows humor . . . my Prague irony.

Zdena Salivarová Škvorecká, Josef Škvorecký, and Bohumil Hrabal, Ithaca, New York, 1989

*

I have always had the advantage of never attaining a real education or genuine knowledge, so I have had to wager all on experience. For the simple reason that I am a bit slow, my education has never been smelted, changed into something qualitatively different, and propelled beyond in a leap. Because I read a lot, I cite a lot, and when I am quoting, I forget to say from where and whom. I am really a robber of corpses and a plunderer of noble sarcophagi. This is in fact my real character; being always on the lookout for what can be pinched from writers and artists, living or dead, I am an innovator and improviser; and then, like the fox dragging its tail behind, I cover the tracks which would lead to where the deed was done. I have thoroughly pillaged the graves of Louis-Ferdinand Céline, Ungaretti, Camus, Erasmus of Rotterdam, Bernard Malamud, Ferlinghetti, and Kerouac. *The Pearl on the Bottom,* I have scratched out from the eyes of Jacob Boehm, as well as the beautiful thought that man cannot rip himself out of his epoch. The perpetual states of melancholy, I have stolen from Leibnitz—or was it Nietzsche? And from the tombstone of Roland Barthes, I pilfered "Art makes celebration of knowledge," and that is just to give an example. In fact, my sound thoughts are always pinched, including Plato's notion of begetting in beauty. Even what I had written well on my very own had always been told to me by others; in fact, I pick

the pockets of restaurant and pub guests in the same way as if I swiped their overcoats or umbrellas. I am, of course, really good at lying about situations in which I have never been, pretending to have read books that I never have, giving testimony about events that never occurred, making oaths that are perjury, hogging credit for deeds that someone else has done, giving eyewitness accounts of incidents that I never saw; I am a whore who goes to bed feinting love; I am a rotter and trickster; lying, like water to a fish, is my natural element; for purgatory to be large enough to hold my sins, the hardened criminals and vandals will have to be taken up to paradise; so my turn will finally come before I am cast into hell. Above all, if only that purgatory, heaven, and hell were real! If only this world were more than that Czech children's game of heaven, hell, and purgatory. If nothing more than this should be true, then I am saved; then I have not lived in vain.

Looking back on that famous life of mine, how, to be accurate, it has run through my fingers, I am filled with faith in the existence of life everlasting. At this moment, I have not the feeling, but the certainty, that I find myself at the other side of things, at the registry of eternal life, from which there is no escape indeed. It is like looking into the spring sun, a blinding as pleasant as that of the much-loved alcohol. This eternal life is nothing but a beautifully dreadful monotony in which the same flageolet waltzes are played over and over. Death, then, is something which does not concern me, because it is a pleasant frontier; it suffices to bow one's head and enter there from whence man came by birth. Every day, encountering the possibility of death, I am very close to that sweet secret behind which the kingdom of light is found. Because I am no longer afraid, I no longer avoid the danger of death; I don't take it into account. I desire only to dwell in the bondage of light. The old world does not retreat from me but rather advances towards me. The devastated cemetery is the triumph of light. My present is irrevocably lost in favor of a return to the beginning. This world is lost to me now, and I am returning to where I have never been. All my life I have lied unintentionally, because I have lived in a world which is nothing but a lie; yet, at its very extremity, it is possible to see the truth of light. I love sclerosis, forgetfulness, and inadequate deeds; with pleasure, I see and observe in myself the coming of imbecility; I see how I am depleting the stock of my renowned memory; I am happy that I am getting nearer to debility, the peak of human existence. No danger exists for me; I have no reason to warn anyone against the assault of doubts and errors; all the advice I was ever given, and all I myself gave, proved to be vanity and more vanity; at their own expense, every man and every society desire no more than to rush headlong into disaster; only after falling and hitting the bottom is there a positive result, can one perceive the true nature of light—the light in the darkness when it is late. And because it is late, the truth is also gained; the truth is always more than fiction of any kind. Fiction is that very beautiful postponement of knowledge. Of course, fiction is always more than any world view or any political idea. The epilogue is always more beautiful than the promising prologue. Old men are always in the foreground, because they have within their hands' reach their youth, inundated by light . . .

This essay is comprised of excerpts from the samizdat version of the author's autobiography, *Kdo jsem.*

The little house in Kersko where Hrabal passes most of his time

Bohumil Hrabal with poet Karel Maryško, early 1980s

Epilogue

Bohumil Hrabal was born on March 28, 1914, in Brno. He grew up in Nymburk, a little town on the banks of the Elbe River, where his father was employed as a brewery agent. In 1934 he entered Charles University in Prague, but his law studies were interrupted when the Nazis closed all Czech universities during World War II. He received his degree in 1946, but never practiced law. During wartime, Hrabal found work in a notary's office and a railway station, and was later employed as an insurance agent and traveling salesman. In 1949 he went to work at the steelworks of Kladno, where he remained for four years. After a serious accident, he became a packer in a paper-recycling plant and finally a stagehand and supernumerary at the S. K. Neumann Theater in Prague.

Hrabal has been writing since the late thirties—first poetry, and then prose which he characterized as "total realism." He put together a first volume of poems in 1948, but the radical changes in cultural policy following the communist takeover prevented him from publishing until 1956, when two short stories came out in a limited edition. That same year, Hrabal married Eliška Plevová; she died in 1987. Hrabal's literary career blossomed at the beginning of the sixties, when the effects of the Soviet Thaw reached Czechoslovakia. The publication in 1963 of his first book, *A Pearl on the Bottom,* brought him instant fame and popularity in his native land. Hrabal has been a professional writer ever since, though after Warsaw Pact armies put an end to the Prague Spring of 1968, he was not allowed to publish until 1976. He wrote some of his most important works during this period, including *I Served the King of England* (1971) and *Too Loud a Solitude* (1976). These books as officially published, however, differ in many respects from the original versions, which were circulated in samizdat editions or printed outside Czechoslovakia, and Hrabal has continued to have problems with censorship. In 1989 the political climate improved dramatically, and Hrabal's original texts will now gradually be published in uncensored versions.

Hrabal lives and works both in Prague and in Kersko, a village near Nymburk, the town of his childhood. He is one of his country's most successful and most published authors. Hrabal's works, widely translated, have won awards in Czechoslovakia, Hungary, and Italy.

—Susanna Roth

BIBLIOGRAPHY

Hrabal's works have been officially published in Czechoslovakia in censored versions; they have been published uncensored in the samizdat and abroad. Since 1990, any works officially published in Czechoslovakia have been uncensored as well.

Fiction:

Hovory lidí (title means "People's Conversations"; anthology) Spolek českých bibliofilů v Praze [Prague], 1956, Československý spisovatel, 1984.

Perlička na dně (title means "A Pearl in the Abyss"; short stories), Československý spisovatel [Prague], 1963.

Pábitelé (title means "The Palavers"; short stories), Mladá fronta [Prague], 1964.

Taneční hodiny pro starší a pokročilé (title means "Dancing Lessons for the Older and Advanced Pupils"; novella), Československý spisovatel, 1964.

Ostře sledované vlaky (novella), Československý spisovatel, 1965, translation by Edith Pargeter published as *Closely Watched Trains*, Grove, 1968, published in England as *A Close Watch on the Trains*, Cape, 1968.

Inzerát na dům, ve kterém už nechci bydlet (title means "For Sale: Selling House I Don't Want to Live In Any Longer"; short stories), Mladá fronta, 1965.

Automat svět (title means "Cafeteria World"; short stories; includes "Pábitelé" and "Fádní odpoledne" ["A Dull Afternoon"], introduction by Emanuel Frynta, Mladá fronta, 1966, translation by Michael Henry Heim published as *The Death of Mr. Baltisberger,* Doubleday, 1975.

Bohumil Hrabal uvádí (title means "Bohumil Hrabal Presents"; anthology), Mladá fronta, 1967.

Postřižiny (title means "Haircutting"), Československý spisovatel, 1976.

Městečko ve kterém se zastavil čas (title means "The Little Town Where Time Has Stopped"), Comenius [Innsbruck], 1978, Odeon, [Prague], 1991.

Morytáty a legendy (title means "Street Ballads and Legends"; novella), Československý spisovatel, 1978.

Slavnosti sněženek (title means "Festivities of Snowdrops"; short stories), Československý spisovatel, 1978.

Krasosmutnění (title means "Beautiful Mourning"), Československý spisovatel, 1979.

Každý den zázrak (title means "Every Day a Miracle"), Československý spisovatel, 1979.

Příliš hlučná samota, Index [Cologne], 1980 (printed from samizdat copy; unreviewed by author), Odeon [Prague], 1989, translation published as *Too Loud a Solitude,* Harcourt, 1990.

Jak jsem obsluhoval anglického krále, Index, 1980 (printed from samizdat copy; unreviewed by author), published as *Obsluhoval jsem anglického krále*, Jazzová sekce [Prague], 1982, translation by Paul Wilson published as *I Served the King of England*, Harcourt, 1989.

Harlekýnovy milióny (title means "Harlequin's Millions"), Československý spisovatel, 1981.

Kluby poezie (title means "Poetry Clubs"), Mladá fronta, 1981.

Něžní Barbaři (title means "Tender Barbarian"), Index, 1981 (printed from samizdat copy; unreviewed by author), Odeon, 1990.

Městečko u vody (title means "The Little Town Near the Water"; contains "Postřižiny," "Krasosmutnění," and "Harlekýnovy milióny"), Československý spisovatel, 1982.

Poupata (title means "Buds"), Mladá fronta, 1970, new edition, 1990, Sixty-eight Publishers [Toronto], 1982.

Proluky (title means "Vacant Sites"), [Prague], 1986, Sixty-eight Publishers, 1986, Československý spisovatel, forthcoming.

Život bez smokingu (title means "Life without a Dinner Jacket"), Československý spisovatel, 1986.

Svatby v domě (title means "Weddings in the House"), Sixty-eight Publishers, 1987, Československý spisovatel, forthcoming.

Můj svět (title means "My World"; anthology), Československý spisovatel, 1988.

Tři novely (title means "Three Novellas"; contains "Ostře sledované vlaky," "Taneční hodiny pro starší a pokročilé," and "Obsluhoval jsem anglického krále"), Československý spisovatel, 1989.

Vita nuove (Latin for "New Life"), Sixty-eight Publishers [Toronto], 1987, Československý spisovatel, forthcoming.

Films:

Perlička na dně (title means "A Pearl in the Abyss"; contains *Dům radosti* ["The House of Happiness"], directed by Evald Schorm; *Podvodníci* ["The Imposters"], directed by Jan Němec; *Automat Svět* ["Cafeteria World"], directed by Věra Chytilová; *Romance,* directed by Jaromil Jireš; *Sběrné surovosti* ["Salvaged Cruelties"], directed by Juraj Herz), Barrandov Film Studio, 1965.

Fádní odpoledne (adapted from his short story "A Dull Afternoon"; directed by Ivan Passer), Barrandov Film Studio, 1965, released in the United States as *A Boring Afternoon,* 1968.

Skřivánci na niti (title means "Skylarks on a String"; directed by Jiří Menzel), Barrandov Film Studio, 1969, released, 1990.

Ostře sledované vlaky (adapted from his novella of the same title; directed by Jiří Menzel), Barrandov Film Studio, 1967, released in the United States as *Closely Watched Trains,* Sigma III, 1968, released in England as *Closely Observed Trains,* 1968, translation of film script by Josef Holzbecher published as *Closely Watched Trains,* Simon & Schuster, 1971, published in England as *Closely Observed Trains,* Lorrimer, 1971.

Postřižiny (adapted from his work of the same title; directed by Jiří Menzel), Barrandov Film Studio, 1980.

Other:

(Editor) *Výbor z české prózy* (title means "Selections from Czech Prose Writers"; anthology), Mladá fronta, 1967.

Toto město je ve společné péči obyvatel (title means "This Town Is Under the Communal Care of Its Inhabitants"), photographs by Miroslav Peterka, Československý spisovatel, 1967.

Domácí úkoly z pilnosti (title means "Homework out of Diligence"; biography), Československý spisovatel, 1982.

Kdo jsem (title means "Who Am I"; autobiography), samizdat version, [Prague], 1989.

Herbert R. Lottman

1927-

Autumn 1989—A new book project. A book about France, of course, because if you live in France and write cultural history you should be working on *French* cultural history. One of my most consistently productive sources is the secondhand-book trade of Paris, not excluding booksellers whose shops are wooden or metal cases clamped to the stone parapet along the Seine river. I'll find a number of books here which are lost or available only on microform at the Bibliothèque Nationale. More, I'll discover titles which I never knew existed, memoirs by secondary figures which throw light on the protagonists of my history. These finds can make the difference between a twice-told and a lively story; at the very least they become helpful footnotes. One more time I'll be praised or blamed as a literary detective, and a few more French historians will wish that I'd go back where I came from.

It's a lovely Indian summer afternoon. Some trees still have their leaves, the mild breeze is deflecting exhaust from the frantic traffic on the riverside boulevard. I stop to look at the Seine, and recall the time when the trays of books in a language strange to me took second place to the views I could catch between them. In another instant I am back in that time, and I don't know what process of thought clangs the gong to remind me that I took this walk for the first time just forty years ago.

To salute that memory, I postpone my book hunt for some minutes, the time it takes to mount the steps to the Pont des Arts, for there are no books on the bridge (no automobile traffic either). Forty years ago I'd stand in the middle of the bridge and tell myself—before writing the same thing to my mother and brother and friends—that I now dominated the world's most glorious cityscape, a museum of monuments still utilized: the Ile de la Cité with Notre Dame, the medieval towers of the royal palace, the Louvre of the Louis across the bridge. From where I stood, turning toward the steeple of Saint Germain des Prés church, my view also took in the vital organs of Left Bank Paris, its publishing houses and literary magazines and cafés. André Malraux and Jean-Paul Sartre and Albert Camus were seated at desks or at

Herbert Lottman with brother, Evan (left), and parents, Betty and George Lottman, about 1937

café tables there, with the Malrauxes and Sartres and Camuses of the next generation.

Do I feel the same way about these things now, I who am usually too busy to stroll onto this bridge? For one thing it's not the same bridge I described in my letters home, for that one was demolished after a barge struck one of its pillars, at which time we learned that the elegant lacework construction, the first bridge to be cast in iron, was irreparable. Nor is the Louvre the same, having become part of a development plan of ambitious politicians; the gracious Renaissance courtyard at the far end of the Pont des Arts is now usually closed to the public for one or another invitation-only affair. Not even the French Academy at this end of the bridge is the same, or perhaps it is my perception of it that has robbed it of its magic; now I know that its members won their seats by flattery, and are busy corrupting the next generation. Camus died, then Malraux, then Sartre, and no culture heroes popped up to replace them. So much has changed in this supposedly unchangeable city; don't I have to ask, what about me?

While thinking about that one, I return to the sidewalk to continue my book hunt. Today, for the first time, I find a book *I* wrote in one of the secondhand trays.

On November 8, 1949, the U.S. Department of State was pleased to inform me that I had won a Fulbright grant, giving me an academic year in Paris. In the interests of economy one traveled by sea then, and they booked me onto the SS *Washington,* a vessel with which U.S. Lines was obviously not trying to compete with the Cunard Queens.

My scholarship had the singularity of going to someone who didn't know the language of the country to which he was being sent. "It would be preferable, not to say necessary, that you work on your French this summer," the educational officer had advised when sending me application forms the previous June. "The idea is that you be sufficiently proficient to operate in a French university. . . . I gather that you are at present studying the language." It was still early enough in the Fulbright program for such a gentle offer to be conceivable.

I was indeed studying French; I was enrolled in French I, a required course at the Graduate Faculty of Philosophy of Columbia University, where I had begun a master's in modern British literature. *British* literature. After majoring in English at Washington Square College of New York University, I was full of Joyce, Yeats, and Eliot and wanted more (and never mind that the first two were Irish and the last American). My Fulbright should have taken me to Britain, for I had become obsessed by Q. D. Leavis's *Fiction and the Reading Public,* a tongue-in-cheek analysis of popular fiction, and I should have liked to pursue the study of high-, middle-, and lowbrow taste with contemporary examples. When it became clear that everybody was applying for Britain—the language comes so easily—I was offered the opportunity to try for France.

France! No matter that I lacked the language. I had actually begun to study it in primary school (a private school in mid-Manhattan called the Franklin School for Boys), although in high school and then in college I turned to Spanish, for we were told that Latin America was our future. But France! And what had Paris to do with the French language, after all?

Had any notable member of the Lost Generation bothered to learn it? When a friend suggested to Hemingway that if they were going to remain in Paris they'd have to become French, he replied, "Who would want to stay?" I grew up with the between-the-wars myth of Paris as paradise for Americans; it had always been in the back of my mind that I would someday partake of that moveable feast, if only for dessert. And there was Joyce.

Concerning Joyce, I was a hero-worshiper. I knew his history, and much of his geography: where he had lived (in Paris, notably), which restaurants and cafés he had preferred. At the tailend of my college years, a James Joyce Society met regularly in the back of the Gotham Book Mart on West Forty-seventh Street in Manhattan. People who hadn't done much more than rub up against Joyce came to tell us about it, and of course we were able to rub up against *them.* Even an Irishman who was on the outs with Joyce might be invited to talk; I'm thinking of Oliver St. John Gogarty, surgeon, poet, playwright, sometime novelist. And of course he was the model for "stately, plump Buck Mulligan," introduced in the first line of *Ulysses.*

That was enough to draw me into his writing course. Gogarty liked my stories, for by then I was composing earnest fiction squarely in the tradition of authors I admired. They included not only modern Irish masters but British contemporaries such as Evelyn Waugh and Graham Greene. Gogarty wasn't put off, confessing that he was not sufficiently acquainted with modern literature to be able to trace my sources, and thus was prepared to accept my work as original. He considered my writing "sensitive" and "fresh"; I achieved effects with economy of scene and character.

I got him to recommend me for this and that. Later I think he tired of my requests, and more or less asked me to get off his back; a visiting Irish poet could take just so much of the American university way of life. Poor friendly Gogarty. I don't think that I abused the patience of any of the other historic Joyceans I met. All I wanted was to bask in their aura.

> Ah, did you once see Shelley plain,
> And did he stop and speak to you
> And did he speak to you again
> How strange it seems and new

Lines from Browning—I've forgotten the context—which have always hit home. My first wanderings in Paris were to streets Joyce had walked. I also had a copy of Elliot Paul's *The Last Time I Saw Paris,* and my

Fulbright year was lived out only steps from the Rue de la Huchette, which Paul described house by house. It was my guide to the people of France.

Luckily no one expected much of me in Paris. No one even asked to see my 314-page typescript, "Readers and Reading in France," the product of my Fulbright year. My chief finding was that, unlike the American stress on a book's best-seller potential, the French approach was hierarchical; a book was good because an eminent peer said so, or a literary academy gave it a prize. (In 1989 my *Gustave Flaubert* won the William the Conqueror prize given by a prestigious French jury. It didn't become a best-seller.)

The Fulbright people did send me to a Sorbonne language institute with a longish name including the word *perfectionnement,* which of course implied that one possessed something to be perfected. I attended a few classes, found other Americans there, but even their exchanges with the instructors went over my head. My French came to me as I went about my research, and in reading *Le Figaro* daily and *Le Figaro Littéraire* weekly.

Anyway, Paris in winter is damp. Somehow I learned of a two-day bus trip to the Riviera, and managed to book passage for the Mardi Gras carnival in Nice. Among the few pieces of evidence of that time to have survived is an exchange with David Greene, who had taught English at Washington Square College, and who was then compiling an anthology of the Irish Literary Revival. He wanted to reprint part of Samuel Beckett's Joycean novel *Murphy;* Beckett had been a friend and perhaps a secretary of Joyce but had since disappeared from the literary scene; could I track him down, and learn what he was up to? Even Beckett's English publisher had lost him.

I got your letter only this week [so I replied to Greene in March 1950—I know this because my draft survives on the back of the envelope containing his letter to me] since I've been on the Riviera escaping the damp weather which has (I hope) terminated the Paris winter. Met some interesting French people, including a lovely Parisian girl with whom I have been having adventures which remind me only of your 3-minute classroom summaries of the Lost Generation novels two winters back.

I can't for the life of me remember interesting French people except for that Parisian girl, and I know that my adventures were not out of a Hemingway novel. My experience was limited to Washington Square girls, who in those days were not as much study-oriented as scouting for husbands who looked like winners. As an English major I had to make do with the scrub team, but even mothers of second-echelon girls worried about an English major being supported by a widowed mother's salary as an office manager.

I obtained Beckett's address from Maria Jolas, an American in Paris who with her husband Eugène, founder of *transition,* had been close to Joyce. Beckett told me that he was still writing, but in French; he also had a novel ready in English (that was *Watt*) but no publisher. This was Beckett before Beckett, but already one hell of a recluse.

But I shall not engage in total recall, or else I may be taken for Leon Edel running poor Henry James ragged. My other bad example is a finicky biography of Faulkner whose author filled a couple of thousand pages spread over two volumes thanks to this kind of spectacular material. "They [Faulkner and a friend in Paris] visited Shakespeare & Company—but never saw Sylvia Beach . . . They did not see Ernest Hemingway, who frequented it, or another American celebrity of Paris, Gertrude Stein." Each of the people Faulkner did not see is indexed at the back.

The index to my autobiography should be even longer. For I didn't talk to contemporary greats, French or foreign, even when I spotted them out front at a café table. I was convinced that I had nothing to say to them, and of course I was right.

I remained a voyeur. Thus I was in Dublin for Bloomsday 1950, commemorating June 16th, the day during which *Ulysses* unravels. I went everywhere Joyce did, even to the coastal fort he had shared with stately, plump Oliver St. John Gogarty in student days. I got a healthy serving of seagull droppings on my one good suit as I stood admiring the River Liffey, perhaps as I recited

riverrun past Eve and Adam's

—the opening words of *Finnegans Wake.* Should I have remembered the warning on the final page: "A gull. Gulls."?

As seen by my generation, the principal occupation of our parents, and theirs, was to efface all evidence of their Old World origins; what they transmitted to us was an absence of culture. My mother was my last surviving parent and, as a youngest daughter, virtually the last survivor in her family, and I confess that I didn't try very hard to make her talk. She seemed evasive about her parents and their lives in Russia as if they had been bandits, and I don't think that they were. No one seemed to have kept papers, even immigration papers. My mother's family came from Odessa, where she was born in 1901, two years before they left for America (which is why she had no accent). Her brother Robert (who lost most of his accent) became a successful painter in New York, doing Cézanne still lifes by night, by day commissioned portraits of the likes of Charles Lindbergh; a teacher at the influential Art Students League, he had several paintings at the Metropolitan Museum of Art. I used to stand before them proudly, before they went out of fashion and into a basement.

Of course I should know more about that clan of talented Jews from Odessa. For there was not only Uncle Robert, but Uncles Arthur and Irving, who designed—clothing? curtains? And their sons, and the sons of Aunt Mary who composed or painted. At twenty my mother was singing on the amateur stage; she and a friend were a sister duet on radio, such as it was in the 1920s, and at least once she played in a semi-professional musical comedy written by my father.

By the time I knew what was up, my father was one of the kingmakers of Tin Pan Alley, New York's popular music district. The show-business weekly *Variety* later referred to him as "the legendary Broadway press agent who cradled many of today's top radio, tv and film humorists and scripters. . . ." "The late great Lottman," one of his disciples called him in another *Variety* piece, mentioning also his talent as a lyricist. He wrote the revised lyrics of "Anchors Aweigh," which remained the standard version through the Second World War. But his main business was promoting the stars of radio and stage, popular singers and musicians.

He looks very Broadway in a photograph taken at his desk: he leans way back in his chair, in shirtsleeves, loosened tie, gray fedora perched on his head, newspaperman style; there is a cigarette in his fingers. I remember the desk, which stood next to the large window overlooking the most strategic site on his Broadway, Lindy's delicatessen restaurant. He was "addicted" to working after midnight (so I learn from the memoirs of columnist Ben Gross, *I Looked and Listened*), sipped Canadian Club whisky from a silver hip flask (I remember that). He "pounded out copy" on an old typewriter—but weren't they all?—"while a bootblack shined his shoes and assorted Broadway characters in the room ate, drank, chattered, rolled

dice, and played hot jazz records on a portable phonograph."

I remember being punished a lot, getting slapped around. Was it ever for a spelling error? My father was a perfectionist, but I suppose that if I had been punished for that I should not have chosen his way at the age of six.

The announcement of my birth—was it so current then?—was produced in the form of a newspaper front page:

IT'S A BOY AT LOTTMANS
Unusual, Remarkable Child Makes Debut

Mr. and Mrs. George D. Lottman
Get First Taste of Parenthood

Boy is Named Herbert

The accompanying "story" sets the precise time of "one of the 'events of the century'" as 6:45 A.M. on August 16, 1927, my weight at 6¼ pounds. Actually I was Herbert *Roger* Lottman, Roger being the son of the legendary millionaire Otto Kahn. Roger was becoming a legend in his own right as a playboy turned band leader, although Otto told my father that he was being paid to keep Roger's name out of the papers. Not long before my birth, Roger Kahn and my father traveled together to England, sailing (I discovered when reading through a collection of historic front pages) on the day Lindbergh landed his *Spirit of St. Louis* in Paris. Kahn piloted a small plane over the channel to land at the same Le Bourget airport, and a photograph I possess shows my father and his playboy client standing on the field in front of Lindbergh's plane.

My father's middle initial is a shorter story. He was born on October 4, 1899, a few days after the New York ticker-tape parade for Admiral George Dewey, the Spanish-American War hero, on his return from conquest and pacification of the Philippines. So patriotic parents—my grandmother from Germany, grandfather from the Baltic coast which was then part of the Russian Empire—registered my father as George Dewey Lottman.

When I was writing my biography of Albert Camus, a secretive man, I was forced to employ the techniques of investigative journalism for what had started out as literary biography. In tracing Camus's family I was able to find official records of his paternal ancestry, which Camus himself had been unable to locate while working on an autobiographical novel (left unfinished at his death). I learned that

Camus's grandfather did not come from Alsace (as Camus thought and wrote) but from southwest France, like the cognac brandy of the same name.

I could do that for Camus; I could not do it for myself. I know more about Flaubert's mother and father and their mothers and fathers than I do about my own family. Even if some foundation should wish to finance my research on the Lottmans, I would have to turn down the offer; I would not know where to begin.

I don't have the first issues of my first newspaper, but much later, in January 1939 when I was twelve and a half, the sixth-anniversary issue of the paper (which for reasons I have forgotten I called *The Humor*) reported that back on January 4, 1934, I had celebrated "our second year of service"; if true, I was five years and five months of age when I began printing *The Humor* (printing with a pencil). My guess is that I was really six and a half. Eight issues have survived, dating from 1935 and 1936, each on standard 8½-by-11-inch paper folded once to make four small pages. The earliest, dated June 17, 1935, when I was getting on to eight, proclaims that "We print all the news we like," which news then concerned my father's show-business clients, our new housemaid (who became my joke and news editor), then ("Flash & Extra!") my return from a hospital after an appendectomy (names of day and night nurses given). If my conception of news was rather down-home at first, by November 1935 I was reporting Mussolini's war in east Africa ("Ethiopia is giving Italy the razz."). We also learn from these issues that my favorite radio star was Jack Benny, my favorite movie star Dick Powell. I rave about Chaplin's *Modern Times*. One of my reporters was Timothy J. Hagerty, in private life our short-legged Boston terrier.

I wish that I could say that these relics show promise of genius. They do reveal a fascination with the techniques of journalism. In the June 27, 1936, issue of *The Humor* I demonstrate the use of eight different kinds of pencil. Pencils were important in my life as in that of my father, and when he died I inherited a drawerful. They lasted, lasted longer than any other inherited thing, because after a time I ceased to use them. In the middle of the 1930s, when we lived on West End Avenue in Manhattan, calling cards were printed for me (as editor in chief of *The Humor*). My letterheads also mentioned my brother Evan, three-and-a-half years my junior, as star reporter.

Fascination with the tools of the trade hasn't left me. My blood moves faster when I enter a printing

"Humor *Editor Interviews Jack Dempsey*," *Herbert Lottman, age eleven, 1939*

plant, I mean a real one, where they still use metal type and real ink.

As for Evan, when he was old enough, say eight or nine, he looked for a way of his own to express himself. Perhaps in revolt against a tyrannical brother, he decided to operate a radio network, using a cardboard microphone. He has since done worse, going into movies, editing some of the big films which take readers away from books. Fortunately his wife Eileen writes novels, including movie tie-ins which become best-sellers around the world; she is the Lottman who appears up front in the bookstores.

The sixth-anniversary issue of the *Humor* was impressive, for it was printed as a proper newspaper. In it I interview ex-champ Jack Dempsey (then running a restaurant across Broadway from my father's office); I also ask people on the street what they think of beggars, and then interview a beggar. A schoolmate, Harold Prince, contributes a piece on how milk is bottled. I wonder if the Broadway producer he became kept a copy.

Soon after that anniversary issue we moved to south Florida. I suppose that the doctors ordered this for my father, and he tried to run his Broadway business from under a palm tree, a losing proposition. He had loyal clients and was able to tinker, but communications were not what they are now.

I can document my junior-high journalism, for a copy survives of the mimeographed paper of which I was elected editor in chief; it is as didactic as most of my productions of that time. "The years we are now spending in school," I explained to fellow students in an editorial in May 1941, "we will later find out, are the happiest years of our lives, regardless of homework and tests." It was certainly through my father that I became associated with a genuine adult newspaper, published a couple of times a week and mostly given away free. The editor of this *Miami Beach Mirror* gave me a column of my own in which I could say anything I wished, and perhaps its title was mine: "Mooning over Miami." I followed the Broadway columnists in style, my pedantry tempered by expressions like "oughta."

In a column in July of that year I called attention to dirty beaches. "It wouldn't take so long each morning for a couple of lifeguards to put their tractors to use and get rid of the debris. We know they're not responsible for the seaweed coming up on the beach, but at least they can try to remedy the situation a little!!!" The lifeguards took this badly and their chief strode into the newspaper threatening to punch me. It took some time for the editor to convince him that the columnist was only thirteen years old.

We lived in the estate area of what was called North Beach, among coconut palms. Our outings included eighteen-hour trips to the Everglades on Florida's western shore. We'd hire a small cabin cruiser with a two-man crew and fish and munch cold chicken and hard-boiled eggs as we sailed among the thousand islands of that marshland. I don't know what's left of the Everglades, but in those days there were flocks of flamingoes close at hand, unafraid. Much later, an adult, I tried to capture that lost world in a story; it gave me a subject which my dreary urban existence lacked. This didn't suffice to make a story worth keeping, for I don't seem to have kept it. Had I found it, it would only be another relic of a dispersed childhood, with significant but unconnected memories, for I cannot pretend that I grew up in the Everglades. But why can't I remember more about the places where I did grow up? A photograph published in the *Washington Evening Star* on September 6, 1939, three days after war was declared in Europe, documents a high point of my preadolescence. This picture illustrates a story headlined

MARY PICKFORD VISITS D.C.
BRIEFLY ON WAY TO FESTIVAL

and shows the legendary star posing as I kneel with my camera beside her plane. I am in short pants, my father (a press agent for Mary Pickford's husband, the band leader Buddy Rogers) looks on. What mattered to me was not this fortuitous encounter or even the airplane ride from Miami to New York, but the purpose of the trip: a visit to the New York World's Fair. I suppose that everyone who ever attended one of these universal exhibitions is prepared to say that it was grandiose, unique. But surely we can agree that in our century, at least, the 1939 fair was special, coinciding as it did with a time preceding immense change, and somehow finding ways to preview that change.

Jump to December 1941. I am now fourteen, back north, settled in a poor cousin to Miami Beach called Long Beach, Long Island. With a mimeograph machine (my father's?) I come out of retirement to launch *This Month*, which begins as a two-column, single-spaced paper typed on stencils. The first issue appeared at the beginning of that month, just before the Japanese attack on Pearl Harbor. My brother, who was by now ten, contributed "Why I am Glad To Be an American," featured on the front page, with a page-two piece on "Why I Like My Dog." The

"Snapping Mary Pickford as my father looks on":
Herbert at age twelve

grammar in all these stories—even Evan's—is impeccable. Newspaper writing doesn't evolve much; I was writing at least as well as I do now.

I dealt with preparations for war, the need to tighten belts. In March 1942 I saw fit to send 2 percent of my earnings to the U.S. Treasury as a voluntary contribution. In that hour when every patriotic gesture counted, the people responsible for promoting the sale of defense bonds didn't let that pass; the press was informed. The *New York Herald-Tribune* ran a three-column story with a photograph of me at my desk, explaining that the Treasury had returned my donation (which amounted to eighty-four cents) with the suggestion that I use it to purchase defense stamps. The reporter described me with "a pencil tucked behind one ear and ink from his mimeograph machine on his hands," and told of my early beginnings in journalism. "Yesterday he said that he had always wanted to be a newspaperman and hoped someday to write editorials for a real grown-up newspaper." Was I also a press agent? Soon after my father's death that autumn, one of his clients—a hapless borscht-circuit magician—engaged me for what might have been five dollars a week to write press releases in his behalf. Perhaps it was because I had already written such things for my father, although I remember nothing of the sort. More likely this client wished to take advantage of the Lottman name.

Shortly before that, during the summer of 1942, I went to work for Nick Kenny, radio editor of the *New York Daily Mirror*. Presumably this was only a summer job, but I do remember that I was often alone and thus "in charge" of the office. At that time the *Mirror* was the number-two tabloid (after the *Daily News*) and probably held its ground thanks to the most popular of all columnists, Walter Winchell, as well as to its comic strips.

I remember taking copy to the composing room, picking up galleys and proofreading them. I also put together a daily birthday column. Did I stay on when school began that autumn? The October 1942 issue of my own *This Month* reported: "When our Navy sinks Japanese ships in the Pacific, Nick Kenny, Radio Editor of the Daily Mirror, is a very happy man indeed. The ship he served on while in the Navy, the Arizona, was destroyed at Pearl Harbor. The Arizona will be and is being avenged." That was the first issue of my paper published from West Eighty-seventh Street, where we were living in a dim hotel suite—my mother, my brother, and I. There isn't a hint in my paper that my father had died after a long decline and

Making a wartime propaganda film at Benjamin Franklin High School, New York City

what must have been a painful final illness (cirrhosis of the liver, the Tin Pan Alley ailment).

The columnist Ben Gross had gone to visit my father in the last weeks of his life when he was indeed a sick man. "You know," he quotes my father, "the doctor says if I take another drink I'll pop right off." And he picked up a flask of whisky he shouldn't have possessed, saying, "Here's to a merry popping off!"

Gross further quotes George Lottman: "Maybe I've wasted my life and maybe I haven't, because I've got a son—and he's not a Broadway guy, but a brilliant student, a scholar, and he's going to show the world what Old Man Lottman didn't . . ." The son not a Broadway guy was me.

As the war went on my paper became increasingly belligerent, notably in attacks on America's pro-Nazi movements which (incredibly) continued to pursue their activities. Before I was done I had gone out after Communists and their fellow travelers as well. The last issue of *This Month*, my final act of amateur journalism, is dated January 1946, the month I was drafted. "After almost fifty months of uninterrupted publication," I informed my readers, whoever they were, "the manpower shortage caused by Uncle Sam's Selective Service Act is forcing us to shut down for a while." Was I trying to be humorous, or bad-tempered? Had my patriotism been caught napping?

It's true that nothing could have seemed more futile than to go to war when it was over. I had my eighteenth birthday August 16, 1945. Ten days earlier we had dropped the first atomic bomb on Hiroshima, followed by a second bomb over Nagasaki on August 9, and by September 2 the Japanese had surrendered unconditionally. Without the bombs, the Pacific war would have dragged on, and dragged me into it, and perhaps out of life.

By then I had two years of NYU's Washington Square College behind me, with the usual required courses, Spanish as my language, and journalism as an elective. My journalism instructor was Kenneth Davis, who would go on to write novels and biographies, notably of Dwight Eisenhower and Franklin Roosevelt, but I am quite sure that we didn't talk about books, and certainly not about biography, in his class. After basic training I was assigned to a sewing school at the headquarters of the Quartermaster Corps in Camp Lee, Virginia; just in time an army buddy who was using family influence for himself generously offered to speak for me too, and we were transferred to the camp newspaper, a posting which included use of a chauffeured jeep and the opportunity to write feature material, indulging my taste for finicky research into such matters as food procurement and

sewage disposal. And in that anticlimactic army I replaced a master sergeant, who had only shortly before replaced a captain, as head of the Quartermaster School public relations department. That got me elevated to the lofty rank of corporal (Tec/5). "Conducted outside promotional campaigns for army activities, and units engaged on field trips for education and recruiting," my job description read. Were we really trying to recruit? A photograph survives showing me demonstrating our cumbersome M-l rifle, or as the caption in the camp paper has it, I was field-stripping it "to point out the simplicity of mechanism in the rifle."

The GI Bill (educational benefits for discharged servicemen) put me through NYU, where I did the four-year program in three, which I think was customary during the war years. So my Fulbright year abroad needn't appear a total waste of time.

Life—intellectual life—began in my final year at NYU. I was released from the army in January 1947, graduated in June 1948. Between those dates I encountered James Burnham, who—whatever one may think about him as an ideologist—was a prince of a teacher. This former Trotskyist, who by training

Demonstrating the M-1 at Camp Lee, Virginia, 1946

was fiercely anti-Stalinist, in the cold war turned bellicose and bitter. He was thin-lipped and dour, spoke in monotone; his only smile was sardonic. Precisely how much responsibility for my intellectual development, such as it is, belongs to him I can't say, since I was also undergoing a natural change—maturity. Burnham taught esthetics, and that year I passed from middlebrow to highbrow (if only in intention). I discovered *Partisan Review,* of which Burnham was a member of the advisory board. At that time I should have sacrificed ten years of my life to be published in that magazine, whose pages I turned only after washing my hands, and cautiously so as not to bend or tear them. It wasn't until very recently, by which time the intellectual establishment and *Partisan Review* had changed even more than I had, that I was asked to contribute (a book review) to my Rosebud.

I was no longer interested in journalism, for example, but in literature. I'd be a writer, an experimental novelist. Certainly I was working on a novel by then, and produced my first short stories. These manuscripts were discarded when I developed critical faculties and/or when the pile of rejection letters grew as high as my bundle of stories.

Preparing for a master's degree in modern British literature at Columbia University, I see that I also enrolled in courses in American literature (Lionel Trilling's lectures were then the school's summit), Shakespearean tragedy, Dryden, and Pope. In my chosen subject William York Tindall's lectures were true intellectual exercises, for if one could get through Milton and Wordsworth just by knowing one's language, to comprehend William Butler Yeats, Gerard Manley Hopkins, or Dylan Thomas required a certain amount of decoding. Tindall gave a seminar on *Finnegans Wake* which drew specialists in modern languages and linguistics. I was the least qualified of the group, and perhaps the most elated. For my master's thesis I chose to analyze the meaning behind Evelyn Waugh, deciding for myself that his ineffectual protagonists were new heroes appropriate to absurd times; and, although Waugh wasn't sure that he agreed with me, he did reply to my queries. Heady days.

But higher education left a wound. I began to approach fiction as a textbook for my own writing. Earlier in my college career I had got hold of Mortimer Adler's list of the hundred great books and read them all; now I deliberately slowed my reading speed so as to be able to discover the secrets of writers I admired. I never did become a novelist, but my ability to read was affected, and it still takes me ages to get through the most ordinary of books. Another

consequence was an excessive concern for effect. Blind admiration for the minimalist approach of Joyce's *Dubliners* contributed to the somewhat bloodless products of my typewriter. Yet I smiled knowingly when Professor Tindall quoted the scornful judgment of poet Roy Campbell "On Some South African Novelists":

> You praise the firm restraint with which they
> write—
> I'm with you there, of course:
> They use the snaffle and the bit all right,
> But where's the bloody horse?

In my family, the name of the game was not to talk about anything really serious, or so it seems to me now. Does that explain my lack of a horse?

Or was it the fault of the terribly factual age that followed World War II, bringing on the drab technological fiction of the following decades? This was when Graham Greene's novels became editorials. Today the reading of historical novels into which invented heroes have been inserted clumsily has the same effect on me as someone running a fingernail along a pane of glass to make it squeak.

All this to excuse myself for the fiction I wrote and tore up. Perhaps it was not all lost effort. I could not invent a hero, but when I had a genuine one like Albert Camus I could move him through his environment, after recreating environment. As soon as I could find a way I was back in Paris, as scout and agent for an American publisher, Farrar, Straus and Giroux, with a cavernous apartment in a creaky building halfway between the Seine and the literary cafés of Saint Germain des Prés. I missed New York all the same. I had a recurring dream involving the *New York Times,* the overpaged and underpriced paper whose Sunday edition was more of a rite than a read. In my dream I wandered about looking for a copy—so of course I was back in New York, undoubtedly on Saturday night—but without success, although everyone who passed me by had a copy. The frustration stayed with me long after I woke up. By the time I began to go to New York for extended visits, a new management had lightened and brightened the *Times;* gone were those stories which never ended, those verbatim transcripts of just about anything.

And in my first years of residence in this city in which I was to spend the rest of my life, I was too busy with external possibilities—with the Paris-ness of Paris—to think about writing. My job put me in touch with authors—Frenchmen published by Far-

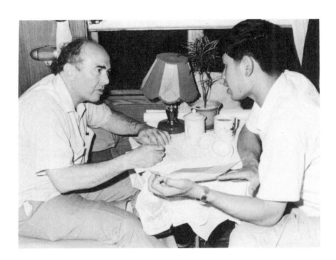

Interviewing an employee of the National Publishing Administration for Publishers Weekly *aboard the express to Shanghai, 1980*

rar, Straus, like François Mauriac, visitors sent to me by Roger Straus, such as Isaac Singer, Susan Sontag, even Edmund Wilson. In my free time I helped the young women who then owned Caedmon Records to find French authors to read from their works. I got Albert Camus and Jean Cocteau to read, but out of shyness I made no attempt to meet them. It was almost déjà vu when I called on Sylvia Beach, not a culture hero of mine but the benefactor of my culture hero. She still lived at famous 12 rue de l'Odéon, even if her Shakespeare and Company bookshop which published *Ulysses* and sold it and so many other contemporary classics had long since shut down. My mission for Caedmon was to obtain a phonograph record of Joyce reading from *Ulysses.*

Photographs of Miss Beach with Joyce, with Hemingway, show a frail New England schoolmistress. In April 1956, when I met her, she was sixty-nine and so wasn't going to be less frail. She was an antique doll with a small high voice and a tendency to deafness which grew worse as time went on. She tried to play the record for me, on first one and then another phonograph, without success. She worried about commercial exploitation of his precious work, and we met again and again to talk about that. It was in the fourth year of our discussion that Miss Beach let me know offhandedly that the record was no longer in her hands. Could I drop by so that she could explain? The apartment was bare, and she didn't have to tell me twice that she had sold everything to a

university. The rights to the recording, it turned out, hadn't belonged to her. But if I lost a record, she (so I thought as I looked at those scarred walls showing where the pictures were) had lost a life. And although I had been a nuisance in her closing years, let me believe that I was also one of those who contributed to her sense of still counting. She died that autumn on a Thursday or Friday, but her body was discovered only on Saturday.

How did I embark upon my second writing career? (The first began in the 1930s with *The Humor;* the third when I started to write books in the 1970s.) While still in college I had sent article proposals to magazines, the way I had been taught in the manual on article writing. Now, in the early 1960s, after years of not trying, I probably indicated a desire to get started to that generous friend Mike Levitas (of the *New York Times),* whose father had run the influential weekly *New Leader.* Myron Kolatch, executive editor of that magazine, began to use my pieces, for which I don't think I expected or received payment. Did Kolatch realize that he was publishing a new writer with a quarter of a century of journalism behind him? On my side I had an opportunity to say what I wanted about European politics and culture in a magazine which also published Stanley Edgar Hyman, Adolf Perle, Hilton Kramer, Jeanne Kirkpatrick, Chester Bowles.

I was to receive similar exposure in the quarterly *Columbia University Forum,* whose young editor Erik Wensberg I had met during a New York visit. He let me deal with matters of particular concern to me, matters which might otherwise have been the subject of indignant letters to the editor. About abusive car traffic in city centers, about what I liked or didn't on the Paris stage, about the Sicilian Mafia, and never mind that the first fees were fifty dollars. Following Wensberg's transfer to *Esquire,* I continued to write for his successor, Peter Spackman. Later, when I was also contributing to more commercial magazines (such as *Saturday Review,* for which I wrote cultural travel pieces), I came to realize that my lengthy exchanges with Wensberg and Spackman were the best editing I ever had.

It was in those years when I was still making stabs in the dark that I connected with *Publishers Weekly,* or rather it connected with me, when one of its editors, Roger Smith, heard that I was going to represent my publisher at the Belgrade Book Fair (in November 1964) and asked me to report on my experience. That became "Selling American Literary Works behind the Iron Curtain" in the January 4, 1965, issue. Another fifty-dollar check, and I was now the foreign correspondent of "The Book Industry Journal." I could write about English-language bookstores overseas, or Armenian printing monks in the Venetian lagoon; nobody was then covering either beat. Before I put an end to my free-lance writing, I had been published in *Harper's,* in the *New York Times Magazine,* in the same paper's *Book Review,* travel, and culture supplements.

Through Roger Straus, my mentor, I met the friendliest of agents, Julian Bach, who helped me take my first baby steps into the world of books. I have a fat file of correspondence with Bach, amply demonstrating the extraordinary patience of that gentle man. Me to him: "You will find that I respond to these uncommercial, no-money assignments with greater alacrity than to more lucrative ones. This is not because I hate money, but because the ten-dollar articles require little work, and are relaxing and amusing to do." I was a dilettante because salaried, and the amazing thing is that Julian Bach stuck with me. I could do a book, but it would have to deal with something about which I felt strongly, and preferably something which could be done in installments. Out of this came a proposal for a personal book on cultural travel, which I could base on trips made over a number of years to not-very-famous places; this was *Detours from the Grand Tour,* published in March 1970 by Prentice-Hall just after the departure of my editor Gladys Carr (followed by the whole trade department). Then *How Cities Are Saved,* an expression of my private crusade for the rehabilitation of old town centers, the point being to show Americans what Europeans were doing. I got a modest Ford Foundation grant to do some new research (the rest was a by-product of vacations or assignments for *Publishers Weekly).* I wasn't a penny richer after publication, but I had found a new reason for being.

I wish I could reconstruct the events leading to my first real book contract, my first meaningful advance on royalties. Dramatically enough, it began in Jerusalem, during an international book fair I was covering in the spring of 1975. A Paris neighbor, Beverly Gordey, then European editor of Doubleday, put me together with Betty Prashker of that house. We lunched outside an Arab restaurant at the Old City's Jaffa Gate, and I made a case for a definitive biography of Flaubert. My expectations proved unrealistic, but back in Paris I sat down with Beverly to talk about alternatives. For Doubleday, at least, Albert Camus seemed a more relevant subject; he had not been written about, which meant that everything had to be discovered. Camus was not my favorite

author, but he had been an exemplary witness to French contemporary history, the Popular Front, the Second World War and Nazi occupation, the excitement of postwar Paris.

The contract was signed with the enthusiastic support of Doubleday's publisher Sam Vaughan (in October 1975), and then the adventure began. Everything was a problem: Camus's family, friends convinced that loyalty required silence, even concerning affairs which showed Camus in a favorable light. There wasn't a single reliable printed source, for Camus made sure that even his friends got his life wrong. I used more journalistic skills than literary ones, knocked on many doors, used the telephone more than my library card. Critics in France would express admiration for my investigative methods; I was the literary detective. The French edition of my *Albert Camus* was one of the first examples in that country of what American and British readers had always expected from their historians. By the time my biography of Philippe Pétain was published in French, readers had learned how to deal with fact-oriented texts and footnotes, and perhaps to enjoy them. Readers, but not all of the traditional critics. "Mr. Lottman seems to prefer interviews," a stodgy literary journal complained, as if I should not have preferred to sit at home taking notes on other people's published research. I have seldom had such an opportunity in France, where scholarship seldom ventures beyond the Middle Ages.

With Peter Weidhaus (right), director of the Frankfurt Book Fair, about 1984

The author in Japan, 1984

In truth I researched and wrote *Albert Camus* in two years. In print it came to 678 pages, with another 51 pages of notes. It appeared to have been a ten-year project, and when asked I didn't dare tell the truth; usually I would say that it had been less than a lifework. My reward was an opportunity to relax with a subject of my making. For *The Left Bank* I looked at Paris as it was in the 1930s and 1940s, from the time when writers and artists became concerned about the wider world beyond their borders, until the early 1950s, when the cold war and bloc rivalry drowned their voices. I wrote about cafés and literary magazines, focusing on colorful heroes and villains. It took a while before I realized that my publishers in the United States and Britain had misread the book, overshot its public (they targeted the Paris-in-the-spring nostalgia crowd). It found better readers in libraries and remainder shops, above all in translations in Europe, Brazil, Japan. In the United States, I think because of budgets committed to computers, many libraries never purchased the book.

Because I had written objectively about Camus, still a controversial personality in France at the time, a French publisher asked me to do the same with another subject no Frenchman could touch without bias, Pétain. By luck I began my research just as the authorities were prepared to grant access to heretofore secret archives; the same happened when I wrote *The Purge,* on the punishment of Nazi collaborators. Largely by coincidence, and a little because the latest generation of French historians spends more time in conferences than in archives, I became the authority on very cruel times, hating every minute of it. I also made enemies among the younger French historians for reasons which should be obvious.

When I returned to my true love, literature and Flaubert, the literary establishment seemed to greet me with open arms; it was only when my biography of the master was published that it became apparent that some a priori convictions (about Flaubert's social and sex lives for instance) had been upset. I received more blame than praise this time for having come in with the definitive biography of the writer's writer. Perhaps there will be more indulgence when my biography of Colette appears.

In 1988 I was invited to open a Florence meeting of Western European specialists of the Association of

College and Research Libraries, but I couldn't be sure whether the *PW* correspondent was wanted or the author. So I introduced myself as Dr. Jekyll and Mr. Hyde. To earn my living I write about the book trade for *Publishers Weekly,* usually within Europe, but sometimes as far away as Argentina, Brazil, Japan, or China. Then, when no one is looking, I disappear into a library to make notes for another book which even American academics sometimes feel is too wordy. My subjects come from France, because that is where I am, and the books I write require long months and sometimes years of research. Unquote.

It's not always smooth going. I've mentioned the sour grapes and the backbiting. I should also say that there are few subjects of equal interest to American and French readers. French publishers have offered me satisfactory advances to write biographies of personalities all but unknown in the United States.

At the beginning of 1985, shortly before her eighty-fourth birthday, my mother moved out of the Brooklyn apartment she had once shared with her mother and two widowed sisters, just across the street from the home of a third (and married) sister; they were all gone before she was. Since she was entering a retirement home, she got rid of everything except papers she may still have thought essential, such as her marriage license, and family photographs, of course. We were also to find a leather-bound album which she had gotten schoolmates to sign on graduation from a New York City public school in June 1915. She had inserted a stunning photograph of herself all in white, with a high white *coiffe* over her heavy dark locks, white flowers, and a white diploma in her hands.

One of her sister graduates had written:

To Betty

Girls are many
Boys are plenty
Don't get married
Before you're twenty.

(She married at twenty-one.) Or:

When you are old and cannot see
Think of the girls of class 8B.

She did live to be old enough not to see, a cruelty, for she then lived only for reading. She had all my articles and books, and we subscribed to *Time* and *National Geographic* for her; my sister-in-law kept her in current fiction. A stroke in mid-life had made her cockeyed; a year or so after entering the home she began to lose the good eye. She watched television through a mist, dozing off, waking to watch again; when I made my weekly phone call from France she never knew whether it was morning or evening. Her heart failed her on December 9, 1988. The will was respected:

I do not want to be taken to any chapel for funeral services when I die.

The only cost involved with me should be for the delivery of my body to the New York University Bellevue Medical Center.

I know my children, relatives and friends will never forget me as I have never forgotten my relatives and friends who have passed on.

There was some correspondence on this subject. She had begun to plan to give her body to science as early as 1959, when she was fifty-eight. Her lawyer gave her the appropriate papers to sign and said that she should also inform her children of her intentions. Did she? I can't even recall. We didn't talk about death. I never found a document or clipping concerning my father's death, and there must have been lots.

BIBLIOGRAPHY

Nonfiction:

Detours from the Grand Tour (travel), Prentice-Hall, 1970.

How Cities Are Saved, Universe Books, 1976.

Albert Camus: A Biography, Doubleday, 1979.

The Left Bank: Writers, Artists, and Politics from the Popular Front to the Cold War, Houghton Mifflin, 1982.

Pétain, Hero or Traitor, Morrow, 1985.

The Purge, Morrow, 1986.

Flaubert: A Biography, Little, Brown, 1989.

Contributor to magazines and newspapers, including *New York Times Magazine, Harper's, Saturday Review, Signature, Travel and Leisure,* and *New York Times.*

Larry Niven

1938-

The Niven File

Larry Niven, 1988

I'm a compulsive teacher, but I can't teach. I lack at least two of the essential qualifications.

I cannot "suffer fools gladly." The smartest of my pupils would get all my attention, and the rest would have to fend for themselves. And I can't handle being interrupted.

Writing is the answer. Whatever I have to teach, my students will select themselves by buying the book. And nobody interrupts a printed page.

I knew what I wanted when I started writing. I've daydreamed all my life, and told stories too. One day the daydreams began shaping themselves into stories. I wanted to share them.

Astrophysical discoveries made peculiar implications, worlds stranger than any found in fantasy. I longed to touch the minds of strangers and show them wonders.

I wanted to be a published science fiction writer, like Poul Anderson and Jack Vance.

I wanted a Hugo Award!

Getting rich formed no part of that. Science fiction writers didn't get rich. (Robert Heinlein excepted. Kurt Vonnegut, Junior, excluded.) I used money to keep score: how many people had I reached?

I had my Hugo Award three years after I sold my first story. Within science fiction fandom one becomes a Grand Old Man fast. Now what?

Now: become a better writer. I'll always have things to learn. I still have trouble writing about the things that hurt me most. In my earlier novels almost nobody got old or sick.

Today? Well, I get allergy attacks. Alcohol, dry air, lack of sleep, or any combination thereof can cause me to wake up blind and in pain, with deep red eyes and puffy eyelids. I have to use a humidifier, or go to sleep with a wet towel. Now you know . . . but you wouldn't have the right to know if I hadn't given the same allergy to Gavving in *The Integral Trees* and Rather in *The Smoke Ring.* I did that for story

purposes, and I had to nerve myself up to it.

Parts of my life are private. My computer erases my early drafts, and that's fine. My mistakes are not for publication.

Born April 30, 1938, in Los Angeles, California, USA.

Father: Waldemar Van Cott Niven.

Mother: Lucy Estelle Doheny Niven Washington.

Raised in Beverly Hills, California. Hawthorne Public School (Beverly Hills); Cate School in Carpinteria.

Entered California Institute of Technology, September 1956. Flunked out February 1958, after discovering a bookstore jammed with used science fiction magazines.

Gainful employment: gas station attendant, summer 1960.

Graduated Washburn University, Kansas, June 1962: B.A. in mathematics with minor in psychology. Half the university was scattered to the winds by a tornado a month after I left. One year graduate work in mathematics at UCLA before I dropped out to write.

First story publication: "The Coldest Place," *Worlds of If,* December 1964.

Married Marilyn Joyce Wisowaty, September 6, 1969. We met at the NYcon, 1967. No children. We reside in Tarzana, California.

I have written at every length. Most of my work is fiction, but there have been speculative articles, speeches for high schools and colleges, television scripts, political action in support of the space program, and seventeen weeks of a newspaper comic strip.

I've collaborated with a variety of writers.

Interests: Science fiction conventions. Computerized games. AAAS meetings and other gatherings of people at the cutting edge of the sciences. The L5 Society. Filksinging.

The author in his office with his wife, Marilyn, 1978

Saving civilization and making a little money. Moving humankind into space by any means, but particularly by making space endeavors attractive to commercial interests.

In 1982 Jerry Pournelle talked me and Marilyn into hosting a gathering of the top minds in the space industry in an attempt to write a space program, with goals, timetables, costs. The Citizens Advisory Council for a National Space Policy has met five times over five years, for harrowing three-day weekends. The attendees include spacecraft designers, businessmen, NASA personnel, astronauts, lawyers. Adding science fiction writers turns out to be stunningly effective. We can translate: we can force these guys to speak English. We've had some effect on the space program . . . not enough, but some.

I grew up with dogs: keeshonds, the show dogs my mother has raised for fifty years. I live with cats. I have passing acquaintance with raccoons and ferrets. Associating with nonhumans has surely given me some insight into alien intelligences.

I've written on computers for nearly ten years. I don't know anything else about computers. What I do is, I buy what Jerry Pournelle tells me to. He's the Users Column for *Byte* magazine. I buy two, to get a spare *and* spare parts, and because *Marilyn* understands and loves computers.

I remember typewriters. I remember typing whole pages to make two or three corrections; I remember Liquid Paper and scissors and Scotch tape. A word processing program is a magic typewriter. Writing first draft is almost as much work as it used to be—the computers don't do *that* yet!—but subsequent drafts are so easy that every time I read a passage over, I find myself rewriting.

My life has changed over the years.

Most photographs show me with a pipe in my mouth. I quit smoking on August 11, 1987, about 6:30 P.M.

Joe Haldeman persuaded me and Jerry to quit drinking during February every year, just to prove we aren't alcoholics. Why February? Shortest month. We switched to January, though, because there's less social activity in January. At this point I'm a teetotaler; the reasons are medical, not philosophical.

Steven Barnes—another collaborator who teaches several varieties of martial arts—urges new exercise programs on us from time to time. There was a Marci Mark 2 weight-lifting system, a torture implement that occupied one wall of our bedroom. There's an hour of aerobics with weights, on a cassette: The Firm Workout. The latest is a Versa

Climber: a device that allows us to climb mountains without leaving home.

We were looking good, until I injured a knee and Marilyn ruptured a spinal disk . . . and then my back went out too . . . For most of a year it was as if our warranties had run out. We've been healing, though. At this point we're both in shape to hike.

Awards: Hugos (or Science Fiction Achievement Awards) for "Neutron Star," 1966; *Ringworld,* 1970; "Inconstant Moon," 1971; "The Hole Man," 1974; "The Borderland of Sol," 1975. Nebula, Best Novel 1970: *Ringworld.* Ditmars (Australian, Best International Science Fiction) for *Ringworld,* 1972, and *Protector,* 1974. Japanese awards for *Ringworld* and "Inconstant Moon," both awarded 1979. Inkpot, 1979, from San Diego Comic Convention. Various Guest-of-Honor plaques.

Doctor of Letters, honorary, from Washburn University, May 1984.

Other novels clamor to be written, if I had the time. I stopped signing contracts (almost) long ago. It doesn't help. A story ready to be written always feels like an obligation.

Thraxisp, A Memoir

John and Bjo Trimble were science fiction fans long before I was. I met them the night I found the Los Angeles Science Fantasy Society.

They're organized.

They've led treks into the desert when it's blooming. On such a trek I discovered a plant called *squaw cabbage:* a green vase with a tiny scarlet flower at the tip. It looks like something seeded from Mars . . . and I examined it in awe and delight while the rest of the trekkers stared at me.

Fans remember Jack Harness discovering the blazing desert starscape on another trek. He stretched out on his sleeping bag and lay there, staring up . . . and they found him in the morning, *on* his sleeping bag, half frozen.

The Trimbles are compulsive organizers. They created Equicon, an annual science fiction convention local to Los Angeles. Equicon merged with Filmcon, which is media-oriented: movies, TV, comic books, posters, role-playing games. Then—

The World Building Project was Joel Hagen's idea. He had made the suggestion to other convention committees. When he talked to John and Bjo Trimble, they said *Yes.*

Joel Hagen is a sculptor. The work he displays at conventions is generally bones: skeletons from other worlds. Sometimes they come with provenances, details on the worlds where they were exhumed, signed by UPXAS, the United Planets Xenoarcheological Society.

Joel chose and assembled the rest of us: Art Costa, Don Dixon, Patricia Ortega, Rick Sternbach (all artists), Paul Preuss and me (writers of fiction), and Dr. William K. Hartmann (astronomer, artist, writer of articles and fiction).

At Equicon/Filmcon, in April 1981, the Trimbles gave us eight hotel rooms plus a big lecture room on the mezzanine. The World Builders Room was to remain open twenty-four hours a day. We eight artists and writers would spend as much of the convention there as we could. Actually we were more than eight; Rick Sternbach's wife Asenath was present most of the time, Marilyn kept wandering in, and there were others.

Most of us arrived Thursday night. We gathered on Friday morning and set to work.

I feared that we would duplicate the results of another world-building consortium, Harlan Ellison's Medea-building group. The World Builders chose a tidally locked habitable moon of a superJovian world, like Ellison's Medea. (Nobody used the term "brown dwarf star" yet.) But we changed some parameters to get something different.

Due to orbital elements chosen by Dr. Hartmann, *Thrassus* (too Latin! I changed it), *Thraxisp* is heated by both its sun and the superJovian planet. It's too hot for life except at the poles and in the seas.

Life would crawl out onto the land at each pole. Life thenceforth would travel separate evolutionary paths.

So Saturday we split into two groups.

I got tired of saying *crawl.* "My creatures will *fly* onto the land!" I cried. Flight first, then lungs . . . our flying lungfish would eventually nest in trees, then evolve legs and design a civilization. The volleks would be natural pilots. Okay, Preuss, top that!

"Mine will *roll,*" Paul gloated. His team designed a sand dollar. It rolled onto the land mass at the south pole and became a miner. The tunneks became a race of sessile philosophers, sensing their world with taste and seismic effects, getting their nourishment by chemical mining, consuming nothing organic.

The room was open to all. Convention attendees could wander in at any time. At set times we would

*With a Pierson's puppeteer (a Niven creation),
Boston, 1989*

lecture on our progress. At all times the artwork would be on display, and somebody would always be there to talk.

There was a globe of Thraxisp. There were paintings as seen from the surface, with the brown dwarf hanging tremendous in the sky; Joel was making and refining sculptures of the volleks and tunneks and their more primitive ancestors.

Convention attendees did wander in, but not many. We could have used more action.

But *we* were having fun.

What we were evolving was two races of natural space travelers.

They would have everything going for them. The tunneks would work on understanding physics. The volleks were natural pilots and explorers. For mines and chemical sources we had tunneks and the Teakettle: an asteroid-impact crater on the equator, facing directly toward the primary: a confined region where the ocean boils gently at all times, precipitating interesting salts and chemicals into glittering hills. Thraxisp's gravity is low; it has to be, because

otherwise the gas torus effect will give it too much atmosphere (see *The Integral Trees*). That makes escape velocity low. We gave them an endless variety of moons to explore, all easily accessible to the most primitive spacecraft. And first contact with alien intelligence would come for both of them before ever they left the atmosphere!

By mid-Sunday, the end of the convention, we had hoped to introduce human explorers. My memory says we didn't get that far.

We didn't get as much crowd as we earned. The movie fans weren't interested. The Trimbles were disappointed.

But we eight continued to work.

Bill Hartmann wrote up the convention and published in *Smithsonian* magazine, March 1982, with some of our illustrations. The money was shared. Our plan was to share every nickel of fallout, 12½ percent each.

The thought of an eventual book must have been in the back of every mind. Now we dared speak of it, and now we dared make more elaborate plans. We sent human explorers to Thrax, aboard the Ring City taken from my "Bigger Than Worlds" article. The artists modified it extensively. We set up a loose plot line, in blocks of short story embedded in artwork of intense variety. Volleks would meet the Ring City in orbit in primitive comic-book spacecraft. The payoff would be the discovery, by inference, of the tunneks, whose existence the volleks are hiding. We assigned each other blocks of text.

More material emerged. The tunneks became musicians: they built great wind-operated pipe systems from careful deposits of slag. We have the recordings. We argued back and forth about designs for Ring City. Elaborate maps emerged, and sociological studies too.

We gathered—never all eight of us together—at universities and conventions to display our work.

We gathered (only five of us) to correlate notes, and to try to sell a book on the basis of what we had. We didn't have enough, or else it wasn't organized enough. The publisher's representative was interested but not sufficiently.

Here we stalled.

What happened?

Too many artists, not enough writers. Five and a half artists, two and a half writers, counting Hartmann as split down the middle. That's good for building a convention display, but bad for a book. It turns out Paul doesn't like the short story form; *that* didn't help.

Too much ingenuity. Ideas scintillated back and forth, and each had to be considered . . . added to the canon . . . memorized by all . . . worked into the larger picture . . .

In a normal collaboration, each of two people has to be willing to do about 80 percent of the work. With eight of us, and with the enormous complexity the project attained, organization took far too much of the effort available. We'd each be doing 80 percent of the work . . . for 12½ percent of the take.

Granted that the project was a true kick in the ass, a mind stretcher, the kind of awesome world building the mundanes can't even dream about, an experience to shape the rest of our lives. It's still true that each of us could earn more, faster, more surely, by working alone.

I've no reason to think that this ever crossed anyone's mind but mine. I've never asked.

And on the gripping hand . . . with eight successful writers/artists working on a long term project, isn't it obvious that one or another would get involved in something else? Other collaborations or other obligations, or personal problems, or something to bring in quicker money . . . It was my first thought when Joel conned me into this. We tried it anyway.

Somebody was lured away, and it was me.

The first major step on the road to success: learn how to turn down bad offers. The second major step: learn how to turn down good offers. This can be very difficult. I say this in my own defense: Jerry Pournelle and I worked these rules out as a basic truth; but I was better at using it, or else I needed the money less. Jerry is still trying to dig out from under too many obligations, all these years later.

But I was snowed under when it was Thraxisp time. I was working on a book with Steven Barnes and a book with Jerry and at least one of my own. That one could be slighted—none of my publishers have ever complained about lateness, Ghod bless them—but the rent is always presumed due for my collaborators. Fair's fair.

This was how it ended—

November 18, 1986

Generic Thraxisp Participant
Dear Generic,

Paul isn't interested in blitzing Thraxisp. I haven't been able to reach Dr. Hartmann by phone.

Me, I would need to be re-inspired. We are the three writers in the Thraxisp Group, and it is we who would need to write text.

So. My position is this:

1) We've had a learning experience. It was pleasant and educational too.

2) The trick is to make money by having fun. But none of the writers is available to turn Thraxisp into a book. It follows that we can only make money by selling individual contributions.

3) The artists have busted their asses at this; and I include Dr. Hartmann as both writer and artist. The artists may sell their artwork and keep the money, no strings attached. (I don't know of any piece of artwork that was a collaboration. If such exists, work your own deals.)

4) The writers may sell whatever they write in future, no strings attached, using the Thraxisp system as a communal idea pool. This includes fiction and also articles. (Bill, you sold an article with illustrations and split the money with us all. Thank you. I hope that the ethics of changing the rules now don't bother you; but give us some input.)

I presently have no such stories in mind; but such might arise in future.

Artists may also make and sell new material, no strings attached.

5) I don't know what to do about existing text. Some of the text was done in solo flights, and those blocks should belong to the author; but I suggest that any of the eight of us may quote from any of the text, making it a communal pool.

6) Obviously, illustrations are available for fiction and articles. I suggest that the artists and writers can cut their deals in the usual fashion.

7) Whatever happens, I suggest we keep each other informed.

8) I don't plan any more eight-part collaborations. The only thing wrong with this bag of snakes is, it was too big!

I'm well aware that the one who ran out of time to work was me. It's embarrassing . . . and I don't want to go through that again either.

Best wishes,
Larry Niven

The true heir to all of this is an annual event called *Contact.*

At *Contact,* all of the invited guests are "soft" scientists—biologists, anthropologists, sociologists—or science fiction writers with an emphasis in the "soft" sciences. There are lectures, there are displays—not like the usual convention Art Show, but more of an anthropological museum display. At night there are films suitable for a college class. The badges are neat. They feature Joel Hagen's alien skulls.

Contact was Jim Funaro's idea. Seven or eight of us carved out details while sitting around a big table in the bar at a Westercon. Joel Hagen and I were there. At the first *Contact* Paul Preuss was also among the guests: three out of eight veterans of the World Builders Project at Equicon/Filmcon.

Contact includes the Bateson Project: a world building exercise. The paying guests get to watch ten to fifteen very good minds shaping worlds in the fashion of the World Builders: artwork, sociology charts, a globe or two, sculpture. At set times the participants lecture on what they've accomplished.

At the first *Contact* the guests had to produce their worlds from scratch. Didn't work. Anthro-bio-sociologists break laws of physics without noticing.

At the second Joel Hagen handed us a sculpture, a thing that was mostly legs . . . and no anus. We made Joel put one in. We called it a *squitch* and extrapolated a world.

Ideally the *Contact* guests need a world to start with. Jim invites a hard science fiction writer or two (Poul Anderson, Jerry Pournelle, me) to make one. He arrives Thursday night with a stack of notes and maps, and lectures on the physics, orbits, climatology, etc. Then the life-sciences people take over.

It's always been two teams. One handles the aliens. One team designs a human culture; and that can be weirder yet. On Sunday they run 'em together, on stage.

Ending is much too strong a word.

Thraxisp hasn't disappeared. We have all the material for an elaborate franchise universe.

Each of us has learned. Cooperation is not easy for professional dreamers. Keeping a dream world consistent isn't easy for anyone. We gave our creatures biology, history, cultures, art forms, vehicles and habitats.

We learned how to play. It's damned few of our five billion who are really good at that.

Biographical Sketches

Milford Writers' Conferences: Tradition says that a novice writer learns nothing from a writers' conference.

I knew this. I attended the Milford Conferences hosted by Kate Wilhelm Knight and Damon Knight; but for fear of losing my ability to write, I skipped every other year. Presently I dropped out, or was dropped; my memory won't tell me which.

The Milford conferences were serious. Each attendee brought several copies of at least one manuscript. During the day the others would read it. The attendees would gather in a Vicious Circle to offer comments, criticism, suggestions.

Of three stories I took to Milford (and Madiera Beach, when the Knights moved there) only one was improved. That was "For a Foggy Night."

It's still true that the Milford Conferences were different. My urge to write did not die because I went to Milford. On the contrary, I always enjoyed myself; I always went home inspired, one way or another; and I met people I'd wanted to know since I was a little boy.

James Blish brought the first section of a novel, *A Torrent of Faces,* and described what he had planned for the rest. An asteroid is due for collision with

Larry Niven, 1978

Earth . . . an Earth inhabited by a trillion people, with no margin of error for any such catastrophe. Bombs are placed to blow away pieces of the rock; lasers fired from the Moon are to boil away some of the surface; but too much of it will touch down . . .

My turn. "Suppose you fire those lasers at just one side of the body? Boil one side. Vapor pressure, law of reaction. Couldn't you cause it to miss the Earth?"

Blish said, "I hope not."

It took me a moment to join the laughter . . . to realise that I'd suggested a way to shoot down the plot for his novel!

But Blish did what a professional would do (and I learned by seeing what he did). He made the laser just powerful enough to shift the impact point of the meteoroid from Chicago to a place not so heavily populated . . . and it still destroyed too much.

Arthur C. Clarke brought a Questar telescope and set it up on the Knights' porch. It was early afternoon and we all took turns looking at Venus.

Many years later, during a radio interview in Los Angeles, Arthur was asked, "Who's your favorite writer?" You know the answer to that, surely. You can't name one, or many; you'll offend all the rest.

He said, "Larry Niven." And apologized to Jerry Pournelle, that night at a Pournelle party.

Jerry tells a similar tale, and in fact lots of us can do so. Arthur Clarke is the kind of man you want to kill someone for, just so he knows.

I'd discovered **Lester Del Rey**'s juveniles at the same time as Robert Heinlein's. Here he was in the flesh, generating wicked arguments on every possible topic.

I met **Piers Anthony** at the Madiera Beach conference, but we never got to talking. We got a dialogue going many years later, when I sent him a fan letter after reading *Omnivore*.

Gordon Dickson and others talked about working for an agency for reading fees. There was mention of a novice writer whose wonderful characters never got involved in anything like a story, and another who mistook funny hats for characterization. They never got the point, and the readers never stopped caring . . . and could never tell anyone to quit.

Harlan Ellison wanted unqualified praise. Any suggestion that a story could be improved was met with verbal vitriol. The circle of critics saw a lot of that.

This grated. If a story didn't need fixing, why bring it? Then again, he brought very good stories, and his suggestions for improving others' stories were pointed and useful.

Years later, my whole attitude flipflopped.

I sent "Inconstant Moon" to Damon Knight for *Orbit.* He rejected it.

Damon Knight was then one of the foremost critics of speculative fiction. The other was James Blish. Algis Budrys was making a reputation; Spider Robinson didn't exist. And *Orbit* was definitive: it was the literary end of the spec fic spectrum throughout the New Wave period.

What I wrote was never New Wave; but there's never been a time when I didn't want to expand my skills. I thought I'd made it this time. A solid study of character; no visible hardware; a love story. New Wave for sure, even if I was writing in complete sentences.

I recently unearthed Damon's long rejection letter. He made a good deal of sense, more than I remembered. Even a Hugo Award winning story can be improved.

At the time I was furious. I questioned his critical skill. This story was perfect, and only an idiot would have questioned, etc.

Maybe a writer needs that much arrogance. Else he'll never send out his first story, never make his first sale.

The Famous Writers School taught me how to know when I was a writer. I knew it when I saw the check.

It was signed by **Frederik Pohl.**

Fred bought my first four stories, and many others, for the Galaxy chain. The third was a novella called "Relice of Empire." He retitled it "World of Ptavvs," got Jack Gaughan to do a stack of interior illos for it, and paid in peanuts. He also took it to Betty Ballantine (the science fiction arm of Ballantine Books) and suggested that it could become a novel.

Fred has figured large in my life.

He was an usher at my wedding.

At my first science fiction convention I was a lost neofan; but a writer too, because Fred Pohl knew me.

Early on, he suggested that I write stories about odd astrophysical domains: very hot and cool stars, hypermasses, Hal Clement's kind of thing; we'd pair them with articles on the same, and paintings . . . That notion fell through, but he set me to looking for the odd pockets in the universe.

When Fred left the Galaxy chain, someone should have warned me to go with him. His replacement, Ejler Jakobssen, was a recycled editor from "pulps" days. Ejler rejected a story months after "buying" it (saying he'd take it, but not sending a check). He "bought" "The Flying Sorcerers" as a four-part serial, demanded references for all of the Tuckerized friends in the book (which ruined all the jokes for me), then rejected the first section! *Then* rejected the rest. I'd heard horror tales about the days of the pulps. Now I got to live through them.

William Rotsler was part of the LASFS crowd when I joined. He's easygoing, curious about his fellow man, easy to get to know. His life follows his whims.

He collects epigrams for what will someday be an enormous volume; meanwhile he sometimes sends them to *Reader's Digest.* ("Everything starts as someone's daydream." Larry Niven, fifty bucks for five words.)

He's a photographer . . . of "fumetti," of bottom-budget movies, of naked ladies. (Models, that is. Naked ladies? "She gets the benefit of the doubt, just like you, dear.") At science fiction conventions his tendency was to escort supernaturally beautiful women, "Rotsler women."

If things get dull at a science fiction convention banquet, look for the cluster of interested, amused, excited people. Bill Rotsler has gotten bored. So he's started drawing . . . on his notepad, the tablecloth . . . When things were slow in starting at a banquet some years back, Bill began illustrating the butter dishes. The restaurant must have been dismayed at how many butter dishes went home with the guests. Mine was a dialogue:

"What does a collaborator do?"

"He adds his name to a work which would not otherwise have the luster."

But I didn't grab my favorite. It's "The Memorial Vincent Van Gogh Coffee Cup," with the handle for an ear and a bandage drawn on the other side!

Once upon a time his whim had him making badges. He made a great many of them. Some were for sale, for charities. Some, personalized, were for friends. So there were badges labeled *Not Larry Pournelle* and *Not Jerry Niven.* I wore *Jerry Pournelle's Voice Coach* for awhile, and when I'd got my fair share of fun out of that, I gave it to Jerry's wife. I wear *LARRY NIVEN, Friend of the Great and Near-Great* to conventions. (Which are you? Well, if you're standing close enough to read the badge . . .) I no longer wear *Have Sex Outside My Species* because it's been too long since *The Ringworld Engineers,* and because I once forgot to take it off when I left the hotel.

You can identify inner-circle fandom by the Rotsler badges.

I met **Tom Doherty** by walking into the Ace party at the World Science Fiction Convention in Florida. Tom had just taken over at Ace Books.

He met me at the door. He knew my name. He had a good smile and (I tend to notice) an impressively large head, roomy enough for the brain of a blue whale. He was talking to Adele Hull of Pocket Books, and he started to tell me how good she was . . . and caught himself. It occurred to him that he shouldn't be praising the opposition in front of a solid author.

I said, "I have to tell you, it probably will never cost you a nickel."

"Why not?"

Oh my God. He didn't know! And I realized that I was going to have to tell him. Who else would? So I did. "Nobody deals with Ace Books unless all the other choices are used up. Nobody expects royalties; the advance is *it.* Overseas money is never reported . . ."

Tom Doherty is a careful businessman. He didn't take over Ace without checking first. He checked back for two years and found no complaints lodged against Ace . . . not because there weren't any, as he thought, but because the whole field had long since given up on ever getting money due from the old Ace Books.

The encounter with Larry Niven was his second awful shock of the day. He had already met Jerry Pournelle that afternoon.

"I'm Jerry Pournelle, President of SFWA, and we want to look at your books!"

Tom wound up paying several hundred thousand dollars in back fees to authors.

After he and James Baen parted company with Ace, Tom formed his own company, Tor Books. Then Jim dropped away and formed Baen Books. In this field we tend to train each other.

I see Tom fairly frequently. Once we met at a Boskone (annual Boston convention) and he took me and Marilyn off to Loch Ober, along with his editor, his wife, and his daughter. He talked four of us into ordering lobster Savannah.

The lobster is cut open along the back; the meat is cooked, chopped and mixed with herbs, then put back. Lobster Savannah looks like it could *heal.* These beasts ran three pounds each. I started talking to my dinner:

"Doctor McCoy will see you now."

*(Front row) Ray Bradbury, Larry Niven,
Julius Schwartz; (back row) Sarah Shaw,
Bob Shaw, Jack Williamson*

"The Federation doesn't think you can defend yourselves without our aid."

"Now, wretched bottom-feeder, you will tell us of your troop movements!"

By dinner's end I had arranged a mutual defense treaty with the baked Alaska. And by the time we reached the hotel, I had been dubbed *Speaker-to-Seafood.*

The last time Marilyn and I were in New York, I came to realize that Tom had bought me five meals! though he was only present at two!

I was told early: when you eat with an editor or publisher, that's who pays the check. It's surprisingly easy to get used to such a tradition . . . but enough is enough. Hell, I'd never even sold him a book.

N-Space started with a phone call from Bob Gleason, one of my favorite editors. He and Tom had got to talking over a dinner . . . and it emerged that Larry Niven was going to have been a published

author for twenty-five years, real soon now. Why not publish a retrospective volume? So Bob called.

It sounded good to me.

In May 1989, Tom Doherty and Bob Gleason stayed at my house for a few days before the SFWA Nebula Awards. We did a fair amount of work on the book. And I fed Tom Doherty by *cooking* several meals.

I even picked up a restaurant check once, by previous negotiation. He tried to back out afterward, but I wouldn't let him.

We called **Don Simpson** the Eldritch Doom because of the things he kept in his room. He's an artist and inventor, of that breed that never gets rich, because he invents new art forms. By the time anything could become successful, he'd be on to something else.

He had a wonderful time with some glass engraving equipment.

I'd been leaving Michelob beer bottles all over the clubhouse: the old lovely vase-shaped bottles too tall to quite fit in a refrigerator. At my fanquet (the banquet given for a LASFS member who has made a professional sale) Don presented me with a beer bottle engraved with Jack Gaughan's illustration of one of my aliens. I got him to do two more for me, then a Baccarat decanter and some Steuben crystal . . .

He was in the LASFS then. Later he moved to San Francisco, but I don't think he gave up his habits.

Frank Gasperik was an oddity. When I met him he was a biker and a hippie and a science fiction fan. Among bikers he carried a guitar and called himself The Minstrel. At science fiction conventions he sang filk.

Jerry and I put him in *Lucifer's Hammer* as Mark Czescu. We put his song in too. He makes a good character . . . though he tends to take over a book, like kudzu.

We put him in *Footfall* too, as Harry Reddington, and commissioned a ballad from him. By then Frank had been through major changes. He'd been rear-ended twice within two weeks while driving two different cars, neither of which had headrests. His insurance company was giving him the runaround and his lawyer told him he'd look better on a witness stand if he didn't get well too quick. So he was avoiding major efforts to walk normally. It's all true . . . and Jerry and I screamed at him separately and together until we made him see that he wasn't being paid enough to stay sick!

We were working near the end of *Footfall* at my house when Frank phoned about another matter. I told him, "We're at the poker table deciding Hairy Red's fate."

"Give me a heroic death," he said. So we killed him.

Dan Alderson is classic. At Jet Propulsion Laboratories they called him their "sane genius." He designed a program used by most of the free world countries for deep space probes. Computer nerd, sedentary, white shirt with infinite pens and pencils in a plastic holder in the pocket. Diabetic.

Characteristic cry: "Weep! Wail!"

From Dan came the germ of a short story, "There Is a Tide." He worked out the exact instability of the Ringworld; it took seven years. I went to him for numbers for the Ringworld meteor defense.

He was Dan Forrester in *Lucifer's Hammer.* The list of what Forrester would need after Hammerfall is his, because Jerry asked him.

He's the hero of one of Jerry's tales of asteroid colonization.

He likes Known Space. He's published intricately plotted outlines for stories that would vastly extend Known Space if they were written.

Judy-Lynn Benjamin Del Rey entered the field as an editor under Fred Pohl at Galaxy Science Fiction. When Fred quit, she continued with Ejler Jakobssen for awhile. She wound up at Ballantine Books and became one of the most powerful editors in the field.

She was a dwarf. One got over noticing that. She was charming, intelligent, enthusiastic, competent. She was tactful within limits: she generally wouldn't lie to an author.

She liked stuffed animals. When I introduced her to the cat-tail (see *World Out of Time*) which Takumi Shibano had brought me from Japan, she fell in love with it. Takumi got me another, and I passed it on.

She wanted to chop hell out of *A Mote in God's Eye.* Jerry and I wouldn't have that, so the book wound up with Simon and Schuster and Bob Gleason. In later years her comment on that decision was, "I don't want to talk about it."

She never bid on books at auction. Thus she lost *Footfall* to Fawcett . . . and got it back when Ballantine bought Fawcett!

Let me tell you about the last time I noticed her height.

We were walking along a Philadelphia sidewalk, talking: me and Marilyn and Judy-Lynn and Lester, who is kind of short himself. Suddenly I was sitting on the sidewalk, dazed, looking up, with blood dripping down my nose from a wedge-shaped notch in my forehead. I saw something massive and metallic hanging over the sidewalk at eyebrow height.

In Philadelphia they put construction equipment where it can bite pedestrians. If I hadn't been looking down I'd have seen it. As it was, I had to go into the construction site and borrow Kleenex and a Band-Aid.

David Gerrold came to the LASFS in peculiar fashion. He came as a big name pro, unknown to all, who had never published in any magazine nor sold any novel. But he had written the script for a *Star Trek* episode, "The Trouble with Tribbles."

This should be remembered: there had been no bad *Star Trek* shows. Nothing like the first season of *Star Trek* had ever been seen. Gene Rodenberry had lured real by-Ghod science fiction writers to write scripts! One season was all it took to alienate them. They weren't used to seeing their precious prose rewritten by inept hacks or (in one case) Gene Rodenberry's secretary.

David was a novice. *Everybody* rewrote "Tribbles," and he took it for granted. From listening to David and others I have gathered that the best stories see the most rewriting. Everybody wants to have had something to do with building a good show.

Marilyn and I invited David and a date over for dinner one night. He turned up alone. In the course of conversation, we discussed writing a story together . . . and kept talking, and looked through a dictionary for definitions for "As A Mauve," and kept talking . . .

David did more of the first-draft writing. He types like a jackrabbit: lots of speed, lots of typos. The story ("The Misspelled Magicians") grew to the size of a two-part serial. I chopped it back to size before we extended the story.

It was fun. We'd take turns at the typewriter. I remember him jumping up from the typewriter, startling me, shouting, "All right, I've got them into a riot! You stop it."

I read what he'd written. I said, "Stop it, hell—" and wrote the riot.

David wrote fast and wordy. I found I was expected to do the cutting. I should have cut deeper; but it felt *wrong* to be chopping at another writer's precious prose. I didn't develop the necessary savagery until the second rewrite of *A Mote in God's Eye.*

We've worked together since. David was story editor for the Saturday morning animated show *Land of the Lost.* The fun went out of it when invisible executives began to interfere with the first script. They chopped out our best character. They were about to take the river out of "Downstream"! I washed my hands of it . . . and then they put the river back . . . And when David told me that he needed help with more scripts, I saw a neat convergence.

I could do the first drafts. David as story editor could decide what changes were needed, and as my collaborator he could then *make* them. I need never worry about the changes in my precious prose. So we did two more.

Steven Barnes stands about five eight or nine. He's black. He's in perfect physical condition. He's smiling. He's probably talking (though he listens good too) and as he talks, he bounces around like he really ought to be tied to a railing, just in case.

Steve isn't exactly your typical fan. Then again, he is. Kids picked on him in high school for an intellectual bookworm. They wouldn't let him be nice. He took up martial arts. He teaches several varieties. Now they let him be nice whenever he wants to.

But . . . he's a science fiction fan. We're *different.* He didn't stop with learning how to survive Conan the Cimmerian.

He wants to know everything that the human body can be made to do. He wants his friends to be healthy and safe. He teaches self-defense classes at the LASFS. He tries out exercise modes, and when he *knows* something works, he passes it on to his friends.

Writing? Oh, *writing!* Jerry Pournelle and I think we're pretty good. We could have made *The Legacy of Heorot* a fine tale of interstellar colonization; but we don't have the right mind-set for a horror novel. What it took was the guy who wants me to see *The Texas Chain-Saw Massacre* for its artistic merit.

Steven's first solo novel (*Street Lethal*) was based on a working love potion, for God's sake! A monogamy treatment. I wouldn't have had the nerve.

The television industry loves him too. Remember a show called *The Wizard?* They were about to drop it. Then they saw Steven's script. It involved a robot suspected of murder.

Suddenly they were talking about this one saving the show! They swapped scripts around to put his in the right place; they found enough money somehow; and when the producer made script changes, the director changed it back and swore it was already perfect. They think he's pretty good.

There's money in scripts too.

You be nice to him, or he'll spend all his time writing scripts.

Jerry Pournelle raised the subject of collaboration, and it sounded like fun to me. Working with David Gerrold had been fun.

Jerry wouldn't work in Known Space, because he couldn't believe in the politics or the history. But he had a thousand years of a future history that uses the faster-than-light drive designed by our mutual friend Dan Alderson. I looked it over. Peculiar. A thousand inhabited planets and no intelligent beings save humans?

Then I realised that the laws of the Alderson Drive allowed me to insert an undiscovered alien civilization right in the middle.

That did it: there was going to be a novel. I had abandoned a novella two-thirds written; I dug it out and resurrected the alien. We spent a wild night extrapolating from the Motie Engineer form, to a dozen varieties of Motie, to a million years of history

With collaborator Jerry Pournelle

and three planet-busting wars. We swore we would write the novel we wanted to read when we were twelve.

Writing is the hard part. Every time we thought we were finished, we found we weren't.

Jerry sent our "finished" manuscript to a friend: Robert Heinlein. Robert told us that he could put one terrific blurb on the cover *if* we made some changes. The first hundred pages had to go . . .

And we did that, and reintroduced characters and moved background data from the lost Prologue to a later scene set on New Scotland, and did more chopping throughout. "There's a scene I've *never* liked," I told Jerry, and our whole relationship changed. This was when we learned not to be too polite to a collaborator; it hurts the book.

And we sent it back to Robert, *who did a complete line editting job.*

I know of a man who once offered Robert Heinlein a reading fee! The results were quite horrid. But in the case of *Mote,* Robert hadn't expected us to take his advice. Nobody ever had before, he tells us. But if "Possibly the finest science fiction novel I have ever read" were to appear on the cover, above Robert Heinlein's name, then the book had to *be* that.

It took us forever to write. We won the LASFS's "Sticky" Award for "Best Unpublished Novel" two years running. It was worth every minute.

Jerry and I had begun work on *Oath of Fealty* when I remembered Dante's *Inferno.* I'd read it in college, twice in quick succession, then daydreamed about a lost soul trying to escape that awful landscape.

The *Divine Comedy* is good fantasy, but only because of the passage of time. It was the first hard science fiction novel. It has all the earmarks: not just because it's a trilogy, and not only for its tremendous scope. Dante used a wide spectrum of the knowledge of the time: theology, the classics, architecture, geography, even astrology. He designed a perfect Easter for his protagonist's trip through Hell and Purgatory and the Earthly Paradise and Heaven. He invented the Southern Cross, as Swift invented the moons of Mars, for story purposes.

I remembered the daydreams, and I remembered that I was a writer now. I remembered that Jerry Pournelle had a strong theological education, and that we'd already written a novel together. I put it to him that we should write a sequel.

Every other book has taken us two to three years to write. Once we got into text, we wrote *Inferno* in four months. Why so fast? Because the territory is terribly unpleasant. We wanted out!

Pocket Books put *Inferno* in a royalties pool with *Mote.* That is, royalties from *A Mote in God's Eye* would go to repay the advance on *Inferno,* because Pocket Books had little faith in *Inferno.* It is understood, in such cases, that second book will at least be published . . . but *Inferno* sat on some shelf for over a year. By the time we noticed and raised some hell, Pocket Books had paid not a penny for *Inferno.*

Inferno has had good critical acclaim. In college courses it has been taught as critical commentary on Dante, which of course it is.

I must add that we should have put it through another draft. We had the time, courtesy of Pocket Books' mistake, and *we didn't know it.*

Since Jerry and I first began writing together, our tendency has been to meet to plot out the book, assign each other scenes, then go off to write them. Near the end of *Footfall* we changed our habit. We wrote in my office, taking turns at the typewriter.

The mood became frenetic.

The more we wrote, the more we saw of scenes that needed to be written. Text in the beginning and middle needed rewriting. The end of the book receded before us like a ghost. Spring became summer . . . yet what we were writing was *superb,* it was *needed,* and the end *was* inching near.

Came the day we worked on the penultimate chapter. We planned a wrap-up-the-threads chapter to follow.

Jerry took his turn. *Will the aliens honor a conditional surrender? The Threat Team dithers. The President makes his choice . . .*

My turn, with the aliens. *Surrender, or all will die! But the Herdmaster must have permission of the females . . .* I was typing fast enough to break bones. *. . . set their feet on the Herdmaster's chest.* I jumped up. "If I don't quit now I'll go into Chayne-Stokes breathing," I said.

Jerry read it through. "I can improve this," he said, and typed, "-30-" (The End).

Laws

From time to time I publish this list; from time to time I update it. I don't think it's possible to track its publishing history. The most recent appearance was in Niven's Laws *from Owlswick Press. In this version I've amplified a little.*

To the best I've been able to tell in fifty years of observation, this is how the universe works. I hope I didn't leave anything out.

Larry Niven at his home in Tarzana, California, 1978

NIVEN'S LAWS

1a) **Never throw shit at an armed man.**

1b) **Never stand next to someone who is throwing shit at an armed man.**

You wouldn't think anyone would need to be told this. Does anyone remember the Democratic National Convention of 1968?

2) **Never fire a laser at a mirror.**

3) **Mother Nature doesn't care if you're having fun.**

You will not be stopped! There are things you can't do because you burn sugar with oxygen, or your bones aren't strong enough, or you're a mammal, or human. Funny chemicals may kill you slow or quick, or ruin your brain . . . or prolong your life. You can't fly like an eagle, nor yet like Daedalus, but you can fly. You're the only Earthly life form that can even begin to deal with jet lag.

You can cheat. Nature doesn't care, but don't get caught.

4) **FxS=k.**

The product of Freedom and Security is a constant. To gain more freedom of thought and/or action, you must give up some security, and vice versa.

These remarks apply to individuals, nations, and civilizations. Notice that the constant **k** is different for every civilization and different for every individual.

5) **Psi and/or magical powers, if real, are nearly useless.**

Over the lifetime of the human species we would otherwise have done something with them.

6) **It is easier to destroy than to create.**

If human beings didn't have a strong preference for creation, nothing would get built.

7) **Any damn fool can predict the past.**

Military men are notorious for this, and certain writers too.

8) **History never repeats itself.**

9) **Ethics changes with technology.**

10) **Anarchy is the least stable of social structures. It falls apart at a touch.**

11) **There is a time and a place for tact.**

(And there are times when tact is entirely misplaced.)

12) **The ways of being human are bounded but infinite.**

13) **The world's dullest subjects, in order:**
   a) Somebody else's diet.
   b) How to make money for a worthy cause.
   c) Special Interest Liberation.

14) **The only universal message in science fiction: There exist minds that think as well as you do, but differently.**
   Niven's corollary: The gene-tampered turkey you're talking to isn't necessarily one of them.

15) **Fuzzy Pink Niven's Law: Never waste calories.**

Potato chips, candy, whipped cream, or hot fudge sundae consumption may involve you, your dietician, your wardrobe, and other factors. But Fuzzy Pink's Law implies:

Don't eat soggy potato chips, or cheap candy, or fake whipped cream, or an inferior hot fudge sundae.

16) **There is no cause so right that one cannot find a fool following it.**

This one's worth noticing.

At the first High Frontier Convention the minds assembled were among the best in the world, and I couldn't find a conversation that didn't teach me something. But the only newspersons I ran across were interviewing the only handicapped person among us.

To prove a point one may seek out a foolish Communist, thirteenth century Liberal, Scientologist, High Frontier advocate, Mensa member, science fiction fan, Jim Bakker acolyte, Christian, or fanatical devotee of Special Interest Lib; but that doesn't really reflect on the cause itself. *Ad hominem* argument saves time, but it's still a fallacy.

17) **No technique works if it isn't used.**

If that sounds simplistic, look at some specifics:

Telling friends about your diet won't make you thin. Buying a diet cookbook won't either. Even reading the recipes doesn't help.

Knowing about Alcoholics Anonymous, looking up the phone number, even jotting it on real paper, won't make you sober.

Buying weights doesn't give you muscles. Signing a piece of paper won't make Soviet missiles disappear, even if you make lots of copies and tell every anchorperson on Earth. Endlessly studying designs for spacecraft won't put anything into orbit.

18) **Not responsible for advice not taken.**

19) **Think before you make the coward's choice. Old age is not for sissies.**

NIVEN'S LAWS FOR WRITERS

1) **Writers who write for other writers should write letters.**

2) **Never be embarrassed or ashamed by anything you choose to write.**

(Think of this before you send it to a market.)

3) **Stories to end all stories on a given topic, don't.**

4) **It is a sin to waste the reader's time.**

5) **If you've nothing to say, say it any way you like.**

Stylistic innovations, contorted story lines or none, exotic or genderless pronouns, internal inconsistencies, the recipe for preparing your lover as a cannibal banquet: feel free. *If what you have to say is important and/or difficult to follow, use the simplest language possible.* If the reader doesn't get it then, let it not be your fault.

6) **Everybody talks first draft.**

BIBLIOGRAPHY

Novels:

World of Ptavvs, Ballantine, 1966.

A Gift from Earth, Ballantine, 1968.

Ringworld, Ballantine, 1970.

(With David Gerrold) *The Flying Sorcerers*, Ballantine, 1971.

Protector, Ballantine, 1973.

(With Jerry Pournelle) *The Mote in God's Eye*, Simon & Schuster, 1974.

(With J. Pournelle) *Inferno*, Pocket Books, 1976.

A World Out of Time, Holt, 1976.

(With J. Pournelle) *Lucifer's Hammer*, Playboy Press, 1977.

The Magic Goes Away, Ace Books, 1978.

The Patchwork Girl, Ace Books, 1980.

The Ringworld Engineers, Holt, 1980.

(With Steven Barnes) *Dream Park*, Ace Books, 1981.

(With J. Pournelle) *Oath of Fealty*, Simon & Schuster, 1981.

(With S. Barnes) *The Descent of Anansi*, Pinnacle Books, 1982.

The Integral Trees, Ballantine, 1984.

(With J. Pournelle) *Footfall*, Ballantine, 1985.

(With J. Pournelle and S. Barnes) *The Legacy of Heorot*, Simon & Schuster, 1987.

The Smoke Ring, Ballantine, 1987.

Story collections:

Neutron Star, Ballantine, 1968.

The Shape of Space, Ballantine, 1969.

All the Myriad Ways, Ballantine, 1971.

The Flight of the Horse, Ballantine, 1973.

Inconstant Moon, Gollancz, 1973.

A Hole in Space, Ballantine, 1974.

Tales of Known Space, Ballantine, 1975.

The Long ARM of Gil Hamilton, Ballantine, 1976.

Convergent Series, Ballantine, 1979.

Niven's Laws, Owlswick Press, 1984.

The Time of the Warlock, SteelDragon Press, 1984.

Limits, Ballantine, 1985.

Editor:

The Magic May Return, Ace Books, 1981.

More Magic, Berkley Publishing, 1984.

Contributor to *Dangerous Visions: 33 Original Stories*, edited by Harlan Ellison, Doubleday, 1967; and *The Craft of Science Fiction*, edited by Reginald Bretnor, Harper, 1976.

Work appears in anthologies. Contributor of short stories to *Magazine of Fantasy and Science Fiction, Galaxy, Playboy,* and *Analog.*

Elder Olson

1909-

At 8:30 in the evening of March 9, 1909, an event occurred which has since been celebrated annually for the last eighty-one years. The scene of that event was a flat in Logan Square, in Chicago. The persons present were Elder Olson, his wife, Hilda (nee Schroeder), old Doc Thompson, who had driven his horse and buggy through a blizzard in order to attend, and a newcomer who, no doubt, behaved in the usual manner of those who have been haled from a warm, safe place where every comfort was supplied into a loud and dazzling world. Others may have been there; I was too upset by my eviction to notice.

I know little of my father and have no memory of him. Those who knew him described him as "a prince." I am told he was good-looking and intelligent, with a warm personality and a phenomenal memory. How well he was educated, I do not know. He was descended from a long line of Norwegian seafarers. His own father was a retired sea captain. My father's generation was apparently the first to break that firm connection with the sea. He himself was an executive of the Canadian Pacific Railroad. People said that he had high hopes for me; he was not to suffer disappointment, for he died at twenty-eight, of a heart attack. He was either of some importance or very popular or both, for a number of executives came to his funeral.

He seems to have left little or no estate, for my mother gave up the flat, took me—then twenty-two months old—to her parents' home, and found work as a salesclerk in a local department store. She had to work very long hours, so I was left mainly in the care of my grandparents and numerous aunts, uncles, and cousins.

My grandfather Wilhelm Schroeder owned two adjacent two-story brick buildings at 1752 and 1754 Augusta Street. My grandparents, my mother, my aunts Lee and Rose, and I lived in 1752, while my Aunt Clara, a widow with two girls and a boy, lived in 1754. Other relatives had homes nearby, so it was a close, almost clannish family with my grandfather the benign center of it all.

Wilhelm Schroeder was a remarkable man. He served his stint in the German army and immigrated

Elder Olson as "Buster Brown," with his grandfather Wilhelm Schroeder

to America. On the ship coming over, he met a German girl from Konigsberg, Karolina, whom he married, and both became naturalized U.S. citizens. In Chicago he set up a lumber yard and prospered. After the Chicago fire—his yard unscathed—he offered free lumber to any fire victims who wished to rebuild or repair. He bought various properties. At one time he owned a stretch of Milwaukee Avenue, then called Plank Avenue because its only paving was planks laid in the mud, for the wagon traffic. Mistakenly, he supposed it would never become valuable, and sold it. He was liked and well-respected in the neighborhood; his influence was such that during a financial panic, he was able to stop a run on a local bank simply by walking in with a moneybag and shouting, "Schroeder *deposits!*" Only five feet five inches tall, he nevertheless possessed great physical strength; I saw him lift, one-handed, a heavy chair by one leg and hold it high over his head when he was in his early eighties. Finding that none of his four sons was interested in his lumber company, he sold it, and retired at the age of fifty.

Seventeen fifty-two and 1754 Augusta Street shared a large common yard holding a big open space and my grandmother's flower-and-vegetable garden. A two-story stable and woodsheds stood in the rear. Each building had its own front garden, and until the street was widened, our side was shaded with cottonwoods. The flats were stoveheated and gaslit (we also had kerosene lamps). Telephones were installed only later.

Here we all lived, then, a tight little clan but friendly with all around us, in a motley neighborhood of Germans, Scandinavians, Jews, and Poles, all perfectly content with one another. I cannot remember a single instance of intolerance. The German "Hungry Five" (a strolling band), the Negro who sold watermelons in the summer, the Chinese laundryman, the Italian barber, the Mexican hawking tamales, the Russian Jew junk man crying "Olrexolionl" (old rags, old iron)—all were shown the same friendliness and respect. If I wondered too much at a strange custom, I was gently rebuked. I remember being upset by the Polish custom of "Switching Day," a day in spring when the boys lashed the girls' legs with green switches until they bled, while the girls squatted, shrieking and trying to cover their legs with their skirts. My grandparents simply shrugged and said, "They do that in their home country." I learned later that the most-whipped girls were also the most pleased, since the whipping was a recognition of their prettiness or popularity.

I was a happy little boy, in the midst of a loving family, playing with my grandfather or my cousins, occasionally baffling my grandmother by sitting rapt and silent in an empty box (dear lady, she could not have known that it was a ship, a dogsled, an automobile, or a balloon-gondola!). I was given a tricycle, a cowboy suit, a policeman suit, and many toys. Nevertheless, I was not spoiled; the family code was too strict for that. I recall throwing only two tantrums. One occurred when my mother bought me a "Little Lord Fauntleroy" suit, blue velvet with lace collar and cuffs. In deference to my outraged masculinity, it

was exchanged for a "Buster Brown" suit, and I got a "Buster Brown" haircut, to be just like the boy in the then-popular comic strip. I threw my second fit on learning—after begging and hoarding streetcar transfers for a whole year—that my Uncle Henry had only been joking when he told me that would win me a goat and a goat-cart. (He promptly atoned by buying me a red, sidewalk racing car [Number 9!], in which I pedaled, I thought, at stupendous speeds.) I loved Uncle Henry, but I did not like his jokes: "Like music, kid?"—"You bet!"—"Here's a cigar band."

At six, I entered the Harvey G. Wells Elementary School, a few blocks away. I was delighted with the classes and with the chance to make new friends. In second grade I wrote my first poem. Elaborately illustrated, it was something or other about a cat. Some months afterward, I came down with polio, then called infantile paralysis. It kept me out of school for two-and-a-half years. During that time we ran through thirteen doctors, all equally ineffective. All prescribed bed rest and absolute immobility. Beginning to have a mind of my own, I decided that they were all clowns, and rebelled: whenever I was alone, I exercised furiously, moving whatever parts of me I could, so that the bed was often soaked with sweat. Bad as my own plight was, I was almost equally pained by the distress of my family—in particular, of my mother. She had always seemed worn and frail to me, though photographs showed her a handsome and blooming girl. My great fear was that she might die, especially since she had a bad cough (in fact she was to live into her eighties). At that time, of course, I could not have known her resources of courage and determination.

I recovered at last with nothing worse remaining than a bad torticollis, which lasted for a year or two. In her desperation my mother had finally turned to Christian Science for aid, and my "miraculous" recovery was naturally attributed to the efficacy of that religion (I knew better!). Everyone in the family now became Christian Scientists. I went back to school. I had read avidly in bed whenever I was not exercising, had done the homework sent to me, and after a few special exams, caught up with my original class, so that I was able to graduate with it.

In the meanwhile my grandfather had died. The Augusta Street properties were sold, and we moved to another property at 3548 Wabansia Avenue, where my Aunt Clara was already installed. I went to Tuley High School, was bored and miserable there and, after two years, transferred to Carl Schurz High, along with my longtime friend Boleslaw Gajda.

Here we both flourished. We took a journalism course, and began writing for the school newspaper, *The Schurz World.* I wrote movie and book reviews, short stories, poems, and a whole serial adventure novel. I set up a column modelled on Keith Preston's in the *Chicago Daily News,* publishing jokes, quips, and poems.

Our English teacher was Mary Cornwall Hill, a bright-eyed, eager, and enthusiastic young woman who gave me my first real sense of the splendors of English literature. I had read all of Longfellow and much of Sir Walter Scott's poetry long before, plus much else, and come away only with a fervent enthusiasm for Poe and Stevenson; now I found myself reading and delighting in not merely Chaucer, Shakespeare, Milton, and other classics, but modern poets like Rupert Brooke and Walter De la Mare. I wrote sonnets by the dozen and haiku by the score. Coming upon a book of English translations of François Villon's poems, I was fascinated by the elaborate and difficult French verse forms, and composed in these as well. My mother bought me a portable typewriter. I clacked away on this industriously. Stevenson had said he learned to write by

"playing the sedulous ape"; I played the sedulous ape myself, carefully imitating writers I admired, to learn both how they had done it and how to do with language anything I might have to do. There was no doubt about it: I was to be a writer—specifically, a poet.

But I had also developed a competing ambition. Back when I was nine, my mother had asked Wilhelm Martin, a friend and a young professor of music, to give me piano lessons. I practiced diligently enough, for I liked music, unhappy only in that practice shortened my regular afternoon boxing and fencing, the only sports that I was any good at. However, in a friend's house some two or so years later, I found a grand piano with an album of music open on the stand. I sat down and began to play. I will never forget that moment; I felt as though someone had punched me in the heart. I stopped and looked at the title of the piece. It was the Mazurka Op. 67, No. 2, by F. F. Chopin. *Chopin?* "Chopin" meant to me only the name of a Polish theater on Chicago Avenue. I did not know that this was the beginning of a lifelong admiration; I merely had to find, and did find, more Chopin. I was eventually, as my technique developed,

"Wife Jerri in her studio, with company"

to play nearly all of his works; and it was from Chopin that I learned many of the rhythms of my poetry. I now took the piano very seriously. In my senior year at Schurz, Mr. Martin told me I was ready for the American Conservatory of Music. I studied there under Cleveland Bohnet, who presently became a close and steadfast friend.

He and other friends took me to, or gave me tickets to, many concerts, chiefly piano recitals or symphony concerts featuring a piano soloist; I was able, thus, to hear almost every famous pianist of the day. Besides, I had ushered in the big Loop movie theaters during the summer vacations and worked at Marshall Field's during the winter ones, so I had some money; my mother refused to accept this, and insisted I spend it on books and records. I toiled at the pieces recorded by great pianists until I fancied I had produced a fair approximation of their performances. Oh, yes, I was going to be a concert pianist. Oh, yes.

Shortly before my graduation from Schurz High, Miss Hill, who as I said was my English teacher and who had given me much (undeserved) encouragement, urged me to send some poems to *Poetry* magazine. I did, and a few days later had a postcard from Harriet Monroe, its founder and editor, which read: "We can't use these, but if you really are only seventeen years old, please come in and let us have a look at you." So off I went to 232 East Erie Street, with a huge loose-leaf notebook stuffed with sonnets, ballades, double ballades, rondeaux, lais, virelais, villanelles, haiku, cinquains, sestinas—whatnot.

I had read descriptions of Miss Monroe as the "high priestess of poetry," and I had seen one photograph of her in somewhat exotic costume that was alarmingly sacerdotal. What I anticipated, thus, thanks to my vast erudition in the works of H. Rider Haggard, was a tall and forbidding woman. What I actually confronted was a small, dainty person; but, despite my surprise, my dominant impression was not of her appearance but of her immense and strictly controlled energy. And she *looked* at me. Because of what I will call an unfortunate exuberance of temperament, I had had a great deal of experience with searching looks, from baffled and irate school teachers and other interested persons; but for the first time I learned what a really piercing look was. Even behind pince-nez glasses, it went through me like a lance. It was a fair preview of the way the Judgment Angel will look at you.

At her invitation, I sat down, handed her my life's work, and she began to read. She managed to keep her gravity for some time, but even her iron control had its limits; she broke into peals of laughter,

took off her glasses, wiped her eyes, and exclaimed, "What on *earth* are 'murmurous mysteries of myrrh'? *Murmurous mysteries of myrrh!*"

Mortally wounded (I thought it one of my very best phrases), I said, "I don't know."

"Then why did you say it?"

"It *sounded* nice." I didn't dare tell her that I had hoped it sounded like my then idol, Rupert Brooke.

She read through the whole mess, commenting now and then, handed back the notebook, and said, "Go home and write some *real poems.* You can, you know. Let us see them. And come back."

I thanked her, and abruptly I found myself outside. I have heard that after a long bout a boxer's trunks can weigh an extra two pounds because of sweat. I should like to know what my clothes weighed at that moment.

A few weeks later—after I had thrown out my "poems," but before I had written any "real poems"—I had a card from her inviting me to a tea at *Poetry* office. It was only the first of many teas: *Poetry* office was a center of culture and of extraordinary people, as Chicago was of railroad traffic. Poets, playwrights, novelists, painters, musicians, artists of every sort, critics and reviewers, all seemed to stream in from every part of the world. Whenever someone particularly interesting came to town, H.M. would have a tea and ask the poets present to read their latest work. I remember that Thornton Wilder, whom I had met earlier that afternoon, came up to me after I read and said enigmatically, "Your hand (he meant my technique) is ready; cultivate your soul."

I soon came to know, even to have as friends, all of the *Poetry* people: Marion Strobel, Jessica Nelson North and her half-brother Sterling North, Eunice Tientjens, George Dillon, Geraldine Udell, as well as many of their friends.

To my astonishment, I was suddenly swept into high circles of Chicago society, where one wore a tuxedo even to informal dinners and tails to formal affairs. I had no such clothing and could not afford it (I had never heard of rental companies); I was stumped and miserable. Our gentle and kindly family dentist, Dr. Maurice M. Kerr, heard of my problem and gave me his whole outfit, which he was replacing. Away I went to a dinner and ball marking the debut of the daughter of Countess Jerace, wearing my new finery. Dr. Kerr's measurements were exactly my own; even so, in unfamiliar array, I must have flopped about like a demented penguin.

For I did not know *how to act, what to do.* The first time I saw the array of silverware at a formal dinner, laid out like a surgeon's instruments before an operation, I nearly collapsed until I remembered "work inward from the ends." I suffered not merely the usual awkwardness of youth; coming from a lower-middle-class family as I did, I suffered also from severe cultural shock. I found an old etiquette book, printed in 1870, in the attic; if I have any "Old World manners," it is probably because of that. I aped the movie actor William Powell in order to seem suave and sophisticated, but Powell or no Powell, I executed the most ordinary social actions with all the grace of a hippopotamus trying to take a pinch of snuff.

I must have been pretty awful, but everybody was very kind, and I was invited and reinvited, God knows why. I had been taught courtesy and good table manners from childhood, so at least nobody had to run away screaming. If I had any other good points, I am unaware of them. I wonder what the devil people saw in me—even more, what they evidently liked. All of them—especially the *Poetry* people—remained my friends until we were separated by distance or by death.

I was publishing groups of poems in *Poetry* and elsewhere, and had won a couple of prizes, so I had enough money to pay tuition at the University of Chicago. I had to drop out in my first quarter because of my Uncle Henry's illness and death, but a few months later, tried again.

Interesting as I found the courses, they did not address the problems that were besetting me. For a curious thing was happening. I had begun writing poetry as some sort of intellectual game; now poems were forcing themselves upon me. I already knew a good deal about forms and techniques; I had been ransacking critical literature since I was seventeen, but clearly there was more—*much* more—that had to be known. I could not be an ignoramus in my own art. I decided that, despite its attractions, the University was not for me. I quit at the end of my sophomore year and got a job in the Merchandise Adjustment Department of the Commonwealth Edison Company. I began paying room and board to my family, only to discover later that the money was merely being put aside for me.

I remained at the Edison Company from 1929 to 1931. Then, feeling that I was getting nowhere, I resigned and went off to Europe. The trip was ostensibly only a tour, but I had the secret idea of studying piano in Leipzig. The poet, however, was gaining ascendancy over the musician, and when I ran into Thornton Wilder in Paris, I told him my plans. He had never heard me play (and never did), but he

had apparently followed my work closely. He waved away my pianistic ambitions impatiently, like annoying smoke. "The woods are full of fine pianists," he said. "You are going to have to be a poet whether you like it or not." He foresaw my fate far better than I did. Three weeks later, playing for some friends in Vienna, I suffered a complete blackout of my musical memory, and to this day can play nothing—no matter how well learned—without a score. Requiem for a pianist. Nature had solved my problem.

I was running out of funds. I returned to the States and started job-hunting. America was now well into the Depression, and persistently as I sought work, I had no luck. Personnel managers were, from their lofty elevation, suspicious either of the sanity or the virility, even, of an adult male (I was now twenty-two) who could spend two years at a university studying *literature.*

Wilder, like Bernard Weinberg, my friend since we had both been freshmen, kept urging me to return to the University. Wilder's idea was that—since no one could make a living by his poetry—I should finish my degree, go on to an M.A., and find a teaching post in some small college where I might "find the leisure to write." Finally convinced, I went back, cracked on full steam, and had my B.A. (Phi Beta Kappa) nine months later.

During that time I had won a number of prizes, but more important things had happened. Harriet Monroe had told me that I was ready to publish a first book of poems; in 1933 she introduced me to H. S. Latham, vice-president of Macmillan Company, her own publishers; and, undoubtedly through her influence, Macmillan published *Thing of Sorrow* in 1934 (it was given the annual award for poetry of the Foundation for Literature in 1935). It was very favorably reviewed by such prominent critics as Mary Colum, Eda Lou Walton, Stanley Kunitz, and William Rose Benét (who included two of my longer pieces in the second edition of *Great Poems of the English Language*). I was pleased, of course, but in truth I had lost any interest I had in a "poetic career" when I was nineteen. I was simply a poet because I had to be, and if people liked my work and wanted to publish it, fine. I would have continued to compose if my work had been ignored or even damned. I had no interest—have never had—in literary politics or literary cliques, both of which I held in contempt. I was merely following Wilder's advice to obtain an M.A. and, if possible, a teaching job. I discontinued my piano lessons at the American Conservatory, though I still played, and devoted myself to my studies. Wilder was then teaching at the University; I took two of his

Daughter Livy with her son, Michael, 1989

courses while I was still an undergraduate. Better still, I took more of his advice: when I asked him to recommend the toughest professors in my field, he suggested Ronald S. Crane and Richard McKeon. I began studying with them at once, and that is one of the most important decisions I ever made.

R. S. Crane was an eminent professor of eighteenth-century literature. I have published a long essay on him *(The American Scholar,* Spring, 1984) and shall shortly write on McKeon, so I shall say little here about these two extraordinary men. They were eventually to become, along with Weinberg, my closest friends.

By the end of my first course with Crane, he had learned that I was a poet interested in literary criticism, and in the same problems that were troubling him. I wanted to know precisely what poets *did* to produce the effects they achieved, for every effect was, as in playing the piano, the consequence of *something done.* In composing I "flew by the seat of my pants," going by the feel alone; I wanted more than that—*knowledge.* Crane wanted it, too, except that he wanted it not to compose but to teach. We spent

many hours in argument and discussion. He was astonished to discover that, while I could analyze and discuss the poetry of others well enough, I was an absolute dummy on my own poems: I could neither say where they came from nor why I had done what I had.

I had told Crane that I wanted to go on for an M.A., but that I needed a program less confining than that provided by the English department—something that would let me study the whole history of literary criticism and as many different literatures as I could. He suggested that I transfer to the Committee on Literature, an interdepartmental arrangement that would make this possible. I did, so that I have only a bachelor's degree in English, the others in that Committee. It was a far stiffer but also a far more rewarding program that we finally worked out. I had already read—in fact, studied—most of the authors in the English program as well as a lot of literary history, and saw no point in doing it all over again.

The first course I had with McKeon was a yearlong one in the intellectual history of Western Europe. McKeon was a philosopher whom the new President of the University, Robert Maynard Hutchins, had induced to leave the Columbia University faculty and come to Chicago. He already had a fine reputation as a specialist in medieval philosophy, but in truth he was a great deal more than that.

The course was really one in the history of philosophy from Plato to the present. It was organized around the perennial problem of knowledge, and McKeon went from philosopher to philosopher, showing the form the problem took for each, the philosophic method entailed, and the workings of the arguments. The reading list was huge, but in my usual fashion I went far beyond it, reading extensively in the *Patrologia Latina* (thank God for Mrs. Lawrence, my tough Latin teacher at Tuley High!), the works of St. Augustine, St. Jerome, Aquinas, William of Ockham, and others. Some of these side-ventures resulted in poems in *The Cock of Heaven,* the new book I was doing for Macmillan; others, in later pieces like "The Ballad of the Scarecrow Christ." I was stunned by the course, and even more so by the tremendous intellect and erudition of the man teaching it. I was to take many another course under him.

I was also taking courses and seminars with Crane and others, and nine months after my B.A., I had my M.A. I also had a job; I was hired as a part-time instructor in English and French at Armour Institute of Technology (later Illinois Institute of Technology). I had even more than that: I had two new passions to add to my passions for poetry and for

Chopin—a passion for philosophy and a passion for logic.

This latter passion was to stand me in good stead when in my second year at Armour, and now a full-time instructor, I substituted a stiff course in logic for the silly and useless course in "Rhetoric and Debate." After a brief rebellion of the students (who ever heard of an English course that was as tough as one in physics or mathematics?!), the course became popular once its value was realized, and I taught it exclusively for the rest of my stay at Armour.

Crane had urged me to go on to a Ph.D., and I was doing just that. My promotion to full time brought a raise from a $900 salary to $1500, and it was now financially possible to move from my mother's house to a university dormitory, thus saving more than three hours of commuting. Bernard Weinberg (also working on a doctorate) and I shared a small two-bedroom suite with a double study-living room on the ground floor of Hitchcock Hall. Here we entertained various visitors—Crane, Norman Maclean, Sir Herbert J. C. Grierson, the distinguished editor of Donne (who became my friend after I had challenged his interpretation of one of Donne's poems), and others. Free evenings were few, however, for both Weinberg and I were overloaded with work. My own schedule was awful; I had to rush from my Armour classes to afternoon and evening seminars, study afterward until 2 A.M., sleep for four hours, and rush back to Armour.

Even so, I found time for other things. Early in the fall of 1936, I met Ann Elizabeth Jones, a pretty and vivacious graduate student in French literature. We were married the following February and presently moved into an apartment on Kimbark Avenue. Our first child, Ann, was born late in 1937. I was now an Assistant Professor with a salary of $1800. I supplemented this income by teaching the summer term for two years, but we were still far from affluent.

Early in 1938 I finished my doctoral dissertation, and it was accepted. I had constructed an original theory of *general* prosody (that is, a theory not restricted to any one language, but applicable to English, French, Greek, Latin, German, Italian, Spanish, etc.) I believe this had never been attempted before.

The final oral exam took place in September. The judges included Crane, McKeon, Clarence Faust, the critic Kenneth Burke, the French scholar and novelist René Etiemble, and some visitors. The examination covered not merely my theory but also some of the many texts in my bibliography, and the questions—particularly those of Burke and McKeon

—were subtle and probing, but I had a fine time. The oral was supposed to last some three hours, but in a little over an hour I was asked to leave the room. In about five minutes Crane came out and said, "You have your degree." McKeon invited all of us to his apartment, where we talked and argued until 2 A.M. I went home to find a party in full swing: a lot of my friends and classmates had arranged it and started celebrating even before the examination had begun. It was a moving demonstration of confidence and affection.

So, after two-and-a-half years, I had my Ph.D., and was promoted to Assistant Professor; everything was proceeding smoothly. Except for one thing, my marriage was a happy one. That "thing" was my mother-in-law, who had determined on hostility before she even met me. Still, it was not she who would eventually wreck the marriage.

Meanwhile McKeon and his wonderful wife, Muriel, had become very close friends of ours, as had the Cranes. Crane, like me, was watching European affairs closely; we both saw the imminent danger of war. I hated Hitler and Fascism. Ever since I had traveled in Germany, I had been uneasy about what I saw developing there. By 1936, I was so furious that I wrote a poem, savage and prophetic, "Munich: New Year's Eve, 1936." I mislaid it somehow, found it decades later, and published it in *Olson's Penny Arcade.* I was not actually in Munich at the time, but the scene was as vivid in my mind's eye as if I had been.

Ann gave birth to a son, Elder. I continued teaching, finished my second book, and wrote articles, book reviews, and more poems. I had offers from several universities, but on Crane's advice did not accept them. Crane had been Chairman of the English Department and McKeon Dean of the Humanities for some years now.

The Cock of Heaven appeared in 1940. On the whole it was favorably reviewed (though some reviewers complained of its obscurity) in *Time* and other magazines and newspapers. No one has understood the basic strategy of the poem. It is a commentary on a fictional text; after the text and an introductory section, the seven deadly sins are dealt with, under their Latin names, followed by a concluding part. The sins are dealt with in the scholastic method (remember, I had been reading heavily in the medieval philosophers!) and the plan was to have the voices of poets and prose-writers, by imitation of their literary styles, echoing down the ages. At the plea of Macmillan readers, who were enthusiastic but puzzled, I supplied a "pony" to assist reviewers, but apparently that assistance was insufficient; reviewers like Randall Jarrell and Louis Untermeyer, both of whom had obviously used the "pony," complained that I had imitated various poets, etc. (How, may I ask, can one suggest various voices without imitating them?) I was amused to see that critics who delighted in puzzling over the poems of Eliot, Pound, and others were annoyed to find something else to puzzle about. I had not intended, of course, to puzzle anyone; I was merely making a poem as it demanded to be made. As a poet I do not think about readers, but about poems. I broke my three-book contract with Macmillan, not caring a rap whether I ever published another book of poetry.

War was steadily approaching. My poem "Ice-Age" reflects that period of anxiety. I wrote other war and prewar poems, including "Horror Story" and "The Statue," which is really about Winston Churchill's political career. With the attack on Pearl Harbor, Bernie Weinberg enlisted in the Air Force, our friend Caleb Bevans joined Intelligence, and I tried desperately, in succession, to enlist in the Army, the Navy, and Intelligence, failing the physical exam each time (I had had a very severe and painful colitis since 1931, which lasted until it was cured by Dr. Philip F. Shapiro in 1948). When my draft notice arrived, I went to the draft board eagerly, only to fail the exam again. *4F!* I was frustrated, for I wanted to serve, and serve in combat. Norman Maclean suggested I join the Military Institute; I did, adding that to my other labors, and spent many hours there drafting an aircraft-recognition manual which was never used.

In 1942 I was invited to teach a summer-quarter course at the University of Chicago. Before the term ended, McKeon came to our apartment, handed me an envelope, and left without a word. Perplexed, I opened the envelope and found a letter of appointment to the University as Assistant Professor of English at a salary of $3500 a year. I left IIT and accepted the appointment.

Although it was understood that I would teach chiefly graduate courses, there were few such, since the war had pretty well emptied the University of graduate students. Full professors, Chairmen of Departments, and Deans were all teaching in the new "Hutchins College," which was, of course, undergraduate. I joined them, teaching Humanities II and Humanities III, two courses that had been designed by McKeon. All of us remained in the College throughout the war. At the war's end, when everyone was too happy with victory and with "Uncle Joe" Stalin to think, I wrote "The Night There Was Dancing in the Streets," foretelling what would be called "The Cold War."

At the University all was going well; at home, very badly. Our marriage had begun to deteriorate early in 1947, and by the end of that year, though we had never quarreled, the situation had become intolerable. The Rockefeller Foundation was funding a professorial exchange program between the University of Chicago and the University at Frankfurt am Main (the Johann Wolfgang Goethe Institute) in Germany, and when Robert Maynard Hutchins invited me to be one of the first team of six to go to Germany, I accepted in the hope that matters might improve in my absence.

I went to Frankfurt in March 1948. There I taught classes in eighteenth- and nineteenth-century political philosophy and a lecture course on modern poetry before a large audience which included some faculty members and their wives. I made many friends, among them the philosopher Hans-Georg Gadamer, the classicist Karl Reinhardt, and the poet Luisa von Kaschnitz. I finished a verse play, *Faust: A Masque,* and at Professor Reinhardt's request, read it to him and his friends in his apartment. The play was repeatedly performed later both at the University of Chicago, where Faust was played by Paul Sills, and at the University of Indiana, as well as elsewhere. The actors have always had trouble with the first part, being carried away by the grandiose diction which in fact is used satirically.

On my return to Chicago, I found things worse than ever. Ann and I were divorced shortly afterward. I did not attend the proceedings, since I had chosen to be the defendant. I had vague plans of traveling west, since I was free until October; however, before I left town I telephoned a very attractive young woman whom I had known briefly in Frankfurt. She was Geraldine Louise Hays, secretary to a colonel, who had earlier been a military secretary in Hawaii and in Tokyo, where she was on General MacArthur's staff. She had resigned and was now living with her grandmother in Stilwell, Oklahoma. She invited me to visit her, and I went, intending only a brief stay, but I remained for three weeks. We were married in mid-September, 1948, and that marriage has lasted.

I was now an Associate Professor, with tenure. Another major university had offered me a full Professorship and the Chairmanship of the Department of Comparative Literature, but after much thought I remained at Chicago. My new bride was welcomed warmly by all our friends, and soon made more friends on her own. Our daughter Inez Olivia ("Livy") was born in 1950, and a second daughter, Shelley, was born eleven months later.

Meanwhile, a number of visiting professors came to the University. Allen Tate, Cleanth Brooks, and Kenneth Burke all brought their wives for the year's stay; we entertained them all, and were entertained in turn. Tate, living across the street from our house at 5540 Kimbark, would come over frequently with his then wife Caroline Gordon to play table tennis with my wife and to grumble because the crushed ice in the mint juleps we served had not been crushed in a leather bag (instead, I ruined many a kitchen towel). One night they brought to dinner with them their houseguest, a young man who behaved so oddly that I thought he had had too many of my old-fashioneds. He was the poet Robert Lowell; I found out only on the next day that he was entering upon another cycle of madness. I had been ignorant of his illness until then. I was sorry that I had taken him back to the kitchen and quietly given him hell (he responded by taking a "vow of silence," which, by the way, he did not keep).

Tate and Brooks, as members of the New Critics, were rivals of mine in literary criticism, but that did nothing to disturb our amity. Kenneth Burke ("KB," as he wanted to be called) had been my friend ever since my doctoral oral, and his wife Libby and Jerri were friends at once. On that earlier visit he had been impressed by the fact that Crane, Maclean, and I had all been studying the *Poetics* closely. In response to pieces we had published he had written an article in which he called us, for the first time, "Neo-Aristotelians," thereby unwittingly contributing to a persistent misunderstanding of my critical theories. Even though literary theory now focuses on vastly different issues, perhaps it is time to set that misunderstanding straight, for the problem of methodology is a perennial one.

I was never *exclusively* an Aristotelian, Neo or whatever. I certainly think the Aristotelian method a sound one, one capable of extension to forms which have emerged since Aristotle, and I am prepared to defend that view, for I have so far found no cogent argument to the contrary. But I was and am a *pluralist,* in the sense of one who holds that there are many valid critical approaches, and I have used them—those of Plato, Longinus, and Hume, for example—in my classes, my lectures, and my critical writings. My essay "The Dialectical Foundations of Critical Pluralism," written about 1935 or 1936 though published much later, should make this clear. In it I investigate the bases of the various critical

systems and their different dialectics and the subjects of their concern. It is a difficult essay, but no one ought to discuss my theories until he has mastered it.

It is time, too, to dispel the myth of "the Chicago School," for as both McKeon and I have said and written, there was no such thing. It is entirely the creation of outsiders. What really happened was this. Allen Tate made me two proposals: (1) that I let him make a selection of my old and new poems and write an introduction to the volume, (2) that I let him select and introduce my critical essays. I thanked him, and rejected both; however, I told Crane about the latter one. Crane had a different idea: why not publish a volume of critical essays by a number of us, which he would edit and introduce?

I acceded to this, but on hindsight I think it was a very bad idea. The resultant volume, *Critics and Criticism: Ancient and Modern,* gave the impression, by the mere *collection* of our essays into a single volume, that we were some sort of united front, unanimous on all matters, especially on Aristotle and the *Poetics.* In part, too, I think this was fostered by Crane's Introduction, temperate and qualified as it is. I did

Daughter Shelley

not see that Introduction before the book was published; I would certainly have made some objections if I had seen it.

If indeed we shared certain assumptions, we drew very different conclusions from them. We were different men, of different temperaments and talents. Though we undoubtedly influenced one another, such influences moved us in diverse directions. In our private conversations Crane and I, and McKeon and I, debated constantly. I had studied much of Aristotle under McKeon, but not the *Poetics*. I cannot flatter myself that his interpretation of that work would be identical with mine, despite all that I learned from him. I am no philosophical genius, as he most surely was. No, if there was any real unity among us, beyond friendship, it was, as I have written elsewhere, "the unity of a log fire in which, by their proximity, the logs stimulate and inflame one another, while each burns with its individual fires." Each of us is responsible for what he himself wrote, and for nothing else.

The University of Puerto Rico invited me to serve there as visiting professor for the academic year 1952–53, and I took my little family with me. Zenobia Jiménez, wife of the Spanish poet Juan Ramón Jiménez, attended a seminar I gave to the faculty, of which she was a member, and one day she took me to meet her husband. Our conversation was somewhat halting, for he knew little English and I could read but not speak Spanish, but with Mrs. Jiménez's assistance, we managed somehow, and met frequently thereafter. Jiménez gave me a book of his poems, and I gave him the most recent copy of *Poetry* magazine, which contained a group of mine. He was greatly taken with them, asked for more, and said that he intended to translate them into Spanish. Whether he ever did or not, I don't know; I do know he wrote to Ezra Pound about me, for he showed me Pound's response, headed "St. Lizzy's Bedlam" (St. Elizabeth's [mental] Hospital). Pound wrote, "Who is this Olson? Anything alive above the eleventh vertebra?" (Some years later, after Juan Ramón had been given the Nobel Prize, Pound wrote me a card: "Intrusted in sompn sides yrself? Juan Ramón won some kind of prize, I fergit what." We had a brief but busy correspondence, in the course of which he wrote, "D'you work in the deanery of your beanery?")

Archibald MacLeish came to the University of Puerto Rico, as did the movie star Myrna Loy. MacLeish, whom I had met earlier at a *Poetry* tea, spent some four hours with me, discussing poetry and the techniques of radio verse-drama (he had written some fine ones). Francisco Ayala, the brilliant writer and editor, was founding a new journal, *La Torre,* and asked me to contribute. My "Dialogue on the Function of Art in Society," in Spanish translation, appeared in the first issue.

On our return to Chicago, Arthur Cohen and the poet Cecil Hemley told me they were establishing a publishing house in New York and asked me for a book of poems. I had not published a book of poetry since 1940, or thought much about it, but I complied. The book appeared under the Noonday Press imprint in 1954 as *The Scarecrow Christ.* I was meanwhile working on a book about the poetry of Dylan Thomas. I had followed his work since 1934, had lectured on it both in Chicago and Frankfurt, and was struck by the fact that, although almost everyone admired his poetry, nobody seemed able to interpret it. I had met Thomas either in 1950 or 1951, and we had got along well from the start. He looked like a plump, grubby schoolboy—he himself, stealing from Charles Laughton, said that he "looked like an unmade bed," but he was one of the funniest people I ever met, with a sharp, sometimes perverse wit. We never discussed his poetry, except that once I asked him why he never read from his "Sonnets." He shook his head and said, "Too abstruse." We met six or seven times; our relations were always civil, indeed, cordial; I have great difficulty still in squaring my image of him with his reputation as a "roaring boy." He died on the Monday of the week when he was due to read in Chicago. I had planned to show him my chapter on the "Sonnets," since he had told several people that "no one would ever break their code." He did not know that I was writing about him, nor that I was a poet.

My interpretation of the "Sonnets" has sometimes been criticized severely—dismissed, most recently, by Daniel Jones in *The Poems of Dylan Thomas* as "ludicrously complex." According to Mr. Jones, the sequence is one poem unified by a "single sustained metaphor," which, however, he does not identify. For my part, I find it ludicrous to suppose that obscure and highly complex poems can have a simple explanation. Kenneth Rexroth wrote me a long letter about my interpretation, commending it and informing me that he had actually seen some of the books I had mentioned as possible sources— notably, Joshua Sylvester's translation of Du Bartas— in Thomas's possession. Others have said the same thing. My book, *The Poetry of Dylan Thomas,* appeared in 1954 and was given an award by the Poetry Society of America as "the best critical book on poetry of the year." In the same year, I was made a full Professor.

Two wealthy Chicago women had come across a one-act prose play of mine, "The Illusionists," and offered to back it on Broadway if I made it into a three-act piece. I warned them that a three-act play could never have the same effect as a one-act, but they insisted, and I rewrote it as "A Crack in the Universe." After they had had their fill of meddling with it and with me, they lost interest. I put it away and forgot about it. I had no great dreams of making Broadway.

In 1956 I was invited to New York to participate in a program arranged by John Chancellor, a trans-Atlantic telephone conversation on Shaw, celebrating the one hundredth anniversary of his birth. (I suppose I was invited because I had given many courses on Shaw and other dramatists, with heavy emphasis on dramatic technique.) My partner on the American side was the producer, director, and actor Guthrie McClintic: our respondents in London were the critic-novelist-playwright St. John Ervine and the actor Peter Ustinov. The hour-long conversation, edited to a half-hour, was to be broadcast in both America and England. When we had finished, McClintic said, "You seem to know a lot about drama—have you ever written a play?" I admitted that I had. "I'd like to see it." I sent him "A Crack in the Universe." Some months later he came to Chicago and telephoned me to meet him. He was enthusiastic about the play, wanted to produce and direct it, and told me the probable cost of production—$250,000—as well as what my royalties would be. I thought the third act needed more work, and after some discussion he agreed. When I at last sent it to him, he was dying. The play was finally produced by the Stevens Dramatic Institute in New York and published in *First Stage.* Another of my pieces, the radio verse-play "The Carnival of Animals," won a joint award of the Columbia Broadcasting System and the Academy of American Poets in 1957.

Roger W. Shugg, Director of the University of Chicago Press, wanted to start a poetry series, and asked me for a volume. I gave him *Plays & Poems* and also took Howard Nemerov to him. In 1958 I gave a series of lectures at Wayne State University; these were published as *Tragedy and the Theory of Drama.* Most reviewers clung to their notion that this was more of Olson's Aristotle. They were wrong again. The tragedy book was based on the method of David Hume, as the Thomas book had been on that of Longinus. Professor James L. Battersby is the only person I know to have observed these differences of critical method.

Over these years I was also appearing on television, giving a half-hour reading of my poems on WGN-TV (this directed by William Friedkin, who later became a film director), discussing poetry with the actor Hans Conried, giving readings and making records at the Library of Congress, etc., etc. I also read—but mostly lectured—pretty well over the country, in universities from Oregon and Texas clear across to New York and Virginia. At the University of Indiana, I was Mahlon Powell Professor of Philosophy, then School of Letters Fellow, then Visiting Professor of Literary Criticism, and finally, Patten Lecturer. The Patten Lectures were published as *The Theory of Comedy,* and these were indeed intended to supply an Aristotelian theory of comedy. I was careful to arrange these performances so that they did not interfere with my classes at Chicago. My *Collected Poems* came out in 1963. Some reviewers remarked that the book should have been called "Selected Poems." They were right; I was careless in choosing the title.

The Rockefeller Foundation called me one day early in 1966: would I be willing to teach for a year, as Rockefeller Professor once more, at the University of the Philippines? They would pay all the expenses, all transport for my family, the children's schooling, etc., and supply a house and a car. I had had several Filipino students sent to me by the Foundation and got along well with them, and the offer was very generous; I would, of course, receive my university salary as well. So off we all went. Everyone in the Philippines was very cordial. Our girls, now well into their teens, were happy at boarding school, Livy in Tokyo, Shelley in Baguio. My wife Jerri, painting busily, had her first solo art show. I gave honors courses and a faculty seminar, plus lectures at the University of the Far East and at Los Baños. Vacations were long and frequent, and we were all able to see much of Southeast Asia. At the end of our stay, General Carlos Romulo, then President of the University, presented me with a Distinguished Service Award. Working our way slowly westward, we visited many countries, finally settling the girls at schools in Switzerland.

In 1971 I was made Distinguished Service Professor; so was Weinberg. We were both due to retire in 1974, but Edward Levi, then President of the University, asked us to remain an extra three years. Weinberg had been on the faculty for some years as Professor of French literature and Chairman of the Romance Department. He was not to live even until the normal retirement age of sixty-five; he died of a heart attack in 1973. We had had an unclouded

Elder Olson, "the old man in his study"

friendship of forty-six years. He was a superb scholar and critic and an absolutely perfect friend, always helpful, always a delight to be with. When I published *Olson's Penny Arcade* in 1975, I dedicated it to the memory of him and his parents, who had treated me as a family member from the first. The book was given the Midland Authors Award. The following year I published a volume of my critical essays, *On Value Judgments in the Arts and Other Essays.*

Retirement loomed again in 1977. I was offered a two-thirds appointment (the limit was mandatory), the schedule to be at my convenience. This could have continued till I dropped in my tracks, but I rejected it. I did not want to hang around "dying on the vine." My mother and my Aunt Rose had died, and there were no close relatives living in Chicago. Crane had died back in 1967, apparently at the same time I was writing to him from Switzerland. Many other friends—Muriel McKeon for one—had died, and many had dispersed. There was little further to hold us in Chicago beyond my love for that city, which my wife did not share.

We sold 5540 Kimbark, which I had owned for thirty-five years, and moved to Albuquerque, New Mexico, where we soon bought another house. Through the kindness of Roger and Helen Shugg, who had moved to Albuquerque when Roger was appointed Director of the University of New Mexico Press, we were introduced to many of their friends, most of whom became our friends as well. We had hardly settled in when the University of Houston invited me to serve as M. D. Anderson Distinguished Visiting Professor for the academic year 1978–79. I went alone, leaving Jerri to arrange the house to her satisfaction. It was our first long separation, though I went back during vacations and she visited me in Houston. During that year, I also went to Phillips University in Oklahoma to head an Aristotelian Conference, where I spoke on the *Poetics* and on Euripides' *The Bacchae*. In Houston I interviewed my old friend Kenneth Burke on television.

Back again in Albuquerque, I taught for a semester at the University of New Mexico. I was invited to return, but decided instead to devote my time to studying and writing. Except for a trip to the University of Missouri with Jerri, that is exactly what I have done. The trip was at the invitation of the poet David Ray, my friend and former student and a professor at the University, to do a reading and a radio interview. I had been publishing a good many poems in various magazines—*The New Yorker, Poetry, New Letters,* and others—and I gathered some into my *Last Poems,* published in 1984. McKeon, who died in 1985, is one of the dedicatees. I called the book *Last Poems* partly because I thought it unlikely that I should make another collection, but more truly because fitting separate and diverse poems into a book has always bored and annoyed me. I am basically a narrative and dramatic lyricist—evidently because I find other people more interesting than I find myself—and for that sort of poet, who can speak in no one character and seldom in his own voice, the resulting diversity of mood and character can cause difficulties: one poem can easily ruin the effect of the one following. It is a miserable problem, and I am

tired of it. Since *Last Poems,* I have continued to write and publish essays and poems—one was given the Mary Elinore Smith Prize by *The American Scholar*—but I do not plan to collect them. There are, besides, a good number of uncollected pieces in verse and prose, but I have made my last book.

Age is more likely to bring decrepitude than wisdom; still, without claiming to be wise, I should like to say certain things that I take to be truths, ignorance of which has made so many lives miserable. In my opinion, the deadliest enemy an artist can have is the *desire for fame.* It is said that when Einstein first came to America he was greeted by huge cheering crowds. He asked Charles Chaplin, standing beside him, "What is all this fame worth?" And Chaplin, who had had his share of it, said, "Nothing. Absolutely nothing." Moving in artistic and academic circles, I have naturally met many famous people. I cannot say that any of them seemed happier for their fame; many, in fact, were discontent with it. Dame Edith Sitwell told me, fretfully, that while the world knew her as a poet, she would have been a great pianist, "except that my family made me study the harp instead—it hurt my fingers." E. E. Cummings complained to me that the world had not recognized him as a painter "more gifted and original than Picasso." T. S. Eliot was unhappy because he thought his plays undervalued. W. H. Auden was bored stiff with adulation. And so on. The only people I know to have been content with their fame were Wallace Stevens and a few scientists and scholars; they were unconscious of it. When an artist is ambitious for fame, it is the person who is ambitious, not the artist. That is mere personal vanity, and has nothing to do with art. The artist's only ambition is to make his work as excellent as possible.

Immortal poems? *Immortal* poets? Eyewash. Some poets and poems are simply more durable than others, for reasons that may have as much to do with the caprices of taste and interest in succeeding generations as with the quality of the work. A poet has no more right to expect his work to last than a child building a snowman. And suppose it *does* last; posterity, when it pays, pays in checks the recipient can never cash. The poet who pays attention to awards—or to critics and reviewers—is letting other people write his poems for him. Something *lasting?* Try nuclear waste.

Looking back on my life, I am struck—and pained—by the many debts I owe to so many people: to my mother, my family, teachers, friends—debts unpayable, unless love and gratitude constitute some sort of payment. I am sorry about all the *I*'s in this account; their recurrence is perhaps unavoidable in autobiography, but it should not cloud the fact that many people have played important parts in my life and work. I think that everything one does is only the eventual result of the hidden, perhaps unwitting, collaboration of many hands and many minds. It is wrong to claim exclusive credit for it, if it is anything creditable.

I have had for the most part a busy, happy, and fortunate life. Now I need only continue to work and write and, in Ben Jonson's fine words:

> . . . make my strengths, such as they are,
> Here in my bosom, and at home.

BIBLIOGRAPHY

Criticism:

General Prosody: Rhythmic, Metric, Harmonics, University of Chicago Press, 1938.

The Poetry of Dylan Thomas, University of Chicago Press, 1954, 2nd edition, 1961.

Tragedy and the Theory of Drama, Wayne State University Press, 1961.

The Theory of Comedy, Indiana University Press, 1968.

On Value Judgments in the Arts, and Other Essays, University of Chicago Press, 1976.

Poetry:

Thing of Sorrow, Macmillan, 1934.

The Cock of Heaven, Macmillan, 1940.

The Scarecrow Christ, Noonday Press, 1954.

Plays & Poems: 1948-1958, University of Chicago Press, 1958.

Collected Poems, University of Chicago Press, 1963.

Olson's Penny Arcade, University of Chicago Press, 1975.

Last Poems, University of Chicago Press, 1984.

Plays:

The Abstract Tragedy: A Comedy of Masks, in *First Stage* (Lafayette, Indiana), Summer 1963.

A Crack in the Universe, in *First Stage,* Spring 1972.

Editor:

American Lyric Poems: From Colonial Times to the Present, Appleton, 1964.

Aristotle's Poetics and English Literature: A Collection of Critical Essays, University of Chicago Press, 1965.

Major Voices: 20 British and American Poets, McGraw, 1973.

Contributor to *Encyclopaedia Britannica, Critics and Criticism, New Yorker, Poetry,* and other publications.

Natalie L. M. Petesch

1924-

THE LAUGHTER OF HASTINGS STREET:
AN AUTOBIOGRAPHICAL MEMOIR

no response

There are seven persons present. Only a few wooden chairs remain in the room, the sofa bed having been moved to the other room where our parents used to sleep, where we children would sleep that night, making room for the coffin. The coffin—no more than a wooden box covered with black cloth—fills the room. In it lies my mother, dead only a few hours. Under the enveloping shroud, her body—if one had dared to look—would be still slender and youthful: she is thirty-five. Her face, however, is much changed; her face reflects the shock of her sudden death. It is discolored by purple and yellow streaks, as if an uncontrollable flash flood had ripped through her body, and the effects of the storm now lie upon her, little or nothing having been done to cover the ruin.

Our Uncle Joseph lifts me up so that I may see her where she lies. My terror shames me. I am more fearful of touching her bruise-colored, saffron cheek than of her Eternal Leavetaking, which has been vaguely described to us. This final departure will not take place until the following day. Meanwhile, we children are to have her with us here, all through the night.

At last, overcoming my terror, I kiss her. Her eyes remain closed. No flicker of response: she has begun to ignore me.

Natalie L. M. Petesch, age three or four, Detroit, Michigan

the laughter of Hastings Street

I have sometimes thought it a pity that we in the Detroit ghetto did not have a Walker Evans among us to memorialize our woe. But the truth is that the woe of Hastings Street during the Great Depression was not the silent, starved, melancholy brooding of Southern children. No: the poverty of the Detroit black ghetto was far more carnal, strident, gritty, meretricious. From the entropy of their despair flowed forth much wine. . . . And laughter: laughter everlasting. And perhaps that is why Walker Evans ignored us: our *merrie deathes* lacked subtlety. How evoke Pity and Terror if the protagonists are laughing? I hear it yet—the laughter of the black folk

Mother, Anna Goldman Levin, about 1928

as she would allow me (great trust, evidently, was placed in her discretion). And unlike our family, Marguerite received Sunday's *Detroit Times*. Here, lying on the floor, with the smell of incense rising from Marguerite's screened four-poster, with the tolling of the bittersweet, hallowed laughter, and the sound of tinkling ice in glasses coming from the kitchen, I learned to read—by connecting the ballooned dialogue with the brightly colored cartoons.

Marguerite never knew, I think, the richness of her gift to me. It was not until I entered Bishop Elementary School that those cartoons full-of-grace were to prove my salvation. Over the years those cartoons have become more sacred to me than Shakespeare; for without them, I would not have understood him: he spoke not in the tongue of Hastings Street. And from time to time now I consider how the Puritan children learned their alphabet along with their knowledge of Sin and the Devil. And I think that the Puritans were truly an inspired people to have done so: for Sin was all around me as I learned to read, and thus it was much easier for me later to distinguish between the operatic antics of Maggie and Jiggs, and the desperate laughter of Marguerite and her Devils.

in steerage and after: Anna and Samuel

Like millions of others, Anna Goldman had come to America in steerage, her pilgrimage to the new land interrupted only by her uncertain passage to Detroit by way of Ellis Island. Alone in Detroit (except for her sisters who were even poorer than she—they already having borne many children), what had she hoped for in the great promised land where everyone was free? And what sort of life had she left behind her? She has left us no biography; but there were rumors of a betrothal back in Russia, a *mésalliance* (*his* family had broken off the engagement, it was rumored). So it was to be Samuel's good fortune to inherit this cast-off prize—he, too, having left Russia for America at about the same time. The two unmarried immigrants became the natural and lawful prey of the professional matchmakers—a trade still being carried on with vigor at that time, and with considerable justification: it was the common belief that the best Security for two lonely immigrants lay in marriage (who ever dared speak of "happiness" or "marital bliss"?). Of "bliss," certainly there could have been little or none. Within two years of their union, children came, as they always did in those days—first my sister, then my brother—these births followed almost at once by heavy debts and life-

around me—a laughter so deep, so hungry, so full of longing, the wrack and throb of it might break your heart: a self-consuming fiery catherine wheel, it was, the joy of a survivor.

Born there among the black folk of Hastings Street as I had been, the youngest child of Anna Goldman and Samuel Levin—both illiterate immigrants—this laughter is one of my earliest memories. Perhaps this was because until I was about five we lived in rooms just across the hallway from Marguerite. With her maplewood color and American Indian hair, Marguerite was lighter of skin than we so-called Caucasians. It was from her side of the hallway that I first heard the laughter of Hastings Street: like the ringing of bells in the village belfry, the laughter that rang forth from her rooms defined the social event of the hours: whether festival or funeral rites.

For reasons that are still obscure to me, I was permitted—in spite of Marguerite's well-known reputation—to visit her apartment across the hall as often threatening illness. The attacks of "painter's colic" Samuel suffered from turned out to be not painter's colic after all, but tuberculosis—and the disease was immediately transmitted to Anna. According to somewhat-fragmented accounts of their shared quarantine (perhaps subsequently embellished by Anna's sisters), Uncle Joseph—the very same Joseph who had lifted me up so that I might kiss my mother in her coffin—had devised a harsh but apparently effective treatment for the newlyweds. For the penniless and desperate couple afflicted with "consumption" (in a world without antibiotics), Joseph built a square, one-room cabin on some land he owned outside Detroit. Here (it is recalled), either because he could not afford a real bed, or beds were too expensive, Joseph simply threw down a mattress on the floor for the young couple. And here, without benefit of bell, book, or candle, he insulated them from their world; here they received much nourishing food: fresh eggs, butter, and milk from a nearby farm (the food was passed through a window). And *Rest:* blessed repose for Samuel from house-painting and its toxic fumes; repose, too, for the weary young mother already fighting for her life. Someone else (who, I do not know: one of her sisters, doubtless) was caring for their two children, and the lagging burden of their last child (myself) was still some years away in the compassionately blurred Future. Yet one's imagination clouds over at the bitter thoughts they may have had in that wooden hutch as, shackled together by illness, they lay on their mattress, awaiting death or health, as God disposed. When they were finally declared well, and released from their eighteen months' incarceration, they could not have known that they had just enjoyed the only real vacation either of them was ever to have.

neither slavery nor involuntary servitude shall exist. . . .

According to British historians, slavery was finally abolished in England in 1834. But here in the United States, nearly one hundred years later, my father—himself a refugee from impressment under the Czar—practiced slavery. Child labor, when practiced within the inescapable circle of the family, is difficult to control by statute. And if it had been illegal, how would either my brother or I have known it was? And what nine-year-old would have filed a complaint? Ironically, our very intelligence made us more vulnerable: we were useful and exploitable. So we were forced into service early on, taught bizarre skills of chicanery, deception, fraud: how to conceal the dissolution lurking in the sprouted potato with its nightshade eyes, the impending rot of the flowering onion; how to sell the imperfect, the broken, the spoiled, as if it were every child's birthright to impose upon others the cracked egg, the rusted can, the fat-lined chop, the swollen chicken. . . . Taught, in short, pitiless survival: because these were Depression days, and many there were who went shoeless and hungry.

One tries to take comfort in the thought that such servitude no longer exists. Perhaps not . . . and yet—it may be that even worse things are happening to children now, which someday as Survivors they will tell us about. In the *New York Times* only recently I read of a three-year-old girl in Thailand found tied to a stake in the ground; she'd been taught to stuff bags of opium. In the photograph, she is smiling into the camera.

But let us walk through a typical working day for my father and me in those times, a day revolving as it

---

To My Mother

Who
never owned
a washing machine
a dishwasher
a Hoover cleaner
or a fur coat.

Who
never drove an automobile
Nor once left Detroit
after arriving there
from Russia.

Who
died there
At the age of 35
Without learning to read or write.

Dedication in The Odyssey of Katinou Kalokovich, *1974*

always did around The Store. Just as in China one speaks of the historicity of The Wall, and as perhaps in Heaven one speaks of The Gate, in our iconology, we spoke of The Store.

We have now moved to East Vernor Highway. There is no public transportation to The Store, so we must allow time to walk to Hastings Street.

In the darkness of a Saturday morning my father shakes me awake—for perhaps the second, or even the third time. Childlike, I am pretending not to have heard his alarm clock go off, nor to have heard his ever-sharper command, repeated now with a certain harsh and rising pitch which may soon become rage: *"Up! Out!* It's time to go!"

No one greets us as I stagger into the kitchen (my stepmother, a woman already old, who has reared five sons and a retarded daughter all alone in America, is still asleep; she will come to The Store later). It is a morning in Detroit for the wintering sparrows to freeze and fall. Hardly awake, I begin to layer myself in sweaters, two pairs of cotton stockings, heavy galoshes—whatever comes to hand. Because I know that the windows of the unheated Store will be frosted over at this hour, and that the front of The Store (where we work) will not be even slightly warm until about eleven o'clock, when at last my father will pause for a few moments from the selling of early morning bread (Taystee and Silvercup), of milk, soap, and cigarettes, to build a fire in the back room. The heat from this small stove will hardly touch us out here at the front of the store, facing Hastings Street, but it will keep the white Leghorn chickens in the back room from freezing to death.

Meanwhile, it is still dark. My father has just finished shaving: I can tell that by the smell of the candle he uses to augment the ceiling light on these dark winter mornings (he says he needs this concentrated light because of his smallpox pits). I see the brooding wick, still smoking slightly, where he has pinched it shut. Minutes later, we begin our forced march to The Store.

The Store is my father's lifeboat during the tidal wave of the Depression. It is of almost supernatural importance: on it our lives depend. So one would not even dare to wonder what others might be doing on this Saturday morning: preparing for music lessons or swimming lessons or even just sleeping, sleeping until they are awakened by the certainty of breakfast, prepared by an invisible hand carrying out "love's austere and lonely offices," as Robert Hayden so beautifully puts it.

Instead, I concentrate on my breathing: my own warm breath, it seems, returned to me again and again through the scarf that covers all my face except my eyes, is what is keeping me alive until we reach Hastings Street. It is not, in miles, so very far: it is only in my child's mind that it seems an endless tundra. . . . But now, at last, we have again survived the trek, and have reached the restaurant next door to The Store. Indoors, at the counter, we sit on high, white stools. I am still young enough and silly enough to spin the seats around just for the fun of it: but I am instantly told to *Quit that!* Quickly we take our coffee and rolls. But my father is already complaining aloud (though not especially to me) that it is turning daylight, there may be people waiting outside for a loaf of bread, etc. And he is already heading for the door while I am trying, unsuccessfully, to malinger over my hot coffee. When, finally, I loosen my grip on the warm, thick cup and move as slowly as is humanly possible out of the comfortable restaurant with its smell of cooking and its haze of steam on the windows, I see that my father is right: first light has come to Hastings Street: the ghetto is quickening to another Saturday morning.

And so our day begins—merely one of hundreds, of thousands, spent in longing for the day to end. The following year, as my tenth birthday approaches, I am promoted in earnest to Worker, First Class. I learn to dress Leghorns, skin rabbits, scale fish, slice meats, and above all to smile and smile like the true villain I am at the endless stream of customers listening to our sirenic call: to buy food, yes, to buy as much as possible, more than they can afford: ribs for barbecuing, and chickens for picnics on Belle Isle, and enough potatoes for an Army, and cigarettes, and later on—when War was already looming on the horizon and The Store had its long longed-for revellers' license—much wine and beer to evoke the laughter of Hastings Street. It was not to be until the clouds of war had become a firestorm that I finally fled from slavery, breaking the chains that bound me.

But that is still seven years of servitude away.

in America begin responsibilities

Samuel had come to the promised land for the same reasons as Anna—to find a new life. But what were the fatal differences between Samuel's story and those heroic accounts I later heard of immigrant parents' "enduring traditional values"—of their love for their family, of their eagerness to educate, if not themselves, then their beloved children? (With Samuel's consent my stepmother once burned my books when I was caught reading instead of scrubbing down the basement steps.)

Only once in his life did my father ever speak to me of his "youth," when, after not having seen him for nearly twenty years, we spoke together briefly, perhaps an hour in all. He was recovering from a heart attack. And eager, finally, to communicate *some*thing, he spoke to me at last in a tumbling scroll of memories, filled with bizarre and shocking details: of his mother's death by starvation; of his induction into the Czar's army; of his dramatic escape; of his internment with smallpox at Bremen while en route to America; and, finally, his pyrrhic arrival—illiterate, humiliated, disfigured—at Ellis Island.

He spoke of how he had gone to work in the promised land: first, cutting blocks of ice in an icehouse, then a twelve-hour night shift at Ford's auto factory; how, in an effort to improve his lot, he became a house painter; then how he married my mother, Anna Goldman, and soon after his marriage became—somewhat to his own surprise—a sort of riverboat gambler of Hastings Street, playing poker all night with sharks and bootleggers, shills and

The author in Cambridge, Massachusetts, 1951

gulls . . . until, suddenly, a Death alert: long months of tuberculosis and, at last, after what had seemed to him the interminable months of his incarceration in the Hut, the Turning Point. He gave up gambling, borrowed a few dollars from some trusting soul, and rented The Store on Hastings Street.

This was the only break in the long silence between us. This account seemed to me at the time of immense literary (and even historical) significance; so on the train back to Austin, Texas, where I was working on my Ph.D., I wrote down the details of Samuel's hegira right away, lest I should forget anything. The story of his Houdini-like escape from the Czar was published many years later in the short-fiction collection *Soul Clap Its Hands and Sing.* But originally, it was not a short story: it was a chapter in the second volume of my projected Kalokovich trilogy—*The Odyssey of Katinou Kalokovich.* While writing this chapter, I worked particularly hard to "explain" to the reader the almost-inexplicable ferocity shown by Jacob toward his daughter, Kate. Perhaps as a consequence of this special effort on my part, a friend who read the manuscript of this novel felt that this one chapter so extenuated Jacob's "crimes" that I had, in effect, weakened the impact of the heroine's struggle. So I decided to delete it from the novel, and "In America Begin Responsibilities" remains today a short story about Jacob's flight to the promised land. Should I have suppressed this account altogether, remained silent after all, and left Samuel to Heaven? No: let it now be said: nearly two generations have passed away—aunts, uncles, my brother, too, all gone into the world of light—and I now believe that Jacob was too kindly treated in my fiction (he makes another appearance in *The Long Hot Summers of Yasha K.* during the Detroit race-riot scene). And this was because a true picture of his labyrinthine cruelties would be beyond the scope of fiction—it would cross over the threshold into pathology. And since I have no expertise in that realm, I must let go at last, and leave him, if not to Heaven, then to history.

I fall in love with a Scottish gentleman

At thirteen, when I entered Northern High School, I promptly fell in love with a Gentleman. I didn't know he was a gentleman, of course. I did know he was different. Archibald MacDonald was my first experience of the Other Side of the Tracks. He dressed elegantly, he spoke pure English, his after-school activities were astonishing: tennis and golf. I had never even seen a tennis racquet or golf club,

The author's first year in Austin, Texas, about 1956

except in movies. Nor had I ever had a conversation with a boy who spoke English correctly: Archibald spoke English like one to the manor born. He was trying to decide whether to be a physician, an architect, or a scientist (I was trying to decide whether I should wear silk stockings like the other girls). He had been *abroad:* it was the first time I had heard that word. And he appeared, amazingly enough, not to dislike the strange, awkward girl, barely five feet tall, so lackluster and biologically unsound that the school nurse exclaimed as she peered at the school scales, "You so skinny—you don't weigh much as my dog!"

Archibald MacDonald was a Presbyterian. Although I had been informed by several members of my family that I was Jewish, I had an unshakeable conviction that I was a Baptist, because my best friend, a girl of twelve and a church-going Baptist, had taught me The Lord's Prayer. Now I pondered how I might become a Scotswoman. But whatever my limitations—whether in religion or *avoirdupois*—Archibald seemed rather fond of me, and my high-school years were much brightened by his presence. I wrote him letters he never received and received letters from him he never wrote (it was an equitable exchange: unbeknownst to myself I was learning to write epistolary novels). I filled my diary with rapturous dialogue in which I always managed to think of the right thing to say at the right time. I began to

wear tartans, hoping I would touch his clannish heart. Alas, the only thing we had in common was the biology lab: so I tried desperately to need help (although biology was one of my favorite subjects). But Archibald was no fool, and he was not fooled by my tactics.

Since I was now a heady thirteen years of age and more than ready to imitate the romantic heroines I had read about (I knew all about those terrible-wonderful things that happened to a girl when she *fell* in love), it turned out, later, to be the luckiest thing in the world for me that Archibald was no Steerforth but an honorable gentleman. Since he had no real interest in me, he pretended none; neither did he snicker. Surely I must have turned pale every time he sat down beside me; he must have known he was my Hero. Nevertheless, he treated me as if I were a human being who happened to be in his biology class, not as a peasant girl who has just met her first Gentleman. For this is Archibald honored: *honi soit qui mal pense.*

a chattel is returned to its rightful owner

Meanwhile, I was having other things to consider. While these fires of True Love were smoking and crackling, life at The Store had continued. In the presence of my fellow students I never mentioned the work I did during the long hours when I disappeared from sight: I was leading a double life, for sure. The solution was simple. Shortly after graduation I ran away from home to meet whatever Life there might be beyond Hastings Street. Until my father caught up with me—legally I was still a minor and therefore subject to parental discipline—I bluffed my adolescent way through a surreal succession of jobs for which I had no training, each job more incredible than the last. When at last my father recaptured his chattel (with the help of two brawny pistol-packing police officers), I was promptly stowed away—by my owner's authorization—as an "incorrigible minor" in the Detroit House of Correction. I was released the very next morning, however, when the house physician discovered I was still *intacta,* and I was declared, therefore, not a delinquent after all.

the Cave

Like any sensible slave, I soon ran away again: but this time I fled to Wayne University. And as Heaven had apparently decreed, I ran straight into the class of a classical scholar who, on the first day of the first class in the first literature course I had ever taken, read to us aloud excerpts from Plato.

There was no doubt in my mind that George Farrell had seen the dirt from the Cave on my hands: ashamed, I hid my hands in the pockets of the cheap new jacket I had bought for my introduction to Learning and Respectability.

But it was hardly a matter of weeks before I had shed the shoddy new jacket, along with the hard-earned lesson of Respectability acquired in my chattel days, and was ready to quit the world (to borrow a phrase from Browning's "Fra Lippo Lippi") to follow George Farrell (who, after Pearl Harbor was bombed, at once became not a scholar, but a warrior) wherever in the war-wracked world he would have led me. Unfortunately (or fortunately—depending on how one views such things), we were not allowed that decision; instead, we were to be separated by thousands of miles. And when, four years later, the war was finally over, each of us had begun a different life.

Nevertheless, that was not what was important. What was important was that, in spite of the war, this experience remained sacred. Because George Farrell knew Literature, and he had said I was a Writer. Who was I to gainsay him? After all, he was God, and I was seventeen.

I become a scholar

Fourteen years were to elapse between the description of Socrates' death during my first hour in a university classroom and the completion of my bachelor's degree at Boston University. During those years, two whispered admonitions followed me wherever I went: You must get out of the Cave, You must be a Writer. So, armed with the handwritten list of Great Books which Farrell had written up for me, and mindful of his command to be a Writer, I methodically checked off, day after day, year after year, the masterpieces he had thought were necessary for any young Writer to read. And I continued to write.

By the time I received my bachelor's degree, my marriage was breaking up, and I had my daughter, Rachel, to consider—then five years old: she and I had one more year to wait before she could attend public school (there were no classes for children until first grade at that time). What was a Writer to do? With my new degree I could get a job teaching five classes a day in a junior high school—a heavy schedule for someone dreaming of being a Writer; but what was even more awesome was something I had noticed while doing my practice teaching: that somehow those smart kids knew I was incapable of

sending anyone downstairs to the principal's office to be "disciplined." *(Disciplined?* I asked myself, recalling my father consigning me to the discipline of the State. *I'm* supposed to send kids somewhere to be *disciplined?)*

Meanwhile, during these rather chaotic years I had written six novels, one of them a thousand pages long, in unabashed adoration of *The Brothers Karamazov.* It was about three sisters and was called *Souls Divided:* could self-delusion go further? And whenever during those years I had had to change residences, and was obliged to carry these boxes of manuscript from one place to another, I would gaze long and penitently at these boxes of seemingly wasted effort.

But—to my great joy—not wholly wasted. The newly appointed chairman of the English department at Brandeis University, J. V. Cunningham, was heroic enough to read *Souls Divided,* and as a result I received a graduate fellowship to Brandeis. In addition to tuition, I would receive seven hundred dollars for the year's expenses (it was to be a one-year program for the M.A.). This was the first of two of the most important events in my adult life (the other

With daughter, Rachel, Pittsburgh, Pennsylvania, 1978

was winning the University of Iowa School of Letters Award for Short Fiction, in 1974). . . .

But I was not at all prepared for scholarly studies: I had never written a research paper on a literary subject. And here I was studying with the renowned Irving Howe! with the poet J. V. Cunningham! I knew nothing about criticism—either the New or the Old. When I showed my new friends from the University of Pennsylvania and Cornell the edition of Shakespeare I had bought for Cunningham's course—a George Lyman Kittredge edition, but *without footnotes*—I drew down a firestorm of laughter (again I hid my Cave-sweated hands). I still own that particular edition of Shakespeare, and I will keep it until I die—as an act of contrition or, if you will, a hair shirt—lest I forget.

Enrolled with me that inspiring year at Brandeis (if I recall, it was only the second year of their graduate program in English) were such gifted writers as Linda Pastan and Ronald Sukenick. Sukenick used to give me a ride to Brandeis in his battered old car (I lived in Somerville), and, from time to time, as we headed into the long Boston winter, we would agree with a rueful laugh that the rich *were* different from us: they had better cars.

By the end of the academic year at Brandeis I had become convinced that only a Ph.D. would remove the last tell-tale marks of the Cave. Again Fate stepped in to lend me a hand: Alexander Sackton, a visiting professor whose courses in Milton and in the Jacobean drama I had been taking, recommended me for a teaching fellowship at the University of Texas at Austin. I was to receive twelve hundred dollars a year, and would teach two classes a semester. It sounded like the opportunity of a lifetime to me—and it was. Texas saved me from Everything.

why I am a Texan

After nearly a decade of living in Massachusetts, I had begun to feel—rightly or wrongly—that in spite of its rich cultural advantages, in spite of its well-educated population and its many talented artists, the internationally famous *milieu* which was so close to where I lived remained an invisible fortress of inherited privilege. And so I left behind me the culture it had taken Massachusetts over three hundred years to create, and took the train West—to a state that was still perceived by many Eastern intellectuals (and particularly by my fellow graduate students) as a foreign country, inhabited by cowboys and Indians.

I was not unhappy to leave. On one occasion I had been denied access to the Athenaeum Library

With son, Nick, at home, Pittsburgh, Christmas 1983

unless I paid a ten-dollar fee (I did not have it); on another day, while studying at Brandeis, I was denied use of the Boston Public Library because I resided in Somerville. These denials had come to seem epiphanic.

My decision to leave—whether impelled by Reason or Instinct—proved to be a fortunate one. When I had settled into Austin as a teaching assistant and candidate for the Ph.D., I discovered to my astonishment that I had been turned from a pumpkin into a person. I now had the first job of my life in which I did not carry other persons' dishes from restaurant tables, nor take care of other persons' children, nor dust other persons' floors, nor type other persons' intellectual yearnings. I was thirty-two years old.

I wept as I walked out of the elevator on the nineteenth floor of the Main Building and unlocked with my own key the door to my own office. I wept as I looked out the office window at the campus, with its Spanish architecture. It seemed to me I had never seen anything so beautiful as these tiled rooftops in the brilliant sunlight of a Texas morning. I put my briefcase down on the big oak desk near the window; the lines of the natural wood seemed as warm and expressive as an intelligent face. That first morning I divided my time between looking out the window and admiring my new desk—filling it with generous stacks of hopeful, white typing paper.

And then *(the wonder of it!)*, everywhere in Austin, people were being gracious to me, were trying to help, were offering suggestions, were showing me the Southwest . . . showing me love. *Out of the Cave, out of the Cave,* our chairman, Mody Boatright, seemed to declare as he praised my teaching, and seemed thereby to add (the Bible notwithstanding) a cubit to my stature.

I've written elsewhere about my love for Texas.[1] And it's true: Texas gave me the first real financial security I had ever known. (I could pay the rent—sixty dollars—every month.) But above all, Texas, more than any other place I had lived, made me a Writer. In Texas for the first time I understood Hopkins's "Pied Beauty": I loved the landscape, the amazing flowers, the desert fauna, the shape of the clouds, the very color of the sky: everything moved and stirred me. The very speech of Texans seemed to me a new kind of music. And even what seemed to me palpable errors—attitudes held over from the War between the States, the gargantuan world of Lyndon Baines Johnson, the Texas of wheelers and dealers—evoked a creative response: not rage, but a sort of doomed hilarity, some of which, I think, came through in my first published fiction collection, *After the First Death, There Is No Other.* After all, if one lives where everyone agrees with what you think, it doesn't necessarily energize your work: one needs, perhaps, some grit-in-the-eye to make one grateful for all the wonderful things to be seen once you've winked the grit out. But perhaps one has to have been born on Hastings Street, and heard the despair of its people, to have loved Texas as much as I did.

Austin at that time was still a small town full of sunshine, flowers, and open spaces where one could slip easily from indoors to outdoors, following only the course of shadows, not the blazing sun. The trees hummed with cicadas; the houses hummed with watercoolers (air conditioning was not yet universal). My daughter, Rachel, and I lived in a furnished Quonset, only a few blocks from the university—rented to us by a wise and sympathetic woman who foresaw my needs better than I did (I had been walking around for seven or eight hours that hot

summer day in August looking for a place that would be close to the university, and also close to an elementary school for my daughter).

And thus began an undertaking that proved more arduous and yet more valuable than I could possibly have imagined. Because I had never thought of myself as anything but a Writer, I had underestimated the hard work that goes into becoming a professionally trained academician. After many humbling attempts, I learned, finally, how to write research papers. But now the difficulty was that I had grown to love Austin so much that I was reluctant to leave it: so I spent four lingering years taking courses—just long enough (it luckily turned out) to meet my husband, Donald Petesch, who, though born in Iowa, had grown up in Texas. I still envy Don his nomadic but formative years in Bay City, Kaufman, San Angelo, Waco, and Dallas.

When at last he and I tore ourselves away from Austin, Don had his M.A. in Sociology, I had (almost) a Ph.D. in English, and we were thinking about having a child, who would turn out to be Nicholas,

Poet David Ray, Texas, 1977

[1] "The Writer's Sense of Place," *South Dakota Review,* Autumn 1975.

born to us a year later—the year I taught at San Francisco State University.

But we had hardly set foot out of Texas before we began to feel homesick. It turned out there had been nearly nothing about Texas that did not inspire me to write about it, whether it was comical stories like "The Girl Who Was Afraid of Snow," or sad stories like "The Exile" and "Be Not Forgetful of Strangers," all of which later appeared in fiction collections such as *Soul Clap Its Hands and Sing* and the award-winning *Wild With All Regret.* All told, I've written dozens of stories about Texans, and three novels that have Texas as their central *milieu.* What Don and I further discovered was that, almost as much as we missed the bluebonnets on the highways and the thrum of the thistle-throated cicadas, we longed for the rise and fall of Southwestern vowels. For it had come to pass that no speech elsewhere on the planet stirred us so much as Texans telling us stories—whether in a style wildly caracolling and picaresque or in the slow reverberating drumroll of tragic loss. So, ever since Don and I left Texas, and people have asked—as folks will do—*Where are you from?* I try not to glance at Don as I lie and say, *We are Texans. . . .* For how can one be even an honorary Texan if one was born on Hastings Street? Ah, but that is the mystery of Texas. It's a place where if you love it, it loves you back: and because, like the ancient Delphic rites, those who trust in these mysteries know what it is they pray for.

David Ray rescues the author from despair

It was perhaps a predictable coincidence that, one summer while Don, our son Nick, and I were making one of our frequent trips to Texas, trying to recapture our golden-age-in-Austin by swimming in Barton Springs, wandering with old friends through the Commons, walking under the shade trees in the Rosedale neighborhood, we should meet the poet David Ray and his wife, Judy, also a writer.

Winning the University of Iowa School of Letters Award for Short Fiction in 1974 had not turned out to be the open-sesame I so fondly hoped for. Three years had passed, during which time I had written two novels (*Duncan's Colony* and *The Leprosarium*) and a collection of short stories (*Soul Clap Its Hands and Sing*), none of which my agent could sell. My 650-page documentary novel of the civil-rights movement was also still unpublished. It was at this time of despair that David Ray offered to read—the generosity of it is still overwhelming—*all* my unpublished manuscripts. From among these he would be

looking for fiction that might be suitable for publication in a special issue of *New Letters.* Then, later, perhaps he would submit this special issue to Mort Weisman at Swallow Press for Weisman's consideration. Not only that—but Dave said he would work with me throughout this process as my editor. From the many manuscripts I brought him, Dave selected two novels, *The Long Hot Summers of Yasha K.* and *The Leprosarium,* both of which were later accepted by Mort Weisman and published in a cloth edition by Swallow Press/Ohio University Press under the umbrella title *Seasons Such as These.*

In celebration of our friendship, Dave, Judy, their daughter Sapphina, Don, our son Nick, and I all went swimming at Deep Eddy (an appropriate metaphor it seemed at the time). Thus when the summer was over, and once again Don and I prepared to take leave of family and friends, instead of our usual tearful farewells, we headed back East in joyful triumph. David Ray had thrown me a life buoy at Deep Eddy, and I would survive.

a flashback to Selma, Alabama, 1965

I had returned to the University of Texas after a year's teaching at San Francisco State University. I now had a husband in graduate school, a daughter at Lamar Junior High, a two-year-old son, and a full-time teaching position at the University of Texas. Life was getting serious!

Along with this middle-class Respectability came the usual *angst* and quiet desperation. *I* could sit on a Thoreauvian pumpkin (with paper and pencil, of course); my children could not. So, as so many writers had done before me, I continued to labor for several years in the vineyards of freshman composition and sophomore surveys, while trying to count my blessings instead of the inexorable passing of time.

Meanwhile, the world was changing. We could see the lightning and hear the thunder in the distance. Rosa Parks refused to give up her seat on a bus; Martin Luther King, Jr., was jailed. Marchers on the Edmund Pettus bridge were being beaten. Gathering ourselves quickly together, Don, my daughter, and I, along with another faculty member, drove to Alabama to join the marchers to Selma. For our small group these were soul-shaking historic events from which, nevertheless, we were returning unharmed. But just as we were leaving Alabama and crossing the state line into Mississippi, we heard that Viola Liuzzo had been shot to death.

The tragedy of this mother of five having sacrificed her life for the civil rights of others struck me hard. The subject gripped me and shook me and refused to let me go: a novel about a woman like Viola Liuzzo (Angelina) and her love affair with Yasha Kalokovich, both of them working in the civil-rights movement, began to take shape in my head. It was to be an historical novel of Detroit as well, of Malcolm X's rise to prominence, of Martin Luther King, Jr.'s, nonviolent revolution, of the long, hot Mississippi summer when Schwerner, Chaney, and Goodman were murdered, and, finally, of the death of my heroine, Viola-Angelina. The ideas for this book intensified my quiet *angst* to an unbearable degree, so that when Don had finished All-But-Dissertation, I did not renew my teaching contract at the University of Texas. I set to work instead on this novel. I worked on it two years, completing the final chapter in Gainesville, Florida. My agent then sent the manuscript to more than thirty publishers. But in spite of the fact—I now think *because* of the fact—that cities were burning with race riots, and Martin Luther King, Jr., stood but one year away from his assassination, no publisher would take it. It was not until David Ray personally took on the responsibility of editing it for *New Letters* that it was published in a

much-shortened version as *The Long Hot Summers of Yasha K*. But without Dave's help, perhaps no part of this civil-rights novel would have come to light: it would, perhaps, simply have crumbled to dust in an attic somewhere.

And I often wonder now at the publishing world today. I wonder whether the thousands of American writers practicing their sullen craft will be lucky enough to find someone to help them as David Ray helped me, or to find a publisher like Mort Weisman who continues to sustain the literary traditions of the past, regardless of the bottom line: where, indeed, will these writers find the idealists of yesteryear?

them glory-days: Pittsburgh

Most of us who were writing poems and stories during our first years in Pittsburgh had either endured the Depression personally or had seen their parents battered by its mailed fist. And although we agreed that we had had uncommonly good luck to have survived thus far, nevertheless none of us had been very active in consuming the world's resources:

Poet Paul Zimmer with his wife, Suzanne, and their children, Erik and Justine

Don and I, for instance, arrived in Pittsburgh with not much more than our boxes of books, accumulated during over twenty years of education, along with thousands of dollars of debt to the Minnie Stevens Piper Foundation (which, in its old-fashioned Texas way, would make loans to graduate students but also, in its old-timey way, insisted on being repaid). So, for many of us in those early literary days in Pittsburgh, moving to our first real academic job was a step toward long-deferred dreams: of financial security, of freedom-to-write, travel, friends—the ideal life. And it was our great good luck that we did find friends; we did write poetry and fiction. We even had our own "Bloomsbury"—about five or six of us met at each other's house to read aloud from our works-in-progress. It was in this group that I heard the early Paul Zimmer poems, those deeply philosophical poems full of whimsy, introspection, and melancholy disillusion—the philosophy, in short, according to Zimmer. And nearly all of us who were lucky enough to hear Paul's award-winning poems went on to win awards of our own: Corinne Demas Bliss received the Missouri

Natalie and Donald Petesch, Andalusia, Spain, 1986

Breakthrough Prize for her short fiction; Ed Ochester received the Devins Award; Anthony Petrosky won the Walt Whitman Award. All these friends were, of course, very talented writers, but it's not my intention here to praise their literary work: one has only to read their published works to recognize their intelligence, their imagination, their charm. But the point is that Zimmer had all those qualities and something else too. According to verifiable reports, he was an all-but-unbeatable Ping-Pong player. And it was in the basement of the Zimmers' home on Hobart Street that these passionate Ping-Pong tourneys took place. Zimmer versus Petesch, it was (sometimes Don, sometimes our son Nick on the opposing side) competing with high gusto, with hilarious trust, with an admiration for each other's prowess that can only be called Love. So now when I conjure up the glory-days of our first years in Pittsburgh, those years when Zimmer was somehow the fulcrum of our little Parnassus (after the Zimmers left Pittsburgh, we were never quite a cohesive group again), I think—not of the thousands of hours of writing that our combined efforts totted up to; nor of our frequent disappointment with publishers who stubbornly refused to recognize that we were all geniuses-at-work; nor even of our rare moments of triumphant prize-winning—I think, rather, of the Zimmers' Ping-Pong table.

There we are, Sue and Paul, and Justine and Erik, and Nick, and Don and I—and we do not even know that we are all still young yet. The Zimmers' basement is not really what is known in Pittsburgh as a full basement; it is rather narrow, and the Ping-Pong table in its center, along with our seven figures, quite fill it up. We, the spectators, stand around the table and watch the game: there is a light overhead, and the round white ball is *hit,* and *hit,* and *hit.* To me—standing there mute with some strange joy—the sound now resembles a fledgling bird in his nest, determined to be heard, now an antique clock ticking patiently beside me to remind me that this life is beautiful and real and passing.

And when somebody actually *wins* a game—so Providentially have these matters been designed that somebody always wins—then we have an excuse to share a celebratory beer and then afterwards wend our way happily homeward, secure in the knowledge that many good lines will be writ that night.

We are all grown up now, too busy for basement Ping-Pong. And well I know that integrity and passion are never the monopoly of any generation: every day I am astonished at the intellectual commitment and power of the gifted new writers writing today. But when I talk to our contemporaries, writing now in the full glory of their stunning gifts, I'm tempted to ask them, not *Who is your publisher?* but rather, *Can you play Ping-Pong like Paul Zimmer?*

a non-epilogue

An epilogue suggests that something is finished. In writing this memoir, I've become aware that I've only begun, that I have not mentioned the many other persons who helped me at one time or another—an invisible phalanx—without whose kindnesses I would never have crossed over even to the other side of Hastings Street: only a few of those wonderful people have been mentioned here. But in closing I would like to say that this memoir is not meant to be a lamentation, nor even a final laying to rest of childhood ghosts, but an encomium of praise and gratitude to those who showed no greater love than to lay down their own manuscript to take up another's.

BIBLIOGRAPHY

Fiction:

After the First Death, There Is No Other (short story collection), University of Iowa Press, 1974.

The Odyssey of Katinou Kalokovich (novel), United Sisters, 1974.

Two Novels: The Leprosarium [and] *The Long Hot Summers of Yasha K.,* University of Missouri—Kansas City Press, 1978; published as *Seasons Such as These,* Swallow Press/Ohio University Press, 1979.

Soul Clap Its Hands and Sing (short story collection), South End Press, 1981.

Duncan's Colony (novel), Swallow Press/Ohio University Press, 1982.

Wild With All Regret (short story collection), Swallow's Tale Press, 1986.

Flowering Mimosa (novel), Swallow Press/Ohio University Press, 1987.

Justina of Andalusia and Other Stories, Swallow Press/Ohio University Press, 1990.

James Schevill

1920-

YEARS OF BECOMING

To Margot:
Although she does not appear as yet in these
"Years of Becoming," she illuminates them by
her constant presence in the writing.

James Schevill

Born June 10, 1920, at the end of the frontier in Berkeley, California, I grew up in a family that seemed to me legendary in a town struggling to shape its independent western myth.

My mother was a restless poet and painter who refused the conventional restrictions in those days confining women to home and church. Eager to absorb all artistic techniques, she studied woodcarving, and created Assyrian lions rearing against a castle on a panel atop our front door. The side panels she carved with gracious flowers, as if indicating the impossible peace and quiet that the lions of her heart would prevent within our redwood canyon home.

In my father's large study, fronting a huge bay tree, thousands of books in many languages blocked the light in towering, densely packed bookcases. A long table dominated the large rectangular room on which a black, yellow-eyed cat slept atop my father's papers. His other constant companion was a mocking, bright-eyed French poodle, Mark, who preferred this serious sanctuary to the noisy activities of us children outside. When he felt abandoned, Mark would saunter off down the hill to my father's office in Wheeler Hall. When he arrived in Wheeler, Mark would never deign to climb the stairs to my father's third-floor office. Proudly, he waited by the private faculty elevator until someone would permit him regally to ascend to greet my father in triumph.

In his study, my father dreamt and edited precisely the dreams of Don Quixote and Sancho Panza in four volumes, producing the best scholarly text, after years of increasingly corrupt texts, as close as possible to Cervantes's Spanish. His complete edition of all of Cervantes's work, coedited with his close friend in Spain, Adolfo Bonilla (who died

James Schevill with his wife, Margot, 1989

halfway through the project yet my father kept his name on the edition), was published in Madrid and financed by the great patroness of the University of California, Phoebe Apperson Hearst, William Randolph Hearst's mother. Often my father would tell stories of his occasional visits to Mrs. Hearst's mansion in Pleasanton. She kept there, he said, a small table by the front door covered with small, splendid Chinese antiques from Gump's in San Francisco. As her guests departed, she would point graciously to the table and say, "Won't you please take one?" I still have two of these gifts that she gave to my father.

When I was born in 1920, our street, Tamalpais Road—named in Spanish after the mountain in Marin County, the home of the Tamal Indians—was mostly country. The tawny, steep hills, covered with sun-dried grasses that fed the virulent Berkeley conflagration of 1923, concealed only a few houses. In the west, a glittering mirage at sunset daily, glowed San Francisco Bay, where a ferry was still the only way to commute to "the city" as we called it reverently. The bridge came later in the 1930s. In the eastern valleys behind us, the wild land was just beginning to be divided into the corporate agriculture and the burgeoning industries of future years. Below us bloomed the botanical gardens that were being transformed into the University of California, designated to be the official fountainhead of western culture.

My father, Rudolph Schevill, was brought out from Yale in 1912 to create a Department of Romance Languages. Born in 1874, he had attended Yale University, and then received his Ph.D. from the University of Munich, specializing in French and German, and writing a thesis on "August Wilhelm Schlegel and the French Theatre." When he appeared for his final oral examination at three o'clock in the afternoon, he was required to wear, as he often mentioned with amusement, a rented swallowtail coat, white tie, too big white gloves, and a stovepipe hat—this in sharp contrast to the examining professors who wore, as my father said, "the oldest clothes they possessed, the kind that never had a pressing in all their worn existence." After teaching at Bucknell, where one of his students was the immortal baseball pitcher Christy Mathewson (badgering my father to describe Christy, he would say over and over "a friendly giant, with no real gift for languages, who sat in the last row"), he returned to Yale. After a year of teaching German at Yale, his growing interests in Spanish literature caused him to take a summer trip to Spain. He fell in love with that country, taught himself Spanish, and converted himself slowly into a Cervantes scholar and Professor of Spanish literature, a feat of love difficult to imagine today when our universities train and assign scholars to their specialized channels.

Also, two of my father's brothers achieved distinguished careers, William as a portrait painter, and Ferdinand as a historian and one of the original faculty members of the University of Chicago. Sons of a German immigrant family fleeing from the European revolutions of 1848, they were all born in Cincinnati, Ohio. Their father, Ferdinand August Schwill (the spelling was changed when my aunt Elsa married William on the condition that the spelling would be altered so it wouldn't always sound in English like *swill*), had fled from his birthplace, Koenigsberg in East Prussia during the Revolution of 1848, on the wave of young immigrants seeking new freedom in the United States. He was one of those restless, ambitious new Americans, with a broad range of scientific interests, who was condemned to be an unsuccessful business man. Before my father's birth, in partnership with a Frenchman, he set up a tobacco factory. I grew up with and finally wrote a short story about the family legend of my grandfather investing all his money in a cigar-making machine that exploded during its first public demonstration, spitting tobacco scornfully onto the faces and formal clothes of the assembled investors dreaming of their wealth-to-be. After that, undaunted, my grandfather pursued a "promising silver mine in Colorado," before settling down to a minor business career in a Cincinnati store.

My mother's family was another immigrant mixture of Irish Robinsons, dedicated to law and order, and English Shrewsburys, eyes uplifted in the search for God and theological correctness. My Irish great-grandfather Robinson became a colonel in the Union Army, commanding a regiment of Maryland volunteers into the Battle of Gettysburg. After surviving that stream of blood he retired to become chief of police in Hoboken, New Jersey. There, he cultivated the peaceful flowers he loved in his split warrior soul in a greenhouse that he built.

Mother's Erwin family created eminent lawyers whom she honored for legal brilliance and power of security, and, indeed, urged me at times to become a lawyer for financial ease. Still, she revolted against this conservative background out of her own instinctive artistic gifts. Mother's father, James Erwin, codified the New Jersey laws. Her older brother, also a James, followed in his father's tracks, becoming a distinguished judge. As might be expected, the younger children rebelled in different directions. The youngest brother, Hobe Erwin, achieved a reputation as an interior designer, half of the New York firm of Jones and Erwin. Summoned to Hollywood as an art director, he designed several of Katharine Hepburn's early films and spoke longingly to my mother of his frustrated love for Hepburn. Finally, his aesthetic interests and his hatred of Hollywood fakery persuaded him to return to his beloved New York interior design business. Although the business no longer exists, his wallpaper designs are still marketed under the title: Hobe Erwin: "A Touch of Elegance."

As a result of her heritage, my mother was a special mixture of aristocratic Republican conservatism and anarchic, artistic impulse. Her parents wanted her to be the new kind of upper middle-class lady that was civilizing the country with high social standards. Deep in the Episcopalian religion, into which I was duly baptized, they trained her to the impeccable standards of a would-be lady. Inevitably, they sent her to Wellesley College, where she had an even more impeccably mannered classmate masking her rigid principles who became Madame Chiang Kai-shek. At Wellesley Mother's extroverted nature flowered. She acted and studied Shakespeare, which spurred on her innate poetic gifts. She was courted by many men who admired her aggressive red hair and her tall, statuesque beauty. When she graduated, after being courted fervently at properly chaperoned campus tea parties and dances, there was a handsome future engineer in her life who attracted her physically and who would provide the American dream of security. She couldn't make up her mind; maybe she loved him, maybe it was too soon to settle into a family and marriage. After graduating, she fled to Arizona to teach English in high school and to coach the women's basketball team. In Arizona she fell in love with the desert, its powerful dawns and sunsets, and the Indian traditions, especially the Navajos and the sense of duality in their myths. This began her lifelong devotion to Navajo myths, which resulted in several books. Mother had grown up with a sense of opposites in her immigrant background, and she could never reconcile her sense of one trinitarian Episcopalian God with her sense of many powerful natural gods whom the Navajos venerated in their ancient tradition. When Mother discovered the Navajo religion in Arizona, the gates of natural wonder opened to her, and she began to pour out poems in praise of her new discoveries. On every rock in Navajo country a god loomed. Particularly the figure of Coyote in Navajo myths had a satirical mockery that pleased Mother's Irish sense of humor. In Arizona the proud, still-yearning, pragmatic figure of her engineer began to fade, although he continued to appear sporadically throughout her life in her treasured dreams as she learned to record them.

When Mother met Father on a trip to California, he thought they were a perfect match. He was ripe for marriage, in his middle thirties, but he was Napoleon short, five feet five inches, and she was almost five ten, a tree target. She wasn't so sure at first about him. After all, he was a good deal older and probably still a virgin, as was she, despite the engineer. In those days sexual innocence was to be preserved until marriage inflicted its awesome, demonic responsibilities. Still, he was a gentle, kindly man, a learned man speaking many languages which she admired as she spoke only one, a scholar already embarked on an important career, and a professor with tenure and a high salary because of his administrative responsibilities. Mother, who was a romantic anyway, convinced herself that she was in love. After their marriage, two children followed in quick succession: to her firstborn she gave her family name of Erwin as if in defiance because she couldn't use her maiden name the way feminists do today; to her second boy she gave the name of Karl Bitter Schevill, a name against which he revolted. Karl was named after my father's brother-in-law, the New York sculptor Karl Bitter. Born in Vienna, Bitter fled from the Austrian army as a youth, when he was refused permission to attend art school. (There was a law in the Austro-Hungarian Empire that drafted young men for two years of military service, but if the soldier was highly qualified artistically, the second

Great-grandfather Colonel Gilbert Proud Robinson, in his Civil War uniform, when he commanded a company of Maryland volunteers for the North at the Battle of Gettysburg

year of service could be spent in art school.) With no money in his pockets, Bitter managed to find a ship in Hamburg on which he could work his way to New York. After landing in New York, he apprenticed himself to an ornamental sculptor and soon learned how to make all kinds of ornamental decorations that led to his being hired by the Vanderbilts for sculptural work in their Newport and North Carolina mansions. In time he became a well-known sculptor himself, who created the Pulitzer Fountain outside of the Plaza Hotel and the Carl Schurz Memorial in New York. However, the name of Bitter did not suit my brother Karl, as school chums ragged him sarcastically by calling him "Bitter."

I was born five years after Karl, and my parents assigned me four lofty names when I was baptized with holy water by the Episcopalian bishop: James Shrewsbury Erwin Schevill. As soon as I became aware of whispers, I decided that I did not want to be a British Shrewsbury religious zealot. I even quailed beneath the punning nickname of "Shoes" that my brother Karl called me in his private joke of brotherly humiliation. Erwin, I accepted as a token of love for my mother's family, but Shrewsbury never! Even in school, I battled to conceal this name from the records. Three names were bad enough, but four! Later, in high school when I began to read Shakespeare, and learned of the Battle of Shrewsbury in *Henry IV,* I wavered a little. Perhaps warrior ancestry was not so bad, but, still, Mother and Father, how could you possibly think I could cope on the American frontier with such a pride of names?

Ghost Voice: Rudolph Schevill

Well he certainly is fantastic, like his sequence of poems: *The American Fantasies.* A legendary family on a mythical street, indeed! Little Jimmy we called him. He was the third male child, no daughters to create a female oasis in our run of children. Our home was more like canyon solitude than the frontier mythical street that Jimmy claims. We lived on the edge of a canyon thick with bay, laurel, and pine trees, and cut by a thin stream trickling down to the haven of Cordonices Park. As the house grew larger and larger, my wife and I built our separate worlds. By adding an immense "Big Room," which she commissioned from the southern California architects Greene and Greene, Margaret created a proud center for the grand parties and the musical salons she loved to give. With her impeccable taste, she filled the room with Chinese scrolls on the immensely high walls, in which three sets of towering twelve-paneled, laddered

windows opened onto the canyon garden. An adjacent, circular, blue bathroom featured a large—almost swimming pool size—bathtub in which the children loved to splash. Still, Margaret's architectural dreams could never be fulfilled.

Once, visiting my brother Ferdinand in Chicago, Margaret had met Frank Lloyd Wright and been swept off her feet. In his impetuous, imperial way, Wright urged her to run away with him and promised to build ideal cities for her. Flattered into a haze of wonder, she left me and lived with Wright for nine months. I was left to play the role of a guilty, abandoned father forced to take care of two rambunctious boys. Why had I secluded myself so deeply in the world of scholarship? Had I not become an abstraction instead of a man? One day I would threaten her with losing her children; the next day, I would promise loving forgiveness if she returned. I did love her creativity, her feminine grace so refreshing after my quixotic, bookish world. Hearing my grief, my brother Ferdinand argued his friend Wright into submission. Fearing the loss of her children, what could Margaret do but capitulate? On a day of weeping and mutual guilt-sharing, she returned to me, and we resolved to build a new life. A year later, Jimmy was born, the child of our reunion, a birthtime of reconciliation that we concealed from Jimmy.

Ghost Voice: Margaret Schevill

After Jimmy was born, I dreamt only occasionally of Wright and his genius. Later in my life, when I was divorced from Rudolph and living in Tucson, I visited Wright in his Taliesin-West home. Now we were only friends, but still close underneath the surfaces of our marriages. He designed for me one of his distinctive, small Usonian houses, open to the mountains and the sun, that I wanted to build outside of Tucson. I never had the money to build that house, but I often looked at the plans with desire and memories.

Despite our reconciliation, Rudolph revenged himself on me unconsciously by falling in love with a blackhaired, beautiful graduate student his short size, Isabel Magaña. She could babble his romantic Spanish as I could not. Still, I do not consider my marriage a failure. Always I admired and was fond of Rudolph. Fondness should not be a damning word in the world of love. Our three boys were born out of love and respect. Of how many marriages can it be said that they were based on admiration and respect?

Parents, Margaret and Rudolph Schevill, as a young married couple

Seeking a profession, I converted the lower basement of our house into an art studio, where I could paint and draw with fellow artists from nude models, and where I could teach art to children. One day, Jimmy, who was developing into a passionate basketball player (despite his poor hornrimmed eyes he would shoot for hours at a hoop we erected over our garage), became aware with his neighborhood chums that a naked woman was posing in the basement. Startled, I looked up from my drawing to discover three wide-eyed boys with gaping mouths staring from the garden through the windows at the model. What to do, as they scurried away, frightened like little animals? I rationalized with my artist friends that we were the new Bohemian age, devoted to a new kind of art education. So we invited the boys in, with the consent of the model, pressed pencil and paper into their perspiring little hands, and forced them down to draw. End of story. Art education does have its advantages with children, exposing them to sensuous life that they would otherwise learn only by snickering gossip.

My art school prospered. I studied children's art, learned how deficient the pragmatic American educational system was in terms of art education. I traveled to Vienna to observe how the famous Professor Cizek conducted his art classes for children. I was accused of wanting every child to become an artist, a misconception about school art programs that is often expressed by doubtful adults who want "success and financial security" for their children. When I discussed this idea with Professor Cizek, he said with a smile: "No, no, my children become automobile mechanics, businessmen, good housewives, teachers, and so on. One is a great violinist. There are few real artists among them, but they are all happier men and women because they have had this opportunity." In Berkeley, I worked with the foremost child psychologists at the University of California to develop art programs that our schools needed. If children have not been inhibited, or if they regain their confidence, they will paint their moods, their dreams, their visions of the inner world so important to their individual development. I got my children to paint incredible fantasies to develop their imaginations "The Black Madonna," "The Snake Who Lives behind the Rainbow," "The Baddest Boy in the World," "The God of the Woods," "The Queen of the Moon and Her Star Ladies." In this way, my children learned how to make their own experiences more comprehensible to themselves, and they adjusted better to life. Would that our public schools could learn to function this way. We helped to change the Berkeley public schools in this regard, but not enough. Eventually, the schools relapsed to the pressure of the old traditional ways, focusing rigidly on reading, writing, and arithmetic, to the exclusion of the arts.

Still, with my husband's help, we were building a communal, frontier street, where new American dreams flourished. Perhaps this is what Jimmy means by a "mythical street." A variety of distinguished people came to live there as the community grew—a physicist, a Greek scholar, a newspaper publisher, a lawyer, an engineer. Contrary to the specialized interests and groups that developed later, excitement flourished in the clash of ideas. Peggy Hayes, the artistic sister of the sculptor Alexander Calder, lived up the street. She assisted me enthusiastically with my children's art classes. Her athletic sons, Calder and Kenneth (or Bunny as he was called), became close friends of my Deadeye Dick Jimmy, pushing him on to sharpen his basket-shooting ability.

My love of parties turned into an annual magical New Year's Eve neighborhood party at our house at which all children were permitted to stay up past the

"Father posing with his brothers and sisters in their early and late years: (from left) Rudolph, Marie (who married the sculptor Karl Bitter), Elsa, Ferdinand (the historian), Albert, and William (the portrait painter)"

midnight witching hour and gape at their parents' antics. Peggy Hayes's husband, Kenneth, a banker whose family lost their bank in the 1929 stockmarket crash forcing Kenneth to become a traveling salesman yet a man who never lost his infectious good spirit, led the dancing, whirling Peggy and me around the floor. At one New Year's party, Alexander Calder, in a red-checked lumberjack's shirt, danced us ladies around until, dripping with perspiration and afraid of staining our long dresses, he stopped abruptly, stripped off his shirt, reversed it, put it on inside out, and continued whirling us around madly!

With the dreams of power go the dreams of death. We remember the fires on Tamalpais Road, the flaming tragedies that were adventures too, holding us together. In 1923, when Jimmy was only three years old, the terrible Berkeley fire burned over the hills from Orinda, driven by the wind. The water mains were inadequate to defend the city, and the water supply was down that year because of the lack of rain. So the fire spread rapidly. Quickly, Rudolph evacuated me and the children to safety downtown on

the east side of the campus. Determined to defend the house, Rudolph gathered his students and posted them on the roof to fend off sparks. Since our house lay in the canyon hollow, it was miraculously saved from the fire that burned down the hills on both sides around us. Surrounded by flames, our house stood in the middle seeking its own survival. A campus joke persisted for years about the many degrees Rudolph handed out that year as a reward to his courageous students.

Another severe fire threatened our house when Jimmy was some eight years old. Early one morning towards dawn—the indeterminate time when ghosts swirl through the Berkeley fog before it lifts with the sun—I woke to smell smoke, and poked my head sleepily out of the window. A grey cloud of smoke fingered with flames was pouring out of the basement. I rushed the children out to the street. Rudolph called the fire department and ran into the basement to battle the flames. That day I gained a new respect for his courage. When the firemen arrived, they rushed into action like a team from a

Mack Sennett comedy, hacking and drenching the side of the house with a fury that drove Rudolph into a frenzy. He had almost put out the fire that was caused by faulty electrical wiring. His face streaked with soot and water, he was suddenly confronted by comedians who, ignoring his protests, began to pour their powerful jets of water into his study. His precious books and scholarly souvenirs endangered, Rudolph began to swear at the firemen, unconsciously cursing them in his beloved Spanish as well as English. As I listened with astonished delight, I felt a small hand tugging at mine. It was little Jimmy seeking maternal shelter, amazed at an angry, cursing father whom he had never seen before, performing linguistic furies he couldn't understand.

James Schevill

What I remember is not the urgent details, but the terrible pressure of events told and retold. I remember the spirit of fire that seemed to hover over our house and that was often discussed at our family dinner table. I remember that my oldest brother, Erwin, died shortly after the Berkeley fire as a result of the terrible influenza epidemic that swept the country. It was a death from which my mother never recovered. Erwin was twelve when he died, and I was only three, but we had a strange, close relationship. My second brother, Karl, was always the superior athlete in the family, who had his own friends and was quick to ignore me when I tagged along. Erwin was a sensitive dreamer and my mother poured her affection into him unconsciously, to Karl's resentment. Erwin wandered through the canyon, naming every bird and tree in his notebook, writing his journal. In school his marks were superior. Perhaps a future botanist or writer, my parents thought. Unlike Karl, the extrovert, who made friends easily with his attractive looks and his social abilities, Erwin, like my father, favored his solitude. When I tottered after Erwin on his canyon voyages, he often let me accompany him (so I was told) because I was too young to pester him. So I came to enjoy and appreciate his solitude too. I learned to admire his superior contemplation and his instinctive wisdom about the natural world. Although he taught me a deep appreciation of nature, alas, I failed to absorb a real knowledge of the biological and botanical names that distinguish animals and plants. The reason was not only that I was too young; I was born with a certain kind of memory that responds to visual objects, fixes on them with tenacity until they reveal their structures, but a memory that is relatively poor

on names and dates. From my dead brother, though, I learned how the power of solitude relates to creativity. Solitude is the inner strength required to contemplate, and accept creatively, the perilous transformations of one's identity that occur because of the inevitable environmental restrictions one confronts in life. From Erwin's short, radiant life I discovered early the tragic meaning of death and the joy of solitude.

Ghost Voice: Erwin Schevill

I am one of the many who die in the midst of promises without fulfillment. Nevertheless, it is wrong to say that we, who die young, die without experiencing the joy of life. The day I died I was sitting up in bed, laughing, talking eagerly to my doctor and my parents. I had no intention of dying and then I was dead! My youngest brother, Jim, never learned his capacity for solitude from me. It was his heritage and his own poetic abilities that came from many sources. It was not unjust that I died from influenza, a dangerous word that now troubles few people because of the invention of antibiotics. What I do regret is the uncanny power that a ghost assumes in time, haunting those who are left behind to the creation of their own family myths. My mother could not face the fact of my death. The Chinese believe that you live eternally through the succession of children. Not only the Chinese. What did I represent to my mother? Certainly not the mere promise of creativity. She had plenty of that in her own gifts. Was it because the firstborn is always the first miracle of birth, the most difficult, and therefore the most miraculous birth? Perhaps, to a certain extent. The first loss can sometimes be the greatest loss. But I think it was also her vision of masculinity. For some strange reason, her vision remained rooted in her family name that she gave me as first name—*Erwin*— I was her vision of masculine seduction and promise more than my brothers.

In any case, when I died and was cremated, she could not bury my ashes. She kept my ashes in a box in the basement of our house to make sure that my ghost would remain in her home on the edge of our canyon. One day, after several years had passed, my youngest brother, Jim, playing around the house, poking into odd corners and closets where secret treasures always seem to lie, stumbled on the box in a corner of the basement. It was tightly, securely wrapped, of a curious weight as he felt it. With the curiosity of youth, he trundled off with the box to our father, asking eagerly, "Look, Papa! A treasure box!

"Mother with her first son, Erwin"

What's in it?" A ludicrous situation! Father mumbled some ridiculous answer and prepared to confront Mother. It wasn't until later that Jim learned about the ashes in the box. By then he knew that ghosts were real presences in dreams, that ghosts like to haunt architecture, particularly if they have been involved in the architectural creation. My father forced my mother to bury the ashes. They went through their own grieving private burial service. So I, Erwin, became the first Schevill to lie in the Berkeley cemetery where my mother's ashes now rest next to me. My father's ashes lie a hundred yards away in a second plot next to where his second wife's ashes will lie.

James Schevill

Living your youth under the shadow of a dead older brother who lingers on as a ghost is like running free into the wind and discovering another invisible runner ahead of you. Often, it is a spur, not a restriction. Whenever the subject of my dead brother came up, in precious pictures or in guarded conversa-tions, I never felt as though I was being reduced to an also-ran. Instead, I grew up with a feeling of wonder. Who was this mysterious presence who had vanished, young, so full of promise? Why did his ghost remain so powerful in our family life? In the nearby elementary Hillside School, my parents commissioned a lovely Spanish-tiled water fountain in Erwin's memory. When I went to that school I walked by it every day, feeling proud. There was Erwin's name on it—immortal! Even kids I didn't like had to drink from that fountain. How could they know the triumph I felt seeing enemies and friends alike drinking from that fountain!

I was a strange mixture of would-be athlete and awkward, subdued introvert in school. For a time I was failing badly in arithmetic. It turned out that, sitting as far out of the action as I could in the back row, I was copying the problems down wrong, and needed glasses badly. I acquired hornrimmed spectacles, which marked me forever. I broke them innumerable times to my parents' despair. Glasses were not safe in those days, and my eye doctor warned me to be careful playing sports. What could I do? I was playing in the wake of my brother Karl's five years older, superior athletic skills and his prowess in the Knoll Athletic Club. The Knoll Athletic Club was a singular institution named after a large wooded lot on top of a hill overlooking the bay. It was owned by a wealthy lawyer, who permitted the neighborhood kids to use it. My brother Karl and his friends were the founding partners. As time went on, I and my younger friends were permitted to fill in the fringe positions as secondary athletes and servant laborers. The servant labor became important when the ringleaders decided to build secret tunnels leading to a sacred underground clubhouse. The construction of this secret labyrinth was marked by an incredible conspiracy.

When I was finally permitted into those tunnels and that clubhouse flickering with candles and the stern authority of older boys, I was scared and awed. Were these tunnels really safe? How did they get all that lumber for the shoring? Was it right to keep all this activity secret from our parents? If you want to get into a group, you have to learn to accept customs and obey orders. Break those customs and orders, and you become the group's enemy. You'll never play any sport with the Knoll Athletic Club unless you can prove yourself a team player. Boys need a sense of challenge, risk. Crawling into that clubhouse, I felt privileged and uneasy. At that time the Knoll Athletic Club was making its presence known in Bay area juvenile athletic leagues. We played football, basketball, and junior league baseball. My brother was fast as a rabbit and could run through opposing teams without a hand touching him. He was a natural leader in sports and could play any sport with distinction as he proved throughout high school and college.

Somehow, it was only in shooting a basketball that I could excel and I continued to practice my outside shooting doggedly after school because it was the one thing that insured my participation in the Knoll Athletic Club. I was years ahead of my time as a three-point outside shooter in a time when every basket counted only two points. In baseball I was a relative flop. When drafted into the junior league baseball team, I was stationed somehow at third base where I achieved notoriety for the most errors ever committed in one game, failing miserably both in blocking the ball and heaving it over to first base where it seemed to arrive either on the bounce or high over the first baseman's frantic leaps.

At the age of nine, with my father on sabbatical, deep in his Spanish scholarship, my parents exiled me and my brother Karl to a private German school in Davos, Switzerland, where Thomas Mann conceived his novel *The Magic Mountain.* For me, it was anything but magic. I was a California boy, accustomed to sunshine and fog. Suddenly I was on an imperious, beautiful mountain, covered with snow and ice. Ice skating and skiing were anathema to me. Speaking in German was like stammering through a muffled curtain of words. I came to live in terror of ski jumping. One day, with other boys and an accompanying master, I found myself watching a typical winter competition. Jumpers swept gracefully high over my head, hurtling gracefully through the clear winter air and slapping down on the steep runway. Suddenly, one jumper suffered an accident and landed in a splinter of ski and falling flesh a few feet away from where I was standing. His cries of pain pierced my isolated brain and I knew something terrible had happened. He had broken his back. An ambulance came and carried him away, and I began to have nightmares about his fall.

About this time I began to suffer from asthma too, doubtless my own body's way of protesting against being snatched away from home and my familiar sports to a winter paradise that seemed a kind of beautiful Hell to me. The only other thing I remember about this school in Davos was that my brother Karl came down with scarlet fever, a dreaded scourge at that time that forced him into an isolated hospital room in total quarantine, where I was only permitted to visit and see him through a glass window and watch him being fed his milk diet—the current

dogged medical belief being that such a diet was the only way to fight scarlet fever.

At the age of thirteen, again, convinced that I needed a better, more selective education to cover my California slovenliness, my parents decided once more to send me away to a private school, this time, Fountain Valley School outside of Colorado Springs in Colorado. Another winter paradise with the towering grandeur of Pike's Peak soaring high in the Rockies to the west. My brother Karl was a champion success at the school. He had even become a glider pilot in his senior year! In his junior year he was a daredevil mechanical engineer, joining his fellow student daredevils in wiring intricate alarms that triggered falling waterbuckets when unsuspecting victims, students and faculty alike, entered their condemned rooms. The wise headmaster, convinced that the only way to deal with such rebellious miscreants was to promote them out of their criminal acts, appointed them to the student council and to the coveted responsibility of flying the only glider on campus. Immediately, the rebels became officials, clamping down strongly on would-be rebels in the lower grades.

To my astonishment, I discovered that I was the youngest boy in school. I was there on a scholarship, so I had to study, although the only thing I wanted to do was read. Not that I was reading exactly what I was supposed to read. I was becoming aware of sex, masturbating more and more in my lonely room, digging in the library for any books that were remotely concerned with sex. If I couldn't become active with the women I desired because of my confinement in a boy's school, at least I could be a sex-reader. In this goal, of course, I soon found myself scorned by the older boys. Either they would scorn me, saying I was too young for such prurient material, or they would act out the masks of sexual experience with bravado, implying that they would sell me really potent sexual material if I would pay them for it. As the youngest, solo boy in the school, I was an awkward target. Although, in any school or fraternity, it's proper to haze, razz, initiate—whatever form of ritual passage it may take to gain the essential seniority of power—there is little merit and no prestige in initiating one isolated boy. So I learned to exist by myself on the fringes of society, perhaps a beneficial education in itself, although I couldn't see the merits of it at the time. In classes I was an average student and remained that way through high school and college. I could get by because I was intelligent enough and an avid reader, but I didn't have the kind of retentive memory that makes for continuous high grades. As I have said, I was slowly discovering that I had a different kind of creative memory. Somehow, literal facts such as dates and names were elusive to me; instead I had a strong intuitive memory of strange details of places and people. I caught singular associations, the beginning of a metaphorical ability that was to lead me to poetry.

In the communal bathroom in the morning, boys lined up waiting for the next open shower, I noticed how the young, blond housemaster-teacher flaunted his naked masculinity in front of us boys. Morning after morning, there was no doubt that he was in his element in the shower room. The love of youthful flesh was his desire, even though he never manifested it directly. Behind his back, the older boys joked about him mercilessly. It was my first experience with the homoerotic world that made me more interested in reading classical literature and discovering the intricate sexual levels of Greek civilization.

By the end of the school year, no matter what the cost, I resolved never to return. Of course, I was being unfair to the school, which had some fine, dedicated faculty who helped me to see the merits, particularly, of music and English. Unfortunately, the school was in its early growth, and I was the victim of an inadequate, small enrollment. Too many of the kids came from wealthy parents who had spoiled them. Often, behind the scenes, these kids flaunted their wealth to my discomfort, since I was on a scholarship with relatively limited parental support. So I withdrew even further and made no attempt to make friends. I wanted out into the free world. If I had stayed, I might have adjusted to the wider range of students that enrolled later to make the school's reputation. When my poor father arrived to give the commencement speech, for which he had been invited as my brother was graduating with honors and success in both grades and general student activities, I let my father have the bombshell: I was leaving! He fended me off by saying that I had all summer to think it over. During the joyous commencement activities, I was like a wasp on the outer rim of the events, diving in to sting my father whenever I could. As my father talked on in his commencement address to the battery of proud parents and happy students about the problems and aims of education in public and private schools, such as this one in which I·was incarcerated, I sat in a rear row seat by myself planning my escape.

Oddly, that year, Francis Froelicher, the headmaster and founder of the school—a distinguished and kind educator with high standards for a broad, humanistic education—decided to spend the summer with his family in Inverness, California, a small town north of San Francisco on Tomales Bay, where my family had a summer cottage. When I heard this news, I was convinced that my parents had joined in a secret plot against me to force me to return to Fountain Valley School. Such are the wild fantasies of a thirteen-year-old boy, turning fourteen, thrashing out into the world. Somehow, that summer proved a turning point in my life. My parents had arranged for an attractive teenage girl with theatrical ambitions, Olivia de Havilland, who needed a summer job, to work for the Froelichers. Olivia and her sister, Joan Fontaine, became friendly with my family in the small town of Los Gatos, where we used to go to visit friends and for occasional vacations. There, I played with these girls, mostly the kind of usual childhood activities in those macho days, where I would assert my masculine ability to throw a stone further than they could or climb a tree higher. They would soon turn away to pursue some superior private activity such as reading a book. Consequently, I became more interested in reading literature of the spirit, rather than the literature of male action such as Tom Swift, Baseball Joe, and The Motor Boys, to which I was addicted.

This special summer in Inverness, I was invited to join a youthful group reading Shakespeare, led by Olivia and her boyfriend, Peter Whitney. Aside from the usual school plays, this reading of *Twelfth Night* was the first serious theatrical activity in which I participated. I can still remember the first professional play my parents took me to in San Francisco— William Gillette's famous stage triumph as Sherlock Holmes. The climatic scene when Holmes is trapped in a pitch-dark room and, suddenly, a match flares up in a startling, melodramatic effect, remains imbedded in my mind. But *Twelfth Night* was my first initiation into the theatrical power of Shakespearean verse spoken aloud. When Peter poured his heart into the opening lines of the lovesick Duke, "If music be the food of love, play on," I was hooked. Despite being the youngest in the group, I was cast as the clown, Feste. As I soon discovered in my innocence, this was no mere part. How could I bring off the famous song that ends the play, when Feste, alone in the garden, sings poignantly his summation of life, "When that I was a little tiny boy . . ."? I felt like a little tiny boy, and I had to pretend I was a big clown. My ambivalence choked me and I hoped Olivia would coach me in the songs, but she was too busy with her job.

My parents hoped that the summer presence of the Froelichers and this Shakespearean venture would help me to change my mind and return to

Fountain Valley School. Instead, as Feste, I perceived the idiocy of adult conduct in the world, as the ladies mischievously plotted against the unctuous, overbearing steward, Malvolio, and tormented him into submission. I, Feste, would not be subdued, even though I would have submitted gladly to Olivia, as she read her lines with melodic ambitious fire. The final song forced me awake out of my Shakespearean fantasies into the real world. Since I was too scared to sing it, I read the lines lamely with the result that I ruined the ending. To this day, when I go to *Twelfth Night* with a reverent expectation that no one accompanying me can understand, I wait for that final song to be sung beautifully, to bring tears to my eyes and a lift to my heart. All too often I hear an actor good at clowning who can't sing and fakes the song. Only once have I heard a perfect singer and a good clown in the role and then, suddenly, the play ended at the right pitch of emotion. What I learned that summer was the real power of drama that was always in my nature, and that I would always aspire to from that moment on.

My parents must have wondered at my sudden, eager dedication to Shakespeare and *Twelfth Night,* but they were upset and saddened by my stubborn determination never to return to Fountain Valley. I simply kept repeating like a blockhead clown, "I will not go, I will not go." In the end, they had to let me go to public school, to Claremont Junior High School in Oakland, which had an affiliation for teacher training with the University of California, so my father thought it was the lesser of all possible educational evils. As the summer ended, so did a certain family relationship. When a boy protests too much, and forces his parents to give up, the boy suddenly finds himself standing outside the family in a new way. Against their better judgment, the parents give up grudgingly. And the grudge stands now between the parents and their child. The boy, with his new, hard-won independence, doesn't know where he's going. The boy has created his own dramatic action, and now he has to live it. Life was the essence of theatre, and performance was the essence of life. That was the lesson I was learning that would shape my life forever.

Ghost Voice: Margaret Schevill

What Jimmy couldn't recognize, and what I could not acknowledge to him at the time, was my growing depression as a woman. I wanted to be a poet and an artist, and instead I was mainly a housewife and a mother. In my despair, I begged my husband to let me go and become a patient of the

psychiatrist C. G. Jung in Switzerland. I learned about Jung from my close Berkeley friend Dr. Elizabeth Whitney, Peter's mother, whose two other children, Jim and Frances, were also friends with my children during our Inverness summer vacations. Elizabeth had been an early patient of Jung's. She became the pioneer medically trained Jungian psychiatrist in California. I turned to her for help with my depressions. Were these periodic depressions driving me insane? Was I losing my husband's and family's love? Why had I turned over so much of my children's upbringing to a devoted English nanny, Miss Edith Handyside, a warm, moralistic spinster lady who transformed herself into a substitute mother, offering her generous, frustrated maternal love to my two remaining boys? Could Jung's new psychology assuage my guilt at the death of my oldest son? Sending Jimmy and Karl to boarding school in Davos, Switzerland, while I went off to study with Jung had seemed a good solution to me, but it hadn't worked out well for the boys. Then, Fountain Valley had been fine for Karl and turned him into the likeable, extroverted success he was destined to be. But stubborn little Jimmy, the rebel, was the thorn motivating much of my guilt. He mirrored so many of my features, I didn't want to see myself in him.

I went to Jung, as if on bended knee for relief, and my eyes and heart opened. Jung was a charismatic master. Sitting face to face with him—a technique he adopted differing from Freud who sat behind his patients lying on a couch—my tears and my heart flowed out, and I learned how commonplace my problems were. I was a mistress of extroverted sensation, as he called his theory of the key aspects of human personality—extroverted and introverted sensation, intuition, and thinking types. American restlessness and rootless extroversion flowed out in all directions. If only I could learn to channel this energy, I could change my life, achieve a new marriage. Guilt was something I had to learn to cast out. I began to write down and study my dreams with Jung, in an effort to understand the disassociated patterns of my life. Jung forced me to draw my problems too, and I became freer in my art, learning to float colors on the page instead of restricting them to conventional forms.

The stage designer Robert Edmond Jones was also a patient of Jung's. Beset with his androgynous sexual problems of identity in an age that denied homosexuality so strongly, Robert and I would go boating on the lovely lake at Küsnacht, and he would pour out his problems to me as I poured out my problems to him. Küsnacht was a quiet little village on the lake near Zürich, where Jung lived, and Robert and I had peaceful, airy rooms in the Hotel Sonne on the lakefront, where I spent hours writing and drawing the ducks and proud white swans. Robert talked eagerly to me of his desire to achieve a new poetic theatre amidst the sterile, commercial restrictions of the American stage. He was a friend and partner of Eugene O'Neill and was designing all of O'Neill's productions. In a fever of excitement, he would talk about the poetic stage that the English designer Gordon Craig was fostering. Also, Robert had an exciting vision of how the new adventure of films—the quick movement, the close-ups, the rapid succession of brilliant images, and the developing soundtrack of interior voices—could be eventually combined with the stage, ideas which he would later express in his influential book *The Dramatic Imagination*. Later, Robert would pass on his ideas to my son Jimmy and become Jimmy's first mentor in the theatre. In those rapt Küsnacht days, drifting on the lake amidst the white swans, we confided in each other so closely that we became like brother and sister. Once, in the evening glow, he stopped rowing with a shout of joy, and began to sketch me. I treasured that sketch and kept it forever. Was I really such a proud, glamorous woman in white dress, white hat seeking to seduce the world?

A strange matriarchy surrounded Jung; British ladies who venerated him, his powerful wife, Emma, who was also a psychologist, and who became my friend. Most of all, I grew close to Toni Wolff, Jung's psychiatric assistant in the Zürich hospital, whom I learned had also been Jung's mistress. Toni had sacrificed her own life as a woman to remain close to Jung. Emma, Toni, and Jung were a powerful trio, rare people who had come to terms with their impulsive desires, and who had shaped their distinguished careers both inside and outside society in unconventional ways. With Jung I learned a new sense of the unconscious mind and how it relates to art. In recording and discussing my dreams with Jung, I grew deeply interested in the symbols of different civilizations, and how different images repeated themselves in what Jung called universal archetypes. With Jung I felt exhilarated. His mind flowed clearly above national boundaries into the ideal, connecting images of great societies. To me too, Jung was a powerful, attractive sexual male and I fell in love with him in a way—a large, strong man who loved woodchopping, building, sailing, cutting stone, but who radiated gentleness from the scholarly solitude that was his delight. He never denigrated his master, Freud, yet he stressed his belief that sexuality

was merely one deeply important aspect of the body and mind. Religiously, Jung was a free, open spirit, despite his strict, conservative Swiss Protestant upbringing. He quizzed me extensively about my knowledge of Navajo and other Southwest American Indian mythologies, and I think I contributed strongly to his growing fascination with these Native American cultures. I was proud when I gave him one of my painted reproductions of Navajo sandpaintings and he hung it enthusiastically on the wall of his study. No, Jung didn't cure me, but he taught me I had to work constantly on curing my own depressions, work to find my place as a woman in this masculine world.

James Schevill

In the ninth grade I began the independent life I had chosen in the Oakland public schools. I commuted for almost an hour each way from my Berkeley home on the old streetcars, soon to be sacrificed to the greed of cars and the growing automobile industry that was determined to dominate American society and force out the streetcars and most forms of public transportation with fantasies of "freeways" to escape from home boredom. The best thing I acquired in the public schools was an awareness of other races, black, particularly, as the Oakland schools had a large number of black kids. In a public school classroom you had to get along or get out. The teaching was very uneven, determined, sticking closely to the rules, but on the dull side. Without too much effort, you could coast through the courses as I did, hanging on the edges—a skeptical kid glad to be amongst fellow skeptics, resigned to the fact that teachers were like gates in fences. You had to get through them somehow to be released into the enjoyable life of the senses that schools were mainly forbidden to teach.

In public school I soon discovered there was a particular menace known as a teacher's pet. This was the most despicable of all the kids, which, in a more mature form, was what Nixon and other similar politicians came to call a "candyass." A pseudo-toughness was what we were condemned to emulate. We were prepared to enforce the proper distance between teacher and student. Any student who became an "asskisser," as we called them sneeringly, was immediately ostracized, banished, sentenced to exile by eating his or her brownbagged lunch in solitary isolation, or, worse, to become the victim of cruel, practical jokes such as doctored sandwiches with unspeakable contents sneaked into their lunches.

As for teachers, every time a young, green male or female student teacher arrived to begin a fatal career and started by writing his or her name boldly on the blackboard, the minute their back was turned to us we let them have it with wads of spitballs. To survive or not survive—that was the teacher's immediate trial. One male teacher, a rugged baseball player, triumphed by pivoting deftly and hurling the spitballs back at us with accurate, deadly effect. One woman teacher gained equal acclaim as a good sport by holding a spitball up to the light, analyzing it scientifically, scornfully in detail, and then demanding that every single member of the class in turn define the nature of a spitball with intellectual precision. Suddenly, we determined anti-intellectuals were forced to become intellectuals and admire, for a brief time, the possibilities of the brain.

Of the teachers I remember, in odd ways, only three. My Latin teacher was a pleasant, spinster lady with a grey bun of hair, who tried her best to inculcate some sense of Roman culture and language into a group of kids who thought that Latin was either a kind of music or a formal term for people to the south of us. Alas, she met her downfall when she took our entire class to see Eddie Cantor's film *Roman Scandals* under the illusion that if it was a popular musical, at least it might inspire us with the power of classical architecture, costumes, and the Latin language even if it could only be seen on signs. Instead, our mouths dropped open with sensuous delight when we saw Cantor as a slave jester being sold amidst a bevy of glamorous, longhaired slave girls chained up in the market place. All of these slave girls (Lucille Ball was one of them) were covered with swatches of incredibly long blonde hair down to their knees over seemingly naked bodies. This hairy disguise seemed even more sensuous to us ardently juiced-up teenagers. Despite hisses and commands from our poor teacher, we began to whistle and jeer with delight until we were nearly ejected from the theatre. After that pitiful experience, the shaken teacher retreated to academic rote grammatical instruction. Our continuous pleas to see another Roman musical were met with a scowl and a shake of her wounded head.

The second teacher was my high school physics teacher who saw immediately that I was a dangerous student in physics, with faulty memory, inadequate mathematical background (in those days there were no pocket computers and I could be seen painfully adding and subtracting with my fingers), and a propensity to disaster with the essential classroom equipment. For some reason he carried me in the course. Finally, he gave me a *C* instead of an *F*, which,

with my other balancing grades, fulfilled a science requirement and enabled me to get into college. At the time, I panicked with the sudden realization that this had become a crucial course in my life. Unless I passed, I couldn't go to college. My rebellion against my parents and academia would meet a deservedly bad end. For a short time, I even tried studying to pass that course, but kept flunking the tests, which the teacher seemed to make deliberately hard. By all rights, this bald-headed, kind, tough little man should have flunked me, sent me to the oblivion I deserved. He never let up on me and gave me a respect for the integrity of physics before the bomb that I still possess. Probably I pleaded with him, opening my hardened little heart to expose my perilous situation as I should have done, but I don't remember doing so. In my adolescent public school daze, I was trying to be a superior adult cynic, but all I could achieve was the silence of my confused isolation soon to burst open in the explosion of World War II. Still, he saw some spark in me and gave me a break. It was the first and last time I ever jumped with joy, stamping the floor with delight, when I received a *C*. More important, this was the first time I began to appreciate the qualities inherent in real teachers such as my father, my uncle, and this physics teacher—how compassion and judgment are essential components of a good teacher faced with intransigent material.

The third teacher, a veteran, prideful man dedicated to his profession and always impeccably dressed, had some kind of hidden power I could not admit. This is the only way I can explain what happened. He inspired warfare in my soul. I felt that he ruined poetry for me, but, in retrospect, he may have been the traditional wall on which I began to scribble my rebellious graffiti that resulted later in my poems. In any case, he made me dislike poetry and turned me away from it to music for several years. Since he was in charge of all English teachers and considered to be outstanding in his profession, this was a particularly bad encounter for me, and my parents couldn't understand my rebellious mutterings. What he did that turned me off was to write his own poems constantly on the classroom blackboard and then analyze them metrically to show how he achieved his effects with the kinds of traditional forms he was using. It wouldn't have been so bad if he had just read his poems. Hearing the struggling efforts of a poet to capture unusual sounds is always sympathetic. But his metrical analyses of his poems on the blackboard, with official notations of syllabic stresses, was terribly academic and boring. My spirit, tuned to jazz and popular music, cried out in dismay that this

"As a rebellious teenager (right), with brother Karl and Father"

tum-ti-tum-ti-tum regularity could be poetry. If this disciplined traditionalism, this pseudo-Keats or imitative Tennyson glide was poetry, I wanted to do something different with my sullen sixteen years. His reverent reading of other poems didn't help much. Again he would give a dry, metrical analysis, and the sound, the real rhythm of the poem, would be lost. Why is it that so many English teachers have no training in reading poetry out loud? He read poems in his soft, flat, tum-ti-tum-ti-tum voice as if he were reading from a metrical dictionary rather than from an emotional action. However, his dogged metrical lessons remained in my rebellious soul as a technical resource in the musical desires that I was developing.

In my senior high school year I began to study voice with Mynard Jones, a well-known Bay area singer, choral conductor, church organist, and teacher. A tall, chubby, imposing man with a rotund belly hardened by a singer's powerful diaphragm, he glinted at you out of glasses with a patient smile that soared deep from his Welsh ancestry. As I had a very light baritone voice, somewhat constricted by my asthmatic problems (indeed my parents hoped that my singing would help me with my asthma and it did),

I wondered at first whether I should study singing. My brother was away at Harvard, triumphing as a rare tenor in the Harvard Glee Club. He was even singing tenor solos in the Bach B Minor Mass in rehearsals with Koussevitsky and the Boston Symphony Orchestra. How could I match that with my inconspicuous baritone? Still, he was east, I was west. Why not try? I had been taking piano lessons without great improvement except in my admiration for my handsome, sexy woman teacher. But singing! Suddenly, dimensions of theatre, the whole unique world of opera, opened before me. Theatre and film had always attracted me, but I was too shy, too confined to the herd instinct, which meant sports, jazz and pop music, and films, to think much about live theatre.

Jones was a sensitive man who saw my latent creativity, so he began teaching me a little harmony and general musicianship in addition to singing. Best of all, coming from a Welsh background, he was a close friend of some of the leading Welsh singers in the San Carlos Opera Company, who visited and stayed with him on their annual tours. Welsh, I was soon convinced, was a society of fantastic, trumpet-like voices, and completely unorthodox behavior, which was confirmed in later years when I met and heard the poet Dylan Thomas.

Particularly, I became a fan of Mostyn Thomas, the leading dramatic baritone of the company. One day Jones made me sing for Thomas, despite my recalcitrance. That did it! Somehow Thomas praised my potential and autographed a picture of himself costumed fiercely with beard and helmet: "To James, with the hope of a fine future career." Tacking that picture proudly on my wall, I became an opera fan forever. So opera began for me my involvement in theatre. The San Carlos Opera Company was the cheap, popular, touring opera of its time. With inexpensive, tattered sets, minimal pale lighting, a skimpy orchestra, and unknown singers, it reigned supreme in my mind. There was something distinctive and endearing about the singers as I got to know them personally. Many of them had magnificent, untrained natural voices which they projected enthusiastically without much sense of style. Paid the minimum, they were used to existing on the edge of survival and had no time to bother with a unified ensemble performance. Every performance was a delightful miracle of happenstance. When the time came for an individual to sing, he or she simply let loose a flood of sound that attempted to eclipse any unfortunate partner on stage. Once, the leading tenor playing Canio in *Pagliacci* actually yanked the curtain around his small, sturdy frame, pranced in it, and then chewed on it at the climax to his aria, much to my delight.

When Jones took me backstage into the grease and grime of reality and raw sweat, far from being disillusioned, I was in seventh heaven. The deep bass, whom I admired as a sinister Mephistopheles in *Faust,* was a true back-alley devil. In his dingy dressing room, his battered, upended suitcase served as his private bar, out of which he lifted triumphantly his whiskey bottle, and drank straight, not bothering with a glass. And the greasepaint on Mostyn Thomas's face in his dressing room where he welcomed us—Thomas whose baritone parts I strove to emulate in the shower every day—that tragic greasepaint seemed to mark the world of dramatic imagination these mad, free spirits were serving with joy.

Singing gave me access to new worlds. One world, strangely enough, led me back into the Episcopalian church, if only in physical presence. Jones was the organist and choirmaster of the leading Episcopalian church in Berkeley. In return for my singing every Sunday in the church choir, he deducted a large part of my singing lesson expenses. We sang a lot of good choral music in his church choir, and I

came to appreciate the power of that kind of vocal sound. During the sermons, when I was troubled by the bland, suburban, comfortable approach to religion, I studied the music that we were singing. Or I let my mind wander about my troublesome destiny. In these circumstances, religion seemed a Sunday discipline rather than the passionate encounter that music, particularly opera, could be. One day, pleased with a hymn that I had written for him as a harmonic exercise, Jones surprised me by reproducing it, rehearsing it with the church choir, and performing it in church! I began to compose some songs too. Was there a chance I could become a composer as well as a singer?

It was 1936, in the middle of the Depression. My mother was reading John Steinbeck's stories and novels about poverty and agricultural problems in the Salinas Valley; also Robinson Jeffers's stirring verse narratives with their sense of classical tragedy and cosmic disaster. My father was still immersed in Cervantes, although he was emerging more frequently from his study to involve himself actively in the Spanish Civil War that had burst out suddenly. One night I heard my father, who had been elected head of the West Coast Committee for the Defense of the Spanish Republic, speak with the Spanish Ambassador to the United States, Fernando de los Rios, before a rally in San Francisco sponsored by Harry Bridges's Longshoremen's Union to raise funds for the Spanish government. Many years later, in an elegy for my father, I included the following account of the meeting:

> I wait for my father to speak in a waterfront union hall filled with huge workers smoking, laughing, drinking, shouting. To my awed teenage eyes, every foot wears a heavy shoe, every muscled arm can bend an iron bar or smash a nose. Speaking to these men is like addressing lions . . . To my startled eyes these powerful men are the champion weightlifters of the world.
>
> Suddenly, my father and de los Rios appear trapped in formal tuxedos! I gape in terror. They look like dolls in formal costumes standing before roughly dressed demons. When they speak, surely straw will come from their mouths! Restless, the workers listen to passionate appeals for democracy, unions, civil rights in Spain. De los Rios condemns Lorca's recent murder by Franco's Civil Guard, the threat of Franco's military dictatorship to Europe in general. Workers stand cheering, passing the hat for donations. Suddenly, to me my father's

absurd rented tuxedo becomes Don Quixote's armor attacking the windmills.

Later I learn that the absurd tuxedos are on their way to a formal civic dinner to raise money for ambulances for the Spanish Republic. I begin to understand my father's unique dedication to Cervantes and the cause of Spanish freedom; why my father wrote at the end of his Cervantes biography: "Spiritual poise and the triumphant heroism that greets the unseen with a cheer . . ." My father marking the scholar's stance in his absurd tuxedo; my father to be blacklisted for these efforts by the Un-American Affairs Committee.

"Clothes are only a costume, son, to create the role that you must play in the theatre of life."

Running blindly to maturity in sweatshirt and jeans, I could only learn by experience the white speech of ghosts. Now, in dreams, I walk with you, father, through the Prado staring at Goya's Black Paintings, the dark fantasies that rule our destinies. I hear with you the ghostly voice of St. Theresa challenging death: "Muero porque no muero."

"Spanish, my son, is the language of romantic opposites, the balance of cruel death against redemptive death that will not die."

My father's romantic, factual stance, five feet four inches tall like his hero, Don Quixote, blending honor with chivalry, where the difficult discovery of sane words shapes the insane battlegrounds of history.

My last year in high school was a fade-out rather than a progress. My parents were drifting apart. I could sense it, as they were living in separate bedrooms, pursuing their own private interests. I was graduating from high school too young, barely seventeen years old. There was no distinction in my record, just a sliding through. My active participation on the basketball team had foundered in my junior year. I broke too many pairs of glasses, and there was no way to play in safety with glasses as is so common in basketball today. Also, beset by sporadic asthma that made minor colds a severe test in breathing, I conferred with the junior varsity coach and we agreed that I should stop playing. As a result I became more of a recluse, although I tried to play wildly, and with wild scores, on the golf team in order to retain some desperate measure of athletic participation. In my increasingly frequent colds, which often confined me to my room for a week at a time with my asthmatic complications, I immersed myself in books. Books of

any kind. I became a quick, avid reader of paragraphs rather than complete narratives. I fled from book to book as if my search for quick breaths had to be reflected in rapid reading. Somehow the kinds of books I read didn't matter so much. If one book didn't stimulate my fantasies, I turned rapidly to the next book. My room was covered with books! Yet my fantasies were very physical, full of adventure and the desire for women. Suddenly I was fighting a health malady that scared me. At times the doctor would have to come in the middle of the night and give me a shot to ease my breathing and make me sleep. The relief at those times was so acute that I can still remember the bliss of that sudden sleeping oblivion. The night world became for me both a trauma of expected breathlessness, as the asthma was always worse at night, and a strange anticipation of blissful relief from pain with the blessed shot.

One advantage prevailed in this health crisis. With medical excuses, I could escape from high school faster now by car, as I had earned a driver's license at the age of sixteen, and my parents were lenient in letting me use the car because of my health. In his blunt fashion, my brother Karl taught me to drive the hard way. In our rickety family Ford, he drove me up a steep Berkeley hill, stopped halfway up at what seemed to me a vertical incline, and said, "You drive now." Although I was terrified, I didn't dare express my fear, so his sink or swim tactics worked. In fact, I became grateful to him because, with the ability of a born teacher, he simplified his driving instructions with a few pointed remarks that focused on the physical necessity to synchronize clutch and gear if I wanted to drive well. "If you can find that rare balance between clutch and gear when you shift on a steep hill," he grinned, "you can do it anywhere. I'll teach you how to double-clutch too."

Now, I possessed that teenager sense of road power and drove frequently to school. Car power, I'm afraid, led me several times to cut school in the afternoon and go to the movies. I was a mesmerized movie buff, and along with opera, these preoccupations seeded my future theatrical interests. To see movies in those days, you entered large palaces, 1920 pseudo-Baroque estates. You walked up huge staircases on red carpets to balcony heavens, where "the Children of Paradise" sat in French theatrical history. Even the toilets were large and spacious "chambers," not closets. Usually, before the enormous velvet curtains swirled open, the cathedral sound of thunderous organ music playing popular songs shook the new temple of fantasies. Where could you hide better from unwanted problems? A newsreel or travelogue, even with the pompous voice of Lowell Thomas or similar narrators, seemed to bring the world closer together, even in the midst of rising dictatorships which didn't invade the screen too much except in terms of brief, comic, satirical interludes. The fillip of cartoons added the relief of essential caricatures to the newsreel's supposed reality.

The movies themselves came in doubles like two-scoop, lavish ice cream cones. That was the reason to arm yourself with popcorn and candy—to receive the energy necessary to endure a lengthy double-bill. On the screen, as I slouched in the rear in my solitary seat, what I learned, along with the other solitary viewers indulging their fantasies (it was astonishing how this new medium of talkies enhanced the stubborn isolation and the individual fantasies of American lives), was the singular nature of *personality.* Personalities became the new sources of success, personalities leaping from films into newspapers, magazines, and advertising billboards. Clark Gable, Jean Harlow, W. C. Fields, Mae West, Norma Shearer, Leslie Howard, Gloria Swanson, William Powell, Myrna Loy—the immortal list of astonishing faces

"Mother, in her Navajo clothes"

and clothes dominated my gaping eyes. When I saw Leslie Howard on stage in San Francisco as Hamlet I could hardly believe he was real. All of these glamorous, witty *stars*—it was wonderful to see such romantic illusions. Wealth triumphed in the end—that was the continuous message glittering in those architectural wonders.

Like all young moviegoers, I was being trained to the art of personal glamour. One was not meant merely to admire people anymore. A community of people didn't exist. What was new was the individual eye trained to the individual personality. Average people were restricted to everyday jobs of boredom. These personalities, viewed in enormous close-ups that showed no wrinkles or misplaced hair, promised for everyone a life of sophistication, laughter, and secret sexual satisfaction beyond belief. Since movies weren't able because of censorship to expose much flesh or show much explicit sex (the famous Hays Office rule was in effect: if two persons are shown in bed in decorous night clothes, one person must keep his or her leg on the floor at all times), the bold screen personalities concentrated on *suggestive behavior.* If you attended the movies as often as I did, you soon thought of yourself as a secret master of suggestion. I became a connoisseur of the veiled, smoldering look, the petulant mouth, the rapacious sneer, the comic laugh, and the provocative leg.

Sometimes, the movies pretended to a new realism. To be sure, the nature of photography could convince you that you were there when you were not there. But then the inevitable personalities would seduce you again and carry you away to the land of the suggestive wink, the sleek evening gown and the handsome tuxedo, the speedy, polished car, the relaxing ocean liner, the land of luxurious living with endless available machines to which every American aspired.

Occasionally, my father, and my uncle when he was visiting, would take me to the raucous comedies of Laurel and Hardy, their special favorites. Once, they burst into fits of uncontrollable laughter and an usher appeared sternly warning them to restrain themselves. I slunk down in my seat as if to show that I wasn't one of these crazies. Oh, I had to admit to myself I liked Laurel and Hardy, Chaplin, Buster Keaton, those great comedians, but at sweet sixteen I wasn't ready for masterful slapstick, I was spellbound by the sexy personality world. So, more and more I ignored high school as I graduated. High school was too dull, too unglamorous. In my isolation, I even skipped the high school senior dance. How could I wear a tuxedo like a movie star? Where were the girls mature enough to wear romantic evening gowns? Such were my uncomfortable delusions as I prepared eagerly to enter the University of California. Maybe, in the university, with my musical abilities, I could enter this new world of personalities that was triumphing internationally. The fanatic, ludicrous appearances of Hitler and Mussolini on the international scene (Stalin was not really known much publicly as yet) only confirmed that ridiculous, grotesque gestures had no chance against the righteousness of glamorous personalities. In this ignorance I prepared for college, a freshman on the threshold of what I hoped would be a pathway into the world of personality success.

That summer, while waiting to enter college, something happened to me that seemed at the time only a singular episode. One day four of us teenagers, two boys and two girls, gathered at my family's summer home in Inverness and took off, as we occasionally did, on a long drive to Petaluma to the movies. "Going to the movies" was the chief way to get better acquainted with girls and I was beginning impulsively to seek female company. Exhilarated after the movies by a clear and beautiful night with an almost full moon, we decided abruptly to drive to Mount Vision, hike to the top, and wait to see the sun rise. Somehow there was little discussion. We were aware of how our parents might worry, what they might think, and what they might do. Maybe there was a romantic, sexual thrill at the bottom of our sudden desire, but we were old summer friends, the children of summer families, not lovers. Why were we so determined to witness dawn breaking?

Keats ended one of his sonnets we read in high school: ". . . like stout Cortez when with eagle eyes / He stared at the Pacific—and all his men / Looked at each other with a wild surmise— / Silent, upon a peak in Darien." That night all four of us were involved in a "wild surmise." What is it that youth really seeks in its sudden, whimsical, idealistic acts? Youth wants an awareness of wonder, a feeling that life contains special moments of revelation. If what we were doing was foolish without our parents' consent, we had forgotten about common sense. We were acting, mesmerized, by an elemental urge. Traditional communal cultures have always valued dawn and sunset in ceremonial ways. Clock measurements in such societies are always secondary to natural phenomena. Yet we Americans follow the clock doggedly, even inventing the *alarm* clock to govern our lives. When weathermen report the time of sunrise on television, it is always de-emphasized in small print

compared with other weather information. If you announced in the newspaper that a group was contemplating a dawn-watch on top of the highest building in town, few people would come unless it were turned into a lottery.

Why, then, did we four young people make such an impulsive choice in the waning summer of 1937? Perhaps we wanted a certain reassurance. The times were difficult, our college careers uncertain, the Spanish Civil War emphasized the totalitarian threat of war in Europe. On top of Mount Vision, then, waiting excitedly for the sun to rise, we were not only summer vacationers responding to youth's desire for romance and adventure. We felt ourselves at a crossroads in time. Vibrations of disaster were soaring through the world and we were reflecting them in our solitary way. In a state of jubilation with only a little beer and no drugs, we wanted to see the dawn rise as an invincible spectacle that would always emerge out of the night. An invincible spectacle, we knew, was hard to come by. We had tried that summer to find it in all kinds of popular activities and public events, and because of a sudden metaphysical impulse, we were seeking it now in the mythical order of time.

If we could only hint to each other of these feelings, we were struck dumb with awe as the sun's arc slowly widened on the eastern horizon. The view from east to west on top of that mountain was infinite, and we couldn't help feeling there the full majesty of space. Rarely in a lifetime can one feel a mystical connection such as we felt: the discovery that you have a soul for light; that you have witnessed the world make a spectacular ascent into dawn; that after this moment of illumination, you will never again deny the essential relationship between man and nature that urban density tends to kill; that anyone can feel the mysterious healing powers of nature if you open yourself to these revelations.

That night became for me, unconsciously, an opening into the sources of poetry, a view into the depths of natural metaphors that would help to transform my future. The four of us felt the necessity to speak and sing aloud. We stammered out our feelings in fragments of poems and songs that we remembered. When we returned to our summer homes in Inverness in the harsh light of morning, the fury of our scared parents and the punishing restrictions they imposed could not prevent our secret exultation: our little gathering of friends had witnessed the reality of wonder. Wonder is not an essence that our pragmatic American society recognizes, and we were suddenly the possessors of this unexpected, proud knowledge. We knew that wonder is something that we must always search for, the sense of wonder that is always possible, even in a threatened world despite our insecure futures. Somehow, we had discovered an elemental resource that would help us forever—that life without this sense of wonder remains incomplete and unfulfilled.

My entrance into the University of California that fall, after a summer in the country, was like entering an exciting factory, where you are very cautious at first about stepping on something dangerous. The thousands of students lined up for classes seemed destined for some kind of regimented pigeon-hole education. When I was a kid, my father's best friends had come from many different departments; the university had seemed an eager part of the community. Now the university seemed more and more specialized with less concentration on under-graduate teaching, which was swamped with large lecture classes. Departments were more turned in on themselves and professors tended to consort only with their fellow specialists. The university seemed to be leading the way into the future of mass education, participating in its own idiosyncratic way in the growing mass movements that were beginning to command this decade.

Somehow, I sensed that my college career would be splintered by the force of events. Too many things were changing rapidly in my family life and in the world for me to believe that I was entering an academic shelter for four years. So I approached my classes warily with the required liberal arts spread. Since I was thinking of a possible career in music, I took sightsinging and counterpoint, a German class, a class in Romantic Poetry (naturally after our night on Mount Vision), and an odd course in Paleontology, the only science course I thought I could pass to fulfill the science requirement. Still, these classes were a decided cut above my high school classes. I began to learn, and became more deeply involved in my voice lessons and in the world of opera. That fall I attended all of the operas during the San Francisco Opera season. After hearing Flagstad and Melchior the previous season, I was stunned again by the power of their voices in *Tristan* and *Lohengrin*. Also, that fall I heard a marvelous production of *Fidelio* with Flagstad and a perfect villain, Ludwig Hofmann, with a sinister voice as Don Pizarro. Most of the operas were staged in a rather old-fashioned way, but Herbert Graf's direction of the prisoners emerging from their dark confinement in *Fidelio* made a distinct impression on me of the dramatic possibilities of the stage. Fritz Reiner conducted all three of these operas with

"Father, around age sixty-five, at the time of his retirement from the University of California"

masterful effect. In the Italian repertory, I became particularly enamored of a new French soprano, Vina Bovy, and the American tenor Charles Kullman in *La Bohème*. Ezio Pinza, whom I had admired in earlier seasons, became a kind of model for me of the singing actor, whom I aspired to be. Pinza always seemed to transform the stage when he appeared, not only in the majestic range of his bass voice, but also in the astonishing, virtuoso dramatic characterizations that he achieved, when I would gasp, thinking, "Is that really Pinza?"

Socially, in college I was trying to participate in the new Age of Personalities that had become the American Dream, so I joined a fraternity, Alpha Delta Phi. Again I was following in my brother's successful social footsteps, although he had transferred to Harvard and I was no longer under his direct influence. Fraternities and sororities dominated the social life of the campus. If you had the right kind of personality, these organizations were the approved way to success. The alumni of these groups connected you with major job possibilities. If fraternities were like private clubs defending their secret laws, what was wrong with that? The fabric of American society was based on private associations from business clubs to country clubs.

The problem with fraternities, as I soon discovered, was that you had to conform. Freshmen had to kow-tow to upperclassmen. A certain undefined racial and economic superiority prevailed. Jews were mostly segregated in one fraternity. Blacks were almost nonexistent. Wealth enabled one to give favors and exert power. Despite the fact that the fraternity I was in was supposed to have "a literary tradition," the dominant talk was of girls, sports, parties, and booze. To be sure "study hours" prevailed in the evening, but they served merely to maintain a certain grade standard. They had nothing to do with love of education. In the fraternities, the group sense of enjoyment and enjoyable personalities prevailed against any intrusion of real cultural or educational values.

Hazing was common practice, and paddling with a long paddle indented with holes was the standard way upperclassmen maintained their rule over restless freshmen. My first paddling, which occurred after some minor insubordination brought on, no doubt, by my sullen resistance to the "gung ho" spirit of enforced brotherhood, caused both pain and humiliation. "Lower your pants, bend over, hang on to your balls!" came the order. Five stiff blows on the buttocks, and I staggered out of the room trying to restrain my tears. The pain lasted several hours, as I wandered around in a fog, cutting one of my classes, struggling to come to terms with my hatred now of the sadists who were enforcing this discipline.

During the early spring, Initiation Week proved to be the real test of endurance, whether you had "the stuff it takes," as we were told, to be a fraternity man. In the case of our freshmen group, this involved a week of being submitted to endless, humiliating chores coupled with daily brainwashing to see if we were worthy to become members. The brainwashing focused on military techniques that I was to encounter later in the army. In an upstairs council room, we were forced to sit at attention in silence on benches, in a state of extended sleeplessness for several nights. Frequently, we were lectured on our bad attitudes and our probable failure unless we were willing to change. This continuous ordeal so brainwashed one of our group, that he was caught fleeing out the window on his way to enlist in the navy, convinced that his college career was shattered because he had failed the fraternity inquisition. After the week was over and we had endured the slave labor, the

enforced sleeplessness, the cosy fraternity rules and songs that we were supposed to learn, our final initiation ceremony was supposed to be a grand turnaround. The tormentors were now beaming hosts extending the secret grip of brotherhood, welcoming us to success, thrusting food and drink into our exhausted hands, permitting us to meet similar beaming, successful, grey-haired alumni who were still bound to their youthful memories of Initiation Week ritual punishments and achievements.

Most of my new fraternity brothers were decent, well-meaning people, soon to be successful in their chosen professions. Why was I so naive in reacting against these fraternity games so strongly? It seemed to me that fraternities gave exactly the wrong kind of support to the educational community. Any real educational community was supposed to create at least the possibility of wonder and pride in its imaginative and scholarly aims. Whereas, fraternities and sororities were mainly ways of stressing and achieving social and economic power in colleges and universities. Clearly, they existed on campus mainly to provide a business-oriented, managerial society with a network of social, hierarchical connections and future job opportunities.

Of course, the relatively few fraternities and sororities that have survived on college campuses in the 1980s are greatly changed. The general hazing of Initiation Week is no longer permitted, and these organizations are no longer permitted officially to discriminate. In general, however, the fraternity system that prevailed for many years was fraternally and culturally antidemocratic and fostered the kinds of privileges and materialistic money values that had nothing to do with Whitman's humanistic sense of "brotherhood." In my growing disillusionment, I stayed away from the fraternity as much as possible, eating only occasional lunches there. Since I was sleeping at home, it was relatively easy to distance myself from the fraternity, even though I felt a little uneasy. What was it that compelled me to a certain outsider status? Why couldn't I transform my solitary personality and enjoy the social mix that was, after all, shaping our society?

At home I was becoming more and more aware of my parents' estrangement. One day, returning home unexpectedly, I met my father in the front hall with his attractive former graduate student, Isabel Magaña. She seemed embarrassed and I wondered why, but my father was then in his early sixties and too much of a dominant family figure to imagine him straying. So it was a profound shock early in the summer of 1937, to be summoned formally by my parents into the Big Room. Our periodic family conferences were almost always held informally in the kitchen, or father's study. What had caused this serious formal encounter in mother's Big Room that she had built to fulfill her artistic passions?

Uneasily, my parents seated me in front of the large black-painted fireplace, and I knew some disaster was impending. Suddenly weeping, unable to control herself, my mother poured out the bitter words: "Your father wants a divorce!" Father began to defend himself by admitting that he had fallen in love with Isabel Magaña. Mother countered, "It's not love, it's a temporary passion for a young woman. I want him to take time to consider his folly!" I sat there stunned, listening to their arguments that stammered back and forth through their mutual tears. Why couldn't I cry too? I could barely focus on what they were saying as Mother kept insisting on "your father's folly"—a word that I would never forget—and Father kept insisting doggedly that he wanted a divorce now. "I won't give it to him now," Mother cried, "I want him to wait until he comes to his senses!"

Folly! Senses! Amidst the tears, the laments, and the pleas, I sat there, shifting back and forth in my uncomfortable seat, wanting only to get up and flee. What could I do to solve this love triangle? "Don't blame him!" my mother continued. "He doesn't know what he's doing!" "I don't want to blame either of you," I muttered, caught in the middle. So, my first year in college came to an end, and I had no idea how my future was about to change forever.

In the summer of 1938, with a friend, John Partridge, along for companionship, I accompanied my mother to Switzerland. In her depression, she had resolved to work with Dr. Jung again. She had made an agreement with my father that he would wait a year for his divorce. Time, she was convinced, was on her side, if only she could work her way into a healthier state of mind. The time was not ripe. In Paris, where we stopped on Bastille Day, people were dancing in the streets without any sense of the impending war. As we crossed the border into Switzerland, the trains were already undergoing blackout rehearsals. If no one else in Europe, except the Nazis, was prepared for war, the Swiss were ready. They were calling up reserves, training troops constantly, mining tunnels against invasion.

While I was studying voice and German in Switzerland, dreaming of becoming an opera singer, glad to be away from college, I was sentenced to poetry by a singular event. Rilke says that you must absorb experiences and memories deep into your blood before they can ripen into poetry of any depth. Newly eighteen, a naive American suddenly in the midst of European turmoil, what did I know about depth? I began studying singing and German in Zürich, while mother was working with Dr. Jung. We lived in the small Hotel Sonne on the lake near Jung's home in Küsnacht, and I commuted by ferry or train several times a week to Zürich for my lessons.

I studied voice with Albert Emmerich, the eminent bass-baritone from Vienna, who was desperately trying to avoid returning to his homeland since it had been annexed by the Nazi state. During my lessons the phone would often ring. The Nazi consul in Zürich was summoning Emmerich back to the "Fatherland" to sing. Emmerich gave a long list of engagements, many of them false, that he had to fulfill before his return. With a compulsory, mock "Heil Hitler!", he would bang the phone down and curse the Nazis. When I saw him play Mephistopheles in Gounod's *Faust,* his quicksilver, leering face, peering out of the gloomy light, convinced me that he was indeed a demonic actor. How could this balding, smiling, forty-year-old, with the changing, rubbery face, who kept hitting me in the stomach demanding more diaphragm support, transform himself in so many mesmerizing ways? As Sarastro, in Mozart's *Magic Flute,* he was the epitome of ancient, sacred dignity. Emmerich was a student of the great Italian baritone Antonio Scotti, and he believed in floating the tone effortlessly, bel canto-style. Struggling vainly for this pure tone, I tended to admire more the Devil of transformations. Emmerich was a great actor-singer with a good voice, not a great voice. But he was a great teacher and I was learning as much about theatre as I was about singing.

German I studied with Frau Wassermann, the attractive widow of the recently deceased German novelist Jakob Wassermann. Her brother was Oskar Karlweis, the comedian, whom I later saw with open-mouthed admiration for his agile gestures, as the cunning Jakobowsky, out-maneuvering the anti-Semitic Polish colonel, in Franz Werfel's successful Broadway play about refugees escaping from Hitler, *Jakobowsky and the Colonel.* Frau Wassermann, whom I always thought of reverently as *Frau,* a woman of universal experience never to be reduced to a mere first name, gave me poems, especially love poems, to read and memorize in German. What a way to learn German!

Lovesick, I followed her eyes and lovely, expanding breasts, as she read the poems aloud so I could hear the correct rhythmical phrasing and proper pronunciation. I began to dream about her at night, but it was a loveless time. She liked me, even encouraged a certain intimacy in her loneliness and dreams of immigrating to the United States. After their invasion of Austria, the Nazis had confiscated her money and property deriving from her Jewish husband's huge pre-Nazi reputation in Germany, when his novels had been considered the equal of those by Heinrich and Thomas Mann. Poverty-stricken, living in a small room with the few personal treasures she had managed to salvage, she was intent only on surviving in the Zürich refugee turmoil. All I could hope for, despite my longings, was her dedicated, passionate teaching. She liked me, and our lessons were a time when she could relax from her frantic efforts to support herself through journalism.

During our lessons, Frau Wassermann didn't say much about politics. She preferred to concentrate on poetry, as if the manic nationalistic rhythms that had ripped apart her life could be subdued by poetry's enduring classical forms. Unlike my unfortunate high school English teacher, she read the classical forms passionately as if they were living emotions. Occasionally, in a fit of sudden rage, she would express her

disdain of the Nazis: "They have no poets! Not one! How can you speak poetry when you have to say 'Heil Hitler!' in military uniforms!"

In the Zürich streets, as the crowded banks filled with secret, international money, I became aware of a new word—*espionage.* Spies from the Nazi, Fascist, and Communist countries were feared everywhere. My teachers would sometimes look out the window or check their mail to express their fear of being spied upon. I felt as if I were living in a tense atmosphere of intrigue. A Swiss student, also studying with Emmerich, informed me that he was training constantly in the army reserve forces and likely to be called up at any time. In the art galleries and museums, I saw the work of the great refugee German painters, particularly the expressionists whom the Nazis had barred from exhibiting as "degenerate artists." It was clear that, hypocritically, the Nazis were selling these paintings on the international market to gather funds for their own nationalistic concerns. In the opera house, I attended the world premiere of Paul Hindemith's *Mathis Der Mahler,* and applauded strongly as Hindemith's bald, gnome-like figure took his curtain calls. Why could this innovative music be

The author's daughters, Deborah and Susie

performed only in exile? Ironically, the Nazis seemed to be defeating their nationalistic aims by exporting German culture to Europe and the United States, and forbidding it at home.

In the late summer of 1938 I took a brief trip to Salzburg to visit the music festival. Salzburg was deceptive. Nazi banners and signs were everywhere. The people seemed almost happy about the Nazi "Anschluss." On a main street, however, there were large signs, *Judengeschäft,* pasted on the windows of a store, and the lonely, worried, trapped face of the owner inside, a haunted face I later incorporated into my long dramatic poem *The Stalingrad Elegies.* In the park, I saw a huge display box of incredibly distorted racial photographs. These ludicrously exaggerated hooked noses were the types I was supposed to hate. In the middle of the display box—I couldn't believe my eyes! There was the broad nose and the scowl of Joe Louis! I was supposed to hate blacks as well as Jews! Then, I remembered, of course, the German resentment of Louis because of his championship fights with the German heavyweight Max Schmeling. A newly typewritten notice in the park indicated that Jews were no longer even permitted to walk in the park. In a fit of anger, I tore down the notice and stuffed it quickly in my pocket, looking around with sudden fear to see if I was being watched.

A limited international representation still prevailed in the music festival, although Toscanini was conspicuously absent in protest against the Nazi takeover. I heard Ezio Pinza give another great singing and acting performance as Don Giovanni. The great German pianist, Edwin Fischer, played with solitary aloofness and majesty on another program. Wilhelm Furtwängler performed the Bruckner Seventh Symphony in intensely slow perfection, and I saw him later on the street, riding off in lonely isolation glowering from the rear seat of his open sedan driven by a chauffeur. How was it possible that such marvelous performances could still exist under the new Nazi tyranny? Was I seeing the end of German musical culture delayed only by a few older men forced to compromise with their new Nazi masters? Did they have to compromise despite their positions of musical power? *Collaborators* was a hateful term I was beginning to hear and think about.

In Munich, I witnessed a rare encounter with the Nazis. I traveled to Munich to see the world premiere of Richard Strauss's new opera, *Friedenstag* (Peace Day). Strauss was said to have cooperated with the Nazis for a time because of a Jewish daughter-in-law. Although born in Munich, he had feuded with his native city and premiered his famous operas else-

where. This occasion was supposed to be a great reunion between Strauss and his native city, where his father had played French horn in the opera house. Why was Strauss now, as an old man, producing a new opera with the provocative title of "Peace Day" in a time when Hitler was clearly preparing for war? Walking through the city before the evening premiere, I passed the memorial to the Nazi "martyrs" of the abortive putsch that Hitler had staged in Munich in 1924, and the rigid, motionless, "Honor Guard" stationed there sent tremors of fear through my body.

The Nationaltheater, the state opera house, was sold out that night, with a long line of people standing in line, waiting hopefully for unavailable tickets. Strauss's aged figure, topped by a fringe of white hair, was visible prominently in a box, as he and his wife kept greeting friends. Brightly lit by spotlights focused on a huge red swastika flag that signaled authority, the center box was conspicuously empty. The Nazi leaders were deliberately boycotting this occasion to show their contempt for Strauss's theme of peace. Even though the opera was set in medieval times, it was clear from the audience's frequent applause that many people appreciated Strauss's symbolic message. After the performance, Strauss and his favorite conductor, Clemens Krauss, and the fine cast led by Hans Hotter and Vioreca Ursuleac, took seventeen curtain calls to standing ovations, which could only be considered a defiance of the Nazis. Leaving the theatre, hearing the buzz of excited conversation about Strauss's daring gesture against Hitler's warlike policies, I came to have a different feeling of respect for Strauss's previous, enigmatic conduct with the Nazis. Here was a man who had become almost a recluse amongst the Nazis, but he wouldn't let his genius, in the end, be co-opted by their tyranny, since he knew that his Germany would disappear in the inevitable war that was approaching.

Ghost Voice: Albert Emmerich

Jimmy, the would-be American singer. He had a thin voice that I tried to make thicker. Somehow he had a sense of poetic phrasing and a love for drama that made me keep trying to teach him despite all the obstacles. He was all tied up in knots. That's why I kept hitting him in the stomach to loosen him up. Americans are as tight as drums. They always seem to be on the move and they don't know where they're going. Jimmy was eighteen years of American naivete and shyness. Once, I brought him backstage with me. I thought his eyes would pop out of his head as he ogled the ladies in their make-up and bright costumes. When he saw me pat one on the rear in operatic comradeship, he wanted to do that too. He was starved for sex. What a puritan country is the United States! What could I do there if I could find engagements? Every time Jimmy came for a lesson, he ogled my wife. As a Viennese, I take that as a compliment. My wife is a big, shapely lady with dark eyes. When she offered Jimmy a cup of tea, Jimmy's hand would tremble when he brushed hers and she would laugh teasingly. Then he would sing for me a Schubert song, and you could hear Jimmy's sexual frustrations surging through his blocked tone that I was trying to liberate. Jimmy! Support! Support! Breathe as if you were a free man! And I'd hit him in the stomach again . . .

With Jimmy I had a fantasy of escape. I hated to say "Heil Hitler" to the Nazi authorities, instead of "Grüss Gott." "Why don't you come to New York and sing at the Metropolitan?" Jimmy would ask. "You arrange it. You be my American manager," I'd joke, "but what'll I do in New York? If I have to look at skyscrapers all the time, I'll get a stiff neck. And I don't speak English. I sing German and Italian, and fake Russian—that's what I sing." "You can learn to sing in English too." "Jimmy, you don't understand. I'm trying to teach you how to sing and act the words at the same time. The gesture of the phrasing is just as important as the melodic line. A great singer sings along the line of the words as if the language is a cutting saw. If you don't hear the language, if you don't hear every syllable correctly, you don't hear the proper phrasing of the music. How can I hear my German language in New York, let alone sing English? Do you understand?" "I think I understand . . ." "Good, let's see if you understand. We'll sing Schubert's *Death and the Erl-King.*"

I try to show Jimmy the difference between the pleading and the commanding voices in Schubert's great song, how the magnetic body must transform with each voice. After we finish, I say sadly: "This is why I'm afraid to go to the United States. I need my German for darkness and my Italian for sunshine and warmth."

So I never went to the United States. I was forced to sing poor performances in German opera houses as the Nazis corrupted our language and the style of production with their cheap rhetoric and their gaudy sense of spectacle. Despite my age, during the last years of the war, I was forced to serve in the army on the eastern front, where Hitler tried to become a new Napoleon and succeeded only in becoming another victim of Russian winter. In the last year of the war, our cities bombed to ruins, myself ill in a hospital, I dreamt of Jimmy, the would-be singer. I dreamt that we would have to create a new language after the war. Jimmy and I, eager student and fervent teacher, would have to create a new international singing language together. In the midst of the stupid racial hate, in the shattered buildings and the shadows of new horrifying weapons that every war seemed to develop with voracious appetite, our new language would sing along the line of the words, words and music acting together to achieve a new harmony, an instinctive understanding, a fresh sense of the heart singing free from war and false super-patriots carrying the banners of nationalism. When I awoke, of course, I realized it was a wondrous dream, but I preferred the dream to the reality in which I was forced to live.

James Schevill

With Emmerich and Frau Wassermann, I was beginning to get a new sense of the reality of good teaching, unfettered by institutional restrictions. Here were proud, sensitive people struggling desperately, in the midst of tyrannical experience, to communicate the power of music and language. But the only way I could really learn about the darkness of Nazism was to experience it directly one fall day in October 1938 that changed my life. An American friend of mine, Jack Kent—later to become a distinguished city and regional planner—was studying at the University of Freiburg in Germany, and invited me to visit him. This was the city where my uncle had received his Ph.D. in history in the late nineteenth century and his enthusiasm for this old medieval town made me anxious to see it before such visits became impossible. I agreed to bring with me some extra American dollars that Jack needed, despite the Nazi restrictions on bringing foreign money into Germany. By report the Nazis weren't as yet searching tourists with American passports. Still . . . I resolved with youthful bravado to hide the money in my jockstrap for security.

Crossing the Swiss border into Germany at night, I could see batteries of lights blazing in the distance. Day and night, the Germans were building their Siegfried Line as a bluff to counteract the supposedly impregnable French Maginot Line. As it turned out, of course, the German generals planned a tank attack around the Maginot Line to invade Holland, Belgium, and France. At the border, the Nazi customs official who entered the compartment and demanded my passport, caused my heart to skip a beat. Sitting skeptically in a movie theatre, you see the head and face of brutality as a stereotype. Impossible, the face of evil is not like that. But when I saw a thick-necked, barren shaved head with gimlet eyes and a thin, sneering mouth that promised cruelty, I felt a flush of fear like a tidal wave. The money in my jock strap seemed to burn my groin and bulge too obviously. The shaved head held out an imperious hand demanding proper identity. Examining my passport sharply with increasing contempt, his eyes switched back and forth slowly from my features to the passport's photograph as though he wanted to make sure what Americans looked like. Then, he proceeded to examine the passport, page by blank page slowly, as if some incriminating evidence might reveal itself. When he asked if I was carrying any money or forbidden gifts, I stammered out that I couldn't understand German—advice that I had received from several travelers. I was petrified that he would start searching me because he was taking so long in confronting me. Finally, he turned away, sharply turning his back on me as if I were too small fish for his official bait. When the train arrived in Freiburg, I was still trembling.

At the station, Jack and I had a joyous reunion. On the way to the inexpensive, small hotel room he had booked for me, we conversed eagerly about old hometown friends and events as though Germany did not exist. The old Gothic buildings and narrow streets were reassuring. Here was an ancient university town of culture and tradition which seemed to exist beyond the Nazis. As we turned into the street where my hotel was located, we saw a fire at the end of the street and men in uniform bustling around, keeping back the small crowd that was gathering. Approaching curiously to see what was going on, we were restrained by a group of policemen who had suddenly appeared. In the distance we caught a glimpse of an elderly man and woman being pushed into a car by some uniformed men. "Who are those men?" I asked Jack. "I don't know," he answered. "They're not police. It looks as though those people are being arrested." "Let's get out of here," I said, feeling nervous about the money in my jockstrap.

Somehow I felt lonely and abandoned in my hotel room that night. I had given Jack the money and he had left, after we had arranged to meet again in the morning. Why didn't I feel relieved after giving him the money? Something about the fire and the men in uniform had made us uneasy. We should have celebrated our reunion, but that evening there didn't seem like much to celebrate. Better go to bed

and start fresh in the morning to see the town and the university. Still I couldn't sleep . . . I tossed and tossed in the hard, uncomfortable bed. Through the thin walls, I heard a couple arrive in the room next door. They were giggling, laughing, drinking, some kind of officer and a woman he had picked up. I heard her question him about the fire. "Just a minor operation," he answered. "It's none of your business." She didn't like that, but he wouldn't tell her anything more. He was eager to get down to business and laughed her into bed, stilling her questions. Soon I could hear the sound of bouncing bedsprings and passionate grunts. Passion against burning, the fire outside versus the fire inside. Was there some fated connection between the strange fire we had witnessed in the street, and the purchased passion I was hearing inside? I couldn't sleep that night, and it was morning before I drifted into wild dreams.

The next morning I woke to Jack's excited hammering on the door. His words tumbled out so rapidly that I had to slow him down before I understood him. What we had witnessed, what we could not identify, was *Kristallnacht,* the night all over Germany when Goering's SA troopers had been assigned to attack Jewish stores and burn synagogues in retaliation for the crazed Dutchman Van Der Lubbe's murder of a German diplomat in Paris. At the end of the street we had seen the old Freiburg synagogue burning. The old couple, who were being pushed into the car by uniformed men, were the rabbi and his wife being arrested by SA troopers. And the officer I had heard with the prostitute was undoubtedly an SA officer indulging his passion after the fire.

Walking into the street where the sun was now shining clearly and coldly on a bright fall day, we turned instinctively down the street where the synagogue had been situated. The street contained only a few pedestrians. A couple of policemen were standing idly on a corner. No storm troopers were visible. Astonishingly, a wooden fence had been built around the burned-down synagogue during the night, as if to conceal what had happened! I felt as though I had been hallucinating. These events were a nightmare. The Germans were a civilized people. My grandparents were German immigrants. Such brutal actions were impossible. But we could see passing German citizens stealing uneasy looks at the peculiar, neatly built wooden fence, as if they were looking at some unbelievable event. Later that day, we heard from other American exchange students at the university about the attacks against the Jews that had happened throughout Germany. From now on, there could be no mistaking what the Nazis intended to do with the Jewish population.

When I was alone in my hotel room, a deep silence prevailed. The whole town seemed to have gone to sleep as if to avoid dealing with this nightmare. Suddenly, overwhelmed by a strange mixture of guilt and anger, I wrote the first poem I had ever written in my life. At the time, of course, I didn't know it was a crucial poem. I had no idea that from this point on, my life would be dedicated to poetry, and that my intent on a musical career was now forever changed. All I did was to scribble out a bad, angry poem, which I kept somehow. I soon learned that it was a false poem written out of a rage that made it simplistic and literal. I hadn't yet earned the right to speak about the fate of the Jews. What I had discovered, though, was the reality of poetry, that words could reflect emotional responses in a direct, powerful way. From that point on, I began to read and respect poetry in a different way. Poetry was not just a series of refined, expert aesthetic structures. With its unique power of compression, poetry could reflect the raw experiences of life in a way that transformed and transcended the printed page. It was not enough to cleanse myself of my confused, tumultuous emotions. Poetry was more than that. It was a grappling with corrupt language, corrupt actions. It was a way to attempt to discover the truth, even if the truth was never really discoverable.

Back in Switzerland, my mother was puzzled by the change in my personality. While she was shocked and understood my reactions to the evil events I had observed, as a poet herself she read my poem correctly as a beginning, poor poem about a shocking encounter. She could never really know how I was changed forever. Indeed, even though I began reading and devouring poetry and plays avidly, I could not know for several years that I had discovered in poetry and drama the art of making over my life.

Walking with the Dutch novelist Henk Meijer, Newport, Rhode Island, 1974

BIBLIOGRAPHY

Plays:

High Sinners, Low Angels (music by author; arranged by Robert Commanday; produced in San Francisco, 1953), Bern Porter, 1953.

The Bloody Tenet (also see below; produced in Providence, Rhode Island, 1956), Meridian, 1957.

Voices of Mass and Capital A (music by Andrew Imbrie; produced in San Francisco, 1962), Friendship Press, 1962.

The Master (also see below), produced in San Francisco, 1963.

American Power: The Space Fan [and] *The Master* (also see below), produced in Minneapolis, 1964.

The Black President and Other Plays (includes *The Bloody Tenet, American Power: The Space Fan, The Master,* and *The Black President*), Alan Swallow, 1965.

The Death of Anton Webern (also see below), produced in Fish Creek, Wisconsin, 1966.

This Is Not True (music by Paul McIntyre), produced in Minneapolis, 1967.

Lovecraft's Follies (produced in Providence, 1970), Swallow Press, 1971.

Oppenheimer's Chair, produced in Providence, 1970.

The Pilots, produced in Providence, 1970.

The Ushers, produced in Providence, 1971.

The American Fantasies, produced in New York, 1972.

Emperor Norton Lives!, produced in Salt Lake City, 1972, revised version produced as *Emperor Norton* (music by Jerome Rosen), San Francisco, 1979.

Fay Wray Meets King Kong (also see below), produced in Providence, 1974.

Sunset and Evening Stance; or, Mr. Krapp's New Tapes (also see below), produced in Providence, 1974.

Cathedral of Ice, edited by Peter Kaplan (produced in Providence, 1975), Pourboire Press, 1975, reprinted in *Plays of the Holocaust,* edited by Elinor Fuchs, Theatre Communications Group, 1989.

Naked in the Garden, produced in Providence, 1975.

The Telephone Murderer (also see below), produced in Providence, 1975.

Year after Year, produced in Providence, 1976.

Questioning Woman, produced in Providence, 1980.

(And director) *Mean Man I,* produced in Providence, 1981.

Edison's Dream, produced in Providence, 1982.

(And director) *Mean Man II,* produced in Providence, 1982.

Cult of Youth, produced in Minneapolis, 1984.

(With Adrian Hall) *Galileo* (adaptation of play by Bertolt Brecht), produced in Providence, 1984.

(And director) *Mean Man III,* produced in Providence, 1985.

Collected Short Plays, Swallow Press/Ohio University Press, 1986.

(And director) *The Planner,* produced in Providence, 1986.

Time of the Hand and Eye, produced in Providence, 1986.

(And director) *The Storyville Doll Lady,* produced in Providence, 1987.

(And codirector with cast) *Shadows of Memory* (two plays, *Ape God,* about Dian Fossey, and *The Radiator,* about Djuna Barnes), produced in Edinburgh, 1989.

American Fantasies (a production in German of Schevill's short plays and performance poems), Rostock, East Germany, 1990.

Mother O or The Last American Mother, produced in Providence, 1990.

(And codirector with Barbara Blossom) *Sisters in the Limelight,* produced in Providence, 1990.

Poetry:

Tensions, Bern Porter, 1947.

The American Fantasies, Bern Porter, 1951.

The Right to Greet, Bern Porter, 1955.

Selected Poems 1945–1959, Bern Porter, 1960.

Private Dooms and Public Destinations: Poems 1945–1962, Alan Swallow, 1962.

The Stalingrad Elegies, Alan Swallow, 1964.

The Buddhist Car (also see below), Walton Press, 1968.

Release, Hellcoal Press, 1968.

Violence and Glory: Poems 1962–1968 (includes "The Death of Anton Webern"), Swallow Press, 1969.

The Buddhist Car and Other Characters, Swallow Press, 1973.

Pursuing Elegy: A Poem about Haiti, Copper Beech Press, 1974.

The Mayan Poems, Copper Beech Press, 1978.

Fire of Eyes: A Guatemalan Sequence, Copper Beech Press, 1979.

The American Fantasies: Collected Poems, 1945–1981, Swallow Press/Ohio University Press, 1983.

The Invisible Volcano, Copper Beech Press, 1985.

Ambiguous Dancers of Fame: Collected Poems, 1945–1986, Swallow Press/Ohio University Press, 1987.

Editor:

Ferdinand Schevill, *Six Historians,* University of Chicago Press, 1956.

(And author) *Break Out! In Search of New Theatrical Environments,* Swallow Press, 1973.

(With Edwin Honig) *Wastepaper Theatre Anthology* (includes *Fay Wray Meets King Kong, Sunset and Evening Stance; or, Mr. Krapp's New Tapes,* and *The Telephone Murderer*), Pourboire Press, 1978.

Contributor:

Fifteen Modern American Poets, edited by George P. Elliott, Rinehart & Company, 1956.

The New Modern Poetry: British and American Poetry Since World War II, edited by M. L. Rosenthal, Macmillan, 1967.

Where Is Vietnam?, edited by Walter Lowenfels, Anchor Books, 1967.

Some Haystacks Don't Even Have Any Needle and Other Complete Modern Poems, edited by Stephen Dunning, Edward Lueders, and Hugh Smith, Scott, Foresman, 1969.

Reader I New Letters, edited by David Ray, University of Missouri, 1983.

The Treasury of American Poetry, edited by Nancy Sullivan, Doubleday, 1984.

Other:

Sherwood Anderson: His Life and Work, University of Denver Press, 1951.

The Roaring Market and the Silent Tomb (biographical study of the scientist and artist Bern Porter), Abbey Press, 1957, 2d edition, Bern Porter, 1968.

The Arena of Ants (novel), Copper Beech Press, 1977.

Performance Poems (recording), Cambridge Records, 1984.

Author of radio plays, including *The Sound of a Soldier,* 1945; *The Death of a President,* 1945; *The Cid* (adaptation of the play by Corneille), 1963. Contributing translator to *Classic Theatre Anthology,* Anchor Books, 1961. Former editor of *Berkeley: A Journal of Modern Culture.*

Schevill's papers are housed in a manuscript collection at the John Hay Library, Brown University, Providence, Rhode Island.

Arturo Vivante

1923-

I was born upside down, wrong side up, head last, and nearly died in the process. Luckily the midwife, who, two years before, had delivered my brother, saw in good time that mine was going to be a difficult case and asked for an obstetrician. My father called the best in Rome, and I was saved.

My first memory is of my father on the roof terrace of our house in Castel Gandolfo, from which you could see Rome and the sea, saying to my mother, "What a beautiful sunset." Or was it of my brother crying when he hit his head on a grotto in our garden?

My father was a philosopher who right to the end of his life thought he would make a living from his books. My grandfather, a law professor in Rome, soon saw this wasn't likely to happen, and, in the hope that his son could become self-supporting, bought him a country estate in Tuscany, a few miles outside of Siena. I was four when we moved there, and I remember leaving the old station in a taxi, skirting the walls of town along a curving road, and two vans arriving with our belongings. They were so tall they couldn't get through the gate of our front yard.

The place was rather remote, and Siena, though a pretty town, wasn't the lively center it once had been. It was, in fact, dormant. Tourism, which before the First World War had livened the town up and which was to liven it up again after the Second, was—with fascism and the Depression—down in the thirties. The university, though one of the world's oldest, had only the faculties of medicine and law. The hospital, also ancient, was the single busy place except for the market on market days. The schools, most of them converted from monasteries and convents, retained their original bare, ascetic look. On winter evenings the town was positively grim. Stark, too, with its narrow, windy streets. As if the cold and frozen Middle Ages weren't enough, the walls were pasted with death notices, and you were quite likely to meet men in black hoods—members of the medieval confraternity of the Misericordia—leading a funeral procession. The morbidity rate in Siena was among the highest in the nation. Owners of the nearby villas—stodgy, titled people—for the most part passed their time in a club, playing bridge or billiards.

Arturo Vivante in his father's arms. His brother Paolo on right, 1925

My mother would have preferred Florence. Much. But she wasn't used to having her own way, and raised no objections to the choice of Siena.

To make up for its lacks, she and my father—both of whom had grown up in Rome and liked company—invited friends, old and new, usually painters and writers, to come and stay. In contrast to Siena, a town crowded within its walls, with streets that the sun reached but never really bathed, our house—Villa Solaia—was sand-colored, the color of the sun, and had an open, spacious atmosphere. Though lived in all year round, it had been built in the early 1800s as a countryhouse, with plenty of doors, two loggias, large windows, and high ceilings.

281

In front, below the terraced yard and garden, were several gigantic evergreens, old as the house—three pines, with sparse branches and colossal, scaly trunks curved toward the top by the west wind; five cypresses, which, like huge dark flames, waved in the wind and sometimes were bent by it almost to the point of breaking and kept in that constrained position till its force abated, when always they returned to point straight upward at the zenith. Those cypresses, I soon climbed them all and found bedlike resting places in the tufted needles that, at various levels, had collected. My mother was apt to change her mind about company and claim she wanted to be alone. The guests, she said, were fine—very dear, congenial, and all that—but everyone had the right to a bit of solitude. "Soon they'll go and we'll be all alone, *cocchino,*" she would tell me, and pat my knee. But when they finally did go—and sometimes they stayed for months—she would often fall into a silent, somber mood. And we looked forward to a visitor, for then—at least at the front door—she would be forced to smile. We depended on her smile. Guests brought it on, and a hundred other things, of course—a brood of newborn chicks, fluffy and golden in a basket, looking up at her in unison, or the sun shining on a newborn leaf, or perhaps a letter. Not my father's jokes, I'm afraid, or his attentions. But a newborn leaf! An urge to draw it, or paint it, or embroider it (she said threads came in a greater variety of colors than did pigments) would assail her, and for a happy day it was a communion between her and the leaf. She was a painter born. She never had an exhibition, though. She didn't care. She was too modest and at the same time too proud. Beyond worldly contest. A woman busy with the children and the house, and with her husband, who kept calling her—to read a paragraph he had written, bring up a word he was looking for, or some problem connected with the publication of a book, a letter he had received no reply to, his hopes for a huge peach orchard he had planted, the heavy financial situation connected with the estate. She was never too busy to listen, never resentful of being interrupted, always ready to put away her work, though with a sigh. Most of her canvases were hidden in closets when they should have been hung—not just in the house but in a gallery for everyone to see.

One day, in third grade, we were asked to write an essay on why we loved our mother. While everyone said they loved their mother because she did so much for them, worked so hard, looked after them so well, gave them presents, and so forth, I simply said I loved her because she was so lovely and good and

dear. Much to my and the other students' astonishment, my little essay was singled out by my teacher as the best. That was my first literary success. The next, in fifth grade, was a poem I wrote about the stars. My father liked it so much he read it aloud and showed it to friends and to my teacher, who had the class listen to it. That early encouragement set me on a course that I still keep. Of my early influences what can I say? My father's appreciation and my mother's help were probably the most important. As a painter she looked more at what she was painting than at the canvas. I tried to do the same while writing. Even before that I remember her bedtime stories, how they held me, especially those that she said were "from the truth." Later she would sometimes help me with an essay. Through her I learned how one detail, accurately drawn, or one right word, can bring life to a picture.

In the early thirties, when my two brothers and I were children, if we saw an airplane flying over our house we would wave, then run into the house to tell my mother about it. "It was flying really low," we would say, hoping to stir her. "Perhaps it was Uncle Lauro." We would watch her. But her face wouldn't brighten. Her eyes, which we had known to be so lively, looked at us dully. The fascists had done this to her, we told ourselves, and hated them with a rich, deep hate.

In October 1931, Lauro de Bosis, her youngest brother, thirty years old, had taken off from the Côte d'Azur in a small airplane and scattered antifascist leaflets over Rome. From the terrace of his home on the top of an apartment house near the Piazza di Spagna, his mother—my grandmother Lillian—had watched the plane flying around and around, and the leaflets showering down from it, some falling on the terrace itself. She knew it was he both from the leaflets, which she had helped print, and from the manner of the enterprise. She had seen people on the street below eagerly picking them up, reading them, folding them, and putting them in their pockets. Then the plane, in the twilight, had headed west, toward Corsica, and no one ever saw it or my uncle again.

I came on my mother in the kitchen the day she heard that he was missing. Leaning against a table there, she told me about it. It was late evening. We remained silent in the gloom. My brothers and I were going to a small country school near Siena. For children under ten—I wasn't quite eight at the time of Lauro's death—we were sharply aware of politics. Lauro had written a half-dozen pages in French, under the title "The Story of My Death," the night before the flight, and sent them to a friend with the request that they be published if he should not come back. "Tomorrow," the document began, "at three o'clock, on a meadow of the Côte d'Azur, I have an appointment with Pegasus. Pegasus—it is the name of my airplane—has a russet body and white wings. Though he's as strong as eighty horses, he's as nimble as a swallow. Drunk with gasoline, he bounds through the skies like his brother of old, but if he wants to, at night, he can glide in the air like a phantom. I found him in the Hercynian Forest, and his old master is going to bring him to me on the coast of the Tyrrhenian Sea, believing in good faith that he will serve the pleasures of an idle young Englishman. My bad accent hasn't awakened his suspicions: may he pardon my deception. All the same we are not going to hunt chimeras, but to bring a message of freedom to an enslaved people across the sea. To do away with metaphors (which I had to use to leave discreetly vague the origins of my airplane), we are going to Rome to scatter in the open air these words of freedom which for seven years have been forbidden like a crime. . . ."

Arturo Vivante, England, 1937

I knew parts of it by heart, and for me the words were a purification from the sodden propaganda I saw on the walls and had to hear at school. They made me indignant, too; I remember tearing to pieces the registration card I got at the beginning of the term, because it had a picture of the fasces on it.

Our classmates were the children of neighboring farmers, who, like my family, had no use for fascism. The only fascist I remember at the school, and the first one I think I ever met, was an inspector who came from Siena to sell us party bonds. They cost ten lire each, or about half a dollar, which was a laborer's day's pay at the time. The inspector told us that when we were twenty-one we would get a dividend from the bonds, and that we each had to buy one. He would come back the next day for the money. The next day, he returned, and he collected from everyone except a strong, freckled boy who said his father had refused to give him the ten lire. For minutes, in front of the whole class, the man swore and shouted at him in a ruthless way. It gave me an excellent idea of the kind of people fascists were. The boy—he must have been eight or nine years old—stood by his desk without saying a word. He didn't cry. He only flushed a little.

The next school we went to—a junior high school—was in Siena. We had a bay horse, Graziella, or Gracie. A smart young farmer, who entertained my brothers and me with stories of his sentimental conquests and plots of films that he had seen, drove us into town each morning and brought us back home in time for lunch. There were plenty of fascists in Siena. The town was theirs as the countryside never was. The moment we entered the city gate in our caleche and saw the dignified old walls pasted over with sheets of paper—usually pink and printed in block letters—we felt as if we had crossed into enemy territory. Our horse would trot fiercely over the paving stones, up a winding street, past a newsstand with the sad headlines of the thirties on a rack, past a small Anglican church, to a stable, where we left her.

There were few tourists, and the Anglican church, which had been built before the First World War, was shut. Its minister was still in Siena, though. We used to see him, in his black suit and clerical collar, wandering about the town, a shepherd looking for a flock. Then his church was boarded up. One day, my mother saw him, still wearing his Protestant minister's clothes, in the cathedral, praying.

From the stable we would walk across the center of Siena to the school—formerly a convent—at the south end of town, then through two very long corridors, the remodelled sides of a cloister, to the classrooms. Though the school was a state and not a church school, my professor was a swarthy, thunder-browed priest who lived alone in an apartment up the street. In the three years I had him he became very attached to his class. He knew not just our names and capabilities but our nicknames, characters, moods, and dispositions. Sometimes he became furious with us and shouted. When he had finished, a deathly silence would settle on the class. Once, he was so impressed by what he had achieved that he seemed awed. He looked at us for a moment and said, "What tension!" I didn't think he was a fascist, but in the Ethiopian War, when Addis Ababa fell, he rushed into the classroom with the news, his cassock flying and his long underwear showing around his ankles. The class rose and cheered. I watched with scorn, kept quiet, and felt disappointed in the man.

The government was trying to turn Italians into warlike people, and soon military training was added to our curriculum, already burdened by two periods of gymnastics. As though this weren't enough, the authorities tried to ingratiate themselves and at the same time indoctrinate us by getting us out of classes right in the middle of a lesson. We might be translating a passage of Italian into Latin when suddenly the bell would ring, the class would be dismissed, and we would hurriedly assemble in the halls. Then the head boys would arrange us in threes and march us out of the school, with the professor of gymnastics, who by now had become very important, in the lead. On these occasions our priest wouldn't come with us. He seemed almost offended by the interruptions. Hands clasped behind his back and his hat on, he would go off on his own at a quick pace. We never knew where we would be led. If we were lucky, we would just march down the main street, march back, and be disbanded. More often, though, there was some surprise—like a speech broadcast from Rome. Then, in a square in which not just our school but all the schools of Siena had assembled, after a long wait we would have to listen to a mixture of voice and static carried at an incredible volume over the loudspeakers. Packed so tight we weren't able to sit, we would await the end with aching feet. Sometimes a fascist official would clap his hands in the middle of a phrase, or chuckle as though something funny had been said. It wasn't easy to leave the formation or to get out of these shows. But one morning—we had started on a march and were heading toward the center of town down a narrow street—I found myself so close to an ice-cream store that I just made a sharp left turn and went inside.

There was a woman serving at the counter. "You've got some sense," she said to me.

I was good at writing but the worst in my class at gymnastics. So bad was I that the gym teacher, who had trained us for months for an exercise in sixty movements that was to be performed at a big rally at the end of term, told me to stay home. From home, I heard bells ring and sirens screaming, announcing that the rally had begun; the fascists always made a lot of noise on these occasions. I turned my back to the city and went for a long walk in the woods. It was a comfort to hear the sound of the cicadas.

If my family had a hero it was Shelley. There was a bust of him in my grandmother Lillian's house in Rome. Her husband, my grandfather Adolfo de Bosis, a poet, had spent a good part of his life translating him into Italian. My father admired him perhaps more than any poet, and met my mother in that way. Both of them spoke English fluently, and my mother almost without an accent, for her mother, Lillian, was American, from Springfield, Missouri. She was a tall, upright, silver-haired woman with large bony hands, spotted by time; simple and gracious, quite beautiful in her mauve or gray long dresses and her shawls. As a girl of six she had come to Rome with her father, a Methodist-Episcopal minister who founded a church there. Later he went back to America but she stayed, married Adolfo, and lived in Rome. He died in 1924, some months after I was born. In 1921, during the fascist march on Rome, he was on his terrace and saw the men on the street below. According to my mother, someone who was standing near him said exultantly, "Here is the new Italy!" He nodded gravely and said, "Unfortunately." For the fact that his death and my birth almost coincided, for everything I heard about him from my mother, and for his poems, I have always felt very close to him. To us children, my grandmother seemed the picture of virtue—any virtue, but mainly, perhaps, justice. If my brothers and I quarreled over a toy, she would seize it and say, "Grandma's," and leave us gaping at her. It never entered our minds to question her, much less to wrest the toy from her hands. Her hands. They were too big to be clever. Not cunning hands but good, strong hands that tried and did—washed children, dressed them, knit, cut, wrote—moving always with a little effort, like big instruments. They were not as wieldy as my mother's hands, which seemed to have in them a quick, creative sense and moved almost without effort, by themselves. Still, I admired my grandmother's earnest efforts. My grandfather was from Ancona, in the

Marches. In the summer we would go to an eighteenth-century tower on the sea ten miles south of Ancona which he had used as a studio. My mother felt right at home there, more at home than anywhere else. If she resembled anyone at all it was the women from near the tower. Slender and tall, their faces weathered by the sun and wind, one saw them on the mountain slope carrying bundles on their heads. She never carried bundles on her head, but had the same resistance, the same grace.

My father's family was Jewish. His father—Cesare Vivante, born in Venice, eminent lawyer and law professor in Rome—was an energetic, trim man with a goatee, reputed never to have lost a case. All Italian law students used his textbooks, and they had been widely translated. If someone talked during his lectures, he would ask the other students to throw him out, something they did with glee. The people he employed around the house were all quite remarkable and devoted to him. There was Mikhail, a lame Russian chauffeur, to whom the air of the steppe still seemed to cling, who would go to great lengths to amuse my brothers and me—pretend the carabinieri were after him, for instance, shout at them and accelerate; the mock chase made the dull streets near my grandfather's house seem exciting avenues of escape. There was Vincenzo, a Neapolitan cook—an artist from whose kitchen ascended the most appetizing smells. There was a suave waiter. And there was Adria, the housekeeper. She was a handsome woman in her early forties, with straight, glossy black hair knotted into a chignon, dark, flashing eyes, and a mouth that seemed always ready to put in a word, or laugh, or kiss. On one of our visits, the house was so full that I was put in Adria's room and slept on a cot next to her bed. One night I went to bed later than usual. A few minutes after I had put out the light, it was switched on again, and, wincing, I saw from between my lashes Adria coming in. She loosened her chignon in front of the mirror and let her hair drop to her shoulders and below them. It covered so much of her back she seemed to be wearing a shawl. Then she went to sit on her bed and began undressing. Intently, I watched her unfasten her stockings, peeling them off her thighs. They were huge, as in a Modigliani, except that their color wasn't at all the brick red, the burnt sienna, the terra cotta of a Modigliani nude, but white, nun-white. A moment later, she noticed I was looking at her. "You are watching me, eh, you little scamp," she said, and switched off the light. This was the first erotic experience that I can remember—a visual one.

My grandmother on my father's side, Lia, was the daughter of Graziadio Isaia Ascoli, an illustrious philologist and linguist, who my father described as rather stern. He was made a senator, as some learned people were in those days. Graziadio—his first name—means "thank God" in Italian, and if occasionally he couldn't meet his class, his students would say, "Graziadio *non c'è*." Lia was a sweet, small, slender woman who went about in long, many-buttoned dresses and looked at you with shiny, pitying eyes. For breakfast she gave us cookies and not the coarse country bread we were used to at home. In the car, she always insisted on going slowly. Unlike her husband, who sat at the head of the table and—had the occasion ever arisen—would have resented being left out of the conversation, she had that marvellous quality some people possess of letting you forget they are there, until a word or some passing remark draws your attention to them. After she died, in the early 1930s, once in a while you noticed her absence—and missed her of a sudden—in exactly the same way you had noticed her presence at the table.

My father was especially keen for us to learn English. Every summer, an English or American young woman would come to stay at our house and tutor us, so that we spoke it without or almost without an accent. Then in the summer of 1937, further to improve my English, I was sent to Wales to stay with friends, as my elder brother had the previous year.

The house our friends—a married couple—lived in was in Porthcawl, a seaside resort with a good harbor in South Wales. I had never been out of Italy before. The outlandish town, the sea, the holidays, the summer, all added to my gaiety. The year too. England had begun rearming and there was a sense of awakening in the air. "In Bristol," I remember the husband in the family saying in a quiet voice and with a subdued smile, "they are building over a hundred aeroplanes a month." The threats and taunts and boastings of the fascists were fresh in my ears, and it made me very happy to hear this. Everything made me happy. I watched the seagulls wheeling, wild even as the robins on the lawn seemed tame. In Italy, except for the pigeons in the public squares, birds didn't come close. I watched the waves thunder against the pier with a violence I had never witnessed, then rebound to meet and quell the onslaught of the next. And I did many things I had never done before—flew kites, went roller-skating, paddled in the pools left by the tide, found an abandoned baby seagull and nurtured it till it flew away, visited a lighthouse and made friends with its keeper, explored a cave draped with stalactites. The cave, from which issued a stream, was in Brenknockshire, about forty miles inland. Nourished by the sunlight, ferns and moss lined the cave's walls for quite a way. The shimmering of the leaves, the ferns, the swirling current cast on the gray stone ceiling a thousand shifting shadows. We went there by car, accompanied by Sheila, a friend of the couple I was staying with. Sheila had come down from London for a week. I was fourteen and she was twenty or so, fairly tall and quite solidly built. She had lustrous black hair, very red lips and an attractive jauntiness about her, beautiful even more than pretty. I was quite cheerful then, much more than now, quite talkative too, a bit short for my age, but very strong, with lots of black hair and dark brown eyes which when I laughed my mother would say looked like blackberries shining in the sun. I wasn't a precocious boy; quite the contrary. I knew very little about love. Oh, in Italy I had played and danced with girls and walked with them arm in arm along lanes and country roads, no more. Having grown up in the country near Siena, I was good at climbing trees, at jumping across ditches or from rock to rock in rivers, and at skipping stones along their surface. So I felt right in my element here. Sheila, on the other hand, being a London girl and having grown up in the city, was having difficulty with the rough bed of the stream, even though the boulders seemed to me simple, easy stepping-stones, nothing at all to negotiate. She made very slow progress, almost always bending over, using her hands, sometimes even her knees, and looking at each stone as if it were a challenge. With anyone else I would have felt an irresistible desire to laugh, she got into such awkward positions. But not with her. I was ever at her feet, telling her where to step, pointing out an easy foothold, being or trying to be most helpful. Probably I wasn't. Probably she would have done better without me, but I couldn't leave her. If her body was cramped into all sorts of odd positions, so was my spirit by her, or rather swayed. I was under her sway, her spell, and I felt privileged, very lucky indeed, to be able to help her, though whether I was helping her or not was, as I say, open to doubt. The other two, living by the sea as they did, on a rocky coast, didn't find the going hard, and on our way out of the cave left us behind. Sheila and I were in the open, but still had to climb out of the stream, and the rocky bank was steep—a height of five or six feet. Too much for her. She tried but couldn't make it. So I pushed her up. She was wearing a skirt, and we were both of us having difficulty—she climbing, I raising her. I had to get a firmer grasp, not on her skirt, which tended

At Villa Solaia, his family home in Siena, Italy, 1950

to slip, but on her bare skin. I clenched her legs above the knees, and still not being able to heave her, in order to push her more effectively, I moved my hands up. Unsupported by me for an instant, she slid down a few inches, into my bare arms. I had a strong hold now around her soft, warm, smooth thighs. There they were, my hands, that had never known such texture, flat on her bareness, pressing, embedded, sunken in her, close to the quick of life, and there she was, above me, but not yet up. I felt as though all my strength were failing me, being diverted downward, away from my hands which were much more instruments of feeling than mere hoists. Then somehow— with one last heave perhaps, or more likely because she had found something to pull on—she was over the top. I don't think she knew what I felt or what I'd felt. She regarded me as just a boy, a serviceable lad, which only increased my emotion. We joined the others, and they started talking about the beauty of the cave and caves in general, stalactites and stalagmites figuring prominently in their conversation. As for me, I had become speechless, and remained so for the rest of the trip.

"What's the matter, Darling? You are not saying anything. Are you disappointed?" the wife said.

"No," I managed to say.

Back in Italy, nasty little articles and editorials against Jews were beginning to appear in the newspapers. One decree after another was promulgated: no books by Jews were to be published; Jews were not to employ non-Jews, or hold property, or go to public schools. Since my mother wasn't Jewish, my brothers, my sister, and I were considered only half-Jewish. To avoid expropriation, my father transferred the property to us, and we continued going to school. But it was clear that matters were deteriorating. My father said we shouldn't live in a country where we didn't have equal rights. For us it was time to leave. We got our passports ready, had some money transferred to England, and leaving the house and the land in the care of our bailiff, maids, and farmers, in the fall of 1938 we took a train and went to England, as refugees. My grandfather chose to stay in Italy.

My mother and father with my eight-year-old sister, Charis, settled in a small cottage amid tall woods in Surrey; my elder brother, Paolo, who was very studious, was invited to stay at the house of a scholar, Robert Trevelyan, and his wife. My younger brother, Cesare, and I went to stay with the couple—Howie and Mary Jones—I had stayed with the year before, in South Wales. We went to a day school in Bridgend, where I soon got into a fight with a tough school boy whose name I still remember, Tommy Tucker. I couldn't box and got a black eye, though I wrestled him to the ground. My young brother fared better. A boy asked him, "Do you like Mussolini?"

"I've never tasted him," he replied.

They thought it was hugely funny.

The next term, in January 1939, I was sent to boarding school at King's School, Worcester. It was right by the cathedral and the river Severn. I remember its flow and the cathedral's lofty arches and sunset-pink stones, but most incisively I remember the caning. I had never been beaten before—in Italian schools it wasn't allowed, and my parents had never raised their hands against me. The indignity of corporal punishment, they were surely against it; and yet they were actually paying for me to be here. "Come and see me after prayers," said one of the monitors, and when I knocked at their door, "We've decided to give you six with the cane." For what? Leaving my desk in disorder. I appealed to the housemaster, and was let off—this time. Days later, when I least expected it, the three monitors and

others lured me to a squash court, pounced on me and beat me up. What I should have done was go to the station, get on a train, and go home. But boys are patient even as they are impatient; they can suffer in silence even as they can cry. And so I stayed the whole term and went back the next and was beaten—three or four times. But at least I had put up a fight; I hadn't submitted; I had made some sort of protest. And I'm glad, because what I've always hated most in myself is my tameness, and because I've always thought that authority is cowardly—not disobedience. There is in my family album a photograph of the boys of my school. The boys don't seem like the big, cruel boys I thought them. They seem nice and are smiling. So am I. I look happy. But if I stray away from the picture, I see them wielding a cane; I feel the welt that is left on the skin, and the mark that is left on the mind. Which is the true picture—the one in my mind or the one that the film has recorded? I don't know. I only know that I can't accept those smiling faces.

On a moonless, starless night in December 1939, four months into the war, my parents, my two brothers, my sister, and I advanced along the sidewalk warily, a tight-knit little group. No chink of light showed from door or window. Sometimes a car went by with covered, slitted headlights. We grazed the walls and shop windows, and groped at each doorway, hoping one might open into a restaurant. We were staying in a hotel near Russell Square, in three little rooms at the end of a long, long corridor. The hotel was so huge one could nearly always get a room. That, I think, was its main advantage, and the reason we had gone there. Murky and dimly lit, it provided little contrast to the blackout outside. Rather, it seemed to partake of it. The lampshades in the lobby were like hoods. Only directly under them was there sufficient light to read a paper by. The darkness from the street entered as you entered, weaved its way around the heavy lampshades, and, hardly mitigated, spread along corridors and halls into the rooms. We had, from our schools and places, all convened in London for a family reunion. The hotel must have had a restaurant, but we certainly didn't want to eat there, so we had gone out. We had walked around a great deal. I think we were quite lost. But we weren't so much trying to find our way as a place to eat. How different this town was from Rome, where practically every other doorway was a cafe or *trattoria* that, war or no war, stayed open late into the night. Here everything was closed or seemed to be. We stopped a passerby and asked him if he knew of a restaurant.

"I'm afraid you won't find anything open at this time here," he said.

My father drew a tiny flashlight and a watch from his pocket. It wasn't even eight. My God, there must be something. We moved along from door to door. Suddenly one gave. I remember the feel of it. It was a leather-covered door, fat and cushiony. It swung open as we pressed it, and it disclosed light. Light refracted by crystal chandeliers. Light broken up and shining. Rivulets of light. It lit us up. It bathed us. We looked at each other and felt we were really seeing each other now. We were in a restaurant—the Holborn. I don't think I have ever seen a restaurant quite like it. The place had a glow the chandeliers couldn't account for. It came from a fire—a robust flame that rose from an open burner in full view of the tables. With its wavering light, it lit our faces orange and made the shadows dance. A white-bonneted cook busied himself about it. And there were copper pans so highly polished they brought the shield of Achilles to my mind. The tables were beautifully laid with white linen cloths, fine dishes, long-stemmed slender goblets, silver, napkins folded in the shape of cones. The waiters plied between the tables, carrying full platters high on their palms. Although the room did not appear crowded, there were a great many guests, some of them lovely women with bare shoulders, long gowns, and hats with sweeping curves. And there were wreaths of smoke, like lightest clouds unfolding, and a mingled sound of voices—almost tuneful—and warmth, and softness, and an indefinable perfume in the air. The atmosphere was dreadfully inviting. So inviting it seemed almost forbidden. We stood at the threshold, looking at my father. Would he really let us eat here? Wasn't this a bit too good for us? He didn't seem to think so—without the slightest hesitancy, he brought us in toward the headwaiter, who was coming over. Waiters, especially headwaiters in black ties and dinner jackets, have always made me feel uneasy. As they come to meet me, I half expect them either to refuse to seat me or to seat me at a table near the door. Once seated and presented with a menu, I often find myself ordering an expensive dish—one that will meet with their approval and not one I really want, like eggs fried in olive oil or a Welsh rarebit. Not so my father. He was quite rich when he was a young man—went to the Ritz in Paris, climbed the Alps, took private dancing lessons. He seemed perfectly at home here. A slightly built man in a blue suit, he moved nimbly, and the waiter didn't so much lead as accompany him to a table—the one my father wanted, central, near the fire. He ordered wine with our

meal, and soon it was being poured from a wicker cradle. My brothers and I had never seen such niceties. We laughed, and I remember my father rather discounting the practice. Our table was round—about the size and shape of the one we had at home in Italy. The wine too was about the same—Chianti. It might have been from our own vineyard. As for the food, it seemed perfectly grand to me, used as I was at school to eating only bread, margarine, and jam for supper.

"When the English set themselves to it, they can cook as well as anybody," one of us said.

"Better," my younger brother said, finishing his Yorkshire pudding.

"And you get dessert every day," I said.

The waiter, who kept refilling our water glasses, suggested plum pudding, and soon, with a flaming blue halo and the smell of spirits hovering around it, a plum pudding was brought in.

Later, after coffee, the check came. We felt apprehensive round the table. Did my father have enough money? He had. He produced a strange white bill such as I had never seen before—a five-pound note—and got some change, which he left on the table. He made no comment on the price. He just smoked a cigarette and watched the smoke, contemplatively. When we left, the headwaiter gave us good directions. It wasn't very far to Russell Square.

In January 1940, King's School, in order to avoid air raids, was evacuated from Worcester to Criccieth, a little town on the west coast of North Wales. There was a castle and, below, on the esplanade, a hotel the school took over. There were fierce storms, with raging seas and waves that battered the shore, wetting us with spray as we watched from the road. I visited various castles, and climbed Moel Hebog and Mount Snowdon. In the late spring the war suddenly flared. Holland, Belgium, and France were invaded. There was talk of fifth columnists. All male enemy aliens between the ages of sixteen and sixty-five, Jewish refugees from Germany and Austria included, were interned. On June tenth, listening to the radio in the common room, I heard that Mussolini had thrown Italy into war. The other boys looked at me, while my eyes shone with shame. The next morning, being over sixteen and now technically an "enemy alien," I was interned. A policeman, gigantic in his uniform, came into the classroom and called me out. I followed him into a Black Maria waiting outside. There was no jail in Criccieth, and so I was driven to a neighboring town—Portmadoc—where there was one. A real old country jail—three cells off a small

Mother, Elena Vivante, 1957

courtyard behind the police station. The cells were empty. With barred doors wide open, they seemed to be waiting for someone to occupy them. I was locked up. I sat on a wooden bunk in the dimness. Silently, I wept and wondered where I would spend the night, and when night came, where the next day. An internment camp near Liverpool, as it turned out. I remember a soldier—a guard—on a turret throwing me a pack of cigarettes. I thanked him and picked them up, though I didn't smoke. After two weeks, we boarded the *Ettrick,* a Polish liner taken over by the English when the Nazis invaded Poland. The ship was loaded with German prisoners of war—most of them airmen—and interned civilians: sailors from Italian freighters caught in British waters, and German, Austrian, and Italian refugees, and other Italians who had been living in England. Perhaps three thousand men altogether. I still wore my school blazer, with a pair of blue jeans I had bought from an Italian sailor for a few shillings when my own flannel slacks had torn. For a while after leaving England, none of us knew where we were going. At one point, perhaps because of a submarine lurking nearby, the ship veered.

"Oh, look, we are going back to England!" I exclaimed.

"If we go back to England I kick you," a German refugee said.

"I love England—I hope we go back," I replied in anger, in spite of my excitement at the prospect of crossing the ocean.

Soon the ship was on her former course. What was her destination? One such ship had gone to Australia; another—though at the time I wasn't aware of it—had been sunk, and the Germans and the Italians on board had fought each other in a mad scramble to be saved. Nearly all had drowned. For a long time, my mother thought I was on that ship. But the *Ettrick* kept sailing west, and it became apparent that we were going to North America—to Canada probably. My father and elder brother had also been interned, but since they'd been living in a different part of England—near Oxford—they were sent to the Isle of Man.

It was nice on the ship. After the internment camp, I felt perfectly free. I was on deck most of the time. Diminutive though the space allotted to us was, it seemed quite sufficient. Here I could feast my eyes on the sea's wideness. Even in the cabin, which I shared with a dozen others, I didn't feel cramped. But I knew it would soon be different—another camp awaited me in Canada. It would end, this interlude. I stayed on deck as long as I could. One night, halfway across the Atlantic, I saw for the first time the northern lights. An astronomer—another Italian refugee—tried to explain the phenomenon to me. I caught a word or two: electrons, cosmic rays. The lights shimmered, danced in the immense silence of the starry night. The ethereal curtains waved—diaphanous, mystic. Seeming to follow some unearthly rhythm, they quickened, glowed, then almost disappeared, only to reappear more intense—they seemed to fade and to reassert themselves in turn. There it was, the aurora borealis. And it was going on and on, nearly half the sky's vault taken up with it. In Italy, in England, you might wait years—a lifetime—and miss it. But here in mid-ocean it blazed spectacularly.

Then, days later, a few birds, and, like a mauve cloud, Newfoundland. The ship entered the Gulf of Saint Lawrence. Was there a river with a wider mouth? At first, the banks were so wide apart they couldn't be seen—then, indistinctly, a cape, a headland. Like open arms, the banks welcomed you. Far away gleamed a white church spire, and rows of white specks—the houses. The river narrowed, and still it was wider than any I had ever seen. Tall, rugged, rocky cliffs rose on each side, pine-terraced. And in the clear summer day, the water mirroring the blue of the sky, the living green of the pine trees, the ancient gray of the rocks, the absence of buildings anywhere near, gave me a gleeful feeling that nothing could mar. Darkness came, and, according to one of the sailors, we were at least a whole day from the city of Quebec—a reckoning that, since we were going at a good clip, testified to the great length of the river.

As for me, I didn't want to get to the end of the journey. I stayed up on deck, sitting on the good wooden floorboards, my eyes on the riverbanks, which now were dark shadows under the night sky. Each moment spent on deck was a moment saved; each moment spent down in the crowded cabin seemed wasted. Let them play cards and crab and tell their pointless stories. A few hours before, while it was still light, I had heard one of the German airmen commenting on my age—I was the youngest there—to an Italian sailor who knew a bit of German. *"Jude?"* the airman said. "No, no," the sailor replied for me as I turned away. A little later, a slick, obtrusive Italian civilian had asked to borrow half a crown, which was almost all the money I had. And I had given the big, shiny silver coin to him. Why had I? And why, Jewish or not, hadn't I replied yes to the airman instead of walking away? I hated myself for taking the easiest course. But now on the deck I was away from them all. It was lucky for me that they preferred to be below—lucky and amazing. Amazing, too, that the guards didn't mind my staying up here. They must have figured that no one could escape, that no one could jump overboard and reach shore. The river was several miles wide in most places; the current was probably strong, the water cold. Yet it was July, and sometimes the ship came pretty close to one of the banks, though in the dark it was hard to tell just how close.

I was a good swimmer; a few weeks before my internment, I had won a long-distance swimming race at my school. Could I make it to shore? Long I wondered, till it was too late; the coast receded. We landed in Quebec. From the way we were hustled down the gangplank and onto a train, I was brusquely reminded what we were. The train sped through thick forests. We arrived in Montreal at night and got off at a secondary station. There were ten buses waiting for us. We followed the lights along the river, strange and resplendent after the blackout I had got used to in England. We crossed a bridge and came to a camp, on Saint Helen's Island, in full view of Montreal. I looked at the lights on the river, a neon light advertising linoleum, its long reflection bare of its paltry message, and farther, the lights of the city. Farther still, on Mount Royal, the Cross, studded with lights; nearer, the searchlights that lit up the camp as though it were going to be filmed. The military police had us all lined up in the yard of the camp—a fortlike, bracket-shaped building that had been turned into barracks. The guards were shouting orders, making us stand motionless at attention, threatening instant death if we moved. Motionless, I stared at the lighted Cross. Above, the stars were shining. Where was God? Up there on that Cross, or farther up, in the stars? In the stars most likely. In the silence, with the tension at its peak, the guards holding their rifles in both hands, and a sergeant-major telling them to shoot between the eyes anyone who moved, a man to my right—a burly, bald man who sported a big moustache as if to make up for his shiny pate—let out a shriek that seemed to tear the sky, and fell to the ground in epileptic convulsions. Two internees fainted at the sight. Never had I heard such an unearthly cry. The guards too and the sergeant-major looked shaken. And surely it was eerie, this involuntary movement that had defied and made a mockery of the order not to move. Soon the silence returned, but the cry still seemed to fill the air. We were counted and given a number. I stared so hard in front of me and wore such a serious face and looked so young, that the sergeant-major kept asking

Father, Leone Vivante, 1966

me questions: how old was I, what was I doing here. . . . Later that night, another NCO, a veteran of World War I, shaggy, hoary, used me as an interpreter with one of the seamen. Some of the things he wanted me to translate verged on the offensive—that, for example, the Italians had "caved in" at Caporetto—and I hated to be of any use, and wished I only knew one language. Group by group, we were herded into a shower room and made to undress. The ugly, ponderous bodies of some of the men made a strange impression on me who had never seen anyone naked but boys and children. We were given blue clothes with red stripes and circles, and later we had our heads shaved. The Canadian camp commandant, a major, appointed one of us—a servile, impudent man—camp leader. We resented his having been made camp leader without our being consulted. It was strange, and in some ways oddly reassuring, to see some of them, rabidly fascist, clamoring for democratic procedures—elections—when it came to appointing a leader. But they didn't see their inconsistency, or at least they wouldn't admit it—one thing was what happened to us, another what happened in Europe, they told me, and swore. I was put to work in the infirmary and slept there. One hot night, a sentry on a watchtower saw me crossing the open doorway inside the room. "Halt!" he shouted, pointing his rifle at me. I froze, and at last a guard came up the steps and the sentry put the rifle down. On rainy days, the water formed all sorts of puddles and channels on the uneven ground of the yard. I loved to walk across them, felt I was walking in a country laced with rivers and lakes. I felt like a giant. I had seven-league boots. Later, I left the confinement of the infirmary. My father, who along with my brother, had been released and was home in England, sent me books. I read poetry, *War and Peace, The Brothers Karamazov, Crime and Punishment,* and *Les Misérables.* The last enthralled me with all its escapes. Jean Valjean was the embodiment of freedom, freedom's flag flying. On the anniversary of their march on Rome, the fascists at lunch sang their national anthem, expecting everyone to stand up. When I didn't, their leader jeered at me, but an antifascist who sat near me and who had fought in Spain against Franco, said to me, "Bravo." Winter came. I spent my time shovelling snow, building military huts just outside the camp, reading, sliding down an icy slope we made in the yard and writing applications for release. Month after month I proclaimed my antifascism and hoped to be let out. At last, after a year, Ruth Draper, the American actress, who had loved my uncle Lauro and was a close friend of my family,

came to Canada for a Red Cross tour. In Ottawa she met Prime Minister Mackenzie King and asked him if I couldn't be released. The next morning, I was free, with Ruth as sponsor or guardian.

I found myself with people my own age, first at Montreal High School, where a teacher—Mr. McBain—appreciated my writing even more than my priest-professor had in Siena, then, after a few months and an exam, at McGill University. But two years in a strict boarding school, and one shut in an internment camp, stood between me and the other students. I was both older and younger than they were. Years ahead and at least three behind. Time to forget—that is what I needed. Forget and return to the time I had pushed Sheila up the river bank in Wales, and the time I used to walk arm in arm with girls from nearby farms in Siena.

From the age of ten on I had continued writing poems, which I transcribed neatly into hardcover blank notebooks. I got some encouragement, but not enough, I decided, for me to embark on a literary career. I would go on writing, but to make a living I had better do something else besides. I knew I had to shun mathematics. It had come near to ruining my boyhood. Often I'd had to take extra lessons and follow my teachers from number to number and, what was even less understandable to me, from letter to letter. To smooth the lesson, I nodded in understanding at things I did not understand, while my mind roved out of squares and rectangles into the infinite spaces beyond. A friend, and my parents by mail, encouraged me to study medicine. I had a beloved uncle in Florence who was a surgeon. McGill had an excellent medical school. I read *Arrowsmith.* I heard Fleming speak. Medicine had little or no mathematics. I thought I was fairly intuitive and might make a good doctor. Medicine seemed more humane than the humanities, and I turned to it and studied it with enthusiasm—first premedicine and then one year of medicine, at McGill. So the war years passed. One summer I worked picking fruit in the Niagara peninsula, another in a forestry lab far north of Ottawa, another at Saint Mary's Hospital in Montreal as a lab intern. That was when I met Maggie, a student nurse. I first saw her in the operating room. From behind the glass partition I watched her, and for a moment our eyes met. Her mouth and nose were covered by a mask. Her hair was capped. Her hands were gloved, she wore a loose white gown. Only her neck was bare. Her eyes, large and long-lashed, reached me through the glass partition, held me for a moment, and then let me go. I saw

Nancy Vivante in a 1968 drawing by Arturo Vivante

her better after the operation. She had brown wavy hair. Some fell, light and springy, on her forehead, which was high. After that day, while I went about the hospital, from time to time she appeared before me like a lucky number. Then, just recently, she had come into the laboratory to bring me a test tube with a sample to analyze. I thanked her, and she went, but not before she had given me a searching look and a smile. It made me look for her from the windows of the lab which faced the nurses' home, toward lunchtime, and from the window of my bedroom toward evening, when she might be going out. I didn't see her, but she came with another sample after two or three days. "It's nice to see you," I said. "I wish you'd bring me a test tube every day."

Again she looked at me directly and smiled—a playful smile, not teasing like the lab girls'. We said a few words, enough to find out our names. They called me Willie at the lab, for some reason. "I'll call you by your real name," she said. She had an intimate way of talking.

The evening of that day, I called the nurses' home. I heard the sound of steps and the name "Maggie" shouted, then, after a long pause, her voice

saying hello. We made an appointment for seven-thirty the next day.

I called for her at the nurses' home. Soon she came down. With white gloves, high heels, silk blouse, and lilac lips, she seemed much smarter than any girl I had ever taken out. Downtown we went to have our fortunes told by a lady who read tea leaves. With an unkind smile of disbelief, I listened to her telling me my future—that there was a long journey very soon. Maggie wouldn't say what the lady had told her. On our way back, she said, "I never see you with the other interns."

"Do you know some of them well?"

"I used to like Dr. Powers—not any more."

"Who do you like now?"

"Now I am going out with you," she said, and gave me a little push.

We reached the nurses' home. "Well, good night," I said, looking at her by the door. I was ready to turn around and go, as I had always done before when I had taken a girl out—as I half expected I would always do.

"Good night," she said, and kissed me—oh, so naturally engaged me in a kiss. I put my arms around her not so much to hug her as to find support.

It was the summer of 1945. The war had ended. I was supposed to go back home, to my family in England, whom I hadn't seen since 1940. But now I didn't want to leave. Finally, though, in the early fall, after starting my second year of medicine, I sailed back, on a freighter that took ten passengers, the *Manchester Progress.*

In the cabin next to mine there was a little girl of four with her mother. They were on their way home from Singapore, where the Japanese had interned them. I was with them in the lounge when we entered the fog banks of Newfoundland and the ship's horn began blowing. It reminded the little girl of the sirens that announced air raids, or perhaps the roll calls in the camp. Every time it blew, she screamed and hugged her mother for shelter. Hard as her mother tried to explain to her that there was no danger of air raids and roll calls, the child couldn't help crying each time the horn blew. Her little windpipe accompanied the huge, monstrous one of the ship, and the low note and the high note mingled to make a strident duet. Loud, long, and dismal bellows the foghorn made. They came at regular intervals, making the silent pauses seem short and irrelevant, only long enough to make her recover her voice for the next sound. She didn't get used to the horn. It seemed she never would. It seemed she would go on and on till she screamed herself to exhaustion. It seemed cruel—it seemed cruel that now peace had come, there shouldn't be peace for her. For her the war had not ended. It was still going on. Echoes of it, out of time, out of place, like a swarm of wasps, still pursued her. Her mother was carrying her out of the lounge, ineffectually trying to console her, when I asked her mother if she would let me try. I went down on all fours and placed her on my back. "I am a pony now and you are a lady on horseback." I remember one of the passengers telling me I would get my trousers dirty. I neighed angrily at him. I went around the lounge once, then I stopped. "Go on," she said.

"Not till I hear the signal," I replied.

"What signal?"

"The horn blowing, that's my signal."

She sat still and silent. I could sense that she was deep in thought.

"The horn," she said perplexedly. "Is that your signal?"

"Yes."

It was due to blow now at any moment. I waited, she waited, her mother waited. We all looked at each other, waiting. Rarely, I think, have I gone through such suspense. Then it blew, and I trotted forth, and she wasn't crying. At the end of the sound, I stopped.

When the horn was about to blow again, I got set and repeated the sequence. This we did two or three times. At each signal I sprang forth like a racehorse when the starting gate is lifted. She loved it. If I felt that she was about to fall, I would bring an arm up and steady her. At the next interval—the fourth or the fifth, whichever it was—I got up and we held hands. I told her the pony was tired. The suspense—for me, at least—was even greater this time. But when the horn blew at last, she was smiling. Later, if I remember correctly, we had another run. She was laughing. By showing her how to put a finger in front of her mouth and blow on it, buzzing and humming against it, I even got her to imitate the sound of the horn. That, perhaps, was my first medical success, of a sort.

Farther east, a good way across the Atlantic, with the waves and the wind sweeping south, a little bird landed on deck. From Greenland? Iceland? After a rest, it took off again to resume its flight southward, to Bermuda? The Caribbean? The Azores? I watched in tremulous flight, now high, now low with the wind, till it was out of sight.

We finally landed in Liverpool. My mother and Cesare—my younger brother—were there to meet me. Long, tight hugs, and kisses. She hadn't changed much, but he had. He was taller than me, but his voice was the same, and so like mine. We took a train to London and went to the little house I'd never seen, on Duke's Lane, Kensington, a pretty eighteenth-century house, and at the door was my father, and my sister, Charis, slim, tall, and pretty. I couldn't recognize her. They had spent most of the war years there. They showed me a little vault in the basement that long ago they had cleared of coal and made into an air-raid shelter. During the blitz, an incendiary bomb had pierced the roof of the house and fallen on my parents' bed, but they were safe down in the shelter. My father had put the fire out. Later, a V-2 had exploded so close it had blown the front door off its hinges. My elder brother, Paolo, was in the British army—had been for years, since his release from internment. First he served in England, then on the continent. Soon he was due to resume his studies, at Oxford, where he had been awarded a scholarship. Cesare had received one for Cambridge and was finishing up there. My mother had worked in a government kitchen, then for the BBC, then doing art work for Harrod's department store. My father had spent some time in an intelligence office, then he had written a book, *English Poetry and Its Contribution to the Knowledge of the Creative Principle,* that later Faber and Faber published. T. S. Eliot was his editor there. I liked to hear especially the little things my mother had to say. At the government kitchen she told of an undernourished man, the sort of person who never gets a break. When she was at the counter, she always gave him an extra large helping of pudding. This was usually tapioca. She marvelled that the customers should like it. The poor old fellow would always look for her from the entrance. Their eyes would meet in a sort of understanding that brought a smile to both. His smile would broaden into a delighted grin as she laid an extra spoonful of the pudding on his plate. He would nod thankfully, a little like a horse to whom a lump of sugar has been given. As she told me, she would imitate the nods. At the kitchen she soon got the reputation for being smart and strong. Any hard job would go to her. "Ask Helen, she has brains." "Ask Helen to unscrew that jar; she's strong." She wasn't heavy or big, but she had a spare, strong frame, and keen, bright eyes. It was tiring work at the kitchen, but she liked that job better than the next one she got as a typist and Italian translator at the BBC. There she had a boss—like herself, an Italian refugee—who was a pretentious and exacting person. Though she earned more money than at the kitchen, she often came home in a dejected mood. But one day something happened to cheer her. She had worked after hours in her office, as she often did. It was a wet, cold, misty day. She said she had done a little shopping, and, coming home, inexplicably, her sense of direction had failed her in the Underground. By some odd circumstance, she had taken the wrong line. She had finally got off, at a station she had never heard of. In East London, was she? She walked down the deserted platform, distraught. A sense of loss seized her. As she related her experience, she brought her fingers to her forehead and her face took on a disoriented look. The tunnel, the ads, she said, began to appear disproportionate, unreal, the platform so long she couldn't hope to walk the length of it. She had a feeling that this was perhaps death, that, without knowing it, she had died and never again would she regain the surface of the world. The wet streets, the mist, the gray sky seemed infinitely desirable. Halfway along, she came to a flight of stairs. She climbed up eagerly, but it brought her to another platform. There, too, there was no one around. She waited, trying to collect herself. Suddenly, a train rushed in and came to a stop. The doors opened. Should she get on? She hesitated; in a moment, the doors slid shut. Immediately, she wished she had stepped in—anything was better than this station. To her amazement, the train did not move on. Instead, it slowly backed up till the head car was near her. Then it stopped, and the trainman, leaning out the window, called to her, "Girl! Come here!" Quickly she went over. He shook hands with her. "Where do you want to go?" he asked. She said to Kensington Church Street. Calling her "Dear" and taking his time about it, as if he had plenty to spare, he told her that this was her train, opened the doors for her, and gave her full directions. Following them, heartened by them, she had absolutely no trouble reaching home.

"Imagine, the train backing up and stopping just for me, and that kind man calling me 'girl'—at my age!—talking to me slowly, softly, surely. I felt completely safe, taken in hand. And he certainly knew the way as well as anybody could possibly know it."

We left for Italy, not all together, I first, to catch up with my studies. I flew to Geneva, then took the train to Milan and Florence. After crossing the Apennines, it was good to see olive trees and cypresses again. In Florence the train stopped long before the station. I had two heavy bags, one laden with medical books. A lanky man, without my asking him to, carried it for me. It seemed light in his hand. He refused a tip, just smiled without a word. I stayed at the Helvetia, the nicest of hotels, owned by a school

With children: Benjamin, Lucy, and Lydia.
In Wellfleet, 1968

friend of my father. I walked to the Arno River. Only the Ponte Vecchio still stood. The accesses to it were in ruin. Florence, joyful city, gashed. The railroad to Siena had not yet been repaired. I took a truck with benches nailed to the floor. From Siena, leaving my luggage in town, I walked and ran to our old house. Up the drive someone saw me and whispered, "Isn't that Arturo?" and someone else said, "He's back." "Arturo is back," somebody else shouted. By the time I got up to the house, the maid, the cook, the bailiff were outside the door to meet me, and hug me, and kiss me.

The house hadn't suffered much during the war. German and Allied troops had used it as barracks, but the farmers around had put away all our valuable things—hidden the silver, buried a statue, put antiques and books in their own houses. Now everything was back in place, and the only traces left by the war were a gatepost which a tank had knocked down, a black patch in the tiled floor of the drawing room where the Germans had set up a stove, and bits of coal strewn over the front yard. It was hard to believe that not so long ago the place had been clicking with boots, resounding with orders. My grandfather had died of old age in the house. The German troops were there, but they didn't harm him. In fact, the German army doctor went to his funeral. My surgeon uncle in Florence had died of septicemia, before penicillin had come into use. A school friend had also died, the one whom the fascist inspector had insulted. Our horses and car were gone, taken by the Germans retreating. Siena itself was almost unscathed.

Soon my parents and sister arrived in Italy, by ship. The bailiff went to meet them in Naples, his socks stuffed with bank notes so no one would steal them.

It was 1946, and Italy was recovering from the war. Nearly all the bridges had been destroyed. A great many were still broken down. But more often than not they were being rebuilt. Even from our garden wall I could hear—down on the main road at the end of our drive, where a stone bridge had been blown up by the Germans—men unloading, hammering, shouting, and swearing. They evoked Christ and the Madonna so often that they seemed their constant companions. "Swearing," my father said, as if to excuse them, "is the only way some people have of being in touch with the divine." Along with all the repairing there was a sense of regeneration, of healing. More than that, with the fall of fascism and the advent of the republic, there was an air of freedom—freedom just born, freedom much

awaited. No more did the postage stamps have the faces of the king, or Mussolini, but smashed chains.

My grandfather had left each of us some money, which though much reduced in value by inflation, was still a sizable amount—enough for me to pay for medical school. I visited the University of Florence, but my surgeon uncle having died, there was little advantage to my studying there, and I decided to go to the medical school in Siena instead. Most of the classes were held in the hospital, one of the oldest in Italy. Some of its walls were frescoed and hadn't been painted in five hundred years. A young man I knew, back from India where he had been a prisoner of war, was in the hospital with a fever and pain in the lower right chest. The doctors didn't know what he had. They made tests, they X-rayed, they gave him penicillin, but the tests were inconclusive, the X-rays no help, the penicillin useless, and he didn't improve. His cheeks became hollower, his eyes looked larger. A certain fear too seemed to discompose them. He was literally wasting away. I delved into a large textbook of medicine and became convinced that he was suffering from an amebic abscess of the liver. I told the doctors, but they discounted my opinion. I insisted but they wouldn't listen. Finally though, with little time left, the doctors had a consultation. The chief of surgery was present. That same day he operated on him. An amebic abscess of the liver was found and drained. He quickly recovered.

In June, my brothers returned from England, and for the first time since December 1939, when we had all had dinner at the Holborn, we sat together around a table. I mentioned the restaurant to my family then, but the memory of it had faded from their minds. "Don't you remember?" I said. "We were groping our way along the sidewalk in the dark, when we came into this place all brightly lit and glowing. A flame was blazing on a grill; the chef wore a white bonnet; they served the wine from a bottle in a wicker cradle. . . . Surely you remember."

No, they didn't. Obviously, the Holborn hadn't made the impression on them it had made on me—the night not seemed so dark, the lights so bright.

"Strange," I said. "For me it was the best restaurant, ever."

"Poor boy," my father said, quite touched.

In the fall of 1946, I transferred to the University of Rome, for Siena, beautiful a town though it is, had something confining for me about it. Perhaps it was my unhappy memories of school there. In the three years I spent in Rome as a medical student, I rented rooms from Santa Costanza to Trastevere, finally settling down near Piazza di Spagna, only a few blocks from where Keats had lived, and Shelley, and Leopardi, and Elizabeth Browning, and Dostoyevsky. I got to know the city well and the countryside around it. I was young and free. To meet the spring, late one winter I went to Naples and Capri, then sailed to Sicily. I walked amid flowers by the Greek temple of Segeste, saw the immense strewn ruins of Selinunte, the golden temples at Girgenti, and came back by train along the coast of Calabria, Lucania, and Campania, I gazed at the bays that endlessly followed each other, till I came to the Greek temples of Paestum, then to Amalfi, Positano, and Ravello. In the warm, thin sand between Terracina and Sperlonga, with the sea shining behind me and in front of me the orange groves of Fondi, I lay naked and alone, the soft golden sand beneath me, and above me the blue sky. Nobody saw me as I found my hollow shape and mated the golden sand, penetrated and clasped her, and delved in the cooler depth, and kissed her—her lips the mold of my lips—and loved her—her form the mold of my form—till I felt I had wedded the earth.

I studied medicine hard, conscientiously, but little by little my first love—writing poems—took more and more of my time. I showed them to Giovannetti, a literary man, who admired them, and to Livia Durante, a woman in her sixties who had been a famous beauty and was still quite beautiful. They certainly encouraged me, those two. For a long time they were my only audience. I graduated in 1949, and before I had even interned in a hospital, I was inducted into the army. After a few months training in Florence, I was sent as a medical sublieutenant to join a regiment in the Alps. For months I followed troops across mountains. One evening, two motorcyclists who had run off a mountain road were brought to me on a hooting truck. They were in a shambles. Everything about them seemed broken and bloody. Inexperienced, with trembling hands, I readied my poor equipment, when my orderly said, "But, Doctor, I think they are dead." And in fact they were. I felt shamefully relieved. In the fall, I spent a few months as an assistant in the military hospital of Udine. Throughout my life I've found little joy in assigned work and its dreary routine. More important, and more memorable to me, has been what I did after hours, when I was on my own, wholly absorbed in my writing, "hidden in the light of thought," or with someone I liked. There in Udine, I lived in a cold rented room, but in December I met a young woman and we basked in each other's warmth. The

monotonous day turned into a beautiful night; the sad, icy bed became a cradle of joy. That I want to remember, and little else of that town.

For a long time I wished I could live in Venice. Suddenly and strangely my wishes were granted. The medical officer there broke a leg, and I was sent to replace him. I arrived in Venice toward sunset—the best possible time, when the marble of the city acquires a rosy tinge, a color so delicate it seems ever on the verge of fading. A time of no fast colors, of shadows on the move, of bright and brief reflections, comparable only to sunrise but gentler and without slumber. On one side of the vaporetto, the Grand Canal was a deep, dark pool in which the houses waved, and on the other—the sunset side—slate-colored, blue-red, the blue ever gaining on the red till it was violet by the Doges' Palace. Then the red completely disappeared and the lagoon became a dark, deep blue that darkened further as the lights were lit. I got a room at the military district headquarters, in an old palace where Petrarch had once lived. The navy was strong in Venice, not the army, and I had little to do. I devoted more and more time to poetry, and in 1951, toward the end of my military service, I published at my own expense a collection, *Poesie.*

Out of the army, I went back to Rome. For a few months I was a resident at the Salvator Mundi, an American hospital there. I made friends there with a nurse nun. We talked about religion a lot. Soon the mother superior became aware of our friendship and transferred her. I never saw her again. I wrote her, but if she ever got my letter, she didn't reply. Then the helplessness that all doctors experience when confronted by a patient with an incurable disease made me choose research.

I was awarded a Fulbright Travel Grant to go to New York. I did some work in pharmacology at the State University of New York and at New York University for a year. I loved New York, especially after five o'clock when I mingled in the life of the city. I found a small, inexpensive apartment in Chelsea, west of Tenth Avenue. From it I could hear the horns of the ships and of freight trains. The colorful cars with beautiful names, like Lackawanna, Chesapeake, and Santa Fe, trailed in front of my kitchen window over a bridge on Twenty-eighth Street. It was a vantage point from which to appreciate the vastness of the continent and ocean. And it was the first home of my own. I bought a typewriter, and wrote till late, poems, a play, a novel I began. Sometimes Vivian Reade, a young woman I met on a Westchester train—I shall never forget how she came down the aisle and sat next to me—would come and visit. A food editor at a magazine, rich, light-spirited, and winsome, she would arrive by taxi or in her Jaguar, laden with food samples, and each time it was a feast. Before leaving for Italy, I saw Boston, Maine, flew to California, and on my way back by train saw the Grand Canyon, New Orleans, and Washington. It was hard to leave.

In Rome again, I went on doing medical research at the university, but the poverty of my ideas was soon apparent to me. It didn't justify my experiments, certainly not the vivisection, and after less than a year I quit. As I left the university and went home—a small apartment on Via dei Greci, near Via Margutta, the street where many artists have their studios—I felt very well—light-footed, buoyant, weightless. This always happens to me when I give something up; there are a few minutes, before my thoughts turn to new things that will have to be done, during which I am only thinking of the things I won't have to be doing any longer. It is a moment of freedom. For a while I joined a city hospital, then left that too and set up a little office in my apartment. I would be just a general practitioner and write in my spare time. Few patients came—neighbors and some people that the American Consulate sent me, mainly veterans for pension visits. My desk was covered with poems, stories, plays I wrote, and my novel. Hurriedly, unwillingly, when a patient came, I would remove them to make room for my medical equipment. After the last patient left, I would write till nine in the evening, then go over to the studio of Fazzini, the sculptor, on Via Margutta. He had a few assistants, one of them Laura Ziegler, an American of whom I was an ardent, and hopeless, admirer. At that time they would be about ready to break off for dinner, and I would go with them to "Carlino," a trattoria.

I was altogether absorbed by my novel *One Arm Akimbo,* about a defiant young woman in New York City. I finished it, and hopeful, confident, I sent it off, but it was rejected. Three short plays fared no better. My book *Poesie* had received little notice. My latest poems had a narrative tone. It seemed natural to write a short story. Before long I had written several. I sent them to England and America, for I wrote mainly in English now. And they too came back. But I persevered. In the short story I had found my form,

Arturo and Nancy Vivante, Wellfleet, 1982

"Lightning that mocks the night, brief even as bright." Hidden, in disguise, some of my verses found refuge in stories. Poets, especially nineteenth-century poets, were my teachers, and, among novelists, the Russians, and Stendhal, Balzac, Hardy, and Lawrence; among short-story writers, Maupassant, Chekhov, Katherine Mansfield, Mary Wilkins Freeman, Ada Negri, Katherine Anne Porter, Dorothy Parker, Carson McCullers, and Salinger, to mention but a few; among playwrights, Ibsen and Tennessee Williams. On December 1, 1955, the *Manchester Guardian* published a short story of mine, entitled "The Snake." I got five guineas for it. The next year, Giorgio Bassani, then editor of *Botteghe Oscure,* published two of my stories. I wrote more and more. Soon I had written at least a dozen stories, set in Italy, England, and Canada.

In Siena, the returns from the four-hundred or so acres that went with the house weren't sufficient for its upkeep, and so we sold some of our land, and my mother began taking in paying guests—usually friends or friends of friends from England and America. People came not so much for the country, or the town, or the house, or the food, or the Chianti wine, as for the conversation that took place around the dinner table. For there was fervor in the way she talked. She was the main attraction of the house. Fanned by her, the conversation flew, took unexpected turns, met never a dead end. The subject might be anything—politics, the Pope, Piero della Francesca, a guest who had just left. Anything. The oval dining table, which could be, and often was, enlarged to seat about twenty people, lent itself, and the wine helped. The guests discovered in the house a genuine atmosphere in which the timid lost their shyness, the bold found their match, and truth was like a Ping-Pong ball balanced on a jet of water and rolling, rolling, while everyone aspired to send it higher. One of the guests was Dwight MacDonald, the literary critic. One weekend that I was home, I showed him a short story. He liked it, took it to the *New Yorker* magazine, and it was accepted.

In Rome a slim brunette in a tight black jacket and a wide plaid skirt, with a pensive air about her, came to my office. A patient sent by the American Consulate. Her name was Nancy Bradish. She had a minor ailment for which she returned after a couple of days. Before leaving, she looked at some of my books and began to talk about poetry. It was close to the end of my office hours, and I asked her if she would like to have a cup of coffee with me around the corner. We became friends. She was on vacation after working on a research project in Cambridge. She had

studied politics at Radcliffe and was quite literary. She left for America. But the next year, she was back in Rome and found a job at an American college in Italy. We became closer and closer, took trips together, to Siena, the sea, the Abruzzi, and later, for Christmas, to England by car, a little prewar green Fiat convertible I had bought. Returning, we crossed the Alps in it. It was a daring venture in which she accompanied me not without fear, but we made it safely across. I felt as though the Alpine pass had married us. In April we were officially married at the Campidoglio in Rome.

It was 1958. The story the *New Yorker* had accepted was published. Two more followed in quick succession, and more were accepted. I signed a first-reading agreement with them, for which I was given a thousand dollars. Nancy and I lived in the little apartment on Via dei Greci. My practice had been very small, but now, unaccountably, it began to increase. At the same time, I was writing more and more stories, correcting proofs, trying to keep up with the correspondence. Nancy helped me. She had a really good ear for the language and was an excellent speller. She would carefully go over each story. Even so, and despite her help, things were becoming hectic. It didn't seem fair to my patients that I should spend so much time on my writing. I was making more money from it than from my practice. I had to decide between one and the other. I couldn't do both. Then Nancy began feeling unwell. In September she had a miscarriage. With a few telephone calls I gave up my medical practice. I got an American visa. We left the apartment and drove to Siena. After a month we flew to America, where my work was being published and where I felt my future lay.

We first went to Quincy, near Boston, where Nancy's family lived, and met her warmhearted mother, her affable father, her quite remarkable sister, who worked in a bookshop. They had a summer house in Cape Cod with a fine view of the ocean. After a few days there, we went to New York. How good it was on a bus to see an attractive woman reading the latest issue of the *New Yorker* open on her lap at my story. For a moment I felt that this, and not Rome, was my town. We found a one-room apartment up high in a hotel. In Cape Cod I had picked a milkweed pod and put it in my suitcase. When I opened it here, the ripened plumed pappi lifted like smoke toward the ceiling, dozens of them; some took to the window and spiralled upward, free. At the *New Yorker,* I met my editor, Rachel MacKenzie. She became more than an editor—a friend, a guide, one who enlightened me again and again with her comments and suggestions.

In the spring we returned to Cape Cod to the cedar-shingled cottage hidden among pines, close to the sea and the pale, glistening blades of grass on the sand of East Orleans. I would write late into the night. Self-oblivious, wholly absorbed in my stories, often I would be surprised to see that it was already dawn. I wrote about my own experiences, about what happened or might have happened, and sometimes what might have happened actually did take place in my stories. My sensations were free, my pen unconstrained. The better a sentence was written, the more truthful and convincing it seemed. At times, if I wasn't sure about a sentence, I would read it as poorly or matter-of-factly as I could, and if it still sounded good despite the bad reading, I'd keep it. Reading it really well, I thought, might disguise its faults. Often the right word came to me unexpectedly, and the same with ideas. I tried to make notes of each one. Originality, I knew was elusive. Even perversely elusive perhaps. It rested on a moment that might never return. A bright moment, a moment of insight.

How wonderful to be able to observe the day to day progression of the spring. The lilacs, whose thin, curving branches had, when we arrived seemed so brittle and stark, now had buds. The daffodils were ready to unfurl. We sowed some grass seed, and soon tiny, thin spears appeared, almost colorless at first. The pollen of the pines settled everywhere, even on the book I was reading, on puddles, and on the sea. Raccoons, one night, came out of an inactive chimney; skunks waddled about; a woodchuck hurried across the unpaved road; rabbits bobbed up; and a flicker early in the morning sharpened its beak on a pail. The terns and red-wing blackbirds chased me if, inadvertently, I went near their nesting grounds. The pine warblers hovered above us when Nancy watered the lawn. The chickadees splashed in a tray of aluminum foil. This, we decided, was the time to conceive; now, when everything seemed to be bursting with life. So we made love and we hoped, and early the next year, in Boston, where we moved from the Cape in the fall, our daughter Lucy was born, in 1960.

Later that year, the three of us flew to Italy, stayed at my family home near Siena, then found an apartment in Florence, on the top floor of a palace in Piazza Santa Croce. In the distance we could see Giotto's tower, "the lily of Florence blossoming in stone," farther, across the river, San Miniato; farther

The author, 1985

still, to the north, Fiesole. Nearer, swallows and pigeons made an aerial dance across the square. Nancy went with Lucy to America to look after her mother who had fallen ill, and for months I was left alone. I wrote a story, "Bachelor Days." There was a statue of Dante on the square. One day, after looking at him a long time, I dreamed of him. He spoke to me and when I told him he was famous, he seemed very surprised. I showed him his picture on a 10,000-lira note. About this dream I wrote a story, "Dante." Alone, I took a trip to Greece. In Athens I went to a small hotel. The only available room was in the attic. I walked up. When I opened the window, I saw the Acropolis, and I don't suppose a window was ever opened or a curtain drawn on anything more splendid. About Greece I wrote a story entitled "The French Girls of Killini," one of my longest. Returning to Italy, I went to Venice and wrote "Venetian Rendezvous." Any place I've lived, almost every place I've travelled to, every important phase of my life, and nearly every person I've loved, I have written about.

In 1962, Nancy's mother died and about her I wrote "Transatlantic Call," and "The Little Ark." We spent two months in the Caribbean; the rain forest in Puerto Rico suggested the short story "Run to the Waterfall." Approaching Saint Thomas, Saint Martin, Saint Kitts by plane, the islands seemed, like their namesakes, to hover in the air. In 1963 my mother died. I wrote about her several stories, on her life and on her death—"A Gift of Joy," "Of Love and Friendship," "The Conversationalist," "Young Days," "By the Bedside," "The Room," "Last Rites," "The Art Teacher," and others. In 1964 my daughter Lydia was born, in Boston. She has some of my mother's traits, and this makes me think of the words of Glaucus in the *Iliad:* "Aren't our generations like leaves? The wind takes them in the fall, but they burgeon again in the spring." That year, we bought a house in Wellfleet, Cape Cod. In 1966 my son Benjamin was happily born. That same year, Little, Brown published my novel *A Goodly Babe,* about marriage and birth. The next year, they published a collection, *The French Girls of Killini and Other Stories,* and, in 1969, my second novel, *Doctor Giovanni,* a love quest in post-war Italy. The novels also came out in Italy, and Heinemann published *A Goodly Babe* in England.

My father died in 1970. I wrote about him some of my best stories—"The Orchard," "The Holborn," "At the Dinner Table," "The Chest," "The Soft Core," "The Bell," "A Gallery of Women." In my many years at universities and in the company of literary people, I have never met anyone who liked poetry more than my father, or, for that matter, knew more about it. I remember him watching the sunset, absorbed in light, a man whom beauty had always held in sway, and I remember him reciting poems, enunciating the words in all their clearness, slowly, in a voice that seemed ever on the verge of breaking yet never broke and that seemed to pick each nuance of rhythm and of meaning, in the realm of the spirit a man of high aims and wider grasp. Even in the last years of his life, beset by illness though he was, he would read poetry day and night. Often I would listen to him with attention and pleasure. It was the only comfort I could bring him. But even as a listener I wasn't quite what he wanted. What he wanted was the company of women. Even Giulia, the maid—an elderly, illiterate woman, who listened to the poetry with composure, her hands clasped in front of her— was for him a better audience than I was. He had always liked women far better than men. A philosopher by nature and vocation, he saw them as the embodiment of tenderness and he thought they were

more intelligent, superior. If challenged, before his memory had deteriorated, he would bring up the names of Emily Brontë, Elizabeth Browning, Anne de Noailles, the mystic Jeanne Marie Guyon, and Diotima. They struck certain notes, he said, that were not inferior to any man's. Among modern writers, he was fondest of Willa Cather and Carson McCullers. Also, with a smile he would mention Dorothy Parker and Katherine Anne Porter, and, from an earlier period, Mary Wilkins Freeman. Of the Italians, he liked Ada Negri. Though in his library there were thousands of books by all sorts of authors, which here and there he had underlined neatly in pencil and annotated in shorthand at the back, now he preferred reading books by women. Sometimes he spoke of women in fiction as if they were real. My mother, too, at times was for him alive, in the next room, arranging the flowers. "Go and call her," he would say, and I would go from his room wondering what to bring to him. One day, looking for a book he might like, I found Theodore Dreiser's "A Gallery of Women." I saw his shorthand notes pencilled at the back, which to me were hieroglyphics but which had numbers opposite them referring to the pages he liked best. And I brought it to him and read him some of those stories, his hand from long ago guiding me from woman to woman. And I asked him about Diotima, and read him the dialogue of Plato in which she appears.

"She must have existed," he said. "There are truths that cannot be ascribed to her interpreters."

And then I read him Emily Brontë's "No Coward Soul Is Mine." Slowly, gradually, my introducing woman after woman to him—fictional and real— became a role unforeseen, unexpected. I warmed to it. It reconciled us. He saw me, I think, no longer as obscure but as a stagehand who disclosed scenes and people to him he looked forward to seeing. I peopled his austere room with characters living and dead—for him all of them living—while I myself kept in the background.

In 1972, Nancy's father died and about him I wrote "The Cedar." There are some strange coincidences in our families, which I mention here because, according to Nabokov, they provide a pattern historians could trace to advantage: Nancy's mother and my father had birthdays in common, so did Nancy and my sister, and so did I and her sister. We felt as though we were almost fated to meet.

In the sixties and seventies I was writing short stories in profusion—fifteen to twenty a year, of which the *New Yorker* took an average of about one in four—enough for us to live on. In 1968 I was offered

Wellfleet home, 1989

and I accepted to be writer-in-residence at the University of North Carolina in Greensboro, and we went there for a year. There I wrote my stories "The Diagnostician," and "Trip South." From then on I taught, with few interruptions, at a number of universities and colleges—Boston University, Purdue, Brandeis, the University of Michigan (where my second collection of short stories, *English Stories,* was published), the University of Iowa, where Flannery O'Connor had been a student and where I met Barbara Briant, student, teacher, and writer, to whom I am tied by a deep friendship, the University of Texas at El Paso, where I wrote "The Gran Quivira," the University of Idaho, and for a much longer period—ten years—Bennington College, where I wrote several stories with a Vermont setting. Except for the year at the U of NC and a year at Purdue, my family stayed in Wellfleet, where I would return for vacations. Many of my stories are about love. I believe in unexclusive love, and that, as Shelley says, "If you divide . . . love . . . each part exceeds the whole." For better or for worse, and to my chagrin sometimes, I have followed that precept, and I don't see how I could have written as I did otherwise, for nearly everything I write stems from experience and I almost always have prototypes for my characters.

We continued going to Italy, to my family home, Solaia, until it was sold in 1974. My parting from it is told in my story "Last Days." In 1975 we spent a year in Rome, near the Pantheon, and, before leaving, I found a small apartment in Bomarzo, a village north of Rome, in Etruscan country that suggested my stories "A Place in Italy" and "Night in the Piazza."

In 1979 Scribner's published my third collection of short stories, *Run to the Waterfall and Other Stories.* That same year I was awarded an NEA grant. In 1980 I published *Writing Fiction,* a collection of essays, the fruit of my teaching experience. Utah University Press, also in 1980, published my father's *Essays on Art and Ontology* that I translated. I have also done some drawing. In 1985 I was awarded a Guggenheim Fellowship. Nancy and I went to Bellagio, on Lake Como (Rockefeller Foundation Residency). In 1988 I published a verse translation I did of the *Canti* of Leopardi, one of the greatest of poets, and one who is not well enough known in America. In

1989 I was given an award in literature by the American Academy of Arts and Letters.

I retired from Bennington College in 1989, but I still teach part-time at the Writing Program of MIT, and I continue writing, mainly short stories, here in Wellfleet. In May 1990 Sheep Meadow Press will publish a new collection of them, *The Tales of Arturo Vivante.*

So now I teach only once a week and live at home with Nancy. The children, in their twenties, often come to visit—Lucy from Cleveland, Lydia and Benjamin from New York. My brother Paolo, who has written books on Homer and who has finished teaching at McGill, visits with his wife, Vera. And there are many friends. Paul Resika, the painter, summers in the next town. I work around the house and read and write. And sometimes I just follow the footprints of the sandpiper on the beach, a script that never tires.

BIBLIOGRAPHY

Fiction, except as noted:

Poesie (poetry), Ferrari (Venice), 1951.

A Goodly Babe, Little, Brown, 1966.

The French Girls of Killini and Other Stories, Little, Brown, 1967.

Doctor Giovanni, Little, Brown, 1969.

English Stories, Street Fiction, 1975.

Run to the Waterfall and Other Stories, Scribner, 1979.

Writing Fiction (essays), Writer, Inc., 1980.

The Tales of Arturo Vivante (selected and with an introduction by Mary Kinzie), Sheep Meadow, 1990.

Translator:

Leone Vivante, *Essays on Art and Ontology,* Utah University Press, 1980.

Poems: Giacomo Leopardi, Delphinium Press, 1988.

Other:

Contributor of over seventy short stories to the *New Yorker,* and others to *Manchester Guardian, Botteghe Oscure, Vogue, Southern Review, Cornhill, London Magazine, New York Times, Greensboro Review, Bennington Review, Confrontation, Canto, Antaeus, New Letters, TriQuarterly, Yankee, Santa Monica Review, Amica, Milleidee, Formations, Agni Review, New England Review, Massachusetts Review, Shenandoah, Review of the Arts,* etc. Many included in anthologies. Contributed travel essays to *Vogue* and the *New York Times.* Plays performed in Provincetown and Bennington include "Evening Light," "The Moon Doesn't Care," "Live Well," and "Curtain Flutter."

Vladimir Voinovich

1932-

HOW I LIVED AND WHO I WAS
(Translated from the Russian by Carleton Copeland)

It seems to me that a man's whole life may be described either very briefly or, just the opposite, at great length. And if you can't be brief enough or run on too long, then it may be best to describe not a whole life, but individual parts of that life—perhaps not even the most important parts.

I will begin simply and from the beginning. I was born September 26, 1932, in Dushanbe, the capital of Soviet Tadzhikistan, a city to which destiny had brought my parents not long before this date. My father was a journalist and worked as managing editor of the republic's newspaper. My mother worked for the paper at first too, and wherever else she could find a job, but later, after graduating from the institute, she became a schoolteacher and taught mathematics. My mother's nationality was Jewish; my father was a Russian of Serbian descent.

A Parisian woman of Russian and Tatar blood was astonished to learn of my roots, and asked me how I could consider myself a Russian writer—to which I answered that I do not consider myself a Russian writer, I *am* a Russian writer.

What I know of my ancestors on my mother's side goes back no further than my grandfather, who was a miller. I know much more, however, about my father's side. My surname comes down from a certain Voin, who was first mentioned in Serbian chronicles in the year 1325. What Voin did for a living, you can judge by his name, which means "warrior" in Russian. The race that descended from him produced many soldiers, including generals and admirals, and there were some—two admirals among them—who served in their time in Russia.

An old encyclopedia tells us that the most famous of these admirals, Count Marko Ivanovich Voinovich, began his service during the time of Catherine the Great "in the Archipelago, where he was distinguished for his bravery." He was the founder and first commander of the Russian Black Sea fleet. To this day, the main pier in Sevastopol is named Grafskaya, or "the count's," in honor of Marko

Vladimir Voinovich, 1988

Ivanovich. And many more of my ancestors were sailors. This tradition died with my great-grandfather, who was a sea captain. But there were people of other professions in our family too—writers, historians, diplomats.

My road seems much longer than it really is, perhaps because I have encountered too much along the way. During the course of my not-so-very-long life, I have actually witnessed two epochs, and even two histories. I passed my early childhood in conditions that might have existed a hundred or even a thousand years ago. Thinking back, I recall the dusty Central Asian, medieval city of Khodzhent, soon renamed Leninabad, where my parents brought me from Dushanbe when I was about three years old.

Some signs of the new age were already in evidence. A railroad had been laid, there were automobiles in the streets, and over our heads flew U-2 biplanes—awkward, slow-moving, but nonetheless airplanes. Whenever one appeared above us, we children would spill into the yards, dancing, jumping, and chanting, "Aeroplane, aeroplane, put me in your pocket. Pocket's empty—look and see—a cabbage in the cockpit . . ." Then we would make wishes. Today there are so many airplanes that if their appearance had anything to do with the fulfillment of wishes, all the hopes of mankind would long ago have been realized. Automobiles, as I have said, were also to be seen in Leninabad, but they were as if strangers from another place, another time.

The most common sights in the dusty streets, yards, and bazaars of Leninabad were still camels, oxen, donkeys, stray dogs, irrigation ditches, a blindman with a face marred by smallpox, a leper with a bell dangling from his neck, teahouses, Tadzhik men in quilted robes and galoshes over bare feet, Tadzhik women with faces covered by veils of horsehair.

If you had to go, say, to the railroad station, you didn't hire a taxi, but a carriage with a folding leather top. Petty tradesmen took chewing gum from yard to yard on donkeys—five kopecks for a piece of pitch, ten for a piece of paraffin. The same donkeys bore sweets of every kind: toffee, *petushki,* and most delicious of all, something called *meshalda*—made perhaps of beaten egg whites and sugar and something else—snow-white, doughy thick, and sweet as sweetness itself. The donkeys carried milk, coal, firewood, and you name it—sometimes in two-wheeled carts, but more often in sacks thrown over the animals' backs. Knife grinders, ragmen, magicians, and beggars all made their rounds on donkeys.

The yards were full of all sorts of smaller animals: pigs, goats, chickens, cats, and dogs. As far as I can recall, the dogs were all strays, and yet somehow domesticated. They lived with everyone and, when the weather turned bad, came in and lay in the hall. But they showed a certain delicacy in this regard, and no sooner had the weather cleared than they went back out into the yards.

From time to time the dogs were hunted down. Villains of both sexes drove through the city, their cages crammed with the unfortunate whining and howling animals, which, so it was said (and of course it was true), they boiled for soap. These loathsome people, dogcatchers, would leave their carriages and cages at a distance and chase around the yards with lassos. The dogs somehow knew in advance of the dogcatchers' approach and came running to the people for a place to hide. They would burrow into the furthest corners, their tails between their legs, and tremble faintly. This was a real and genuine animal fear of death.

All the dogs in the yards, regardless of breed or sex, were called Bobka. A reddish female Bobka always hid with my family, and always long before the appearance of the dogcatchers. There was also a very large, carefree male Bobka, who happily carried us children on his back.

We lived in a long, one-story building with small apartments and a yard for every two families. Electricity was unknown. We had a big kerosine lamp, which in time formed an enormous black spot on the high plywood ceiling. In front of the building were barns in which the residents kept their livestock, firewood, and coal, and beyond the barns was an outhouse of the most ancient and primitive construction. There was of course no shower and no bath. Grandmother took me to the women's bathhouse, and Mama bathed at home in a zinc tub.

At first there were five of us living together: Grandmother, Grandfather, Mother, Father, and I. Then my father disappeared. I didn't realize this in the beginning, because as a journalist, he had dropped out of sight before, sometimes for long periods. But eventually, when I saw how my father's absence dragged on, I began to ask Mama where Papa was. "Papa is away on business," she said.

Time went by, I grew, and my father's business trip seemed as if it would never end. I already barely remembered him. I remembered only that he was some sort of VIP, that he rode in a car with the top down and had a driver by the name of Borisenko. One day Borisenko had taken me for a ride too, and he sang a song that I liked very much: "Hey, little apple, don't roll away. Hey, drop in my mouth, and don't go astray." But even better than a drive in the car, I loved to ride with my father on the back of his bicycle. Time passed, my father did not return, and his image in my mind's eye began to erode. Finally, there was only one thing I remembered well—he had a birthmark on the left side of his face, above his upper lip.

We lived on Embankment Street, so named because it stretched along the bank of the Syr Daria River. Between the street and the bank there was still a cobblestone pavement, which gave way to a meadow and, beyond that, the river itself, walled off from the meadow by an earthen barrier to protect against flooding. This meadow was often used by cavalrymen as a training ground. They rode horses, jumped hurdles, and split branches, waving long sabers that flashed in the sunlight. We children battled one another in the yards, riding on sticks that were transformed as needed from horses into sabers, rifles, and machine guns.

The world still lived by medieval standards. The strength of the army was measured by the number of bayonets or sabers it could field, these being considered the most reliable weapons. Even many years later, when I served in jet aviation, our teachers still mindlessly repeated a saying of Aleksandr Suvorov, Field Marshal in the time of Catherine the Great: "Bullets are dumb, but a bayonet thinks."

When my mother sent me to kindergarten, I saw on the wall a large portrait of Stalin with a little girl in his arms. Under the portrait, and stretching from one side of the room to the other, was a banner that read, THANK YOU, COMRADE STALIN, FOR OUR HAPPY CHILDHOOD. On holidays—February 23 (Red Army Day), May 1, and November 7—the kindergarten was visited by a cavalryman with a long saber at his side. He told us of the Red Army's invincibility and let us touch the saber—without removing it from its scabbard, though.

In kindergarten I had a friend by the name of Galya Salibayeva, daughter of the high-school principal. We were inseparable and always walked hand in hand. When the other kids in the neighborhood saw us, they would jump up and down and tease us with this rhyme: "They kneaded dough, the groom and bride. The dough dried out, and the woman died. The groom wet his pants and cried and cried." This offended us both, but did not affect our friendship. In the first grade we continued to walk hand in hand.

Some forty years later, I asked a friend who was going to Dushanbe to see if anyone there happened to know Galya Salibayeva. Finding her did not present much of a problem, as it turned out that she was married to the Chief Justice of the Supreme Court of Tadzhikistan. She told my friend that she remembered me well, and that made me happy, though a man in my position was unlikely to associate with a chief justice—except as a defendant.

I finished first grade in the spring of 1941. By that time there were only three of us left in the family,

Vladimir (front row, center), age five, in kindergarten at Leninabad, 1937

Grandfather having died three years earlier. No one but my teachers took any time with me. Grandmother couldn't handle me, and Mama was too busy. During the day Mama studied at a teachers institute, and in the evening she worked. When she left for the institute, I was still asleep, and when she came home from work, I was already in bed. Still, between study and work, Mama sometimes managed to stop in, and then we would see each other for a short time during lunch.

This is what happened one day in particular. Mama came home, we ate lunch, and then we went our separate ways—Mama to work, and I into the yard, to the barns, where I straddled Mashka the pig and attempted to master the art of riding. As I was training, my pal Vitka, nicknamed "Louse," came running to say that a man was asking for me.

The man turned out to be some kind of hobo. He wore a ragged old coat with tufts of cotton sticking out, and reddish soldier's boots, worn down at the heels.

"Are you Vova?" the hobo asked me with an odd sort of grin.

"Yes."

"What's your last name?"

I told him.

"Where do you live?"

I pointed to the place.

"Well, let's go to your house."

I took him home, looking around again and again to peer into his face, which was overgrown with a rough, bristly beard.

In the yard, Grandmother was hanging out the wash. When she caught sight of the man I had brought home with me, she gasped, "Kolya!" and, dropping the laundry, threw her arms around the hobo's neck.

I flew out of the yard. My mother was already long gone, but I caught up with her all the same. "Mama! Mama!" I cried, "Come home quick, Papa's back!"

I remember Mama uttered a cry and steadied herself against the wall of a mud house. Then she collected herself, looked at me, and said quietly, "What can you be thinking of?"

"It's true! It's true!" I panted. "It's Papa. He has a birthmark right here."

I remember the gray, twilled suit, bought in the old days, that had waited for Father during the five long years of his absence. Having changed into that suit, Father no longer looked like a hobo, but became instead the dignified and cultured man I had imagined him to be. Yet there was something very

surprising about his behavior. From time to time I was awakened in the middle of the night and would watch as my father gnashed his teeth, jumped up, looked around with frightened eyes, and yelled until he came to his senses.

I thought my father would soon go back to work, and I would soon see the motorcar and merry driver and go riding with Father on his bicycle. But nothing of the sort happened. Father was away somewhere, came home troubled about something, whispered with Mother, and suddenly announced that we— Father, Grandmother, and I—were going away. We would take Grandmother to live with Mama's eldest brother, Uncle Volodya, in Vologda; then the two of us would go on to the Ukraine, where we would stay with Papa's sister, Aunt Anya. I asked, "What about Mama?" Mama would come in the fall, I was told, after she had received her diploma.

I didn't find out what lay behind all of this until much later, and the answer didn't come all at once or from my parents. When my father finally decided to tell me the whole truth, after I came home from the army in the fifties, I already knew in a general way what had happened.

I knew that my father had been arrested in 1936 for the crime of expressing one day, to a circle of three friends, his doubt that socialism could be built in isolation in a single country. My father believed that socialism could only be built after a worldwide revolution had engulfed all the nations of the earth at once. His opinion coincided with Lenin's thought on the subject, but did not coincide with the view of Stalin. And in those days, disagreement with Stalin was tantamount to the most heinous state crimes.

For saying what he did, my father was virtually accused of terrorism and held for two years while his case was under investigation. He was expected to go before a firing squad, but my father, as he concluded later, was lucky. His trial took place in January 1938, immediately following the famous plenum of the Central Committee of the Communist Party, when the commissar of internal affairs, Nikolai Yezhov, was removed for "excesses" and replaced by Lavrenti Beria. Beria was of course no better than Yezhov, but in putting him at the head of the organs of state security, Stalin wanted to create the illusion that law and order had been restored. This was the first Soviet "thaw" of sorts. Instead of a firing squad, my father received five years in camps.

Later he was even more "lucky." There was a wave of rehabilitations on the eve of war, and when my father returned to Leninabad at the end of his camp term, he was even invited to take back his party membership card—to which he replied, "I won't ever go back to your party!" This statement might have served as grounds for a new arrest, and my parents decided that the sooner my father got out of Central Asia, the better—hence the plan for our departure.

In those days, travel by rail still entailed certain hardships and adventures—jumping out for a bite to eat at the stations along the way, lining up at the faucets for hot and cold water, the perpetual fear of missing the train. For me, the journey was my first acquaintance with the achievements of the twentieth century, which seemed nothing short of a miracle—in Moscow, the Metro; in Zaporozhe, the trolleybuses and trams. In Zaporozhe, for the first time in my life, I lived in an apartment with electricity, a watercloset, a bath, and hot water. Before then, I had never dreamed that hot water could be obtained in any other way than by kindling firewood or pumping the primus stove—here you just turned on the tap, and out it came. Yes, this was the twentieth century, but an antediluvian period—now almost forgotten—that did not as yet know nuclear weapons, space equipment, lasers, computers, or radar. Even black-and-white television was still being developed in laboratories somewhere.

It was already summer in Zaporozhe when we arrived there at the end of May. On Sundays the whole family—Aunt Anya; her husband, Uncle Kostya; their two sons, Seva and Vitya; my father; and I—went to the beach on the island of Khortitsa. My cousins were older than I was—Seva by six years and Vitya by four—and they taught me how to swim.

June 22 was very hot. The bugs were eating me alive, which made me cry, and I think this was the reason we returned home earlier than usual. At home Grandmother met us with the news that there was war with Germany. Having said this, she burst into tears. I was dumbfounded. What was so tragic? After all, war as I had seen it at the movies was great, full of interesting things—horses, sabers, gun carriages, and machine guns. Soon even I learned that war in real life was very different from what I had seen at the movies.

During the second half of the same day, the adults went out with shovels to dig bomb trenches throughout the city. Everyone was ordered to paste strips of paper on their windows, and this was supposed to keep the glass from shattering when the bombs began to drop. Strict measures were taken to maintain a blackout. Rumors circulated (and they didn't seem farfetched to anyone) that the police would shoot at windows where they saw any light.

As soon as the second night, there was an air-raid warning. Grandmother and I were sent to a bomb shelter, while the other members of our family took cover in the newly dug trenches. The bomb shelter was in the cellar of the building next door, and it filled up primarily with old folks and children. Many came with blankets and pillows, others with assorted bags and baggage. It was crowded, and spirits were high. Suddenly the lights went out. There were several seconds of silence and a muffled explosion that made the floor rock under our feet. In the darkness someone screamed; someone else began to cry. I didn't cry. It was still a game to me, and an interesting game at that. I simply had no way of imagining that anything could happen to me in this game. I thought the lights would go on again at any moment, but they still hadn't come on when the all-clear was given.

Leaving the shelter, we found that the first bomb to hit Zaporozhe had fallen in the immediate vicinity of our building. It had downed a high-voltage power line and killed a watchman at the nearby kindergarten. In our apartment, we found glass everywhere and the windows all broken to the last pane. The strips of paper hadn't saved them.

The next day, boys collected fragments of the bomb and traded them for various other treasures. But the German bombers flew over almost nightly now, bombs fell, and the fragments were soon worth nothing at all.

In a few days my father came from the enlistment office in an army uniform—to say good-bye. I already knew that such good-byes were for a very long time, and on this occasion I cried, clung to my father, and didn't want to let him go. Retreating Soviet troops were soon trudging through Zaporozhe, and the occupants were ordered to evacuate.

We were evacuated, as was the practice, in freight cars—"hot cars," calf cars, and cattle cars. Each was supposed to hold eight horses or forty men, but there were many more than forty of us to a car. Where we were going, nobody knew; it was a military secret. The adults tried to guess our general direction by the station names. No one told us what the next station would be or how long we would be there. That too was a military secret—perhaps a secret at times even to those who directed our movements. One day we pulled out of a station in the early evening, rode all night almost without stopping, in the morning came to a stop, stuck our heads out, and—it was the same station. There were times when we stopped in an empty field. Anywhere at all, the

Father, Nicolaj Voinovich

train might stand for a day, an hour, or a minute—the length of our stay was unannounced. This made people afraid to leave the train, and men and women relieved themselves indiscriminately in front of the cars. Only when we changed engines or took on water could they risk going a little farther. We rode day and night without a whistle or lights—the blackout applied to both light and sound. The stations were dark too. Finally, I remember rolling into Kavkazsky Station—the beautiful station house, the unaccustomed brightness of electric light, the engines whistling, honking at one another, maybe even for no reason, but from pure joy—that they were able to light up and whistle and honk.

After a week and a half in transit, we reached our point of destination—the city of Stavropol. There we had a wearying three-day wait at the junction on a wide, dusty square in the open air. It was all right at night, but the days were very hot. For some reason there was no water, and we all suffered from thirst. One foolish little girl bit her own chubby lips and drank the blood.

At the end of three days, we faced a journey of the same duration by oxen. We were put in *arabas*—spacious carts with high wheels—and driven off. Our road passed through the steppe. Wherever we looked, on all sides, there was nothing but gray steppe, overgrown with grass, as far as the eye could see. We saw no dwellings—no sign that such things even existed. The sun rose in the morning, swelling ominously with heat, and crawled interminably from one horizon to the other. During the day there was no salvation from the heat. In midday, when the oxen were unharnessed to drink (they carried water with them), people climbed under the carts to escape from the sun, but even there the heat was incredible. Someone in my group died along the way of sunstroke, and a woman in the next cart gave birth.

Thirty years later, passing the same places in a car, I decided to retrace the journey I had made by oxen. It took me no more than an hour, and the steppe did not seem so boundless after all.

We found ourselves at last in a settlement called North-Eastern farm—as distinct from South-Western, which was seven kilometers away. These farms made up our collective, or *kolkhoz*. The *kolkhoz* office was in South-Western, as was the elementary school, which was set up as rural schools usually were, with four grades in two rooms—the first and third grades in one, the second and fourth in the other. I started in the second grade.

Seven kilometers is quite a distance for a child, and the collective allotted the schoolchildren a large two-wheeled cart and a pair of oxen, which were driven by the eldest among us—namely, the fourth graders. Everything went well until it came into someone's head to play a joke and harness the oxen in the wrong way. In order to understand the situation, you need to know that oxen are the most obedient and reliable of animals, but they do know and love order. They know that only two names exist for all oxen—Tsob and Tsobe—and a team must always include them both. You mustn't yoke two Tsobs or two Tsobes together. Moreover, you have to know *how* Tsob and Tsobe are harnessed: Tsob always stands on the right, and Tsobe on the left. In this order, they know their job. Once in motion, if you decide to turn left, you rap Tsob on the back with a stick and say, "Tsob!" Tsob will begin to push against Tsobe, and the oxen will turn to the left. For a right turn, you hit the left-standing Tsobe with your stick, and he will begin to push Tsob. To go straight, you hit both and say, "Tsob-Tsobe." Then, pushing one against the other, the oxen will move straight ahead.

So one day, when we were gathering for the ride home from school, one of the fourth graders had the bright idea to conduct an experiment and harness the oxen in the wrong way—that is, to put Tsob on the left and Tsobe on the right. No one really thought this would be a problem; you'd just give the commands in reverse. But neither Tsob nor Tsobe took a liking to the idea. It violated the established order without creating a new one. Hearing his name, Tsob tensed in readiness to push against his brother on the left, but there was no one on his left. Tsobe found himself in a similar situation. The oxen became visibly nervous. Not understanding the command, they began to jerk and drag our cart from side to side, then went completely mad and, heeding neither word nor stick, took off across the field, making sharp and unexpected zigzags. This frightened the children, and they began to scream. Some were thrown from the cart, while others jumped. The cart was finally overturned, but the oxen ran on, raising clouds of dust, until they were stopped by a haystack. As a result of this experiment, one girl broke her leg, and the others escaped with minor injuries.

After that, the *kolkhoz* authorities deprived us of all means of transportation, and we had to walk to school. But seven kilometers is still a long way to go for a small child. In the winter I think this distance would have been unconquerable, but I didn't have to wait and find out.

Once, while walking home from school alone, I almost stepped on a snake and was so frightened that I ran off without watching where I was going. I thought every snake on the steppe was after me, and I ran, yelling at the top of my lungs, until I dropped from exhaustion. I lay there for a long while. When I got up, it was already dark—all around me was the steppe and no road anywhere. In the end I was lucky, and after walking a ways, I saw a light and heard noise in the distance. It was the *kolkhoz* threshing floor, and there was a threshing machine in operation. A brigade leader by the name of Soroka put me in a cart and took me home. When I recounted what had happened, described the snake that had attacked me and the orange spots over its eyes, my cousins Seva and Vitya just laughed at me—and explained that what I had seen was the most harmless of grass snakes. Harmless or not, my aunt decided that I would no longer be allowed to go to school, and in this way my education was interrupted.

In the area where we lived, people spoke Ukrainian, or rather the mixture of Ukrainian and Russian spoken by almost all Ukrainians on the left bank of the Dneiper, and they called themselves *khokhly*. Since in the Ukraine the word *khokhol* is considered as offensive as *katsap* (for Russian) or *zhid* (for Jew), our people laughed in embarrassment and corrected them: "What do you mean *khokhly?* There's no such people. You're not *khokhly,* you're Ukrainians."

"No, no," the locals replied, "we're *khokhly.*"

I don't know how it came about, but in spite of the collective-farm system, the peasants in those areas were still quite prosperous. Some owned two, three, or even four cows apiece.

The farmers ate nothing that was not hot, fresh, or rich. Present-day advocates of one diet or another would be horrified by what we ate, but I must confess I remember with longing the *gorishki*—balls of dough saturated with garlic and fried in boiling fat—goose cracklings as they sizzled in the skillet, *vareniki* swimming in melted butter or sour cream. And it's hard to believe that the bread we ate could exist on earth—fluffy loaves with a crispy crust that puffed out in places and was coarse, like congealed foam. When visitors asked the locals if they ate black bread, they answered in surprise, "What do you think we are—pigs?" When we first came to the farm, food was very inexpensive, and people wouldn't take money at all in exchange for milk, believing that milk was as free as water and it wasn't right to take money for it.

We were given a separate hut the moment we arrived, and all the members of our family except my grandmother and me went to work on the farm. I did a little work, and even earned several work-days picking beans for castor oil, but they were really just humoring me. It was on the farm that I learned to ride bareback—on an old gelding named Voroshilov. The gelding actually resembled his namesake in the Kremlin, the celebrated Soviet marshal, but he was old, not at all ornery, and would go no faster than a walk.

Toward the end of autumn the collective farm distributed food in compensation for work-days earned, and we received several bags of wheat. Part of the wheat was taken to the mill and ground into flour, and Grandmother was soon baking bread as delicious as that made by the locals.

Winter came on quickly and proved to be quite harsh. Before New Year a heavy snow fell in a howling storm, and the houses were surrounded by snowdrifts higher than the rooftops. Nature is sometimes merciful; after a heavy snowstorm, there is usually space left between a snowdrift and the wall of a house, so the door can be opened. Some of our neighbors went around to dig each other out, all the same.

My grown-up relatives were city folk, unaccustomed to the struggle with nature, and winter took us unawares. We were caught without food or water, and the fuel situation was not much better. We had a stove, but nothing to heat it with. The farm people heated their stoves with *kizyak*—briquettes made of cow dung and straw. But we had neither cow nor dung, so we heated our stove with straw. My cousins Seva and Vitya went out to a lone stack in the field somewhere. The straw was packed very tightly and had to be pried out of the center. My cousins would twist off large bundles, drag them home, and then set out again. The straw made a fire that burned brightly, but died down quickly and didn't give off much heat, and the trip out to the stack was thus a constant and exhausting duty.

Water was a problem too. The wells on the farm froze up and were covered by snow, so water for drinking and cooking was obtained by melting snow. Then the flour ran out. We still had a store of wheat, but in order to make the grain into flour, it had to be taken twenty-five kilometers away to a mill in the village of Takhta. This required a horse, and we were given none. Later they gave us a horse, but the mill in Takhta broke down. We had to cook the grain itself, which we first pounded in a mortar to remove the husks. This dish was known as *kutya*. At first we ate *kutya* with sugar and rancid melted butter (bought the previous autumn), then without sugar or butter, but at least we had our fill. That was all the food we had, though sometimes the farm people invited my grandmother and me over for holidays, and for feasts in remembrance of the dead, and gave us something good to eat.

I had actually learned to read quite early, but it was on the farm that I took a liking to thicker books. True, there were only two such books on the farm: The Gospel According to St. Matthew and *School* by Arkady Gaidar. I liked them both equally and read them over and over, until I discovered that one of the evacuees had brought along part of her home library and would let me share her riches. She asked me over, showed me a small pile of rather worn books, and invited me to pick whichever one caught my eye. I didn't have to think long, and put my finger on the title that appealed to me most—*War and Peace.*

"Aren't you a little young to be reading that?" asked the neighbor lady.

"No," I said, "I'm not."

From that moment on, till I was called up for the army, I read books like a man on a drinking binge. We kept moving from place to place, living at various times in the city and in the country, libraries were

better or worse, and I read everything I could get my hands on. Luckily, what I often got were Russian classics. As it happened, I didn't have to read the books that many generations of children like me were raised on—the novels of Dumas, Mayne Reid, and Jules Verne—and later I found them boring. But even those I did read in childhood—*Robinson Crusoe, Treasure Island,* and *The Count of Monte Cristo*—made less of an impression on me than, say, *War and Peace, Oblomov,* or *Dead Souls.* Since most of the books I read were from the library, the best were always worn, and it is just such tattered, soiled, and well-thumbed covers that inspire longing in me to this day. My eyes pass over the glossy jackets with complete indifference.

I also learned on the farm that all men are mortal. My grandmother told me. I hadn't known before. That is to say, I saw that from time to time people were taken somewhere in wooden boxes and buried in the ground, but I never thought such a thing could happen to me. Now Grandmother said it could. I didn't believe her at first, but then it got me thinking, and I tried to imagine what it would be like. Well, with Grandmother it was fairly easy. She was small, thin, and fair, with a pointy nose. If you put her in a coffin, closed her eyes, and decorated with flowers, she would look right at home. At last, stretching my imagination as far as it would go, I was able to imagine that Mama and Papa might die. But me?

It was summer—a clear, hot day. I walked out into the steppe, leaving the farm behind, and gazed into the distance. The steppe, to the limits of vision, was silver with dry grass that dissolved in a smoky haze on the horizon. A black bird—a kite—hung motionless beneath the sun. I closed one eye and then the other. I opened my eyes, one after the other, and saw what I had seen before—silver grass, a smoky haze, the hanging kite. I closed and opened my eyes together. Everything remained where it had been. Even the kite had not moved from its place. I tried to imagine how all this could exist without me, but the more I thought, and the harder I tried, the more clearly I understood that none of it could possibly exist without me.

As spring approached, the mill in Takhta was repaired, but it now lacked some of its bolters and as a result produced only gray flour. That spring, for the first time in anyone's memory, the local people began to eat black bread, which they had recently held in such low regard. But the farmers had all they needed of most other foodstuffs, whereas we had nothing. So that spring, the grown-up members of our family began to trade things for food—at first on what we considered to be very good terms. We'd give them a jacket, say, or a secondhand skirt or pants, and they'd give us a sack of flour or a hunk of lard. Living conditions deteriorated rapidly, however.

That summer the Germans launched a new offensive, and as fall approached we were ordered to be evacuated yet again. The local people would stay where they were. In fact, many looked forward to the coming of the Germans, hoping that they would break up the collective farms. The farmers gave us a warm send-off all the same, weeping and handing out food for the road, but the people of the settlements we passed along the way (traveling again by oxen) were quite hostile—and of course we were all Jews to them. I remember some men at work in a field who ran up to the road, menacing us with rakes and pitchforks and yelling, "Run, you dirty Jews, run! If the Germans get you, they'll cut your throats!" They seemed about ready to give up waiting for the Germans and take matters into their own hands, but they never did make up their minds.

The second evacuation was, if possible, harder than the first. A significant portion of our journey was through places already visited by the war—demolished stations, burned houses, the roads strewn with disabled tanks, cannons, and trucks. At last we reached a small town in the district of Kuibyshev. Here, after long adventures, I was found by my mother, and toward autumn my father arrived. He had fought for only half a year, was seriously wounded, and after several months in the hospital, came home to his family an invalid.

The war was still at its height. It had already brought so many misfortunes, and the longer it went on, the greater was the people's hatred of the Germans.

"Papa," I said, asking my father a question very common in those times, "how many Germans did you kill?"

My father had never looked at me as fiercely as he did at that moment. He spoke distinctly. "Remember this for the rest of your life," he said. "I never killed a single person, and I'm very proud of that fact."

I remembered. For the rest of my life.

About the same time, in the summer of 1942, my parents and I went to live in the country, while Aunt Anya and her family remained in town. My heart was torn in two. When my parents were gone, I missed them, but when my parents and I went away, I missed my aunt Anya, grandmother, and cousins. I spent the winter of 1942-43 with my parents in the country.

Life was hard, but we weren't destitute. At any rate, we had enough to eat.

The next summer I went to visit Aunt Anya and stayed on. Beginning in the fall, we experienced famine no less severe than that described by survivors of the siege of Leningrad. People bloated and died, sometimes dropping right on the street. Our family suffered too, and we had to scrounge for food as best we could. A military unit was stationed next to our building, and I would go next door and ask the soldiers for potato peelings to feed to a rabbit we didn't have. These peelings were made into pancakes, which we fried in machine oil. My cousin Vitya built a snare, something like a mousetrap, for catching birds. Only once did he ever get anything. The snare trapped a sparrow, which we cooked and divided six ways.

In December my father came for me. When I saw what he had brought me as a treat, I was very

Vladimir, age nineteen, as a soldier in the Red Army, 1951

"On the balcony of our apartment," Moscow, 1971

disappointed. It was boiled lard—something I had never eaten before. But when I tried it, I felt that I had never eaten anything so good in my life.

In February 1944 my parents and I moved to a rural area in the district of Vologda, where Mama's brother, Uncle Volodya, was chairman of a collective farm. Mama was pregnant, and soon after our arrival she bore me a little sister—named, against my wishes, Faina. There on the collective farm, and then on a state farm, I began to earn my daily bread. In the summer I worked on a threshing machine, was a herdsman, a watchman, and did other kinds of farm work. I finished fourth grade, but did not go on to the fifth; the school was a long way off, and I didn't have any shoes.

In May 1945, war with the Germans came to an end, and in the autumn we returned to Zaporozhe. The city had been totally destroyed. Its people were all very poor, and so were we. My parents couldn't feed me and sent me to a trade school to become a joiner, but this profession did not come easily to me. I was suited to mental and not physical labor. After suffering through two years of trade school, I was assigned a job in a factory and had no choice but to go. What I really wanted was to study, but it just wasn't possible. My parents were too poor to feed two children, and leaving the factory was out of the question in any case. All trade-school graduates were required to work four years at whatever job they were given, and anyone who left would face a trial and prison. And those who left weren't the only ones

prosecuted. If you came twenty minutes late to work, or five minutes late on two separate days, the punishment was four months of incarceration.

I studied evenings at a school for working youth. Students were required to work eight hours and then study four, with only one day off a week. I completed sixth and seventh grades in spite of this exhausting schedule, and in place of the eighth, I went to a local flying club, where I flew gliders and practiced skydiving.

I feel I must leave out so many things. My four years as a soldier were an important part of my life, but I'll have to hurry through them. In 1951 I was nineteen and of military age. Army service was unavoidable for me, and I never tried to dodge it. I had done very well at the flying club and passed a two-year course of study in only one year. I wanted to fly, but I had no chance of becoming a real pilot. Flying schools required a high-school education, and I had only a seventh-grade certificate. I knew of a military glider school in the Altai that I was fully qualified for, but I wasn't accepted there either, supposedly on medical grounds: when I went before the medical board, I had a light cold. I refused to accept this decision—went to the enlistment office, sent off letters of protest—and was blocked at every turn. Only many years later did I guess that I was rejected, not because of my cold, but because of my mother's Jewish background. My Serbian family name would also have sounded suspicious to an anti-Semite.

I wasn't accepted to flying school or glider school, but I did get into aviation, and after graduating from a special school, I became an airplane mechanic. To be honest, I wasn't much of a soldier, though I had no trouble mastering the various skills of barracks life. I learned to be out of bed and ready in forty seconds, to lift my legs to the required height, and I didn't confuse my left side with my right. But the idiocy of army life was oppressive all the same.

In my third year, it dawned on me what I wanted to do after my discharge. I had hated working as a joiner, and although I was managing pretty well as an airplane mechanic, that job wasn't much to my liking either. My soul was drawn to more intellectual pursuits, and above all to literature—the very thing I had long resisted, because of my father's example. His literary studies had no doubt brought him some satisfaction, but they had also been a source of much disappointment. I knew that literature, more than any other sphere of human activity, demanded total honesty—and honesty was not in favor. But change was in the air. Stalin died. The "thaw" was yet to come, but there were slight indications of a warming trend. All this had an effect on me, and I decided to try my hand at writing verse. My first efforts were terrible. When I read these early works to an acquaintance many years later, she said they convinced her that a horse, by persistent effort, could become a man.

I *was* persistent. I worked like a horse because I had so many hurdles to jump. My education had been unsystematic, and although I had read quite a number of books, I had absolutely no idea how they were written. In the army I didn't know a single person who could have evaluated my writing and given advice. I had to grope my way, trusting only to feeling and taste. Apparently I had both taste and feeling, because I didn't flatter myself that what I had done was good. I saw that my scribbling had no relation to literature whatsoever. But I also knew that writing was not a simple matter. Hard work was the only way to master it, and I spared no effort.

I wrote something—good or bad—whenever I had a free minute, and often when I didn't. On my night table in the barracks, on the wing of a plane, even behind the backs of other soldiers in formation, I would take down the lines that came to me in a notebook. I decided to train myself by writing at least one poem a day. It might be bad—even awful—but one had to be written every day. One or more. My record was eleven. I realized that an untalented writer would be disappointed again and again, and could make himself unhappy for the rest of his life. So I gave myself a deadline. If I hadn't written anything I could call poetry within a year, I would give up writing.

In three months I had something that resembled verse. I found a man in our unit who had taught literature as a schoolteacher, and I showed him my composition. After reading it, he thought a moment and said, "You know, I used to write poems too, but mine were never this good. You should keep at it. You could do something."

I was discharged in November 1955. When I went to sign up for night school, the first quarter had already ended. I said I had finished ninth grade and wanted to enter the tenth. I was accepted for a trial period and, to my own surprise, very easily caught up with all my classmates—passed many in fact—and graduated with a perfectly respectable record of A's and B's. I applied to the Gorky Literary Institute, the only institute in the USSR to train future writers. I was turned down. I sent them a telegram: "Your answer did not make my day any brighter. I haven't lost heart, and I *will* be a writer." The director of the

institute reportedly said that I should have been accepted on the basis of that telegram alone. I wasn't accepted, but I didn't lose heart either, and I showed up in Moscow without any invitation.

In Moscow I worked as a trackwalker for the railroad and as a carpenter on a construction site. I took classes in the history department at a teachers institute, but I was totally absorbed in my own writing and consequently a poor student. I wrote poetry, but I wasn't getting anywhere with my real interest, which was prose. I thought then, and I still think, that prose is a more complex genre than poetry. Prose has less in the way of visible boundaries, reference points, and rules, and is much easier to get lost in. Poetry is a ride downriver—prose an ocean voyage. Time and again I tackled prose, and all too often I took what I had written and tore it up in despair. I used up hundreds of sheets of paper and threw them all away. My descriptions of nature, people, and events were dull and lifeless. Something essential was missing, but exactly what, I didn't know.

It happened just as it had happened once with poetry. I went to bed one day in the depths of despair and thought, What am I going to do? Why do all my attempts at prose come to nothing? I know life relatively well. I even have an idea what I want to say about it. So why, when I pick up the pen, do I get nothing but amorphous, contrived, and insincere phrases that no one would ever say? I tossed and turned, unable to sleep, and didn't much want to go on living. All of a sudden I heard, as if off to one side, a sound like a tuning fork. Then, clear as day, I saw a

The author with daughter Marina and son Pavel, 1974

With daughter Olga in Maleevka, a Russian village near Moscow, 1975

picture worth describing and the only words that could possibly describe it. I was tired and wanted to sleep, but I realized that if I didn't get this fleeting image on paper, it would depart, slip away, and might never come again.

I leaped out of bed, sat down at the table in my shorts, and wrote, "It was early morning and the grass, drenched with dew, looked sleek and black." You may wonder what it is about this sentence that's so magical, but it had just the magic needed to lead me onward. I sat and wrote. As I wrote one line, I didn't know what the next line would be, but I knew that something would come. A rough draft of my first story was written in several days. Then I spent a long time rewriting, until I got it right. I never have any desire to reread that story. I know that in places it's weak and uninspired, and on the whole I would call it infantile, though it also contains lines that I may never have surpassed. One writer who read it said, "This story will be published, but you'll catch hell for it, because what you write is too close to real life."

He turned out to be right. I did catch hell for that story, and for what I wrote after it, and for what I didn't write, and generally for not being what literary critics and the KGB wanted to see. But my first encounter with the KGB came a little earlier. This is the way it happened: On a misty, frosty morning in January 1959, I was awakened by a loud, almost hysterical knock at my door. Peeking out, I saw my landlady, Ludmila Alekseyevna, once a dancer at the Bolshoi Theater, standing half-dressed in the hall.

"Volodya," she said, sounding terribly alarmed, "there's a man banging at the back door who says he's your friend."

I looked at my watch. It was eight-thirty. I usually got up much later, because I went to bed quite late. My landladies, Olga Leopoldovna Pash-Davydova and her daughter, Ludmila Alekseyevna, had both danced at the Bolshoi and were both now retired. (The mother was past eighty and the daughter close to sixty.) They kept to their old habits and never went to bed before three in the morning. I had grown accustomed to their schedule, and if I happened to fall asleep early, Olga Leopoldovna would knock loudly at my door and say, "Volodya, are you still awake? I came to wish you good night."

Olga Leopoldovna's late husband had been one of the first People's Artists of the Russian republic, and they were among the few Muscovites lucky enough to have a four-room apartment in the center of Moscow. Olga Leopoldovna had shared one room with her husband and a large, regal poodle. Ludmila Alekseyevna lived in another with her husband, newborn baby, and sheepdog Nelka. The third room stood empty, unless you count a mean little Tibetan terrier that always sat in one corner. I occupied the fourth room—if you can call it that, since it was less than four square meters in size. Its only furnishings were a large iron bed, as long as the room itself, and a chair that would only fit sideways between the bed and the windowsill. The sill, which was deep and served as my desk, held a typewriter that I had bought for next to nothing, and all of my unpublished works, collected in a heap. This collection grew slowly but steadily, because I was young, full of energy and hope, and I wrote every day, fanatically, turning out volumes of work.

I had rented the room quite recently, and not even my closest friends knew my address. There was no one who could have come to see me for any reason. The landlady went with me to the back door. All three dogs had burst into the hall and were barking with a vengeance.

"Who is it?" I asked.

"Vladimir Nikolayevich," came an embarrassed voice, "please open the door. I need to see you for a moment."

This was very surprising, and not a little suspicious. Though I was already twenty-seven, I was only a student, and no one yet called me by my name and patronymic. Instead of asking the uninvited visitor to go around to the front, Ludmila Alekseyevna and I set about unearthing the back entryway, clearing away assorted tubs, buckets, and cardboard boxes. We finally opened the door and saw before us a relatively young man in glasses.

"Please, will you take the dogs away?" he pleaded.

"Who are you and what do you want?"

"I'll explain everything in a moment."

The dogs were rounded up, and Ludmila Alekseyevna left the two of us alone in the sitting room.

"What do you want?" I asked him.

"Just a moment and I'll explain everything." He slowly nodded his balding head. Then, lowering his voice, he said hurriedly, "No one can hear us?"

"No one can hear us."

"And the dogs are gone? They can't get in here?"

"No, they still haven't learned how to open the doors."

"Ah, yes, the door opens the other way. And no one can hear us?"

"I don't know," I said, raising my voice, "whether anyone can hear us or not, but I don't intend to speak in whispers. Now what do you want?"

"Just a moment, just a moment. I'll explain everything. Are you sure no one can hear us?"

Until then I had never come in contact with employees of the KGB and had no idea what one would look like. I had never thought about it at all, to tell you the truth, but I had no doubt as to my visitor's profession.

"Vladimir Nikolayevich . . . are you sure no one can hear us?"

"No, no one can hear us."

"Good, good, very good. I believe you. I've come to talk to you on behalf of the student literary society."

"And what might that be?" I asked.

"Oh, just a student society. Affiliated with . . . with . . . with Moscow University. We get together, read poetry, discuss things. You're sure no one can hear us?"

"What do you want from me?"

"Oh, nothing, nothing. Nothing in particular. We'd simply like you to give a reading for us. We've read your verses in *Evening Moscow,* and several of our members heard you read in Izmailovsky Park. So we'd like very much—are you sure no one can hear us?—to invite you to read."

"When?" I asked.

"Well, right now, right now."

"Now?" I asked incredulously. "At eight-thirty in the morning? Don't the students have classes?"

"Well, of course they do, Vladimir Nikolayevich, of course they do. But a few of our members would like to speak with you in advance. You're sure no one can hear us? We could go right now; it's quite close."

"Do you mind telling me why I should?"

"Well, we'll iron out some of the details. Maybe you'll agree to do a reading. I hope you don't have any objections."

He filled me with revulsion and with an unexplainable fear. I had to get rid of him somehow, and to my own surprise, I suddenly said that I read only for money. This was an outright lie. Though I had given several public readings as a member of the literary society Magistral, no one had ever offered me any money for them.

"What do you mean, money?" he said, taken aback. "We're a student society. We don't have any money."

"Well, if you don't, you don't, but I won't read for free."

"No, no, no, Vladimir Nikolayevich . . . You're sure no one can hear us? Come now, how can you ask for money?"

This began a long and senseless disputation. He simply couldn't understand how a student—and only a beginning poet, not a professional—could be so greedy, and for some reason I stood my ground and demanded payment. Seeing that this upset him, I was even more insistent, but financial gain had nothing to do with it. I was simply trying, in this irrational way, to ward off a danger that I sensed, but didn't fully understand. My preoccupation with money evidently threw him. He even lost interest in whether anyone could hear us or not and spent a long time arguing, not very persuasively, that I should read for free, though he would have lost nothing by agreeing to my demand. Why he was so flustered, I can't exactly say, but it was probably because our conversation had

deviated from the course mapped out at the planning stage. When I had finally had enough, I stood up, rather rudely asked him to leave, and went to open the door.

"Wait, wait, wait," he hissed, nearly in hysterics. "Vladimir Nikolayevich, are you sure no one can hear us? I certainly hope no one can hear us. I didn't properly introduce myself before. Let me introduce myself a little differently." He was instantly transformed. His face took on a haughty, self-satisfied expression, and he reached imperiously into his inside jacket pocket for his papers.

"Don't bother," I said. "I can see who you are."

Pain and disappointment mingled on his face. He evidently thought he had carried off his role with great artistry and skill. "How did you know?" he asked, his voice falling.

"It wasn't difficult," I said. "I don't often read detective novels, but I do on occasion, and all the detectives look just like you."

"They do?"

I could see that my words had hurt him. Later, having made the acquaintance of several of his

At a farewell party with wife Irina before being expelled from the Soviet Union, December 1980: "Very sad!"

colleagues, I observed that the majority are very thin-skinned. This sensitivity is a remnant of the humanity that was in them at birth. Whatever general or personal theories they live their lives by, however they justify their activities, they still feel despised. There are some, on the other hand, who are not thin-skinned, and these are the most dangerous.

"Well, well, so you figured it out, you figured it out." There was disappointment in his voice. "Well, let's go then," he said, neither asking nor ordering.

"Let's go then," I agreed.

Let me be very clear. Although I spoke in a highly disrespectful and mocking tone, I was actually scared to death. I have probably never been so frightened before or since. I was just starting out as a poet, and I thought I could do good work. But at the same time I always had the feeling that some fateful turn of events would prevent me from realizing my potential. Either I would be diagnosed with a rapidly advancing and incurable illness, or be hit by a car, or something else of the sort would happen.

I was a true Soviet, but that didn't mean I was fond of Soviet rule or believed in Marxism-Leninism-Communism. In fact, I didn't believe in any of this and considered all Soviet propaganda to be empty words for idiots. Like the overwhelming majority of people that I had met in my life, I hated all the Soviet gibberish, despised the political lessons, meetings, rallies, demonstrations, elections, and voluntary work. I did my best to avoid all of that, but at the same time I didn't ask for trouble. Many years later I realized that for me this was precisely what it meant to be Soviet.

Whether it was in the army or on the job, the administration and party leadership always knew that I would engage in no ideological activity. They never invited me to join the party and never even tried to recruit me as an informer (not even in the case at hand). I was that passive, completely harmless member of society whom the authorities find neither useful nor threatening. Those young people who took a serious interest in Communist theory and immersed themselves in Marx, Lenin, and Stalin were far more dangerous to the regime, and the Soviet authorities eventually realized this. A man who takes the theory seriously will sooner or later compare theory with practice and end up rejecting either one or the other, and then both. But a man who is not deluded by theory will see the existing practice as a normal and immutable evil, and he will somehow adapt.

I maintain, therefore, that I was Soviet through and through. This also meant that nothing the authorities could do or say would have surprised me,

which was precisely what made me incapable of any significant protest. My concept of legal rights was virtually nil. Although I spoke with my guest in an ironic and unpleasant tone, we immediately came to a tacit agreement on what was most important. I was frightened, and fully accepted the possibility that I might disappear forever and no one would ever know what had become of me. It never occurred to me that, having committed no crime, I might protest against being abducted in this way. I never checked my visitor's papers or questioned his right to take me wherever he pleased.

When we stepped into the corridor, my landlady was there, now fully dressed. "Volodya," she said, trying not to look at my escort, "will you be gone long?"

I turned to him and asked loudly, so that my landlady would know who he was, "Will I be gone long?"

"No, no, of course you won't!" He resumed his air of embarrassment. "He'll be back very, very soon."

I thought how cleverly I had let the landlady know where I was going. I imagined how the police would twist my arms as they threw me into a black van waiting for me at the curb. But there was no black van, and my escort indicated that we would go on foot. This surprised me, but I went along. On the way, he was no longer ingratiating, but spoke in a condescending manner. He asked me why I wrote such sad verses. Aware that I could be shot for writing sad verses, I disagreed and said that, while my poems were sad, they contained elements of an inner optimism. I saw from his face that he was unpersuaded. He looked at me as he would at a young man gone astray—someone to be pitied, but shot nonetheless. We walked and walked through a maze of winding alleys, and I asked him sarcastically (at least I thought I was being sarcastic) if we were lost.

"Yes, yes, it's possible," he said, obviously worried. "We might be lost. No, I take that back. We're not lost after all." He pointed to a sign that read,

STATE SECURITY COMMITTEE COUNCIL OF MINISTERS OF THE USSR

"There, you see," he said again, as if priding himself on his knowledge of the surrounding alleys. "We're not lost after all."

I have no memory of the doors we passed, of elevators or corridors, or whether they asked either of us for identification. I remember only that we entered an office with a large but rather plain table, behind which sat an ordinary man of average height in a gray suit. He shook my hand, told me his name and patronymic, and addressed me also by name and patronymic. Then he offered me a chair and said, "What do you think, Vladimir Nikolayevich—are you a good Soviet?"

I felt a little relieved. If they hadn't made up their minds whether I was Soviet or not, it meant they might not shoot me immediately. I assured him fervently that I was.

"Of course you are," he said, "I never doubted it for a second. You're a good Soviet, and we need your help. You help us and we help you. If you help us, then we'll help you." He rubbed his hands and fixed his eyes on me in anticipation of something pleasurable. "Well, let's hear it."

"Hear what?" I asked, sincerely perplexed.

"Let's hear what you know."

"I don't know anything."

"Come now, Vladimir Nikolayevich." My host smiled and exchanged glances with my escort, who was sitting in the corner. "You must know something."

"Well, something perhaps, but I don't know what you're interested in."

"We're interested in everything."

"I don't understand," I said.

"Vladimir Nikolayevich"—he threw up his hands in a gesture of exasperation—"You're a good Soviet, aren't you?"

"Yes, of course I am, but I don't understand what it is you want."

Then he told me: he wanted a full account (you help us and we help you) of where I went and who I associated with. I never doubted his right to ask, but I also knew I should avoid answering questions. I told him that I went nowhere and associated with no one.

"Oh, come now, come now, come now"—the man who had brought me came to life. "You went to an art exhibit, didn't you, and looked at abstract paintings?"

So that was it! Even though the exhibit had been completely official, and there had been no warning from anyone to stay away, I was supposed to understand, as a good Soviet, that it was better not to look at abstract paintings. I didn't ask how they knew I had been at the exhibit and not turned away from the abstract paintings, but the quality of their information raised the hope that they knew something else—that I had thoroughly disliked those paintings. I was more than happy to tell them so.

Irina, Olga, and Vladimir in Austria, 1984

"No normal person could like them," the older man remarked profoundly, and his younger colleague seconded the opinion.

"No, no, they're a profanation of art."

"And what do you think of Pasternak?" asked the older man.

I said I didn't think anything about Pasternak, which was perfectly true, since I didn't begin to read and think about Pasternak until much later. I was partial to Simonov and Tvardovsky among Soviet poets, and Sholokhov among the prose writers, and this was pretty much their idea of what would appeal to a normal Soviet with healthy tastes.

But they were still dissatisfied, and the older man made a seemingly offhand remark, which he repeated thereafter with increasing frequency: "You be careful, or you'll have only yourself to blame."

At one point, he suddenly broke off the conversation and darted out of the room. No sooner had he gone than the younger man walked over to the table, picked up an ordinary wooden ruler, and returned to his place. Holding the ruler like a pistol, he began aiming it at me, grinning mysteriously, but saying nothing. The older man came running back and started in again: "You help us and we help you, but if you don't help us, you'll have only yourself to blame." Again, nothing very concrete.

"All right, who are your friends?" he asked.

"I don't have any friends."

"And what about Litovtsev and Polsky?"

I studied with Litovtsev and Polsky at the institute, and we read our poems to one another. To deny that I knew them would have been unwise. I said, "Oh, yes, Litovtsev and Polsky. We go to school together. All three of us write poetry, and, well, we see each other sometimes."

"What do you talk about?"

"Well, poetry, for example."

"And what else?"

"Nothing else."

"Nothing else?" He was raising his voice more often now. "You don't even talk about women?"

"No," I said angrily, "I'm a married man with a daughter, and I don't talk about women!"

"Well, well, well!" remarked the young man ironically.

"All right," said the man at the desk, "we'll leave women out of it. Do you talk about politics?"

"No," I said.

"Not at all? Do you mean to say you have no interest in politics?"

"None," I said, and at the time it was the simple truth.

"How can you be a good Soviet and have no interest in politics?"

"That's just the way it is," I said, gradually losing my temper. "I'm a good Soviet and I have no interest in politics."

"All right. Women don't interest you, politics don't interest you. How are your relations with foreigners?"

At this point I completely lost control and shouted, "What foreigners? What nonsense is this? I don't know one single foreigner!"

"Come now, come now, come now," the young man mumbled from his corner. "What about the Israeli diplomat?"

"Oh, hell!" I even spat, I was so annoyed. Or maybe it just seems that I spat.

The story of the Israeli diplomat went like this: One day, after crossing Kuznetsky Bridge, Igor Litovtsev and I stopped in at a bookstore, and Litovtsev discovered that they were selling a collection of poetry by Avram Gontar.

"Who is this Gontar?" I asked.

"You don't know? He's a very good Jewish poet. We have to get a copy."

We stood in line, paid our money, and the cashier gave us two receipts, but when we took them up to the counter to claim our books, we found that they were already sold out. A curly-headed man in front of us had taken the last four copies.

On first returning to Moscow: with writer B. Sarnow (left) and actor V. Smechov, who is reading aloud from Voinovich's book Putem vzaimnoi perepiski (In Plain Russian), *1989*

Overhearing our conversation with the saleswoman, the curly-headed man immediately turned around and said that if we were interested in Gontar, he would be happy to give us each a copy, and he held out the books. We said we couldn't, he insisted, and the five of us stepped outside. (He had two little curly-headed boys, between the ages of four and six.) We took the books, but at that point the man began pressing Litovtsev to explain why Soviet policy was anti-Semitic. Litovtsev mumbled something. As a true Soviet, and truly ignorant about politics, I rushed to his aid with the assertion that the USSR had no such policy. The curly-headed man said that, as a secretary of the Israeli embassy, he knew what he was talking about, and he continued to press Litovtsev, ignoring me altogether. He told Litovtsev that he should be ashamed not to know the Jewish language and Jewish culture. I said Litovtsev was not a Jew, but a pure Russian, and for a Russian, he knew Jewish culture well enough.

I don't know what the Israeli took me for—perhaps a commissar assigned to keep an eye on Litovtsev—but he obviously didn't want to talk to me and kept his back to me the whole time. Despite my assurances, the man persisted in trying to shame Litovtsev for not acknowledging his Jewish heritage. Litovtsev mumbled something in response, and it was clear from what he said that in fact he was ashamed. The diplomat's children were pulling him by the arms. He resisted for quite a while, but finally gave up and got in his car. The Israelis drove off, and Litovtsev and I continued on our way.

My outbursts were becoming more frequent. I said to the man at the desk, "Why do you even bother asking? You've been following me around and know everything anyway."

"And just what—just what makes you think we've been following you?" came the voice from the corner.

"How would you know about the Israeli, if you hadn't been following me?"

"All right," said the older man irritably, "we know what we know. But why didn't you come and tell us yourself?"

"Why should I?"

"Why? You're a good Soviet, aren't you?"

"Yes," I said proudly, "I am a good Soviet. But I didn't think I had to come running to you every time I met someone on the street."

"Come now, you could see that this provocateur was spouting Zionist propaganda. Oh, that's right,

you're not interested in politics. You're only interested in poetry. So who's reading at Rodnik these days?"

"Where?" I asked.

"The literary society at your institute—it's called Rodnik, isn't it?" The older man looked at his colleague.

"Rodnik, Rodnik," the younger man said with authority.

At this point I began to breathe easily again. They seemed to know everything about me, but there was something they didn't know after all. Enjoying my advantage, I said, "You do know, don't you, that I've never been to Rodnik in my life." I noticed that this answer demoralized them considerably. The older man looked sternly at the younger, who seemed to shrink back guiltily.

"Then you don't know who their student leader is?" asked the older man.

"I have no idea," I answered quite truthfully.

"All right," he said, in some confusion, "what do your professors talk about in their lectures?"

"That," I said slyly (and the answer still pleases me) "is a question I have trouble answering even on exams."

"Why is that?" The older man didn't get my joke.

"Because," I said, rubbing it in, "if you *have* been following me, you should have noticed that I'm never at the institute, and when I go, it's usually to collect my stipend. And if you'd gone to my group leader and checked my name on the attendance sheet, you would have seen nothing but 'absent, absent, absent.'"

Here the interrogation ended, but they were not quite done. The older man said that, on the one hand, he believed I was a good Soviet, but on the other, he had his doubts. And if I had misrepresented or omitted anything, I would have only myself to blame. He said I should think it over and come back the following Tuesday. "And while you're at it," he said, "bring your poems along. We'll look them over and see what we can do to help. You help us and we help you. But if you don't help us, you'll have only yourself to blame."

Then they asked me to sign a statement that I would divulge nothing of what had passed between us. As a good Soviet, I did this without a murmur of protest, and when I left the offices of the KGB, I ran and, like a good Soviet, told my friends everything that had happened.

And this is what I learned: Since I rarely went to the institute, it turned out that I had missed quite a sensation. The student leader of the literary society

Vladimir and Irina Voinovich, New York, 1988

Rodnik had been arrested for writing anti-Soviet poetry. I actually knew him, though I hadn't known he was the leader of Rodnik. I even knew a little of his poetry. He had cornered me one day and recited some, and there were two lines that stuck in my mind:

> *And those whom we exalt today*
> *Will swing from lampposts on the morrow.*

I didn't like those lines; as a good Soviet, I didn't care for such things. I don't like them as an anti-Soviet, either.

Thinking back on that first encounter with the KGB, it occurs to me how ignorant I was about legal matters. Anyone with a minimal understanding of legal rights could have told me that I had made a whole series of the grossest errors. First, as soon as I knew he was KGB, before we ever left the apartment, I should have checked his papers. Second, I should have refused to go anywhere without an official summons. Third, during my interrogation I should have demanded to know why I had been brought in and insisted that a record be kept of the proceedings.

As for the statement I signed, I'm not sure, but I think it was illegal.

If, however, I had been that clever—if I had demonstrated a familiarity with the law and a developed sense of legality—the KGB would have made a note of it, and in a sense my fate would have been sealed, unknown to anyone. I was an authentic Soviet man, who didn't believe in Marxism-Leninism, or in laws, or truth, or legal rights. In my relations with the KGB, I chose the most idiotic line of action, and this was the approach that proved most correct.

Many years went by, and my situation changed dramatically. From the very lowest rung, I moved far up the social ladder, though not all the way to the top: I became a member of the privileged caste of Soviet writers. My outlook on the world slowly changed. I became aware that, as an individual and a member of society, I had certain obligations and rights. I already knew quite a bit about Soviet law and put that knowledge into practice, but the more scrupulous I was in observing the law, the more problems I had.

In the end I was banished from the caste of writers and deprived even of what meager opportunities I had had as a carpenter and a student (the opportunity to work, for example, even if the pay was minimal). First in practice, and then by official order, they took away from me the title of "Soviet Man" and declared me an enemy of the Soviet system. And they were perfectly justified. Having grasped the idea that the Soviet Union does have laws, I forgot something that I had always known instinctively—that there are no laws in the Soviet Union. It is not the written laws that are important, but the unwritten rules of conduct.

And the rest in a nutshell: My novella *My zdes' zhivem* (We live here) was published in 1961 in the most prestigious of Soviet magazines, *Novy mir*. In September 1962, at the height of the "thaw," I was unceremoniously received into the Soviet Writers' Union, as a Soviet writer of great promise. Twelve years later I was expelled from that union, as an anti-Soviet writer of unfulfilled promise. As an elder colleague once correctly diagnosed, what I wrote was "too close to real life." As a consequence, my books were banned for a number of years, and I found myself under constant KGB supervision. In December 1980 I was expelled from the Soviet Union, and a half year later I was stripped of my Soviet citizenship by an order of Leonid Brezhnev. I have lived in West Germany ever since. Fifteen years after my expulsion from the writers' union, their decision was reversed as incorrect. For now, the order depriving me of Soviet citizenship remains in effect, probably because fifteen years have not elapsed since the day it was signed.

A portion of this essay was excerpted from Voinovich's *Antisovetskii Sovetskii Soiuz.*

BIBLIOGRAPHY

Fiction:

My zdes' zhivem (novella), Sovetskii pisatel' [Moscow], 1963.

Stepen' doveriia (historical novel about Vera Figner), Politizdat [Moscow], 1972.

Povesti (novellas; contains "My zdes' zhivem," "Dva tovarishcha," and "Vladychitsa"), Sovetskii pisatel', 1972.

Zhizn' i neobychainye prikliucheniia soldata Ivana Chonkina, YMCA-Press [Paris], 1975, translation by Richard Lourie published as *The Life and Extraordinary Adventures of Private Ivan Chonkin,* Farrar, Straus, 1977.

Ivan'kiada, ili rasskaz o vselenii pisatelia Voinovicha v novuiu kvartiru (novella), Ardis, 1976, translation by David Lapeza published as *The Ivankiad; or, The Tale of the Writer Voinovich's Installation in His New Apartment,* Farrar, Straus, 1977.

Pretendent na prestol: Novye prikliucheniia soldata Ivana Chonkina, YMCA-Press, 1979, translation by Richard Lourie published as *Pretender to the Throne: The Further Adventures of Private Ivan Chonkin,* Farrar, Straus, 1981.

Putem vzaimnoi perepiski, YMCA-Press, 1979, translation by Richard Lourie published as *In Plain Russian,* Farrar, Straus, 1979.

Antisovetskii Sovetskii Soiuz, Ardis, 1985, translation by Richard Lourie published as *The Anti-Soviet Soviet Union,* Harcourt, 1986.

Moskva 2042, Ardis, 1987, translation by Richard Lourie published as *Moscow 2042,* Harcourt, 1987.

Shapka (novella), Overseas Publications Interchange [London], 1988, translation by Susan Brownsberger published as *The Fur Hat,* Harcourt, 1989.

Khochu byt' chestnym (novellas; includes "Ivan'kiada" and "Shapka"), Moskovskii rabochii [Moscow], 1989.

Plays:

Tribunal (comedy in three acts), Overseas Publications Interchange, 1985.

Contributor of short stories and novellas to *Novy Mir* and *Nauka i religia.* Author of poems, feuilletons, movie scripts, and plays based on his novellas "Shapka," "Khochu byt' chestnym," and "Dva tovarishcha."

Paul Weiss

1901-

AUTOBIOGRAPHICAL COMMENTS
(Selected and organized by Dr. Robert L. Castiglione)

The philosopher in mid-lecture: Paul Weiss, 1986

Preface

On arriving at the last eighties, still occupied with ideas that seem to be new and important, I find it to be more and more difficult, and even distasteful, to write about myself. Consequently, I have for quite a while resisted the invitation to contribute to this valuable series. But I have found a good compromise. I have invited Dr. Robert Castiglione, who has just completed a biography of me, to accept the difficult task of going through my writings of some sixty years and extracting quotations which will together provide a concise, illuminating account of my life and some of my salient opinions.

Dr. Castiglione has shown me his selections. I have suggested some changes and have recommended omissions, so as to bring his account within the allotted scope and to keep it focussed on the most revealing thoughts. He has had the freedom to select what he thought important, and to overrule my suggestions and comments. I think what follows is better than anything I could now provide, or could produce by making my own selections from what has been previously done.

Paul Weiss

Selections

I was born on Avenue D in New York City. My father was a Hungarian from near Budapest. He had been a wandering tinker and left for America to escape service in the army. My mother was a German, from Eisenach, the daughter of a small manufacturer of sausage containers. She was a servant girl when he met her. I was the third . . . child . . . (six boys in all), the first having died before I was born, another but younger brother when I was very young. I was three years younger than the oldest, and five years older than the next.[1]

When I was about six we moved to Yorkville. My earliest recollections begin about this time. I remember that my father had to take off a day from work and go to school when I was in the second grace. I was apparently misbehaving. He took me out of my seat and spanked me before the entire class. I was transferred to another school where, awed by the larger boys, I immediately began to behave myself and was soon doing quite well in my schoolwork. I skipped two classes and was graduated at thirteen. I think the trouble in the earlier class was my showing off before the girls; the new class and school were solidly male.

My father, Samuel, was a little under six feet (I am five feet, [three] and one half inches, down from five feet, six inches), swarthy, black-haired, strong. About the time we moved to Yorkville he became a coppersmith. Previously he had been a tinsmith, and a construction worker (he had worked at the construction of the World's Columbian Exposition in 1892); a little later he became a foreman in a boiler factory, supervising some half-dozen to a dozen Bohemians and Hungarians making large copper drums for beer manufacturers. My mother was a little more than five feet, with red hair. He was quiet, she talkative; he had hardly any interests, going early to bed every night (he worked from eight to after five, I think it was, and half a day on Saturday). Sunday afternoons were spent with his Hungarian cronies, playing cards at a coffeehouse; Sunday morning was spent reading the newspaper. He read Hungarian and German, but had difficulty with English. She, on the other hand, took every opportunity to see operas, plays, and to read the latest books. I thought her too noisy, and liked him more, but in retrospect I can see that she was a lively, imaginative, intelligent woman who had married a man who could not match her in spirit or intellect. But he was steady, hardworking, with firm moral standards. He had a broomstick with three knotted leather thongs hanging on the back

door of the kitchen. He used it on the boys occasionally, but never when we did not deserve it. I never resented his using it on me.

We lived in a railroad flat on what is now York Avenue at Eighty-sixth Street from about the time I was eight to about the time I was seventeen. It was heated by a stove in the kitchen. There were five rooms—the kitchen where we really lived, three bedrooms, one for my younger brothers, one for my older brother and myself, and the third for my parents. Beyond them was a "front room," with our only good furniture. This was closed at all times except for use by my father on Sunday mornings, when we were allowed to come in and fool around with him for a while, and when, which was very rarely, we had visitors. But if we heard a fire alarm, we could without permission run into the front room to look out.

Most of my time was spent on the street. It was comparatively quiet, mainly Jewish and Italian families on our side, and some Irish families, and a few high brownstones occupied by professionals, on the other side. A gangster's family lived across the way. When the gangster was killed, there was a large funeral procession many blocks long, with a number of carriages containing nothing but flowers; this was one of the outstanding events of the time. Around one corner were tenement houses, many stories high, filled with immigrants more recent than my parents. We occasionally bought things from the stores there, but for the most part we kept aloof. Around the other corner were Irish, of whom we were terrified. A half-dozen streets down was a Bohemian district; a dozen streets up was an Italian. Though I wandered all over the city, and skated as my fancy dictated, I never wandered far into Harlem, or into the Italian district.[2]

After I was graduated from P.S. 77 at Eighty-sixth Street and First Avenue, at the urging of my elder brother I entered the High School of Commerce, taking courses in commercial drawing, commercial Spanish, shorthand, typewriting, bookkeeping, practical arithmetic, chemistry, and English. My work was not good. It got worse every year. By the time I was in my third year, I was working during the summer as a kind of secretary-stenographer-bookkeeper in a fountain-pen company—Salz Brothers—and my mother encouraged me to keep working there.[3]

I think that when I was a young man I was what some psychiatrists would call 'manic'; I was beset with a multiplicity of thoughts, darting in many

"After a day of teaching and writing I would at unspecified times try my hand at painting—and later at drawing," 1967

directions, which I could not bring into focus or order. Even today, I may have to go through as many as a half-dozen heavily rewritten drafts before I have something like a coherent account, over which I will have to work some more in order to take care of errors in syntax, to remove confusions and contradictions in thought, and to increase the clarity of the discourse. Today the thoughts are not as many or as vagrant as they once were, but they still take me in many different directions, if only for short periods.[4]

I had left school when I was about sixteen. I was without focus, without money, having learned little and been inspired less by the subjects offered in a commercial high school. For some six barren years I occupied a dozen minor posts in minor businesses. During that time I read voraciously in a rather undisciplined way, buying and studying a wild miscellany of books on life and death, nature, science, logic, poetry, becoming no clearer, wiser, or even better focussed in the process. Somehow, though, I hit on the idea that since proverbs epitomized the wisdom of the race I could come closer to the bone of truth by reflecting on proverbs. I remember hurrying to the library after the day's work was done, pulling down large collections of proverbs, and then reading and studying them until the library closed. In a way the proverbs satisfied me. They had an air of sufficiency, of finality, of bedrock, and seemed to turn everything else into a derivative or commentary. They also left me discontent. It was startling and dismaying to find that every list contained contradictory observations, all apparently equally sage and sound.[5]

A drawing by Paul Weiss, 1979

When I was about sixteen I tried to enlist. As a strong pacifist I can find no excuse except my being caught up in propaganda, in not having much sense, or perhaps even in making a vain display, knowing that I would not be accepted, though I do not think the last was a factor. When I went to work in various minor posts . . . I did allow and even participated in multiple sleazy, not altogether ethical activities carried out by the firms with which I was connected, including the partnership I had with my brother. . . . [W]as I not cheating for my own gain? I was in a way, though it was my older brother who called the tune and dictated the policies. But I did participate and I did share in the profits, and in that sense I was culpable.[6]

Still restless, vaguely searching for something I did not know how to name or recognize, I spoke one day with a Japanese salesman who worked for the same firm. With some hesitation I told him of the things I had read and had been bewilderedly thinking about. With a confidence that awakened mine, he told me that I was interested in philosophy.

To think, during that period, was to act. Without delay I enrolled for philosophy courses in the evening session of City College. To the surprise of the registrar I enrolled for three courses of philosophy to be taken at successive hours three times a week. I was in class from seven to ten. After that I rode home on the subway. The ride took over an hour, giving me time to read my next assignments and other things. I remember being quite sleepy when I set off to work the next day; I believe my office work was found to be increasingly unsatisfactory. But I did not mind; I had found what I was looking for. I was then twenty-two.

City College at night was, at that time, a depressing place, even for one imbued, as so many were, with a passion to know. Tired, earnest, anxious men and women, after a hard day's work, came together in badly lit rooms to hear incidental remarks uttered by weary instructors. The classes were so large, the membership so fluid, the texts so inadequate, the attention so flagging, that it is surprising that any one of us learned enough to pass the examinations or had the energy to write the required essays. I had the good fortune, however, of encountering in two of the classes Eliseo Vivas . . . at that time an eager, energetic, excitable, and exciting student. We two were somewhat violent defenders of opposite, partial truths which we hurled at one another with fury, to the delight of John Pickett Turner, our teacher, and to the surprise and annoyance of the other students. I think we were quite trying, though for the most part we were oblivious of the effect we were making or of the fact that we were taking up so much of the class time and the teacher's attention.

During this period I was at once excited and abstracted, avid for knowledge yet incredibly dogmatic, at once willing to study and unwilling to keep quiet and listen—faults which pursue me until today. I wrote constantly, though somewhat disconnectedly, interspersing time at the typewriter with reading of every kind. At City College there was a small prize [the Kenyon Prize in Philosophy] offered for an essay written in a course during the year. The contest was open to students in the evening and day sessions. Apparently no one in the evening had yet found the leisure or the need to enter the competition. I did. The novelty of the entry was a factor in the decision to have me share the prize with Milton Steinberg. At the end of the year, without too much conviction, my instructor suggested to me that I ought to become a day student.

It did not occur to me until much later that this was a casual remark. It was enough, though, to prompt me to give up my job and enroll in the day session of City College. I soon found that all I had to do was to rent an inexpensive room, earn my food and rent by teaching English to foreigners and children some half-dozen hours a week, and I could spend the rest of the time studying, writing, and discussing. It is easier now than it was for me then to understand the astonishment of John Pickett Turner when he found that I had followed his advice and entered the day session, and particularly that I had decided to begin by taking a course with Morris R. Cohen.

I had heard but little of Cohen by then. And I did not know that his logic class was the meeting ground of seniors who, with considerable justification, prided themselves on being quicker, abler, and better read than the others. All I knew was that I had read Mill's *Logic* during the summer and had been much impressed with it. I wanted to find out more. I did.

Cohen was a remarkable man, in the multiple senses of that term. In appearance and in personality he was unforgettable. Frail, carelessly dressed, he had an enormous domelike head, quick alert eyes, a sharp angular nose, a lean, incisive, nimble mouth, and a jutting jaw. Iconoclastic, quick as lightning, with an amazing amount of information at his fingertips, Cohen was the master of all the students he encountered.[7]

A critical intellect such as Cohen's, even when backed with a sweet kindness which came to expression again and again through the interstices of his sharp dialectic, awakens respect and admiration. Even awe. It teaches one that every reality, no matter how important and respectable, can be a datum for an investigation, and must, if it is to remain worthy of respect and attention, withstand the biting effect of disciplined, searching inquiry. But the critical mind has little time for creative wonder, and can give no occasion for it. It quickens thought but tends to stop the imagination. In my own case Cohen had this effect. But in compensation he stimulated my appetite for the study of logic, and above all aroused my interest in two men somewhat unknown at the time, one living, the other dead, Alfred North Whitehead and Charles Sanders Peirce.[8]

Toward the end of my junior year I met Victoria Brodkin. She was the youngest child of four; her mother was a widow who could not write her own name, but managed to have all her children well-educated. For a time two of them, the son and Victoria, were placed in an orphan asylum, with no effect apparently on the son, but with permanent ill effect on Victoria. Her life there was traumatic, and was always remembered with shock and hurt. Victoria went to Hunter College, where she did not do good work. But she was imaginative, free-spirited, very intelligent. When, on graduation, I decided to go to Harvard to study with Whitehead, about whom I had heard but whose writings, particularly on extensive abstraction, I did not understand and no one apparently could teach me (and also to avoid going to Columbia, where most of the young City College philosophers went, but where they seemed to continue the incessant arguing which characterized them at City), she took a job as a schoolteacher. I borrowed something like seventy-five dollars and went off to Harvard, not quite sure just what to expect.

At that time, Harvard was a place for rich undergraduates, and for graduates who came from colleges all over, but rarely from City College. In any case, I was an oddity; I was poor, badly dressed, with a New York accent, a loud voice, poor manners, somewhat smelly, half-educated, but evidently hardworking and not stupid. No one could make much sense of me; none of my teachers apparently had had much or any acquaintance with the sons of Jewish immigrants from the Lower East Side.[9]

. . . a classmate from City College, Nat Berall, sent me a picture of myself from around 1926. I was astonished to see that I was rather handsome. I had thought of myself as relatively homely. When I wrote

"At my home with Dr. Akio Kataoka, professor of physical education at the Institute of Sport Science, University of Tsukuba, Ibaragi-Ken, Japan, 1987. He is the translator' of my Sport: A Philosophic Inquiry *into Japanese, and is now translating some of my others."*

to him and said that I thought that at the time I was crass, gross, a misfit, he said that I was mistaken. Did I come to that conclusion only after I had been at Harvard, where I was surrounded by rich undergraduates, a Wasp faculty, and was identified by them as *outré?* Perhaps. If so, my portrayals of myself at Harvard must be understood to express in part what I took to be the evaluations of the students and faculty about my manners, dress, ethnicity, and appearance, and not what was true in fact.[10]

By tutoring undergraduates, it was possible for me to get through the year just ahead of the bills. But all that was incidental. My eyes and mind were elsewhere. I had encountered greatness.

Whitehead was a man unlike any I had ever met. Rosy-cheeked, with unbelievably vivid blue eyes, courteous, gentle, above all eminently civilized, probing, perpetually ruminating, Whitehead was singularly uninterested in argument or dispute, with making himself personally evident, with a need to

defeat or overcome. Our first meetings were almost comedies of error and frustration. Though his enunciation was precise, his speech crystal clear, and his language simple, I literally could not grasp a single word in the hundreds he uttered the first day I came to his class. His British speech was beyond my grasp. He told me later that when he first spoke with me, he could not understand a word I said. He had never heard an East Side New York accent, such rapid speech, with so many of the endings of words blurred or omitted. He had been in this country only three years then, and never had had the occasion to hear anyone talk about ideas in such a language or with such a manner. But he never let on. He was kindness itself. I learned about it much later when teacher became teacher and friend.[11]

. . . Evelyn [Mrs. Whitehead] . . . [was] soon . . . urging me on all the colleagues and all the colleagues' wives, until I think she made a nuisance of herself, and did not make them want to have much to do with me. But all that was to the side. In most subtle ways, with kindness and thoughtfulness, shrewdly and sensibly, she constantly edged me toward more and more civilized behavior. I was intrigued by her; she was opinionated and lively, widely read in literature, with independent views and forcefully expressed opinions on politics, people, and literature.

Victoria came to Harvard a year after I did. We were married soon after. She there had a brilliant career, coming out with the highest marks in her graduate examinations, and being sought out by Whitehead and other . . . [distinguished thinkers] again and again. Her opinions were shrewd and bold; she had a brilliant mind . . . she was perceptive, original, daring, mature, radically honest, and easily the intellectual equal of anyone with whom we came in contact.[12]

One learned much, perhaps even more from conversations with Whitehead at his open house on Sunday evenings than one learned in his classes or from his books. Here Mrs. Whitehead and he spoke easily and freshly on whatever topic happened to come to the fore. They were at once charmingly witty and sage, at home in history and literature, politics and religion. The talk ranged on every dimension of existence, all participating—undergraduates, graduates, and colleagues—to the degree that they wished and could. There one grasped what it meant to be a civilized person in speech and in interest, to be appreciative of one's fellow being.[13]

To listen to Whitehead was to be challenged not only in idea but in spirit and in value; it was to feel oneself tested not by him but by absolute standards of integrity. Rarely did he speak directly in answer to a question. Rarely did he stay with any topic for a length of time. His way was that of half-sentences, not altogether clear, but each adding something to its predecessor, until an insight, having no evident bearing on the remarks he had previously made, would stand out in sudden light. What he said was frequently subtler and more profound than a direct answer to one's questions could have been. I used to come home after an evening with him somewhat beside myself with excitement, carrying on a train of thought which more likely than not had little to do with what he had remarked, but which had been stirred and awakened by his insight and creativity. I would visit him years after when I should presumably have grown in knowledge, surety, and wisdom only to find myself still a screechy [piece of] chalk . . . writing trivialities on an uncleaned blackboard.[14]

By now I have forgotten most of the things I heard then and before. What remains behind, hardly touched by time, is the effect of the quality of mind and character, the impact of greatness, the feel of a Whitehead. With the years I have come to have less confidence in his philosophical system, though I think it to be the shrewdest presentation of the currently dominant Cartesian-Lockean view. But the spirit and the values he pointed to in thought and act remain unaltered, a still-attractive goad and guide.[15]

When I was an undergraduate at City College, Morris Cohen published [Charles Sanders Peirce's] *Chance, Love, and Logic,* and we had this as a text in one of his advanced courses. . . . When speaking to some of the graduate students [at Harvard] I learned that the Peirce papers were being edited by Charles Hartshorne. At that time I was single, had a great deal of energy, and decided to go up and see whether I could be of some help to Mr. Hartshorne. I found Hartshorne in a room put aside for him in Widener Library, surrounded by all of Peirce's papers, some piled high on his desk. He was very glad to see me, apparently because nobody had seen him for months. He had been working on these papers for a number of years; I don't know exactly

Paul Weiss, 1987

the condition they were in when he received them, but by the time I came they were piled high without much order. Some piles were marked "not to be used" or "unpublishable." . . . I volunteered my services to Hartshorne. He immediately turned over to me all the writings in logic, saying that he had not had training in logic and that, since I was specializing in this field, I would undoubtedly be able to make judgments about them that he could not. There was no thought at that time of my being an editor; it was Hartshorne's own idea to make me—some time later, after I had been working on these papers—a coeditor. I received nothing for my work on the Peirce papers at that time, and before the end of the term I went home. I had passed my preliminaries and therefore had been freed, according to the Harvard system, from the need to take examinations in any of my courses.[16]

Hartshorne and I were both deeply moved by Peirce. Here was a man who, in the face of hardship and neglect, had devoted himself to a life of philosophizing. It is hard to conceive how, unheralded and ignored, suffering economic, social, and finally physi-

cal handicaps, Peirce could work hour after hour, day after day, year after year, on papers which he could not reasonably hope to see published. He said of himself that he had the persistence of a wasp in a bottle. The figure is singularly apt.[17]

While I was looking for a job [in New York City] to help me over the summer [of 1927], I received a telegram from C. I. Lewis offering me five hundred dollars to come back to work that summer on the Peirce papers. I did not get any pay, if I remember rightly, for any of the work that I did on the Peirce papers during the year, but the next summer I was paid again, and I think a little later received a sum of money in connection with some of the later volumes.[18]

On receipt of the doctorate, I received a second-level scholarship for traveling abroad. Victoria and I went to Berlin, and there, on the urging of Jacob Klein (later dean at Saint Johns), who was a splendid companion and friend to both of us, went to Freiburg for a term. I there heard Heidegger, whom I did not understand very well, and who, when I approached him, brushed me off with a scornful look, because of

A painting by Paul Weiss, 1970, now located at the home of Dean Jude Dougherty of the Catholic University of America

my ignorance, German, or appearance.[19] We returned to Cambridge, Massachusetts, where I had a post as a one-year instructor at Harvard and at Radcliffe. I taught logic at both places. My teaching at Radcliffe was a disaster. I had been told by some young teacher that one merely went over to Radcliffe, said one's piece, and walked out.[20]

It was a relief to all [I think] when I was offered a position at Bryn Mawr. I had not known that Mrs. [Grace] de Laguna, the head of the department, had already consulted with the Whiteheads and that they had recommended me. But, as she quickly told me, they already had a Jew in the department, and she did not think that it was possible to have two. (I notice that the most liberal of places always sees every group but white Protestants to make up a segment in which there cannot be more than a few members. They will not allow a department of more than two or perhaps three Swedes, Hungarians, Greek Catholics, Buddhists, no matter how brilliant, how divergent their interests and background and personalities; but there is no limit to the number of white Protestants that can be tolerated, all the way to the limit of having only these.) . . . She told me that they could not employ a foreigner. . . . After a night's struggle with her conscience, she decided that it was possible to hire a northern Jew since this provided a sufficient contrast with the already-hired southern Jew (Milton Nahm).[21] ([Years later I became] head of the department at Bryn Mawr, succeeding Grace de Laguna. I was a poor head of the department. Not only had I not been getting along too well with my colleague Milton Nahm, but I was too brusque, too quick, too insistent, too much in a hurry to change things, presumably for the better, too thoughtless to be much more than an irritant to him and to the more junior people.)[22]

Victoria decided to remain in Cambridge to finish her work for the doctorate (never completed), and I went alone to Bryn Mawr. She became involved with someone else, and when she told me of it I was terribly upset, never entirely recovering until, over the years, I managed to push the matter to the back of my mind. . . . There was a large correspondence between us, most of which—perhaps all—was destroyed. My upset allowed me to be almost seduced by a student, a situation from which Victoria rescued me. Once we had managed to get back to a normal life, there were no recurrences, no recriminations nor references. I know that the above account is lacking in detail, and might even be said to be coy and evasive, but it contains as much as I think is pertinent to understanding me, my personal problems, and my marriage.[23]

Victoria was very unhappy in Bryn Mawr. They would not give her a job, and she had few friends. I loved [Bryn Mawr]; my students were exceptionally keen, hardworking, already on my side. They liked me and I liked them, and to this day can count as friends those I taught even in the first years.[24]

When . . . [the Peirce papers] were out of the way, at Victoria's suggestion I gave up writing articles and began work on *Reality*. She read every word of it, and made me explain and clarify what was not evident to her. Unfortunately, she was too intelligent, and much that she understood others did not. At any rate, the book never did sell very well.[25] [Whitehead] was not very favorable. He thought it was obscure and thought that perhaps I ought not to publish it. Then, of course, I did revise it, and he was happy that I dedicated it to Evelyn. But he himself found very little to commend in the book itself. As I look back, I think it's a stronger book than he allowed it to be. I grant that it is quite obscure.[26] I still think there are splendid things in it. But like most of what I have written in philosophy since then, it did not make contact with the larger philosophical community.[27]

My rise [at Bryn Mawr] was rapid; I was a full professor at top salary—at that time fifty-two hundred dollars—by the time I was thirty-seven. . . . I was publishing; I had just finished a book; the Peirce papers were out of the way; I was (by 1939) the happy father of two children who, although not always in the best of health, were bright and attractive. My teaching was a pleasure; I had many friends among the students, though few among the faculty. . . .[28]

Every year [from 1931 to 1945] I think I went to Cambridge, sometimes during term time [to see Whitehead]. In the summers my family and I spent weeks with him and Evelyn at Billerica with the Pickman's, where the Whiteheads stayed. The Pickmans asked the Whiteheads whom they'd like to have come, and the Whiteheads said they'd like us with them. We'd see the Whiteheads in the afternoon, and we'd spend every evening talking in a quasi-philosophical, intelligent, civilized way.[29]

In 1945 I received a call from Brand Blanshard at Yale. He needed someone to substitute for him for a term while he underwent . . . surgery.[30] I came to Yale as veterans were returning from the war. They were older men, some of whom had attended Yale before, and now had returned, sobered, serious, matured, after some experience in the armed forces. I made a great impression on them, in part perhaps because I was seen to be somewhat irregular in my ways, thinking, and speech. I found out later that a number had written to the dean and other university officers urging that I be kept.[31]

It is hard to believe at the present time, but in the 1940s and a good part of the 1950s Yale was rather anti-Semitic. It had had Jewish students, mainly from New Haven, but all, I think, were excluded from the eating clubs, fraternities, and senior societies. There had been a number of distinguished Jewish teachers in the law, medical, and graduate schools, but there had never been a Jewish full professor appointed to the undergraduate school. Those who had been appointed to the graduate and other schools did not teach undergraduates as a rule; and, if they did, they were not members of its faculty.[32]

In my first year I had a graduate student, Eli Karlin, twenty years of age or so. He was brash, bright, independent. Convinced that I was the greatest philosopher since Aristotle, he told everyone that he was my disciple, and that I was a philosopher of exceptional stature. He wanted me to start a periodical devoted to my thoughts. I did not approve. But I did say I would be willing to start a periodical devoted to aspects of philosophy that were being neglected today, providing that I could be assured of financial backing. He told me that his family would guarantee the finances. Somewhat naively I accepted the assurance and launched the *Review of Metaphysics* the next year [September 1947]. It was hard to interest people in a periodical with that title—deliberately chosen, in fact, as a challenge to a positivistically dominated philosophical world. It took some five or six years before the periodical was able to pay for itself.[33] I alone was the editor and made all the editorial decisions; the managing editor was in charge of seeing the periodical though the press, the bookkeeping, and the circulation/advertising. As soon as he learned how to do the job well, I would ask him to leave so that another young person could learn how a periodical was published.[34] [By 1950 it] became clear to me that there [also] was a place for a society where the great problems of philosophy were treated as of primary concern. With that in mind I called a meeting of the Metaphysical Society of America—an institution which is still flourishing. . . .[35]

Victoria died of lung cancer in 1953, at the age of forty-seven. She had become a heavy compulsive smoker in her later years. . . . I had planned to go to India with Victoria on a sabbatical supported in part by a grant. With some misgivings, but with the approval of my children and at the urging of my colleagues, I decided to go, and break the pattern of

my life with Victoria.[36] Victoria was an exacting but imaginative parent. . . . [She] saw through fraud and incompetence with a penetration that could startle. . . . Never did I have a moment's doubt about her magnitude, and not only I and my children suffered a grave loss on Victoria's death, but all who knew her. She was a person whom no one ever seemed to forget meeting and being affected by in a lasting way.[37]

When I first began to dine at Silliman [College], I met Richard Sewall. We soon became good friends. We had lunch together at least once a week for the twenty-odd years I was at Yale. No two people could have been more dissimilar in obvious ways. He was the son of a minister, quiet, careful, at work for almost his entire career on a life of Emily Dickinson (his book on that life won a National Book Award [in 1975]). When he became master of Ezra Stiles [College], I left Jonathan Edwards in order to take up residence there, helping him with decisions on new fellows and the like. At lunch we would discuss or interchange opinions, on literature primarily, but also on university politics and issues, personalities, and students. He knew a great number of students, and was also on good terms with a great number of the faculty. . . .

Yale had invented a Scholar of the House program—I think it was Dean W. De Vane's idea. Excellent students could offer a project which they would carry out in senior year, free from all classes, but under the supervision of a faculty member. I had students in the program very early. . . . By the time Richard Sewall took charge of the program—the third director, I think—it had developed a good routine. He improved it further. Students and their directors met once a week at dinner; one of the students would read from his work in progress; this was discussed by the others. Sewall had me come every week, whether or not I had a student in the program. I functioned as a kind of devil's advocate, raising difficulties and pointing out directions not considered by the student or his director. We made a good team, I think.[38]

I was due for retirement in 1969. . . . I wanted . . . [an appointment] of at least five years' duration. That was the offer I received from the Catholic University of America.[39]

I have not been particularly conscious of myself as a Jew. This is due in part to my not being active in the Jewish community, in my not being religious in practice, in my not discriminating amongst those I take to be friends. I never have a second thought when I am invited somewhere; it does not occur to me that I am being invited by a Jew or a non-Jew, though I do note, almost unconsciously, whatever Jews are present. I do not make more or less contact with them than I do with others. If I were to make a list of those with whom I am most friendly, I would find a larger proportion of Jews, I think; but that will be due in part to the fact that they have made more of an effort to be friendly with me. This is particularly true, I believe, of the students I taught at Yale, but not of those I taught at Bryn Mawr, or those I am teaching [now at Catholic University].

My friends in Israel and I, I believe, share an unspoken awareness of our common history, particularly of the Holocaust, though we do not speak of it, and though I do not feel any particular attachment to them because, or so far as, I and they are Jewish. I do not share their view that Israel is the place all Jews ought to be, and that we can expect to have a virulent anti-Semitism aroused in this country one of these days, perhaps soon. I have no hesitation in taking myself to be in the same common situation with them, to share in the same history, and to be subject to the same great turns in the course of the world. I don't think that my thoughts are Jewish in any particular way. I never write with a sense that I am Jewish, that what I say may have Jewish overtones, or that I have a distinctive outlook that permits me to say something those in other groups would not or could not. I do not think that I see anything from a distinctive Jewish angle. One reason I am glad I am a Jew is that I am able to dispel (at least for myself) the myth that there is something special to see from a Jewish position. Were I one with the majority, I would wonder what mysterious power the Jews had that they could achieve so much over the centuries. But I do not note anything that has been intellectually gained by my coming to problems from the position of one who was born to Jews, grew up in a semi-orthodox home, was bar mitzvahed, and found it most congenial to marry and be involved with Jewish women—though I never did hesitate and had no problems when I in fact was involved with those who were not Jewish.[40]

If I believed in a God, I would suppose him to be struggling to get to the stage where he was worthy of being worshipped. The world he was supposed to have created is so poorly organized that he must have been thinking of something else at the time. I would love him the way I love another, wanting nothing but good for him. I would be content with whatever he was able to give me, and not lament the fact that he could do no more at the time. I would think that his

A self-portrait with a head above it, 1980: "I painted to learn what painting involved. When I reached the point where I was convinced that I would never be a first-rate painter, I quit."

love was a blundering love, not altogether adjusted to the beloved. He would want nothing but good for me, but would not be able to give it to me, any more than I could give him all the good he would need. Instead, he would want me to make myself as excellent as I could, he supporting me as much as he was able, consistently with my being myself and doing all the work. We would help one another, I feebly and he somewhat more, but less than he might since he would be so involved in getting to a stage where he was worthy of my and other men's faith in him. The extant religions would be seen by me to be anticipatory, celebrating the last days, the Second Coming or the coming of the Messiah, the day of final judgment, the coming to be of a new de-temporalized era. He would then be worthy of worship but would have no longer any need of us, thereby making unnecessary any further time.[41]

It is sometimes said that a belief in God allows one to face death with confidence or ease of spirit. I find that I am at ease because I do not entertain the prospect of continuing in some way after death. A divine judgment faces one with a possible outcome that may not be to one's liking; if death ends one's existence absolutely, that prospect is eliminated. I do not eliminate it in order to feel at ease, but I find that my living and dying without reference to such a prospect is accompanied with a feeling of contentment.

If I do not have such a belief, how could I write *The God We Seek?* The book was an adventure in sympathetic understanding. I tried to understand what religion means to religious people, and the meanings that language, faith, God, and so on must have if a religion is to be more than a delusion. That the work has been praised by religious people and by theologians makes evident that it is possible to provide sensitive and even illuminating observations about what occurs in fields with which one has little or no acquaintance.[42]

Granted—as I do—that life in this world is all that is to be expected, there is nothing better to do than to live it at its fullest. To do this one must (*a*) be perpetually alert, curious, aware of the distinctive nature of everything. Bores can be interesting, as Chekhov showed; criminals are to be observed carefully, as Dostoevsky did; silences, emptiness, a hole in the ground all reveal nuances, contours, differentiations, intensities, and depths to the attentive. (*b*) One must also be kind, considerate, thoughtful, aware of the needs, appetites, feelings, difficulties, and limitations of others. A sensitive awareness without sympathy tends to make one so detached as to be inhuman; a sympathy without awareness ends in sentimentality. (*c*) One must be creative, if only in one's way of being attentive and kind, or in the giving of oneself so as to produce what is excellent through the maximum use of what is available. Creativity allows one to bring energies into focus, and ends with material organized and revelatory to a degree it was not before. (*d*) One must relax, let go, separate oneself from the fruits (as the *Gita* says), so as to be able to flavor what is present and to be open to the next experience. And (*e*) one must build on what one has achieved, using this as the occasion and ground for other achievements. Creativity without relaxation tends to be frenzied, overurgent, disorganized; relaxation without creativity ends

with a passivity filled out only by what happens to impinge.

It would be sad to see a grown man involved in modern politics, did one not hide from oneself the emptiness of his life, his lack of leisure time and reflection, his concern with details and positioning. For one who would live a rich life, the politician, even if he is a scoundrel, or just a routinized person in a position where he can exert some power affecting the welfare of others, is a phenomenon just as interesting as any other. But it is depressing to think what his life might have been.

Novelists and playwrights seem most ready and able to enjoy the different types of humans that there are and could be imagined. Dickens is a superb observer and inventor of distinctive human types; I think he surpasses Balzac and even Shakespeare here, while lacking the ability of the one to see men in contexts, and the ability of the other to understand great heroic or villainous figures.[43]

There is a barrier I must overcome before I can write about my emotional experiences. I find that, when I try to write a story, I become so emotionally heated in thinking out the feelings and thoughts of a character that I quickly stop. I think I would find that if I raked my memory and tried to relive what I had undergone, I would open myself to emotions which get in the way of my trying to think about basic philosophic issues—and that is what I want most to do.[44]

It is not uncommon in the West to laugh at philosophers. In recent times, those who teach philosophy join in the laughter. They want to have philosophies, preferably ones sanctioned by history and in a schematized form. They too think that no one should be a philosopher, forgetting that those they admire were philosophers. The philosophies they adopt are in fact the residua of the living thoughts of great philosophers.

I have spent my life trying to be a philosopher. I was able to do this through a series of fortunate accidents. Firstly, I had a job (at Bryn Mawr) for fifteen years where I was off the beaten track; secondly, I had helped edit the Peirce papers and therefore had the needed scholarly stigmata; thirdly, I had my higher degrees from Harvard. In the absence of all three, and in the absence of the sudden expansion of enrollments of men coming back from the war, I might not have had a job at all, or might have been denied the opportunity to have graduate students and therefore to explore my ideas and the writings of great thinkers with them. But perhaps

Paul Weiss receiving an honorary degree at the convocation in his honor at Boston University, March 17, 1989. Also pictured are John Silber, right, president of Boston University, and Robert Neville, dean of the School of Theology.

none was absolutely necessary if I really was earnest about being a philosopher.[45]

Life is like a twenty-yard dash. One has hardly started when it is all over. It is hard to tell the winners from the losers. The rewards are of little consequence. Most men will never know that you had been among those present. Each finds himself in it before even knowing that he had entered it. Nothing is gained by stopping short. And nothing much is gained by going a few more yards.

The comparison breaks down, of course, with the recognition that men run races of different lengths, under different circumstances, in different terrains, and that the object of a good life is not to get to the end but to live properly all the while.[46]

Once a man has ventured into public view, or even placed himself in a position where he is to become, or wants to become, a public individual, he no longer has a strong claim on what he has written, published or unpublished, private material or public. He does not know just what parts of his writings will prove important or unimportant, what will throw light on what he had already done, what will help others see what he perhaps never saw. Having once accepted the role of contributor of something for public consumption, he is obligated, I think, to provide every possible clue he can to what he meant and to its value. That means that he must leave the material, finished and unfinished, polished or not, personal or semipersonal, for those who follow after to judge. If it is thought to be useless or corruptive, it will be up to those others to determine what is to be done with it. No man can properly judge what will be of value and what will seem to be trivial to those who approach the material from another perspective, at another time, with other values.[47]

Textual Sources of Autobiographical Comments

1. *Philosophy in Process,* Volume 7: 1975–1976, Southern Illinois University Press, 1978, p. 198.

2. *Ibid.*, pp. 199–200.

3. *Ibid.*, p. 201.

4. *Ibid.*, p. 234.

5. "Persons, Places and Things," *Moments of Personal Discovery,* edited by R. M. MacIver, The Institute for Religious and Social Studies, 1952, p. 48.

6. *Philosophy in Process,* Volume 9: 1980–1984, State University of New York Press, 1986, p. 389.

7. "Persons, Places and Things," pp. 48–51.

8. *Ibid.*, pp. 51–52.

9. *Philosophy in Process,* Volume 7, p. 204.

10. *Philosophy in Process,* Volume 11: 1986–1987, State University of New York Press, 1989, p. 339.

11. "Persons, Places and Things," p. 52.

12. *Philosophy in Process,* Volume 7, pp. 204–205.

13. "Persons, Places and Things," p. 53.

14. *Ibid.*, pp. 52–53.

15. *Ibid.*, p. 54.

16. "Paul Weiss's Recollections of Editing the Peirce Papers," an interview by Richard Bernstein, *Transactions of the Charles S. Peirce Society,* 6:3–4 (Summer–Fall 1970), pp. 161–162.

17. "Persons, Places and Things," pp. 54–55.

18. "Paul Weiss's Recollections of Editing the Peirce Papers," p. 162.

19. *Philosophy in Process,* Volume 7, p. 210.

20. *Ibid.*, p. 211.

21. *Ibid.*, p. 211.

22. *Ibid.*, p. 214.

23. *Philosophy in Process,* Volume 11, pp. 309–310.

24. *Philosophy in Process,* Volume 7, pp. 211–212.

25. *Ibid.*, p. 212.

26. "Recollections of Alfred North Whitehead," an interview by Lewis S. Ford, *Process Studies,* 10 (Spring–Summer 1980), p. 55.

27. *Philosophy in Process,* Volume 7, p. 212.

28. *Ibid.*, p. 213.

29. "Recollections of Alfred North Whitehead," p. 45.

30. *Philosophy in Process,* Volume 7, p. 213.

31. *Ibid.*, pp. 214–215.

32. *Ibid.*, pp. 216–217.

33. *Ibid.*, p. 220.

34. *Ibid.*, pp. 221–222.

35. *Ibid.*, p. 221.

36. *Ibid.*, p. 223.

37. *Philosophy in Process,* Volume 7, Part 2: 1977–1978, State University of New York Press, 1985, p. 81.

38. *Philosophy in Process,* Volume 7, pp. 222–223.

39. *Ibid.*, p. 224.

40. *Philosophy in Process,* Volume 7, Part 2, pp. 210–211.

41. *Philosophy in Process,* Volume 8: 1978–1980, State University of New York Press, 1983, p. 171.

42. *Philosophy in Process,* Volume 10: 1984–1986, State University of New York Press, 1987, pp. 19–20.

43. *Philosophy in Process,* Volume 9, pp. 184–185.

44. *Philosophy in Process,* Volume 10, p. 374.

45. *Philosophy in Process,* Volume 9, p. 105.

46. *Ibid.*, p. 455.

47. *Philosophy in Process,* Volume 7, p. 20.

BIBLIOGRAPHY

Nonfiction:

Reality, Princeton University Press, 1938, reprinted, Southern Illinois University Press, 1967.

Nature and Man, Holt, 1947, reprinted, University Press of America, 1983.

Man's Freedom, Yale University Press, 1950, reprinted, Southern Illinois University Press, 1967.

Modes of Being, Southern Illinois University Press, 1958.

Our Public Life, Southern Illinois University Press, 1959.

Nine Basic Arts, Southern Illinois University Press, 1961.

The World of Art, Southern Illinois University Press, 1961.

History: Written and Lived, Southern Illinois University Press, 1962.

Religion and Art, Marquette University Press, 1963.

The God We Seek, Southern Illinois University Press, 1964.

Philosophy in Process, Southern Illinois University Press, Volume 1, 1966, Volume 2, 1966, Volume 3, 1968, Volume 4, 1969, Volume 5, 1971, Volume 6, 1975, Volume 7, 1978, State University of New York Press, Volume 7, Part 2, 1985, Volume 8, 1983, Volume 9, 1986, Volume 10, 1987, Volume 11, 1989.

The Making of Men, Southern Illinois University Press, 1967.

(With Jonathan Weiss) *Right and Wrong: A Philosophical Dialogue between Father and Son,* Basic Books, 1967.

Sport: A Philosophic Inquiry, Southern Illinois University Press, 1969.

Beyond All Appearances, Southern Illinois University Press, 1974.

Cinematics, Southern Illinois University Press, 1975.

First Considerations: An Examination of Philosophical Evidence, Southern Illinois University Press, 1977.

You, I, and the Others, Southern Illinois University Press, 1980.

Privacy, Southern Illinois University Press, 1983.

Toward a Perfected State, State University of New York Press, 1986.

Contributor:

Proceedings of the Seventh International Congress of Philosophy, Oxford University Press, 1931.

American Philosophy Today and Tomorrow, Furnam, 1935.

Approaches to World Peace, Harper, 1944.

Perspectives on a Troubled Decade, The Conference on Science, Philosophy and Religion in Their Relation to the Democratic Way of Life, Inc., 1950.

Moral Principles of Action, Harper, 1952.

Moments of Personal Discovery, The Institute for Religious and Social Studies, 1952.

Philosophy and History, New York University Press, 1963.

Editor:

(With Charles Hartshorne) *Collected Papers of Charles Sanders Peirce,* six volumes, Harvard University Press, 1931–35.

(And founder) *Review of Metaphysics,* 1947–64.

Jonathan Williams

1929-

CLOCHES A TRAVERS LES FEUILLES

LETTER TO ANSEL ADAMS

Dear Ansel,

A friend in Asheville phoned the other day to tell us that, mirabile dictu, Harry Callahan was coming to Western Carolina University in Cullowhee to show slides and some of the new color prints. We went over.

You would have joined us in moaning ruefully at the mess the campus has turned into. You used to enter from the old highway along the Tuckasegee River. An augury of time to come was the building of a Burger King right where you turned into the grounds. Lately, there's a four-lane bypass on the other side of the campus. The two conspicuously ugly big buildings are for administration (white) and sports (black). The art department is like all the others: redbrick never seen, surely, by anyone called an architect. Acres of bulldozed red clay dotted with brick boxes, looking like a low-security reformatory for towheaded, callow, and recalcitrant youth.

Harry was in good form and spoke so clearly and simply that probably very few understood what he was saying. He began by recalling how important your visit to the Detroit Photo Guild in 1941 was to him. It was the first time he had ever seen "real" prints. It was your small contact prints that moved him. "In Michigan there were no mountains, so I had to look close at the ground." Great remark. You also spoke to them of music and its connections with photography. Harry insisted that photography really saved his life. "I was a guy who couldn't fit into a job. Suddenly I had something to do that made me feel like a person."

The slides were a pleasure, including early color work from the 1940s I'd never seen. Callahan was photographing walls *before* he'd ever heard of Siskind—how different they are, of course. Anyway, when he talks there's no artspeak or bafflegab. The only abstract noun he uses is *stuff.* "I didn't know anything about art history or composition or stuff like that."

Jonathan Williams, Stokes County, North Carolina, 1988. Photograph by Roger Manley.

One has to smile. This is a guy whose eye is so formal, so immaculate, so cool, that he hardly ever misses. A glorious clarity demonstrated over and over hundreds of times. The music that came to mind as the images flashed was John Lewis's piano. Bill Evans's too, but Evans is less focused and less sharp than Harry.

Bushwhacking is a great American pastime of the moment (the man's substance seems that kind learned exclusively at country clubs, post-Andover, post-

339

Yale), but at least your old pal Ronnie Reagan has gone back to swing in the banana trees of Bel Air and Hollywood. Salut!

LETTER TO FERDINAND RUGE

Dear Ferdinand,

I think it was the fact that I knew your birthplace, Dahlonega, Georgia; that it had seen a gold rush in Andrew Jackson's day; that a federal mint had been built there to deal with the coinage—all this decided you to exert so much strenuous effort in educating me at St. Albans back in 1944. (Years later, in 1961, I actually visited Dahlonega. Had the famous breakfast at the Smith House, then headed for Amicalola Falls State Park, climbed up onto Springer Mountain, and began my walk up the Appalachian Trail to the Hudson River at Bear Mountain, New York.) You were certainly the first to warn me of the moral and physical dangers of *ankyblepharon*, that fine neologism (of surely your making) which indicated getting your eyeballs frozen to the right or left from looking at what other people were writing on their exams.

Becoming editor of the *St. Albans News* in 1946 was a ground for much of what I have done since, had one

Middle Creek Falls, Scaly Mountain, North Carolina, 1951. Photograph by Francine du Plessix.

but known. You must have spent nearly as much time in the office as Tony Morley and I did, putting the paper together. So if I begrudged all that time it took to get a story straight (the who, when, where, why, and what of it all), because it meant I missed tennis practice, or time in the art room, and had to grab a hamburger at the Alban Towers drugstore instead of going home to the Westchester for dinner, then you missed a lot too. Students often forget that faculty advisors have wives and children and real lives to lead.

Grammar and spelling have nearly fled the republic by this date, 1989, but they hadn't when you held sway on Mount St. Alban: "Woolley is bully but Lester is bester," as the familiar couplet went. (I seem to remember now once meeting the son of that mentor of orthography, John A. Lester. If I have it right, his name was Jack Lester and he was the Librarian at Haverford College.) I never have forgotten your demand for precision, fact, and clarity; and for the virtues of descriptive and expository prose. One of your more dreaded exercises was a paper of one thousand words simply describing a postage stamp, one with a bald eagle on it. I can still remember the fun of writing: "Resting on the tarso-metatarsi . . ." Learned stuff.

The design of Jargon Society books and the rigors of my literary style would have been much less mature without your scrutiny and help in my late teens. Let me thank you again. And let me thank you for that classic distinction between two schools of Greek philosophy which you so often regaled us with in class: "A Stoic's vat brings de babies; and a Cynic's ver you vash de dishes."

LETTER TO ANTHONY JEFFERSON MORLEY

Dear Klark-Ash-Ton,

I suppose that not many now crawling about on Planet Unearthly would know why I addressed you as such back in 1945? Clark Ashton Smith, one of the mad, piping, acephalous shuggoths who pranced in the primal slime of H. P. Lovecraft's prose style—where are the oddballs of yesteryear? Actually, I once did meet Mr. Smith, a refined and placid gentleman, living nicely in Carmel, California. There was a collection of his sculptured heads of the Old Ones from the Extra-Dimensions Sacred to Great Cthulhu out in the sunny garden.

It's good to ruminate over things from forty-five years ago, especially how important it was to have you for a friend at St. Albans, someone with whom not only to share Howard Phillips Lovecraft, but Albert Pinkham Ryder, Odilon Redon, Robinson Jeffers, Kenneth Patchen, Henry Miller, Jan Sibelius, Aldous Huxley, C. S. Lewis, and the others. What you had to share with me was even more important: a Quaker conscience that reminded me that other minorities besides the aesthetic ones existed, and that one was obliged to think about black people and poor people and old people and actually do something about them. Few of our classmates had these humane concerns. I learned a lot from your jolly, energetic character, and it was always a treat to be in the company of Father Felix, Mother Isabel, and the two sisters (one of whom we wickedly insisted on calling The Sick One) who seldom tolerated our adolescent nonsense.

How many times have we met since the Class of 1947 set out on the Great Road of Life? I remember a time in New York, a time in the Sangre de Cristo mountains in Colorado, a time in St. Louis, some earlier times at Haverford College. Still, you sit there in Minneapolis as vivid and much of a friend as ever. I get to see John Davis and Stanley Willis from STA days pretty regularly. Maybe circumstances will change and we'll have more time to froth in nuclear chaos at the center of Outer Cosmic Infinity and chew the Lovecraftian fat in the Dark Cave of N'ith on the Plateau of Leng at the hour of charnel feeding, blah blah blah. Love,

LETTER TO JAMES ———

Dear Jim,

Here I am engaged in constructing a bit of autobiography in what I hope is a more useful way than customary; i.e., by addressing those living and dead who have been of major importance to me in a sequence of imaginary letters. Norman Douglas did a wonderful book on his life (my copy is in England, I cannot remember the title). His method was to reach into a goldfish bowl that held the calling cards of his friends and acquaintances over fifty years. One card would produce a whole chapter. Another would elicit a comment like: "Baron von Krautbutt. . . . hmmm, I can't remember one bloody thing about this, apparently, boring person."

It's weird that you and I have not been in touch for nearly forty years, for you most certainly were the first love of my life. How clearly I remember the occasion of setting eyes on you at Bill Hayter's Atelier 17 when we were both students there in the autumn of 1949. *Alors, la vie bohème* in Greenwich Village in the City of Joe DiMaggio (and Jackie Robinson and the Boys of Summer across the East River). Touching knees under the table at the White Horse Tavern, where Old Ernie served such excellent porter and ale. Good-night kisses in the alley near the place at the intersection of West Fourth Street and West Twelfth where I had a room for eight dollars a week that even Vincent Van Gogh might have considered shabby.

Of course, what I remember most was that long weekend in the Flower District, in the loft you shared with your brother. He was away visiting the parents on Long Island. Four days in bed, staggering out rarely for pizza or Liederkranz and Bermuda onion sandwiches and ale at McSorley's Tavern. There wasn't much about eroticism left unlearned by those two enchanted young Celts during those four nights.

What happened? Well, I met your ditzy brother Joe, and his literary blarney and sultry person quite seduced me. But, not for very long. Never take very seriously anything people say who think that either Rainer Maria Rilke or Hart Crane is the greatest of all poets. Aye, Joe caused some grief. The last time I ever saw him was 1966 in Paris at the Deux Magots, with a tiny Japanese woman said to be his wife. More blarney, perhaps.

Forty years. It would be amazing to know what happened to you or to see you again. Did you become an artist? What romance came into your life? Where have you lived? It's a funny old world, as our English cousins say. Love,

LETTER TO GAIUS VALERIUS CATULLUS

Dear Stud,

It's great how you stick in one's conk, like some crapulent cocklebur, to be fancy about it. The poet of outspokenness, exhilaration, exasperation. The fact that you were a Gallic hick who spent some time in the Big Town and then went back to the villa at Sirmione on the Lago di Garda has always made it easier to write poems here in the Appalachian outback, increasingly befouled by tree-choppers and Floridian dummies.

It's fun to try to imagine you in the flesh. Rome was falling apart at the seams in those days. Maybe it was no more civilized than Boise, Idaho? It took tough language to cope with all the shitheads. Maybe you weren't too different from Jerry Lee Lewis, Little Enis, Elvis, Little Richard, Richard Pryor, or Robin Williams—just about crazy enough to get your licks in. A bad dude with a pile-drivin' ass and a hoe-handle hard-on.

Your enthusiasts keep trying to see that the stuff is alive on the front burner. The bright kids of every new generation love to figure out what "pedicate" and "irrumate" mean! Zukofsky, Frank O. Copley, Reney Myers, and Robert J. Ormsby, they've done wonders. Whether they call him Meantool, or Big Dick, or Pricko, that scumbag Mamurra, Caesar's Chief of Engineers, that "monstrous, menacing Mentula" remains vivid. I would like to serve Senator Jesse Helms so well in words, he'd be despised two thousand years from now. Thanks for striking the first match.

Back in the 1960s when I did my *lepidum novum libellum, Sharp Tools for Catullan Gardens,* for an Italian translation (it came out *Affilati attrezzi per i giardini di Catullo),* I had the sound of the bop hipsters in my head. Now I hear the likes of Mojo Nixon, the profane and potent redneck songster. If he (and I) were doing LXXXV from the *Carmina,* it would maybe come out:

> I love and I hate
> and, good buddy, that's all she wrote

Shake it!—and don't brake it . . .

LETTER TO HUGO WEBER

Dear Hugo,

Even though I knew you for only a few months during my abortive semester at the Institute of Design in Chicago (spring 1951, it was), you often come to mind. Your class in graphic design was a lifesaver. That severe intensity of yours seemed very un-Swiss. A pleasure to study with a man who had assisted Maillol and been friendly with Hans Arp; who could talk about Jan Tschichold, Klee, Schoenberg, Frank Martin, and Max Bill. I still remember a party at your loft where I drank about four times more bourbon than necessary and started a diatribe against the commercial, lowbrow attitudes of most of the faculty at the ID. I was just about to get slugged in the mouth by the irascible Art Sinsabaugh, when I had the good sense to run to the john and throw up. And

then pass out amongst the coats on a bed in a dark room.

Sadly, you've been dead a long time now. But how much I admired your paintings and those drawings in oil on paper, those ones of Mies in particular. Too few know this work. Still, whenever I get together with Emerson Woelffer or Harry Callahan or Aaron Siskind or Harold Cohen, we get excited when we talk about our friend Hugo. Yours ever,

LETTER TO KENNETH PATCHEN

Dear Kenneth,

There are still watercolors on the walls here and plenty of KP books on the shelves to keep you close to heart. Just about forty years ago I paid my first visit to you and Miriam and left that "Yellow Clown" by Rouault for you to keep for awhile. The little red cabin by the pond on the lane out of town is firmly in place in the mind's eye. And your introducing me to George Lewis and Barbellion and Ruthven Todd and Trakl and Lee Bell and John Cage and Varèse and Bob DeNiro and Bill Russell and so many others. You even mentioned that a poet named Louis Zukofsky with a wife named Celia and a boy named Paul had a shack down the way they used occasionally in the summer. It took me a few years to find out about them, but you said clearly: "The Three Little Bears, they're OK people."

There are more dark clouds over the fretful earth now than there were then. Less Angels and more Monsters. Less poets with fire, wrath, and compassion. If anyone ever had the blues (of the empyrean sort) and the glory of simple joys, you did. To have shaken your hand firmly and to have seen the light in your eyes make many things still seem possible. Next spring I will go up to the Patchen Festival in Warren, Ohio, and read them some of your poems and some of mine. Hope Miriam will also be there. Love,

LETTER TO AUGEAS, KING OF ELIS, GREAT SON OF HELIOS BY NAUPIADAME, DAUGHTER OF AMPHIDAMAS

Mon Cher Père Ubu,

Heraklitos could not say it better: SHIT HAPPENS. What this means is that shits run the country, everybody's buying and selling shit, everybody has shit-for-brains, and that this time Hercules is not coming to either the Peloponnese or to Mother Earth with muck fork in hand. He couldn't use the neigh-

Kenneth Patchen, San Francisco, 1954. Photograph by Jonathan Williams.

boring rivers Alpheus and Peneus—now they're just part of Shit Creek too.

Now, in addition to radioactive waste, we waste entire generations and seem somehow surprised when we turn around from not busily shovelling the shit to see them dead of crack or AIDS or neglect, lying there on the doorstep, or standing there with gun in hand. That's when it's too late to shoot the shit, man. Shit-Man, the state-of-the-art Golem.

Just a generation ago the Collier Brothers, your progeny, of course, seemed amiable and rare eccentrics. Their virus got around in a hurry. Little did I realize that my mother was a Collier. But I realize it now. Much of life is spent cleaning the maternal houses, apartments, and condominiums. Throw out one box of stale crackers and you suddenly find a little cache of four more. How many more single shoes with no mates are lurking in the basement; how many unused leather handbags from Garfinkel's in Washington, D.C., bought in the 1940s, are disintegrating in the attic? We need one thousand Shakers to come help clean just one house on a mountainside in the Southern Appalachians. But, there are no Shakers, except maybe two ancient ladies up in Maine. So, how about it, Augeas? You were once the wealthiest man on earth, you lazy sod. We pay minimum wage: $4.25. Get your thumb out! If this house ever gets clean, there is even hope for the planet! Russell Edson says it best: "The things you took for granted do not take you so." *Gardyloo!*

LETTER TO KENNETH REXROTH

Dear Kenneth,

It's a bright winter morning in the Hog River Valley of Connecticut. I just went to see Dr. Lederman, my

West Hartford podiatrist, to see if my feet still work. (The arches have slumped from all this traipsing about on two continents, and I now sport a pair of fancy orthotic devices.) My idiosyncratic appendages still work, says Harvey. We all have to get used to chronic discomforts. He's right: lunkheads in the universities, lunkheads in publishers' offices, lunkheads in the guvmint.

One thing you said during a hike out in the state park west of Mount Tamalpais still sticks with me. You said that you wanted to know enough about fending for yourself that you could be dropped by parachute into any situation and environment and you could survive it. Sounds great, but it's still tough stuff. I mean, being dropped into the Circus Maximus in Rome to join the Christians being fed to lions is bad enough—being dropped into Fernand Point's kitchen at the Restaurant de la Pyraminde in Vienne and being asked to prepare a quick sauce de champagne is almost worse. Poets aren't much more canny than the next stiff. Yet, lions or sauce notwithstanding, you remain a model and a paragon of much that I adhere to. What a pleasure to hike with a man who knew the name of every flower, every tree, every rock, every bird, every cloud formation; i.e., a man at home in his homemade world. A man who dressed like a poet (whatever that means). A man who had traditional tailors in London and Paris make him working suits (say, for reading poems to audiences in so you didn't look like a tire salesman or a fruit salad) or walking suits (for strolling over the Pentland Hills of Dumfriesshire to evoke the spirit of Robert Louis Stevenson in).

Whenever I visit anyone in their home, I want to know what kind of books and records and pictures they have. Books of Kenneth Rexroth's translations from the Greek and Latin and Chinese and Japanese and his poems and his essays remind us that we were all born in Elkhart, Indiana, all dropped by parachute into a society of ignorant scissorbills, and are lucky to survive as long as we do. I wish we could walk this afternoon in Marin County, California, talk about the doings of sexy boy and girl poets, and compare the virtues of zinfandel from Geyserville in the Napa Valley and Gigondas from east of the Rhône. And, of course, I would hope for a couple of vintage anecdotes, like the one about the time the representative from Black Mountain College came to interview you. You later wrote to me and referred to the unfortunate lady as a "frigid, dirty-pantsed nymphomaniac." Anyway, she walked into your apartment in the Fillmore, looked at the walls and said: "Oh, Mr.

Rexroth, do you paint?" And you said: "Of course not, girl, my cheeks are just naturally ruddy." Love, old friend.

LETTER TO BASIL BUNTING

Dear Basil,

You are so connected in spirit with Brigflatts Meeting House and the River Rawthey, and to Corn Close cottage, for that matter, that you seem here as much as ever, merely sitting off in the "Vodka Lounge" nodding over Joseph Wright's *English Dialect Dictionary*, or strolling down by the Dee.

The CD player in the library has brought an infusion of Bruckner to the Dale—this may not be particularly happy music to your ears, but there are some splendid recent recordings: the *Fifth* by Horenstein; the *Sixth* by Sawallisch; the *Seventh* by Riccardo Chailly; the *Eighth* by Karajan; and the *Ninth* by Giulini. Fear not, we still get down to Chopin and Liszt regularly, and we don't ignore Peter Warlock. A very lively, sadly short-lived American harpsichordist named Scott Case has committed all of the Scarlatti sonatas (555, is it?) to compact discs. One hopes to hear them all while in earthly residence!

Basil Bunting, Oughtershaw, Langstrothdale, Yorkshire, 1983. Photograph by Jonathan Williams.

Unabashed people and new boys and girls still inhabit the territory, and they revere both what you did and the unyielding strength of your position in a literary world filled with company men from Oxbridge and all those other gentlemen's clubs for the preservation of mediocre sentiment and lukewarm music. The dalesmen who put one stone to the next and make the dry walls in Swaledale and Dent, they still have the craft to build them. Peewit and curlew still cry along the rivers. The peat of the water is as dark as the tone of your vowels. We often toast your name with Lagavulin from the Isle of Islay. Cheers, man! Here's for more ears, fishermen, and poets; and eyes that do their own doing. Love,

LETTER TO EDWARD DAHLBERG

Dear Edward,

"O, my friend, there is no friend." That's an observation you quoted that sticks like a burr. Bunting said that if you kept straight, you would have no friends but catgut and blossom in season, as you picked away at a Japanese banjo in the hōjōki in the piney woods. Creeley surmised that only by selling insurance would you ever have more than two friends. Dire predictions from two hyperborean bards!

But, you're probably right. There are some fifteen hundred names on my mailing list, but when I start counting serious/playful readers and serious/playful friends, the totals come in at less than one hundred souls. I can hear you raging: TOO MANY! And that's right too. What has happened during the last decade is that time for reflection, for the quietude required by poetry, and the attention you crave from other people, they've all disappeared. Soon both conversation and writing will become offenses, and one will do himself and others the most credit by staying home, weeding the garden, and reading Epicurus to the cat. There were reports that in your dotage you would wander about Santa Barbara holding heated, one-sided discourses with peppertrees and rowans. Another instance of your vatic soothsaying.

How's the poker in the Elysian Fields? Five-card stud, deuces wild? Or, something more rarified like "Australian Rat Fuck," a finesse game John Chamberlain introduced to the table at Black Mountain. I like to imagine your table including Cabeza de Vaca, Sir Thomas Browne, Heraklitos, Sherwood Anderson, Billy Bartram, and maybe the old Kansas City pugilist, Piano Mover Jones? Love,

The author in Washington, D.C., 1961

LETTER TO PROFESSOR WILLIAM HARMON, UNC–CH

Dear Willyum,

Was scanning the back jacket of Michael McFee's new book from J. Greene's Gnomon Press and was amazed at what I read there, i.e., that J. Williams, Gentleman Sportsman and Sultan of Sweat, is not good enough to earn a place in the batting order of the Tarheel Academicals Baseball Club. Yep, quite amazing. Makes me feel truly outré.

Once he gets past Preacher Ammons (who hasn't really hit the fastball for quite awhile now), I can't imagine our pal Wallace Gould having much trouble with those guys, even at his age.

Why don't you get some of your company folks like Louis Rubin and Annie Dillard to get me one of those Bollweevilgen Awards from up North? Then I can spread it all over the cover of every book I ever write and people will think I am really something? WINNER OF THE BOLLWEEVILGEN AWARD!!! Well, chomp my tallywacker, that trifflin' Williams boy has finally amounted to somethin'—and him sixty-one years old!

My problem, being on the outs with Corporate America, is that I can't do enough for guys like you. I can't publish you because I keep finding Outsiders like Thomas A. Clark and Simon Cutts and Thomas Meyer and Richard Emil Braun and Mason Jordan Mason who need it much more than you to keep both dignity and heart together. I can't help get you a reading at Brown. I can't help you get a better job at Berkeley or anywhere else. I don't write about you in the *Georgia Review*. Only poets who can do such things write good poetry. What I write is designed to be of no consequence in the brain factories, and let's hope it stays like that until times change a lot and the barbecue from Red Pig #2 in Concord, North Carolina, becomes the official snack-of-choice at the Modern Language Association. Hang in there,

LETTER TO LORINE NIEDECKER

Dear Lorine,

I got a phone call from someone at the Academy of American Poets the other day, wanting your phone number. I had to tell them that, unfortunately, LN has been dead for twenty years. So, the Establishment knows about as much as it always did. Better buy your own bird seed, don't count on a grant.

Of course, the fact is you probably never applied for a grant in your whole life, or asked anybody for a dime, or even presumed on another's privacy to the extent of asking them to pause and listen to a poem of yours uttered out loud. The Self-Effaced Miss Niedecker. What a calm thing it was, to read your poems and write you letters. So little ever got in the way. You put the bird seed dutifully out in the snow. We depended on it and kept pecking away.

When we went to visit your grave several springs ago with Gail and Bonnie Roub, Karl Gartung and Walter Hamady, Black Hawk Island and the Rock River did not appear to have changed much. A water world with red-winged blackbirds and fast clouds. But no poet. Love,

PS: I wish I could tell you something about Paul Zukofsky, but I can't. Occasionally, the *New York Times* reports that he is conducting a concert with the Julliard Orchestra. It's music I am unfamiliar with, on the whole, and I fear I am not going to Gotham or Gehenna to hear it. When I went backstage to see Paul after a violin recital at the University of Illinois

awhile back, the meeting seemed of very, very little consequence to him. *Tant pis,* grunted G. Flaubert. Me too.

LETTER TO CLARENCE JOHN LAUGHLIN

Dear Clarence,

Well, at least you are spared Jesse Helms and all manner and number of Republican crooks and greedies, plus even a reformed Klansman in the Louisiana legislature. Things, naturally, are no better in our shop-till-you-drop pejoracracy.

There are still some photographers around with at least three eyes to see with. Some of the names who would interest you are: Guy Mendes, Roger Manley, Shelby Lee Adams, Paul Kwilecki, John McWilliams, Kay Du Vernet, Lucinda Bunnen, Virginia Warren Smith, Martha Strawn, John Weiss, Denny Moers, Elizabeth Matheson, John Lawrence, and Keith Smith. Most of these are Southerners—I don't range the continent like I once did. Not that I ranged it like you did. There's still never been *anybody* in the U.S.A. who has seen anything like what you saw. And, sadly, there is so much less to see.

You would have loved visiting the Land of Pasaquan outside of Buena Vista, Georgia; and meeting the bizarre and affable creator of that realm, Eddie Owens Martin, ST. EOM. He would have offered you a gigantic spliff of homegrown Mary Jane, some fine collards, cornbread, and lemonade, and told you stories until you were storied out, and out of film.

I am almost sure that you must have been to that locally guarded, secret cemetery near Charleston, South Carolina, called Magnolia Umbra? Wonderful name in itself. And surely a major feast for the personal eye of CJL. Some of the greatest tombs in America. Regency, Classic Revival, Gothic, High Victorian, and Just Plain Autochthonous. If there is teleportation beyond the grave, do by all means make arrangements to travel to Magnolia Umbra. I can't offhand remember any images of it by you, and that's puzzling. . . . A letter in today from a young enthusiast in Asheville speaks of Afro-American funeral rites and monuments in the Deep South, and asks if I know the grave of Cyrus Bowen in Sunbury, Georgia. I must tell him I don't.

The book I have been struggling to finish for too long is now firmly in hand and will not make yet another protean escape. It's the one on Outsider Artists (visionaries, eccentrics, weirds, wackos, etc.) and is called *Walks to the Paradise Garden*. That's a variation on the title of Delius's interlude from the opera, *A Village Romeo & Juliet*. (People don't know, or forget, that the Paradise Garden in question is a pub frequented by the lovers.) Most Outsiders are simply trying to make Paradise in the backyard. Or the front yard. Some homemade place that's safe and pretty. Anyway, Roger Manley and Guy Mendes have contributed great photographs and we are about to give a publisher an astonishing book. It will be dedicated to you.

I am writing this from Hartford in Connecticut. You were the first to tell me about Mark Twain's superb brick house in Hartford and we've been to see it twice. About ten or twelve miles to the southwest of here is an institution called the Avon Old Farm School, a place with an amazing atmosphere. Again, mostly redbrick and limestone. The architect (a woman I know nothing about with the delicious name of Theodate Pope) created an English assemblage of buildings in a somewhat Mediaeval style and then added touches of the Arts and Crafts movement. It is stunning. Whenever I see anything this special, I always ask myself if Clarence saw it. The answer is usually: yes! Love,

LETTER TO JOEL OPPENHEIMER

Dear Big Daddy Jello,

Since you left us in saddened condition on this baleful planet, the bottom seems to have dropped out of the bottom. A year now since we sent out an initial eighty-three copies of *Names & Local Habitations* (the complimentary and review freebies). Guess how many reviews? Two, old buddy. TWO—count 'em, Yussel! One by Rich Blevins in Pat Smith's mag, *Notus;* one by Tom Patterson's paper, *Arts Journal*, out of Asheville. Don't ask me about the *New York Times*. Don't ask me about the *Village Voice*. I don't know the answer. Bertholf, the other day over at the Poetry Collection in Buffalo, said there was suddenly zero interest in Olson scholarship and anything to do with Black Mountain. Nobody's using the stuff. So, the yups and the bores are drying up the water holes and the lines of force. The siege may be a long one— "bring plenty of dynamite, it looks like a big mother," as Woody Allen suggests in *What's Up, Tiger Lily?*

Fret not, the *terre à terre, goyische* forces of Jargon will not desert you! During 1990 I'll be in touch with Teresa and see how the script is being put together by the committee or whatever they call themselves. We'll

publish the *Selected Later Poems* in 1991. I can already see the jacket, featuring a stunning black-and-white image by Lyle Bongé. And maybe some more inside too. He has a great series of lines and splatters from Manhattan pavements that look like angelic letters from the Kabbala.

Doc says he expects to have a real good year, but it's too early in the year to think about the blessed Mets—even for you to think about them! Are you the only Mets Freak in the Elysian Fields? Love, Old Putz.

LETTER TO CHARLES OLSON

Hombre!

It's interesting, how often we encounter each other in dreams. The latest, just a couple of weeks ago in Highlands. The only person I see more is Anton Bruckner. He might look like a particularly ugly specimen of mangel-wurzel, but he can boogie with the best of them when he gets that brass band to open up the heavens and bring down the house.

There's no particular news. The condition of poetry and the nation is squalid. That's not news, that's the way the world ends. T. S. Eliot scholarship is down the drain from what one hears. I can just about stand

Charles Olson, Black Mountain College, 1954. Photograph by Jonathan Williams.

that. I am much more bemused that Charles Olson scholarship seems to be languishing at Storrs and at Buffalo. What interests kids these days, except money, is sunk in mystery. "Soon all will become Elvis, because Elvis is Perfect Being," quoting Mojo Nixon, the latest white-trash orphic-avatar and country-rocker. Well, let's hope it all happens. Perfect Being or not, it won't be hard for Elvis to be better than the mind of George Bush or the poetry of Robert Penn Warren, both brought to us courtesy of Eli Yale University. A Church of Elvis has been established in Portland, Oregon. (Jesus of Nazareth may be gone by the end of the millenium.) *Rolling Stone* this week reports that a rocker named Elvis Hitler is touring the land. What a clever conceit: join the two most famous people of the deplorable twentieth century into one astonishing personality. "Please don't step on my blue-suede, storm-trooper shoes!"

There were two things you put down on paper for me that I will never forget. One was part of your inscription of my copy of *Call Me Ishmael:* "o, jonathan, to be furious is to be frighted out of fear!" The other was the advice to us, your students at Black Mountain: "There are four legs to stand on. The first, be romantic. The second, be passionate. The third, be imaginative. And the fourth, never be rushed."

I caught a rare glimpse of Charles Peter in Buffalo last week. A solid-looking man of obvious intelligence. What he knows of, or cares about, poetry, I have no idea. There's a bit of your look around his nose and mouth. I asked about Kate. She seems to be running a bed-and-breakfast place on Deer Isle, Maine. Who would have guessed that—or much else—in 1990?

Paul and Nancy Metcalf are driving down on Friday for lunch here in Hartford. Time being the tireless, dark avalanche that it is, Paul is nearly seventy-five now. Still writing his distinctive, honest, polymorphous narratives and finding very few citizens inclined to pay them any mind at all. Wait till new year!

Maybe in the next dream meeting we'll be back in Griffith Stadium, D.C., where we saw Jim Lemon hit three solo homers off Whitey Ford one spring evening, with Dwight David Eisenhower also in attendance? I still remember the Chinese restaurant (the one at Ninth and Mass Avenue) afterwards, where you single-handedly devoured a gigantic baked fish. You wouldn't like the way people eat and drink these days. Afraid of everything, void of passion, unable to enjoy. Here's mud, and proprioception, right in your

eye! How I miss your bulk and your blarney. Love, Big O.

LETTER TO THOMAS MEYER

Deer Cat,

Since you've seldom been more than fifty feet away for coming up twenty-two years, it's not surprising how few letters of mine you've received.

Maurice Sendak is certainly right when he says when you reach sixty, you go a little bit nuts and start trying to do everything in the world all at once, just in case you don't make it to sixty-one. *C'est moi.*

It's interesting that *Feng Shui,* the Chinese art of placement, is very much now in the Western air. Quoting a blurb: "This ancient Chinese practice, based on principles from design, ecology, architecture, mysticism, and common sense, applies not only to the layout of a building but to the arrangement of furniture within a room, to the best design of offices and public spaces—in short, to any arrangement of man's environment. The goal of *Feng Shui* is maximum harmony with the natural order, which, achieved, will bring financial prosperity, good health, and happiness."

So, many gains have been accomplished by dint of a lot of southern-fried *Feng Shui* and attentiveness these past twelve months. The clearing out of the beck at Corn Close; the planting of hundreds of bluebell bulbs, snowdrops, and crocuses down the bank to the river; getting my archives for 1979–89, on deposit at the Poetry Collection at the University of Buffalo, sorted out for appraisal by James Jaffe; getting the houses and property here in Highlands insured and inventoried by a responsible insurance person; getting a couple like Bill and Connie Richardson living on the place as caretakers, interested in all the plants and animals and birds; getting my mother to write a proper will, and getting me to write a new one as well; getting the basement cleaned out in preparation for the new Jargon office, Outsider Art gallery, alcove for guests, and exercise room with hot tub—all this is encouraging stuff. The joys of having a pot to hiss in, plus the proper place to put it.

Anyway, should Hesse Jelms or Velen Hendler or some irate De-Constructionist from Yale decide to put out a contract on my worthless head, you should have firm title to the contents of the houses here in Highlands and to everything that is ours at Corn Close. The Frederick Sommer photographs, the big

Ansel Adams, the three David Hockney drawings, the Bill Traylor, the Edgar Tolson, the Howard Finsters, the Kitaj pastel, the Tom Phillips, the oriental porcelains, the library should keep all wolves too far away from your door for you ever to notice them. Obviously, the point is for you to keep everything in place as long as you want to. Having willed the buildings and land to the Jargon Society, my hope is that they can figure out a way to preserve this place more or less as it is, with a custodian in charge and various budding caitiffs of the sort we like to be offered a temporary place to escape the Mammonites and Yobbocrats. Lawd nose, it would be a fantastically more interesting site than the boarding house of Thomas Wolfe's mother in Asheville. Something on the order of "Plas Newydd" in Llangollen in Wales, where the Ladies of Llangollen entertained the artists of their time and made their unique collections.

Being in somewhat wistful mood, it remains to say that this companionship of ours has left us in similar boats: each with little but each other and each with his work to get done. It's been no help to you in some ways that you have been saddled with a "controversial" figure, someone as deliberate, eccentric, and irascibly zany as JW. Still, no one these days gets invited to the Brain Factories of Yupdom, nor would they want to be. And one can't count three magazines one would like to publish in, even for no payment at all. One makes a private world, and keeps it clean; and keeps good eats on the table and decent drink for the stray pilgrims; and keeps the weeds out of the gardens. But, not all the weeds à la Gertrude Jekyll. The butterflies like the stinging nettles. Love from The Pumpkin (his mark),

Robert Duncan, Point Lobos, California, 1955. Photograph by Jonathan Williams.

LETTER TO JAMES JAFFE

Honored Editor and Bibliographer,

Here it is, Superbowl Time! It might keep one more interested in the actual game if one picked the Broncos and gave 14 points? Even you might want some of that action? But, to be a bit more realistic: San Francisco 35—Denver 10.

I'm racing the clock to finish a series of real and imaginary letters to constitute something in the way of an autobiography—this for that series from Gale Research called *Contemporary Authors Autobiography Series.* They ask for circa ten thousand words, so, being the inveterate letter writer that I still am, I am directing these epistles to the likes of Catullus and Herr Doktor Professor Anton Bruckner and Clarence John Laughlin, just to let them know how both they and I are doing. I couldn't face yet another retelling of why I dropped out of Princeton in the sophomore year and parted company forever with the gilded and gelid youth; or, "The Christmas Dinner That Marlene Dietrich Cooked for Francine du Plessix and Her Hillbilly Swain in 1951." I am calling the piece "CLOCHES A TRAVERS LES FEUILLES," from Book One of Debussy's Images Pour Piano. Have been listening to the account of the work by Arturo Benedetti Michelangeli, with his extraordinary finesse evident at all points—tickling the ivories indeed.

Since I love lists, here are a few that might fill in various chinks:

MY TEN DESERT-ISLAND DISCS:

Jean Sibelius: *Fifth Symphony* (Serge Koussevitsky)
Sergei Rachmaninoff: *Second Piano Sonata* (Vladimir Horowitz)
Charles Mingus: "Jelly Roll Jellies"
Anton Bruckner: *Eighth Symphony* (Wilhelm Furtwangler)
George Lewis: "Over the Waves"
Maurice Ravel: *L'Enfant et les Sortilèges*
Gustav Mahler: *Third Symphony* (Jascha Horenstein)
Frederick Delius: *The Mass of Life*
Gabriel Fauré: *Requiem* (John Rutter)
Earl Scruggs: "Foggy Mountain Breakdown"

TEN MALE OBJECTS OF EITHER UNCOMMON, UNREQUITED, OR FOOLISH DESIRE:

Brandon de Wilde
Robert Duncan
Michael McClure
Duke Armstrong
John Browning
Rob Kanak II
Joe Kadlec
Alex Gildzen
Larry Fisher
Jeffrey Jones

TEN FAVORITE PLACES TO EAT:

Restaurant de la Pyramide, Vienne, Isère (Fernand Point)
Ridgewood Restaurant, Bluff City, Tennessee (Grace Profitt)
Stars, San Francisco (Jeremiah Tower)
Chez Nico, London (Nico Ladinis)
The Oyster Bar, New York City
Bistro at the Maison de Ville, New Orleans, Louisiana (Susan Spicer)
Lexington Barbecue, Lexington, North Carolina (Dwane Monk)
Paul's, Winston-Salem, North Carolina (Paul Perello)
Auberge de l'Ill, Illhaeusern, Alsace (Messrs. Haeberlin)
Yang Sing, Manchester (Harry Yeung)

TEN FAVORITE JAZZ PIANISTS:

John Lewis
Thelonious Sphere Monk
Herbie Nichols
Jimmy Rowles
Errol Garner
Jelly Roll Morton
Art Tatum
Duke Ellington
Bud Powell
Red Garland

TEN MEMORABLE SPORTSMEN, FOR BETTER OR WORSE:

Larvelle "Sugar Bear" Blanks
Slammin' Sammy Snead
Slingin' Sammy Baugh
Big Bill Tilden
Ancient Archie Moore
Dick "Dr. Strangeglove" Stewart
"Say Hey" Willie Mays
Michael "Air" Jordan
Elroy Face
Alpha "Cotton" Brazle

Williams (center) with Ronald Johnson and Tom Meyer, Gotham Book Mart, New York City, 1976

TEN IMMENSELY SATISFYING, IMAGINATIVE READS:

Ruth Rendell: *A Judgment in Stone*
Peter Straub: *If You Could See Me Now*
H. P. Lovecraft: *The Shadow Out of Time*
Bruce Chatwin: *On the Black Hill*
Stephen King: *Salem's Lot*
John Valentine: *Puppies*
Vladimir Nabokov: *Lolita*
J. R. R. Tolkien: *The Lord of the Rings*
William Least Heat Moon: *Blue Highways*
Ed McClanahan: *The Natural Man*

TEN PLACES ONE MIGHT WISH NOT TO SEE AGAIN:

Manhattan Island
Odd, West Virginia
Birmingham, England
Buffalo, New York
Charleroi, Belgium
Carcassonne, France
Disney World (and Florida as well)
Los Angeles, California
Egypt, Georgia
Egypt

TEN PLACES TO VISIT BECAUSE OF THE ART:

Colmar, Alsace, for Grünewald's "Isenheimer Altar"
Firenze, for the Botticellis
Cookham in Berkshire, for the Stanley Spencer
    Museum
Washington, D.C., for the Albert Pinkham Ryders
Oxford, for the Samuel Palmers in the Ashmolean
    Museum
Charlottesville and Monticello, Virginia, for Thomas
    Jefferson
Borgo San Sepulcre, for Piero
Owatonna, Minnesota, for Louis Sullivan's bank
Hauterives, Drôme, for the Ideal Dream Palace of the
    Postman Cheval
Nancy, Lorraine, for the Museum of the Art Nou-
    veau
Toblach, Austrian Tyrol, for the landscape of dolom-
    itic alps that Gustav Mahler saw daily while com-
    posing *Das Lied von der Erde* and the *Ninth
    Symphony;* i.e., nature helping to shape art

TEN MOVIES:

The Wizard of Oz (Victor Fleming)
Fantasia (Disney)
La Belle et le Bête (Jean Cocteau)
Monsieur Verdoux (Chaplin)
Les Vacances de Monsieur Hulot (Jacques Tati)
The Wages of Fear (Henri-Georges Clouzot)
Pixote (Hector Barbenco)
Stop Surprise (Jean-Daniel Cadinot)
Stevie (Hugh Whitemore)
Blue Velvet (David Lynch)

Well, one could go on and on. These days, should one's autobiography include ten fast-food abominations, one's ten favorite malls, ten unfavorite TV sitcoms, ten most-decorticated rock groups? Leading the determinedly hermitic life most of time, I can't quite get with the likes of the Butthole Surfers. But, I do love Les Négresses Vertes; and I like Mojo Nixon a lot. His "Elvis Is Everywhere" will become the new national anthem when the King takes over from the Gentle Nazarene.

Next week I'll study your suggestions for the contents of *Blackbird Dust*. I have some additions to propose to give these essays more range than they now seem to have. For instance, I want to knock out a quick one on walking in the Black Forest, to put with the piece on the Wye Valley and the piece on Eire. The problem, of course, is finding a publisher who will show the slightest enthusiasm for these texts. I have asked Herb Leibowitz and David Wilk to give me their ideas. The list will be short. If we can reach five between us, we'll be lucky. Eat yer collards!

LETTER TO SERGEI VASILYEVICH RACHMANINOFF

Dear Maestro,

As we say these days in the dumbed-down Urals, the good news is that your music endures. As long as Pletnev and Gavrilov are about, the piano music is in good hands. Ashkenazy has done the symphonies brilliantly. And let's not forget that amazing performance of the *Fourth Piano Concerto* by Michelangeli. I have seven or eight attempts at the *Third Concerto*—even Earl Wild doesn't seem to get it entirely. It remains perhaps the one piece in all of the music I know I simply cannot hear often enough. The bad news is that Volodya is dead at eighty-six. I continue to measure my life by hearing you in Washington, D.C., in 1942, and by hearing Horowitz there in

1943. How could an aspiring Southern middle-class hick have had any idea of transcendental playing before I heard you two? "Mad Vlad" continued to stagger one and all until the end. Real devil stuff; or, *diablerie, si vous voulez*. The Scriabin, the Schumann, the Scarlatti, the Rachmaninoff, the Liszt. That he couldn't play Beethoven or Mozart doesn't bother me much at all—I don't take much pleasure in either. It's a shame that he never bothered to record the Ravel that he played at home for over half a century. The composer reports that he liked it, though it wasn't quite the way they were used to playing Ravel in Paris. *Tiens.*

Do you know that amazing thing Horowitz said? "There are three kinds of pianists. Jewish pianists. Homosexual pianists. And bad pianists."

I pour four ounces of pepper vodka into a crystal glass and drink your health. Think of your being buried there in Valhalla, New York, along with Herbert Lehman and Lou "The Iron Horse" Gehrig! *Salut!*

WILLIAM C. WILLIAMS M. D.
9 RIDGE ROAD
RUTHERFORD, N. J.

Sept. 8/56

Dear Williams:

Don't let the "glum days" get you, I for one would feel lost without the genius of your publications. It's a strange thing about "the new", in which category I place what you do, at first it shocks, even repels, such a man as myself but in a few days, or a month or a year we rush to it drooling at the mouth as if it were a fruit an apple in winter. Whatever it is you publish everything is not successful. BUT to get and not miss the rare excellence that is a chance that has to be taken. What you are doing is tremendously important to me. I don't swallow everything I see even of what I see of yours but in it or among it I get what I cant get otherwise.

Use what you like of what I wrote about DEATH OF 100 Whales and be sure you sent a copy of the broadside. The finest thing about you, and not the only thing, is the topography, the entire appearance of what you print, it is distinguised and attractive. Nuff said.

Sincerely yours

Williams

A note of praise for the Jargon Society from William Carlos Williams, 1956

LETTER TO ELVIS ARON PRESLEY

Dear King,

Mojo Nixon says there's only one person left on earth (the Evil Anti-Elvis: Michael J. Fox) that don't have no Elvis in him. I hear it—in the deep heart's core, like us poets say. If you'll spare us from George Herbert Walker Bush and James Danforth Quayle, I'll chomp the gray, withered, tobacco-stained tally-wacker of Jesse Alexander Helms, Jr., from this day forth, forever more! Answer my prayer, Good Buddy! Hey, I just heard Carl Perkins do his original of "Blue Suede Shoes." Great stuff—after all, he wrote it. But the way you covered it: every broad in the Republic thought you were ready to hump her, and every rednecked stud-asshole was ready to take it up the butt for the first and only time, world without end, etc. Nomads got gonads too—they don't just belong to the Rich Folks. Thank you, man!

LETTER TO MICHAEL HENY

Cher Ensorceleur,

Everybody's been travelling. I just received a couple of letters from you that missed me in Cumbria towards the end of October. And a very nice letter from Miz Natasha. Please thank her. (I can't quite decipher her last name, is it Mouge? And is her address: 1616 JPA, Charlottesville, Virginia 22903? What is JPA?) She says: "I wish I could make Michael as happy as you do." Gee whiz—that brings a tear or two to the eyes. One is completely disarmed.

I had, earlier on, been thinking to deliver a brief sermon on Social Deportment and all that. Viz., when visiting your aesthetical elders, don't act like Labrador puppies and paw each other endlessly, and then retire to your room to pick the guitar and whisper and whisper and whisper and all that. But, maybe that's nothin' but BORING and nothin' you need to hear from your crazy old mentor. So, enough of that.

Anyway, Most Esteemed Suburban-Bumpkin, let me try to catch you up on the latest. January seventh we flitted up to darkest Buffalony. They were all in shock from a loss by the Bills to, I think, the Cleveland Browns. Some miserable dude dropped a catchable ball in the end zone in the last seconds of play. That would have won it. *Alors* . . .

The Amherst campus of the State University of New York of Buffalo looks like a place in South Africa for confining people of color. I mean serious max-securi-ty! For five days Tom and James Jaffe and I opened boxes, sorted, and filed all the Jargon/JW archive material from 1979-89. James is making an appraisal. We doubt that the powers that be at SUNYAB will want to purchase this addendum to their holdings, and that's for two reasons: (1) the present curator of the Poetry Collection gets along with me about as well as Jesse Jackson does with Jesse Helms; plus, there's the fact that he specializes in people like Robert Duncan, Charles Olson, Robert Creeley, and Lorine Niedecker. That material is already in their hands . . . (2) the University at Buffalo Foundation hasn't finished paying for what they already have held for ten years—why expect them to change their somnolent ways? Anyway, after work in the Poetry Collection, we retired to the splendors of the Red Roof Inn, munched crudites from Wegman's, drank liquor, watched basketball games (Duke/Georgia Tech was a classic), and occasionally staggered out into the cold and snow for dubious grub.

Jaffe drove us over to Rochester and we had a brief, very pleasant time with Keith Smith (artist, photographer, bookmaker) and his boyfriend, Scott McCarney, an interesting bookmaker in his own right. We all dined with Dale Davis and her new husband Michael in Fairport. Dale is one of the last firebrands and torchbearers of poetry. Mention Lorine Niedecker and her Italian blood positively smoulders. Michael was presiding over the kitchen and we couldn't find out much about his work as an art critic and teacher. Good cook: a rough venison pâté; roast leg of lamb with haricot beans and a highly refined ratatouille; Keith brought a rum/pecan pie. The claret flowed, and so did the single malt whisky later on.

Got up at daybust to slither over the snows to the Rochester airport to catch a plane for Hartford. The 0700 flight was cancelled (one somehow wonders if that flight ever runs?). They sent us to Philadelphia, where we sat for two hours; and then on to Hartford. U.S. Air has a very odd conception of what a "Danish" is. Gary Knoble met us in a hired van so all and sundry minions of Hog River Music could go down to see the exhibition of Coracle Press at the Yale Center for British Arts in New Haven. James Sellars, composer of *The Turing Opera,* which he and Tom have been working on for six years, now presides over a household consisting of Gary (chief breadwinner and a vice president of The Hartford Insurance Company); Robert Black (the world's most avant-garde double-bass player—he is constantly trudging out into the snow to drive to Boston in another blizzard to play another gig); Finn Byrhard

(Danish musician and James's factotum—"FINN, what's happened to the bird seed, I don't have anything for lunch!" "FINN, I can't find the Stravinsky score!" "FINN, call up David Hockney and tell him I need to talk to him about HAPLOMATICS."); and a new twenty-two-year-old waif they keep in the attic named Todd Merrell. Todd is true New England blueblood. Governor William Bradford is a direct ancestor. He's in the process of escaping both parents and conventional music schools. Wants to study with James, but another mouth to feed, body to clothe, and bright mind to put up with seemed to be putting a mild strain on the delicate balance of four gay men living together in what Leonard Bernstein calls the "Bordello d'Amore." All things (and persons) are shared at Hog River Music. The four gents share one bank account. There is a vast drawer with communal socks and communal underwear. People nearly go nuts on occasion (as they do in more usual arrangements), but it is a fascinating experiment and everyone is so lively that they entertain bemused friends and guests and colleagues on a nonstop, virtuoso basis. Gary and Finn are first-class cooks. Lest I forget: I liked an off-the-cuff comment by

Maestro Sellars about handsome young Mr. Merrell. I turned it into a metafour:

Todd

twenty-two year old body
ninety-five year old mind
four year old sexdrive

So, a nine-day sojourn in the Hog River Valley. Act I of the opera is complete, and that represents about two-thirds of the music. Now comes the expensive business of getting all of that copied to present to an opera company capable of performing it. I mostly stayed in our attic eyrie and read novels. I'd never quite managed to digest Forrest Reid before, but did nicely with one of his novels of childhood, *Uncle Tom.* Got through three of Jonathan Valin's. His memorable detective, Harry Stone, is one heap-big shamus. It all occurs in Cincinnati, a place seldom graced by gory fiction. Try *Day of Wrath* and *Dead Letter,* available in your favorite drugstore or paperback shop. And if you want to read a workmanlike, very honest account of the trials and tribulations of two

Jonathan Williams (left) and Tom Meyer, Philadelphia, 1985. Photograph by David Lebe.

gay English teenagers in Mrs. Thatcher's dreary country, try Mike Seabrook's *Unnatural Relations.*

One of the excellencies of life at the Bordello d'Amore (a.k.a. "Grace Noodle Mansion"—it is precisely the sort of stock-broker dwelling that Wallace Stevens once lived in a few blocks away) is the formality of the evening meal (with Gary usually slaving over the cookstove, his wonders to prepare: the best chiles rellenos ever, wonderful boeuf bourguignon, paella, etc. He keeps a serious wine cellar. And an astonishing array of marc, eaux de vie, brandies, cordials, and single malts). As I said, the household is seldom without guests. One of the regulars is a delightful, portly Irishman by the name of John McDonaugh. Every civilized residence should have a John McDonaugh, just as it should have a Vietnamese Pot-Bellied Porker as a pet. John owns a deposit of coal and makes a living selling it to the inhabitants of Hartford. He has an extraordinary speaking voice and is in great demand to tell the story of Peter and the Wolf and pieces like Vaughan Williams's *An Oxford Elegy* and the Sitwell/Walton *Façade Suite.* What a jolly man.

One Thursday afternoon the five of us not struck down by the flu got into the ancient Volvo station wagon and drove down to New Haven for me to give a talk and a reading at Ezra Stiles College. Every visit I offer to wash the blessed vehicle but am always met with disapproval. The consensus is that the body would fall into many pieces if not cemented by all that mud. The sponsor of the Yale event was an undergraduate magazine, *Zirkus,* edited by an extremely brainy nineteen-year-old from Indianapolis named B. Gregory Hays . He wrote the one-and-only review of *Dementations on Shank's Mare* (I think I sent you a copy last year?) and seemed to know things about my style that I certainly didn't. The venue was the Master's House at the college, the master being a charming Turkish professor of engineering by the name of Turan Onat. Is that something spelled backwards? Tea in the afternoon with me blathering on about poetry and publishing for thirty or thirty-five people. A break to get a few scotch-and-sodas under the belt and visit Culter's record shop. (The catch included CDs of the Busoni piano concerto, the two Ives piano sonatas, the last two Martinu symphonies, three symphonies by Eduard Tubin, Riccardo Chailly's Bruckner Seventh, a session by Ralph Peterson's Quintet, and, for very necessary comic relief: *Leroy Anderson's Greatest Hits.*) I'll bet you didn't know Mr. Anderson studied at Harvard with Walter Piston and Georges Enesco, and once planned to be a

professor of Old Norse? Anyway, back to Professor Onat's quarters for a reading. It went nicely enough, all except "Who Is Little Enis?" The Andover/Yale tradition seemed to find this unduly vulgar and sex-besotted. Gee whiz and gosh all hemlock, as we used to say in the countryside. I asked Greg if he'd taken courses with H. "Boom Boom" Bloom and those dire De-Constructionists of the EngDept? No way, he proclaimed, he was a classics major. The other very keen undergrad was a smiling small person named Rhys, who turned out to be half-Japanese and half-Jawja Cracker, from a hamlet named Register, Georgia. (I note on the map it very close to Emit and to Egypt, Georgia.) He was studying anthropology. And, happily, sex was not entirely from his person. He confided that he knew what all those verbs meant in Catullus's headier poems. Good lad. The reading done with, a small band of us retired to the Old Heidelberg to drink beer and eat pasta.

So, back on the mountainside we are, with lots of rain and workmen putting deep ruts in the driveway as they labor over the renovation of the basement. A snazzy hot tub has been ordered and by April, perhaps, all will be wonderful in the nether regions: Jargon's computer office, gallery space for photographs and Outsider Art, alcove for discerning guests, and the exercise room for aching backs and sagging guts.

A long letter, but why not? You're one of the few people I know who seems to enjoy either reading or writing "personal" letters. These days there are few townies who want to give you even ninety seconds on the telephone. They are already thinking about what happens when they slam down the receiver. And what is that? What indeed?

It's good to hear that Charles Rowell is so good. That Mr. Jefferson's university on the hill affords you two excellent teachers is a rare thing. Toast your luck with a bottle of Chateau Montdomaine's merlot. Love,

LETTER TO JOHN CLEAVELAND, MAYOR OF HIGHLANDS, NORTH CAROLINA

Dear John,

No actual complaints for a change, except that I don't see enough of your mother's pie on my fork.

But, two things do occur to me. (1) Is there no way to control the deprivations of the telephone company? The broad-cutting policy is bad enough, but the disgusting mess they leave is even worse. Next time you're driving down the Dillard road, just observe the rape and pillage from the ski lift right on down to the Georgia line. The worst of it is from below the Middle Creek bridge. The edge of the creek is trashed, that beautiful stand of rhododendrons just before you get to the Arnolds' property is completely smashed by trees just left to rot. Then there's more desolation right across from our entrance. I have been driving up and down the Dillard road since 1943, and it has never looked worse. Somebody has to take some responsibility. I'd be willing to help pay for a plane ticket to Frankfurt so that the president of Contel of North Carolina, Incorporated, could take a train down the Rhine Valley and then go into the Black Forest to see how one manages telephone lines in a way that doesn't ruin the landscape. Actually, the guy in charge of the highway department needs to go too. Those machines they use to chop the verges of our roads are horrible. There's nothing finer than a Carolina hemlock to look at with half the trunk ripped off.

(2) Being what I believe would be described locally as, politely, a Bleeding-Heart Liberal, let me make the community an offer. I'd be willing to devote one day a month to work with a volunteer group in and around Highlands. The town would set this up and be in charge; i.e., this would be less disruptive than setting up a private organization and causing more bickering. I think a number of people would be willing to join in, doing whatever is most necessary. Twelve days a year is more than two work weeks, but I could afford that and would be glad to join others to "improve" the scene. (There are some cold-eyed cynics like the composer John Cage who say: "Please don't try to help save the world—you'll only make things worse!") My manual skills aren't brilliant but I could at least help out. Literary skills might be part of the effort as well? Lest the Highlands plateau be trashed entirely, new plans need to be put into place to control the litterers and polluters and despoilers, those with no respect for their neighbors and for the unique place they happen to live in.

Good wishes,

BIBLIOGRAPHY

Poetry, except as indicated:

Garbage Litters the Iron Face of the Sun's Child (engraving by David Ruff), Jargon Society, 1951.

Red / Gray (drawings by Paul Ellsworth), Jargon Society, 1951.

Four Stoppages: A Configuration (drawings by Charles Oscar), Jargon Society, 1953.

The Empire Finals at Verona (collages and drawings by Fielding Dawson), Jargon Society, 1959.

Lord! Lord! Lord!, Jargon Society, 1959.

Amen / Huzza / Selah (preface by Louis Zukofsky, photographs by Williams), Jargon Society, 1960.

Elegies and Celebrations (preface by Robert Duncan, photographs by Aaron Siskind and Williams), 1962.

Emblems for the Little Dells, & Nooks & Corners of Paradise, Jargon Society, 1962.

In England's Green & (A Garland & Clyster) (drawings by Philip Van Aver), Auerhahn, 1962.

LTGD (Lullabies Twisters Gibbers Drags) (covers by R. B. Kitaj), Jargon Society, 1963, reprinted with new introduction, Design Department, Indiana University, 1967.

Lines about Hills above Lakes (prose; foreword by John Wain, drawings by Barry Hall), Roman Books, 1964.

Petite Country Concrete Suite, Fenian Head Centre Press, 1965.

Twelve Jargonelles from the Herbalist's Notebook (graphic design by Ann Wilkinson), Design Department, Indiana University, 1965.

Four Jargonelles from the Herbalist's Notebook, Lowell House Printers, Harvard University, 1966.

Paean to Dvorak, Deemer & McClure, Dave Haselwood, 1966.

Ten Jargonelles from the Herbalist's Notebook (graphic design by Arthur Korant), Graduate Graphic Design Program, University of Illinois, 1966.

Affilati attrezzi per i giardini di Catullo (selected poems in English and Italian; translations by Leda Sartini Mussio, drawings by James McGarrell), Roberto Lerici Editori (Milan), 1967, published as *Sharp Tools for Catullan Gardens* (introductory note by Guy Davenport), Fine Arts Department, Indiana University, 1968.

Eight Jargonelles from the Herbalist's Notebook (graphic design by Dave Ahlsted), Design Department, Indiana University, 1967.

50! EPIphytes, -taphs, -tomes, -grams, -thets! 50!, Poet & Printer (London), 1967.

A French 75! (Salut Milhaudious), Dave Haselwood, 1967.

Futura 15: Polycotyledonous Poems, Edition Hansjoerg Mayer (Stuttgart), 1967.

Mahler Becomes Politics . . . Beisbol (silk-screen prints by Kitaj), Marlborough Fine Arts (London), 1967, revised and enlarged edition published as *Mahler*, Grossman, 1969.

Les Six Pak, Aspen Institute, 1967.

Descant on Rawthey's Madrigal: Conversations with Basil Bunting, Gnomon Press, 1968.

The Lucidities: Sixteen in Visionary Company (drawings by John Furnival), Turret Books, 1968.

An Ear in Bartram's Tree: Selected Poems, 1957–1967 (introduction by Davenport), University of North Carolina Press, 1969.

On Arriving at the Same Age as Jack Benny, Finial Press, 1969.

Ripostes (silk-screen print and design by William Katz), Edition Domberger (Stuttgart), 1969.

Six Rusticated, Wall-Eyed Poems (graphic realizations by Dana Atchley), Press of the Maryland Institute of Art, 1969.

The Apocryphal, Oracular Yeah-Sayings of the Ersatz Mae West (lithographs by Raoul Middleman), Press of the Maryland Institute of Art, 1970.

(Editor) *Edward Dahlberg: A Tribute* (prose and poetry collection), David Lewis, 1970.

The New Architectural Monuments of Baltimore City (lithographs by John Sparks, typography by Robert Gotsch), Press of the Maryland Institute of Art, 1970.

Blues & Roots/Rue & Bluets: A Garland for the Appalachians (photographs by Nicholas Dean, graphic realizations by Atchley), Grossman, 1971, enlarged edition, Duke University Press, 1984.

Strung Out with Elgar on a Hill (plates by Peter Bodner), Finial Press, 1971.

(With Thomas Meyer) *EPitaph* (typography by Asa Benveniste), Jargon Society, 1972.

(With Meyer) *Fruits Confits* (decorations by Ian Gardner), Jargon Society, 1972.

The Loco-Logodaedalist in Situ: Selected Poems, 1968–1970 (embellishments by Joe Tilson), Grossman, 1972.

Adventures with a Twelve-Inch Pianist beyond the Blue Horizon (photographs by David Colley), 1973.

(Editor and contributor) *Epitaphs for Lorine: 33 Poets Celebrate Lorine Niedecker*, Jargon Society, 1973.

(With Meyer) *Gone into When* (seven epitaphs), William Katz, 1973.

Imaginary Postcards (Clints Grikes Gripes Glints) (drawings by Tom Phillips, typography by Benveniste), Trigram Press, 1973.

Much Further Out Than You Thought (prose; drawing by Furnival), *Parnassus*, Spring/Summer 1974.

(Contributor) Ralph Eugene Meatyard, *The Family Album of Lucybelle Crater*, Jargon Society, 1974.

Five from up T'Dale (prints by A. Doyle Moore), Finial Press, 1974.

Hasidic Exclamation upon Stevie Smith's Poem "Not Waving but Drowning," University of Connecticut Library, 1974.

My Quaker-Atheist Friend (drawings by Gardner), privately printed, 1974.

(Editor and author of preface) Lyle Bongé, *The Sleep of Reason*, Jargon Society, 1974.

Who Is Little Enis?, Jargon Society, 1974.

Gists from a Presidential Report on Hardcornponeography, Jargon Society, 1975.

How What? Collages, Texts, Photographs (prose; illustrations by Dawson), Mole Press, 1975.

(Contributor) *The Land: Twentieth-Century Landscape Photographs*, Fraser, 1975.

Pairidaeza (lithographs by Gardner, typography by Ronald Pearson), Jargon Society, 1975.

A Wee Tot for Catullus, Moschatel Press, 1975.

A Celestial Centennial Reverie for Charles E. Ives (drawing by Willard Midgette), Donald B. Anderson, 1975.

gAy BCs (drawings by Joe Brainard), Finial Press, 1976.

In the Field at the Solstice, Finial Press, 1976.

A Blue Ridge Weather Prophet Makes Twelve Stitches in Time on the Twelfth Day of Christmas (illustrations by Carolyn Whitesel), Gnomon Press, 1977.

(Editor and contributor) *Madeira and Toasts for Basil Bunting's Seventy-fifth Birthday*, Jargon Society, 1977.

An Omen for Stevie Smith, Sterling Memorial Library, Yale University, 1977.

Super-Duper Zuppa Inglese (and Other Trifles from the Land of Stodge) (drawings by Barbara Jones), Aggie Weston's Editions, 1977.

Untinears & Antennae for Maurice Ravel, Truck Press, 1977.

A Hairy Coat Near Yanworth Yat, North Carolina Wesleyan College Press, 1978.

(Editor and author of introduction) *"I Shall Save One Land Unvisited": Eleven Southern Photographers*, Gnomon Press, 1978.

The Delian Seasons (illustrations by Karl Torok), Topia Press, 1979.

Elite/Elate Poems: Selected Poems, 1971–1975 (photographs by Guy Mendes), Jargon Society, 1979.

Glees, Swarthy Monotonies, Rince Cochon, and Chozzerai for Simon (drawings by Furnival), DBA Editions, 1979.

Portrait Photographs (photographs and prose commentary), Gnomon Press, 1979.

Shankum Naggum, Friends of the Library, North Carolina Wesleyan College, 1979.

Homage Umbrage Quibble and Chicane (drawings by Furnival), DBA Editions, 1980.

Jonathan Williams: A Poet Collects (exhibition catalog), Southeastern Center for Contemporary Art, 1981.

The Photographer's Art, Kent State University Libraries, 1981.

Get Hot or Get Out: A Selection of Poems, 1957–1981, Scarecrow Press, 1982.

The Magpie's Bagpipe (essays; edited by Meyer), North Point Press, 1982.

Niches Inches (New & Selected Poems 1957–81 for British Consumption) (introduction by Eric Mottram, illustrations by Torok and Furnival), Dentdale, 1982.

Ten Photographs, Aggie Weston's Editions, 1982.

The Fifty-two Clerihews of Clara Hughes (illustrations by Glen Baxter), Pynyon Press, 1983.

Lexington Nocturne, Keith Smith, 1983.

Dear World, Forget It! Love, Mnemosyne (letters), DBA/JCA Editions, 1985.

In the Azure over the Squalor, Ransackings & Shorings (quotes), Gnomon Press, 1985.

Letters to the Great Dead (prints by Furnival), Openings Press, 1985.

Lord Stodge's Good Thing Guide to Over 100 English Delights (prose), DBA Editions, 1985.

The Concise Dentdale Dictionary of English Place-Names, Otis Editions, 1987.

Rivulets & Sibilants of Dent (illustrations by Torok), Topia Press, 1987.

Aposiopeses, Granary Books, 1988.

Dementations on Shank's Mare, Truck Press, 1988.

(Editor of Festschrift) *DBA at 70,* Jargon Society, 1989.

Quote, Unquote (illustrations by Baxter), Ten Speed Press, 1989.

Uncle Gus Flaubert Rates the Jargon Society in 101 Laconic Presale Sage Sentences, University of North Carolina Library, 1989.

Eight Days in Eire (prose; photographs by Mike Harding), North Carolina Wesleyan Press, 1990.

Metafours for Mysophobes, North and South Press, 1990.

No-No Nse-Nse, Perishable Press, 1990.

Quantulumcumque (drawing by McGarrell), French Broad Press, 1990.

Blackbird Dust (essays; photograph by Siskind), Jargon Society, 1991.

In a New Light (essays), Aperture, in press.

Work represented in many anthologies, including *New Directions in Prose and Poetry,* New Directions, Volume XVI, 1957, Volume XVII, edited by James Laughlin, 1961; *The Beat Scene,* edited by Elias Wilentz, Corinth Books, 1960; *The New American Poetry, 1945–1960,* edited by Donald Allen, Grove, 1960; *Beat Poets,* Vista Books, 1963; *Erotic Poetry,* edited by William Cole, Random House, 1963; *A Controversy of Poets,* edited by Paris Leary and Robert Kelly, Doubleday-Anchor, 1965; *Poets of North Carolina,* edited by Richard Gaither Walser, University of North Carolina Press, 1965; *The Voice That Is Great within Us,* edited by Hayden Carruth, Bantam, 1970. Author of recording *Get Hot or Get Out,* Watershed Foundation, 1985.

Contributor to *Evergreen Review, Contact, Vogue, Nation, Aperture, Black Mountain Review, Monk's Pond, Kulchur, Origin, Jazz Monthly* (St. Ives), *Poor. Old. Tired. Horse.* (Dunsyre, Lanarkshire), *Vou* (Tokyo), *I Quattro Soli* (Turin), *Cimaise* (Paris), *Art International* (Zurich), *Cultural Affairs, Art in Society, Craft Horizons, Poetry Review* (London), *Parnassus: Poetry in Review, Prose,* and other periodicals. Contributing editor, *Aperture.*

For a comprehensive bibliography of Williams's writings see *Jonathan Williams: A Bibliographical Checklist of His Writings 1950–1988,* compiled by James S. Jaffe, with introduction by Guy Davenport, Haverford, Pennsylvania, 1989.

Cumulative Index

CUMULATIVE INDEX

For every reference that appears *in more than one essay,*
the name of the essayist is given before the volume and page number(s).

INDEX

INDEX